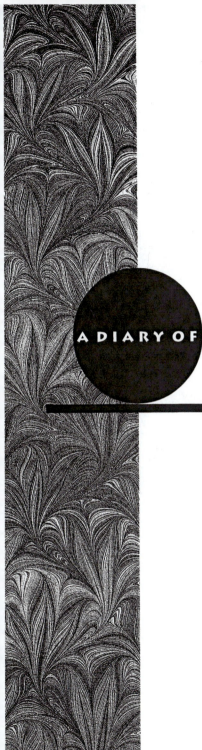

A DIARY OF DARKNESS

A DIARY OF DARKNESS

THE WARTIME
DIARY
OF
KIYOSAWA
KIYOSHI

Foreword by

MARIUS JANSEN

Edited and with an introduction by

EUGENE SOVIAK

Translated by

EUGENE SOVIAK *and*

KAMIYAMA TAMIE

PRINCETON UNIVERSITY PRESS

PRINCETON, NEW JERSEY

intellectual property, including the Paris Convention, Madrid Protocol, the Trademark Law Treaty, and the Berne Convention. More than 175 nations are members of WIPO. WIPO is headquartered in Geneva, Switzerland, and its home page is http://www.wipo.org.

There are also a number of international agreements and treaties that affect intellectual property. Among them are the following:

- **Berne Convention for the Protection of Literary and Artistic Works (the Berne Convention).** The Berne Convention was created in 1886 under the leadership of Victor Hugo to protect literary and artistic works. It has more than 145 member nations. The United States became a party to the Berne Convention in 1989. The Berne Convention is administered by WIPO and is based on the precept that each member nation must treat nationals of other member countries like its own nationals for purposes of copyright (the principle of "national treatment").

- **Madrid Protocol.** The Madrid Protocol came into existence in 1996 and allows trademark protection for more than sixty countries, including all twenty-five countries of the European Union, by means of a centralized trademark filing procedure. The United States implemented the terms of the Protocol in late 2003. This treaty facilitates a one-stop, low-cost, efficient system for the international registration of trademarks by permitting a U.S. trademark owner to file for international registration in any number of member countries by filing a single standardized application form with the PTO, in English, with a single set of fees.

- **Paris Convention.** One of the first treaties or "conventions" designed to address trademark protection in foreign countries was the Paris Convention of 1883, adopted to facilitate international patent and trademark protection. The Paris Convention is based on the principle of reciprocity so that foreign trademark and patent owners may obtain in a member country the same legal protection for their marks and patents as can citizens of those member countries. Perhaps the most significant benefit provided by the Paris Convention is that of priority. An applicant for a trademark has six months after filing an application in any of the more than 160 member nations to file a corresponding application in any of the other member countries of the Paris Convention and obtain the benefits of the first filing date. Similar priority is afforded for utility patent applications, although the priority period is one year rather than six months. The Paris Convention is administered by WIPO.

- **North American Free Trade Agreement (NAFTA).** The NAFTA came into effect on January 1, 1994, and is adhered to by the United States, Canada, and Mexico. The NAFTA resulted in some changes to U.S. trademark law, primarily with regard to marks that include geographical terms.

- **General Agreement on Tariffs and Trade (GATT).** GATT was concluded in 1994 and is adhered to by most of the major industrialized nations in the world. The most significant changes to U.S. intellectual property law from GATT are that nonuse of a trademark for three years creates a presumption the mark has been abandoned and that the duration of a utility patent is now twenty years from the filing date of the

Originally published as *Ankoku nikki: Shōwa jūshichinen jūnigaīsu kokonoka—Nijūnen gogatsu itsuka*
Copyright © 1980 by Hyoronsha

English translation copyright © 1999 by
Princeton University Press
Published by Princeton University Press, 41 William Street,
Princeton, New Jersey 08540
In the United Kingdom: Princeton University Press,
Chichester, West Sussex

Library of Congress Cataloging-in-Publication Data
Kiyosawa, Kiyoshi, 1890–1945.
[Ankoku nikki. English]
A diary of darkness : the wartime diary of Kiyosawa Kiyoshi /
foreword by Marius Jansen : edited with an introduction by Eugene
Soviak ; translated by Eugene Soviak and Kamiyama Tamie.
p.   cm.
Includes index.
ISBN: 978-0-691-14030-8 (cloth : alk. paper)
1. Kiyosawa, Kiyoshi, 1890–1945. 2. World War, 1939–1945—
Personal narratives, Japanese. 3. Journalists—Japan—Diaries.
I. Soviak, Eugene, 1927– . II. Title.
D811.5.K54313 1999
940.54'8252—DC21   98-20063 CIP

Publication of this book has been aided by the Japan Foundation

This book has been composed in Janson

Princeton University Press books are printed on acid-free paper
and meet the guidelines for permanence and durability of the
Committee on Production Guidelines for Book Longevity
of the Council on Library Resources

http://pup.princeton.edu

Printed in the United States of America

1 2 3 4 5 6 7 8 9 10

CONTENTS

FOREWORD

This is the translation of a diary that begins on the first anniversary of the Japanese attack on Pearl Harbor and runs until the author's death at the age of fifty-five a few months before the end of the war in 1945. It is a unique document. The author notes that his friends express their doubts about the wisdom of keeping it under conditions of wartime surveillance. He explains, perhaps in case of its discovery, that he records it as a resource for a future history of the period. He did not live to write that history, but his diary, in the immediacy of its entries, probably provides a better account than any history could.

The diary first became known when part of it was published in 1948. Its description of the obtuse truculence of Japan's wartime leadership, presented in cryptic, matter-of-fact notations of personal encounters that are supplemented by reflections on the pathology of Japanese society, caused a sensation. The complete text was published in three volumes in 1954, when wartime wounds were still fresh in readers' minds. It was entitled *Diary of Darkness*, as appropriate for what was now referred to as Japan's "Valley of Darkness."[1] The diary was republished in 1979–1980 and again in 1989. It is considered the most thoughtful, perceptive, and courageous account kept by a Japanese liberal during the war.

Kiyosawa was a journalist, commentator, diplomatic historian, and intimate friend of some of modern Japan's most sensitive and interesting intellectuals. His career did not follow the usual pattern; he was simultaneously insider and outsider among the intellectual elite. Born in 1890 to a farm family in Nagano Prefecture, he encountered Christianity in the "nonchurch" movement of Uchimura Kanzō and then emigrated to the United States at the age of sixteen. There he pursued his education at Whitworth College and the University of Washington before taking up employment as a journalist for Japanese American papers in Tacoma and San Francisco.

After his return to Japan at the end of World War I, Kiyosawa wrote on politics and foreign affairs for several newspapers, including the influential *Asahi shimbun*. After he criticized the murder of a prominent radical who was being held in police custody, he was subjected to right-wing attack and left the paper. He made a number of trips to Europe and America and continued to write on politics and foreign affairs for business-oriented and liberal journals,

---

[1] Thomas R. Havens, *Valley of Darkness: The Japanese People and World War Two* (New York: W. W. Norton, 1978).

among them *Chūō kōron* (The Central Review), whose publisher and writers often appear in this diary. He also published widely on Japanese–American relations. His was a balanced, rational view; he had had the immigrant experience of prejudice, but he also had a firsthand knowledge of the political vitality and industrial power of America. His studies of Japanese–American relations are praised by a contemporary authority, Kitaoka Shin'ichi, as extraordinary in quality and still relevant. They were not, however, welcomed by the militant nationalists who controlled the world of print as war with American approached. Kiyosawa remained a freelance writer.[2] From his informed perspective, Kiyosawa judged the bellicose obscurantism of wartime Japan as evidence of a deep national pathology. Incessant talk of "national spirit" as sure to prevail over the less highly motivated enemy flooded the air waves at the same time that shortages of food and consumer goods became more critical each day. He himself was distrusted and ignored, while self-important and self-appointed experts played to popular prejudices they had helped create. He and his circle of friends, which included the postwar Prime Minister Ishibashi Tanzan, knew better, but they found themselves increasingly beleaguered. Public statements could go no farther than Aesopian formulation of doubts.

The Japanese society Kiyosawa describes is one that seems almost beyond repair. Bureaucratic regulation extends to specifying dress appropriate to wartime "spirit." Ordinary people, given minor regulatory responsibilities, preen themselves and become petty despots. Thievery replaces honesty. As the crisis deepens it becomes difficult and finally impossible to sustain life without ignoring laws and regulations. Government becomes more intrusive and "socialistic" while denouncing socialism. Kiyosawa and his friends sense revolution in the offing, but they have foreboding that they will fare even worse in that day.

Kiyosawa did not survive to see Japan in surrender and in reconstruction. One can imagine that, his experience and judgment recognized at last, he might have played a role in that recovery. Instead his diary notations, with their stark reminder of a darker past, have helped to shape his country's present and, one hopes, its future.

Marius B. Jansen
Princeton University

---

[2] Kitaoka Shin'ichi, "Prophet without Honor: Kiyosawa Kiyoshi's View of Japanese-American Relations," in James W. White, Michio Umegaki, and Thomas R. H. Havens, eds., *The Ambivalence of Nationalism: Modern Japan Between East and West* (Lanham, MD.: University Press of America, 1990), and *Kiyosawa Kiyoshi: Nichi-Bei kankei e no dōsatsu* (Kiyosawa Kiyoshi: Toward discernment in Japanese-American relations) (Tokyo: Chūō kōron, 1987).

TRANSLATORS' NOTE

The text used here is the second edition of the *Ankoku nikki*, published by Hyoronsha in 1980 with explanatory and bibliographical notes, preface, and introduction by Hashikawa Bunzo. Due to the extreme length of the original, we omitted a portion of the entries, which we felt were not indispensable in sustaining the distinctive character of the *Diary*. Given the scope and richness of the remaining material, we do not feel that this significantly injures the integrity of the work itself. We tried always to sustain a balance representing the extraordinary range of Kiyosawa's wartime activities, but in our editing we gave priority to his critical judgments and recurrent ideas as they progress through the entries. For example, we largely eliminated daily one-line weather reports, retaining them only when their significance is more than purely meteorological. Similarly, after a few representative inclusions, reports of Kiyosawa's apparent service as marriage go-between are excluded. We made only a few minor changes in the original format. In many instances we chose to conjoin into a single unit entries that are closely related in content but often spatially separated in the original. We hope that this reduced some of the unevenness of flow and especially the disorientation that the cascade of entries can sometimes induce in the reader. If we failed in this we can only plead the intractable nature of diaries as a genre.

It was customary for Kiyosawa to insert newspaper clippings throughout the *Diary* to which the entries are responses. These increase in frequency and length as the *Diary* proceeds, and the corresponding entry invariably makes clear the theme of the article. In all such instances we cited the publication in question in the entry.

We follow the Asian style of surname before given name and use the Wade-Giles rendition of Chinese personal and geographic names.

Colleagues in both the History Department and the Department of Asian and Near Eastern Languages and Literatures at Washington University were remarkably generous with both their time and their specialized knowledge as we prepared the translation. Most particularly, without the saintly patience and computer virtuosity of Bette Marbs in the History office through countless revisions, we never would have completed the manuscript. Our appreciation is profuse. We are greatly indebted to Sachiko Morrell, our East Asian and Near Eastern librarian, for indispensable assistance throughout, especially in unraveling language puzzles that sometimes seemed to defy decoding. We are most appreciative for the gracious kindliness of Ikeda Mariko throughout the preparation of the work, and especially for granting permission to reproduce family photographs.

INTRODUCTION: THE LIBERAL CORNERED

When the liberal journalist-critic Kiyosawa Kiyoshi (1890–1945) began his war diary, he could hardly have imagined it would emerge in the postwar period as a "classic" valued for its detailed insights into wartime Japan. It was, after all, for his own eyes only and merely firsthand impressions to be incorporated into a future, fully polished work. That purpose was declared in the *Diary's* opening entry. But with Kiyosawa's unexpected and premature death in May 1945, it would survive as a work in its own right, and in fact as a kind of final, "inadvertent autobiography," encapsulating along with its methodical chronicling of events a lifetime of liberal writings devoted particularly to the advancement of amicable Japanese–American relations. It may be that the *Diary* came to achieve more in itself than the grand projected history of the Pacific War it was merely to document, judging from the pessimistic forebodings regarding Kiyosawa's future that haunt the entries.

The timing of the author's serious commitment to a war diary, in December 1942, undoubtedly coincided with the anxious publication of his most recent and major scholarly work, the *History of Japanese Foreign Relations* (which Kiyosawa's contemporary expositor Professor Kataoka Shinichi deems the finest prewar work of its kind). It had become increasingly clear to Kiyosawa that scholarly and, most particularly, diplomatic studies were now forbidden zones of inquiry. Under the invasive quasi-militaristic regime, this would be especially so if such work was the product of a well-known liberal journalist and free-lance critic known for his outspoken and abrasive judgments. The scope of his prewar career as diplomatic historian and "American specialist" would now be drastically limited, fraught with the threat of official censure and possibly even arrest or detention. In this constricting environment supposedly dictated by the war, the *Diary* would become the last place where it was possible to give free reign to his personal judgments in almost daily assessments of the conduct of the war on the battlefields and at home. It would also provide an indispensable record for future reference, treating subjects that could not be written about elsewhere and serving as a corrective to probable postwar glosses on the war period.

The *Diary's* importance to Kiyosawa is clearly evidenced in the regularity with which it was kept. Until his unexpected death just a few months before the war's end, Kiyosawa was an exemplary, untiring diarist. Even when the *Diary's* flow was interrupted while Kiyosawa traveled the hinterland on officially sponsored lecture tours, the lapsed entries were always dutifully restored. To the end, it was obviously a refuge for untrammeled and often bitter criticism of the war effort in the suffocating atmosphere of ideological fanaticism and hysterical propaganda that he complained disfigured these years. Throughout its pages Kiyosawa would reaffirm his liberal convictions, which had publicly evolved in the prewar years in, by his own count, some thirty volumes of argument and polemic.

What emerged from this intense dedication to the meticulous reporting of the calamitous impact of the war was a multilevel overview of the disintegration of Japanese society as the imperialist gamble failed militarily. Given Kiyosawa's preceding journalistic career and increasing prominence as a diplomatic historian and social critic, one might have expected an account focused on the reactions of his immediate sympathetic intellectual circle. Like Kiyosawa himself, that small band of like-minded malcontents maneuvered precariously in what were the last, contracting pockets of free speech and opposition to the war. While this beleaguered group was indispensable and vital to Kiyosawa's intellectual activity and well-being, however, the *Diary* embraces an all-inclusive social coverage. The sentiments of the local barber are as worthy of notation as the weighty musings of former and current foreign ministers to whom Kiyosawa had personal access. Representatives of every social stratum voice their understanding, and more often misunderstanding, of events. "Kaleidoscopic" might best describe the restless sweep of Kiyosawa's focus, from the street level to the upper echelons of leadership, from the capitol to the countryside, from the thriving and arrogant farmers and laborers to the cowed and hard-pressed intelligentsia. The whole panorama of devastation wrought by total war is evidenced here in merciless detail.

But if the *Diary* offered some consolation to an all but silenced Kiyosawa, the sudden compression of his former professional world of words posed a serious threat to the continuation of his prewar life-style. Confronted by the specter of possible arrest, some of his earlier works already blacklisted, the newspapers reduced to propaganda organs, distinguished journals emasculated by official subversion, he saw the outlets for his writing all but hermetically sealed off. Of course this also now meant that severe inroads were made into his income. There were, to be sure, still a few publications willing to include his editorials—usually under a pseudonym. *Tōyō keizai*, with which Kiyosawa had already been associated and itself constantly under the baleful gaze of the authorities, was one of these. There was still the odd commission—a history of the Tokyo Electric Company, private subsidies for research groups of which Kiyosawa was a member, part-time employment at the Foreign Ministry, and what he deemed niggardly honoraria for his speeches and lectures—in amounts below the level of a worker's daily wage, which only accentuated the debased status of intellectuals. Even on occasion a smoked salmon was not an unworthy honorarium in times when the desperate preoccupation with food became literally more painful every day.

Yet almost as if in foreknowledge of the war and its likely consequences, by the early 1930s Kiyosawa had taken steps toward financial and thereby critical independence. He invested in a restaurant (the Silver Star), a well-established confectioner (Fuji Ice), a stock portfolio, rental houses in Tokyo, and a villa and considerable landholdings in Karuizawa. With the mounting privations occasioned by rationing, the black market, the inflation of food prices, and the inadequacies of agricultural production, it would unexpectedly be the last of these properties that would become more and more critical for survival. Kiyosawa found his time and energy increasingly consumed in the hastily acquired skills of farming. It is apparent from the *Diary* that Kiyosawa came to acquire with some pride an enviable degree of competence in this field work and, by his own confession, a decided taste for it. Several times he fantasized an ideal life-style in which "one would farm when it was clear and read when it rained." As the impact of a worsening war situation enveloped the homeland with the visible evidence of malnutrition and emaciation, when friends suddenly became physically unrecognizable, food became the obsessive subject of discussion, even to the exclusion of political upheavals and battle defeats. Kiyosawa wondered grimly how the majority of less advanced Japanese could endure the terrible personal costs of an increasingly hopeless, self-destructive war. There was, too, a still darker dimension to his reflections: namely, the specter of what he felt was the frightening inevitability of revolution; a revolution that promised only ambiguous, and probably completely destructive, consequences for private property holders and the middle class, among whom he counted himself.

But far more demoralizing than mere economic and career worries was the perpetual menacing atmosphere of hysteria in which Kiyosawa and his confreres tried to maintain some semblance of independent judgment and expression. Constant care had to be exercised, particularly in public, against incurring the deadly label of "pro-American" or "defeatist" or "un-Japanese." Somewhat sheepishly, Kiyosawa frequently remarked on his restraint in public utterance, especially when there was obvious official surveillance of his lectures or speeches. In the later pages of the *Diary*, he acknowledged that his damning of the American bombers that threatened his own property with fiery destruction was at least in part for the benefit of his neighbors. Friends aware of the *Diary*'s existence anxiously warned of the danger of its exposure and the dreaded consequences to follow. There were intimidating instances everywhere of arrests after far less provocation in a time when even asking questions could prompt seizure by the police. Indeed, recurrent rumors of Kiyosawa's arrest or detainment only deepened this miasma of unremitting uneasiness that overshadowed his war years. On occasion both he and Ishibashi Tanzan (a far more recklessly outspoken antiwar critic) speculated on the probable reasons for their having escaped the worst consequences of their liberal reputations and their continued, thinly disguised publications in journals still willing to risk official censure or worse. One almost has the sense that despite, and even because of, the element of peril, the *Diary* represented an important psychological act of resistance and defiance in Kiyosawa's "prison of silence."

There were also deeper, darker, personal dimensions to this interior exile to which Kiyosawa had been banished. Along with their tireless reportage of

application (rather than seventeen years from the date the patent issued, as was previously the case).

(See Appendix A, Table of Treaties.)

THE INCREASING IMPORTANCE OF INTELLECTUAL PROPERTY RIGHTS

While people have always realized the importance of protecting intellectual property rights, the rapidly developing pace of technology has led to increased awareness of the importance of intellectual property assets. Some individuals and companies offer only knowledge. Thus, computer consultants, advertising agencies, Internet companies, and software implementers sell only brainpower. Similarly, some forms of intellectual property, such as domain names and moving images shown on a company's web page, did not even exist until relatively recently. Internet domain names such as www.ibm.com are valuable assets that must be protected against infringement.

The Director of the PTO has stated that almost five percent of the gross domestic product and more than four million Americans are involved in intellectual property-based enterprises. Additionally, more than fifty percent of

U.S. exports now depend on some form of intellectual property protection; these intellectual property exports are greater than U.S. exports of the automobile, agriculture, and aircraft industries combined.

Moreover, the rapidity with which information can be communicated through the Internet has led to increasing challenges in the field of intellectual property. The day after the movie *Titanic* swept the Oscars, more than fifty web sites offered illegal or pirated copies of the film. Books, movies, and songs can now be copied, infringed, and sold illegally with the touch of a keystroke.

The Office of the United States Trade Representative has estimated that U.S. industries lose between $41 billion and $61 billion annually from piracy, counterfeiting of goods, and other intellectual property infringements.

In many cases, the most valuable assets a company owns are its intellectual property assets. For example, the value of the trademarks and service marks owned by the Coca-Cola Company has been estimated at $68.9 billion. Thus, companies must act aggressively to protect these valuable assets from infringement or misuse by others. The field of intellectual property law aims to protect the value of such investments.

TRIVIA

- The value of Microsoft Corporation's trademarks is estimated to be $65.1 billion.
- For businesses in the food or luxury goods sector, the value of their brands and related intellectual property is estimated at between seventy percent and ninety percent of the total value of their businesses.
- The Department of Commerce has stated that the combined copyright and trademark industries represent the second fastest growing sector of the U.S. economy.
- The Business Software Alliance concluded that software piracy cost the United States 109,000 jobs and $91 million in lost tax revenue in 1998.

events and typically caustic asides, the *Diary* entries reverberated with expressions of Kiyosawa's embittered chagrin at being denied a way of serving the nation, leaving him to improvise a role (or roles) in times that had no use for him. The chance circumstances of wartime provoked some somber reflections on his own mortality and what amount of time would be allowed to him for future accomplishments. As the war tortuously dragged on, he reluctantly confessed that he was no longer engaged in preparing really serious major works, although gestures were being made in that direction (a diplomatic history ranging from the Washington Conference to the beginning of the Pacific War was in the works). This acute recognition that he could ill-afford to fritter away precious years of possible creative productivity prompted almost defiant, self-reassuring declarations of renewed purpose: He would energetically devote his unnumbered remaining years to changing traditional Japanese thought patterns, which he hoped were now being profoundly shaken and even repudiated with the ever more disastrous reversals of the war. He would write history for the enlightenment of the inevitably more liberated postwar generations since the present war would be either unintelligible or defensively misrepresented. He would even announce himself as the inspired successor to the democratic theorist of the Taisho period, Yoshino Sakuzo; he would be the Yoshina Sakuzo of the Showa period. He felt the strongest obligation to identify the "irresponsible theorists" (Tokutomi Sohō in particular) whose rabid fulminations helped precipitate the war. Indeed, this may have been the complementary compulsion to his passion to contribute to the peaceful diplomatic conclusion to the present war and more grandiosely the eradication of all war. He was among the few if any to the very end who dared to submit to the Foreign Ministry proposals anticipating Japan's postwar status and future.

Kiyosawa's projections of the new society that must emerge from, for him, the inevitable defeat in war incorporated all his criticisms of prewar Japanese society and the Pacific War and were particularized as a kind of bill of indictment in the *Diary*. Absolute freedom of speech must be a fundamental principle of new social structure. Freedom of opposition must be absolutely guaranteed. The petrified edifice of the Japanese educational system must be completely recast. Healthy national development would follow the dismantling of the former social order, which had called forth imperialist aggression as a national policy. Brute force as national style must be repudiated and knowledge given the highest priority. The long-violated constitutional rule of law must be resolutely reaffirmed and zealously maintained. The grotesque archaisms of the historical past and the recent pseudo-modern past must finally be renounced. There must be an end to the feudalistic obsession with vengeance, the ridiculous invocation of "divine winds," the inflated exhalation of the ethic spirit, the mindless surrender to sacrificial death individually and en masse, the bifurcated mental categories of material and spiritual—all of which had deformed the conduct of the war and would continue to deface any reconstituted postwar society.

All of this was linked to Kiyosawa's persistent outraged indignation over the victimization of well-informed and potentially useful intellectuals on the presumption of their questionable and probably lip-service "patriotism." Obviously with himself foremost in mind, he would continually bemoan the irrational exclusion of intellectuals from the ranks of war advisers and specialists despite their invaluable qualifications. American and international experts like himself were maliciously dismissed as disputatious and subversive malcontents since they failed to fulfill the rigid conformist demands of the official definition of "patriotism." Indeed, for Kiyosawa, it was the intellectuals of his cast of mind whose dispassionate analyses and objective judgments were the desperately needed contributions to any effective management of war. One of the unforgivable failings of the wartime leadership was its arrogant indifference and often vindictive hostility to these "real patriots." But aside from the self-serving nationalist ideologues, for Kiyosawa the war was the climactic degradation of the intelligentsia who had sadly failed to forestall the war in the first place and now failed to serve it constructively, as he imagined he should, or resist it courageously, as almost none did. The status of intellectuals had declined to an all-time low under a regime that expressed only suspicion and contempt for scholarship, research, and knowledge and settled for nothing less than blind submission to the most insufferable nationalist cant.

One may assume that Kiyosawa's notions of patriotism were formulated in a broader international context. Twelve years of his early life had been spent on the American West Coast in journalistic apprenticeship. In addition to return visits to Japan, he had wider experience of the Asian continent as well as Europe. While adjudging himself no less a fervent patriot than the most bellicose jingoist, he had in fact escaped entirely the worst excesses of prewar nationalist hysteria. But as the *Diary* entries often testify, he would declare his fundamental attachment to his homeland even as he concealed the irrational, emotional sources of his passion and loyalty. Even the imperial house itself could still elicit his genuine awe, especially when the emperor offered to visit the war front to revivify dwindling national morale. In a Japan he saw tottering on the threshold of revolution he deemed the imperial institution as the only remaining resort for sustaining a national unity ominously disintegrating in the face of impending, calamitous defeat. In all probability not only would the empire acquired at such horrendous cost now ingloriously disappear, but the very future of Japan itself now inspired the grimmest misgivings. But perhaps then the moment for the ascendance of the "true patriots" would finally arrive in a more liberated and promising postwar world. Ironically, what Kiyosawa could not do individually, alone, however mightily he exerted himself, the war that he so vehemently detested was doing for him: profoundly challenging the values, institutions, and behaviors of Japan's first phase of modernity, which were the targets of his pitiless attacks throughout the *Diary*.

If the war-induced breakdown of Japanese society occurring before his very eyes offered hope of a new order more in keeping with his lifelong critique of the preexisting structure, this dissolution was also fraught with revolutionary peril. These changes might be welcome and desirable, but they aroused uneasy ambivalence about the prospect of their ultimate enactment in revolutionary upheaval. The *Diary* entries are replete with descriptions of prerevolutionary symptoms foretelling not only revolutionary changes but revolution itself. Class warfare incited by low-ranking bureaucratic officials and military officers was everywhere manifest in their denunciations of a self-serving capitalism pitted against the workers, in the deepening tensions between the rich and the masses, in the universal condemnation of property holders and the idle middle class, in a rampant nouveau riche flaunting its black market profits, in the swaggering self-importance of farmers and workers glorying in their new preeminence in local politics, in the rapacious expropriations of private property by the military and bureaucracy, in the appalling collapse of social manners. For Kiyosawa all of this portended an updated version of the historic "bottom overturning the top" (*gekokujo*), which historically characterized Japanese "high feudalism." Conflicting comparisons with the prerevolutionary conditions of the French and Russian revolutions left little doubt in his mind of the inevitability of revolution after defeat.

Still less in doubt was his assumption that socialism would be the by-product of the war and its revolutionary denouement. Once again the potential vehicle of Japan's sociopolitical regeneration hardly lessened Kiyosawa's constant gnawing anxieties over his personal financial solvency in such a radicalized future. Perhaps by way of self-consolation, he concluded that while the fate of private property might be in question, it was already seriously threatened and violated during the war; though it would no doubt be subjected to more stringent regulations, it would not be eliminated altogether. It was not that Kiyosawa feared or abhorred revolution, but rather that he forecast that, lacking great objectives, it would be purely destructive, not creative, and without the cultural benefits conferred in the French Revolution.

Disastrous defeat abroad and revolutionary chaos at home are not the only menacing premonitions that overshadow the *Diary*. Inseparably linked to both are Kiyosawa's uneasy forebodings over the dubious readiness of the Japanese people to take power into their own hands and, more importantly, their ability to exercise it intelligently. The classic intellectual's dilemma is posed repeatedly in the entries: the very people he yearned to enlighten and activate to redeem the gross follies of the war and shocking shortcomings of the system are the same people about whose capacity to act responsibly he suffers the deepest uncertainties. For Kiyosawa was only too painfully aware of how little actual direct personal experience of the war itself the Japanese had, even at the eleventh hour, despite the most trying privations at home and the loss of sons on remote battlegrounds. Systematic official deprivation of the most basic information relating to the war reduced their understanding of what was happening to pathetic simplisms and the degree to which this exposed the blatant incompetence of national policies. Not be until they were personally assaulted by the horrors of modern warfare at home in the form of unchallenged American bombers overhead and incinerated cities beneath them would they perceive the enormity of the price the war exacted. They would grasp the national calamity in the offing and repudiate the regime whose last indecent demand on their massive suffering was now "one hundred million honorable deaths." A benighted Japanese people awash in obfuscating, homiletic propaganda were not the most reassuring candidates for future self governance. The overindoctrinated victims of a long-entrenched authoritarian system and its conditioned reflex educational apparatus led Kiyosawa to the conclusion, no doubt particularly disturbing to himself, that only more war trauma would release the Japanese from their thralldom. There would be no profit whatsoever for the people from the carnage and sacrifices of the war if there were no resultant fundamental changes in Japanese national behavior. It would be unfortunate, if not tragic, if the war ended before the people were forced to acknowledge the gross ineptitude and wanton callousness of Japanese leadership. Kiyosawa was ensnared in the no-man's-land between extravagant hope and reluctant pessimism, and death cheated him of ever knowing which posture would be finally vindicated.

In their furious onrush, the *Diary* entries are in continuous, interrelated motion on several levels of analysis simultaneously. There is the stimulus-response reaction of objective reportage of specific event after event, almost always immediately accompanied by the typical critical aside (no doubt the kind of exasperated rebuke he longed to hurl at the leadership). There is also the deeper evaluation of the society that produced the incredible folly of the war and the even more incredible malfeasance of its leadership. There is, at the deepest level and interwoven with the others, an ongoing indictment of Japanese "national character" itself. The war, for Kiyosawa, was only a particularly virulent stage of the emergent prewar "pathology" already beginning to be diagnosed in his earlier works. He had long studied what he considered the steady political deterioration in political leadership, from the statesmen giants of the Meiji period with their visionary breadth to the increasingly dominant military-bureaucratic pygmies of the Showa period with their unyielding fanaticism and self-righteous complacency. What had evolved was a maniacal system of all-intrusive statism now centered and embodied in a lethal coalition of bureaucracy and military, which had joined forces at the time of the Manchurian Incident. At its wartime peak it was merely a politics of *diktat* whose ultimate demand was to serve and die without murmur. This duo now reigned supreme, giving full vent to its worst vices—most particularly, its obsession with all-encompassing regulation. The "logic" of the state rationalized its claim to monopoly of all relationships between people. In effect, hyperregulation of every facet of life was the characteristic feature of the system. But this stranglehold of perpetually multiplying rules thwarted wartime productivity rather than advancing it and self-destructively alienated intellectuals, businesspeople, workers, and farmers. It only engendered what Kiyosawa called the "paralysis of formalism." Nomenclature was compulsively revised and tables of organization juggled, but to no apparent advantage.

Inspirational mottoes, bombastic slogans, and mystic incantations were the invariable substitutes for disciplined critical thought or a realistic grasp of brutal wartime realities. Most of the ills seen in their most exaggerated form in the war were the deplorable result of this fixation on formalism and legalistic, bureaucratic nitpicking.

At best or worst, the military-bureaucratic leaders were virtuosi in manipulating the national mystique to the forcible exclusion of all other demurring voices; the supremacy of the "Japanese spirit," the preeminence of the spiritual over the material, the divine status of the Japanese nation, the preordained colonial mission of the Japanese race were among the commonplace aspects of this tedious litany. A sterile but pervasive irrationality ruthlessly implemented through a mechanistic bureaucratism had reduced Japan to a politics of mindless fanaticism. It was also the leadership's petrified and only technique for dealing with their own incapacity to accommodate the whirlwind wartime changes. An utter and appalling lack of adaptive flexibility in the face of shifting circumstances betrayed an official mindset devoid of perspective and analytical imagination. And even more ominous for the ultimate outcome of the war was the lack of any reassuring evidence of even the slightest self-examination or self-criticism on the part of this leadership. They were more and more at the erratic mercy of rampant lower military ranks, self-serving bureaucratic underlings, and newly empowered greengrocers. Even catastrophic war had failed to stimulate any challenge to the smug self-satisfaction of a mentally constricted and nigh illiterate officialdom.

Those simplistically categorized as not "Japanese-like" were maliciously ostracized. Precluded was any tolerance, still less constructive exploitation, of promising dissenting ideas. Overbearing majors and colonels were now the arbiters of the lives and discourse of writers and thinkers. The almost pathological secretiveness in frantically withholding specific details of the course of the war betrayed a fearful distrust of the people because of the knowledge, as Kiyosawa sarcastically observed, that when the people were informed they would "do the right thing," and this was what was dreaded most. Even the most tentative consideration of postwar possibilities was savagely condemned. Essential research on the world structure that would follow the war was outlawed in favor of ever larger doses of hysterical spiritual mumbo jumbo. And most deserving of Kiyosawa's wrath was his oft reiterated and highly personalized plaint of the failure to employ really qualified specialist advisers. Before the war these had been not only ignored but silenced, and they remained mute throughout the war. The West, by invidious comparison, had no qualms about employing in the interests of the war specialists of any ideological persuasion, and this only underscored the self-blinded folly of Japanese wartime leadership. In the end the war had only produced an overextended, ramshackle empire, which merely exposed the dubiousness of Japanese leadership in Asia and the painful disqualification of Japan as the ruler of other peoples. The final confirmation of the poverty of the official mentality as

Japan staggered into collapse and defeat was the atavistic invocation of national suicide.

Throughout, for Kiyosawa, it was education that was at once the hateful source and potential remedy for the outrageous folly of the war. That folly compelled its reconstitution hereafter through the fullest cultivation of the "independent thinking" that he so much admired in the American educational system. It must nurture a maximum breadth of perspective and informed flexibility of mind—precisely what was so woefully lacking in the current leadership and Japanese people in general. The existing educational system had perpetuated and reinforced an incongruous amalgam of the least admirable traits of the traditional mentality and modern technics, and the *Diary* is an exhaustive catalogue of the consequences of this unfortunate union. By now the vicissitudes of war had brought into profound doubt the behavioral characteristics and values that were Kiyosawa's unwavering focus of attack: passive submission to authoritarianism, rarity of moral courage, habitual simple-minded formalism, self-sacrificial resignation, reflexive emotionalism, arrogant anti-intellectualism, endemic equivocation, a philosophy of death but none of life, and self-regarding insularity that negated any empathy for others. As Kiyosawa generalized it, neither prewar nor wartime Japan had mastered the modern ways of thinking nor retained the best of its traditions. How else could one account for the bizarre juxtaposition of modern technological warfare and divine winds and other assorted irrationalities? Now, with the old regime self-indicted and self-discredited, there could be hope for a completely reconceived educational system dedicated to unlimited intellectual individuality, to the unqualified endorsement of science, to the fullest validation of scholarship and culture, to the reconciliation of the dangerous mental categories of "material" and "spiritual," to the empathetic identification with other, non-Japanese modes of thought and styles of behavior.

Given the meticulous attention to detail, the self-revealing thoughtfulness of his reflections, and the acuity of observation Kiyosawa invested in the *Diary*, some sort of intellectual justice should have entitled him to see the final end of the war he so detested and the resolution of his speculations and prophecies, and perhaps even vindication of his passionate critique of Japanese society and the war. There still should have been many years of his typically mordant reactions to the even more momentous historical developments that ended and followed the war—the atomic bombings, the American Occupation, perhaps even the beginnings of the ensuing "economic miracle." What would the postwar order signify for a Japan always hypersensitive to global power balances and now, devastated and defeated, returned to an ambiguity of status not unlike its position when it first entered the nineteenth-century "modern world"? Even before the sudden silence of the *Diary*, Kiyosawa had forecast a Japan as the "Greece of Asia," though a colleague predicted the "Egypt of Asia" as the more likely outcome of the war. But the continued pursuit and exposition of such tantalizing themes were to be denied him. His ordinarily robust physical constitution undermined by several years of malnutrition, he succumbed to pneumonia a week after the last *Diary* entry. The *Diary* had ended abruptly in the same darkness in which it had begun. Whether its sequel would have been a liberated and approving record of light, we are regrettably deprived of ever knowing.

1942

December 9 (Wednesday)

Because I had the desire to leave a written account of recent events, I am going to keep a diary again.

Yesterday was a commemoration day for the Greater East Asian War. In the morning the radio began with a message from Finance Minister Kaya Okinori, and from beginning to end it was an emotional outcry. I did not listen in the evening, but there was a broadcast to the effect that America is a devil and England an evil spirit, and even my wife turned off the switch. Is it possible to carry on the war without an appeal to the emotions? Okumura Kiwao, vice-chief of the Information Board, at a board meeting proposed that there must be hostility toward America and England. The broadcast expressed these proposals.

Officials assembled for the purpose of grading sweets in Tōkyō City and sampled the famous confections. How carefree the officials are.

Because of the liberalism and individualism in England and America, they would not have been expected to stand firm. Our leaders now talk about the resolution of England and America.

I hear that because the term *hyō* in *hyōron* is outrageous to government officials, the Dainihon Hyōronka Hōkokukai (Greater Japan Critics Patriotic Association) has been changed to Genron Hōkokukai (Patriotic Press Association). So neither notices nor invitations come to me.

What everybody is talking about in the first year of the Greater East Asian War is the fact that the promotion of war consciousness is insufficient. (Okumura, Yahagi, of the Headquarters Information Board, both do this— *Nichinichi*, December 9.) How can we raise this consciousness higher than it is now?

Everything is a matter of official position. Politics is carried on for the benefit of the officials. The provincial bloc. (The problem of hiring and firing officials.) The problem of the war.

On December 8 a meeting to express gratitude to the army held at the Kabukiza at Kibanchō was filled to overflowing. The term "continuous decisive battles" has newly emerged.

Tokutomi Iichirō, who exerted the greatest power in precipitating the outbreak of the war, in the first year of the war is saying, "On the one hand, in Japan there is the Japanese spirit, and on the other hand, in America and England there is the American-English devil." Again he says, "Regarding the ancient phrase, 'The morning air is sharp, the evening air recedes,' as for the Anglo-Saxons, 'The morning air is dim and the evening air flourishes.'"

The evils of the political parties, the evils of the officials, after all, are the result of education.

From morning until night Prime Minister Tōjō gives speeches, pays calls, consoles people on the city streets, and does the work of five or six people. As a result, opinion of him is extremely favorable. His holding the highest responsibility as prime minister is evidence of what the people are seeking.

are also given the time and opportunity to develop your thesis/dissertation plan and get it approved before you formally start working on your research project. You can take advantage of these critical steps to make sure you are on the right track and will be doing fine with your guided research project. These steps will be further discussed in the next chapter.

Matching your approaches with your objectives

Research is often more complicated than what you have learned from your research classes. It is unlikely that you can simply and exactly follow a flow chart in your textbook when you are working on your own project. Many factors can affect your decision in every single step of your research. Some of them would even prescribe the basic features of your thesis/dissertation. For example, many student researchers have been functioning as the research assistants (RA's) to some faculty members. Due to their involvement in the faculty research projects, they often have access to the faculty's data sets. And more often than not, they not only have the permission but are encouraged to use such data sets for their theses or dissertations. If you decide to take advantage of such an offer, then your research is likely to be using secondary sources of information, and your thesis or dissertation will form an integral part of the faculty's research project.

If you do not have access to any existing and substantial data set, you will have to start from scratch to collect first-hand information for yourself. This does not necessarily mean you will have a tougher job than those who are making use of existing data sets. Rather, you have the advantage of laying out a data collection plan according to your research interests and objectives. And if you take your thesis/dissertation as a learning process, you will be trained more extensively than just focusing on the kind of intensive data analysis. For example, if your data collection involves human subjects, you will be cautioned as to how to protect the rights of participants and deal with the human subjects review committee of your institution.

Secondary data analysis is not necessarily an easier approach to your thesis or dissertation since you are likely to face more demanding analytic tasks than when you present your first-hand data. All or most of the straightforward information has been presented by the principal investigators, and probably all the simple analytic procedures have been applied on the data by these investigators or by their research assistants. Now that you have decided to use these data sets for

18

CHAPTER SUMMARY

The term *intellectual property* is generally thought of as comprising four overlapping fields of law: trademarks (protecting names, logos, symbols, and other devices indicating the quality and source of products and services); copyrights (protecting original works of authorship); patents (grants by the federal government allowing their owners to exclude others from making, using, or selling the owner's invention); and trade secrets (any commercial information that, if known by a competitor, would afford the competitor an advantage in the marketplace). Patents must be issued by the federal government, while rights in trademarks are created by use of marks and rights in copyright exist from the time a work is created in fixed form. Nevertheless, registration of trademarks and copyrights offers certain advantages and benefits. Trade secrets are governed by various state laws, and registration is not required for existence and ownership of a trade secret. Trademarks and trade secrets can endure perpetually as long as they are protected, while copyrights and patents will fall into the public domain and be available for use by anyone after their terms expire.

As our world becomes increasingly reliant on technological advances, greater demands and challenges are made on IP practitioners. The field is an exciting and challenging one and offers significant opportunities for hands-on involvement by IP professionals.

CASE ILLUSTRATION—POLICIES UNDERLYING INTELLECTUAL PROPERTY LAW

Case: *Mazer v. Stein*, 347 U.S. 201 (1954)

Facts: Parties engaged in the manufacture and sale of electric lamps created statuettes used as the bases for the lamps and sought to register the statuettes as works of art.

Holding: The statuettes were copyrightable. The economic philosophy behind the clause empowering Congress to grant patents and copyrights is the conviction that encouragement of individual effort by personal gain is the best way to advance public welfare through the talents of authors and inventors in "science and useful arts." Intellectual property fields afford encouragement to the production of literary or artistic works of lasting benefit to the world.

CASE STUDY AND ACTIVITIES

Case Study.   Your firm's client, Watson Inc., owns an entertainment park in Nevada called Fantasy Fun Adventure. The park has more than 100 lushly landscaped acres and includes a variety of rides, amusements, and a water park. Some of the rides feature intricate mechanical dolls, such as the Wonder Dolls, and others are more exciting roller coaster and log flumetype rides. Many of the park's activities feature a well-

Throughout the Greater East Asian War the most representative person is the vice-chief of the Information Board, Okumura. I love reading the statements of Information Board Vice-Chief Okumura. The reason is that his statements are representative of the ideology of the present. Okumura's intelligence represents the Japanese people. I dare say that he is not widely known in the world.

December 11 (Friday)

Sensitivity toward language is the special characteristic of these times. Far East is forbidden and becomes East Asia, and this resembles the obliteration of English and American.

Yesterday I stopped at the house of Hanzawa Tamashirō. I did this after attending a party at the home of Kurahashi Tōjirō. The same gentleman said the present was a war of capitalism with the "reds," and he said he went to the main office of Mitsubishi and told them that. The discontent of the capitalists is extreme. If we consider that Kobayashi Ichizō is talking about the radicalization of the bureaucrats, the capitalists are extremely hostile to this.

December 12 (Saturday)

It is a world of the right wing and ruffians. The streets of Tōkyō are full of handbills with the anti-Communist speeches of the rogue called "Akao Bin," and the newspapers write in large print of the comings and goings between Tōkyō and Ōsaka of Sasagawa Ryōichi, the head of the National Essence party. The truth is that such people are in charge of the situation.

The vulgar tone of the radio no longer makes listening possible.

Two or three days ago those of the Information Board of the Police Office came and inquired as to the effectiveness of the anti-enemy propaganda against America and England. They want to hear criticism against the policy being conducted by the vice-chief of the Information Board, Okumura. I said it was necessary to replace Okumura.

The reverses during the Greater East Asian War have been centered only upon those who hold extreme opinions and the intelligentsia not being allowed any share of responsible participation in the war.

December 13 (Sunday)

At midday yesterday I went to a meeting on the Foreign Relations Compilation *Chronology*, and I also went to a gathering with Takeuchi Katsumi. In the evening I invited Hasegawa Nyozekan, Ishibashi Tanzan, Shimanaka Yūsaku, Ōta Eifuku, and Akiyama Takashi. The theater was filled to overflowing. The restaurants everywhere were "sold out," and we came close to missing our evening meal. It has reached the point that the newspapers merely chattering about "be aware of present conditions" does not lead the people to an awareness of present conditions (*Nichinichi*, "Commentary").

Even such people as Ishibashi say that the coming year will be terrible. Everybody will feel more and more the pressure of the crisis situation.

On the 12th, in the middle of the night, there was an air raid warning. The news of a desperate sea battle in the Solomon Islands was transmitted from town to town. The bureaucracy is unified only on the matter of the destruction of the black market. However, they pay no attention to production.

December 14 (Monday)

The capitalists are shouldering the heavy burden of increasing production. Notwithstanding that, they are bound by legal regulations and restrained by controls and are filled with discontent. On the capitalists' side there are those who call the contemporary bureaucrats "reds." This is true of Kobayashi Ichizō and it is true of Hanazawa Tamashirō. The capitalists at last have come to return evil for good. This morning Fujiyama Aichiro said, "Reject the mechanization of people!" and wrote about idealistic equalitarianism. Class warfare between the capitalists and working class and among the young has come to the fore.

Last night I visited Ōkuma Makoto and we talked about matters of history. I was pessimistic on the contemporary state of affairs. Ōkuma said, "When I listen to such people as Yahagi—head of the Information Board—on the radio, he says America in the past was fine, but in its modern polity it is mistaken." And Ōkuma feels the same, but as for the Okumura clique, it says that America is completely unacceptable. And that being so, Ōkuma said there was no path for resolution.

December 15 (Tuesday)

Yesterday I attended the Monday Board of Directors meeting of the *Tōyō keizai* (The oriental economist). Itō Masanori also attended.

It is said that at a gathering of the Newspaper Reporters' Association, Okumura, vice-chief of the Information Board, stated, "From next year onward the quantity of newsprint will be negligible. You all will cease being newspaper reporters and will even tour the provinces making speeches on the realization of the Holy War for the Information Board." After this, Okumura went on the offensive against *Chūō kōron* (The central review), saying that it would receive the least amount of paper. Moreover, a commander named Horiuchi said that *Chūō kōron* would be put out of existence. Is it any wonder that free discussion becomes the toy of young officials such as these?

December 17 (Thursday)

In this morning's newspaper it was reported that the stock exchange has been put under official control. The socialism of the state progresses increasingly. From the capitalists' side there will probably be denunciations of communism, etc. Nevertheless, one should be astonished at the strengthening of the range of power of the government. Moreover, this government is in no way unified. Here is the problem.

December 21 (Monday)

The Patriotic Press Association came into existence. This was not communicated to me. Patriotic writing, thirty years. They did not even bother to notify me concerning this matter. However, once before I did not respond to them.

On the evening of the 17th Iwanami Shigeo, Abe Yoshishige, Fujiwara Chinpei, Hasegawa Nyozekan, Baba Tsunego, Ishibashi, and others assembled together. For Iwanami, sincerity is everything, and I said that Saigō was a fool. He asked, what is so important about this law-abiding spirit? Professor Fujiwara said that the Japanese Army was trouncing the enemy in the Solomon Islands. He says he cannot bear his pleasure over this. Iwanami said with violent anger, "If Japan does not spread righteousness in the world, these victories are worthless." Indeed, this is all simple-minded.

On the 20th I finished writing "A History of Recent Japanese–American Relations." It is about a thousand pages. I still have to make the effort to revise it.

December 22 (Tuesday)

The day before yesterday I had a meeting with Kobayashi Ichizō about writing a history of Tōjō.

Mitsui and Mitsubishi were unable to collect even one million in bank capital funds. These capital funds were water value. The Patriotic Press Association did not come to recruit me.

I heard that Kiyosawa Ichiji, from my native place, has finally been conscripted and is departing on the 23rd. Because he is the only man who is the breadwinner, I can say my family line may be completely destroyed. The problems of trying to increase production are clearly evident even in this one example.

For Ozaki Yukio, the court decided upon penal servitude for eight months for lèse majesté but suspended execution of the sentence for one year.

According to Bertz (a German), the German people do not understand the term "vengeance" of the 47 Ronin. It takes on an unfortunate meaning. He said he changed the term to "duel." Westerners do not understand the *sami-*

sen, and they dislike the sound made with a plectrum. They also do not understand *nagauta*[1] and *gidayu*.[2] He said that compared with these, *yōkyoku*[3] was fine.

December 23 (Wednesday)

I hear that Ōkuma has kindly agreed to write on the Bakumatsu period (1853–1868). At least the Bakumatsu period section will be outstanding.

December 26 (Saturday)

Through yesterday I completed the draft of the "History of Japanese–American Relations." It looks as if the entire work will come to seven hundred pages.

Darlan has been assassinated. The Japanese pity France. However, there is no certainty that France cannot later become the most fortunate country in Europe. France has escaped the disasters of war. History will judge.

A Japanese air raid on Calcutta. According to the newspapers, because of this sort of thing, the Indian people will become attached to Japan. An ideology is difficult to change on the basis of experience.

December 27 (Sunday)

Okamura Kesayoshi was here in the morning, and Kasahara Kiyoaki came in the afternoon.

Because there was no paper for my "History of Japanese–American Relations," Senda of the Kokusaku Kenkyūkai (National Policy Research Society) proposed it be shortened; I am in difficulties because I have already completed the work. He said he would also leave off the index. I am insisting on the original plan.

It has been decided that the Foreign Relations *Chronology* will be issued by the Chūō Kōron Company. There was a telephone call from the head of the publishing department, Fujita, concerning the publication. With this my mind was put to rest.

I have heard that Baba Tsunego receives no communications from the Patriotic Press Association. Both I and Baba are excluded.

Counselor Miyakawa from the Japanese Embassy in the Soviet Union talked on the 25th. He explained that in the collision between the Soviet Union and Germany, the most important problem was that of the power in the Dardanelles Straits. Politically this is certainly true, yet ideologically one cannot omit the power politics and opinions of the Nazis regarding Bolshevism.

The towns and streetcars are full of drunks.

December 28 (Monday)

Wang Ching-wei returned to Nanking. I daresay his visit on this occasion probably concerned the problem of participation in the war. This is what formalism comes to in politics.

Patriotic Press Association! Don't belittle yourself. Solicitations for membership do not come to either me or Baba Tsunego. If we are not critics, who are the critics? Is it possible for these people alone to shoulder the great responsibility of this war?

For three days from the 25th, the thirty seven members of the Increasing Prosperity of Filial Piety Society under the society's leader Minagawa Haruhiro conducted a purification ceremony at dawn. In front of the palace grounds they made up a group in white kimono and white hakama prostrating themselves on the ground. Truly, this had the look of the Bakumatsu Restoration period. At the center was a student from elementary school. He was called Kazama Masamori. I doubt whether this sort of teaching has any kind of influence in Japan.

December 30 (Wednesday)

On the 29th a merger was established of Mitsui, Daiichi, Mitsubishi, and Daihyaku. The Communist movement is succeeding more and more. And it is only one step ahead from here to ownership of the country.

In front of the tobacco shops and train ticket windows there are queues like long snakes.

Why is it that men become drunk and women do not become drunk? In the West this is not always the case. In the evening if one rides the train after 8 P.M. the drunks are many and their messes are everywhere.

1943

January 8 (Friday)

On the 31st I stayed at Atami's Sannō Hotel, and I returned home in the afternoon. The *Japan Times* has changed its name to the *Nippon Times*. The *Tōkyō nichinichi shinbun* (Tokyo daily news) changed to the *Mainichi shinbun* (Daily news). Also, Batavia has changed to Jakarta, and Marei, Malaya, to Marai. This change of names is the easiest sort of self-satisfaction.

Does culture develop on the basis of interchange, or, along with that, does it develop by way of preservation of its purity? If it is the latter, the political strategy of the Nazis is ultimately the best policy. I understand that Germany has already prohibited the literature of Dostoyevsky.

January 11 (Monday)

On the 9th the Nanking government declared war on America and England. It declared Japan's return of such things as foreign settlements and extraterritorial powers. China, without doing a thing about this, obtained the harvest. It is a Chinese victory. Wang Ching-wei with these gifts will be able to return to his former employer at Chungking whenever he wishes. The ignorance of the Japanese government and those related to it is revealed on all sides.

A Japanese interpreter who works at the Italian Embassy asked a high official whether he should translate a telegram from Berlin. He said that he was told, "Have you ever put any faith in a German telegram?" (an actual story of Baba Tsunego).

Ashida Hitoshi, reminiscing about the subject of elections, said, "I have never been pressured by foreign governments. However, the Japanese government attempted to rob me of my political life. I can never forget that fact."

The rows of pine trees along the Tōkaidō are to be cut down (*Central Japan News*). Even the metal strips at the bottom of doors will be commandeered.

The animosity toward the intelligentsia is also an attitude of rejection of scholarship. The truth is that those who do not know critically attack those who do know.

The inadequacies of school education, however, are clear. It is certain that there is the necessity for individual training. University graduates are taught only indulgence.

Yahagi, the chief of the army's Information Board, went to the Uchihara Agriculture Training Center and lectured on political policy to the agricultural villages. What he said was very much to the point. However, formerly this kind of speech properly belonged to the sphere of the premier.

January 12 (Tuesday)

Among the intellectuals, Information Board Vice-Chief Okumura is held in extremely low esteem. Dr. Imai Toshiki (professor at the Imperial University)

personal freedom (*Meiji Political History*, 1:358, 370; 2:130). In the following year, Meiji 14 (1881), Saionji began a newspaper called the *Eastern Liberal News* (*Reformism*, 2:184).

Liberalism 2:245 (Principles of Representative Political Parties), Meiji 23, 8, 23 (August 23, 1890)

Formation of the Rikken Jiyūtō (Constitutional Liberal Party) 2:247. Afterward referred to as Liberal Party (p. 254).

February 2 (Tuesday)

Premier Tōjō, who was bedridden with a cold, got up for a session of the Diet. Tōjō stated that "In war there are two occasions for defeat. The first is when the army and navy are divided, and the second is when popular sentiments are divided. However, one cannot imagine either of these possibilities." And he emphatically stated that even if those who destroy this unity are the highest officials, they cannot be pardoned.

I hear that Tōjō is frequently angry. Even in the Sūmitsuin (Privy Council) he gets angry, and it is said that Minami Jirō stood up and said that everyone has the motive of loyalty. If one relies upon the talk of Lt. General Sakai Kōji, Tōjō loves logic and his mind is fine, but he has the tendency to be excitable.

The newspapers are reporting an extremely serious battle in the South Pacific. Hitherto there has been extreme secrecy about the war, and now desperate battles such as Guadalcanal and New Guinea are being made known by the correspondent of the *Mainichi shinbun*, Kodaki Yūjiro (February 2).

His are precisely the words such as exist in old chronicles.

Yesterday there was a great naval victory off Rennell Island. We should rejoice! We should rejoice!

February 4 (Thursday)

The German Army at Stalingrad has been completely destroyed. In the ten-year commemoration of the Nazis, the dictator Hitler did not appear. The war front in Africa goes badly for the Germans. The English and the Turks have concluded a new alliance.

Premier Tōjō says that Japan will be victorious in war without fail. Yet it appears that among the masses there is still a feeling of uncertainty.

February 5 (Friday)

In the Diet Premier Tōjō stated, "Because I myself have faith in the loyalty of the Japanese people, there is no need for martial law." As for the Diet, it is all followerism, and it talks extravagantly of "rigid enforcement." When one tries looking at rigid enforcement, are the results worthwhile? Why don't they try this in the interests of practical education and see? If one comes this far, whatever one does it is the same. However, under no circumstances will the Diet members probably learn from experience.

February 6 (Saturday)

At the time of the Sino-Japanese War, Foreign Minister Mutsu Munemitsu gave his consent to the English demand that the war not be extended to Shanghai. The fact that China used Shanghai in the war was not criticized.

An account of Lt. General Sakai recently reported that, Hitler met with Ōshima (Hiroshi), Japanese ambassador in Germany. The meeting was unofficial. Hitler reminisced:

1. At the time of Dunkirk he was about to invade England, but he did not have enough ships.
2. He thought about whether or not he should attack Russia. He never thought about anything so much.
3. He did not think that the Allied forces were that weak. He thought Germany would be secure if it were able to stand on its side of the Don. However, even with this it was possible to pursue them.

Rōyama Masamichi returned from the Philippines and there was a warm welcome for him. [He said], (l). this is the degree of peace that will be achieved in the Philippines. The problem is that the free American Army is issuing money in the amount of about 35 million pesos in paper (total currency amount 100,000,005,000 pesos). And this has become the basis for the inflation. (2). Because the great plan of the Greater East Asia Co-prosperity Sphere is not understood, there will be problems.

February 8 (Monday)

It is my fifty-third birthday. In the evening I ate *sekihan* (red rice). How long will I live and what will I do?

I hear that the Foreign Ministry responded to Baron Shidehara (Kijūrō), saying, "The selection of important items in Kiyosawa's *Chronology* is crude." This does not please me, but to me it is a fine gift. In trivial matters I can be extremely inept; however, as a scholar I must be accurate. I intend to try harder.

As to the aforementioned, I pulled out things that should be included in the *Chronology*, and those things that I asked Baron Shidehara about he sent to the Foreign Ministry and requested they be investigated. This was the answer. This is enough to reveal the arrogant attitude of the young people at the Research Office.

I bet Itō Masanori on whether or not Germany will be crushed during the present year.

known cartoon character developed by Watson Inc. called Fluffy Buffy Bear. The park sells a variety of books, stuffed animals, and videos featuring Fluffy Buffy Bear. Due to the park's success, Watson Inc. is considering building another park in Georgia and is conducting confidential market and customer surveys to determine the level of interest in a new park.

Activities.   Identify the trademarks, copyrights, patentable matter, and trade secrets Watson Inc. might own. In what way could Watson Inc. use its character Fluffy Buffy Bear to increase revenue?

ROLE OF PARALEGAL

Because of the increasing array of intellectual property (IP) that can be created in our high-tech society and the increasing ease with which it can be infringed, intellectual property law is a growing practice area. Ten years ago, few law firms had intellectual property law departments, and intellectual property matters were handled by small firms that specialized in the field. Today, nearly every large law firm has a department devoted exclusively to intellectual property, and IP professionals are courted and valued. The *National Law Journal* has reported that attorneys in the field of intellectual property law were the highest paid of all legal specialties. Every legal newspaper and journal contains advertisements for IP paralegals, and in many cases, specialists in the field of intellectual property law are paid more than their counterparts in other fields. For example, the *National Law Journal* reported that compensation for intermediate attorneys in intellectual property was the highest of all practice fields, outstripping some areas by nearly $30,000 annually.

Among the tasks commonly performed by IP paralegals are the following:

- assisting in trademark searching to clear marks for use and preparing, filing, and monitoring trademark registration applications, maintenance, and renewal documents;
- preparing, filing, and monitoring copyright registration applications;
- assisting in patent searching and preparing, filing, and monitoring patent applications;
- drafting license agreements for licensing of trademarks, copyrights, and patents;
- preparing employment agreements and noncompetition agreements;
- assisting in intellectual property audits to determine the extent and value of a client's intellectual property; and
- assisting in protection of trade secrets by developing and implementing policies for protection of trade secrets.

Many of the issues presented in intellectual property law are cutting-edge issues: protection of Internet domain names; copyright piracy on the Internet; downloading of music from Internet file-sharing sites; importation of counterfeited or "knockoff" goods; and development and patenting of wonder drugs. Thus, the field is exciting and presents unique

February 10 (Wednesday)

The vice-chief of the Information Board, Okumura, says that the Japanese propaganda directed overseas goes extremely well. These people are ignorant of the psychology of the enemy, but I think that the self-confidence is on the side of the enemy. We probably do not ever learn anything. It is to be regretted.

Masamune Hakuchō stated, "Writers are a bad lot! I hate to attend their gatherings. The other day I rode in the same automobile with Kikuchi Kan, and for Kikuchi just the fact that in the present war the Philippines became ours is something of great moment. And he said with three or four years of patience America and England would be utterly crushed, and with this he became completely elated."

Masamune said that because writers do things for the sake of their livelihood he could sympathize. However, for people who do no more than this he had no respect.

Miki Kiyoshi also stated, "Writers are awful. What they see is only the emotional side. There is a great deal of talk, but there is nothing to get hold of."

Even an officer such as Homma Masaharu viewed putting women above men with extreme gravity. Under the military administration of the Philippines one of the first things that was done was to stop coeducation. Miki Kiyoshi says, "Spain provided the churches, America provided the schools. And Japan must provide agricultural employment."

February 11 (Thursday)

It is Foundation Day. The rising sun was brilliant. Ah! Heaven! Let Japan be fortunate! Let Japan be great! Let the Imperial Family be eternal! I love my homeland! I have lived, have grown up, and will die only in this country and am tied to its fate!

On the 10th there were two meetings. The first was a regular meeting of the International Relations Research Society. There was a report by Nakajima Kenzō on Malaya.

1. At first we thought of the overseas Chinese merchants as Chinese. As a consequence the fate of a great many people is unclear. And then we demanded a donation of 80 million dollars. This was done on the basis of the ideas of a very small number of people. However, there was no bank. And because there was no way to provide security, this money could not be raised. Even now it is all entangled. This was a defeat. This is a form of wartime taxation.

2. The Malays always ask, (1) When will the military government end?

They feel antipathy to the color khaki. (2) The English made the Malay people English-like. This was a mistake. The Malays say that it would also be a mistake for Japan to make them Japanese-like. They think that having had the medicine effective for the English, this will not necessarily be effective for the Malays.

3. Mitsuchi's view of Premier Tōjō—Tōjō is a charming man. Tōjō likes to appear where he does not have to be. In such places as the Sūmi-tsuin, his anger soars.

February 14 (Sunday)

The newspapers are filled with details of such things as the parachute assault on Palembang and the victory at Singapore. They also include the memoranda of a general called Heath. While other things are suppressed, they like making a great fuss about military successes.

February 17 (Wednesday)

On the 16th I played golf. It's been two months since I last played. The results were not very good. Golf nowadays could be called batting the ball. When I asked how it would be if one called the golf bag a batting-training bag, everyone laughed. Tennis is accepted, and even the English word "tennis" is in the Japanese language. This is the childishness of contemporary ideas.

The fact that Rostov has fallen appeared in Monday's newspapers. After continuing the theme of the subject of the "violent attacks of the German Army" and the "defeat of the Red Army," there is a report such as this.

February 18 (Thursday)

From a speech at Fukuoka on the 17th by chief of the Information Board, Yahagi, it is sufficient to grasp his understanding of America. That is to say, Yahagi misused the statement by Roosevelt to Churchill that "Americans believe in England." He spoke of the "divine wind" and "dark clouds." And if this is made known to England and America by dispatches, they will probably despise Japan.

The students who come to help with the *Chronology* say that a single bowlful of rice does not fill the stomach.

The night before last, when I went to the Enjushun restaurant, I had had only one bowl of rice gruel. Even I returned home and ate again.

The result of investing all effort into vital production has been the regulation of small businesses, and this will produce 170,000–180,000 unemployed people.

February 19 (Friday)

Premier Tōjō stated that in the fall election it would not do to use the nomination system. He also declared that bureaucrats and police could not direct the election. With this government declaration, for the first time there is discussion of this issue. Previously there was not a single person who argued against this. This is "free speech" in Japan.

It appears that Tōjō thinks he should like there to be as much fairness as possible. As regards that, injustice will probably occur in the matter of "maintaining the status quo."

Japan is coming to have the common sense of a primary school student's level. Ah! It is complete foolishness! Given this, if the nation can go on functioning smoothly it will be extraordinary.

Because there was some sort of discussion in the *New York Times* (two or three days ago), in a Diet speech Okumura said it was a technique of the American government to give tacit consent. I realize again how hopelessly stupid he is.

February 20 (Saturday)

The minister of propaganda, Goebbels, gave a speech on the great trials that were coming for the nation (the 18th), and he indicated the threat of Bolshevism. He noted: (1) the fact that Germany will not attack England; (2) the fact that Germany had underestimated the military power of the Soviets was frankly confessed; (3) the fact that Hitler will not prevail for a while. There are many questions here concerning Goebbels having had to make this speech.

The German people know for the first time that even the German Army can be defeated. It is a fact that those things that have been kept secret until now have for the first time been revealed. When this point has been reached, Germany will probably not be able to hold out.

Satō, chief of the Army Affairs Office, as usual took the responses in the Diet seriously. He said that no matter how high the official, he would punish antiwar and antimilitary statements. The military is a dictatorship.

In the central areas of China, progressive warfare has begun. China will probably launch attacks. This will probably require the long presence of several tens of thousands of troops.

In the Diet Greater East Asia Minister Aoki said that Chiang Kai-shek would absolutely not be made an enemy. Premier Tōjō also said that he is only to be subjugated. It appears that China is also saying the same thing. If one reflects upon it, at the time of the Japanese–American negotiations China was most violently opposed to their cooperation.

Consequently, the present war will probably most effectively teach us whether or not military power is able to resolve problems.

February 22 (Monday)

The culture of the *Naniwa-bushi*⁴ is being turned into reality. The Greater East Asian War is the revenge idea of the *Naniwa-bushi* culture. The newspapers call America *Meriken* and England *Anguro*, and again, during the Washington trip of Madame Chiang Kai-shek they made every sort of insulting report. They think this sort of thing is necessary to the success of the war.

Why is it impossible to fight in the interests of high ideals; to appeal to the world masses and to reason? Alas!

Yesterday's *Asahi* had a critique of my *History of Japanese Foreign Relations* by Furukaki. Half of it was approving and half was disparaging. In the final analysis it is a fact to say that the things related to America were of insufficient depth.

Trees everywhere are being cut down with abandon. It is for the purpose of building boats. When something is begun, the ones who always carry it to extremes are the Japanese. Even now there is danger that they will do things without considering mechanical power and other things. There probably will be floods. Indiscriminate deforestation will probably occur.

Investigate it scientifically! What quantity is necessary?

February 25 (Thursday)

The Greater East Asia minister, Aoki, and the chief of the Military Affairs Office, Satō, made statements in yesterday's Diet and announced, "Respecting the independence and original ideas of the Nationalist Government, there will be no interference in its internal administration." Satō said, "America also is without war objectives." Why such statements are made I do not understand, but

1. The opposition of China continues, and this is an extremely troublesome matter.

2. The fact is that there is the question whether in the responses and questions from the Wang government on the Nationalist flag problem there was a backlash.

3. The fact that America is a powerful enemy is probably at last fully clear. If an appropriate political policy had been taken from the beginning, both the China Incident would have been settled and the Greater East Asia War would probably not have occurred. Because they lack understanding until there is an encounter with reality, I am terribly worried. Of late, if one discusses this only the weak points appear.

The Greater East Asia War is the triumph of feudalism over enlighten-mentism.

There is a small magazine called *Chikakiyori* (The contemporary scene), put out by a lawyer named Masaki Hideri. The January and February issues are surprisingly antimilitary, cynical things. The existence of something that goes this far in wartime circumstances is amazing, and one should be aston-ished at the courage of the person who wrote it. He is a born democrat, and his writing is extremely skillful.

March 2 (Tuesday)

Two or three days ago I visited Baron Shidehara.

1. Someone in the Kizokuin (House of Peers) inquired of the foreign minister, Tani Masayuki, about the existence or nonexistence of postwar plans. Tani said he was in the midst of vigorously studying this. The same question was put to the Greater East Asia minister, Aoki. He colored, and it is said he answered, "How can there be postwar plans while we are now in the midst of war?"

2. The wife of old Prince Matsukata Masayoshi frequently talked to Baron Shidehara about her discomfort at the dances of the Rokumeikan[5] period. It was very hard to attend these when everyone else was in bed.

3. Shidehara, an intimate of Denison, related his (Denison's) account of a trip to Egypt and back. He reported that until the time of the Sino-Japanese War it was worrisome to speak of a right wing and a left wing; rather, there was the confrontation of a National Essence party and a Pro-gressive party. However, with the Sino-Japanese War they became con-joined. It was exactly like the two branches of the Nile converging at Khar-toum and from this flowing to the Lower Delta. On the one side there was greenness because of the living things, and on the other side there was the whiteness of the minerals. In just this way Japan was joined together. Be-cause Denison also said he regretted the Westernism of Japan, he resem-bles Boissonade.

March 4 (Thursday)

Anger is being inculcated in every direction toward America and England. The *Mainichi shinbun* reported that the ladies of Otemachi in Akita ken made effigies of Churchill and Roosevelt, and girls and little children pierced them with spears. These are merely feudal ideas of revenge and not at all a new world order. People with no better ideas than these lead the nation.

On the other hand, the shift of political policy toward China is complete. Is there any difference in this from liberal foreign relations?

March 10 (Wednesday)

I heard a discussion of Maeda, who was a special correspondent of the *Asahi* newspaper.

    1. The foreign minister of Turkey had an interview with Ambassador Kurihara Tadashi and said that the Axis countries have no chance of winning. He said how would it be if Japan (1) returned Singapore to England, and (2) returned the Philippines to America?

    2. There were negotiations by the Turks to sell quinine to Japan. Japan raised problems about the price and all sorts of other things. Thereupon American Ambassador [to Turkey 1942–1945] Laurence Steinhart paid the entire amount to the Turks under his own name for American use.

    3. The war will reach its peak in August or September.

    4. Italy will not yet fall into ruin. The reason is that opponents of Mussolini have not appeared. Genoa and Milan are completely in ruins. Moreover, before the war Italy only had 30 million tons of oil. Now there is probably nothing left.

March 14 (Sunday)

The Foreign Relations *Chronology* is making progress. Perseverance will conquer. From every direction people are coming to us spontaneously. Due to the illness of Hirukawa of the Meiji section, a person under Ōkuma named Onitsuka (Masaji) had kindly taken on the task.

    This morning's newspaper says that the enemy will probably be sending air raids from the continent. As to that, how do they propose to destroy the enemy?

    Each day I fret about the ignorant so-and-so's whose conduct of politics have brought us to this point.

March 16 (Tuesday)

In the evening paper I learned that Premier Tōjō went to Nanking. The reason was a return courtesy for the Japanese visit of Wang Ching-wei. However, talks have already been concluded on the unconditional return of foreign settlements, and probably he went for the purpose of negotiations and conciliatory diplomacy toward China.

    The most important points are that, although Tōjō conducts actual foreign relations, it is a fact that he will inescapably make such concessions, and circumstances have been pushed to this point. I hope that on the basis of this the people will become a little wiser intellectually. However, politically speaking, on the basis of this China only brings out the Japanese weak points, and it is clear that there will be no effect of any kind.

March 17 (Wednesday)

Tokutomi Sohō explains the true nature of the Anglo-Saxons in the *Mainichi* newspaper. I agree with this man's discussion of Japanese history, but how well does he understand Anglo-Saxons?

However, he still writes interesting things (*Mainichi*, March 17).

In the past wasn't he an exponent of Europeanization?

An account of Horiuchi Kensuke (recently, the first part of the present month).

> The emperor deigned to speak with Premier Tōjō, stating, "Ambassador Ariyoshi told me that the Westerners in China all devoured the feast on the plate. However, the Japanese even ate the plate." Deeply impressed, Tōjō took himself home and, assembling high-ranking officials, transmitted the imperial will and announced a change in Japanese China policy.

At any rate, if it is unavoidable to make such concessions, then the current concessions will probably have to be recognized. However, referring to the emperor in a shift of political policy—something also frequently done in the Diet—is extremely risky. Is this not a reverential return of responsibility to the emperor?

March 18 (Thursday)

Advisers have been established in the Cabinet. All of them are businessmen, and, moreover, the youngest of these is Toyoda Teijirō, who is fifty-nine. Where does the world of the "young" exist nowadays?

At the same time it shows clearly that the attempt to carry out the dream of bureaucratic absolutism has failed. However, it is also clear that with the impoverishment of the people and the enrichment of the few, the opportunity for revolution is being invited. The fate of this country will not be peaceful.

An investigation system that I previously advocated in *Chūgai*[6] has been implemented.

March 20 (Saturday)

I have heard that in America they have set up meetings on Thursdays to discuss postwar affairs. If one discusses postwar matters in Japan, one is criticized as being a defeatist, or one may be punished.

This morning's *Yomiuri* took up the problem of Jewish financial power in America. The simpleminded who divide the world into Jews and anti-Jews are incapable of any solution at all. Those who talk about the Jewish question are those who are unable to discuss world problems in their complex forms. This crowd states that Morgenthau (treasury secretary) forcibly led America into war. It is because there are simplistic theories such as these that we are in trouble.

March 22 (Monday)

It is said that the American war costs for one day are 250 million dollars.

After a long absence, Hitler returned to Berlin and delivered a speech. The fact that he has not appeared publicly has generated various rumors. This is the first time since November 8 of last year. According to him, the total German Army casualties were 542,000. One wonders how the German people now listen to the words of Hitler. I would like to know that.

In our country we are taught how to hate the enemy. For example, the Stars and Stripes is trampled underfoot. The objectives of the war must be more elevated than such emotions. With antiquated ideas of revenge, it is not possible to establish a new world order. It will serve no purpose if there is not the establishment of high ideals and if America obstructs the realization of these ideals.

The newspaper dispatches every day are reporting that Anglo-American meetings concerning the postwar are progressing. This, despite the fact that Japan and Germany are still fighting.

March 23 (Tuesday)

Yesterday evening there was a conference of the Foreign Relations *Chronology*, and Takeuchi Katsumi was in charge. This man at least is a person of talent. Also attending were such people as Nobuo, Tamura, and Yoneda.

In the *Mainichi* newspaper a certain lt. general discussed his ideals on the war. It is fine if such people discuss matters of actual warfare. This is because they are specialists. However, what are their qualifications for discussing ideals? The low quality of ideas at present is because of such leaders.

April 7 (Wednesday)

During the period March 23 to April 4, I stayed in Shikoku. I gave lectures on behalf of the Communications Ministry and the Economic Club.

On the trains it was truly impossible to have lunch. Fortunately, I was carrying bread and I ate that. At a first-class inn at Matsuyama—called Kidoya— and the place where Soseki visited, I was unable to have lunch.

Among the towns in Shikoku, Matsuyama, Kōchi, Tokushima, and Taka-matsu are all castle towns and they have a planned quality. I discovered that even the Japanese have a capacity for planning. The scale is small, though.

April 10 (Saturday)

Nakamura, a Chūō University student, has returned from China. He said that anti-Japanese feeling in China, especially North China, is widespread. He said that in Peking it is dangerous for a man to walk alone at night, and the railway at Shan-hai-kuan, Tientsin, is always blocked. In the case of Hsu-chou, he said, old people and children are killed and their flesh eaten.

April 23 (Friday)

Karasawa Toshiki has been elected to the office of vice-chief of home affairs and Machimura to chief of the Police Bureau. I am acquainted with both men. Both of them are excellent gentlemen. They are open-minded. The best thing is the fact that Okumura has resigned.

April 24 (Saturday)

Okabe Nagakage of anti–metric law fame became minister of education. This is the sort of recruitment typical of Tōjō. His opposition only to metric laws shows the trivialism of the man. He is formalistic and cherishes the past. The Education Ministry is full of nonprofessionals. This is so of General Araki and even so of Hashida Kunihiko. I cannot help worrying about the interests of the nation. But I am helpless.

It is reported in this morning's newspapers that because on April 18 of last year Japan gave the death sentence to the Americans who bombed the impe-rial capitol, America is saying that Japan was barbarian. And so it appears that protest, objection has come. How the public opinion of America and others is worsening can be imagined. It is just like the hostility toward Germany in the previous First World War. How all-important this public opinion is for the final completion of the war, the present leadership does not comprehend at all. This is because there is only "powerism."

In Japan, writings on the outbreak of the war cannot be published, and also regarding such things as the prisoner of war problem the people are denied all knowledge. And yet the newspapers attack the secretiveness of America. I wonder if this is the level of knowledge of the Japanese masses?

In a new age, protection of free speech must become the foundation of government.

April 30 (Friday)

• The morning radio becomes more and more vulgar day by day, and its foolishness is enormous. No! It is only the repetition of this kind of thing. Yesterday morning the one named Kakei Katsuhiko performed a sort of prayer. At the beginning he read a prayer, and then later he ended by calling out three times, "Growing prosperity," "Growing prosperity," "...." This is the behavior of the leadership of fanatics.

There is a limit to spiritualism. Even if one says that one has penetrated the spirit, after the penetration, as there is no concrete plan of what to do, it comes to nothing. With this we are brought to a standstill.

• It has been decided that my *History of Japanese–American Relations* will be put out by Nihon Hyōronsha (Japan Review Company). Previous arrangements were completed on the 28th.

• With the help of Kiyosawa Satoru we rebuilt the roof.

This, the world of stars, anchors, face, black market, and queues.

A ditty that is circulating says, "In this society there is nothing but the army, the navy, the big shots, and the black market. It is only fools who stand in lines."

It is reported that the Soviet Union has cut off its diplomatic relations with Poland. The Soviet can also see the omens of war, and it is disadvantageous that she be restricted by the problems of Poland's national boundaries. In this she probably thinks the assistance of England and America will not be enough. These are the reasons there is the muddle.

May 1 (Saturday)

The Japanese people are too nervous in considering diplomatic problems. International relations are not something that shifts and changes from right to left with such speed. With respect to the aggravation of Soviet–Polish relations, Mutō Sadaichi is already thinking of anti-Soviet strategies. Didn't this man think that Japan, having taken Singapore previously, would be able forcibly to humble England and America?

Tani has become ambassador to China. Yukawa has been elected to the House of Peers. This is a victory of the Tōjō group, and this is a Tōjō personnel arrangement. As usual, Tokutomi Sohō is engaged in attacks on England. I will not discuss the contents. I merely doubt he has the qualifications to discuss England. The arguments of people such as he do not buy the favor of the world. There is no need to say that Tokutomi has the greatest responsibility for the war.

ROLE OF PARALEGAL (cont'd)

opportunities for learning and growth. Additionally, there is a great deal of client contact, and playing a part in a client's selection of a new name or mark for a product, bringing a new product to market, and protecting that property from infringement or misappropriation by others is interesting and exciting.

Along with these unique opportunities for learning and growth come concomitant duties of ethics and confidentiality. In many instances, clients disclose highly confidential information to attorneys and paralegals. Plans for marketing, newly discovered inventions, new product names, new songs, methods of doing business, and plans to sue another company for infringement may be disclosed by clients so that the legal team can help obtain protection for the client. Although it may be tempting to share such interesting information with others, attorneys and paralegals are under strict ethical duties to maintain the confidentiality of client work. They must not take files home from the office without appropriate notice or permission, discuss confidential client matters in social settings or even in office building elevators, or leave files where they are accessible by others. When in doubt, they should avoid disclosure.

In sum, intellectual property is a growing, exciting, and dynamic area, offering unique opportunities and challenging work. The field changes on nearly a daily basis, the issues are interesting, and IP paralegals are valued members of a legal team devoted to ensuring that clients receive the broadest possible scope of protection for their creative assets.

INTERNET RESOURCES

Federal statutes governing intellectual property:	http://www.ll.georgetown.edu and http://www.findlaw.com
Trademark and patent information, forms, and fees:	http://www.uspto.gov
Copyright information, forms, and fees:	http://www.loc.gov/copyright
International treaties and agreements:	http://www.wipo.org
General information on intellectual property topics:	http://www.findlaw.com and http://www.megalaw.com

Tokutomi Sohō and Miyake Setsurei have received an award from the Geijutsuin (The Arts Center).

And now Hasegawa and Baba are hard-pressed to survive.

May 2 (Sunday)

The enemy countries make intense use of each and every one of those who are well-versed in the affairs of Japan. For example, there are such cases as the use of Grew and Dooman, former counsellor to the American Embassy in Japan, as minister to the embassy in Moscow. Japan keeps such people at arm's length.

May 3 (Monday)

The naming of the Aleutian Island Attu as Atsuka and Kiska as Narugamijima is based upon bureaucratic thought patterns that rejoice in changing names and is evidence again of not treating the war seriously.

Shiba Sometarō hoped to travel to the Philippines but was stopped midcourse. If one relies upon what has been recently revealed since he was an officer of the Rotary Club, it is said he was opposed by the military, who thought him an American supporter. I was told this story yesterday by the said gentleman, who had come down from the countryside. It is rare that such people as the aforementioned gentleman are "nationalists." They are old-type patriots, and to criticize such people because of their stance is formalistic. I wonder why Japan does not make use of America specialists with regard to America?

Compared with the enemy, which uses Cripps and Grew, which makes use of anybody who has knowledge, on this point it is to be regretted: we are inferior.

May 11 (Tuesday)

It is said that Easter ceremonies have been revived in the Soviet Union. This indicates the defeat of ideology and the triumph of traditional customs. It is the liberation of the people.

May 15 (Saturday)

On the 12th I heard a lecture by Ambassador Nomura. He said that until about August or September the United States was eager to negotiate. It was a talk at the University Professors' League. Afterward, Nomura said to Professor Komatsu, referring to me, "Because this man is an American specialist he probably thinks, 'The speaker is just telling us a story.'" His mind is excellent and it is obvious that he is already above the crowd. He probably has a future.

The Axis armies have withdrawn from northern Africa. Both the telegrams from Germany and the public discussion here write about this as if it were a preplanned movement. War is something that at great effort brings forth rationalizations. Such a young critic of military affairs as the one named Saitō Tadashi was wrong even from the beginning in his observations, yet he is, naturally, still popular. Consequently we grasp the general trend of the times.

The newspapers are transmitting reports of the invasion of Attu Island by the enemy's army. It is a matter of enormous sacrifices. Previously it was ordered that Attu be changed to Atsuka and Kiska to Narugami-jima, and in the statements of Imperial Headquarters these names were used. Now it is still reported as Attu Island! These are probably conclusions assuming the time when the island is retaken.

It reveals the childish delight in changing names. Those with the intelligence of children are conducting politics!

The leader of the Axis armies in North Africa received a testimonial and has been made Field Marshall. This is General Arnim. I daresay that he has probably been specially elevated. This is the psychology of Westerners, but on our side even the newspapers do not write anything at all about this.

May 16 (Sunday)

In the morning Kanō (of the Higashi Chōfu Police Department) came to call. It was because he wanted to discuss the outcome of the Tunisian battlefront. They probably selected men to be asked these questions. I told him that (1) there was no chance of peace between Germany and England, America and the Soviet; (2) consequently the fighting would continue; (3) however, a nation, like a human being, has limits of endurance; (4) and, after all, Germany will be defeated; (5) and this would be the climax of the year.

According to him, the right wing is saying, "Tōjō is just like Konoe. He probably won't last longer than this year." The right wing is dissatisfied with such things as extraterritoriality power rights in China. Again he said, "If the young naval clique relied upon the declarations of Tōjō, a withdrawal from even Kainan Island would come about." Saying this was regrettable, they made a proposal to the chief of the Military Affairs Bureau, and the chief of the Military Affairs Bureau told this to Minister Shimada Shigetarō, and he conveyed this to Tōjō.

I hear that Yamauchi went out in the usual kimono and was forced to return home and change into *mompei* (trousers). Eiko goes about wearing pants. Schoolgirls' clothing is best for movement. Can Japan be rescued from its formalism?

May 17 (Monday)

Yesterday, besides Mr. and Mrs. Obama Toshie, such people as Mrs. Kataoka and Mrs. Okamura Kesayoshi came to visit and there was much commotion. We served strawberries that had been grown in the family vegetable garden.

1. According to the tale of Kataoka, industrial workers are working as much as twenty hours a day.
2. The heavy industries are far behind the textile industry. The textile industry will not accept impossible assignments. However, the heavy industries are made to accept such assignments, and in consequence, working beyond their capacity, there is no rise in their efficiency.

We see through the nationally prescribed textbooks that the Mombusho has no fixed views and staggers about (Tōkyō nichinichi, May 17).

May 20 (Thursday)

They say that the wheat harvest is extremely bad. It is said that at best the production decrease is 30 percent and generally it is 50 percent.

The distress of food problems. In the history of the world is there an instance of the government of a single country falling into the hands of such a group of low-grade, stupid people?

In an account of Professor Tanaka Kōtarō, who has returned from China, as for the Chinese people, even more important than what they say about the abolition of extraterritoriality in actuality is their hope to be able to get food. Last year in the neighborhood of Shanghai thirteen or fourteen hundred regularly died of starvation. This was the account of Tachibana.

The Town Council Bureau of Tōkyō City gave a banquet of thanks. Although of late I have been ignored in such things, I did participate in the banquet. At the gathering there were remarks from someone connected with the Ministry of Education. He said, "Country people are saying that as regards the change of course in Guadalcanal, the excuses of the military are excessive. Why is the government incapable of trust in the Japanese people?"

It is said that on the island of Attu there are ten of the enemy to one of us, and they have five hundred aircraft. In a lecture at the Japan Club, Commander Akiyama said, "The Japanese Army is falling into isolated helplessness." Why do the authorities not increase provisions adequately? However, it is a fact that the destruction en route by submarines is considerable, and the soldiers occupying the island have only the military equipment they brought at the beginning. I sympathize with the desperateness of their fight. Ah! Whose crime is this?

May 21 (Friday)

I asked Tamura Kōsaku to look at the Taishō section of the *Chronology*. Indeed, he is meticulous and has an excellent memory. He made various suggestions.

In a talk with Onizuka Shoji he said that at a lecture meeting of the Foreign Office, Yasuoka Masanori stated, "No matter where the Japanese go, they are thoroughly hated. After a decade problems will probably arise again." I wonder if the thing known as Imperial Way-ism of Japan engenders the admiration of a single foreigner? What comes of preaching the sermons in the style of Kakei[7] by those who go to foreign countries?

May 22 (Saturday)

Yesterday there was the report of the battle death of Admiral Yamamoto. I talked with Usui Yae and the principal of the elementary school in Shinshū, Kamiya, at the Japan Club. Learning of this in front of the Asahi Newspaper Building, we were aghast.

Of late there has not been such momentous news. Yamamoto was opposed to the Japanese–American war. As vice-minister of the navy he rashly resisted the army's war on American leadership, and for a time he was even called unpatriotic. He publicly opposed the army. However, once national policy had been settled he would fight without protest and launched the opening attack, that is to say, joining what was to him a detestable conflict. According to the story of a schoolgirl en route by bus to play golf, her mother learned of Yamamoto's death on the radio and was unable to eat her supper. According to Akira's account, the radio announcer finally broke into tears. The Jiyū Gakuen (Liberal Academy) student who reported the incident said she also broke into tears. Thus one can grasp the feelings of the people. As to these reactions, together with the preceding Guadalcanal and Attu reverses, there is widespread sentiment of dark foreboding about the future course of the war.

To Masamune Hakuchō, country scenery is splendid. Even though he has lost a child, he accepted it fatalistically. He said that the Japanese people are not anxious about the future course of the war. I think this is probably so. The stupid Japanese people have a kind of fatalism.

May 23 (Sunday)

It is said that Yamamoto's shrine will be erected at Nagaoka.

"He shouldered the responsibilities of the nation, and even when confronted by an army of one million he did not complain."

How does the army, which only complains, view this? What do they think about this? This expresses popular sentiment regarding Yamamoto and also popular sentiment regarding the navy.

In the *Yomiuri* a lt. general named Nakai Ryōtarō said, "Emphasize leadership in soldier power." He argued, "Military rule puts aside the liberalistic constitutional theory, which is not pervasive among the people, and military rule exercises leadership in total war mobilization." We have never had such military leadership as we do now, and yet, if it is still said that this is not sufficient, then there are weak points in the fundamentals. However, for this man there is absolutely no such self-reflection.

Among the people we have known, there is no single brilliant America specialist who has served in the role of government adviser. Each and every consultant is someone who has previously come to his own personal conclusions. This being so, they are incapable of correctly interpreting the state of affairs. This selection of advisees is the greatest weak point of the Greater East Asian War.

Of the detained anti-American activist residents in America, there are 2,199 Japanese, 1,715 Germans, and 242 Italians. This is sufficient to understand that there are a larger number of Japanese detainees in proportion to Japanese residents.

May 24 (Monday)

The novel *Sasameyuki*[8] (Tanizaki Junichirō) in *Chūō kōron* has been very popular, but its continued publication in the magazine has been stopped. There was a publisher's announcement stating, "Viewed from the standpoint of the various demands of the present decisive stage of war, considering that it may exert undesirable influences, we are sorry but we cannot continue it" (the June number).

The death of Admiral Yamamoto was an extreme shock. However, the constant repetition morning and night in the newspapers and radio is rather disgusting. The present leadership does not understand psychology. However, the great mass of the people might just prefer it this way.

Starting with the right of supreme command, we will end with the resolution of the right of supreme command. We are not formalistic. However, the need for formalism is particularly true in a country that cannot change with the times. The authority of supreme command is an example.

It is a problem of morale. In this Japan is completely deadlocked.

The officials of the Interior Ministry are changing quickly. Even if someone like myself lives an entire lifetime, I will not fully comprehend a single problem. What does this crowd understand?

A communiqué from Lisbon reports that Roosevelt previously requested the loan of a Siberian airfield from Stalin. A communiqué from Berlin also smacked of such matters, but it is probably German propaganda. The ignorance of the Japanese might seize upon this. Or else, it may be the propaganda of the Japanese themselves. Beginning with Ōshima there is a large element that hopes for a war against the Soviet.

May 25 (Tuesday)

Yesterday at the International Relations Research Society meeting Inui Tadao read a plan for a new world order. This is a new world order plan centered upon the East Asian Co-prosperity Sphere. It appears that in no quarter was anyone impressed with it. That is to say, it is because circumstances are difficult. It is fine to seek to liberate the world, but if that be the case, is it possible to recognize the independence of all races in East Asia? For example, if as a result of a popular ballot the Koreans desired independence, then what?

At least the left wing carries on research. Even in their historical research they enter unexplored lands. From the materialist point of view. However, as regards the right wing, they do no research whatsoever. They do not contribute a single thing to world culture.

May 26 (Wednesday)

Because the Ina-sun Education Society of Shinshū wished to invite Fuse Katsuji, I conveyed the request to him yesterday while we were having lunch together. Previously the Thursday Society had invited Admiral Yamamoto Isoroku when he became vice-minister of the Navy, and we were invited to the party where he gave his greetings, saying, "Here I am with my undistinguished face." At that time I also delivered a salutation.

A close friend of Mitsui named Kodera reported, "Businessmen are saying that the observations of scholars are totally worthless." It is not that the scholars are worthless, but that those who behave as scholars are worthless.

On the 25th at the Yokohama Municipal Park Concert Hall, Yahagi, chief of the Information Board, lectured on the theme that the victory of the Axis side was certain, and if the war continued at length, all the better. The points he made were, "The production level of America is 60 percent of what they say." "The fact that aircraft accidents were constantly occurring in America was a result of the mental inferiority of the workers, and by such defective products they intentionally reveal their opposition to the war." "Soldiers are not tools but spirit! They are souls! American soldiers are crudely made and overproduced." "The present year is the peak of America's production." What Board Chief Yahagi said about the problems of rubber and quinine was the same thing said before the war by the military and by Nakano Shōgō. Indeed, ensuing realities will probably reveal whether or not these opinions are correct.

May 27 (Thursday)

I wrote a letter to Admiral Koga (commander of the Combined Fleet). It was for the purpose of encouragement.

Kasahara Seimei says that the allotments to such things as restaurants will probably disappear in the fall of this year. It may be so.

The Russian Revolution came because of a food famine. This is also true of the First World War in Germany. Is there any assurance that if the same fate came to Japan, riots would not occur? In any case, revolutionary changes will not be avoided.

May 30 (Sunday)

In the *Jikyoku zasshi* (Current affairs journal) a man named Nomura Shigeomi said that my *History of Foreign Relations* stated the opinions of America and England, and we must generate intellectual plurality domestically. He does not indicate the whys and wherefores of his criticism. Where is the proof that his viewpoint is correct? If it can be said that my viewpoint is more Japanese, is it not a different viewpoint? The problem is, will Japan be made great by his ideology? The people responsible for the war are of this type. However, the right wing, for the time being, necessarily thrives.

The Komazawa Golf Course has become a training ground for soldiers. I hear that previously they asked permission. Now they do not. After the soldiers rest there are cigarette butts and bits of paper scattered everywhere. Golf course employees cleaned up these messes. Thus, even though this is done, golf approximates a social crime.

Since there is pause in my work, I am reading a book on golf. *Talks on the History of Japanese Foreign Relations*, by Kyoguchi Motokichi, is extremely interesting. He has written a great deal on things unknown to me. To be exhaustively informed in history is especially difficult. Where do Nomura Shigeomi and others of that crowd obtain such definitive judgments?

May 31 (Monday)

Yesterday there was a report that the entire Japanese Army on Attu died with honor. It was a public announcement by the Imperial Headquarters at 5:00 P.M. When one looked at this morning's newspapers it was stated that at the end around 150 or 160 survived; the wounded killed themselves, and those still able fought savagely and died. If this were not something related to the military, questions would arise and probably become social problems.

1. If one relies upon a communiqué of the Information Board chief, Yahagi, he said that the head of the same military force, General Yamazaki,

did not request the aid of even a single soldier more. Why didn't headquarters voluntarily send reenforcements?

2. It was to be expected that the Japanese would know what the enemy would do. This is particularly so regarding the extensive preparations in Alaska. That being the case, why were they left isolated and helpless just as they were, without any prior or later assistance in this regard?

3. For an army renowned throughout the world for its incomparable courage, is not this total destruction a defeat in terms of strategy?

4. As there is no criticism of strategy, it becomes a matter of no self-criticism at all, and consequently it is perfectly reasonable that so many failures occur.

5. The one that will come next is Kiska. It is said that there is roughly one entire division there. Dying-with-honorism will probably rob these people of their lives. Is this beneficial to the nation? Hereafter, on this point, there will be inevitable problems. However, this sort of matter will not become a question for the masses in general. Ah! The benighted masses.

The English Labour party rejected the entrance of the Communist party by a vote of fifteen to two. For the thought style that talks about liberalism as the hotbed of the Communist party, does this not reveal some sort of commentary?

Don't create so many military martyrs! The commander of the Amazaki corps, Field Marshall Yamamoto, the coxswain Sakuma, the Nine Martyrs of Hawaii, each and every one, must be regretted. These show the severity of warfare.

June 1 (Tuesday)

The sacrifices on Attu are sad. I feel uneasy in a different sense. The more the war turns against us, pressure throughout the country will probably intensify.

Every newspaper is full of statements declaring "Revenge!" "Send Military Equipment to Achieve Revenge!" (*Mainichi* editorial), "Remember May 29!" (*Yomiuri*).

June 3 (Thursday)

Morning, there was a speech by Tokutomi Sohō on the radio. He said that Perry had the intention of occupying Japan. Building such an image of him is preposterous. He said thanking Roosevelt for his intervention in the Russo-Japanese War was a foolish thing. America is a war-loving nation. America is a country without benevolence or virtue. The content of his talk consisted of such judgments.

He also lectured recently, at the time of the death of Admiral Yamamoto, and now it is the age of the Tokutomis. Tokutomi is a counterfeit scholar and a social flatterer. He is one of the greatest deceivers of Japan.

It is a fact that in the Meiji Government, "Even those who were outcasts, if they repaid their crimes, the government dealt with them reasonably and justly" (*History of the People*, contemporary period, Iwakura's letter). Because of this such people as Enomoto were pardoned. In the Shōwa Restoration—in the period of the Greater East Asian War—one absolutely could not be pardoned.

June 12 (Saturday)

I went on a lecture tour to Ōsaka, Kobe, Nagoya, and Kyoto and returned home on the 11th. At the same time I had a meeting with Kobayashi Ichizō.

1. First of all I was surprised at the maldistribution of commodities in the Ōsaka area. Some things are abundant. Exports have stopped and nothing is sent to regions within the country.

2. There is no sugar in the hotels. There is no salt. This is common in the first-class hotels. There is no butter in the Oriental Hotel. Those who eat near me spit up phlegm and it is unpleasant. It is a world completely ignorant of politeness, of manners.

3. In Ikeda city there are no postcards. I couldn't find any ordinary postcards. I feel there is widespread sloppiness among people.

4. A relatively large number of people attended the lecture meeting. Without stating any conclusions, I talked about the international situation centering upon the European war. Because there were business people in the audience it seems they did understand the basic things I was saying.

5. A man named Mutō Sadaichi put forth a fulsome attack on mission schools and Christianity in the *Yomiuri shinbun*. In the Soviet Union worship is allowed and freedom of religion exists. Is it likely that at this time he intends to stir up unrest in Japan? A person like Mutō is an originator of the war. What is the *Yomiuri* doing honoring such people? (It is said he also attacked Rikkyō University.)

It is said that Kawamura Yūsen is saying that the students of the Business School of Aoyama Gakuin generated a strike. It is said that the personal activities of the school's principal Sasamori lean too much toward Christianism. It is said that he tried to stop the students but had a heart attack and died as a result—the igniting of Christian prohibition—an ideological expression of the Greater East Asian War. Mutō attack (*Yomiuri hōchi*, "The Japanese Sword," June 12).

A speech by Kobayashi Ichizō related, "When I was acting as minister, a commander of the navy came to me and stated, 'Kindly carry out your intentions. We will by all means back you.' Because of this relationship with the navy we became aggressive on the problem of the vice-ministership of Kishi.

However, as the problem progressed the navy pulled out completely. In such a situation it appears they think it would be unpleasant to have a direct confrontation with the army.

"I intended to impeach the 'reds' in the Privy Council. That is to say, someone was made to ask, 'Is it true that Kobayashi is evading taxes?' With this I was determined to expose, root and branch, a secret red plot before his Majesty. As regards this, Ikeda did not approve and nobody else endorsed it either.

"Because I judged that the situation was worsening, I proposed my resignation to Konoe. He asked me if I preferred membership in the House of Peers or the Privy Council. I said that having to attend the Privy Council frequently would present difficulties. It is a fact that I wanted to retire."

The industrialists on the whole firmly believe the current power structure is "red," and they move on the basis of its instructions.

June 13 (Sunday)

According to the *Mainichi shinbun*, in the locale of Karuizawa they are repossessing the golf course, and it appears that they are trying to open up the villas to industrial workers. If they were to be for the wounded one could understand, but what are they doing giving these to workers? In accordance with the deepening of the war, one sees "revolutionary" signs. That is to say, it is "red." Someone like Representative Koyama Ryō is typical of this. It is the left wing turning into the right wing.

In Kansai one sees signs that for the ordinary stores "Business hours will be from 8:00 A.M. to 5:00 P.M.," but these limits did not apply in the case of urgent business. It is the bureaucratization of small businessmen.

It is said that the enemy is reporting that Admiral Yamamoto committed suicide. Because of defeat after defeat—this is what they say—he is alleged to have killed himself.

Suzuki, president of the Planning Board, has investigated the industrial world of Tōkyō and Yokohama, and his report was published this morning (May 12 to 20). He stated, "There is the necessity for a greater degree of effort" in the matter of strengthening the sense of official responsibility in pursuit of realizing a planned economy.

The Italian island of Pantelleria has fallen. The island of Sicily will probably be next. Prospects for Italy's survival are dim, and it is probably already only a question of time. Italy has been at war for three years. One can see in communiqués their "reconfirmation" of the continuation of the war. Reconfirmation!

During my trip the trains were always late. The special expresses were always thirty minutes to an hour late.

I contented myself with a meal of rationed rice and, on the way to Kyoto, May rain.

DISCUSSION QUESTIONS

1. Indicate whether the following items would be protectable as trademarks, copyrights, patents, or trade secrets:

   a vacuum cleaner

   the name of a new type of ice cream

   a company's plans for its future business operations and possible mergers

   a new type of rose

   a new slogan to be used by Burger King

   a new novel by Toni Morrison

2. McDonald's Corporation has filed a trademark application for MCMAGIC MIXERS for new condiment blends. How long will federal protection for this mark last?

3. A patent was issued on January 28, 2003, to Hoffman-LaRoche Inc. for a new type of compound to treat Alzheimer's disease. The application was filed on August 10, 2000. How long will patent protection for this invention last?

4. The novel *Moby Dick* was written in 1851 and its author, Herman Melville, died in 1891. Can a sequel based on the novel be written by another author? Why?

5. The song "Allentown" was composed by Billy Joel in 1982. How long will protection for this song last?

6. In what way do file-sharing services, such as Kazaa, pose a threat to artists and composers?

For additional resources, go to www.westlegalstudies.com.

The cessation of publications continues. Many publications that I received—the May issue of the *Trade Control Society Proceedings*, the April issue of the *Proceedings* of the *Yūsen kaisha*, *Hokoku*, the *Ōsaka biru*—have all been discontinued.

Mito Nariaki said burn European writing and control scholars (Mito Han Collection, 1:214). Should we imitate this today?

June 14 (Monday)

I went to play golf. The Komazawa Golf Course has been turned into a training ground for soldiers and youth organizations. Moreover, it is said that they make use of it without the slightest consultation and without permission. Consequently, the cleaning up is done by the members.

Yesterday Toyota Norio came to call. I hear that Wang Ching-wei is incorruptible, but the administration of the rest of the government is corrupt and venal. When one tries looking into a certain incident, such people as Wang's wife Chen Pi-chun and Hsiu Fo-hai are at the center of it, and it is impossible to advance the investigation.

It is being rumored by *Dōmei* that Premier Tōjō's trip to Nanking was because Hata was having conferences regarding the next premier. What was being heard throughout the country was that because the military on the scene was discontented about such matters as the elimination of extrality and the abolition of foreign settlements, he went there to control the military.

On one occasion Tōjō was summoned to an imperial audience, and it is said that the emperor told him the story that previously, at the time of Minister Ariyoshi's return to Japan, he stated, "The Westerners devoured the feast but went off leaving the plate, but when the Japanese ate the feast they carried off the plate." Tōjō was extremely distraught. He returned to the Army Ministry, related his Majesty's words to the high officials, and said, "We will absolutely put this into practice and will begrudge no sacrifice for this purpose." However, if one views this historically, when the Japanese Army fails militarily in China, accordingly, it makes efforts to gain the popular support of the Chinese people.

Nakaya Tamotsu was released on bail. In the war economy a fine businessman like Nakaya ended up as a criminal.

June 15 (Tuesday)

In the morning rain fell. The rainy season is not over. Yet my umbrella fell apart and now I have none. Little by little, even in our daily lives, we are coming to feel the inadequacy of things in our surroundings.

On my trip to Kyōto-Ōsaka, at the Takarazuka Hotel in the morning there was sugar for the coffee, but the meal was the usual soup and fried clams. The pleasure of breakfast was completely absent. At the Oriental Hotel a little sugar had been put into the coffee. A man at the next table was spitting phlegm and I didn't feel much like eating a meal.

The fact that such places as the Imperial Hotel and the Oriental Hotel are occupied by a crowd ignorant of manners is their special characteristic nowadays.

It is the worker who is unreasonably flattered. Good treatment is something that I essentially stress. But this type of treatment is accumulating the seeds of a future workers' revolution.

The probability of invasion in Italy is something being talked about in every European communiqué. It is probably likely. If this occurs, Italy will probably not be able to survive. If the invasion is successful, there will probably be nothing else but the collapse of Italy. At the same time, on the Eastern war front, the Soviet Union is victorious. The problem is "when."

June 16 (Wednesday)

An account of Ōta. Fifteen hundred apprentice workmen came to the factory of a friend. This because they are recognized as critical war production workers. However, to train them it takes six months, and it has instead reduced the efficiency of well-trained workers. On top of this there are no dormitories; also, there is no bedding and no food supplies. Thereupon, he went to the police headquarters and obtained ration coupons, but bedding cotton was not obtainable in Tōkyō. Going around the vicinity of Kyōto, at last he acquired units for five hundred people and said he provided each person with bedding.

The opening session of the Diet. Enterprise planning and the reorganization of workers—wage raises are suspended, but there may be small increases.

Formalism is expressed in everything. In foreign affairs, in legislation, in politics.

June 17 (Thursday)

Yesterday in a government speech in the Diet, Premier Tōjō did not ideologically attack the position of America and England at all. It is to be regretted. Why did he not take the opportunity to attempt to destroy the political policy of the enemy? We are conducting ideological war, and this is not the way to do so.

Premier Tōjō spoke only of war matters, the continued efforts toward the independence of the Philippines, and cooperation with Thailand.

A story of Tanikawa Tetsuzō. It is said that in Nanking 50–60 percent of the university students are anti-Japanese, 10 percent pro-Japanese, and the rest opportunists. When he inquired about this in Peking it was generally true, but the opportunists were probably more numerous, he said.

In the environs of Peking every day, two to three hundred people die of starvation. We have divided China into three sections: a section occupied by the Japanese, a Communist section, and a Chungking section. However, within these in the Japanese occupied zone there are opportunities for explosion because of the problem of food supplies and other things.

In China the dance halls have been completely closed. Because of this Macao is said to be bustling.

The divinely inspired rhetoric of Japan is in other lands not understood in the least and is merely held in contempt. Our advisers in these locales unanimously recognize this point. However, when I return to Japan things are just as before.

A story of Yanagisawa Ken. China and Thailand are in the same situation. Only six or seven people attend the national policy films of Japan. Nothing can be done about this. Afterward, German films are shown. However, when a film of someone like Eno Ken is shown, people come expressly for this. He said to the Information Board, "Please send something that is nonpolitical."

Yanagisawa told an Information official named Hori Kōichi that the uninteresting things that were now heard on the propaganda broadcasts were ineffective. Hori said please tell what he had been told, with some slight exaggeration, to the Information Board. He related this to the high officials. Then he was told, "Please relate this to the Investigation Bureau of the Interior Ministry." He intends to relate this to them.

The Thai people are talking. They are saying that in the Greater East Asian War the Japanese will get something, but what will Thailand get?

Foreign Minister Matsuoka's arbitration of conflict between Indo-China and Thailand is generating deeper dissatisfaction in Thailand. The Thais are saying that in Japan there is only one-sided information, and that Japan does not understand the other party.

In the newspaper and on the radio there is heavy treatment of the comments regarding the speech of Tōjō collected from Manchuria, Thailand, the Philippines, and others. This kind of childish self-satisfaction will bring about scorn for Japan in the world.

June 18 (Friday)

Yesterday an account of Miyake Seiki. One of his friends, believing that revolution was inevitable in our country, has decided to buy fields and a mountain grove and move close to Asakawa. This friend might be Ōuchi Hyōe.

A story of Shimanaka Yūsaku. A wife of a neighbor was called to the police station and told, "Such things as the use of maids is extravagance. If you have extra rooms, lend them for productive workers. Then you can get by without cleaning."

When one reflects upon the foregoing story, one can understand that radicalized currents are flowing at the roots of society. Previously, I have been saying that with the beginning of air raids, pillage and plunder will be inescapable. Also, I had come to think that there would be revolutionary outbursts because of food shortages. However, it is unfortunate that we are not able to conceive of techniques to escape this.

The deepening of the war—food shortages, outbursts, changes in cabinets, continued vacillation, the coming to the fore of peace discussions, revolutionary changes—something like this will occur.

The Diet still only deceives itself. The people of the nation are really strange. They are content with self-satisfaction. The people are able to believe what they wish to believe.

An account of Katō Takeo, who has returned from Korea. Among the Koreans there is discontent with Japan. The Japanese residents in Korea see this; however, they behave as though they did not know it. He warned of this problem. He thinks that among the American postwar demands will there not be the demand for Korean independence (because this was to be carried out legally)? However, he said that this would probably be something decided by withdrawal based upon the vote of the people.

An account of Shimanaka Yūsaku. Chūō Kōron Company alone was prohibited from appearing at the Army Ministry. It appears that they did not cancel Tanizaki's *Sasameyuki* quickly enough.

For the first time, Foreign Minister Shigemitsu made a response in the Diet. The result was unclear. The gist was that America and England have a destructive political policy, and our country would achieve its purpose by the liberation of Asia. The points that he made indicating the deficiencies of America and England were few.

Love suicide has disappeared in society. The views of male-female morality have changed. That is to say, there is no social necessity for it anymore. Of late, I hear that the crime that has increased the most is rape.

June 19 (Saturday)

Kasahara Seimei is saying that he wants to quit the Ginsei[9] and go to the South Seas. He is an honest man, and the problems of the black market have made him more and more disgusted.

At present, those who have great influence in society are either fools or opportunists.

Noguchi Yonejirō, Tokutomi Sohō, Kume Masao, and there are others. Tsurumi Yūsuke, Nagai Ryūtarō are probably the same as these people. It is a world of "risers."

Murobushi Kōshin mentioned that prior to the Greater East Asian War, with the indirect assistance of the Information Board, Takata Yasuma, Honiden Yoshio, and other scholars were gathered together. It was for the purpose of promoting the beginning of the war. Murobushi was the only one among them who opposed the war. Amaha Eiji was there, but his opposition was merely lip service. Officials are not trustworthy.

On May 16 there was an aerial battle at Lunga Straits. It is said that on the Japanese side twenty planes have not returned. This is the first time that the term "air battle" has appeared.

Prior to the Greater East Asian War, the young military officers spurred on the young heir of the imperial house, and I hear that it was to beg for extreme action by the imperial house.

It is said that those around the imperial prince are wise.

June 20 (Sunday)

The Greater Japan Patriotic Press Association has created the "Japanese World View Society" and the "Japanese Wartime Thought Control Society." The leading member of the former is Lt. General Tsukushi Kumashichi, and members elected were Yamada Yoshio, Kanokogi Kazunobu, and others. The head of the latter is Kanokogi, and from the intellectual world members elected to it were Aikawa Katsuroku, Ichikawa Fusae, Hashimoto Kingorō, and Saitō Ryū. I wonder if anything good is possible from it.

Subhas Chandra Bose has come to Tōkyō. He is certainly an influential Indian. However, how are the newspapers handling this? Both last night and this morning they were completely filled with reports of him. As usual, they do not understand the degree of his importance. Even if he, as a single person, is powerful, what would he be able to do? The Japanese do not have any breadth of knowledge.

Yesterday I heard Kotsuji Setsuzō deliver a talk concerning the Jews. He is an outstanding scholar who gives lectures in Hebrew. It appears that he was at the University of Southern California and knows me. He talked about the history of the Jewish people. It was an extremely rewarding talk. There are close to thirty thousand Jews in Shanghai.

Among the Jewish people there are the Sephardic and the Ashkenazy; the former are of Spanish lineage, and the latter are of German lineage. The Ashkenazy are called "Germans" in the Hebrew language. One stream went from Rome to Spain; encountering fierce persecution, they returned to Babylon. The others traveled along the Danube and went to Germany. Dividing the Jews into major categories, the former make up 10 percent and the latter 90 percent.

The previous evening I saw the Jewish Thesis article of someone named Commander Shioten. It is in a pamphlet of the Professors' League, which is directed by Komatsu Yūdō. It is decidedly childish and subjective in its opinions. It is nothing more than a collection of clippings from magazines in order to concoct a simple conclusion. I am disgusted at the intellectual level of Japan when I think that this kind of childish discussion is listened to with admiration.

This is true, but on the other hand even books such as ours are sold. Though intellectuals are extremely numerous, these people do not appear in public, and this means that the stupidity of the masses flourishes.

June 22 (Tuesday)

Itō Masanori says that what gives him constant displeasure is the arrogant swaggering around of such contemptible people as Tokutomi Sohō, Mutō Sadaichi, and Saitō Tadashi.

In this morning's *Yomiuri*, Mutō discussed Aizawa Tadashi (of Mito han) and admired the Tokugawa proscriptions of Christianity and also engaged in an attack on Christianity. Is this his real belief or is it opportunism with respect to the military? In any case, it is clear that the present war started from ideas, and the war has revolved around ideas.

The "Keihan" (Kyoto-Ōsaka Railway) Line and the "Kyūko" (Express Railway) Line in Ōsaka have been merged. Keen competition between both made for great progress, but what will happen now?

June 23 (Wednesday)

Yesterday I gave a lecture at Meiji Gakuin (Meiji Academy). The result was extremely poor. My unsuccessful and successful attempts are very numerous. This is probably because of physiological reasons.

If one relies upon the *Melbourne News Report*, at the very beginning of the Greater East Asian War it is a fact that "at the time of the invasion against Australia it was the intention of the army to surrender Australia above the Brisbane line." This is something that the minister of labor, Ward, revealed in the Legislature on June 6. But no matter what the intention was, Japan's war power was insufficient (communiqué issued on the 21st by Buenos Aires *Dōmei*, *Asahi shinbun*, June 20, morning edition).

In this morning's *Mainichi shinbun*, Tokutomi Sohō expounded upon the Jewishification of England. Tokutomi and Mutō! They are certainly ideal partners. One can only grieve on behalf of the nation.

Will the Japanese people become greater as a result of this war? If one relies upon the talk of Tanikawa Tetsuzō, in the governing of the outposts there is unanimous agreement that the divine-wind ideas are bad. This is so, but notwithstanding that, such things as dancing are forbidden. One, there is collision of ideas between center and periphery, and two, there are contradictions among those in the field.

June 24 (Thursday)

There is danger in the Mediterranean. The *Asahi* has reported on the views of German soldiers toward Italy.

This spring in Minami-Azumi in Shinshū, they killed all the dogs and presented the hides to the army.

I understand that all doctors are insurance doctors, and they receive their fees from the village office. That is to say, when a patient falls ill the doctor gives him a prescription or an injection. The cost of these is claimed at the village office, and there the village office decides the fees and turns over the appropriate funds. Therefore, they do not merely pay the claim made by the doctors. Everybody is an insurance company member, and payment is made in proportion to taxes.

The core of all such things is the Yokusan organization.[10] This Adult Assistance Group came to the house of Takada and told him to produce all his books and recordings that were English-American. As might be expected of him, it is said that he replied, "Which ones won't do?" and thus saved one part of these. It is said that in the matter of copper and iron they took out even the lamps of the Buddhist altars. At the home of Dōbashi they extracted something like five hundred *kan* (about two tons).

Each of these accounts is a true story. The older generation criticized this as "going too far," but there was nothing whatsoever to be done about it. Such is the power of youth organizations. Particularly the youth of Shinshū have become "Communized," and their activity is pervasive. It is only that they have no wisdom as yet. From here it is only one step to revolution.

Chūō kōron announced that this month's issue will not be published. This is probably related to the prohibition of *Chūō kōron* contact with the Army Ministry.

I met Takahashi of the *Yomiuri* at the Japan Club. When I spoke about Mutō Sadaichi he said the latter was extremely popular, and he said that "The popularity of the intelligentsia is low." However, he said that they check his statements closely. If this is the case, then this is nothing but government censorship.

June 25 (Friday)

At the beginning of *Kaizō*[11] there is a roundtable discussion among the chief of the Information Board, Yahagi, Ōkushi Toyoo, and Saitō Shō. There was an introduction and at the end the author offered polite thanks, saying, "We express our deepest thanks for the fact that just at the time of important military affairs his Excellency Yahagi contributed his valuable time and understood the idea for the present collection." However, have we ever, ever heard such extreme politeness in a roundtable? The contents revealed that while

Rear Admiral Yahagi is aware of the current situation, Ōkushi and Saitō are completely ignorant. Yahagi talked about the real story concerning the dispatch of Dr. Nitobe to America at the time of the Manchurian Incident. Indeed, this was because Yahagi had been in China at length. Yet if one considers his basic thought-style, there emerge conflicts and contradictions.

June 27 (Sunday)

Nakano Seigo, Hatoyama Ichirō, Shiratori Toshio, and others withdrew from the Imperial Rule Assistance Society. At one time the atmosphere was such that Nakano and Hatoyama, who did not approve of this group, had to participate. Now this is not strange at all.

The strange thing is the "atmosphere" and "momentum." Even in America there is such momentum, but in Japan it is especially unified. This momentum is dangerous. There is the fear that because of this mistakes will be disregarded.

Ishibashi lectured for the International Relations Research Society on the problem of large territories. There were statements by Takahashi Kameiki, Ashida Hitoshi, Arita Hachirō, and others. I also was one of the discussants.

I hear that editor of *Chūō kōron* has been suspended. (Shimanaka already talked about the possibility of this.) When one listens to the explanations of the Military Press Corps, it felt that *Chūō kōron* had the strength of ten but only put out the strength of five. This was because of the remnants of a persistent liberalism. They told them to reflect upon their behavior. Thereupon *Chūō kōron* halted all the completed magazines that had been issued, expressed its intention of exercising self-reproach, and decided it will resume publication in August. It is said that the reason was that Kanokogi and his party were not allowed to write for *Chūō kōron* and they were filled with outraged indignation. They quarreled over the fact that Miki Kiyoshi, Tanizaki, and others had been included. In the final analysis, Katsumoto said that it was because *Chūō kōron* had not been wining and dining the Military Information Board. And it is said that their underlying motive was the desire to capture the magazine completely.

The Home Ministry and the Information Board have rather favored *Chūō kōron*, but I understand that everything is decided only by the Military Information Bureau. Majors and lt. colonels are able to influence the freedom of discussion and the lives of writers.

June 28 (Monday)

It is said that German soldiers have moved to northern Italy and are defending the Brenner Pass in the Alps. The conditions in Italy are not clear, and there is the threat of an invasion by the enemy.

According to an account of Yamamoto Kiyoshi of *Daimai* (Ōsaka daily news), special correspondent Ono demanded travel expenses to go Switzerland. I hear that the common opinion in his newspaper is that Italy's position is desperate.

June 30 (Wednesday)

Today, in the morning, I wrote an editorial for *Tōyō keizai*, and in the afternoon I played golf. The movement to confiscate this golf course is in the hands of the Nagano Prefecture Adult Assistance Rule Group. But isn't the problem inadequate labor? How are they going to produce anything taking these fields? Are they selling their names, are they Communists?

The Philosophic Lecture Series of the Peoples' Scholarly Arts Society has been canceled. I hear that the public notices regarding these lectures stated that one should apply to the Chūō Kōron Company, and it seems that someone wrote to the Military Press Corps and its anger is like a blazing fire. I hear that as regards the aforementioned lectures the plan is for a week-long series, and already more than one hundred people have applied. Among the lecturers is a certain professor of Kyōto University (one of the Nishida school), and also Miki Kiyoshi is one of these. This is outrageous!

If one relies upon what Shimanaka says, in the end, it is fortunate that Kanokogi, Nomura, and others were not allowed to write in *Chūō kōron*. It is said that from the August number there will be a total change in the contents. From a magazine that could be oversold it will be made into a magazine that could not be sold at all. I hear that the navy said it is sympathetic to *Chūō kōron*, but if it now clashes with the army the fate of the magazine will depend upon events; therefore, without pleasing itself, the navy will create a magazine that pleases the army. The reaction over the suspension of the July issue was extremely great, and it appears, rather, to have hardened the army. It seems that one objective was to change the company president, but if that were indeed the case, Shimanaka expressed his determination for total self-destruction.

July 1 (Thursday)

From today onward the capital's name becomes "Tōkyo-tō." Again, here one can see an example of the pleasure taken in changing names. Of course, there are bad practices in the *fu* (urban prefecture) and *shi* (municipality). It's true, but are they such that they have to be changed in time of war?

July 2 (Friday)

Japan has returned the allied foreign settlements in Shanghai to China. The Japanese residents in China will probably express their discontent, and the right wing will probably be furious. Besides territorial occupation, what are the Chinese problems that are actual problems? Aiming at territorial expansion and having reached this point, the right will probably be vexed, and then the discontent will probably concentrate on Premier Tōjō.

As regards such people as these—

1. They cannot imagine that for Tōjō, as the representative of the military, there has to be the return of the "International Settlement" and extraterritoriality rights.

2. They cannot possibly conceive that in the end the military policy will do great harm.

3. The world and China will certainly think of these concessions as a sign of weakness.

4. This is also an expression of the Japanese intellectual tendency of placing too much attention on formalism. That is to say, it is a matter of thinking that if they solve formal problems (extrality and other concessions), the Chinese will probably be delighted. What they want is bread. It is not law.

5. However, if these concessions are once made, these rights will disappear forever. Is this indeed in the interest of China and the world? Extrality aside, did the International Settlements do harm to China?

6. Returning the Allied foreign settlements is a mistake even when viewed from the civil war problem of China. However, they must be returned sometime. Returning them now is probably all right . . . as long as we are involved in carrying on this kind of politics.

Yesterday evening the radio announced the emergence of the Five Great Regional Offices. To destroy the *fu-ken* (urban-regional prefectures) block, these regional divisions were created. Indirectly, this is an admission that the government cannot destroy the *fu-ken* block. As a solution they created this system. If ideas become feudalistic, then the nation and regions become feudalistic. Ideas are not isolated.

July 3 (Saturday)

Though today is the day of the PGA Golf Tournament, it rained heavily from yesterday evening. For something like golf it didn't really matter. How good it was for the farmers.

Lately, in a talk with Uchida Nobuya, who has become governor of Miyagi Prefecture, he said, "I have recently heard the story that it took a certain iron foundry six months to go through the procedures of each ministry just to drive a ship's piling. In order to simplify administration, one should simplify these vexatious procedures."

Even in the present state of affairs, this is the way things are done. One understands that slogans are frivolous and nothing but empty *nembutsu* (ritual invocation of Buddha's name).

Imperial Headquarters announced that there is an enemy invasion of Rendova Island in the Solomon chain. I fear that the case of Attu will be repeated.

The day is coming on which the moralistic view of the suicide of an entire army will be questioned not only by the intelligentsia but by the entire military itself. This is because it is in most powerful opposition to self-interest. Again, it is a national loss.

On the one hand, feudalism is being injected, and on the other hand, in carrying it out only ruin is revealed. What form will this contradiction continue to take?

July 6 (Tuesday)

I have a premonition that it will not be possible to play golf as early as next year, and the PGA group shares this feeling.

For Suzuki Bunshirō the present ruling class corresponds to the red faces of the Kabuki.[12] One certainly does have that sort of feeling. Someone has said, "Is it possible to have a total war while thoughtlessly criticizing the common people?"

Arisawa Hiromi requested money from his elder brother, and, buying three *tan* (about ¼ of an acre) of land and a mountain at Asakawa, he improved the farmhouse and became an owner-farmer. This is because of his fear of the upheaval and revolution that must come.

Today at Shimanaka's home in a discussion with certain people I said, "At the moment I was passing the Imperial Palace on a streetcar I lowered my head. At such times I usually pray to the gods for the peace and prosperity of the imperial family. This is not mere gesture. I recall that a reporter named McKesson, in an article in the *Saturday Evening Post*, after an audience he had with the emperor wrote at the time, 'As for the emperor, throughout his life he has probably passed through all sorts of experiences.' While I was recalling such words I truly prayed for the emperor's peace and prosperity."

There is the question of what will happen when the Japanese have no cooperative training and no center called the imperial house. However, this is not a problem of logic, and it is because emotionally I have a feeling of "Japaneseness."

July 7 (Wednesday)

The sixth year of the Sino-Japanese Incident. The radio broadcast this morning said, "The ones who manipulate China are Britain and America. Chiang Kai-shek remains alone, and the Chinese masses are with the Japanese." This kind of thinking, even after six years of war with China, will still not leave the minds of the Japanese people. If Britain and America are destroyed, will the Chinese masses immediately be friendly toward Japan? Do the Chinese have no "identity" at all?

This morning again, as usual, the government had representatives from Manchukuo, Wang Ching-wei, Vargas of the Philippines, and other important people broadcast their praise of Japanese political policy. As long as there is such infantile self-satisfaction, Japan will be ridiculed.

Yesterday evening I was reading H. G. Wells' *The Shape of Things to Come* in Books on the Far East (1934, *Kobe Chronicle*). The themes of his writing are: taking the Manchurian Incident as the beginning point, he said there would be total war with China. Japan would defeat China three times and then, like Napoleon, would itself be crushed. After that, in 1940, there would be war between America and Japan. Tōkyō and Ōsaka would be returned to the hands of "dangerous thinkers," "the last stage of Japan begins," and Japan will be defeated. Wells' predictions indeed were extremely appropriate. Even in the dating of the outbreak of Japanese–American hostilities there is only the difference of one year.

Wells also says, "Future historians will probably question whether Japan was sane or not." At the same time that Japan is carrying out the same plans as those of Hideyoshi, biographies of Hideyoshi are being written by Yoshikawa Eiji and others, and these are selling well. Such people as Toyotomi and Saigō Takamori have never been so popular.

There is no uncertainty about the relationship of these works and the Japanese–American war. This is of the greatest interest. Moreover, the radio . . .

July 9 (Friday)

On the 8th I returned to the capital from Karuizawa. This was because this evening under the auspices of Ashida Hitoshi there was a meeting that centered on Masaki Hideri. Masaki is a young lawyer who is publishing *Chikaki-yori*. His epigrammatical writing is suddenly famous. Those who assembled were Ashida, Baba, Shimanaka, Nagawa Kanshi, Andō Masazumi, and Sasaki Mosaku.

According to Masaki's account, the February and June numbers of *Chikaki-yori* were prohibited. He said that his not being summoned by the authorities was possibly because he is a lawyer. I hear that Nagawa is also a lawyer, and when there is a show of strength the officials become weak. He said that the only thing in their heads is "rising in the world." It appears that one is only summoned once by the Kempeitai.

Masaki says, "The leadership of Japan is on the level of petty bureaucrats." Since he stated his regrets over his ignorance concerning foreign countries, I said, "It is better not to know. I cannot forget the feelings I had at the time of the outbreak of the Greater East Asian War on December 8. I spent a whole day in anguish over whether I as a patriot could fulfill a retainer's integrity, or should I have made the greatest effort to avoid war. This is because I know the conditions of the world and the war strength of America."

Tsurumi Yūsuke is optimistic about the future course of the war. Nagai and Tsurumi write beautifully, but they have no ideas. However, Tsurumi has the greatest kindness for me and says, "If it is necessary, I will always help you."

Even though I am at Karuizawa and improving my house, I always have the feeling of "what will happen if my house is seized."

Revolution in Japan will have to occur. This revolution will probably come by way of feudalistic communism. The result of this will be stealing what others possess. It will not be creation, it will be destruction. This is particularly true in the Shinshū area.

Because Ashida said, "I am trying to make my peace with the fact that no matter what sort of effort we make it makes no difference," I replied, "What you say is true, but I cannot be optimistic concerning the results that will be brought about from these circumstances. That is to say, I am not fearful of revolution itself, but I do not foresee any cultural benefits as a result of revolution. On that point the Japanese revolution will not have objectives such as the great French Revolution had."

July 10 (Saturday)

Yesterday there was a general meeting of the Fuji Manufacturing Company. I decided to put money into it. I can't do anything but borrow money from the Kangyō Bank.

Last night there was a conference of the People's Scholarly Arts Society. At the meeting there was an explanation from the director, Shimanaka, concerning the circumstances that resulted in the suspension of the lectures (philosophy).

"We were told by the Military Press Corps that the membership of speakers of the Scholars' Association was not acceptable. Therefore we stopped the lectures, but this had to do with their relationship to *Chūō kōron. Chūō kōron* was criticized as being ignorant of the times because Tanizaki's *Sasameyuki* of the January issue had as its subject leisured matrons. It was halted twice, but about that time it appears that there was an emotional outcry. Moreover, there was a roundtable discussion in *Chūō kōron* on this issue by Kyōto school philosophers, and this did not please the Military Press Corps. Again, the American studies of Shimizu Ikutarō and others were criticized. The Military Press Corps went so far as to call for the destruction of *Chūō kōron*. Such groups as the Information Board, Home Ministry, and especially the navy seemed not particularly concerned, and this increasingly offended the Military Press Corps. Moreover, the editor made a complete justification, and this, on the contrary, only worsened the outcome. This is because it is said that when the contents of the July number were examined there was not the slightest evidence of self-discipline, and with that the military acted decisively and publication was suspended. Immediately afterward, the public announcement of the People's Scholarly Arts Society appeared, and this agitated emotions. It was not the program itself but simply the speakers list. It was that the members' characters were suspect." He stated that if it was his presence that was creating trouble then he was willing to resign.

Following that, after dining, there were various comments by Tanaka Kōtarō about his visit to China:

1. The masses are largely unconcerned about the abolition of extrality rights.

2. In Japan it is said that Chungking might be isolated, but if the Chinese masses wish peace, there is nothing else for Chungking to do, and if, on the contrary, they wish to fight, they will fight.

3. The treatment of university professors is extremely bad. Some of them are living in janitor quarters. Scholars are being sought, but in these circumstances it is impossible to attract them.

4. In China, the people are believers in natural law. The lack of national power has come about as a result. And the reason that interventionism had been defeated and noninterventionism has succeeded is due to this. China is a country of democracy.

July 11 (Sunday)

There is a communiqué with the message that an anti-Axis army has invaded the island of Sicily. It is something that has previously been expected. It is merely a matter of time before Italy withdraws from the Axis. Already there is a German Army at the Brenner Pass, and there is the threat of an invasion of Central Europe.

If Italy falls we must expect that the English-American fleet that is there will be seen in great force in the Pacific.

Last night I read Chamberlain's *Things Japanese*. It is interesting. Moreover, Hearn argues that Japanese women are a type who absolutely will not appear in a future technological civilization. Together with Longford's[13] writing, it appears that Japanese women are of the greatest interest.

The instructions of the authorities to the newspapers are thorough to the degree that it is amusing. I am keeping the above-mentioned information for later purposes. I was able to find through prohibited items that the Indian People's Army is being rounded up as war prisoners.

The Information Board provided the newspapers certain reports. When one looked at what came out on the following day it was completely changed. When the board raged at this and summoned them for investigation, it understood that the Military Information Bureau made the corrections. The Information Bureau did not know at whom to strike.

July 12 (Monday)

The applicants for flying are coming in great numbers from students. It is a fact that they are being recruited. The situation is that in such places as Waseda University there are already 1,998, and at Tōkyō University, 458 (*Mainichi*, July 11). If it were England using university students there would probably be selectivity and rational use of human resources. That is to say, if one makes all those who have received a university education into fliers this will open up holes in other places. However, no one mentions such things, and the irrationality continues to advance without correction.

An account of Tsurumi Yūsaku. Recently, at a certain meeting a powerful politician of the former Minseitō party came to Tsurumi and asked, "America still has not bowed its head, has it?" Tsurumi did not know how to answer this sudden question. If one were to make thoughtless statements there would be misunderstanding.

The ignorance and illiteracy of politicians tends to this extremity. The Greater East Asian War is threatened by the leadership of the ignorant.

Creating a chronology for the *Tōdenshi* (History of Tōkyō Electric Power Company), which relates to Kobayashi Ichizō, one feels keenly that in the last part of Taishō (1) corruption flourished in the political parties, (2) strikes occurred frequently, and (3) such things as plans for disarmament led to the victory of the military, which had been in the background until then, and right-wing ideas.

When one looks at the telegrams the Japanese people write and the newspapers, it is said that Roosevelt is losing his popularity because the U.S. war situation is poor and he is in a panic to regain popularity. It is proof that the Japanese do not know the American mind. The American people are not sensitive, as are the Japanese, to "war," and moreover, they probably do not think it is the responsibility of Roosevelt. Lt. Commander Horita Yoshiaki of the Imperial Headquarters Army Information Bureau stated in a speech at Ōsaka, "Drawing in the enemy, we will end the war with a crushing defeat." If that is the case, would it have been better not to have taken the initiative in the first place?

From the end of Taishō to the beginning of Shōwa it is all turmoil— it is a period of collapse. The collapse of power, the corruption of the political parties, the awakening of China, on the one hand.

July 13 (Tuesday)

Last night I went to the theater. I joined the subscription group for Taganojō.[14] I invited Nyozekan.

While I was at *Nihon hyōron* I asked how the *History of Japanese–American Relations* was coming. It appears that they could not obtain a special ration, but if they could print it on their allotted paper there would be no difficulty. It is possible to finish the printing by next year. Learning this, I was at ease.

As to the matter of the *Chronology*, there is vacillation on the part of the publishing company. I wish this also to be settled, but . . .

I am not moved by Kikugorō.[15] His is an art of nothing but dancing. His voice is bad and the plot line is always weak.

July 14 (Wednesday)

On those occasions when those who do not know things ridicule and belittle those who do know things, invariable errors occur. Before the Pacific East Asian War the specialists who were available were not only ignored but also silenced.

The reason for the insistence of the Imperial Rule Assistance Association of Shinshū on closing down the Karuizawa Golf Course is that it is impossible to increase production with Konoe, Gotō, and their kind playing golf.

That recreation is necessary for intellectuals is beyond their grasp; and one sees, at the root of this, destructiveness and jealousy.

A communiqué has been issued on the desperate conditions of our army in the Solomon Islands. This is regrettable. The newspapers report that the enemy does not mind making enormous sacrifices. Aren't these the same newspapers that previously denigrated English-American individualism and liberalism and said this precluded even thought of war?

The most exaggerated expressions are popular. There are usages such as "Our marvelously skillful torpedo boats." "The greatest going-it-alone war, past or present!" The war in the southwestern Pacific has never been anything like this. It is the preliminary skirmish. It is evidence of what only a small part of the people are understanding.

There is agitation for disciplining the regulated companies. It appears that the government is making things that many called regulated companies laws. It is a fact that throughout the country there are as many as six hundred government-controlled firms (*Mainichi*, today's paper).

For example, publishing companies pay a 25 percent commission to the "*Nichihai*." No matter what they do, they will be forced to pay. We call them "tunnel companies."

This is being tied hand and foot by formalism. And even at the present time the authorities think only of control and not at all of production.

July 15 (Thursday)

Starting today, for three days, there will be air-raid defense practice. As usual, we will pour all our strength into whether there must be leggings or whether there should be kimono sleeves. This is because the military is the core of leadership.

As regards this, the informed, especially the scholars, react negatively. Starting yesterday there was the meeting of the cooperative assembly (*Asahi*, July 15, evening edition).

An account of Kawai Tatsuo (former ambassador to Australia):

> Premier Tōjō stated in a speech that "you must understand the world situation and you must cooperate with Japan," but in Australia they laughed at this. They said that because we do understand the world situation we take the attitude we do. It appears that Tōjō thinks the war is a tennis match and that he believes that when he takes the score he has won. This was the gist of an editorial in a certain newspaper. It appears that the premier thinks it is possible to separate Australia from the British Empire, but it is not possible to do such a thing.

Previously, at the time of the Tanaka Giichi Cabinet, in fact I wrote that an aggressive political policy toward China would probably be the final act. It was because I thought, due to the defeat of Tanaka, that the eyes of the people would be opened. However, I learned that the people are not self-critical in this way. This is because they are ignorant and do not understand causal relations. Those who think the people will be self-critical this time are those who do not know the stupidities of the past.

If one relies upon the account of Uchida and others, they say that in their native places the people firmly believe that if America is victorious in the war, property will be seized and the people will be killed. This is the extremity of ignorance.

July 16 (Friday)

The primary problem of the Imperial Rule Assistance Association is the problem of dress code. From the 15th, air-raid defense training began, but as usual the problem of clothing is the greatest problem. A critique of air-raid defense day (*Mainichi*, July 15, evening edition).

This clothing problem is the thing upon which current thought is focused. (1) There are the fundamentalists, and, as was stated by a representative from Shinshū, their's is the principle that sees the spirit by way of clothing. They say those who do not dress properly do not have air-raid defense spirit. (2) There are practicalists who say why make such a fuss about it?

The American-British Army, which has invaded Sicily, is indeed advancing as though it were a land without people. Italy has indicated the areas of battle as Naples and Barletta (the Adriatic Sea). There are reports that are transmitting the possibility of an invasion of the central region. The fate of Mussolini presses on. The collapse of Italy presses on.

July 17 (Saturday)

Yesterday evening, after a long while, the Twenty-Six Society met. This time my role was general manager of the society. With Tanikawa Tetsuzō as the guest of honor, Shimanaka Yūsaku, Hasegawa Nyokezan, Baba Tsunego, Masamune Hakuchō, Kamitsukasa Shōken, and Abe Shinosuke also attended, and all of them are people who do not accommodate themselves to the times. (Ashida Hitoshi also came.)

It is said that when the air-raid alarms are sounded, people prostrate themselves, even in the bathrooms of the Maru Building, and press their face to the floor. This senselessness is sheer madness. And, thus, twenty-year-olds walk about arrogantly giving orders.

July 18 (Sunday)

As regards the *History of Civilization* put out by *Tōyō keizai*, Tsuchiya Takao, who had not written for it yet, wrote the "History of Industry," but his treatment of the connections of capitalism and government cannot be published as is. Accordingly, I hear that Tsuchiya eliminated these parts. It is a country in which one cannot write true history. I have also had this kind of experience.

It is said that the applications for student fliers have exceeded twenty thousand.

July 19 (Monday)

This morning Satō Kusashi came, together with Miwako. I hear that on the second of next month he will be appointed to the Philippines. I hear that the civilian adviser to the military is not an impressive post, and he is anticipating returning to the Philippine consulate after two years. He said, "When one goes to the Army Ministry they are all quacking there in great angry voices. I thought, is effective national policy possible, carrying on like this?"

Because of an earlier arrangement, I visited Tamura Teijirō, and together with Higashi Ryōzō we had supper. Tamura is extremely wealthy. It is a fact that he pays around five thousand yen in taxes. Yet we did not discuss national policy, and I felt something was missing.

On the radio every morning they read aloud the sermons of Hayashi Shihei and certain other people. These people lived at a time when there was no knowledge of the facts of foreign countries and they were on in years. Now, one hundred years later, having such people as these embody the "golden rule" is anachronistic.

The people who get off at Karuizawa are fewer than expected. Is this because of the conditions of the times?

If one combines all the regions, the regulated companies have come to number six hundred, and it is said that there is the need for such consolidation. It is regulation for the sake of regulation. It is a phenomenon of the Greater East Asian War.

July 21 (Wednesday)

This morning's radio conveyed the news that his Highness Prince Yi has become an air force commander in chief, and it cites examples of the imperial family taking important positions.

There is no good evidence, despite the propaganda of the radio, that the imperial family is taking on vital positions. At this time of most difficult circumstances, failure on anyone's part will conclude in responsibility assigned to the leaders.

Again, is it likely that the people will be made to feel that the imperial family's appointment to vital posts is because of their real ability?

We are in the midst of constructing a chronology of the Shōwa period for the *Tōden* commemorative volume. In the two or three years before the Manchurian Incident there were innumerable instances of strikes, student agitation, and intellectual crises. There were incidents involving the attempted assassination of His Majesty, the Nanba Daisuke incident, and in 1932 the Korean rebel Li Hōsho.[16] One may probably say that this insecurity and violence were reactions to the Manchurian Incident.

Even now, ten years later, this undercurrent has not been swept away. It is unnatural to think that as a result of the Greater East Asian War nothing will else occur.

The compromise between militarism and communism. I have long had in mind the interpretation that communism is a product of the same frame of mind as feudalism. This fact can be seen in all of its aspects.

Three days after the May 15 Incident[17] there was the granting of honors with regard to the Sino-Japanese Incident (the Manchurian Incident). Since then, during this war that has not yet ended, honors have been given. This is some sort of brazenness. (The Forty-Fourth Recognition of Honors has been announced.)

July 22 (Thursday)

The Diet, insofar as it is related to foreign affairs, moved a resolution of gratitude to the expeditionary armies in the field.

As regards the defendants in the May 15 Incident, the severest sentence was four years (the prosecution sought eight years), and, contrary to that, the assassin of Hamaguchi, Sagoya Tomeo, was sentenced to death. (Sagoya's appeal was dismissed.) This is the way sentences are carried out in our country. (The army's sentence was September 19, 1933; Sagoya's, November 5, 1933.)

July 24 (Saturday)

At long last, yesterday and today, it cleared up. On clear days Karuizawa is the best place on earth. The construction of the storeroom was completed. The result was extremely fine. We bought and stored a variety of things, and now everything is convenient. My foresight is confirmed that things will be unfortunate for the Japanese nation.

I do not go out to play golf every day and am confined to the house. I do the cleaning myself.

In the afternoon I go out to play golf. The results are not pleasing. I only lose the ball. They are cultivating the soil on the course. Why must they now cultivate the soil? There are many supervisors of this cultivation. Is this in the interests of production—to be sure it is not!

July 25 (Sunday)

The fact that the Japanese people do not voluntarily have positive policies for avoiding disasters can be known by way of the recurrence of fires. Hakodate keeps having one fire after another. However, they do not conceive a specific policy for preventing this. The latest great fire in December 1934 destroyed 23,600 houses. Through the agency of education, the Japanese people must definitely be self-critical about this in relation to present conditions.

The virtue of the Japanese is resignation. However, in the end, it is not possible to build constructively from that. While they are not a foolish people, they are not a great people.

Just as the German people always return to the same things, the Japanese people also without fail will probably return to the same things.

In 1934 it was decided that Japan would be called Nippon, and it is now a generally fixed reading. As regards such things as horizontal writing and weights and measures, there is naturally strong opposition to change.

A conversation with Tamura Kōsaku. In the *Mainichi shinbun*, East Asia Research Society scholars are carrying forward studies on the responsibility for the war. Someone named Commander Akita came and said, "Don't you understand the matter? It is Churchill and Roosevelt who are responsible. After all this time, how absurd this business of war responsibility is!" The scholars and teachers have been completely defeated, and the Society no longer exists.

April 28, 1934. Western music was abolished at the Four Great Shinto Festivals at the imperial court.

PART
II

The Law of
Trademarks

There are attacks on the Chinese by the Japanese newspapers, and, as a result, one understands the mental aberration of the responsible parties. If things are not handled on the basis of fair judgments, even beggars will not obey.

In the *Yomiuri* newspaper there are two representative essays on the conditions of the times. The first, by General Hayashi, who writes the "Sunday New Opinion Column," is an essay entitled "Accept the Imperial Will." "First of all the imperial decree, second of all the imperial decree must be completely accepted in one's daily life, and one must put into practice the imperial decree that began the war." And then he said this becomes the way to victory. This is true. However, as regards imperial rescripts, governments in power approach the throne and request expression of the imperial will. Is not the essence of the national polity not deigning to trouble the imperial house? In the case of Tōjō and General Hayashi, they exceed boldness in linking themselves to the imperial rescripts.

The other essay is the usual thing by Mutō Sadaichi, entitled "The Axis's Chances of Victory Are Obvious." He writes as if he were observing the negotiations between Stalin and Roosevelt. Despite the immobility on the island of Sicily and the eastern war front, those capable of such a view still commonly exist. From the beginning, sorry to say, it is these people who do not understand the psychology of England and America. And if they earnestly think they do, they are stupid. And if this is lip service, it is impudent and shameless. However, these are the leaders of contemporary society (essay of Mutō Sadaichi, *Yomiuri hōchi*, July 25.

In Shinshū there is a movement to get rid of absentee landlords. I also am an absentee landlord, but this movement is probably reasonable. However, even in this, one sees the tendency toward revolution.

July 27 (Tuesday)

Mussolini has finally resigned. Italy is collapsing. Even at the Twenty-Six Society everyone was skittish and could not talk about the events of the day. We only kept repeating how disastrous it was.

There is a rumor that Nakano Seigo, Akita Kiyoshi, and Shiratori Toshio have joined forces, and also that Nagai Ryūtarō is joining them.

I hear that among certain people there is strong opposition because Tōjō's policy is compromising and they feel this is bad. There is the possibility that this will become a Get-Rid-Of-Tōjō movement. This is something that can be well-imagined.

The fact that Tōjō controls the military strengthens his position. Because, internally and externally, Tōjō's policy is one of compromise, there might be dissatisfaction.

Today I wrote about the clothing problem in *Tōkei* (*Tōyō keizai*).

July 28 (Wednesday)

I am writing an essay for the English-language *Economist* on Anglo-American relations.

By way of fragmentary telegrams, the Italian political changes are at last coming to be clarified. What should be noted are the facts that (1) martial law has been proclaimed, (2) the telegraph and telephones are not getting through, and (3) the Fascist People's Army has been reorganized and they have established "The National Defense People's Army." The following conclusions probably emerge from these above-mentioned facts:

1. The opposition to the Fascists and Mussolini is rising and intensifying.
2. In a certain sense, instability is reaching a revolutionary degree.
3. The surrender of Italy is only one step ahead.

It is said that the president of the Stefani News Agency has died, but is it death from illness or death from accident? Indeed, one wonders whether or not even Mussolini is safe. The Fascist party for the most part is disintegrating. With this whole-nation-one-partyism is destroyed. It is a fact that for the Italian people fascism is revealing its worthlessness. If one relies upon a Rome dispatch,

1. It is said there is antagonism throughout the country between fascists and antifascists, and because of the appearance of Marshall Badoglio this was swept away.
2. In the end, this dictatorship will not be able to achieve national unity. Of course this is true in Japan.
3. In Japan it is the victims of infantilism like Okumura who are calling the informed and Anglo-English types unpatriotic. The "domestic war" of such people is seriously inviting the animosity of one part of the people.

July 29 (Thursday)

The low tone of the *Mainichi shinbun* is a regrettable thing. On the 29th there was an editorial of this sort. It is of the same tone as the Shiōten clique.[18] It has the same form as the ideas that classify everything as "Anglo-American."

July 30 (Friday)

In a letter regarding his experience after appendicitis surgery, Mizuno Hironori states:

I am extremely irritated that my recovery is slow because not only am I on in years, but also just at this time one cannot get enough nourishment.

Given the fact that babies come first under the slogan of "produce more children," for us elders to obtain even a single measure of milk we obtain certifications from a doctor, neighborhood association, and City Hall. In the end it is a situation in which one out of three of the rations of once every three or five days are spoiled, and, as a result, this is the best of all possible worlds.

Also the future of state of affairs becomes more and more gloomy. Ah! Where is Japan going? Now, the military authorities are flattering advanced students who formerly, at the beginning of the war, they viewed with scorn as enemies and traitors to the nation. This represents the triumph of reason over physical coercion and the submission of Yamato-damashii to science. I feel that even in darkness human beings continuously make progress. The flight of the foresightful Mussolini makes us feel that he is the first of many leaves to fall. One leg of the tripod has been removed. Three-country alliances are risky, aren't they?

For the elderly, like me, our days are numbered, and we naturally pass away, and this serves the nation. But you who love the life before you, I hope that you will work for the rebirth of Japan.

The above is the letter of Colonel Mizuno. I feel so sorry for Mizuno, who has greater talents than his classmates Kobayashi Seizō and Nomura Kichisaburō, who flourish in society.

The weather has not been good until now, and there is anxiety about the harvest. The actual quantity of rice produced this year was 39,750,000 koku, and it did not reach the assigned quota of 40 million koku.[19]

While one sees in this alone the evils of bureaucratic government, there are still those who scheme for the realization of a Marxist, bureaucratic government, and their foolishness knows no bounds. However, the cheers for contemporary capitalists must be corrected.

Mutō Sadaichi has taken up some sort of function in the Imperial Rule Assistance Society. With this his poison will probably flow, but the fact that his essays have disappeared from the newspapers should be rejoiced over.

The defeat of Mussolini seems to have given considerable shock to people in every quarter. It is unfortunate that they did not understand until this occurred.

I hear that a policeman came to a villa in Karuizawa and advised air-raid preparations to be made. Strengthening air-raid facilities in isolated houses in the mountains is police standardization, and consequently I can understand their lack of common sense.

Special delivery fourth-class items are not handled in the mails anymore. I accept the change, but when I sent a manuscript to *Tōyō keizai* I made a mistake and cut the envelope. When our maid Toyo took it to the post office the cut envelope could not be accepted and they requested a new envelope. Even this is an instance of formalism.

One cannot send luggage from Kutsukake Station to one's home. We sent it to Tōkyō Station, and there again we had to change procedure. This sort of thing is also bureaucratic formalism.

July 31 (Saturday)

This morning the weather was fine. The mountain air was pervasive. Here and there nightingales and cuckoos were singing. I heard the voices of the cicadas too. How long will this life be possible?

The Berlin authorities have criticized the newspapers in Italy as having become liberalistic. If the Fascists and dictatorship are deadlocked, liberalism is inevitable. It is said that in Portugal events have developed that approach revolution. However, in adjusting to these circumstances concessions are necessary, and concessions are not popular. One does not think of liberalism as something that becomes powerful so simply. In Japan when I look at the news it is the liberals who overthrow the Fascists, and I can imagine the possibility of the exercise of power by liberal pressure. The truth is forgotten that those who are deadlocked are the Fascists and that there is the possibility of liberalism being resisted. For some time to come, there will probably be political warfare between liberalism and communism.

If he were in Japan, Mussolini would commit suicide. In Italy what is done? When one sees the disappearance of the Italian ambassador in Berlin, it appears that within Italy there have been extreme upheavals and Fascist repression.

Listening to the radio every morning, I always feel the following: Among the great nations of the world, are there similar examples of countries with weakness such as ours and with uninformed leadership? In critical times in international politics they do not understand international politics. Being led by people who do not comprehend the conditions of the world at all is dangerous.

August 1 (Sunday)

The Greater East Asian War is a war in which one sacrifices oneself and exercises virtue.

1. From today onward, Burma has been given its complete independence. The president, Ba Maw, has become the sovereign power. In exchange it has declared war on England and America. This is the same strategy with regard to Wang's political power.

2. There has been a complete restoration of foreign concessions in China, and from now on the foreign concessions in Shanghai and elsewhere are totally under Chinese sovereignty.

3. Soon, independence will be restored to the Philippines.
4. Conscription laws will be instituted in Korea and Taiwan.

Has ceding four provinces to Thailand and the return of foreign concessions and independence of Burma been done according to proper procedures? In any case, since there must be the return of foreign concessions, I have no objection to make to this.

Tsurumi Yūsuke said that Mussolini was imprisoned and eight members of his party have been jailed. It was a matter of a military coup d'état, I hear. When Premier Tōjō first obtained this report he tried to conceal it, but the president of the Information Board, Amaha, forcefully made it public. Tsurumi also said that great numbers of university students of Japan, learning of Mussolini's downfall, are changing their opinions. Moreover, because it is a historical fact that currents of ideas shift in thirteen-year cycles, around 1946 there will be a shift of direction.

When I mentioned I was keeping a diary, Shimanaka said, "It's dangerous!" The Police Superintendent's Office seized the publications of the Chūō Kōron Company, and included among them are writings of mine and of Baba Tsunego. While I keep this diary I cannot help but feel some sort of uneasiness.

Yet in my own case it does not go beyond trying to keep a record for future use in order that I may later write a "history of the present."

August 2 (Monday)

How long will we be able to play golf? Golf in the morning. In the afternoon I work at the *Chronology*.

According to Yanagizawa, two or three weeks ago when he was lunching with Foreign Minister Shigemitsu the latter said, "There cannot be a situation in which peace will be made only by the Europeans, leaving out the Far East area. Don't worry."

August 3 (Tuesday)

I played golf with Kataoka Teppei and others. On the way back we had lunch at my place and they stayed until four o'clock.

I share his opinion that with the Fascist collapse the pressure on Japanese liberals will probably increase. Honest patriots such as the liberals are few. They play no role in the nation, and this is a loss to the nation.

Those who aspired to literature and failed are in the Information Board and Censorate and we cannot expect anything from them. Jealously and hatred are this period's special characteristics.

In Hindenburg's *From My Life* he says, "For Asians there is no virtue nobler than revenge." What are the objectives of the war?

August 4 (Wednesday)

Since the Manchurian Incident, those who inspire the radio and the public are Takayama Kikokurō, Yoshida Shōin, and Saigō Takamori. Each and every one of these was a traitor and sentenced to punishment. This was true of many Mito people. For those who seize leadership in society to inspire a rebellious spirit is to threaten their own lives.

In the evening Kitada Masatake came. He said that he is staying at the home of an Imperial University professor. He related that at Jōchi University Germans dominate, but because they are Catholic they are opposed to the Nazis and Hitler. The reserve colonel officer who is attached to the university is extremely dictatorial, and he always complains and opposes the principal and the German teachers. When the German teachers come out, he severely scolds them with the words, "I have nothing to do with you!" He believes that Christianity has the same ideas as Judaism. He says this is not good for Japan and tells this to the students.

August 5 (Thursday)

Recently a workman came to our house in Karuizawa, saying, "I wonder why this war is going on? Roosevelt and Churchill, who caused the war to start with, are rascals. Isn't it possible to kill off these two?" This is a typical instance of the ideas of the Japanese people in general, who firmly believe that the outbreak of the war was due to these two people.

August 16 (Monday)

On August 9 I left for Tōkyō. On the 15th I returned to Karuizawa. At the request of the Communications Ministry, I went about giving lectures at Fukushima, Sendai, Yonezawa, and Yamagata for the purpose of training new office heads.

On the morning of the 9th at Ueno Station I was robbed of a purse containing more than two hundred yen. I wanted to say that I had dropped it, but there was no possibility of having dropped it, and it would probably be best to say it was stolen. My companion on the journey from the Communications Ministry also had his suitcase stolen.

The confusion at Ueno Station is indeed extreme. Exploiting this, thieves run wild everywhere.

1. According to Kikuchi Eitarō, the office head of Fukushima, when he attended the farewell ceremonies for the war dead at a neighboring village and left his shoes in the entrance, they were stolen.
2. According to Ōkoshi Gunzō, when friends of his removed their shoes in the train, they were stolen.

Conditions are so bad that one may say the Japanese are becoming impoverished and all of them are turning into thieves.

In Fukushima I said that there should not be optimism about the situation in Germany and Italy, but I only implied this. But even at that, the listeners said that this was the first time they had heard such pessimistic talk.

At an agricultural school at a place called Rikusen Ochiai, there is training for new office heads. They are permitted to ask questions. One person said, regarding the state of affairs in Europe, "I am discouraged." They are people who have been extremely optimistic.

Moreover, at the Yonezawa office they ask the question, "How will the Greater East Asian War turn out?" Depending on their persistence I answer, "It is a matter of forcing out a spirit of war weariness in America." So I point out America's weak points. One understands that these are people who have questions regarding the conclusion of the Greater East Asian War.

Also, at the Yonezawa office they ask why Japan accepted the 5, 5, 3 ratio at the London Conference. It is clear that they have heard the account of Japan's humiliation.

In Yonezawa I worshiped at the Uesugi Shrine, a place dedicated to the reverence of Uesugi Kenshin. This matter of worshiping people who have been subjected to various historical criticisms is probably not reasonable. It is probably fine to do homage to people who cannot be criticized, but . . .

On the way home I stopped at the home of Ōkoshi Matao of Shirakawa-machi. He was, as usual, in high spirits. The confusion on the trains while en route is murderous. It is said that people are killed when pushed off the connecting vestibules of the cars.

Rome has been declared an open city. Italy has already declared the whole country a war zone, but this probably indicates the pressure of the Anglo-American invasion of the homeland. At the same time, it probably indicates that the policy of the new government is not a scorched-earth policy.

August 17 (Tuesday)

In the Meiji Restoration educational costs were provided to the children of the aristocracy, and on January 29, 1871, it was decided to limit these funds to students studying abroad. In order to avoid, in the future, self-important people ignorant of the world, there had to be extensive broadening of the overseas student system to include officials and others besides students.

After the present war I believe that capitalism will flourish in Japan. After everything is used up there will be a need to increase products quickly. However, the nation in carrying this out will have no capital funds. It has been proven that revival will not be possible under the direction of officials in the bureaucracy. It may be that efforts will be exerted to have enterprises established by individuals. In December 1871 the government permitted those who maintained canals and roads at private expense to charge levies.

All university and specialty school students have returned their holidays to the emperor and are providing labor service. Because of this, many sacrifice themselves. From this it is enough to understand that this "training" is unscientific.

August 18 (Wednesday)

Played golf with Shimanaka. In a talk with Shimanaka he revealed that works published by *Chūō kōron* had been previously taken off for investigation by the Police Superintendent's Office. As a result, my book—which book is unclear—had one part eliminated, and Baba Tsunego's work *Activist Politicians* and others were ordered to be completely cut and thrown away. And such things as the "lumpen" novels of Shimomura Chiaki were prohibited.

In today's (or yesterday's) *History of the Japanese People*, there is an essay complaining that Enomoto Takeaki did not take his own life. This is probably true if discussed from the view of Bushido. However, Enomoto performed meritorious service with regard to Russia and elsewhere and expended himself for the nation.

Is it better to commit suicide or exhaust oneself for the nation? Herein is the clash of views between Japanism and progressivism.

On August 30, 1875, three thousand yen was granted for the preservation of the Nikkō Shrine. In the Greater East Asian War, the first thing that was done was to cut down the avenue of cryptomerias at Nikkō.

August 19 (Thursday)

The outstanding trait of those who received their education in America is seriousness and sincerity. Those who have a sense of responsibility akin to such people are hard to find. Among the people known to me, they are the most sincere group. They will probably always be successful. Probably in America there is an atmosphere that teaches this sort of sincerity.

In a speech at the Miyagi Agricultural School, there was a man who asked was there no one who could kill Chiang Kai-shek? He said he's the bad one. He said that people should make up some sort of volunteer corps for this purpose. Rather than killing Japanese, the right wing should kill the enemy. However, such people as these are ignorant of the fact that Chiang Kai-shek represents the Chinese masses. They think only of what is before their eyes, and their ideas are not historical.

The island of Sicily is finally being abandoned. This was anticipated and so is not surprising (*Yomiuri hōchi*, August 19).

Krakov is also in extreme danger. Germany's eastern war front is in danger of complete collapse.

In the South Pacific the three areas of Kupang (Timor), Kekuwa (New

Guinea), and Mimika are under enemy air raids, and these have even reached the Chishima Islands.

The newspapers write about nothing else but the increase of production. Akira came back from Aokemi and said that in addition to turning over all metal altar implements, roofing also must be turned in, and I hear that as soon as cement tiles can be acquired this will be done.

The rayon yarn industries have begun their fourth stage of preparations, and they will be finished next month. The objective is the production of scrap iron. When the war is over it is possible that there will truly be no iron objects throughout the country. Even in the commercial side of warfare there are problems. Where will the capital and machinery come from?

August 20 (Friday)

The heads of the official enterprises have been named "Ōchōshi." If one looks at the service regulations of the Ōchōshi, they are: "The Ōchōshi who is the head of an enterprise must be filled with the consciousness that he must bear the burden of the entire responsibility for the execution of production and must carry out the responsibility for increasing war capacity."

If the government has come as far as this, it is no longer amusing and it is the toy of the children. The government thinks if they turn the head into an official and make him take an oath, they will raise efficiency. With the exception of capital, this is the nationalization of everything and would complete the conjoining of Marxist formula and bureaucratic ideology. Has one ever previously heard of officials feeling real responsibility? The newspapers did not identify this company. This is probably in the interest of counterintelligence (*Yomiuri hōchi*, August 20, evening edition).

I bought H. G. Wells' *The Shape of Things to Come* at a used book store in Karuizawa. In it he writes about Japan and states the opinion, "The minds of the authorities approach insanity." One cannot help but feel how sharply he has penetrated the matter. One sees this in the orders commandeering company heads and in listening to lectures on the radio. Hirakawa returned to Tōkyō.

August 21 (Saturday)

On the 20th a treaty was signed for the incorporation of territory by Japan and Thailand. It was the recognition of the incorporation by Thailand of the territory of Terengannu, Kelantan, Kedah, and Perlis of northern Malaya that is under Japanese territorial control and the states of Mong Pan and Keng tung in the Shan Federated States. This signifies three things: (1) Territories such as these are under occupation by Japan, but one never sees a final settlement regarding them. (What sort of Anglo-American criticism will there be? They will say this is thieves sharing among themselves.) (2) These sort of "weak foreign relations" were carried out by the army man Tōjō, who feels that no matter what the circumstances, concessions and cooperation are crimes. At the beginning Premier Tōjō said he valued the independence of Thailand, but he did not mention any territorial concessions. Because Tōjō was an uninformed military man, when he tried to act by himself it was to be expected that it would become clear to him that international relations did not work this simply. Knowledge comes first. (3) There was an indemnity for the purpose of buying Thailand's participation in the war and friendship. (In the treaty document there is no mention of concessions and it speaks of "confirmation.")

Today there was a flood of visitors. Extraordinarily, Masamune Hakuchō said that he had *manju* and brought me some. Mitsui Takao and Kodera Shukichi came by. Seeing Shimanaka's house when they were returning home, Yanagizawa brought a marvelously delicious pie. We had a discussion concerning the state of the war. Afterward, Kasahara Seimei and Okamura Kesayoshi stopped over with us.

Again, Yanagizawa said, "Prince Takamatsu indeed has wisdom. To repay his condescension there were of course those ready to sacrifice themselves for the Japan-Thai cultural enterprise. He is versed in all problems, and it appears that he has a lucid mind."

August 22 (Sunday)

In the morning Ayusawa Iwao and his whole family came. He said, "The businessmen in Tōkyō feel that Japan and America are equals in actual power. There are those who say that as a result it is probably possible to compromise. The stupidity of businessmen!"

Yamauchi Ichirō traveled to Kuibyshev as a courier and went to the home of Ambassador Satō Naotake. He said that the ambassador reported that the Soviet Union was not in fact exhausted after two years of war. And in response to Yamauchi's inquiry as to whether arbitration between the Soviet and Germany was impossible, he said, "Even among influential people in Japan, those who talk about this matter are numerous. The fact that many think that such a thing is possible indicates the ominous state of the international situation and is lamentable."

Ayusawa spoke with a researcher on the Soviet from the Japanese Ministry of Foreign Affairs. Ayusawa reported: "When that person was riding the Siberian Railway, a soldier boarded the train. The female conductor told him 'Your ticket is no good!' The soldier pointed to his medals and service bars and said, 'Let me stay here.' For the female conductor, the great one in Russia was Stalin. And on this train the great one was herself. For her there was no

excuse for riding with his ticket and she expelled him." I said, "I would like somehow to give America a devastating blow. I would like to create complete destruction in New York. Making America experience the suffering of war would be in the interests of the world. Yet the problem is whether or not this is possible."

There is a radio report to the effect that the Japanese Army has at last been withdrawn from Kiska. And it was reported in such a way as to seem that not a single soldier was injured and America made a fool of herself.

On the radio it was reported that Shimazaki Tōson had died. He was kind to me on many occasions, and I had even received some of his works. I recall his slightly down-turned face with its serene, brilliant eyes. I was unable to attend his last party. *This* is an event that has left me aghast with surprise. Until the last, he went on writing and his mind was firm. He is a historical personality.

August 23 (Monday)

It is splendid to attempt to avoid increasing battle deaths uselessly by the withdrawal of the Japanese Army from Kiska. But the technique of reporting this as strange and wonderful in terms of "the divine protection of the gods" and "the divine protection of the spirits of the honorable war dead soldiers of Attu Island" is an irritating denigration of the people.

It is clear that these reports were produced by the army. It is the same in all the newspapers.

All the newspapers report that the success of this withdrawal from Kiska is a result of (1) the divine protection of the gods, (2) the divine protection of the spirits of all of the men who died on Attu, and (3) the skill of military operations.

    1. Is it likely that the spirits of dead soldiers exist only in Japan and not in foreign countries?
    2. Wouldn't excellent military operations consist of advance and attack rather than withdrawal?

To say that the annihilation on the island of Attu frightened the American demon to the core is little more than the newspapers being impressed by their own writing. With this level of intelligence, it is not possible to fight a first-rank country. This is the common-sense level that one gets from the recitations of the romantic tales of the Forty-seven Rōnin or Miyamoto Mushashi.[20]

The daily newspapers and radio search out from the newspapers of Chungking and America items that declare "the undefeatable position of Japan." The pursuit of self-satisfaction based upon flattery is the single military weapon.

The influence on Japan of Marxism has been pronounced:

1. Its mixture with feudalistic ideas.
2. Its interjection of the materialistic view of life.
3. The idea of achieving its goal by way of force, that is to say, power first-ism. Moreover, it has deteriorated into a communism that is not the so-called five-year plan of H. G. Wells.

Obama Toshie said, "Of late all the thieves are wearing military caps and civilian uniforms."

The criminal activities of the black market are widespread, but if they involve contractors for the military or military-employed civilians, customarily both the courts and the police do not investigate them thoroughly. That is to say, they are completely outside the law.

August 24 (Tuesday)

It appears that soldiers have to be constantly praised and that they must praise themselves. Despite the fact that for everyone the Kiska withdrawal is a minus in terms of the war situation, "the unparalleled success of the Kiska withdrawal was obtained by the protection of the gods under the intervention of the emperor and was based upon the determined combined action of the Imperial Navy," or "in actuality the withdrawal is not something that will have injurious effect on our superior strategic circumstances in the future, and, on the contrary, it will increase our determined tenacity in defense preparations." That is to say, what is being said here is that the reason for the occupation of Attu and Kiska on June 7 and 8, 1942, was to strengthen the defenses of the Northeast areas of our homeland. And accordingly, the newspaper's way of treating the courageous honorable deaths of the officers and men of the defending army on Attu is to claim, "To achieve the goal these were the unfortunate risks of military operation."

Indeed, I also had formulated such reasons and had said to withdraw the troops from Attu and Kiska earlier. However, when they keep repeating themselves in this way I cannot accept it.

Do the people probably feel that this level of reporting is reasonable?

1. Did Kiska and Attu prevent the coming enemy attack? The answer is no. These places are not even departure points for airplanes.

2. That being the case, why is it said that the homeland is all-important? The "Foreign Policy Bulletin" of New York (Foreign Affairs Society Report) makes the following statement (issued by Buenos Aires Dōmei on the 14th) (in the newspapers on the 17th):

America and England must prevent the weakening of Chungking's resistance to Japan.

1. England and America have concluded treaties with Chungking for the abolition of extraterritoriality.

2. The dissolution of the International Communist party will strengthen the position in Chungking.

3. The abolition of anti-Chinese immigration laws would provide a psychological influence on the political power of Chungking (although in reality this does not exceed one hundred persons a year).

August 25 (Wednesday)

A Berlin communiqué of the 23rd has reported the withdrawal from Krakov. With this, the German Army is already unable to maintain the eastern front. However, this announcement is exactly the same as that of the Japanese Army (*Yomiuri hōchi*, August 25, special communiqué).

It is probably the German intention to resist on the banks of the Dnieper. However, I wonder if this is indeed possible?

Unexpectedly, Interior Minister Frick has resigned and Heinrich Himmler has assumed the dual role of head of the Elite Army (SS) and chief of the secret police. We interpret this as meaning preparation for internal problems.

At three in the afternoon the Ayusawas came. They were repaying a visit of ours. We were going to eat waffles. A person named Lt. Kagami came along with them. He is a member of the Mitsubishi Bank. He is a graduate of Keiō and had gone to an American university. Comparing Japanese students with American students, he said Japanese students only take notes. He said American students know how to study by themselves and read through original texts. He is a young man with a sharp mind.

August 26 (Thursday)

The Quebec conference is completed. The conference between Roosevelt and Churchill began on August 11 and concluded on August 14.

As regards the conference:

1. There was discussion concerning unification in terms of military matters.

2. The main subject was the military operations against Japan.

The reason the Soviet Union was not invited was that the problem was mainly military operations against Japan.

Due to this, it is clear that Anglo-American offensive military operations will be intensified. Even in the communiqués of the Imperial Headquarters it is recognized that on the islands of New Georgia and Vella LaVella, "it will be difficult to minimize the power of the enemy offensive."

Gradually there are emerging from the government arguments that attribute war responsibility to the productive inadequacy of the home front.

If America and England come to the point of stating as their peace conditions, "Hand over those responsible for the war!" in the same way they did for Italy, what will become of Premier Tōjō and others?

Today was Shimazaki Tōson's funeral, but somehow I couldn't bring myself to attend. It was an extremely lavish affair. Because it was so well attended, I felt it didn't matter if I didn't attend.

August 27 (Friday)

I am reading *Ōkubo Toshimichi* by the Paris correspondent Ikebe Sanzan. (It is a book belonging to Yanagizawa Ken (Kimura Tsuyoshi, editor). He seems to be of great intelligence, and the things he says are definitive. (He has an excellent understanding of Ōkubo.)

Explaining the fact that Ōkubo did not fear the power of the military, he says,

> As to the military, especially the great military figures who were the most popular in society, he finds them his political enemy, and he puts aside both friendship and intimacy. . . . As a result, he rejected decisively fear of the threat of society becoming his enemy, and, establishing the idea of a civilian cabinet, there was no one to compare to him in the outstanding structure of his makeup as a politician. In the end Ōkubo as a politician refused to subordinate himself to the military. . . . His courage was even greater than Bismarck's. . . . And in case Yamagata proposed striking at China once more, who was there to resist this?

Indeed, this is well stated. There have been two misfortunes in Japan since the Manchurian Incident: The first is the fact that there were no politicians who resisted the military. The second is the fact that military people themselves were unable to control the army. And with a Japan seized by animal impulses, these factors finally brought about the war.

The government talks extravagantly about dissemination of scientific knowledge and the preparations for research. For this purpose, the premier assembled the presidents of the imperial universities. In addition, from the 150,000 yen of the Education Ministry's scholarships, 100,000 yen is for assistance for natural science expenses. As usual, for humanistic studies there is contempt.

In regard to the unification of scientific studies, not a single newspaper talks about getting rid of the rivalry between army and navy. The Military Department is completely beyond criticism. In both military equipment and research centers there is mutual depredation and conflict. And even in this grave situation of the nation it is still not possible to handle this feeling of rivalry. I wonder if they are qualified to attack what others do?

The weak point of so-called Japanism is the fact that it is unable to make use of the patriots within the nation. Because of its differing ideas, it drives away even the patriots of the nation. This is its fatal weak point.

I hear there is an announcement stating the establishment of a South East Asia Command and that Vice-Admiral Louis Mountbatten has assumed the post of highest commander. It is the first step in the forthcoming assault against Japan. Every day one is aware of the intensification of the air raids in China and the South Pacific area.

The Meiji Emperor placed his complete trust in Itō Hirobumi. This is the reason why he occupied a powerful position despite the attacks of people from the right wing and the military.

August 28 (Saturday)

The leader of the English labor unions, Asa Deakin, traveled to Stockholm and conferred with the head of the Finnish labor unions, Uori. It appears that they are planning arrangements for relations with the Soviet Union (*Yomiuri*, Stockholm, special dispatch 28th). Their strong point is carrying on negotiations by sending all sorts of people. In Japan, those who are not "comrades" and "Japanese-like" are ostracized.

A "Greater East Asian Writers Conference" was held with much fanfare. It is a patriotic movement of writers. The newspapers are full of articles about it. There are sympathetic writers from Manchuria and Taiwan. There are also critics, but, of course, I did not receive any notice of it.

Even among the most important lines of the Japanese railway system, one-way tracks are numerous. This is because from the earliest time the system was completely the property of the state. One may say that if there is no free competition, development and expansion are impossible. In our nation this is the level of politics.

August 29 (Sunday)

Captain Yamazaki of Attu Island was elevated two ranks to lt. general. Yesterday evening both the radio and the newspapers were full of nothing but this news. That it was at the orders of the military is clear. Yesterday's evening radio programs from eight to nine were changed.

I have already had enough of the great men of the "even-the-gods-weep-for-them style." I wish for a stop to these praiseworthy "human bullet" anecdotes. And in our military operations we must not tread a road that repeats such a tragedy.

And if such tragedies are repeated, I wonder if the people think about the "locus of responsibility." It is impossible to calculate the depth of ignorance.

On the one hand, there is ever-increasing daily encouragement of the sciences, and on the other hand, there is the heightening of ridiculous spiritual-ism. This contradiction is not something that will continue long. It is just like the Tokugawa Bakufu, which collapsed when its basic trends and its political policy collided in contradiction.

The final questions regarding Attu:

1. Did Japan inflict great losses on the enemy? No!
2. Will there be a devastating blow to the enemy's spirit? No!

If this is the case, there is nothing other than to say that for internal and traditional reasons the entire army will commit suicide. Ah! More than two thousand capable, likable young men! I have written this previously, but also, from the standpoint of national resources, this feudalistic, patriotic view must be changed. Of course, the traditional sentiment of the people is not something that will be changed in a short space of time, but . . .

In Ukebe Sanzan's *Iwakura Tomomi ron*, he wonders what would have hap-pened if the Kyōto faction had insisted upon expelling the barbarian because of the provisions of "extraterritoriality rights." This is an excellent thesis.

An account of Yanagizawa. At the time of the Great World War, France decided that if Japan participated it would be suitable to give her Indochina. This fact, he said, was stated in a British document.

In Meiji it was the Satchō[21] clique. In Shōwa it is the period of the army-navy clique.

In the afternoon I visited Kurusu Saburō and listened to his talk about former diplomacy. I had dinner at Mitsui Takao's home. It was a meal with special greens.

August 30 (Monday)

A conversation with Ishibashi Tanzan, who said he met and talked with Arita Hachirō at Lake Yamanaka. I hear that, along with others, Arita is extremely pessimistic about current conditions. He said that if unconditional surrender is imposed it will be impossible to do research openly and there will be prob-lems. If one relies upon what Arita says, those around Premier Tōjō are still optimistic. Probably when one is in that position one is optimistic.

According to the account of Itō, it seems that America is exhausting its entire strength at Rabaul. If Rabaul should fall, a wedge will be driven into the front line. If they reach the Philippines, it will be disastrous for Japan.

While on a train I was reading *A Historical Glimpse of Shōwa Foreign Rela-tions*. I had read it once but am reading it again. As a work of Arita it will survive for a long time. However, this "Greater East Asian Co-prosperity Sphere" idea is half-baked, and even to have it represent the intellectual trends of the times is not logical. Arita does not have a good mind. His strong points are his straightforwardness and tenacity. He is sincere.

Germany has announced martial law in Denmark. One can imagine that now there is the pressing threat that England will invade the continent of Europe. How long will Germany last?

The fact that Germany has begun to mention that "it bases itself on international law" should be noticed. Until now, it has not had such things as international law on its mind.

August 31 (Tuesday)

I visited the bereaved home of Shimazaki Tōson. I can understand that Shimazaki Shizuko was hospitalized because she was exhausted. The transparent eyes of Tōson's picture in the tokonoma were shining. But it was not a scolding gaze. It was a down-turned, self-examining look.

The Mombushō has closed down the Bunka gakuin (The Cultural Academy) at Surugadai. It is said this is because it is "liberal." A system in which this kind of punishment is a single official's decision is frightening. In Japan the constitution does not exist. Shimanaka's second daughter attended the school, and she said that it was an altogether fine school.

Today I am reading Itō Hirobumi's *Commentary on the Constitution*. This is in the interest of my research regarding the conditions that will follow the worsening of the war. The government for its part should carry out such research, but, since nobody there is doing it, if someone else does it there is the fear they will suffer serious consequences. I must be concerned about this.

September 1 (Wednesday)

The former principal of the Bunka Gakuin, Nishimura Isaku, has been arrested for lèse majesté and misleading the people.

It has come to pressure against the "liberals." However, I do not know at all what sort of person Nishimura is, and, as regards the educational goals of the Bunka Gakuin, for someone like myself who respects the rules, I cannot approve, but . . . the crime of lèse majesté is a serious matter. Ōzaki Yukio is a similar case, and Nishimura is the second offender.

The Japanese newspapers are full of details about the German side regarding the Russo-German war. I wonder why? Do we not have neutral relations with the Soviet Union?

Ōtani Risuke has been stopping over since yesterday evening. We went to Tsurumi and Yokohama together. The iron chains of the graveyards have been completely removed. It is said that even the doors of the Marunouchi Building and the iron in the steps of the stairway have been removed. We will probably end up in the postwar without a piece of iron anywhere.

I went to borrow money at the Kangyō Bank. It was to pay for new stock in Fuji Ice. When one borrows, though it is not a great sum, one understands that there will be some sort of complications. In my case the bank has been very accommodating.

The American planes increase in number and come to attack Minami Tori-jima (a part of Ogasawara Island). Because of this, alarms and warnings are issued.

The water pipes are not functioning. The baths have broken down. Even when the tatami become too old we cannot change them. At last our daily lives are reaching their lowest point. Because there are no meals anywhere even when we went out today visiting the tombs, we brought our own lunches. All of this just to go to Yokohama.

September 2 (Thursday)

Together with the worsening of the war, there is curiosity about how the right wing will behave. They are always searching for war and then they get war (*Yomiuri*, September 2).

Of late, it is always being said, "Neither overflowing with optimism nor falling into pessimism," and it is also said, "Neither mocking the enemy nor fearing them." Such words are always added after writings and speeches. I wonder what the middle position in all of this might be. When we study it we are trapped in one position or the other. Is lapsing into ambiguity the mental attitude of war?

It is just a month ago that I began the procedure of a land house mortgage to obtain a loan from the Kangyō Bank. There were numerous troublesome matters, such as official signature documents and family vital statistics. Today, again, because I did not take proof of the additions to my house, I went back and forth to the city hall and court and squandered the afternoon. The clerk said, "Even if you can come tomorrow, you must calculate on spending the whole day."

I understand how complicated things are in court proceedings. It is here that formalism most strongly appears. Even with collateral I had to go through complicated procedures. There must be a change in this kind of red tape where a man loses several days to borrow money.

It's true, but will there probably be a change? There will probably be no improvement in the Japanese people's bad habit of political formalism, with all its documents, intellectual games, and ignoring other people's concerns.

Of late, I am very much disgusted with the Japanese.

I am reading Ernest Satow's *A Record of Bakumatsu Recollections*.[22] The translation is extremely good.

September 4 (Saturday)

From the night of the 2nd, the anti-Axis armies have begun the land invasion of Italy. If one relies upon a telegram from Berlin, it is an invasion of an entire division, but even if it were not a military force of this size, there is nothing but pessimism regarding the Axis armies. Even in Denmark there are revolts. Also the eastern front is bad, and in the Smolensk area the fierce fighting continues to go badly. In the fourth year of the world war, victory or defeat is becoming clear. Propaganda is shifting to statements that the armed forces are strong and undefeated, but because steel is insufficient they cannot grasp victory (*Mainichi shinbun*, "Editorial," September 4).

According to what people are saying, our battleships *Mutsu* and *Nagato* have already been sunk and, moreover, the merchant marine no longer exists. Is this really true or not?

I met with Sakamoto Naomichi. This gentleman was chief of the Paris branch office of the Manchurian Railroad and is knowledgeable.

1. In a meeting with high officials, Premier Tōjō merely said, "To have to admit that Germany and Italy are becoming powerless is unexpected, and we made a mistaken forecast." The high officials were struck dumb.

2. Shigemitsu went to see Hirota and begged aid for a new solution in relations with Russia. Hirota said that he himself couldn't do anything and said to use Tōjō. However, when he conferred with Tōjō the latter did not approve. Because of the former problem (the foreign minister's resignation), he rejected Hirota on the basis of emotion.

3. Hirota is a great figure. But at this late point in time, he said he had no ideas.

4. Hirota thought that by constructing a demilitarized zone between the Japanese Army and Russia, troops could be withdrawn and brought to the China area, but the government would not consider such a possibility at all and maintained the military force just as it had until now.

5. In the view of General Yamamoto Hidesuke, England's strategy is a total assault—first strike at the Burma area and then advance into China. From this area it will advance on Thailand and intercept the Japanese Army.

6. I hear that Matsuoka is extremely pessimistic.

September 5 (Sunday)

It was thought that hereafter farm cultivation could be carried on by whole families, but this was not possible because of the rain. And yet the water pipes do not produce a drop of water. This is because the houses are on rather high foundations. The rain is continuing, but with the water at this level there will probably be an increase in the demand for water, which will be impossible to satisfy. The result of unplanned city expansion.

At times when international relations are the most important thing, the newspapers actually have no reports of international affairs. There is still great faith in spiritual preaching.

Yahagi, head of the Military Press Corps, gave a speech at Utsunomiya, and as usual the newspapers reported it extensively. The fact that the army and navy officers receive treatment accorded premiers in foreign countries is the distinctive characteristic of late. Who is moving this is perfectly clear.

What should be noted are the people here and there who say, "Even in America they have abandoned the last hope for a battle to the death between us." Is this a trial balloon? The fact that there is no such discussion in America I think is more and more clear. Other statements, such as "Conditions within America do not allow for a long drawn-out war," if known in foreign countries would be laughed at. America is probably thinking the war is just beginning.

September 6 (Monday)

Today I borrowed twelve thousand yen from the Kangyō Bank. There were a great many complications. Would it be possible to borrow money without all these complications? There is a need for the simplification of procedures.

I was asked by Ishibashi to do a study concerning postwar problems. There will be difficulties since there are problems I cannot write about. However, Japan must give thought to every possibility, and if there cannot be an atmosphere of free research, the nation is in danger. The present situation is a result of such an atmosphere.

September 7 (Tuesday)

All the newspapers inserted on their first pages last night's radio speech of Captain Akiyama. He admitted severe fighting in the southern regions (*Mainichi*, September 7). Captain Akiyama thought that if India and Australia fall, the enemy will be defeated. I wonder where this conclusion came from.

There is an article in this morning's *Yomiuri hōchi*. It states that Perry came for the purpose of invading Japan.

In Japan there is an uproar to put pressure on Christianity and about the trivial problem of cutting the "long sleeves" of kimonos.

September 8 (Wednesday)

In this morning's *Yomiuri* there was a long essay entitled "Germany Is Invincible" by Ikesaki Chūkō. It was divided into four arguments: (1) military power, (2) productive capacity in war materials, (3) self-sufficiency in food, (4) national spiritual strength to endure the fears and sacrifices of war. Each and every point argued decisively Germany's superiority (*Yomiuri hōchi*, September 8).

To think of attacking America at all is folly. But opposing this is not possible. Regarding this, I have just submitted a letter to a column of the *Yomiuri*.

CHAPTER 2

Foundations of Trademark Law

CHAPTER OVERVIEW

Trademarks surround us every day and help us make valuable and informed decisions about the products and services we purchase. There are four types of marks: *trademarks* are used for goods; *service marks* are used for services; *certification marks* are used to certify some quality of a product or service; and *collective marks* indicate membership in an organization. Some marks, namely those that are coined or "made up," like EXXON®, are stronger than others, namely those that describe or suggest something about a good or service. Not all matter is protectable: marks that disparage a person or that are scandalous cannot be protected. On the other hand, even some unusual devices can be protected, such as sounds and fragrances. Trademarks come into existence through use; they need not be registered with the U.S. Patent and Trademark Office to be protected, although federal registration affords several advantages to a trademark owner.

INTRODUCTION

Although there was some use of trademarks or symbols in the Middle East and Far East several centuries ago, contemporary trademark law can be traced back to use of trademarks during the medieval period in Europe by merchants who sought to distinguish the goods they sold from those sold by others by applying a mark or symbol to their goods. By viewing the mark, purchasers would immediately be able to identify the craftsperson who made the goods and make an informed decision about the quality of the materials. The use of symbols by medieval craftspeople to distinguish and identify their goods is the direct antecedent for the modern

September 9 (Thursday)

Parts of an article that speak of Ikesaki Chūkō's conclusion on the "Invincibility of Germany" (*Yomiuri hōchi*, September 9).

Today—the submission of Italy to unconditional surrender.

In the past, the national debate before and after the Meiji Restoration, the common sense of the Japanese people was expressed by Mutsu in the Sino-Japanese War, and the criticism against Komura's peace settlement in the Russo-Japanese War. And now there is spreading low-level discussion of current conditions. I wonder if the Japanese people have finally descended to this level.

At noon we heard the report from Tanaka Tokichi at the Japan Club of the unconditional surrender of Italy. The news was published in the evening papers.

At the Marunouchi Building newsstands, people are standing in long, long lines, and they are eager to buy newspapers. It appears they received a considerable shock. This was because the announcement came immediately after the propaganda that claimed that the Badoglio government would continue the same way as Mussolini had. This sort of transparent, lying propaganda is continuous, and, moreover, these mistakes continue, the mistakes are repeated, and it is a sad thing!

At the International Politics Association I heard a speech of an officer named Horita. It was a worthless, commonplace sermon. His stating that Germany would absolutely not let go of the Crimea was the only new fact I heard. His conclusion was that Germany has an immovable foundation.

Kaji has returned from Shanghai and will depart the day after tomorrow.

1. The controlled economy is being carried out, but it will probably not be a success.

2. The officials of Japan only oppress the Japanese people, and because of this, capital is fleeing in large quantities to the Chinese side. (For example, the government purchasing ten thousand yen worth of cotton contributes four thousand yen or more to the national debt. However, it provides eighteen thousand yen to the Chinese.

3. The Japanese people do not at all have the qualifications for managing or leading the Chinese.

September 10 (Friday)

Since the surrender of the Badoglio government, the Japanese newspapers have begun to "bad-mouth" Italy. As usual, it is the same old thing.

Shiratori and others are expressing their opinions in the newspapers. The forgetfulness of both the people who shamelessly talk about "the obligation of Italy is ended" and those who accept this position is nothing but astonishing.

Who are the people who concluded an alliance with this sort of country? Which people still rejoice in this? Is anyone happy about this?

September 11 (Saturday)

The attacks of each newspaper on Italy become more and more ferocious.

The betrayal by Badoglio is intolerable. The Japanese empire declares its opposition.

It is said that overseas students from everywhere in East Asia are being guided to Japaneseness. Is it possible for people of our level to lead the people of other countries?

Those who until yesterday cried out "Italy! Italy!" are today even using the culture columns to bad-mouth Italy. It appears that the Japanese newspapers do not even have the common sense and logic of elementary school students.

The Fascist New People's Government was established in Italy. If there is an absolutist mentality, it is impossible to change a government completely. The government always encouraged the emergence of like-minded persons and made use of them. There was no cooperation, there was competition.

The German style of behavior is in this manner. Japan is completely the same. In international politics, however, this has produced numerous sacrifices.

Evening, I went to a People's Scholarly Arts Society meeting. When I asked, "Is the present situation of Japan as it has been, or is it getting worse?" Watsuji Tetsurō said, "It's the worst!" Miki Kiyoshi said this was because of the low level of popular intelligence.

Miki detects the fundamentals of Marxism in the present war, and Professor Watsuji and I say it is nationalism. I said, "Today, where in the world is there any manifestation of the Yellow Peril? Is it not a rivalry of country against country?"

September 12 (Sunday)

The tragedy of Italy was its attempt to become a great empire without having had the actual power to become a great empire.

Lavish indignation is expressed over the Italian betrayal of Japan (in every newspaper—*The Asahi*, the Iguchi essays). Be careful! Wasn't the German–Soviet pact the same thing?

If Italy was an untrustworthy country, those responsible for bringing this alliance about at the start should be punished. And who rejoices over this?

A professor of Hitotsubashi University named Ueda Tatsunosuke says, "Fascism's basic principle of national salvation is eternal" (*Asahi*). However, fascism is a system that has the inevitable character of being unable to bring out the "best brains."

In a conversation yesterday evening it was said, "A death notice of Shimazaki Tōson was sent from the *Geijutsu-in*, and this death notice was delivered to the Shimazaki home." That is to say, Shimazaki had been notified of his own death. However, it is an excellent example of the workings of formalism. The section chief asked Fujita of *Chūō kōron* if in "Tōson" it was *tō* (*higashi*) or *tō* (*fuji*)."[23]

The greatest agony at present is that vulgar discussion cannot be criticized more. Increasingly this is degrading public opinion.

I've heard that General Staff Headquarters has relieved Tōjō of his second position as army minister and they hoped to have someone else take up that position. However, Tōjō will probably not resign easily.

September 13 (Monday)

I believed it would be useless, but I made some inquiries about the *Yomiuri* article on Perry. I did this through Takahashi. It became clear that it had no basis whatever.

It is said that the English and American planes are making their target the dwellings of the middle class. This is widely believed in Japan. Is it true? It is material for later research.

A meeting of the International Relations Research Society opened at noon. Yamauchi Ichirō, who works part-time at the Foreign Ministry, gave a report on his visit to the Soviet. He said that the morale of the Soviet Union was good and its culture flourishing.

> 1. He was bringing important papers, and the Siberian Railway line was filled with students of the railway school who were returning home for summer vacation. Because the conductor requested the students to guard the foreigner's luggage, they alternately kept watch until quite late. Even such people as the porters were kind.
> 2. One-third to two-thirds of those working on the train were women.
> 3. One cannot see any sense of war weariness.
> 4. Everyone thinks there will be a victory over Germany.
> 5. Because they are self-confident, religion is untrammeled. The churches were full.

September 14 (Tuesday)

Yesterday at the International Relations Research Association I insisted that because the Soviet Union is the only possible foreign relations opponent for

Japan, at the least, first of all, be fair in reporting the military mess on the eastern war front, and after that, in the Manchurian area, construct a demilitarized buffer zone and move into China with a great army.

The fact that the Soviet Union makes use of religion indicates the thinness of her ideology. This indicates that the Soviet is one step ahead of Japan, which carries on a politics of fanaticism.

Evening, saw a play at the Yūraku Theater called *Bose*. This was because I was sent tickets by Sōma Aizō. The actors were very good, but the moralizing was extremely tiresome. Tōyama Mitsuru, together with his wife, came to the show. This aged, silent gentleman is a man without learning and does not study, but nevertheless great numbers of people all but worship him. This is probably because of the "passion" in his personality.

September 15 (Wednesday)

Came to Karuizawa. As always, the congestion was murderous.

The fixed market price is unreasonable, and merchants cannot support themselves. The fixed price system abuses these trustworthy people, and it is a system that encourages the black market. Moreover, in a current situation in which bureaucrats have complete power, criticism against the controlled economy is not permitted. And because the government is killing criticism and intends to operate an economy dealing with the masses, it is natural that the problems will increase a thousandfold. The black market is the usual outcome. Without the black market, people cannot live for even one day. Therefore it is called the "people's market price" or the "fixed price of the black market." And in the relation of supply and demand, naturally, there is a market price that can be recognized.

Sugar is from 30 to 40 yen per one kamme (8⅓ pounds), and sometimes it costs 50 yen. According to the account of a service person, his friend bought honey for 200 yen per kamme. Rising prices change rapidly, and just a short time ago sugar was 10 yen per kamme. When sugar was 30 yen per kamme (even this cheap), one full teaspoon was 210 sen (a full teaspoon took about 3 momme, .1326 oz.). Five or six months ago it is said that a suit of Western clothes cost 1,000 yen. A frightful inflation has set in. And indeed the difference between the fixed price and the actual value in the market is tenfold.

September 16 (Thursday)

Yesterday, while on a train, I finished reading Ernest Satow's *Record of Bakumatsu Recollections* (translation). More than in any other single work, the facts of the Bakumatsu period are lavishly detailed in this work. He associated with people from every quarter. Saigō, Ōkubo, Katsu, Nakai, and others were all his friends. He listened to their discussions and made great efforts on behalf of transferring political authority to the emperor. In any case, Englishmen are diligent scholars. Satow, Mitford, Adams, Oliphant, and Alcock all left behind major works for later generations. They were young when they came to Japan, and they studied in this land.

Confronted with the betrayal of Italy, Japan is indignant, but if Italy were asked about this, how would it probably respond?

1. How much did Japan help in this war?

2. Has not Japan, since the time of the Manchurian Incident, taken the position that in a situation in which the old treaties do not conform to the new conditions, it is all right to break them at any time? The present circumstances of Italy are the same.

3. The reform of Italy's political policy is a logical conclusion from the fall of Mussolini. However, the newspapers of Japan self-servingly write hopeful observations. This is the responsibility of Japan itself, and as regards Italy in this matter, it does not share any obligation.

Regarding the *Taiyō-maru*, among the total number of a thousand and several hundred passengers, it was only twenty or so who were saved. In the case of military transport ships, the commander is a lt. colonel in the army, and the ship's captain is under his command. However, these officers know nothing of nautical matters. In the event of an accident on the ship, it is the lt. colonel who gives the orders. Also, in the case of the *Taiyō-maru*, it appears there was conflict over how to deal with the crisis. Both the ship's captain and the army officer died, and it is not easy to know the real circumstances.

Even at the time of the maritime court hearing, it was ordered that the subject of lines of command was not to be touched. The ship's captain is of the same rank as a captain in the navy, but he belongs to the army and is completely under the command of the army. It appears that because of facts such as these, unnecessary sacrifices occur. Talking about these circumstances with others has been completely prohibited. For reasons such as these, there is absolutely no opportunity for correcting such mistakes.

September 17 (Friday)

Throughout the morning today, I worked on the *Chronology* of the *Tōden*, and in the afternoon I played golf with Ichihara.

Mussolini formed the Republican Fascist party and declared its five principles. He did not publicly acknowledge the Italian emperor. However, emperor-centered Japan assisted the Republican Fascist party, and I wonder whether this was logical. I wonder whether the Italian leaders, pressured by the circumstances of the times, think that taking a position contrary to that of Japan will in the end create great problems. When one looks at the newspaper reports, the number of destroyed Japanese planes is extremely small. An example of this is the number of planes sent to raid Buin on Bougainville Island that were destroyed: If one relies on news sources, as against the 176 enemy planes destroyed there were about 15 of ours damaged. That is to a ratio of 10 to 1. If that is the case, I feel that it is unnecessary to say anything "critical." I read a speech made by Churchill at the Guild Hall on July 3.

1. Seeing that America was standing on the precipice of war, these *foul Japanese* [in English] attacked Pearl Harbor with the air of dominating Asia. Until Germany can be wiped out by the air power of America and England, until it is possible to achieve this greatest war victory, if Japan has still not been humbled he swore an oath. England will gather up all of its ships and planes and, turning them toward the Pacific, we will destroy Japan.

2. In Tunisia a 350,000-man German-Italian army is either taken prisoner of war or annihilated.

3. In June new ship construction on the Anglo-American side will replace every ship lost with seven to ten new ships.

4. In addition to the more than 40,000 of our people killed, 120,000 have been wounded by German airplanes. Now the whirlwind is in the opposite direction. In six months of the present year, the RAF has dropped thirty-five times more bombs than the Germans dropped on us. In Dusseldorf alone, one evening, we dropped 2,000 tons of bombs, and the damage was 38 planes. In contrast to that, in the same half year the enemy dropped 1,500 tons of bombs on our country, and the damage was 245 planes.

5. Before the autumn leaves fall, there will be a great offensive in the Mediterranean. (The foregoing was a speech by Churchill when he received the title of "Free Man" of the city of London.) Churchill delivered a speech concerning the fall of Mussolini at the Parliament, July 27, 1943.

6. He does not know what will happen to Italy. However, he did not wish Italy to be placed in a position of upheaval and a state of anarchy, or to be in a position of an enemy not to be negotiated with. The errors such as those made by Germany in ruling many countries and assuming responsibility for their internal politics must not be repeated. As regards Italy, he did not wish to execute the death sentence and lead it to a concentration camp.

Churchill stressed the fact that the true enemy was Germany. He called for generous settlement with respect to Italy, and he encouraged unconditional surrender.

September 18 (Saturday)

The radio reported that today marks the twentieth anniversary of the Manchurian Incident, and there was a commentary on its significance broadcast to the Philippine people by some head of the Manila Saitō Press Corps. As regards this significance, the Manchurian Incident was the first step of the Greater East Asian War. This was the first step in liberating other races. The broadcast said that it hoped the Philippine people would recognize the sincerity of Japan.

The military apparently think that saying such things will impress the Philippine people. Ordinarily, it would be better to be quiet about such things as the Manchurian Incident and the like, and it is customary not to arouse the memories of others. And yet to talk about these things intentionally is foolishness that goes beyond imagination. They do not carry out the least bit of self-examination regarding the present stage and future of the war. Moreover, no matter how circumstances develop, the fact that they have not received an education in which they were trained in self-examination has already become clear. Writing the *Chronology*, what concerns me is the great frequency of fires. In such places as Hakodate, these are extremely numerous, and there is no thought given to the basic techniques for preventing these fires. No matter how deeply there is suffering from war, there will probably be no self-examination. But human beings are not as clever as that.

On this morning's radio it was announced that the head of the branch of the Sanseisō office of Mitsui Bussan (Mitsui Products) has been imprisoned for ten years, and Mitsui Bussan is prohibited from business in the same area. It is said that they violated the regulation system, but what sort of crime was committed I do not know, and irrationality is running rampant in everything. It is because the young officers have extraterritoriality rights.

Every day there is a great deal of fog and we have no clear weather. On the radio I search for the news of the world, but every day it is nothing but the reports of the military.

September 19 (Sunday)

As to the conferring of honors in the Sino-Japanese War, after the final end of the war there was the establishment of a commission of inquiry, and after this, on August 5 (the restoration of peace, April), for the first time there was the conferring of awards. Since the Sino-Japanese Incident, although there is no resolution yet, there has already been the conferring of awards some forty times.

Sometime or other, Kawai Tatsuo said that in Australia there was no response at all to a proposed agreement on a commercial treaty with Japan. In Japan there were the usual office delays, and the other party misunderstood and concluded that Japan disliked the treaty, and there was discussion of the whole matter.

Parliamentary government does not function if there is no conformity to justice. From the Meiji period, Japan has been a battleground of cliques.

At four o'clock in the afternoon, keeping an appointment, I visited with Prince Konoe, and for about an hour and a half I listened to his account of the Japanese–American negotiations. He said there was no way to conduct the current situation. He added, "It is irresponsible." Sung Tzu-wen made a speech after the Quebec Conference and loudly proclaimed such things as the return of Taiwan and Manchuria to China and the independence of Korea. And it is said he stated that Indochina and Hong Kong are also to be considered. I think that Sung's political maneuvers with regard to England and America are extremely skillful.

Konoe wondered whether the military would put forward more repressive political policies in accordance with the worsening of the war.

How would it be if under a new system the premier was elected by the upper and lower houses and, serving for a period of about two years, was allowed reelection?

September 20 (Monday)

Today is Aviation Day, and there is strong emphasis on increased production. On the other hand, the newspapers have taken up the issue of the unification of administration. Reading between the lines, they are printing the hopes on the people's part regarding the uncoordinated placing of orders by the army and navy. (in the *Yomiuri* today, in the Asahi on the 16th and 17th.)

Despite this, the army and navy are robbing each other of materials.

September 21 (Tuesday)

There are typhoons and, from Kyūshū through the entire Chūgoku, severe damage. Probably one reason for this is that warnings are not possible. It is said that there has been an earthquake in Tottori—heaven's anger?—and because very little of this is reported in the newspapers, the real facts are probably beyond our knowing. Somewhat later than this time last year, I went around the Sanin area and the Sanyō area, but I think the extent of the damage now is greater than it was then. As a result, resources are completely unavailable. Ah!

September 22 (Wednesday)

This morning's *Yomiuri hōchi* reported that Perry's Expedition Record was for spying. This is the level of ignorance.

September 23 (Thursday)

Last night on the radio Premier Tōjō made a speech concerning the renovation of the government. His specific plans were reported in this morning's newspapers. These drastic policies involve the withdrawal of the postponed drafting of students, the prohibition of seventeen kinds of work for males, the laying off of government officials, and the regulation of office buildings, private houses, and shops.

The fact that it has reached the point that males under the age of forty cannot be employed in restaurants will have great influence on my relations with such places as the Ginsei and Fuji Ice.

It is probably not possible to regulate public offices; therefore, in the end, only the common people will pay in suffering.

However, in carrying on the war it is natural to reach this stage. It is probably excellent training for the people to think deeply about the meaning of modern war. Moreover, the preparation of buildings and roads is absolutely necessary for the prevention of fires, and this also is inevitable.

It is said the head of the Military Press Corps, Yahagi Nakao, met with Shimanaka and resolved the *Chūō kōron* problem. I have heard recently that for the most part control is becoming the single channel of the Information Board.

Yahagi is somewhat under criticism in his department. For example, the idea for the evacuation of Tōkyō's population was his, but given the circumstances, transportation facilities are inadequate and there has been a return to the original policy of having everyone staying put. We hear that Tōjō has scolded Yahagi. Also, in the China-related political maneuvering, the Information Board is a persistent supporter of Wang Ching-wei, but the core of the government is seeking a union with Chiang Kai-shek, and they have to put forward ideas acceptable even to Chinese opinion.

On March 15, 1908, a police order prohibited face coverings.

September 24 (Friday)

Wang Ching-wei arrived in Tōkyō on the 22nd and left for home on the 23rd. Was it a matter of a loan or preparatory arrangements for winning over Chiang Kai-shek? Inflation is becoming rather severe.

Concerning Japanese propaganda, Kaji said that there were posters that supposedly said "Chiang Kai-shek has failed," but in Chinese the inscription meant "Chiang Kai-shek has not failed." There are probably innumerable such examples.

Military conscription has been declared in Taiwan.

Since Meiji, every government has frequently fought with the military. From the 1880s to the 1890s they were in opposition over the reduction of military budgets. However, in the Russo-Japanese War they were completely without such power. Moreover, because the same people were in influential posts over a long period of time, they were politically experienced. Thus, good politicians were produced. These included such people as Katsura Tarō, Saitō Makoto, and Yamamoto Gombei.

September 25 (Saturday)

According to Nagata, recently there have been frequent burglaries in the houses of Karuizawa.

A conversation with Sekido. In the area of Nagoya, girls are training with bamboo spears, and his wife and daughters are doing this every day. Neither the province nor the city is overly supportive, but the responsible persons of the military division carry this out.

Every household is digging shelters, and because of this there are places where the houses lean over. What happens if a house overturns in a fire? In Tōkyō everybody is made to dig shelters. One example of this formalism is the compulsory provision of fire-fighting straw mats in the mountain villas of Karuizawa.

September 26 (Sunday)

I had a discussion with General Ugaki. It was for the purpose of hearing the facts concerning his tenure as foreign minister. He is extremely youthful looking, and his goals are admirable. It's possible that this man is the one to save the nation. Konoe is brilliant, but he is not courageous and forceful, and for him other military men are impossible. There is the opportunity for Ugaki to rise. No matter who does it, however, it is too late.

September 27 (Monday)

During the day, *Tōyō keizai*; in the evening, a meeting of the Twenty-six Society. At the Twenty-six Society everyone was in agreement on the inevitability of air raids. It was said that when there are large-scale air raids there would be 150,000–160,000 casualties.

The acknowledgment of Fascist power.

September 28 (Tuesday)

At the Foreign Politics Association I listened to a talk by a Foreign Ministry official named Kase Sunichi. He noted that America was aiming at a short war, and that her will for war was thriving. To say that they are aiming at a brief war, even more than being a domestic issue, is really a matter of disparaging the enemy, Japan and Germany.

use of trademarks such as COCA-COLA®, MICROSOFT®, and CREST®. (See Exhibit 2–1 for History of Trademarks.)

PURPOSE AND FUNCTION OF TRADEMARKS

Trademarks perform two critical functions in the marketplace: they provide assurance that goods are of a certain quality and consistency, and they assist consumers in making decisions about the purchase of goods. If a trademark such as NIKE® could be counterfeited and used by another on inferior merchandise, there would be no incentive for the owners of the NIKE mark to produce high-quality shoes and to expend money establish-

ing consumer recognition of the products offered under the NIKE marks. Thus, protection of trademarks results in increased competition in the marketplace, with both the producer of goods and services and the consumer as the ultimate beneficiaries. Businesses benefit because they can reap the rewards of their investment in developing and marketing a product without fearing another business will deceive consumers by using the same or a confusingly similar mark for like goods, and consumers benefit because they are able to identify and purchase desired goods.

The value inherent in achieving consumer loyalty to a particular product or service through the maintenance of consistent quality of the products or services offered under a mark is called **goodwill.** The goodwill associated

EXHIBIT 2–1
History of Trademarks
(from PTO web site at
www.uspto.gov)

The Patent and Trademark Office believes that the importance of trademarks dates back seven thousand years to about 5000 B.C., when drawings showing bison with distinctive symbols on their flanks appeared in the caves of prehistoric man. These were likely some kind of ownership mark, that is, a trademark that identified those particular bison as being the property of a unique owner and distinguishing those bison from the bison of others.

By 500 B.C., a real economic use of trademarks can be documented in ancient Rome, where evidence has been found of bricks stamped with the mark of the brick manufacturer.

There is little to be found about the use and growth of trademarks between the fall of the Roman Empire and the Renaissance. The Renaissance, however, brought with it a celebration of the arts, and trademarks reemerged in a significant way. In about the twelfth century, trade guilds began using marks to identify goods made by their members. In 1266, the earliest English law on trademarks, the Bakers Marking Law, came into being. This law allowed bakers to identify their breads by stamping a mark on the loaf or pricking the loaf in a particular and recognizable pattern.

The first reference to trademark infringement litigation occurred in 1618 when a clothier who produced inferior cloth used the mark of a superior cloth producer and was brought to court in the case of *Southern v. How.*

The origin of American trademark protection came in the sailcloth manufacturing industry. As a result of concerns of sailcloth makers, in 1791, Thomas Jefferson recommended the creation of trademark legislation based on the Commerce Clause of the Constitution. In 1879, the United States finally enacted its first trademark legislation. The first registered trademark was registered under that law. The mark, used to identify liquid paints by Averill Paints, was dominated by the depiction of an eagle.

September 29 (Wednesday)

Today the Ministry of Munitions came into existence, and the Ministry of Commerce-Industry and the Planning Board were abolished.

This is the typical way of doing things. If it were another country, it is to be expected that the previously established apparatus would remain just as it was, a Munitions Ministry would be established, and by this the functions would be unified. However, in the "Japanese character" such a thing is impossible. Moreover, in mechanistic military politics, such a thing is not possible.

That is to say, if one discusses this from one angle, it is a breach of Tōjō's "people rather than machineism." The purpose of the Munitions Ministry was to accommodate the demands for centralized purchasing. If it is no more than this, is there any necessity for a new system? Here is one of the deficiencies of the Japanese people.

The reason Wang Ching-wei came to Japan was that Japan had begun efforts to work with Chiang Kai-shek and propose conditions. Through Sung Tzu-wen, these were published in the American newspapers. Hearing this, Wang was infuriated. In protest, he asked if this was not a violation of the treaty that he himself would handle Chungking negotiations.

These Chungking political maneuvers have occurred many times. Unbelievably, only now have they finally come to be noticed.

Recently, although actually it goes back a long way, newspaper articles and speeches talk about "military-official-people." That is to say, it is the order referred to as *shi-nō-kō-shō*.[24]

A certain person said that in Tōjō's the other day, as usual there were the words "Under Our Great Imperial Majesty," but the pillow-word "Glorious War Results" was not there.

Since it was alleged that the branch store of Mitsui Bussan in Shansi Province violated regulations, the head of the store received ten years of penal servitude, and the company head Mukai left for China, expressing his apology. After returning to Japan he would resign his position.

We can see in this the attitude that only abuses the people without concern for voluntary increases in production by leaving things as they are.

There are differences in air forces. However, with regard to air forces, no matter how many planes we have, they are never enough to be sent everywhere in the world. There are limits to the productive power of Japan. One must think about military operations and foreign relations with this level in mind. Has thought been given to this matter?

At the Foreign Relations Association yesterday, Takashima Heizaburō asked why America hated the Japanese people. Why Japan could be hated is not comprehensible to this intellectual class.

In a speech on July 28, Roosevelt said [quoted in English],

In the Pacific we are pushing the Japs around from the Aleutians to New Guinea. . . . The Japs have lost more planes and more ships than they have been able to replace. The continuous and energetic prosecution of attrition will drive the Japs back from their overextended line running from Burma and Siam and [so on]. We have good reason to believe that their shipping and air power cannot support such outposts. Our naval, land, and air strength in the Pacific is constantly growing; if the Japanese are basing their future plans for the Pacific on a long period in which they will be permitted to consolidate and exploit their conquered resources [this sentence is not in *Kokusai jōhō* (International report) published by the Information Board], they had better start revising their plans now, I give that to them merely as a helpful suggestion.

Having said this, he noted that the Allies occupied the superior position throughout the skies of Burma and elsewhere. Where is Japan's perfect military strategy?

Today (September 29) the death sentence was pronounced on Ozaki Hotsumi. I had met with him only once or twice. I wonder whether he was really a spy. There is no material that either affirms or denies this. Yet it is regrettable that the evidence is not public.

The Greater East Asian War is a great war with extreme ups and downs. Those who write must assume the obligation of leaving behind some sort of record for succeeding generations. That is, I am beginning here a diary of things that have not been written about. This is for the purpose of creating materials for a history of Greater East Asian foreign relations.

Gods! Save Japan.

October 1 (Friday)

Yesterday I went to pick up my bag on the closing day at the Karuizawa Golf Course. While playing, my nine-iron was stolen. It was really unpleasant. Nowadays it is a world of thieves. People have their shoes stolen while they are seated on trains. In the streetcars people have their briefcases stolen. This is extremely common.

In the newspapers and radio, there is talk of nothing but increase in production and airplane output. The desire is for a great number of planes. However, we can't very well expect to say that we have enough planes when we are spread over worldwide war fronts. Aren't these war fronts too widely spread? Roosevelt is saying so—is this a good idea? Since there is no criticism about these matters, sacrifices will probably be extremely great again.

From the outset of the war, the Planning Commission and other bodies were supposed to study (1) the productive power of the enemy, and (2) the industrial power of our country. The fact that at this stage we are now facing confusion is nothing more than an indication that these researches serve complacency.

An announcement in the September 19 morning edition. Vice-Admiral Itō committed suicide by *harakiri* because his strategies were not succeeding. The newspapers praised his virtue in enlarged type. He was buried in a naval funeral ceremony. This is one instance of death itself being venerated as a virtue.

Three men have come from the Philippines: Laurel, Aquino, and Vargas.

Whether MacArthur should have died in the Philippines or, continuing to live, he should have led the American-English armies—of course, the Anglo-American viewpoint.

The Japanese newspapers have not escaped the influence of Marxism, and when it was announced that Stettinius had become assistant-secretary of state, they criticized him as a member of the Morgan clique (*Chūbu Nihon shinbun*). Even in the Berlin dispatches there is no such crude materialism. The difficulties of this crowd are that they only engage in formulas and have no disposition to get out from under these.

October 2 (Saturday)

Yesterday evening I attended a meeting of the People's Scholarly Arts Society and had a discussion with Miki Kiyoshi. The essential points were not clear, but in the final analysis I said that when war came with England and America there was no way for cooperation, and it appeared that he disagreed on the point that there was the possibility of cooperation. He has the habit of muddling objective circumstances with ideals and hopes.

The letters-to-the-editor section of the *Asahi shinbun* is criticizing the excessively cruel domination of the extremist right wing (*Mainichi shinbun*, October 2, evening edition).

Although the Japanese nation is the best in the world, there are no people like the Japanese for doubting their own people.

However, magazines such as *Kōron* and *Bungei shunjū* are receiving complete support from the military. Only magazines such as these have not had a reduction in their paper allotment.

In today's *Yomiuri*, Nomura Shigeomi said the "domestic war" will increasingly be an offensive attack on Anglo-American ideas.

Ayusawa Iwao resigned from the World Economic Research Association. A follower of Ayusawa has been arrested because he is left-wing. As a witness summoned by the Yokohama police, he discovered that he had been under observation for about the past year and a half because he was in contact with Americans and Britains and he was the head of the Tōkyō branch of the International Labor Organization. At the police station he was examined by three assistant police inspectors and policemen, but he was unable to recollect how many times he was beaten. He was abused with extremely harsh words.

And in the neighboring rooms he could hear the sound of someone being beaten.

Ayusawa was abroad from the time of his youth and does not understand Japanese matters. Isn't the appointment of Higashi Ryōzō as managing director of the Fresh Produce Union also the same thing? Having well-intentioned motives of patriotism, such people as he do not understand the psychology of the Japanese, and when they interact with foreigners they are mistrusted. It is too bad.

It was alleged that Ayusawa was dealing in secret information. The disgusting Japanese penchant for informing! It is the usual practice for the military and police to beat and kick those who are concerned about the people. This is common for those caught up in the black market.

October 3 (Sunday)

It is raining. It rains every day; however, nothing comes out of the water pipes.

On this morning's radio it was reported that the Ministry of Railways and the Ministry of Communications have been combined into a Munitions Ministry, and in place of the Ministry of Agriculture and Forestry there is a Ministry of Commerce. (1) These great changes have occurred without any problem; however, (2) the changes in machinery will temporarily interrupt efficiency, and (3) this will be a problem for Premier Tōjō, who talks of "people rather than machines" carrying out these reforms. Actually, changing the machinery is not a bad thing.

1. In tampering with machinery, naturally formalism is the core of the ideology.
2. If there is no change in formalism, the officials who are moved by this focus are not able to separate themselves from their sectionalism.

This second point must be stressed as a special characteristic of the Japanese.

In everyone's mind the great problem of the moment is the unification and reconciliation of the army and navy, and everyone thinks that first of all an operation must be performed in this case. There is no one who says even one word about this.

October 4 (Monday)

Now we are having violent winds from the Kantō area to the Tōhoku area. In these areas it appears that the damage has not been so great, but I think this will probably have an influence on the production of food supplies because the rice plants are destroyed. In this case the "divine wind" is a curse. There is no guarantee that some will not think this is supernatural. I am worried. If the weather does not clear up, there is fear that epidemics will follow.

According to a man in Mitsui Bussan, those who went to the southern regions all returned to Japan in splendid physical condition. However, within the space of one month they inevitably become thinner. The poor complexions of the young people on the trains.

In this morning's editions of the *Asahi* and *Yomiuri* an editorial stated that Chungking must reflect seriously upon itself. The themes were "Looking for Decisiveness in Chungking" (*Asahi*) and "The Position of Chungking" (*Yomiuri*). It was a discussion that enlarged upon the statement of Wang Ching-wei: "The reasons for the anti-Japanese war have already disappeared." It was also a protest against the emergence in Burma of a Chungking army. But it is all too late. It is the perspective of someone whose spirit is seized only by the problems before his eyes.

A Peking communiqué stating that "The rumor of all-party peace talks with Chungking must be strictly controlled" is in all the newspapers. I wonder what the reason is for only silence from Peking and nobody knowing anything.

I attended a meeting of the *Tōkei* (*Tōyō keizai*) directors. The state of the German eastern warfront is bad. If it is a planned withdrawal of the German armies, this is possible; if it is defeat, there is no way to regain their position. The future of the war depends completely upon the possibility of a counterattack on the Danube River. Or, I wonder if there is enough power remaining to counterattack.

The head of the Ōmotokyō[25] predicted current events and the faith's followers are increasing. Their belief has no basis, but it's possible such things could be predicted.

October 5 (Tuesday)

Even when there are no problems, the "strengthening of the controls" is the special characteristic of the Japanese. In this morning's newspaper, discussion was about unification. It stated, for example, "The unification of defense administration is an urgent necessity," "The unification of trade leadership" (*Yomiuri*), "The inevitable unification of propaganda machinery," "The thorough unification of purchasing" (*Mainichi*), and "Repeating unification, the war will be brought to an end." One sees the bureaucratic characteristic in the fact that it was once enough to call it the Transportation Ministry, but now it is lengthened into Transportation-Communications Ministry.

I hear that the harassment of Christianity is severe. For example, it is seen in connection with Aoyama Gakuin and Rikkyō Daigaku (St. Paul's University). It is exactly the same as the Bakumatsu period.

Recently the senior statesmen met with Premier Tōjō. When Okada Keisuke said, "It appears that the war is completely indecisive!" Tōjō became excited and stood up abruptly, saying, "Don't you have faith in certain victory?"

Again, when Wakatsuki Reijirō said, "There is concern over the harvest!" it is said that Tōjō again became excited and replied, "Even if we eat nothing, we members of the cabinet intend to give our lives for the nation!"

Whether he is in the Diet or elsewhere, it appears he is a man who always gets angry. The reason that he surrounds himself with yes-men is that such is his personality.

At the Diplomatic Association there was discussion by the Research official, Iguchi, concerning Italy:

1. At the beginning of the war, aircraft production was around 300 planes a month.

2. Emmanuel II did not approve participation in the war. This was revealed because Italy was defeated.

3. The excessive optimism with which the war situation was reported accounted for Mussolini's defeat.

4. When the president of the Information Board, Amaha, said to the head of the Propaganda Office, Rossi, "Let's fight fiercely!" the latter replied to Ambassador Hidaka, "The Axis spirit will handle it." And he also said, "It is all right to announce this in Japan, but it will not be announced inside Italy."

5. Even the reports from the Badoglio government to Japan do not say, "Hereafter we will carry on the English-American war till the bitter end."

6. The chief of staff of the Badoglio regime went to Lisbon under an assumed name and settled matters in a conference with Samuel Hoare.

7. Because they understood the general state of affairs, they were cautious. However, after sending out warships "to attack the Americans and English," firing three or four salvos, they surrendered, and two-thirds fled into enemy hands. It appears the Americans and English intend to refurbish them and have them patrol the Mediterranean and then redirect the English fleet to India.

8. Germany has three strategies: (1) Prepare for bombing air raids, (2) intensify submarine warfare, (3) peace between Russia and Germany. They are not hopeful for all of these. In the war on merchant shipping, the 800,000 tons at the beginning became in June 150,000 tons. Churchill said this was one-seventh or one-tenth of production.

9. Among such neutral countries as Spain, there is vacillation about establishing a Japanese consul in Morocco, and this has not yet been approved. Portugal was told by England to declare war in order to regain Timor.

October 6 (Wednesday)

Recently I have also said this, but since the Greater East Asian War started there is not a daily newspaper in which there is no writing by army people, majors and lt. colonels. Herein one can understand the bias of the leadership.

The National Policy Research Society attempted to publish writings concerning the Greater East Asian administration. The Greater East Asian Ministry would not allow this. Or else it is possible that the Greater East Asian Ministry will forecast the future, but as yet it has not had the courage to issue a statement.

I hear that because the Ministry of Communications and the Ministry of Railways have been combined, there is a great uproar in both ministries. I am not the least bit surprised by this. Will there be efficiency with this merger? In that case there will be no jurisdictional disputes. In a great war it is probably good for the people to prepare with all their might.

At midday, at the Japan Club, I heard a talk by Colonel Odashima (chief of the Prisoners of War Office) entitled "Concerning the Treatment of Prisoners of War."

1. There were those who were violent toward the prisoners of war in the environs of Seoul, Aomori, and Kobe who leaped from the crowds shouting "hateful enemy." In Taiwan, a soldier went to where Wainwright was standing and said, "This beast is the enemy of our countrymen," and thrashed him soundly, it is said.

2. In all, there are 300,000 prisoners of war, but people within the Greater East Asia sphere are liberated, and of the 30,000 who were not set free among these, adding about 120,000–130,000 whites, there are only 150,000. Ten percent of these are regimental officers. There are fifteen prisoner-of-war camps. Among these eight are in Japan. The figures are something like 30,000 Dutch and 20,000 Americans.

3. In the Russo-Japanese War—shall we refer to it in the Anglo-American style?—there was generous treatment of prisoners. However, in the present war, the slate is wiped clean regarding the regulations concerning prisoners of war, and we have decided "within the limits of not violating international law there would be strict regulation." As regards the provisions relating to the prisoners of war for those who did not conform to the *Kokutai* (the quintessential Japanese national self-definition), it was not possible to obtain imperial approval.

4. The enemy prisoners of war all had faith in victory. There were a great many who predicted in advance the defeat of Italy. They said that Germany also would soon be defeated. At first Japan thought of plans to reeducate them, but because their belief in certain victory was absolute, the idea of educating them was given up.

5. They were not in the least bit ashamed of being prisoners of war. Indeed, they worked splendidly. They work from morning until night without the least bit of rest. It is said if there had not been prisoners of war the heavy industries companies in the Ōsaka and Kobe areas would have fallen apart. Even their efficiency was extremely high.

6. The wage level of the prisoners is from ten to twenty sen a day. When they sharpen circular saws, they finish thirteen or fourteen in one day. In contrast, Japanese workers finish about twenty. However, one in four of the

ones finished by prisoners passed inspection, while none of the Japanese ones were acceptable. And with riveting work, it is said the rate was about 150 pieces a day for the prisoners and 50 for the Japanese workers. They are careful of materials. For example, even when they drop nails they gather them up. Moreover, when they light fires, if half the wood that was ignited remains, they extinguish it and use it the next time.

7. Their racial prejudices are very strong. They do not mingle with each other. The Englishmen shave their beards smartly and are meticulous in appearance. When one talks to certain American fliers they say, "For the sake of my country it would be all right to be a prisoner of war all my life." An Italian warship came to visit Kobe, but its crew was completely lacking in discipline. When the warship raised its flag, only one or two people came out.

Judging from Lt. Colonel Odashima's talk, it appears he expresses some degree of respect for the prisoners of war. But he is completely incapable of sympathetic understanding of the ways of thinking of these prisoners of war. The fact of the emotionalism of the Japanese—for example, they thought it extraordinary that the prisoners were incapable of understanding the nobility involved in the honorable deaths on the island of Attu. The Japanese are totally incapable of standing apart objectively and viewing positively the emotions and thought patterns of other countries. Accordingly, it is not possible for them to look at things objectively. I had this sort of feeling in hearing such an account.

October 7 (Thursday)

I am reading *War and Peace*.[26] It is said that when Nomura and Kurusu handed over the last communiqué on December 7, Hull stated that it was not possible for him to imagine a government that was capable of stating such lies. He had no faith in Konoe. Kurusu asked Konoe, who had begun the China problem, whether even a conference could settle it peacefully. It is my intention to research and compare all of this.

October 8 (Friday)

I heard a talk at the Economic Club entitled "Concerning the Current Situation in England" by a Foreign Ministry section chief, Ōta Saburō. He is a person with an extremely fine mind.

1. In England the conviction that it cannot destroy Germany continues to deepen. Gilbert says the same thing. Consequently, with respect to this there are only two strategies: one, with the Soviet Union as an ally, this will allow them to pressure Germany; two, to nail down America to European problems.

2. English food policy and manpower policy are succeeding. In food resources, bread is unlimited. Milk is extremely abundant. Previously they were only capable of 25 percent self-support, and now they are 48 percent self-supporting.

3. There are two postwar problems. One is the fact that the gulf between property and wealth is becoming smaller. Accordingly, in England, there is no income above five thousand annually. Previously, it was said that gentlemen could not live on less than two thousand a month. The other problem is that what England accumulated in three hundred years was completely spent in three years. Even in such places as India in the first half of the present year, the railway loans have been repaid. It is the same in every country. Consequently, the ties that bind together England and Australia have completely dissolved.

4. On New Year's day, because of high spirits induced by sake, unexpected things emerged. From Casablanca, "unconditional surrender," and "Chiang Kai-shek is not worth being considered an enemy." "Unconditional surrender" is not the English disposition, it is the American disposition. In England there is no such way of thinking.

5. With respect to Germany, make it powerless; the idea to divide Germany is gradually changing.

6. Germany attacks and destroys the strong points of strong countries. This is the Schlieffen military strategy. Contrary to this, England works upon the weak points. This is particularly so of Churchill.

Mizuno came this morning to discuss opinions concerning the American–English–Russian Conference. They were questions proposed by the police department.

The talk in the Marunouchi Building is that after the establishment of the Munitions Ministry, martial law will be proclaimed. Various rumors are spreading.

A certain Diet representative had an interview with Premier Tōjō to state his opinions. When he had done so, the military police summoned him and detained him for ten days, sometimes interrogating him and sometimes abusing him. Previously, Suma, chief of the Information Board, had the same experience of being dragged in by the military police.

October 9 (Saturday)

In this morning's newspaper the changes that were at the core of the Munitions Ministry were published. It is much better to operate the nation without centralized machinery, and taking this as the opportunity, it would be well to abolish it. However, if this is the case, why has there not been a union of the contending Foreign Ministry and the Greater East Asia Ministry? Moreover, what about a plan for a Military Operations Ministry of army and navy?

A magazine with the name *East-West Cultural Circle* was sent to me. It is probably from the magazine's company. Such magazines as *Chūō kōron, Kaizō,* and *Tōyō keizai* are in decline, and probably no one reads them. Such magazines have a great number of pages. Their contents are right-wing extremism, and the military ideology is seen from the contents of roundtable discussions of people such as Lt. Akiyama.

October 10 (Sunday)

The marriage ceremony of the oldest son of Ōta. I attended the ceremony and delivered congratulations. In the evening a typhoon was approaching. Damage to agricultural production will be considerable. On my way home I visited with Akiyama Takashi and Ishibashi. Obama told me that there is a rumor that I was arrested by the police. It was at a gathering of Takahashi Yūsai's including others in his intellectual circle. Is there any grounds for this, or is it simply rumor? There is a rumor that Hanzawa Tamaki has been investigated. Hanzawa was invited by the governor of Shizuoka Prefecture, and he gave a talk to the provincial administration and the Imperial Rule Assistance Society. I understand that there were problems with his talk.

It is said that Premier Tōjō treats cabinet members and others like errand boys. Of late, there is not a single person among the intellectual class who evaluates him highly. Even his declaration of granting territory to Thailand may be merely lip service to his Majesty the emperor, but others were not party to the decision.

October 12 (Tuesday)

The wife of Arita Hachirō passed away and today was the funeral ceremony. On the way home I went to the heart of the city in the automobile of Takahashi Yūsai. I had lunch at the Japan Club and in the evening I went to the Kabuki. The scripts of Kikugorō are always thin. The art of Kichiemon[27] is always impressive. I returned with Obama and his wife.

October 13 (Wednesday)

The Badoglio government declares war on Germany (October 13). It is said that the manuscript of Yokota Kisaburō, with the approval of the entire body, circulated among the Tōdai Professors Committee, and in order to claim doctoral status it went around the Ministry of Education, but it has not been accepted even after close to a year has elapsed. Even if my own manuscript passed, it would probably have the same fate. It appears that the claim for

with a trademark continues to increase over time as additional sales are made of the product offered under a mark and consumers associate the mark with its owner. There is no doubt that the goodwill inherent in a trademark can be among a company's most valuable assets. As discussed in Chapter 1, the COCA-COLA marks have been valued at $68.9 billion, and the COCA-COLA mark is the most recognized mark in the world.

Trademarks thus provide the following functions:

- they identify one maker's goods or services and distinguish them from those offered by others;
- they indicate that all goods or services offered under the mark come from a single producer, manufacturer, or "source";
- they indicate that all goods or services offered under the mark are of consistent quality; and
- they serve as an advertising device so that consumers link a product or service being offered with a mark (for example, when many consumers see or hear the phrase JUST DO IT®, they immediately think of Nike products).

Thus, a consumer who purchases GAP® khaki pants in Dallas is assured that the fit and style is the same as a pair that would be purchased in Philadelphia, and that the item is the product of a single source, namely, Gap Inc.

Trademark law is a part of the broader law of unfair competition or unfair trade practices. Infringement of another's trademark is a species of unfair competition. Other acts of unfair competition include false advertising and infringement of copyrights, patents, or trade names. The law of unfair competition is meant to protect consumers and eliminate unfair business practices. Trademark law is a vital part of the broad protection afforded by the law of unfair competition. The law of unfair competition is fully discussed in Chapter 23.

TYPES OF MARKS: TRADEMARKS, SERVICE MARKS, CERTIFICATION MARKS, AND COLLECTIVE MARKS

There are four different types of marks: trademarks, service marks, certification marks, and collective marks.

The modern definition of *trademark* is that it is a word, name, symbol, or device, or a combination thereof, used by a person (including a business entity), or which a person has a bona fide intention to use, to identify and distinguish his or her goods from those manufactured by others and to indicate the source of those goods. 15 U.S.C. § 1127. A *service mark* is a word, name, symbol, or device, or a combination thereof, used by a person, or which a person has a bona fide intention to use, to identify and distinguish the services of one person from those of others and to indicate the source of those services. Thus, a trademark is used to identify *goods,* such as CHEERIOS®

for cereal, LEXUS® for cars, or JIM BEAM® for whiskey. A service mark is used to identify *services,* such as H & R BLOCK® for accounting services, T.G.I. FRIDAY'S® for restaurant services, and FEDEX® for transportation services.

While the term *trademark* thus refers to some physical and tangible good, and *service mark* refers to an intangible service, in common usage the term *trademark* is often used to refer to marks for both goods and services. Throughout this text, discussions related to "trademarks" will also apply to service marks unless otherwise noted. Similarly, the term **mark** will be used as a synonym for both trademarks and service marks. The federal statute governing trademark law, the U.S. Trademark Act (the Lanham Act, found at 15 U.S.C. § 1051 *et seq.*) itself states that the term *mark* includes any trademark, service mark, collective mark, or certification mark. See Appendix E. 15 U.S.C. § 1127.

academic status of a man named Fuji from Waseda was rejected. It is said that the thesis exams are overscheduled and cannot move very quickly.

I wrote an essay entitled "On the Russo-Japanese War" in *Gaikō hyōron* (Foreign relations review).

October 14 (Thursday)

In *Tōyō keizai* I wrote a report on Philippine independence. Today the independence of the Philippines is established. The Japanese newspapers are full of this report. If America had provisionally granted independence, I wonder whether Japan would have taken this sort of attitude. Moreover, Japan will gain absolutely nothing at all from this independence. The Japanese are people who thrive on sentiment.

October 15 (Friday)

I wrote a manuscript for *Chūbu Nihon*. In the afternoon I work on the *Chronology*, and every morning I work in the vegetable garden. Now when I do farm work I really feel good. This is evidence that I am a practical person.

It is said that two hundred enemy planes came to attack Rabaul. Rabaul is the front line in the inner line of military operations. If this is lost it will be the cause of a wedge being driven into the Mandated Islands of the South Seas.

October 16 (Saturday)

It has been decided to present laws regarding munitions companies in an extraordinary Diet session. It is natural to work hard in order to increase production, but if orders are enacted and, moreover, if laws are established, they think that increased production will be possible (*Mainichi shinbun*, August 16).

The writer Hayashi Fusao wrote a communiqué from Manila regarding the independence of the Philippines. Hayashi is the author of *Saigō Takamori*. However, its true target was not "independence" but "Japanese territory" (*Mainichi shinbun*, August 16). Miki Kiyoshi has also stated that there are many ignorant novelists.

One hears about nothing but the fact of "the nationalized character of companies" or "the rejection of the pursuit of profit." Even the laws on munitions companies are the same. If formalism goes this far, there will probably not be any room at all for self-criticism. It is not good to overemphasize the existent system. No matter how the machinery changes, the Japanese people are the Japanese people. The reason that the Soviet is strong is not Soviet-style organization but its basis in native tradition.

October 17 (Sunday)

Tomorrow is the second anniversary of the Tōjō cabinet. The judgment of this cabinet will be for later historians to decide. However, there is probably no example in the world of a cabinet lacking in intelligence and perception to this degree.

My feeling while working on the *Chronology* (the period around 1940–1941). The military interfered step by step with the Imperial Rule Assistance Society and other things. Domestically they were completely victorious. But whether or not they will achieve the same victory against the enemy is the single remaining problem.

October 19 (Tuesday)

In the *Mainichi shinbun* there was a debate between Tokutomi Sohō and Honda Kumatarō. These are the two men most responsible for the outbreak of the war. In the literary world, Tokutomi; in the diplomatic world, Honda; in the military world, Suetsugu Nobumasa; in politics, Nakano Seigō: these are the leading figures. Both Tokutomi and Honda are completely without objectivity.

Roosevelt is attacking Argentina's repression of Jews. Has America the right to talk about racial problems?

Tokutomi is exhibiting the style, as usual, of a sycophant toward Tōjō. This crowd should be sent to the front line. The complete achievement of public morality is the premise for a regulated economy and socialism. Such things as the water system have broken down, and the repairmen repair nothing.

October 20 (Wednesday)

The newspapers almost every day are discussing the reform of government structure as their central theme. It is a matter of thinking that if orders are issued, these will move the people, that fumbling with the structure will generate good results. No matter how severe the war becomes, it does not change these ways of thinking.

October 21 (Thursday)

I wonder what goal made Japan great. It is not true that it is war itself. People fight because they will achieve something. The passion to chastise and subjugate, is insufficient. In chastising and subjugating, what is one pursuing? In the end it is two aims: thinking that one will spread Japanese things to the world, and because of this there will probably be self-advantage. The Japanese like to interfere. However, they do not do this with any kind of action. For example, yesterday on the streetcar when I tried to put my bag on the overhead net, not a single person would help. Japanese interfere only in intellectual matters.

The English and Americans dislike interference. However, this is related to ideas, and when others are in trouble they offer assistance. An example of this is that when one is preoccupied while on foot, someone will ask, "What are you looking for?" and will try to help. On the trains there is always help. This being the case, the interference is the same. As regards the differences, one returns to the point of asking, "What is the aim?" and one may probably say that it is the differences in customs and dispositions.

October 22, 23 (Friday, Saturday)

In the second-class cars there is always a vulgar crowd of engineering contractors as passengers. At the time of the First World War the so-called new rich brought about great changes in Japan. At present it is the same. The deficiencies of capitalism are certainly to be found in this. However, even if there were socialism or totalitarianism, there would be other evils. The key is only in the advance of education.

This morning there was a letter from my wife. There was a telephone call from Shimanaka. There are rumors concerning my personal activities and he was worried. He advised care in my behavior.

Recently there have been rumors of this kind. I am certain that someone is checking on me. However, I do not go around everywhere making imprudent statements. Since the war started it is natural to think only of victory.

Is there suspicion because of my visits to the homes of Konoe and Ugaki? At any rate, in order not to be subjected to ridiculous misunderstandings, it is my intention to be careful insofar as possible. The fall in Shinshū is cold.

The second son of the Okamura family attends Waseda University. With the cancellation this year of military deferment he is receiving his physical exam. His eligibility is a foregone conclusion. He accompanied me as far as the bus. He is a lively young man. He is extremely optimistic even regarding his departure for the front, and no matter how many bullets fly he says he is the only one who will not be hit. This is everyone's feeling. It is the same as thinking about one's own home when Tōkyō is bombed.

October 24 (Sunday)

If one relies upon *War and Peace*, it appears that America on two occasions hoped for an entente with Japan. Hull spoke of a Japanese, American, and

English rapprochement to Nomura, and Roosevelt also spoke in this manner. However, it was not possible at that time. He would have been an extraordinary diplomat if he had been capable of quick responsiveness. However, the foreign relations of a nation are not something that can be changed along the way. How much the more in Japanese foreign relations.

It is said that in Karuizawa this year, more than the usual number of people are left; however, all the houses are shut up. It seems that a great deal of luggage has been arriving at Karuizawa.

October 26 (Tuesday)

I heard that Nakano Seigo has been arrested by the Police Headquarters. It is because of his overturn-the-cabinet movement.

October 27 (Wednesday)

Yesterday evening Murobuse Takanobu said that the entire world was going back to liberalism and praised the position of me and Ashida.

I learned of Nakano Seigo's suicide in the evening press. I received an extreme shock comparable to that upon the eruption of the Greater East Asian War. However, it's possible it was because I had dinner with him in Rome. At any rate, a thousand emotions, one after the other, boiled up in me. I hated him. His ideas generated the war. Yet confronting his suicide I had the feeling of having allowed a crime. After all, I have the Japanese tradition deep in my mind. Yet reasons for his suicide are completely obscure.

He was a straightforward person. When the war broke out he publicly stated that America would be shattered immediately. However, that was a mistake. Is it likely that his introspective nature was one part of the cause for his suicide? If that was the case, that's fine. Along with that, he dreamed of being like Mussolini and Hitler, but he could not achieve this goal and because of that lost hope. In any case, one must recognize the single fact that he is a typical Japanese *shishi*.

In Rome I said, "From now on it will be a world of your generation. Go to Germany and see what the Nazis are doing. The movement of the Nazis has a practical basis." I presented him with *I Know These Dictators*.[28]

I had dinner with him on two occasions. When I said, "If we make England our enemy, brace yourself!" he replied, "They are an extremely strong opponent. They defeated both Napoleon and the Kaiser, didn't they?" He had not gone to England because he was afraid he would lapse into English ways of thinking. To protect a rigid ideology, he would not listen to other arguments, and this was his weak point psychologically. His attitude was always religious. He feared the "truth," and so in the end he committed suicide.

October 28 (Thursday)

I attended a lecture arranged by Tōkyō City, and in the evening I went to a director's meeting of the Pen Club. I hear that Masamune Hakuchō accepted its presidency. It is unexpected that he accepted the presidency.

October 29 (Friday)

Evening, there was a meeting of the International Relations Research Society, and it was at the same time a welcoming reception for Rōyama. Rōyama wants to withdraw from this group. There will probably be no objection even if he withdraws. Isn't this because it is a time in which there is no warm welcome for research of any kind?

October 30 (Saturday)

In the morning I went as usual to the fields. Of late, I am working about three hours a day, and as a result I am not able to study and am distressed.

According to Yamamoto's account, the will of Nakano Seigo was simple. Because his sword looked dull, he did not commit seppuku but instead cut his carotid artery. It is a fact that the military police were watching his house.

The problem arises as to whether it was suicide or he was killed. If he had been killed, there would be no way to get past this in an autopsy, so one might imagine it was suicide, but it is much too obscure a death.

In the evening editions the completion of a Sino-Japanese Treaty of Alliance was announced. Its motto is mutual respect and equality and good-neighbor friendship. It may be seen as one part of the Chungking maneuvers, but Chungking is definitely unlikely to respond. If this affair had been enacted two years ago, it would have settled the Sino-Japanese Incident, and the Greater East Asian War would not have occurred.

October 31 (Sunday)

I worked in the fields for the whole day. I have been moving plants. In the morning Mizuno of the police came to ask about the new Sino-Japanese Treaty. He related that Chungking would probably not respond.

The fact that the night-soil man applies fertilizer is fine, but he steals precious ginger and persimmons. I am most indignant. When I think that this is the level of morality, I feel contempt for the Japanese.

November 1 (Monday)

From today onward, the Munitions Ministry, the Military Transport and Communications Ministry, and the Agriculture-Commerce Ministry have been newly established. It was said this was the opportunity "for the epoch-making strengthening of the premier's powers." The same report has been published many times [*Mainichi shinbun*, "Yoroku," November 1).

How can people with general knowledge say this sort of foolish thing? However, if they say, "I cannot write but I can type," it is a different story. The lack of conscience of those who write these things worsens the conditions of the times.

This morning when I went out into the fields some man was breaking the branches of the hedge. I yelled at him.

The decline in the morale of the Japanese people is absolutely surprising. The people definitely cannot take on leadership. At the time of war the fact that they are preoccupied with other things, the fact that resources are also inadequate, the fact they are becoming coarse-natured, the fact that their discipline in the moral sphere is weakening—it is from such factors that this manifestation of decline was generated.

One cannot but think about war.

From today onward, new newspaper subscriptions are prohibited.

Someone reports that the Japanese in Manchuria (the military of course) still hoped for war with the Soviet Union and were chaffing for action. I hear that they are devising plans for that purpose.

Mill has written, "I sometimes think that if the things one thought about were suddenly achieved, one would probably lose hope in the extreme. It is a fact that mankind takes pleasure in the future." If they are soldiers they think about war; the police welcome incidents; the newspapers and magazines, in the same way, produce incidents.

Everywhere I go, people are talking about the death of Nakano Seigo. Nyozekan said that because Nakano always wanted to win, he was disappointed with things that did not correspond to his wishes.

From today onward, the newly established ministries will open shop. The newspapers are full of the new appointments.

November 2 (Tuesday)

As usual, in the morning I was a farmer. Ikebe Hidete came to visit. We ate lunch together. We talked together about such things as farmers. It was about three in the afternoon when he left. Afterward I wrote about the Sino-Japanese Alliance Treaty.

The alliance treaty is a defensive alliance. However, this one is a postwar foundation treaty. Its purpose is the Chungking operation. If only this political policy had been in effect two years ago.

It was Tōjō who did not allow any sort of discussion whatsoever on the withdrawal of troops. Now this Tōjō is taking the lead in agreeing to this. Grew's term, "frankly opportunistic," is something that can be used about Tōjō. This is so, but it is natural as contemporary political policy, and this is not really criticism.

November 3 (Wednesday)

Every day I muddle along and don't study at all. The main reason is that the garden takes the cream of my time.

Obama and his wife came to tea. He said Masa (sho)-chan had gone off to war and his wife is crying every day. Her saying, "If the mothers of Japan and the mothers of America talked together, wouldn't the war be quickly put to rights?" is exactly right.

Today is a memorial day for the Meiji Emperor. The fame of the Meiji Emperor is enormous. Those responsible for the Greater East Asian War— both the politicians and the writers—would not have been satisfied with the policies of the Meiji Emperor. One example of this is those who say that the Russo-Japanese War was too "Anglo-American."

November 4 (Thursday)

Together with our maid Toyo, I planted beans for three hours in the morning. She says that last year the available ground was not fully used, but this year it is fully planted.

On October 19–30, at Moscow, the twelve meetings of the Foreign Ministers Conference, made up of America, England, and Russia, were announced. It is of extreme significance. (Besides this, there was also published a public announcement of the Allies.)

As regards this joint statement:

1. "Unconditional surrender" is a victory for America. It is clear that America dragged the meeting into this position.

2. An international organization called the United Nations will be adopted.

3. After the termination of the war the independence of all countries will be recognized (Article 6).

4. It was declared that Austria would be made independent. And by this plan they intend to create internal disquiet in Germany.

The submission to the claims of the Soviet Union (*Yomiuri* special communiqué from Stockholm on the 2nd), complete submission to the Soviet Union (*Mainichi*, special Berlin communiqué on the 2nd), the evident failure of America and England (Buenos Aires special correspondent Imai on the 2nd)—all the newspapers are talking about the victory of the Soviet Union, but in actuality this is not true. Rather, it must be seen that the American position of supporting Russia has obtained a complete victory.

It appears that in all of this many points were excluded (such things as the problem of war criminals).

Just here, my *Diary* for 1939:

I heard a speech of Yoshitomi Masaomi, second secretary in the Soviet Union. He is young but decisive. His opinion was that we should not have war between Russia and Japan. The newspapers are saying there is no starvation. There is also no opposition among the peasantry.

With the Chang Ku-feng [Chang Tso-lin] incident, the Manchurian ministers of state withdrew their money, gathered up their belongings, and decided to go to China. Japan is oppressing the peasants, and the latter sing the praises of the Chang Hsueh-liang period.

1. People are waiting in two- or three-block lines to see *Anna Karenina*. When I said, "You have become tan from waiting outdoors," the other party replied, "It's because we waited so long."

2. When I said that American Indians are naked, the other party said, "Do they have the Soviet system?"

November 5 (Friday)

On October 9, 1942, both America and England announced the abolition of extrality in China, and each handed over a treaty document, America on October 24 and England on November 1. Under these circumstances there is no reason for only Japan to hold out on these. Those who attack Premier Tōjō on this point are not reasonable. Yet even Tōjō himself did know that he was in such a position.

Today the Greater East Asia Conference opened in Tōkyō. Such people as Wang, Chang Ching-hui, Laurel, Ba Maw, and Bose came to attend. Only Thailand merely sent a representative.

It is indeed a cabinet that likes to dramatize everything.

As usual the declarations of Tōjō are commonplace and stilted, and of course we writers cannot endure a single reading of them. His statements are weak and he simply repeats Hitler. Why is it that someone is not allowed to write for him?

The new Philippine Constitution is completely in the American style. The attempt to impose one of Japanese style has been defeated. Yet it is only the preamble that has an article stating, "A world order built upon moral justice."

1. In the Philippines there are many loyal politicians. The legislature is being established first, and the administration of the government later. I wonder how they will be made use of.

2. In the first plan for the ratification of the treaty, it was to be by a vote of two-thirds, and this was changed to a simple majority. Nevertheless, it will be a problematic point hereafter.

3. It was decided that Japan could obtain resources only for the duration of the war. After the war there would be coordination and settlement.

Ōta said that the management of Fuji Ice would be tightened up.

November 6 (Saturday)

I thought I would write for the *Oriental Economist* on the subject of the Greater East Asian War and American responsibility.

It is strange that of late there are still those who are anxious to hear my views—for example, people from the Insurance Association and those who came yesterday. It is probably because the things I said in the past are now brought to mind.

November 7 (Sunday)

I am digging up sweet potatoes and storing them. I worked throughout the morning. My body aches all over and I am in pain.

A proclamation was issued by the Greater East Asian Conference. The newspapers also printed this in bold-face type, and yesterday evening the evening editions put out four pages. It was a commemorative issue. There were also newspapers that wrote that this was the Pacific Charter as opposed to the Atlantic Charter. It was a plan that talked about mutual independence and respect.

However, I wonder what on earth this sort of thing will give Japan. As usual, it is self-indulgence. It is unfortunate.

The battle results of the campaign in the Bougainville Straits are coming out. They are cause for rejoicing, but if one looks at it from the other side, it shows that the enemy's main strength is approaching the front line of Rabaul.

November 8 (Monday)

There is an Allied announcement that in England a Ministry of Recovery has recently been formed. England thinks the war is already won in Germany and is embarked on postwar administration. In regard to a questionnaire that asked, "What is the most essential matter?" 20 percent answered the Second Front, but there was not a single person who said the Greater East Asian War. In America many circumstances are different, but the answers are similar.

Previously, Nakano Seigo and others said, "Those who take sides with Japan will be victorious." This conceit brought about our present misery.

Yesterday I listened for a while to the radio speeches of all of the representatives of the so-called Greater East Asian Conference. Both the speech and English of Chandra Bose were excellent. Ba Maw was also skillful, but he had an accent. However, shouldn't we expect opposition from the right wing regarding utterances in English in Tōkyō?

I hear that the police stand in strategic places on trains and inspect luggage piece by piece. There was even someone who committed suicide in Toyama-ken because of two sho of rice.

The work of the police is not catching thieves but has become that of seizing citizens. This work is easier than catching thieves. Japan should not have pulled England down from the stage of East Asia. If England were here in East Asia, together with Japan, it would be possible to control America. England is no threat to us. However, because Japan ejected England, America and England have joined hands.

This anti-English action was the worst example of amateur foreign relations behavior.

The tragedy of Japan is writing a declaration resembling the Atlantic Charter and the fact that a declaration of independence and freedom for all people had to be issued.

November 9 (Tuesday)

In an investigation of the Patriotic Production Society, a male weighing 13 kamme takes in 1,400 calories a day, and the intake of calories necessary to go back and forth to work is 1,600 calories. However, the present ration is 1,400 calories. Because the average weight of a woman is 11 kamme, they adapt to the ration. However, because the rationing is unjust, the results will be inadequate.

The reduction in the number of industrial facilities is advancing. Six thousand commercial companies have been reduced to six hundred; publishing companies are reduced 10 percent.

The reason the military premiers in the past did not lose their central position was that they held office for long periods and they knew politics. The tragedy of Premier Tōjō is that he rose to an influential post directly from outside the mainstream. When he had been in office for some time, one understood his background. People are resentful of Tōjō, and this is reflected in his China political policy.

your thesis or dissertation, you have to show something new or prove something important that has not yet been demonstrated.

Whether to conduct a first-hand investigation or to make use of existing data depends on your research questions and objectives. When you set up your questions and objectives, you will naturally take into account your position and your available resources. In this regard, no one research approach is inherently better than another. Rather, there are research strategies that match some problems and resources well but fit with others poorly. If you have been playing with certain data sets for a while and are confident about their quality and utility to your project, it might be to your advantage to further dig into them and tease out what you need for your thesis or dissertation. If, however, you have no or little experience with the data sets offered to you and/or you find it very hard to manage them, you might be better off starting data collection for yourself. This happens when existing data sets are too complicated, too "dirty" (i.e., requiring too much time to get cleaned and organized), and/or containing incomplete information essential for your project. In any case, you need to make a careful assessment before you start using an existing source of information.

The particular research skills you have will also be a factor in considering how to go about your project. If you consider yourself a "qualitative person," so to speak, it is unlikely that you will be interested in any large quantitative data set that would require some complex computer equipment to handle. Conversely, if someone regards herself as a "quantitative person," she probably will not be patient enough to spend most of her time collecting data through such methods as case studies.

Your research purpose, however, should be the first factor in considering your approaches. For instance, if you want to elaborate on some new data analysis procedures as the core content of your thesis/dissertation, it would be wise for you to try to make use of existing data sources since otherwise you may not be able to concentrate on what you are really interested in doing. In contrast, if you desire to spend time to obtain new information on some substantive problems, the best way to proceed with your thesis/dissertation is probably to launch a project emphasizing the collection of some first-hand data. In any case, how to go about your project will depend on your research purpose, your time and available resources, and also your familiarity with certain specific research skills.

A **certification mark** is a word, name, symbol, device, or combination thereof, used by one person to certify that the goods or services of others have certain features in regard to quality, material, mode of manufacture, or some other characteristic (or that the work done on the goods or services was performed by members of a union or other organization). Examples of certification marks are the GOOD HOUSEKEEPING® and Underwriters Laboratory seals of approval. Certification marks are, by their very nature, unlike any other types of marks. They do not indicate the origin or source of the goods or services, and they are not used by the actual owner of the goods or services. Rather, the mark is placed on the goods or used in connection with the services of another to certify something about the goods or services. Thus, a toaster that carries the GOOD HOUSEKEEPING® seal of approval signifies to consumers that the toaster has been reviewed, tested, and found to meet certain standards in regard to quality, safety, price, or some other characteristic. The toaster is not made by the Good Housekeeping people. They merely certify that the goods on which their mark is placed meet certain objective and preestablished standards. Similarly, the mark ILGWU INTERNATIONAL GARMENT WORKERS' UNION MADE AFL-CIO (& DESIGN)® certifies that the work or labor done on garments was performed by members of the registrant's union. The owner of a certified mark may lose rights to the mark if it arbitrarily refuses to allow use of a mark by one whose products or services meet its stated certification standards.

A **collective mark** is one used by a collective membership organization, such as a labor union, fraternity, or professional society, to identify that the person displaying the mark is a member of the organization. Thus, the FUTURE FARMERS OF AMERICA® and AMERICAN BAR ASSOCIATION® marks indicate membership in certain organizations.

(See Exhibit 2–2 for further examples of the four types of marks.)

A company may use several marks. An examination of a can of Coca-Cola reveals multiple marks: the words COCA-COLA®, the stylized WAVE DESIGN®, and the slogan THINGS GO BETTER WITH COKE®. All of these marks are used on one product and all are protected by the Coca-Cola Company.

On some occasions, companies use **house marks** to establish recognition in a wide range of products or services. For example, General Mills has registered one mark, GENERAL MILLS® (with a cursive G), for numerous food products, including cereal, biscuit mixes, and mashed potatoes.

ACQUISITION OF TRADEMARK RIGHTS

In most foreign countries, trademark rights arise from registering the mark with a governmental entity. The law in the United States is quite different: trademark rights arise from adoption and *use* of a mark, not from registra-

---

EXHIBIT 2–2
Types of Marks

Type of Mark	Example
Trademark	COMET® (for cleanser)
Service Mark	HYATT® (for lodging services)
Certification Mark	UNION MADE® (for clothing)
Collective Mark	MORTGAGE BANKERS ASSOCIATION® (for membership in an organization)

I wrote a manuscript for the *Oriental Economist*. In the evening I went to a meeting of the National Scholarly Arts Society. There was a talk concerning "Satō Issai"[29] by Nyozekan.

November 11 (Thursday)

I went to a golf tournament. I took third place. I have already lost interest in golf. I would rather be a farmer. This is not the time for golf.

November 12 (Friday)

I am harvesting taro.

November 13 (Saturday)

In a special Berlin communiqué in the *Mainichi*, there was a piece called "The Reasons the English Government Permits Such Critiques," referring to an essay concerning the level of power in Europe. It is an example of the ignorance of conditions in England (*Mainichi*, November 13).

Upon returning home, I heard that the draft notice for Kiyoaki had come. This will be troublesome and I am frightened. This is because he managed the Silver Star by himself.

November 14 (Sunday)

The China Incident started because China did not maintain its treaty. Now, however, because the treaty is abolished, there will be no problem. The Chinese people believed that Chiang is coming back.

The Japanese residents in China are suspicious as to whether this sort of Japanese political policy is a stratagem or the truth. The majority of people believe that it is a stratagem.

Komura Hideaki came. He is the son-in-law of the late Shunzaburō, a neighbor, and had been sent to the front in Manchuria. He is a sergeant.

He said that in Manchuria the temperature is now below zero, and it always goes down about 30 degrees. He served in Kantoshō (Chien-tao Province). On the front line the failings of Japan are talked about in an exaggerated way—for example, the claim that there is no rice.

If the Japanese who are in China can find buyers, they will sell their property and return to Japan. The "China hands" particularly wish to leave.

As a consequence of the war, what the overseas Japanese built in America, South America, China, and other areas can be completely lost.

I explained to Komura the fact that (1) the political policy of Premier Tōjō could not be stopped in order to keep China and others as our allies; (2) because of the allies the enemy was one step ahead, nothing could be done, and I supported this policy.

Because Tōjō is an intellectual liar, no one can believe him. Yet in the matter of telling lies, at any rate, it shows that the concept of military political policy is untenable. And in the final analysis, ideas will probably bring progress.

November 15 (Monday)

When I went to the barber shop previously it was operated by seven people, but now it has been reduced to two people, including the owner. Moreover, it is reported that the draft notice came for one of the remaining two. The owner complained, "If you do not intend to ruin the shop, at least leave me one person!" He thinks he might receive special treatment, having someone at the front. A man named Kasahara of Fuji Ice was also drafted, and the head of the Kobe branch was drafted as well. The present draft is extremely widespread, and with a draft of this extent, how can industry in general operate?

Even within these boundaries it is unreasonable because it is carried out by people ignorant of economic ideas. Drafting factory workers does not raise efficiency. It incites antiwar feelings, and surely there will be an explosion from this group because of accumulated frustration.

In the evening I went to the Zenshinza (Progressive Theater). The first play on the current social situation was very poor. At the recommendation of the Military Defense Center, it has the support of the Information Board. The actors read commonplace, meaningless lines. Ishibashi said, "Do they think that this play will be effective?" It was on a low-class, commonplace level and simply propaganda. This sort of thing will produce no benefit.

The next was *Chūshingura*,[30] a dramatization by Mayama Seiko, and this, as might have been expected, was splendid. It will probably survive for later generations.

November 16 (Tuesday)

I set off for Tōhuku to give lectures. The usual crowds. But in front there was a second-class car and I placed myself there. I had Natsu wait in line, as the ticket gate was opened an hour early and I couldn't make it.

According to a gentleman next to me, letters that come from Kyūshū are frequently censored. There is mutual suspicion throughout the country. The influence of the war.

November 17 (Wednesday)

Today I am reading Seeley's *The Expansion of England*.[31] This is indeed interesting. The English classics are coming into focus for me. The expansion of England took place because it was not built upon war. I wonder how it would have been if Japan had not engaged in war at all with China or Russia and, embracing the balance of powers, had set out on an English maritime political policy.

The failure of France is because she pursued the two rabbits of continent and seas. The circumstances of Japan are just so.

I got off the train at Yokote. There was a large welcoming party waiting. I gave a speech. Yokote does not have any military production, and there is clearly dissatisfaction over the conditions of the times. One can detect this atmosphere from the meetings.

At the Zenshinza, Professor Takagaki Torajirō said, "Take care when you go into the countryside." The fact that my speech was full of admonitions did not please my audience.

The question was asked, "I hear that the war will be ending in the coming year?" Again they asked, "If Germany is defeated, will there only be Japan left?" People here recognize the worsening of the war situation, and it is different from other places.

Here in the country towns, the residents say there are no vegetables. Everywhere dissatisfaction with the rationing is conspicuous. Without question the black market is spreading.

November 18 (Thursday)

Early in the morning I set out for Akita.

At the inn they set up a *kotatsu*[32] for me and it was pleasant. Everything is generous at this inn.

At Akita Station were Nishino Kohachirō and Hitomi of the Sakigake newspaper. Nishino is a man I traveled with to Manchuria and is secretary of the Economic Club. We put our bags in the Ishibashi Inn and were invited to supper by Sawagi Junkichi of the Akita Bank. Good food is plentiful in the countryside.

The people of Akita are open. Because they are not profiting at all from military supplies, they are cool toward the current state of affairs.

In my individual conversations after the lecture, there was the hope of greater participation in the munitions business. Providing only supplies and labor, they were profiting very little. Mutō Sadakazu recently visited and said Germany and the Soviet are reconciled. England and the Soviet are in conflict, and so Japan will gain a great victory. It appears that he spreads such optimistic views. The gullibility of this group is beyond understanding. It is a time in which the deranged are in control.

November 19 (Friday)

The train had little heat. The enlightened are not accustomed to struggling for existence. Even in the inns of Akita there are no *kotatsu* to speak of. It is not that they are inhospitable; it is because the residents do not feel the cold to the same degree. While I was riding in the train, when the car became somewhat warmer, someone opened a window in the ceiling.

When I arrived at Niigata I was greeted by a man named so and so. At a place called the Italy House, several tens of people dined with me, and when I went to make my speech I was observed by two plainclothesmen, one who was watching and one who was taking notes. It is impossible to give a good lecture under these conditions. In the event that campaign speeches and lectures are overseen by people resembling schoolchildren, decent politics and free speech are not to be expected. The destruction of bureaucratic government is necessary, but do the people now have the capacity to govern themselves?

November 20 (Saturday)

Leaving Niigata early, at Nagaoka I changed trains. The direct train to Tōkyō runs only once or twice a day, and the confusion is homicidal.

Masamune Hakuchō said, "I am always threatened by indecision and disquiet. Even if there is victory in the war, it has little relation to me." He means the irksomeness of the neighborhood associations, the irksomeness of the Imperial Rule Assistance Society, and the continuous pressure of the bureaucracy.

The repatriation ship arrived on the 14th, and the newspapers inserted an article "Expose the Tyranny of America!" (*Asahi*, from the 17th). The serialized articles were entitled "Japanese Put into Murderers' Cells" and "Shooting Japanese to Death."

On the train I read Seeley's *The Expansion of England*. I have learned many things from this book. At about seven in the evening I arrived at our Karuizawa villa, and my wife and Natsu were there.

November 22 (Monday)

About noon Yasuda Rihei came to visit. He came as he had previously promised to. In the afternoon we walked around old Karuizawa together. There are many Germans here. They were ordered to evacuate Yokohama and other places, and about 250 are coming here.

November 23 (Tuesday)

Female laborers are replacing men. It is a revolution for Japanese women. They are no longer the slaves they have been until now. Necessarily their status will probably rise and their knowledge will improve.

Everything is bringing revolution in Japan. Sacrifices will be great, but if the Japanese are wise they will probably inevitably achieve this. Because they have reached their limit, there is the necessity for some sort of external treatment. As to the group possessing vigor of spirit becoming pessimistic, on the contrary, it is becoming optimistic.

November 24 (Wednesday)

From Obama a letter came saying that there will be a dinner for the Greater East Asian minister, Aoki, and inviting me to join, so I decided to return to Tōkyō. With all the confusion on the train, I had a second-class ticket but sat in a third-class car.

On the train I read *Newspapers of the Bakumatsu*. It included such things as the Richardson Incident (Namamugi Incident)[33] and the bombardment of Chōshū.

November 25 (Thursday)

I received an invitation from the Greater East Asian minister, Aoki. In attendance were also Obama, Takahashi Kamekichi, Ishibashi, Ishiyama, Hasegawa Nyozekan, Fuse Shōji, and Abe Kenichi.

His official residence was said to have been originally the mansion of Takashima Kokinji. It was absolutely splendid.

Aoki is an excellent official. However, he is not really a politician. Consequently, I felt sorry about asking for the inside gossip one usually gets from other ministers.

He accepts the Greater East Asian Declaration as it is. He thinks the greatness of Japan, victorious in war, lies in issuing such a declaration. But he says a structure has not been built, and Japan is not assuming leadership.

The above-mentioned points are political policy as one part of war. He says this means that in order to be victorious, everyone must make sacrifices. That being the case, this will be obtained by stratagems. However, it is an analysis in which all these elements combine.

He is a person who builds formal structures and is able to believe in them literally. I regret saying this after being entertained, but he is not an outstanding politician. He must be a good businessman. It seems that Shigemitsu is better than he is.

I went with Hasegawa Nyozekan to the used-book district. I bought

Searching for Free Japan.[34] It was 2 yen, 30 sen. This is slightly higher than the fixed price.

At the residence of the Greater East Asian Minister, Aoki, the problem of the postwar structure emerged. Aoki speaks as if he was not enthusiastic and his hands were full with just finishing the war. "If there are peace talks tomorrow, wouldn't Japanese world politics be a question?"

Even at such a gathering of the highest intelligence, everyone tells lies. Hence it is impossible to convince others.

November 26 (Friday)

Today being the commemoration of the final American notification to Japan [before Pearl Harbor], in all the newspapers there were accounts in bold type of Kurusu's talks.

The Japanese-Chinese alliance. From an intellectual perspective, the Greater East Asian Declaration is Japan's greatest victory, and from a diplomatic perspective it is the complete defeat of Japan. It will be necessary to analyze these judgments in the future.

According to the Greater East Asian Minister, Aoki, the representative from Burma asked, regarding the draft of the "Greater East Asian Declaration" how it would be if the fifth article were changed to the "Mutual Development of Resources." I understand that when he was told, "Its meaning is just that," it was left as it was.

In my manuscript for the *Oriental Economist*, at the point when I talked about Theodore Roosevelt calling out the fleet and said, "In the American protests to Japan there is little indication of threat," anything critical about Japan had to be removed. It is said that this was the idea of the translator. It is impossible to make propaganda in this way.

It appears that this crowd thinks if it shuts its ears, other people also will not hear.

It is said that the Gilbert Islands have been taken. It was a frontal assault.

Even at the Twenty-six Society, people will not discuss matters directly. Everybody is telling lies. (Tsurumi is always optimistic regarding the war.)

An account of Kobayashi Ichizō. Things such as politics are worthless. They merely say things that are not straightforward and settle very little. But businessmen completely fulfill their responsibilities.

November 27 (Saturday)

Today is air-raid defense practice day. I stayed home all day and reexamined the *Chronology*. The air-raid training is completely formalistic. We feel the necessity for this, but when we look at it realistically it becomes ridiculous. Because everybody has the feeling that "it can't be helped," they say, "In the real situation it would not be useful at all."

November 28 (Sunday)

A revolution is already approaching us. A deep antagonism toward the rich by the masses and young policemen is expressed.

1. According to Shimanaka, in the restaurant area of Shimbashi the tires on more than twenty automobiles were slashed.
2. My wife heard on the train to Ueda that a policeman said to a person in a neighboring seat, "How extraordinary it is to have coolies on their way to weed in the private villas."

According to Ashida, the crowd that was clamoring for the "Tripartite Alliance" is now being investigated in the police stations. Of late there is a great deal of rushing about on the German side, and it may be there are lavish expenditures. In the accounts of later times, this will probably still be a problem.

Twenty-six enemy planes attacked Taiwan and on the 22nd, and the 23rd, and the 26th, English planes bombed Berlin. The destruction was enormous, and on the English side it is said they announced unconditional surrender terms for Germany. This appeared in the Berlin dispatch. I think the winter bombing damage will be extreme. Schmidt, the head of the German Information Bureau, was wounded. Branch offices of both *Asahi* and *Mainichi* were destroyed. And in Berlin even the theaters have been put underground.

It was decided on November 26 that the government controlled by Mussolini of Italy, the Fascist Republican Government, would be called the Italian Social Republic. This did not appear in the Japanese newspapers. I think this is because there are probably difficulties in calling an ally the "Italian Socialist Republic."

November 29 (Monday)

At noon there was a meeting of the Tōkei International Relations Research Society. I introduced Higashi Ryōzō to Yamada Fumio of the Pacific Affairs Association. Afterward we were invited to an evening banquet by Kuroki Tokitarō. Besides myself and others, there were Hara Nobuko, Sumida Seiichi, and wives at the Kuroki residence. I felt great because of the excellent liquor. Sumida returned home in the middle of the party because he was drunk. Because the hosts are accustomed to giving banquets, the food was really delicious.

In this evening's *Yomiuri* there was something called a report of the circumstances on the outbreak of the Greater East Asian War in *Fortune* magazine. It was written as if ambassadors Nomura and Kurusu first visited Hull and delivered their last notification, and afterward the war broke out. Why do they have to write such big lies? This matter of writing lies is their moral weakness. Wouldn't it be better if they published things as they were?

November 30 (Tuesday)

For the newspapers the incident of American General Patton slapping a soldier and this becoming a great problem is evidence of the defeat of the martial spirit of the American Army. It does not appear to be a situation in which one must necessarily come to this conclusion. One understands their complete ignorance regarding the peculiar sentiments and ways of thinking of America.

When I was about to see off the second son of Shimanaka, who is going to the front, Iwanami, along with his employees, came by. He came to visit the bereaved family of Komura Toshisaburō, but, hearing that my house was nearby, he came to call. We ate lunch together and then went to worship at Komura's tomb at the Tsurumi Sōji Temple.

People who did not compromise their integrity have the influence of great virtue. Iwanami, who came to visit, is also a great man. I see a singular noble patriot in Iwanami.

December 1 (Wednesday)

Early this morning I went to see off Shimanaka Shinya, but with the confusion of the crowds I failed to find him. Students were wrapped from their shoulder over their body with the Japanese flag, and their spirits were overwhelming. Look at their innocence! These people were not there for the purpose of scholarship; it was to raise up rifles. I could not restrain my emotion.

Are there indeed people, men of high virtue, who will eradicate war from the world and rise up bravely? I will at least carry my part of the responsibility on my shoulders.

A discussion by Tokutomi Sohō (*Tōkyō shinbun*, December 1). He regrets conducting the Greater East Asian Conference in enemy languages. Tell that to Premier Tōjō. Tokutomi is not always in sympathy with Greater East Asia propaganda. (This is natural.)

One must always write a "congratulatory prayer" for people who are being sent off to the front. Also, we understand, one says "congratulations" to the bereaved family of someone killed in the war!

Sumida Seiichi said that he has sent off two children to the war, but he felt strange in having to offer congratulations.

Because of this lack of harmony between feeling and expression, all sorts of problems arise.

In the newspapers yesterday, a report of an interview of all the ambassadors at the Vatican in Rome. Afterward, Berlin rejected peace talks.

In the newspapers dated the 1st, Hull rejected peace talks.

It is clear that there are some problems. The Berlin air raids seem to be on a big scale.

The Berlin air raids have gone on from the 22nd to the 26th. The bombs that fell in the first two evenings exceeded those dropped on Hamburg in a week's time (*Asahi*).

December 2 (Thursday)

There was a Board of Directors/Meeting of Fuji Ice. The combined bonuses and shares of the directors are in excess of two thousand yen. Of late there has been a rise in commodity prices, and it is difficult to support outlays with income. Fortunately, there is income from investment, and this is enough to maintain a balance.

In this regard, someone like myself who belongs to the rather wealthy class has been living comfortably. But what of people in general? I think the people who are in trouble are extremely numerous.

Roosevelt, Churchill, and Chiang Kai-shek conferred over a five-day period from November 23 to November 27 at Cairo. The results of the conference were published on December 1. Of course the newspapers did not transmit the entire text, but from them it is clear that the war is probably worsening.

The *Mainichi* merely reported the incident without transmitting the complete text. The *Asahi* report was also simplified.

Mainichi. Aim at obliterating the land of Japan, outlaw the Cairo Conference, attack decisively and plan for this, respond with shattering strategies, and answer with actual power.

Asahi. The Cairo Conference, conclusions of the arrogant enemy, covering up the ruinous war situation, make Chiang dance and zealous strategies.

Yomiuri. (absurd) Cairo Conference, turn Japan into a third-class nation, stripping us of new territories.

In the *Mainichi shinbun* Lt. Colonel Satake, in an article entitled "The Inevitable Victory Position of Germany Is an Iron Wall," stated three times that Germany was in an unconquerable position.

The lt. colonel was in Germany and returned sometime in May this year. One can see that he attacks the production situation in Japan (*Mainichi shinbun*, December 2, evening edition).

Today I handed over the *Tōden Chronology* to Itō.

December 3 (Friday)

Every day the papers are writing on a grand scale of nothing but England's and America's difficulty in attacking Japan. This is self-consolation. One example: They always add inevitably "the puny, piecemeal attacks" of America (in English, *Dōmei*, Buenos Aires, Nov. 29).

Kikuta Sadao came to call. He is an outstanding scholar. He is a professor at Meiji Gakuin and a scholar of the Meiji period.

An account by the same person. The save-the-Bakufu samurai of the Baku-matsu period went off in two directions. They were Christians and newspaper journalists. Because of their background, the journalists were antigovernment. To attack the government, they depended on the foreign residents. Such a person as Black[35] put out a newspaper in Japanese, but the government could not do anything about it.

I have bought *The Recent Decade of World Foreign Relations* by Miyoshi Sadao. It is not a great work but draws slightly upon my *History of Foreign Relations*.

December 4 (Saturday)

In the student military recruitment examination, naval volunteers comprise the greatest number. Because the examining official was army, he inquired, "Why is this?" We understand that there were those who said something about "We like the uniform," "We like the sea," or "the atmosphere," and some answered, "It feels fine."

I hear that the draft laws have even reached Maru of the Silver Star. Now everyone can be drafted. Two or three days ago the age limit in the recruitment law was raised to forty-five.

It is said that the only vegetables available are one or two radishes. My house has enough because we are doing farmers' work.

In the postwar period the nobility will increase, there will be promotions, and the Order of the Kinshi[36] medal will multiply. How would it be if we completely abolished such medals? If we did so, this would probably eliminate those who would want war from obtaining these decorations. In actuality, such things could be rejected on the grounds that while the rest of our countrymen pay only in sacrifices, the bureaucrats and military men obtain profit.

Afternoon, went to the bank and Fuji Ice. It seems that my manuscript cannot be published by Nihon Hyōronsha. I took part of the manuscript home.

December 5 (Sunday)

Military people hate education. However, it is clear that they do not wholly reject education itself because they boast of such things as their silver watches from the Military College.

What is going on when the army praises in the extreme "students" whom they reviled until now? (A discussion between Matsumura and Kurihara.) But the reason they criticize scholars is that even scholarship is bad when it is carried to extremes.

tion. Thus, a person using a mark may have valid and enforceable rights in a mark even though the mark is not registered with the PTO. Such an owner will have priority even over a subsequent user who has secured a federal registration for a mark with the PTO.

The "use" required to establish trademark rights is more than token use; it must be public use. While actual sales of products or services are not required, a certain level of presale activity is required. For example, sales within a company or to personal friends are insufficient to show use, while soliciting and accepting orders is usually sufficient to show commercial use.

Establishing a date of first use is critical for a trademark owner because priority of trademark rights is measured from this date. If one party first used a mark on September 15, 2003, and another first used a similar mark on October 15, 2003, the prior, or **senior, user** will be able to preclude the **junior user** from using a confusingly similar mark.

For a mark to be registrable, it must be based on use in commerce, meaning the type of commerce that can be regulated by Congress. Generally, the use is based on **interstate commerce,** or commerce between states (although it could be based on commerce between the United States and a foreign country). A purely intrastate use does not provide a basis for federal registration of a mark. The requirement of interstate commerce is satisfied if the goods or services are advertised in more than one state, offered to citizens of more than one state, or offered on the Internet, which is considered use in commerce because it is available to a national audience through the use of telephone lines.

Although the general rule is that acquisition of trademark rights stem from use, there is one exception to this rule: the **intent-to-use application.** Until 1989, the United States was one of only two countries in the world that required that a mark be in actual use before an owner could file an application to register it.

After an applicant had begun using the mark and then filed an application, the PTO might refuse registration of the mark on the basis it was confusingly similar to a prior mark or was subject to some other defect. The applicant would then have invested substantial money and time in developing the mark, in using it in commerce, marketing, and advertising, and in applying for registration, only to be told the mark was unregistrable. To remedy this situation, the Trademark Law Revision Act of 1988 allowed persons to file applications for marks based on a bona fide intent to use the mark in commerce in the future. If the PTO determines the mark is unregistrable, the applicant will not have expended any sums other than the PTO filing fee and can readily file another application for a new mark. If the PTO determines the mark is registrable, the applicant must then commence use of the mark in commerce and provide a statement verifying such use to the PTO before the mark can proceed to registration. Interestingly enough, however, once the mark proceeds to registration, priority is measured from the date the intent-to-use application was *filed,* even though that filing date may precede actual use in commerce by more than three years. (See Exhibit 2–3.)

Minimal or token use cannot serve as the basis for securing or maintaining a registration, ensuring that an owner does not reserve or "warehouse" a mark by making only sporadic use of it with the intent to block others from using it rather than having a true commercial intent to exploit the mark for sales. Moreover, the PTO desires to clear its records of unused marks, or "deadwood," so that such unused marks may be available by others.

The use required is "bona fide use of a mark in the ordinary course of trade, and not made merely to reserve a right in a mark." 15 U.S.C. § 1127. Thus, an owner must make use of a mark as would be typical in the industry or trade. If a product is extremely expensive, such that only a few units are sold each year, this

December 6 (Monday)

Flexibility of mind is the necessary qualification for politicians. Nowadays military politicians are completely lacking in this flexibility. Consequently, they cannot bring forth appropriate policy conforming to the times.

Every day the newspapers publish conversations and exchanges and so on from Matsumura and Kurihara, both Information Board chiefs. They warn of the alarming war situation.

The fact that the Japanese are unskillful at propaganda is a weakness that they themselves recognize. In all other aspects, Japanese believe that they are outstanding (*Asahi shinbun*, December 6, dialogue of Matsumura, Kurihara; *Asahi shinbun*, "Kamikaze Ode").

December 8 (Wednesday)

It is the second anniversary of the war. Both the newspapers and the radio were full of past recollections and encouragement and so on. Besides this, they were lavish in instructions.

In two full years the clear fact is just as Sawada said yesterday: the people still have not had enough of war.

Since two or three days ago I have been looking at the December number of *Chūō kōron*. There was a symposium entitled "A Study of Difficulties Ahead." And although the participants were a group of professors from Kyōto Imperial University, it was a strange thing. It claimed that France turned on Tokugawa Keiki, and the "Seikanron" resembled the strategy of America.[37] Again, a professor named Komaki repeated, "The Greater East Asian War is supported by the heavenly gods." The *Chūō kōron* had this tone throughout.

In the Greater East Asian War: (1) there are people who completely make this their aim, (2) there are people who will probably use this as the opportunity for domestic revolution, (3) there are people who will profit by means of this. There is, at the bottom stratum, the mentality that military power will settle everything, and there are the masses who have this fatalistic view of the inescapability of war. For them war must be fought out to the very end.

In the second year of the war, the thing that strikes one's attention is the brazenness of the sneak-thieves. There is not a house that has not had things stolen. Overcoats, and shoes that are placed in the entry hall are taken immediately.

Today's newspapers published a public declaration of the Teheran Conference of Roosevelt, Churchill, and Stalin. It stated, "All the peoples of the world will not accept oppression, but rather they hope for the day on which they will be able to carry on their free lives based upon their own self-determination and conscience." If the statement had not identified the *London Telegram*[38] as the source, we might easily mistaken it for the Greater East Asian Declaration.

Previously we heard words from the Japanism advocates that "Japan will be victorious in the war that she has joined." Nakano Seigo was one person who said so. Even now, this conviction has not been lost.

Mizuno of the police came and said that there would probably be the plundering of food supplies during air raids. Anticipating this, he recommended that the neighborhood associations should organize defense bodies in units. Also, he said that the European side was engaged in the "rejection of peace talks," but there is something that must make them reject these talks. He has knowledge acquired by ear, and he penetrates actual conditions correctly.

December 9 (Thursday)

Premier Tōjō's speech on the radio last night filled the morning's newspapers. As usual he said, "There are glorious victories."

Everybody is saying, "In America there are no war aims." I wonder how it would be to say there are no war aims in Japan? Both the Naval Information Bureau chief and a group who had returned from abroad spoke of the lack of American war aims. This was probably at the instigation of the authorities.

In the speech of Tōjō this was also the case.

It seems that saying there is internal discontent in America is wishful thinking. In the *Asahi shinbun*, Shiratori Toshio spoke of "Jews." He stated the fact that both England and America were driven by Jews. The *Mainichi shinbun* had Honda and Kanokogi Kasunobu relating their feelings about Commemoration Day, December 8. These are the people responsible for the war.

According to Masamune Hakuchō, after I went to Niigata for a lecture, Hakuchō and Saitō went there and stated that Germany had thrown off the burden called Italy and an indestructible resistance would now be possible. Everything is optimistic. Hearing my discussion was an interesting comparison, but I understand that they (Sakaguchi Semmu, *Niigata shinbun*) preferred Shiratori's line of explanation.

It was the same for Mutō Sadaichi's talk in Akita. Because this sort of crowd goes to the countryside, it is not surprising there is an optimistic feeling there.

December 10 (Friday)

At the Economic Club there was a talk entitled "America the Impatient Enemy" by Colonel Takase. It was my intention to attend, but I did not go. There are many people who are saying the recent American offensives are "the result of impatience and aim at a short war." And so it is said that this exposes the American weak point.

This, too, is self-delusion. Didn't America say from the outset she would open an offensive at the end of 1943?

I wrote for the International Relations Society on the problem of the Second World War and racism.

Matsumura, the head of the Information Board (Matsumura Hidezō, army general), gave a speech on the subject "A Letter to Veterans." He cried out against the "Opium War" of England and American "cruelty toward the Philippines." Wouldn't it have been better to attack instead the unjust immigration laws of America? The Opium War is already ancient history.

It is to be regretted that America has attacked and sunk a hospital ship (*Asahi*, December 10, evening edition).

December 11 (Saturday)

The head of the Military Affairs Office directs primary school education, but when military officers are attached to the elementary schools this is completely militaristic politics.

Even now the attached military officers have extraordinary power with regard to higher education (*Yōmiuri shinbun*, December 11).

"Because the individual is strong, the squad (unit) is strong."

"Is this not an individualistic way of thinking?"

The fliers are obtaining their fighting techniques from ancient *kendo*.

The similarity of the Nazi psychology and Japanese leadership spirit. (The praise of war, the absolute nature of real power, etc.) (See the paper in English on political notes.)

Kagawa Toyohiko and Takara Fumiko were summoned by the military police. Because they were members of a peace organization in England, they were instructed to submit a letter that said, "I joined this organization at the connivance of England, but I will definitely leave the society." Moreover, they were told they were sent a letter from the military police.

What happened afterward, I don't know. (It is said that Kagawa was held.) (Later entry.)

December 12 (Sunday)

I went to the funeral of Wakasugi. It was regrettable that I had not asked him about Japanese-American relations. The death of people of talent is grievous.

The foreign minister, Shigemitsu, gave a speech on radio. This was because the 11th was the commemoration date of the military alliance among Japan, Germany, and Italy. He said that Perry came to Japan to oppress us, but such statements only elicit the contempt of the enemy. It is because people who are historians do not believe this sort of thing. Rather, it would be better to bring up the immigration problem.

December 13 (Monday)

I sent my *History of Japanese Foreign Relations* with a letter to Foreign Minister Shigemitsu and pointed out that his speech on such things as Perry and the bombardment of Kagoshima differed from the actual facts of history. I strongly emphasized that our propaganda must be based on actual facts.

At the Overseas Development Association I listened to a bit of the speeches of Azumi Homei and Hayashi Jinnojō.

1. Doesn't the fact that all Japanese returning from America are saying the same thing, that America as a whole seems confused as to its war goals, indicate that they have been coerced by the Japanese government? Hasegawa Susumu told us that a man who was in New York and submitted articles to such newspapers as the *New York Times* was immediately arrested by the police when he gave a speech (at a certain place).

2. Hayashi was violently opposed to the annexation of four provinces of Thailand by Malaya. This was announced by Premier Tōjō.

  1. Even historically there is no foundation for this.
  2. The resident population will not consent.
  3. Malaya is economically incapable of this (the annexed lands are places producing rice).
  4. A great deal of Japanese iron comes from these areas.
  5. How will peace and order be maintained?
  6. How will this benefit Japan?

According to the account of the same gentleman, Malaya is pressed for food supplies. Peace and order will never be able to be maintained. Because the dispatched officials interfered in everything, the general population thinks it better to remain connected with Thailand.

The declarations of Premier Tōjō reflect a way of thinking that regards these territories as spoils.

In today's *Asahi* there is the report of chronic colds. The heating equipment has been replaced in all buildings. Even the windows of the banks have been stripped. The railings of bridges have been carried off.

Probably in the postwar period this will be a country without metal objects. Their replacement will involve great cost. This will become more acute when the air raids come.

It is said that the navy felt relieved with the outcome of the sea battle at Bougainville and the Gilberts. Murayama of Tōkei says that as a result there cannot be any direct attacks upon Japan until fall of the coming year.

December 14 (Tuesday)

German Ambassador Stahmer often meets with Shigemitsu. It is said that he stated, "If Japan does not open hostilities with the Soviet, it's possible that Germany will conclude peace with England." This seems to be a possibility.

Because the general population does not know how ill-informed they are, even now there are those who still clamor for the beginning of war with the Soviet.

Chūō kōron has become utterly astonishing. In the "Study of the Difficulties Ahead" symposium, attended by a group of Kyōto University professors, in their scholarship on the West everything is more or less in the following style: "Biblical Scholarship," "The Meiji Reform of the Calendar Was Unnecessary," "On the Restoration of Scholarship," "As Regards Scholarship, Everything Is Written There if One Reads the *Nihon shoki*[39] "(Noda)," "International Law Is Completely a Strategic Plan of America and England," "There Is Absolutely No Doubt of the Sense of Identity of the Jews," "France Made Tokugawa Keiki Oppose the Imperial Rescript," "*Dōshisha* Is a Plot."

It is interesting that bizarre arguments are carried as far as this. While I was comparing names with actual ranks, I could not bear to put the volume down. When I related this to Ishibashi, he said he feels exactly the same.

In the magazine *Jewish Studies*, even the matter of the fall of the Italian Badoglio government is haunted by the specter of the Jews.

They say that Japanese is being intensely studied in America (*Mainichi shinbun*).

December 15 (Wednesday)

When I listen to the morning radio nowadays, I find it completely insulting to the intelligent. There is the attempt to make the entire nation listen to stuff that has descended to this low level. Even if I do listen, I am enraged.

Has there, I wonder, ever been such a low-level period in the world?

On the commemoration day, the 11th, of the Japanese-German Offensive-Defensive Alliance, what is the reason that only Japan is making such a fuss about it? In Berlin, under the auspices of Ambassador Ōshima, the high officials were invited, but Ribbentrop did not show up. Was this to remind us of the Offensive-Defensive Alliance?

It is said that in America the newspaper reporters are free of censorship (Buenos Aires, *Dōmei*) (published on the 11th).

It seems they already expected the war.

I wrote an essay entitled "Russia and Japan Must Maintain Neutrality" in the *Tōyō keizai* and for the Nagoya press.

I am having stomach trouble. It is very difficult to recover from this. I have never had such stubborn intestinal problems.

December 16 (Thursday)

The ancient Japanese *wakō* (pirates) have a new form now in 1940, 1941.

Right-wing kamikaze-type ideas are circulating throughout the country. Travel to foreign countries is limited by this type of crowd. For example, because Professor Tanaka Kōtarō of Tōkyō University was said to lack the Japanese spirit since he was Catholic, they canceled travel plans that had already been settled. We are in a period of vacillating officials who cancel things previously agreed to. Though ignorant, they are self-confident. It is common talk that they regiment and formalize the various countries in East Asia to which they go. But such people as these will not be obeyed. Hayashi Jinnojō also talks about this matter, and everybody talks of it.

Of late those drawn to be civil administration are truly complete converts to right-wing ideas. Yano, who was made governor of Toyama Province, is one of these people.

I would like to know what intellectuals of the various countries of Greater East Asia will think of Japan.

A man named Tsuchida, who is a graduate of Chūō Daigaku and is at the Naval Paymaster School, came to call. I hear that students there are cruelly beaten. It appears that the business of beating is regarded as an obligation. I understand from others that the school believes that it is one form of training and that by beating they can train professional soldiers.

An account of a secretary of the Greater East Asian Ministry named Hagiwara Tōru. Premier Tōjō does not like people who oppose him. Right now Shigemitsu gives him some advice, but if he were to continue to do so, before long Shigemitsu would be dismissed.

An account of Abe Kenichi. The Senior Statesmen all make idle complaints to Tōjō. Even in the matter of the war situation, Tōjō says, "Put your faith in me!" and does not share his opinions with others and does not seek advice. The only one who supports Tōjō unconditionally is Abe Nobuyuki.

Nakano Seigo therefore planned to support Ugaki.

Sugimori Kōjirō said that Nakano Hideto (brother of Nakano) came immediately after Seigo's death and said he did not understand his brother's death at all.

The government is all worked up, and the Kempeitai are being sent flying about in all directions. Even in the neighborhood of Fukuoka they are arresting innocent people.

December 17 (Friday)

At the International Relations Research Society there was speech concerning the culture of the Orient and Occident by Miura Shinshichi. He is an intense scholar. He thinks that while the Occident makes its foundation Christianity, the Orient is more diverse. In the Occident there is a separation between God and Man, and one advances making efforts to attempt to reach God. Contrary to this, in the Orient, one discovers oneself in the power of nature. In the Occident, the church developed as the core, but because of that there arose the problem of church versus state. In Japan, religion is one with the state. This is the reason that such people as Hitler are envious of Japan.

I met Akamatsu Katsuma after a long absence. I understand from him that the intellectual deterioration of the industrial worker should be surprising. It is said that even the capitalists are saying it would be better to build labor unions and have the workers commanded by their leadership.

While the American side is still thinking about machinery for the guarantee of complete peace, the only problem is that of achieving it (*Asahi*, 18th special edition).

December 18 (Saturday)

Of late, newspaper writing always has one single form. They add at the end words that say, "We must advance to increased war power," and "We must carry out the responsibilities of the home front." This is the manifestation of a national spirit that prefers preaching. There is probably a feeling of some sort of insecurity when these phrases are not used.

It is reported that on the 16th the English again dropped fifteen hundred tons of bombs on Berlin. When the Germans try to rebuild it, it is the strategy of war to destroy it. The same strategy will probably be used on Japan, and when this happens there will probably be very few buildings left standing in Tōkyō.

I went to browse in the used-book market. Books have become very expensive. I bought *Foreign Relations and Foreign Conquest* by Inagaki Manjirō. It was published in 1896. The fact that at that time he predicted the Anglo-Japanese alliance as a consequence of the Sino-Japanese War is admirable. His Western history is also interestingly written.

No matter when it appears, something that has merit still has good points. He is a Cambridge graduate.

I understand there is a movement arising in Korea that asks, "Why do you not give us independence?" Moreover, on the occasion of farewell parties for our volunteer soldiers, sometimes there is jeering and sometimes there is disorder. It is said that individuals are receiving three or four letters from their native towns encouraging volunteering.

December 19 (Sunday)

On the 17th America abolished the Anti-Chinese Immigration Laws (Executive Order of President Roosevelt).

December 20 (Monday)

The Japan Newspaper Society arranged a discussion for Abe Shinnosuke and me. This was for the report of the same organization. When the Information Board heard of it, they said opinions of people who were not at present officials would be better, and they asked us to speak.

Abe said later, "The fact that they chose us is evidence that they have no self-confidence."

I returned to Shimanaka the interest charge of 1,000 yen and 15,000 yen. This was for land in Karuizawa. I presented him all of my bonds, which I had changed from foreign bonds into Nippatsu Company bonds, and on top of this I added cash. We have decided interest will be 5 percent. The return next year would be 1,100 yen.

December 21 (Tuesday)

This morning's newspapers published the fact that the islands of Makin and Tarawa in the Gilberts have been seized by the enemy, and some three thousand were killed. While it was reported that the American losses of late have been extremely numerous, the information on Japanese casualties has been fed out in small quantities. In the case of today's information, speaking of Makasu—a peninsula in New Britain Island—the Japanese people probably received a considerable shock.

In a talk with Okamura of *Dōmei*, he said that in his own circles there is collective agreement that America is a country of individualism and liberalism, and because she detests war, the war in the end will probably conclude in compromise. This is the level of a young person's knowledge.

Admiral Suetsugu, Saitō Tadashi, and others are still the favorites of the period. They are certainly the people responsible for the war. They still enliven the magazines and newspapers. Yamada (*Tōyō keizai*) said, "As for Saitō Tadashi, he still has admiring readers!"

A little while ago, according to an account of a Greater East Asia Ministry official named Hagiwara Tōru, he reported that Phibul[40] was in some measure making ready to flee.

December 22 (Wednesday)

The balance sheet of stubborn foreign relations.

A tax increase plan was published in this morning's newspapers. It aimed at a revenue of 2.2 billion yen at the beginning year level. That is to say it is eight times the revenue at the time of the China Incident. Even up until the present, foreign nations have called Japan such things as poverty-stricken. It is a fact that the people who pay taxes have more and more become animals. However, if one carries on war, of course, this is inevitable (*Mainichi shinbun*, December 22).

There is widespread propaganda from those returning to Japan that American treatment of human beings is devil-like (*Chūbu Nihon shinbun*, "Chūkyō Shunjū," article of the 19th).

Kawai said that with regard to Manchuria we can score sixty points. As regards China, we do not even have the examination qualifications. The maneuverings of Chiang Kai-shek are bad. Also, the Japanese way of doing things in China—

1. When one walks in the Northern Gardens of Peking, they have set up water for air-raid defense. Yet behind these are huge ponds.

The phrase "Ignoring Chiang Kai-shek as the enemy" was born as the result of a cabinet meeting. From about that time the cabinet became absorbed in foreign affairs. Someone asked, what does this "ignoring Chiang Kai-shek as the enemy" mean? Chief Secretary Kazami Akira, hearing this, said, "It is much stronger than ignoring China." Upon hearing this, China became more intransigent.

Obama said that when the point of half-heartedness is reached in the Japanese-American war, there will be a compromise. Even a person who knows the situation well has this degree of optimism. His thinking is that because of increased attacks on the enemy in the Gilberts sea war, the enemy will become exhausted. He thinks it doubtful even that Tōkyō will be bombed.

In Shansi one match costs about two sen, five rin, but in Peking it is one yen, sixty sen, and in Shangtung, about two yen, sixty sen.

I bought Yamamoto Shigeru's *History of Treaty Revisions*. It is a fine book. I bought a dedication pamphlet that was a keepsake of Perry sent by his grandson. The interpretation of Perry differs depending on the level of Japanese–American relations. At the time Perry was the founder of an open Japan.

December 23 (Thursday)

Just as every year, I invited Ōta Eifuku and his wife and others to the Kabuki. A man in the seat behind me stole the cane that I had placed under my seat.

December 24 (Friday)

According to this morning's newspapers, it was announced that the suitable draft age will be reduced one year from the 1944 level. It is clear that about next year this will be lowered again.

If one relies upon the statements of the Army Ministry, the suitable conscription age in America and England is eighteen, and in Germany it is seventeen. Is this indeed so? After the war there is need for research into the matter. There probably has been confusion between "military age" and "conscription."

An account of Obama. China has given Roosevelt something like a $2 million bribe. Japan has given nothing. This is the reason for his anti-Japanism. Such is the level of common knowledge.

I attended the Twenty-six Society. Suzuki Bunshirō said that the food supplies of Japan had reached the low level of the meal we had. He said that the fact one can eat in a restaurant without having a ration coupon is evidence that there is no crisis. Moreover, he said that even in the war things will go well.

Both Suzuki and Obama, who have many opportunities to confer with those who have political connections, are extremely optimistic. It is probably because they have no opportunity to think. It is an example of the need for the advice of thinkers in the world of doers.

Kanokogi Kazunobu is the chief secretary of the Patriotic Press Association and the most representative favorite of the period. I agree with the viewpoint that the American military curries favor with the masses.

Kasama has returned to Japan and appeared at the Twenty-six Society. He also is optimistic and said it was surprising there was so much pessimism in Japan.

December 25 (Saturday)

It is said that the use of the phrase "Greater East Asia Co-prosperity Sphere" in newspapers and magazines is forbidden. The government does not care for the impression it gives of the leadership.

According to the account of Secretary Hagiwara, in Bose's statement to the Chinese masses he added, "In my recent travels to Japan I noticed that Japan has changed its previous aggressive attitude," and the Chinese were extremely angry. Hagiwara said the Information Board does not know what is going on.

While the plans of the government are the globalism and idealism of the Sino-Japanese Alliance and the Greater East Asia Declaration, they naturally restrain such discussion by others, saying, "International law is a stratagem of America and England" (*Chūō kōron* symposium). Here is the real world.

December 26 (Sunday)

The governor of the Kyūshū region (the so-called greater area governor) in a symposium discussion in the *Mainichi* newspaper attacked the Agriculture-Commerce Ministry with respect to the ridiculous oscillations of controls and prices. It is official attacking official, and this is a grand sight.

An account of Baba Tsunego. In Chiba Prefecture there was an incident in which a housewife was harassed by the police over a matter of five sho of rice. Thereupon her husband became furious and killed a police inspector. I understand that Minami Hiroshi announced this to a Sūmitsuin conference, but it appears that Premier Tōjō already knew about it.

March 30, 1934 (*Shōwa* 9), was the eighty-ninth anniversary, and Perry Day has been celebrated in various places. Foreign Minister Hirota's speech was also delivered. (This is one evidence that the evaluation of Perry is divided.)

Those who are optimistic about the future course of the war are awaiting

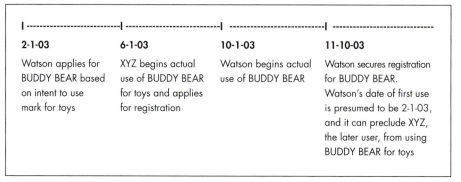

EXHIBIT 2–3
Timeline for
Intent-to-Use
Applications

2-1-03	6-1-03	10-1-03	11-10-03
Watson applies for BUDDY BEAR based on intent to use mark for toys	XYZ begins actual use of BUDDY BEAR for toys and applies for registration	Watson begins actual use of BUDDY BEAR	Watson secures registration for BUDDY BEAR. Watson's date of first use is presumed to be 2-1-03, and it can preclude XYZ, the later user, from using BUDDY BEAR for toys

may be sufficient use if such meager sales are the norm in the relevant industry.

Just as use is required to acquire rights in a mark, continued use is required to maintain rights in a mark. Failure to use a mark for three years creates a presumption the mark has been abandoned. Abandonment is further discussed in Chapter 5.

COMMON LAW RIGHTS, FEDERAL REGISTRATION UNDER THE LANHAM ACT, LAWS AND TREATIES GOVERNING TRADEMARKS, AND STATE TRADEMARK RIGHTS

Common Law Rights

As discussed, in the United States, trademark rights arise from use of a mark. It is not necessary to secure permission or registration from any governmental entity to acquire trademark rights. A party who is using a mark without any such governmental registration is said to have a **common law trademark.** This common law trademark can be enforced in any geographical area in which the mark is used. Thus, if an owner uses the mark CAKERY CRAVINGS in connection with a pastry shop in Portland, Oregon, the owner will be able to preclude later users from using a confusingly similar mark in connection with similar goods or services in Portland and in a reasonable area of expansion beyond Portland.

Federal Registration

Although there is no requirement that a trademark owner apply for or secure federal registration of a mark with the PTO, registration on the PTO's Principal Register does offer several advantages:

- nationwide constructive use effective from the filing date of the application (meaning that the public is assumed to have notice that the registrant has nationwide priority in the use of its mark as of this date);
- nationwide notice to the public of an owner's claim to a mark, thereby precluding a later user from claiming it used a mark in good faith in a remote territory and should be able to continue use;
- the ability to bar importation of goods bearing infringing trademarks (assuming the registration is deposited with the U.S. Customs Service);
- the right under the Paris Convention to obtain a registration in various foreign countries based upon the U.S. registration;
- the right to bring an action in federal court for trademark infringement and recover lost profits, damages, costs, and possibly triple damages and attorneys' fees;

antiwar sentiment in America. However, in neither America or England is there unified opinion, and in this they are worse than the Soviet and China. This is not good, is it? Such expectations have never been expressed in the least about the Soviet and China.

December 27 (Monday)

An order closing down the Okichi Hall.

Shimoda Telegram, the Okichi Hall, Ryōsenji, a famous sight of Shimoda port, Izu, of the Tōjin Okichi[41] was ordered closed as unnecessary under the circumstances of the times.

To close the Okichi Hall is to be expected; however, the fact of Shimoda being regarded as a cursed land is the condition of the times.

There is a dispatch announcing that Harold Lasky is being sent as the Labor representative to the Soviet Union. Lasky is a famous political scientist. Previously, left-wing Cripps had been sent as ambassador. They choose the person suitable for the country. This is the style in which the English handle foreign relations. The people do not complain about this at all.

My article entitled "American Tragedy," which has been published in the *Oriental Economist*, was reprinted in the *Japan Times*. I understand that a letter came from Gō, president of the *Japan Times*, saying that the Foreign Ministry said that it was good. This essay was thoroughly attacked by the Information Board and those with military connections.

An account of Sasaki Mosaku. It is said that *Kōron* is not imported into the Philippines. And the reason for this is that it gives the impression that there are all sorts of factions in Japan, and the tone is extremely narrow.

These sorts of opinions and political policies are emerging little by little.

December 28 (Tuesday)

I wrote a proposal for the establishment of a "Japanese Foreign Relations History Research Society." I am doing something that I have hoped for for a long time; at the same time, it is something that prepares for my future livelihood.

A special dispatch in the evening edition of the *Tōkyō Nichinichi shinbun* said, "Powerful Anti-Japanese Enemy Anger," and it claimed that the Chinese people were stubbornly opposed to Japan (*Mainichi shinbun*, December 28, evening edition).

The foregoing was a dispatch from "Shanghai, the 27th, special correspondent Masui." It made the point that even economically there was the power of resistance, but I cut that part off.

As for other Chinese special dispatches, they all state that the Chinese masses have come to be friends with Japan. However, only in this special dispatch, while there are things held back, is there the report of actual facts. Of course, this was something done with the understanding and censorship of the military. At the end is a conclusion we have heard before—the "nothing but the destruction of the enemy's fighting power." There is no self-reflection.

In the *Asahi* of the same day, it is stated that Chinese youth groups destroyed a dance hall and other things in Shanghai and, gathering up clothing and money, burned these on the main road. Of course, this was instigated by the Japanese authorities. They do not understand that no matter how long they are in China, such behavior becomes the cause of anti-Japanese feeling.

I wonder if there will be the slightest advantage to the Japanese people in the present war. It is extremely doubtful. If there is no fundamental change in education . . .

A story of Obama. China hates turtles. These hateful characters—"ten and one half turtles"—were put in the design of a Savings Bank bond. Ordinarily this could not be seen, but if a magnifying glass were used it was visible. The characters, pronounced as *sepake* in the Shanghai dialect, correspond to "Japanese devil." That is to say, it meant to damn the Japanese. The designer was executed.

If there is this sort of resistance of the masses, there is no hope for Japanese–Chinese relations. Ah! the awareness of the Japanese masses.

December 29 (Wednesday)

I spoke with Kurasawa of *Tōyō keizai* regarding the matter of a foreign relations chronology, and I spoke to Kiyono regarding a history of Japanese–American relations. Somehow, I will pour all my energy into producing these.

In the first chapter of Tokutomi Sohō's *History of the People*, he names Iwakura and Ōkubo as meritorious retainers in the Restoration, and in the preface to the second chapter he states that the *Satchō* and the Bakufu both were in coalition with England and France. He denied the *Chūō kōron* symposium (December issue) that the opposition of Keiki to the decree was due to the urging of France.

December 30 (Thursday)

In an editorial in this morning's *Mainichi shinbun* there is an article on the "Radicalization of North Africa." In the conclusion it states that Jewish power permeates North Africa (*Mainichi shinbun*, December 20, "Editorial").

Capitalism and communism are the two wings of Jewish activism. The *Mainichi shinbun*—this is an editorial of one of the two great newspapers of Japan. It shows the stupidity of the Japanese people. Look at this pretense of knowledge.

Foreign relations cannot be achieved without absolute faith in one's own country. If one says, "what spreads the power of the Soviet is radicalization" (previously cited editorial), foreign relations with the Soviet are impossible. Moreover, to view England and America as the Jewish people makes foreign relations with them impossible. If one asks why English foreign relations are excellent, it is because they firmly believe that their own country will not be radicalized.

Even if one's way of thinking differs, one can be a patriot, and even if one's opinions differ, it is possible to be united with others. But the "patriots" of our country are incapable of thinking in this fashion.

If the war ends before the Japanese people learn the hard experience that Japanese political policies cannot rule other races, this will be rather unfortunate for the Japanese people.

It is a fact that government-operated industry has no locus of responsibility.

The so-called stubborn foreign policy is succeeding. This would be so if it stopped at a certain fixed point.

It would succeed if Japan had stopped at the Manchurian Incident, Italy in Ethiopia, and Germany at the Munich Conference. In Italy's war in Ethiopia, the League of Nations admitted failure and the neutral nations (of the First World War) officially discontinued their economic blockade (June 25, 1936). The problem is whether or not these various nations should have stopped there.

Since the Manchurian Incident, particularly before and after 1936, even economic problems were completely handled by the military (1935, military opposition to the Chinese fiscal reforms, the agreement for the development of North China on October 1, 1936, etc.).

December 31 (Friday)

I wanted to go to Atami, but I could not buy a ticket. I heard that people were standing in line to buy tickets from about eight o'clock last night. Of late I hear that there is a business in tickets, and buyers offer an extra ten-yen tip.

1944

January 1 (Saturday)

An important year has come. The days are coming that will decide history. Yet at the same time I do not have this feeling at all. Nothing is being done yet to prepare for this.

Morning, because I was able to purchase tickets I went off to Atami. I arrived on foot at the Sannō Hotel.

I had supper with Baron Tōgō Yasushi and Tsuchiya Kesazō, and while we were drinking coffee at Tsuchiya's house we discussed the future path of the nation. Previously, the conversations at the Sannō Hotel had a lively flow of ideas and were interesting, but now the discussion of current affairs in a public place is a very dangerous thing.

It is a fact that in every home when people have breakfast they say, "Will we really be able to eat in this way next year also?"

I am reading an English work entitled *Japanese–American Relations before Perry*. It is interesting. It appears that Japan did not treat foreigners cruelly. However, this may also signify propaganda directed toward America, and it needs to be investigated. The clear fact is that shipwrecked Japanese were extremely well treated, and, moreover, in America warships were purposely sent out to pick up shipwrecked Americans. Contrary to this, in Japan the shipwrecked were not picked up at all. The value of what is called "people" differs.

January 2 (Sunday)

As usual, at noon there was a meal at the hotel. They put out an extraordinary spread.

Evening, at the home of Tsuchiya there was a four-way conversation, which included Tōgō Yasushi and Inukai Ken. Inukai was prosecuted in the Ozaki Hotsumi incident and judged innocent.

January 3 (Monday)

In the afternoon I visited Takagi Rikurō. When I discussed the Foreign Relations History Research Center he said talk with Kobiyama of the Manchurian Railway. Indeed, this is a good idea.

On the way home I visited Iwanami Shigeo. He was about to take a walk. We went out together and had supper, and he asked me to stay over. The villa is splendid, and it was an exceptional meal. His first and second sons were there. The eldest son is at the Shibaura Research Center, and the second son is a student of Western history at the Imperial University.

While we drank whiskey-laced English tea, we indulged in big talk. Iwanami values extreme sincerity above all else. I value results above all else. I like Ōkubo and Kido and he likes Saigō. Iwanami's second son feels the same as I do.

January 4 (Tuesday)

I was astonished at the fantastic food at the Iwanami home. In the morning there were rice cakes. Iwanami set off for Tōkyō before 6 A.M. and had a meal with me and his second son. He has a very clear mind.

In the evening newspapers, as the government has settled upon a Wartime Officials' Public Service Ordinance, Premier Tōjō is preaching about this. This so-called Wartime Officials' Public Service Ordinance is terribly abstract. It says, "Try to do your duty with maximum effort and flexibility." This again is Tōjō's usual preaching.

Tōjō views the official as the samurai of the past, and, accordingly, he views the people as the ruled class.

The Greater East Asian War. After the political events of the Manchurian Incident, the military and the bureaucracy joined hands. The war resulted when those who make war their aim and the bureaucratic officials who see only one part (and, moreover, feel they should rule) mingled together and compromised.

January 5 (Wednesday)

Everywhere I go there is talk of the rise in prices of things. According to an account of Viscount Soga, butter is 25 yen a pound. Also, rice is 200 yen a sack, and sugar is 60 yen a kamme. These are the standard prices of the black market. Consequently, there are many farmers and others who make extraordinary profits.

Unlike the usual atmosphere in Atami, now there is a stillness like death. Not one orange appears in the shops. This is completely a result of the regulation of everything. Of course, there is no fish.

January 6 (Thursday)

I left on the three o'clock train and returned to Tōkyō.

According to Navy Lt. Commander Akiyama Kunio, the Americans are calling the Japanese army barbaric (*Chūbu Nihon shinbun*, January 2, 1944). This man says that the Americans focus on the Japanese and call them barbarians. He previously stated, "There are women of leisure who said that the Americans were pitiful," and he does not understand that his statements stress the ideas of revenge and action.

Yankees also do cruel things. An account of Uo. At an island in the South Seas an American submarine appeared and seized the fish caught by fishermen. Then, after locking up the fishermen in their boat, they doused it with oil and set it afire. Fortunately, the fishermen escaped with only burns.

War is a continuation of barbarian behavior.

The symposium of Andō Masazumi, Kawasaki Katsumi, and others was taken by the New Year's issue of *Yomiuri*, but it was not inserted in the newspaper. Isn't the reason that they are regarded as a group opposed to current conditions (*Yomiuri*, "Front Line," January 6, evening edition)?

January, Shōwa 19 (1944). The newspaper tone expressed in the fourth year of the war. While Japan faces the Greater East Asia Declaration and domestically the problem of food supplies and the necessity for the modernization of military equipment, the media world is still getting its ideas from divine inspiration. Is it possible to win the war in this way?

Wherever one goes, there is anxiety about the future of the war.

January 7 (Friday)

There was a New Year's lecture by Ishibashi, and I went to the Keizai Club. Ishibashi said that the views held last year were partly accurate. He said that with regard to the Political Policy for the Maintenance of Food Supplies published last year (December 28) (Self-Supply Food Provisions), people were drafted from the villages and there were now insufficient workers. It is something I heard in Atami, and this year there would probably be a shortfall of thirteen or fourteen million koku.

The government is energetically carrying out the evacuation of the population. Previously, those who left Tōkyō were said to be unpatriotic. Feudal emotions are being pushed to the limit.

Even such people as Ōguchi Kiroku do not listen to anything the officials say. When he had a nose-bleed he accepted a bandage for the first time. But usually he stubbornly says, "This is none of your business!"

There is no longer a place called the Diet, that discusses major affairs and the government has been handed over to the hands of young university graduates. There is no way to improve conditions. The present deadlock was born from this.

January 8 (Saturday)

Everything is extremely grim. It was reported on the 10th and 19th that our submarines in March last year sank 940,000 tons of enemy shipping, more than 10,000 tons a day, but this was the peak, and recently they have become inactive (with the new year they have become active again—in ten days, twenty-one destroyers).

If Germany is defeated, what will happen? Everyone is worried about this. The fact that until now the destruction of Germany has been the first priority of America is clear.

On the Japanese side, it is being said that American casualties are 400,000, but on the American side, they say 130,000.

As usual, I am correcting the *Chronology*. If I go on in this way, will I ever be able to publish it?

About 1938 there was the threat of war with the Soviet Union, and we were venting our anger on both England and America. It is a form of saying "if a horse runs into you, lash out."

Since the Manchurian Incident foreign affairs have shifted completely to the military. This is a development preferred by the general masses. As to whether this is good or bad, time alone will probably clarify.

January 9 (Sunday)

On the occasion of the Meiji Emperor's visit to Tōkyō, his Imperial Decree sought men who would provide honest counsel. The statements of administrators were requested to be the same. However, now such honest counsel is something that is rejected above all else (*Mainichi*, January 9).

As for myself, if I am a specialist, it is in the area of "America" and foreign relations. My approximately thirty volumes are on these subjects. However, in a war that makes America the enemy, my words are completely sealed, and there is no way for me to serve the nation. On top of this, a political policy is being carried out that could cut off my livelihood. Then, how is it possible for the nation to be mobilized?

An illustration of the ignorance of the leadership. Now the evacuation of the population is now being carried out vigorously. Because of this it has reached the point of the government having legal dictatorial power. If it had been done two or three years ago, how much more effective would it have been? At the time there would have been strong objections with emphasis on spiritual resistance. Also, *Mainichi shinbun* talked about this once, but at that time the government suppressed it.

My wife says if we are always defeating the enemy, I wonder why it is being said, "The war is becoming more severe."

While I was at the home of Katō, Miyashita Ushitarō came to call. Previously, as an editor of *Yūben* (Eloquence) and *Gendai* (Today), he persuaded me to write for the magazines. He worked for Kodansha for twenty-one years, but it appears his payment was a pittance. He violently attacked Kodansha. I was also someone who Noma Seiji took care of, but after the death of the dictator it was a confused state of affairs.

Moreover, he heard that there is discontent with rice deliveries based on quotas. Even in the countryside of Hokuriku region they say, "We know, of course, that we cannot lose the war. Yet, there is excessive meddling and we dislike having the hairs of our bottoms plucked."

January 10 (Monday)

There is a telegram saying that Chiba Utako is returning home, and Ishibashi is worried whether or not some sort of problem arose in Hsu Chou.

It is being said that the Spanish visit of Ribbentrop is a false rumor. However, there can be no doubt that Germany is in an extremely difficult position.

I hear that they will accept the *Chronology* at *Tōyō keizai*. However, the problems of printing it are formidable.

When one assigns the question of the good and bad points of capitalism to the students of Jiyū Gakuin, nearly all say there are no good points. Akira says that capitalism is fine. He says that it made America and England rich. There are mistakes on both sides, but the result of this great war is that changes in the form of capitalism cannot be stopped.

January 11 (Tuesday)

In the German–Soviet War, the Red Army has broken through the old borders of Poland. At the same time there is talk of a second front. But it appears that the supporters of Germany are optimistic.

America has appointed pro-German people to the administrative council of Italy. These kinds of appointments are incomprehensible in Japan.

The death of Ciano, former foreign minister, has been confirmed. The danger of living in totalitarian countries.

January 12 (Wednesday)

The *Yomiuri* and *Asahi* are extravagantly playing up the Greater East Asia Declaration. This is clearly the intention of the government. To emphasize this, Saitō Tadashi and Nakano Tomio are asked to write for *Asahi*. These imperialists—when the extreme right wing talks about the "Greater East Asia Declaration," those outside Japan will probably not believe them. It is just like the wolf imitating the bleat of the sheep.

Koizumi Makoto, doctor of science, has returned from Rabaul. He said that the sacrifices in the war are indeed enormous, but he is extremely optimistic about the road ahead. The chief civil administrator, Kasama, also feels the same way. On the front line they say that on the home front there is not a proper comprehension of the war.

January 13 (Thursday)

A story my wife heard from Shimanaka. Shinya joined the Setagaya Regiment, but he was beaten every day, and the shape of his face was changed. Because he was beaten with the soles of studded clogs, he always had fresh

- incontestable status of the registration after five years of continuous use subsequent to the registration (meaning that the mark is immune to certain challenges), assuming appropriate documents are filed;
- the right to use the registration symbol ® with the mark;
- a possible basis to claim priority to an Internet domain name; and
- *prima facie* (literally, "on its face") evidence of the validity of the registration, the registrant's ownership of the mark, and the registrant's exclusive right to use the mark in connection with the identified goods and services.

Additionally, because individuals routinely search the PTO records before adopting a new mark, a mark that is registered or applied for with the PTO may deter a party from seeking a registration for a similar mark, thus avoiding expensive litigation.

In sum, while federal registration is not required to secure trademark rights, registration provides several advantages and enhances the level of protection an owner has for a mark.

Laws and Treaties Governing Trademarks

There are several laws and treaties governing trademarks, including the following (most of which will be further discussed in the chapters to come):

- **Lanham Act.** The federal statute governing trademark rights is the **Lanham Act** (also called the United States Trademark Act and found at 15 U.S.C. § 1051 *et seq.*), enacted in 1946 and named for Congressman Fritz Garland Lanham (D. Tex.), the then chair of the House Patent Committee (which also proposed legislation relating to trademarks) who introduced the legislation.

In addition to providing for federal trademark protection, the Lanham Act also includes statutes prohibiting unfair competition. The Lanham Act has been amended numerous times. Perhaps the most significant amendment occurred with the Trademark Law Revision Act of 1988, which provided the following two critical changes: allowing for a trademark application based on the applicant's intent to use a mark in the future (in the past, applications were all based on actual use of the mark); and reducing the period of protection for federally registered marks from twenty years to ten years (at which time the registration must be renewed). Rules of practice and procedure relating to trademarks are found at Title 37 of the Code of Federal Regulations (C.F.R.).

- **North American Free Trade Agreement (NAFTA).** NAFTA was enacted in 1994 as an agreement among Canada, Mexico, and the United States. NAFTA precludes registration of marks that are primarily geographically deceptively misdescriptive.
- **Trade-Related Aspects of Intellectual Property Rights (TRIPs).** TRIPs, a treaty signed by the United States in 1994, bars registration of a mark for wine or liquor if the mark identifies a place other than the origin of the goods and was first used after 1996. Thus, a new wine cannot use the mark "Napa" unless the product originates in that region of California. TRIPs also increased the period of time of nonuse of a mark that would result in abandonment from two years to three years.
- **Trademark Law Treaty Implementation Act (TLTIA).** TLTIA, effective in late 1999, simplified several requirements relating to trademark

wounds and he said, "It was much worse than hell!" Since he was a particularly gentle person, as a mother she grieved, "Poor thing! Poor thing!"

The polemics of the right wing appear daily in the newspapers, but they are also full of polemics leaning toward the left wing. For example, in the *Yomiuri's* editorial this morning regarding a decisive American battle under the heading "This Year Will Be the Decisive Year for the Enemy," the reasons for American labor disputes were:

> 1. The workers not seeing the emergence of a second front in the support of the Soviet union, have lost hope.
> 2. The self-serving activity of the capitalists is evident.

The latter is true, but the former is the exaggerated thinking of the Marxists. The American workers are not that friendly to the Soviet. Because this writer is fearful of internal divisions in America, he says that this year will be the great decisive stage. Planes came to raid Yen Shui, Gao Hsiung, in Taiwan.

January 14 (Friday)

I was informed by Kurasawa of *Tōyō keizai* that the *Foreign Relations Chronology* would be published by Dai Nihon Insatsu (Greater Japan Publications). What could give me more pleasure than this? I felt very happy.

The chief of the Police Bureau came and told me that the plans for the Rokugō Waterworks, which I had previously prepared, were decided upon in the Ōmori and Kamata wards. This also made me happy. Moreover, the fowl that I had bought earlier produced a single egg.

Yesterday I went to play golf. I went around with Kondō Kōichirō. The artist Kondō's eldest son entered the navy at Yokosuka. He is extremely brilliant.

Beating flourishes even in the navy, and inductees are made to stand on tip-toe for even as long as an hour. He says it is utterly cruel. This is the training imposed on the graduates of the highest educational institutions. According to a story of Shimanaka, a classmate of Shinya committed suicide in a privy.

This is what the officers think is training.

January 15 (Saturday)

I met with Shimanaka and asked him to transfer a special allotment of paper to *Tōyō keizai*. He agreed gladly. After that, I consulted with the chief of the printing section of *Tōyō keizai*, called Takagi, concerning format. Again, I asked Ishibashi for the services of Itō of the "Chronology section" in the *Chronology* work. I expect it will be settled in a conference with Takamori on Monday.

In every newspaper they are putting out articles entitled, "The Unfolding of the Greater East Asia Declaration" (*Yomiuri*), "The Manifestation of the Greater East Asia Declaration" (*Asahi*), "The Five Basic Principles of Greater East Asia Construction" (*Mainichi*). When one sees the term "Director, Patriotic Speech Society" as the title of these writers, it is clear that these are official preparations of the same society. This is probably also a strategy of the government. But when one looks at the writers, they are peripheral to the Greater East Asia Declaration. Such people as Shiratori Toshio, Ōgushi, etc.

I hear that Katō Takeo was asked by the Information Board for a novel related to the "Greater East Asia Declaration."

January 16 (Sunday)

I invited Todoroki, Adzumi, Iwanami Yūjiro, Katō Takeo, and Sumiko to my place.

Todoroki returned on the second exchange ship. He said that the Japanese on the Pacific coast completely lost all their possessions and property. Now even if they are released, they can do nothing for the moment. That is to say, they have been stripped of everything they had.

In America when they hear Japanese make the statements, "Is Japan winning or losing the war?" and "Peace talks in Washington," they perceive this as "unconditional surrender." Rephrasing this in unconditional surrender terms, it must be Japan who acts first.

The fact that Japan shot the American fliers after their capture brought an extreme reaction in America. Roosevelt made use of this, and war bond sales increased. It is said that the results exceeded all expectations.

January 17 (Monday)

I was asked by the former Ministry of Communications to go to Karafuto and Hokkaidō and accepted. I understand this will be the first time that Karafuto will be incorporated into Japan proper.

January 18 (Tuesday)

All day long I wrote about the 1943 period in the *Foreign Relations Chronology*.

January 20 (Thursday)

Morning, there was a telegram from Professor Takayanagi Kenzō of Tōkyō University. When I went there he said he worked part-time for the Foreign

Ministry carrying on propaganda directed toward the intellectual class over-seas, and would I become a committee member? Itakura Takuzō and I had been elected members. I said I would probably do so if possible.

Because the title "part-time" was bothersome, they have decided upon committee member. Because there was the problem of Professor Itakura's work on some biography or other of Fukuzawa Yūkichi, he said he would reply next week.

At the Foreign Politics Association I heard a talk on Germany by Secretary Ushiba. It was completely favorable to Germany. It appears that their food resources are fully adequate. And even though the destruction from the air raids is great, it appears that after one or two months things are immediately rebuilt. He said that even oil was plentiful.

When we find that those who come back from Germany are all optimistic about Germany, it is because the internal situation might be fine. However, the problem is how they compare with the actual power of England, America, and the Soviet. It is said that Ushiba is right wing.

January 21 (Friday)

Yamagata of the Foreign Politics Association told me there was an order not to have any discussion about the Soviet-Polish problem. Might this secretive-ness be the young officials just having fun?

January 22 (Saturday)

Researchers on Jews report that even war colds are a scheme of the Jews. This is the intellectual level of "Shōwa Japan."

Yesterday the Diet opened. Premier Tōjō added a tone of sophistication to his speech because he is so practiced in such deliveries. Considering its con-tent, it can only be wondered how he could go on and on about such a sim-ple subject; however, the tone of the *Yomiuri* is significant (*Yomiuri hōchi*, January 22).

If one compares this tone to the insulting way in which it spoke of Diet affairs previously, one understands how much of an extreme contrast this is.

I ate lunch at the Economic Club. It was twenty-three yen for four people. It was steak and nothing else. Previously, one could eat there for one yen. It is a sixfold inflation. I hear that Professor Kindaichi is paying one yen for a single egg.

I was sent *Peace and War* by Ōta Saburō. It is classified "top secret"? Why is it "top secret"? Is it distrust in the people, is it because they have no confi-dence in their own actions and political policy, or are the young officials doing this to monopolize information?

January 23 (Sunday)

The special characteristic of Japan is that the Japanese do not clearly say yes
or no. In the Japanese history of Sohō in this morning's *Mainichi*, the father
and son of the Mori family spoke to the problem of dealing with the Lords of
Ōu, the son saying, "All in the world is subdued," and the father saying, "It is
all fear and shuddering." It is neither yes nor no.

The attitude of the Japanese government in the debate over an open country or a closed country and at the time of the Siberian Expedition was the
same in each case, neither yes nor no.

It has been decided that the magazines that can continue are *Chūō kōron*,
Kōron, and *Gendai. Gendai* has a symposium on the "Centralization of Administration," and this contains writings by such people as Nomura Shigeomi.
Kōron is recognized throughout society as extreme right wing. On the basis
of developments such as these, one naturally understands how the times and
administration have been dragged along by the extreme right and the military
(*Gendai*, Feb. issue).

This magazine and the most right-wing *Kōron* survive.

How these magazines harmonize with the Greater East Asia propaganda is
of interest.

January 24 (Monday)

In the Diet yesterday Premier Tōjō responded to questions of Tsurumi.
What has become clear in the present war is the worsening of "aggression"
and the "colonization of other peoples." The extraordinary thing is that this
is said by both sides. The objection on the Japanese side was represented by
Premier Tōjō's statements of January 24. A budgetary conference on January
24 (*Yomiuri hōchi*, January 24).

January 25 (Tuesday)

In the morning I worked in the fields, and in afternoon I wrote an editorial for
Tōkei concerning a talk of the Education Minister entitled "An Indictment of
Japanese Behavior in Southeast Asia."

January 26 (Wednesday)

I consulted with Kobayashi and Mitsui concerning the business of the Japanese Foreign Relations Society. Kobayashi said he would be happy to help.
We also decided to seek supporters.

I attended the Twenty-six Society. Of late, in every newspaper they have established a censor, and it is said that every day they bring out the guidelines and compare them with the article. It is said that outside Tōkyō the thought police use the censorship law as a pretext, and there is wider repression.

In the Diet there was a question stating that the English primer is still too British. Education Minister Okabe, an advocate of Imperial-Wayism, was terribly embarrassed and instantly responded that it would be changed at once.

In America there are publications concerning Japanese-American relations and returnees to Japan bring these back. When Konoe told Prince Takamatsu about them, the prince said he wished to read them, and Konoe had them translated by Ushiba. However, the typist was a spy, and when knowledge of this was revealed, he was taken for investigation by the military police. When he was asked where these books went, he said they were presented to Prince Takamatsu and Konoe. I understand that one also went to Baba Tsunego. This was something presented by Konoe. I understand that when these facts became known, he barely escaped prosecution.

Hanzawa Tamaki has retired into privacy because he made unfortunate slips of the tongue in public. No matter who it is, he will not meet with them. It is said that he was pressured into cutting his ties with the Gaikō Jihō and the Foreign Relations Research Center. It was said that when a plan had been proposed to have Komuro Makoto serve as chief editor of *Jihō*, the reaction was, "Wouldn't this plan be the same thing as having Hanzawa serve?" Yes, that is exactly the case. According to the account of the chief of the Kempeitai, I understand that a great deal of money is being printed. It is probably a problem of the interpretation of "great."

I understand with regard to newspaper mergers that Lt. General Atomiya said, "The merger of the *Ōsaka Asahi* and the *Mainichi* is probably just a question of time." This is a story of Kobayashi Ichizō.

January 27 (Thursday)

It is said that on the 25th Argentina broke off diplomatic relations with Japan and Germany. The newspapers argued that it was due to the "pressure of America." This is an example of thinking of a nation's action as coming only from pressures in the background.

January 28 (Friday)

On the 27th the government of Liberia announced its declaration of war on Germany and Japan.

In the afternoon there was a meeting of the English-language *Oriental Economist*. It was decided that hereafter there will be a meeting every month.

Aoki Tokuzō invited the former *Hōchi* editors to the Kinsui restaurant. Only Kuratsuji and Kawaguchi did not come. I have reasons to be grateful to *Hōchi* and Noma. It was at that time I developed my basic skills.

I heard a talk at the Economic Club on Germany by a navy commander named Fushishita Tetsuo. He said, "The internal conditions in Germany are certainly reassuring. However, the consequences that will emerge from the conduct of the war are not clear." He also said these results will be decided on the basis of the total volume of production. Of course, he did not say what these results will be, but he is pessimistic. Germany's labor force is thirty million, of which eight million are foreigners.

January 29 (Saturday)

Despite the fact that the Hess incident has been publicly announced in the English Parliament, in Japan it is "top secret." According to the account of Ambassador Matsuda Michikazu, this is like saying "Recognize the English Empire."

In the evening I was invited to a sukiyaki dinner given by Miyake Seiki. When I went to Suzuki Bunshirō's office there was a certain Tomoatsu, a "China Rōnin," who was formerly a reporter for *Asahi*. He said the Chinese do not refer to the "Imperial Army" and attach the insect radical to the "Imperial" character. This means that when the locust army comes not a single thing remains. Also, in the Nanking area the children engage in mock sword play, and if one asks the meaning of this they reply, "We are strengthening ourselves to drive off the Japanese devils."

If one relies upon Miyake's view, the one who will probably be the savior is Lt. General Ishihara Kanji. Ishihara stresses the restoration of the Diet, free speech, multiple small political parties, and other things.

From Premier Tōjō we have not heard even once ideas concerning postwar arrangements and a new order. If one relies upon his speeches in the Diet, he thinks this would be the same as a thief sharing part of his loot (*Nihon sangyō keizai*, January 29).

Previously, we heard bizarre interpretations of individualism and liberalism from Army Minister Terauchi. Now, again, there are such definitions. One can see how far removed this is from real knowledge.

It seems that the work in the *Tōkyō Record* of the special correspondent of the *New York Times*, Tolischus, is of interest. He was disappointed at seeing the small-sized houses in Japan, the boredom of a geisha party, and, after that, the contents of Foreign Minister Kataoka's European War Mediation plan, etc.

Suzuki Bunshirō said they did not have enough rice at home, and because of this they ate out now and then.

January 30 (Sunday)

In the *Mainichi* there was an editorial entitled "We Must Carry on Resolutely!" Because the American Army attacked a hospital ship, there must be
revenge for this. They are saying that prisoners of war must be killed.

It is said that in Tolischus's *Tōkyō Record* he calls the *Mainichi* jingoistic.

January 31 (Monday)

I attended the directors meeting of *Tōkei*. It was a conference on the publication of the *Chronology*. Ishibashi, who is suffering from arthritis, went to
Ōsaka and did not attend.

February 1 (Tuesday)

I moved my books for the evacuation of the Tōkyō Building. The work on the
Tōdenshi is finished. From today onward I am no longer a salaried man. The
price of things knows no limit. It is said that black-market sugar is now one
hundred yen per kamme. Everywhere there is a shortage of rice.

Enemy planes have attacked the Marshall Islands. It is said that there is a
fierce battle now in progress. Isn't this battle part of the larger invasion plan?
It should be a source of anxiety.

The Soviet Union has announced it is giving foreign affairs rights and defense rights to its various republics (a constitutional reform in the fourteenth
meeting of the Soviet Presidium.) This suggests there are serious problems.
Just as in the Greater East Asia community, the nationalities request respect
for independence in the Soviet Union. By accepting these requests, the Soviet
Union is attempting to unify and merge such areas as the Baltic states and
Poland.

February 3 (Thursday)

Morning, I went to Hakone. It was snowing. It was cold at the Fujiya Hotel.
Takayanagi, Obata, and I, along with Nara, discussed the matter of overseas
propaganda.

Food was good, but the quantity was small.

February 4 (Friday)

Rain is falling. We stayed in the hotel and continued our conference. This
went on until eleven-thirty in the morning. Because this hotel is one of the
best in Japan, the meals are excellent but the quantities small. There is no

other hotel that serves such splendid things. However, even with our modest appetites we were not satisfied.

The steam heat was not on. It is unimaginable why they do not use the hot springs for heating. Is this a matter of the anti-scientific character of the Japanese people? There are many Germans in the hotel.

I went to a grocery store. Dried persimmons are forty sen a piece. In ordinary times they are five or six sen. In the tangerine-producing areas there is not a single tangerine. Dried persimmons come from Fukushima Prefecture, and they are sent to other places. Distribution, unification, and planning are the root of the problem.

February 5 (Saturday)

During the morning we completed our draft. It was based upon an original draft of mine. If this plan is carried out, I will have a considerable role in concluding the war.

The information has been announced that the enemy has invaded the Marshall Islands. This I had already heard on the third from a man named Hata at the Foreign Ministry. Ishibashi Kazuhiko is supposed to be on Kwajelain, and we don't know if he is all right or not. I share the same feeling of anxiety that Ishibashi does.

February 6 (Sunday)

Every newspaper has filled its front pages with calls for unified preparation for the greatest problem since the Mongol Invasion. The *Asahi* has Tōyama Mitsuro as its spokesman, and the *Mainichi* has Tokutomi as its spokesman (*Asahi*, February 6).

Each prefecture has organized large groups of food supply units. I hear that there is military training being given in elementary schools—evidence of the militarization of the country (*Mainichi*, February 6).

I wrote a critique of an American White Paper in the *Oriental Economist*.

February 7 (Monday)

I attended a directors' meeting of *Tōkei*. I wrote for *Chūbū Nihon*. I was extremely busy at this kind of writing, and I could not write anything really structured.

In all this morning's newspapers there were articles aimed at raising hatred toward the enemy directed against England and America. These are probably things written by the Military Section and the Information Board. Those in the *Asahi* were especially strong. They said that in America they are shouting, "Kill the Japanese!" The problem is whether using such ideas of vengeance and seeking sympathy in the world will serve to heighten dedication to the war (*Asahi*, front page insertion, February 7).

February 8 (Tuesday)

Throughout the day I wrote a draft on the "American White Paper," which I must lecture on at the Scholarly Arts Society.

Hired-hand farmers come at 9:30 in the morning and stop work at 11:30; in the afternoon they come at 1:30 and stop at 4:30. During this time they spend about an hour drinking tea. For this they charge seven or eight yen.

February 9 (Wednesday)

Since I had some spare time I spent a surprising amount of time on a single manuscript. This evening's lecture was one example. It was a lecture read aloud. It took about two hours.

I lectured on why America must shoulder the political responsibility for the war.

There was a meeting of military men in an adjacent room. This I learned when the audience dispersed after the meeting.

February 10 (Thursday)

I went to the Foreign Ministry. When I asked Secretary Kase about the plan we had constructed, he said it was no good and, moreover, there was a difference of view from section heads Ōta and Matsudaira. Even if we make up proposals such as these, they are crushed in somebody or other's hands and come to nothing.

Section Head Matsudaira stated that (1) he had meticulously read the American White Paper proposals at the request of Kurusu, but there was nothing to point out. That is to say, what was noted by the White Paper was fact. He said, "It was just like that." (2) Because military action had already occurred during the negotiations, justification of the attack on Hawaii was useless, even though this point was communicated to America. (3) He said that regarding the mid-April proposals of the White Paper, both the Japanese proposals and the American proposals were ambiguous.

The honesty of the officials of the Foreign Ministry ought to be highly valued. Being informed and knowing the other side's position, they are fair in their recognition of actual facts.

However, they do not have the positive spirit to attack the enemy. Regarding this I said, "Theoretically I understand the problems of Japan's position and I am in accord on this point. However, it would be fine if even 20 percent or 30 percent of the Americans thought that Japan also had its reasons, and I made this effort toward that end." It is almost impossible to build a so-called new world order.

This is completely bad!

It looks as if Japanese education has made breadth of perspective impossible.

Evening, I went to a gathering at the Japan-Thai Cultural Center. The topic everywhere is food. Everyone is hungry.

At the Tokiwa restaurant yesterday evening they were out of supplies and no cooked rice was served.

Professor Kuwaki said that today there was not a grain of rice at his home.

As the daughter of Yanagizawa Ken goes to school, she has to bring her lunch, but the maid steals and eats it. He told me that if he complains about this she will leave and nothing is done about it.

At Eiko's Aoyama Jōgakuin (Girls' High School), the students have stopped warming their lunches on the stove. This is because they were immediately stolen.

Because everyone is talking about the pressure of the food shortage, pessimistic statements are being expressed.

In Tōkyō I heard that June 28 is the date on which a prophecy predicts that the war will end in victory for Japan. It is said that until today the fortune-teller has been right. Now, fortune-tellers are the great fashion, and all hopes are hung on them.

Kitada said that a man named "Yoshida," or some such, of the Imperial Rule Assistance Society stated that the situation will reach its peak in about six months from now. He is a young man who lives next door. During that time more airplanes will be built and the enemy will be driven off.

February 11 (Friday)

The English and Americans have announced, at the same time, Japanese mistreatment of prisoners. Regarding this, on the Japanese side it is being announced that the English and Americans are doing the same thing.

The registration of the Japanese people is widening to include the ages twelve to sixty. The danger that even I will be recruited is increasing.

Yamamoto Kiyoshi came to Tōkyō and we went to the Kabuki together. The performance of Onoe Kikugorō was splendid. His lion dance was superb, and also in the role of Gotobei in "Yoshitsune" he was marvelous. Uzaemon[42] also appeared, and it has been a long time since we have had such fine plays.

February 12 (Saturday)

There is an escalation of mutual attacks (12th *Yomiuri*) (*Yomiuri hōchi*, "Record of Worldly Affairs," February 12).

Of late, the *Mainichi* declares that in response to the attacks on our hospital ships we should resort to drastic measures! This means that we should dispose

registration and maintenance. For example, at present, the applicant need only submit one specimen showing how a mark is used rather than three, as was previously required. Additionally, a trademark applicant need no longer state the manner in which the mark is used. Finally, TLTIA established a six-month grace period for filing a renewal for a trademark registration.

- **Madrid Protocol.** The Madrid Protocol became effective in November 2003 and allows trademark applicants or registrants to file a single international trademark application and obtain protection in any of the more than 60 countries that are party to the Protocol. The Protocol thus facilitates efficient and cost-effective protection for marks on an international basis.

- **Federal Trademark Dilution Act.** The **Federal Trademark Dilution Act** protects against dilution of famous marks by preventing use of a confusingly similar mark even on unrelated goods. Thus, the owner of NIKE could prevent another individual entity from using the NIKE mark in connection with doughnuts.

- **Anticybersquatting Consumer Protection Act.** The **Anticybersquatting Consumer Protection Act** was signed into law in late 1999 and is intended to protect the public from acts of Internet *cybersquatting*, a term used to describe the bad faith, abusive registration of Internet domain names, such as the registration of www.juliaroberts.com by one with no affiliation with Julia Roberts.

State Registration

It is possible that a mark may not qualify for federal registration, generally because it is not used in interstate commerce but is used only within the confines of one state, namely, in **intrastate commerce.** Thus, the owner of the CAKERY CRAVINGS mark used solely in Portland might seek to register the mark in Oregon. Each one of the fifty states has its own trademark act. Generally, obtaining a state registration is a fairly expeditious and inexpensive process. Forms are available from each state's secretary of state, located in the state capital, and are often available for downloading on the web site of the secretary of state. The state registration confers benefits only within the boundaries of the state. Thus, the owner of CAKERY CRAVINGS could not preclude another from using the same or a similar mark in Seattle, Washington. Armed with a *federal* registration, however, the owner could preclude the later Seattle user. There is no procedural or substantive advantage of securing state registrations in addition to a federal registration. The federal registration is nationwide in scope and should be sought whenever a mark qualifies for federal registration. (See Appendix B for a summary of state trademark registration provisions.)

CATEGORIES OF MARKS

Although marks can consist of words, symbols, designs, slogans, or a combination thereof, not every term is protectable. Even among marks that are protectable, some marks are stronger than others. In determining strength of marks, courts recognize several categories of marks. In ascending order of strength and protectability, the five categories are generic, descriptive, suggestive, arbitrary, and fanciful or coined marks.

- A **generic mark** is not truly a mark at all but is merely a common name of a product, such as *car*, *soap*, or *beverage*. Such generic terms are not protectable

of prisoners of war (what is becoming of our countrymen in America?) (*Mainichi*, editorial, February 12).

Under the auspices of the English-language *Tōyō keizai*, we were invited to a Chinese dinner. I was impressed with how the restaurants manage to collect the ingredients.

February 13 (Sunday)

I finished reading Walter Lippman's *History of American Foreign Relations*, which I began yesterday. (1) He takes as a premise that Japan and Germany will be eliminated from among the strong countries. America, England, Soviet Russia, and China must become the responsible parties of the postwar world order. (2) As a result, there will be regionalism. (3) America will conclude alliances with the three aforementioned countries.

There have been explanations of regionalism, but there has not been any essay that has formulated opinions so clearly. However, it is clear that it will be necessary not to force America back into her past position of isolationism. Among his opinions, an outstanding one is to state the fact that American policy in the Far East has been consistent because of the security of the Atlantic.

In the evening Tsuchida Seiichi came to call. He is a graduate of Chūō University and is a naval officer candidate. I hear that in two or three days he will become a lieutenant paymaster.

1. Education is defunct, and in half a year students learn nothing at all.
2. It is a fact that there is not the slightest discussion of the state of the war.

Hereafter he will go to the front line as a naval officer. In the light of present circumstances, what indeed will be his expectations of returning alive? How can I not but be moved by this pathetic state of affairs? He is a passionate Christian.

Ishibashi told me that enemy battleships are being brought into the Marshall Islands.

There would be no question of our complete defeat. Ishibashi said rather calmly, "The problem is, how do I keep my wife from going mad?" I was surprised at the attitude of Ishibashi, who spoke dispassionately of the prospect of bad news concerning his son.

In a report in the *Mainichi*, in an investigation of Ōsaka public school students, those who did not bring their lunches were 0 percent. It is said that the Ōsaka Hygiene Inspection Office is in the midst of a study on increasing calories.

Of late, even the "Silver Star" is supposed to provide gruel to its customers. It costs thirty sen a serving, but when customers complain that it does not fill the stomach, I hear that the police station replies, "Nobody has a full stomach; isn't it better than not being able to eat at all?" A story at a meeting yesterday evening. There was a man who said that he goes to three restaurants for lunch. In the present situation, nobody has a full stomach.

February 14 (Monday)

The enemy's propaganda on the abuse of prisoners of war is probably due to the differences in customs. There is nothing like the thrashing and kicking of criminals found in Japan. But when one goes to America and England, human rights are a major issue. At the time of the Russo-Japanese War, "International Law" was a rigorous guide. And if one takes this as a guide, the result will be the humane treatment of prisoners. This was true also at the time of the First World War. Now there is a Japanese reactionary mentality, and because humane treatment of English-American prisoners is termed "Anglo-American style," naturally abuses will probably run to extremes. Colonel Odajima, the Prisoners of War official, formerly stated, "About the time of the Russo-Japanese War there was adoration of the West, but at present it is all 'Japanism.'"

Even in such small matters—the influence is never small—one may see the reactionary character of the present war.

This morning there was a radio speech by Professor Akiyama Kenzō of Kokugakuin University. He lectured bombastically on the kamikaze and the Mongol Invasion.

From morning to night there is propaganda about increasing airplane production. Finally some people are denying the propaganda that states, "The front line is laboring mightily, but there are not enough airplanes. This is the responsibility of the home front."

February 15 (Tuesday)

I went to the Foreign Ministry. The plan that I had previously constructed was not acceptable to Secretary Kase, and it was decided to reformulate it. I spent the whole day there. To the nucleus of the group we added Professor Ueda Tatsunosuke of Shōdai (Commercial College). We had all sorts of discussions but could not work out a plan.

When Professor Ueda listened to the proposals, he immediately said, "This is full of difficulties." He said if Japan did not admit the wrongs of its past failures, the foreigners would not believe it. This is probably the attitude of an intellectual. However, the difficult matter is that Japan would definitely not acknowledge its past failures.

February 16 (Wednesday)

At home all day and I wrote for *Tōkei*, "The Enemy's Propaganda about Japanese Cruelty," and, similarly, for the *Chūbū Nihon* I wrote on the propaganda aimed at foreign countries.

February 17 (Thursday)

I went to the Foreign Ministry. There was discussion of the blueprint of my proposals, and as a result it was settled.

There was a telephone call from the Transportation Ministry. I was told that because the Seikan ferry would be stopped from the 19th for four or five days, I should leave on the 18th. Afterward, Higashikawa came to call. He said that it was possible it would be difficult to purchase tickets. When I asked about it, he said that he was working at the Transportation Ministry and he would rely upon his friends at the Army Ministry. Wasn't I going to lecture to train people for the Postal Service? It is a fact that railway tickets for official business were not to be had from the same ministry but were bought through the army. One should reflect upon the whole matter.

Won't the forcible joining together of the Railway Ministry and the Communications Ministry produce all sorts of bad results? This is one consequence of formalism.

February 18 (Friday)

A newspaper article by Tokutomi Sohō, the person responsible for the Greater East Asian War (*Yomiuri hōchi*, "Book Review," February 18).

Of late the newspapers and radio are becoming more and more spiritual. The crowd that makes completely wrong predictions triumphantly has everything its own way. This is true of such people as Tokutomi and Saitō.

March 6 (Monday) (at Hakodate)

On the 19th I left Tōkyō. It was for the purpose of conducting a lecture tour in Karafuto and Hokkaidō at the request of the Ministry of Communications—the new Ministry of Transportation and Communication. All parties concerned agree that the combined Ministry of Communication and Railways will not operate at all well.

I left Ueno on the morning of the 19th. The train was three hours late. The fact that an express train was late is the usual state of affairs.

The main arteries are single-track. The pros and cons of a national railway system are revealed here. Before the war Japan ought to have completed its transportation facilities. My train was late, and because of this I did not meet the first trip of the scheduled Seikan ferry boat. Just at this time because of the transportation restrictions there was transport for general passengers only once a day. I had to wait in Aomori Station from 2:30 in the morning to 1:00 in the afternoon.

Even in Aomori there were no apples and it was like a dead city. I arrived in Hakodate at close to 6:00 P.M. and immediately went to the lecture hall. I was welcomed by Hakodate Communications Section Head Shimura. He accompanied me as far as Sapporo.

In both Aomori and Hakodate the station employees are coarse and quarrelsome with the passengers. From that point onward, the problem later was the typical rudeness in the train stations. With the sight of snow everywhere filling my eyes, the scenery of Hokkaidō emerged. In the evening I dined together with the regional office head and others. Evening of the 20th.

Morning of the 21st, very few people boarded the train. About two-thirds were left at the station. With a second-class ticket, I took my place in the third class. I lectured at the Otaru Economic Club. Otaru was full of soldiers. I went to Sapporo and stayed over at the Yamagata Hotel.

22nd, I returned to Otaru and gave a lecture at the post office. I stopped off at the Hokkai Hotel. The service was absolutely beyond belief. The women of Hokkaido do not understand etiquette and are unrefined. In the evening I dined with the post office officials.

On the 23rd I lectured at the Sapporo Communications Office. I met with the office chief and others and then arrived at the Jozankei Hotel. It was about ten degrees colder than Sapporo. There were stoves everywhere. It was more comfortable here.

On the 24th I went to Asahigawa and lectured. Afterward, in the evening, I boarded a sleeping car and arrived at Wakkanai at six in the morning. In the most northern part of Hokkaidō the cold is excessive. However, even here, there are stoves and it is easier to survive than in Tōkyō. In the evening a speech. The office members came to see me off and I boarded the boat. There was a wind blowing. It is said that the boat that we were sailing in takes thirty hours from Odomari. On this day it did not depart at once, but we were blessed by the weather and departed in the early morning.

This evening I listened to the radio account of the sacrificial deaths of the courageous soldiers on Kwajelain. It is to be expected that Ishibashi Kazuhiko is among them. I could not control my emotions. While I listened to the snowstorm outside the ship, I mourned the last days of this bright young man.

The 25th I arrived at Odomari. We were welcomed by the members of the Toyohara Communications Office. Here there also were soldiers, and because it was a boat stop it was full of passengers and I stopped over at a place resembling a cheap lodging house. I noticed everywhere the *yukata*[43] were dirty.

Changing my schedule I set off for Shikka. It was close to the border of Karafuto. On the train there were stoves. They were of the old style. There was an abundance of everything compared with Tōkyō. I was able to buy lunch on the train.

I arrived at Shikka at six in the evening. I lodged at the Yamagata Inn. There was a reason why the service of the maids here was better than at any inn I had lodged in. The owner was a woman of education and is sending her son and daughter to Jiyū Gakuen.

27th, I gave a lecture at the Shikka Post Office. The office head had gone to great trouble to buy me a smoked salmon-trout and sent it off to Tōkyō.

At four in the afternoon I was aboard the train and stopped over at a place called [character of placename missing]. I departed the following morning at six and arrived at Toyohara at three in the afternoon. I lectured from five in the afternoon. In the evening, at the invitation of the office head I attended the Ōji Paper Company Club. It was a wonderful banquet. I was surprised at the abundance of electric power. I stayed over there.

The following day I lectured at Odomari.

On the evening of March 1 I boarded a ship and arrived at Wakkanai on the 2nd at three in the afternoon. Everything went smoothly. I rested at the office. We stuffed ourselves with king crabs. It was one of the most delicious dinners I have ever had.

On March 3 in the morning I arrived at Sapporo. We went to the Grand Hotel. Speech in the evening.

On the morning of March 4 I left Sapporo. Until now I had been traveling with assistance. From today onward I would know the weight of my own baggage. As I neared Hakodate (the southern area) peoples' behavior became cruder. At Tomakomai Station I was aware of this. I changed trains and rode in an overcrowded third-class coach to Hitaka Uraga. Okuda Saneharu and Kasahara Yoshikazu came to welcome me. At Okuda's house I had a bath and we had an extraordinary meal. We filled ourselves with fresh fish for the first time in a long while.

Evening, the people of the neighborhood assembled and there was a discussion meeting. The recent tendency is that one cannot speak frankly in all places.

I changed my plans to reach Noboribetsu in the morning and departed instead at four o'clock. On the train a soldier from second class who was returning home sat next to me. I understood that he was going to be a wireless telegrapher in someplace called Erimo. He said they were rebuilding stations repeatedly toppled by the wind.

On the 6th I arrived at Hakodate in the early morning. I went to the Fukuikan on the Yunokawa. I learned later there was space available at Hakodate, so I moved back to Hakodate.

Evening, lecture. I did get a sleeping car ticket and changed my plans to an earlier schedule, boarding a ship in the evening. March 7, I was in an express train for a whole day. Eiko and the maid were waiting for me at Ueno Station. I was back home by 10:30 in the evening.

March 8 (Wednesday)

This diary, which had been sent in care of the head of the Asahikawa Post Office, did not arrive. I received it for the first time in Hakodate, and while I was waiting for it I only noted essentials.

Upon returning I noticed that during a period of about twenty days conditions had dramatically altered. The marriage ceremony of the second daughter of Matsuo was suspended because the Western-style dining room of the Imperial Hotel has been closed. Also the meeting for the 9th of the People's Scholarly Arts Society, which should have been held at the Gakushi Kaikan (University Club), was suspended. Even the Economic Club has cut off meals to nonmembers.

Only Karafuto still has a little dried fish, but even this will probably not last much longer.

We are told that rice is guaranteed for only ten months; however, this will probably raise problems later on. It is said that Hokkaidō is going to produce something like 400,000 koku for Karafuto.

When the boat arrived at the dock in Aomori I was relieved. I believed everything was all right, but there was no evidence that a submarine would not appear. As I came closer to Sendai the snow was disappearing.

> An evening of blowing snow and violent wind,
> in Hokkaidō I listen to accounts,
> of the deaths of our sacrificial heroes
> on Kwajelain.

> Even now I cannot forget his appearance
> in becoming military uniform,
> the long sword of a naval sublieutenant.

> The sages of old were Gods,
> who performed miracles.
> Oh Gods, if you are there,
> appear to the world.

> I would like to mow down
> the thick weeds of silly ideas and politics
> which thickly surround us.

Kazuhiko was indeed a splendid youth.

The confusion on the trains is indescribable. The railway employees understand the term "wartime conditions" as synonymous with unfriendliness. Everywhere there is bickering. Even the sloppiness of the inns is beyond description. In the decades to come, this unkindliness will become the common path of Japan.

March 9 (Thursday)

I visited Shimanaka and he said that he has truly been in agony because he has had continuous business problems since last year. He is thinking of evacuating to Karuizawa. I hear that it is because Fujita, Hatanaka, Sawa, and many other people who have left-wing connections are being arrested.

I am told that there are Japanese prisoners on the island of Kwajelain. However, I hear they are completely passive and silent. The American side is broadcasting these facts. Is Kazuhiko among them or not?

It is probably natural to expect that martial law will come before long.

March 10 (Friday)

Today is a military holiday, and both newspapers and radio are offering prayers for the military. This morning there was a radio speech by General Inoue Ikutarō. In the speeches of late, Hōjō Tokimuni[44] is invariably brought up. He stated that enemy's power cannot merely be talked about in terms of sheer numbers.

In the prewar period Japanese argued that Americans did not become sailors. They ran away. Moreover, they said submarines were uncomfortable and they refused to ride in them. We laughed at the fact that the plans of America were all inflated figures and unrealized.

Now, we must acknowledge their "reality."

The *Mainichi shinbun*, which is one of the jingoistic newspapers responsible for the war, printed a talk by Honda Kumatarō. In it he stated that he was completely of the same opinions as Sohō (*Mainichi shinbun*, March 9).

At the time of the Japanese–American negotiations, Honda came to Tōkyō from Nanking and opposed the settlement of these negotiations. That is to say, he strongly opposed the nonrecognition of the Chiang Kai-shek government. Honda is a man of sharp views. However, he has a single position and explains everything from this angle.

The fact that those who were responsible for the Greater East Asian War boast about their "foresight" and "destiny" without the slightest feeling of responsibility can probably be understood from this speech.

In the future I have the responsibility of identifying such irresponsible theorists.

At the times that are critical for nations, are there not, throughout the world, childish, stupid leaders such as these who lead these nations? Every day I constantly lament this.

A certain professor of the Imperial University (Tatsuno Yutaka) said, "Premier Tōjō has the mind of about a middle-school student, hasn't he?" There are many middle-school students with his intellectual ability.

Current propaganda:

1. Wooden airplanes are being enthusiastically propagandized. Yet I hear that not a single one has been produced. They say that these plans have been completed rather recently. Ōji Paper Manufacturing Company is building a factory in Hokkaidō.

2. There is nothing but propaganda regarding the increased production of vegetables, and with respect to seed there is not even a specific plan. I wish to plant scallions at our place, but they are unavailable.

In Niigata I hear that great numbers of enemy prisoners are dying because of the cold and the food, and that they are being buried.

During my trip to Karafuto and Hokkaidō the most important news was that of the sacrificial deaths of the heroes on Kwajalein and Premier Tōjō's simultaneous assumption of the position as chief of military staff (army chief of staff, General Shimada).

(In the issue of the 2nd in *Dōmei jiji nippō*, there appeared a résumé entitled, "The Tightening of the Supreme Command in National Government.")

From the 5th of March, Sundays will be abolished completely. There will be a revision of the law to enable even students to continue their education on Sundays. To think that increased work time will increase efficiency reveals the mentality of the time.

On a train from Uragawa to Tomakomai, drafted workers came aboard. Their leader made a speech saying, "This thing called the Atlantic Charter was made by Churchill and Roosevelt, and they decided to kill all Japanese. They have clearly stated they will kill both men and women. Are we something to be killed by these beasts?"

The average Japanese believes that Americans will remove their testicles to prevent the birth of children, or else they will be driven off to solitary islands.

As regards total political policy, it is being said that this year will be filled with decisive battles and victory or defeat will be decided (*Chūbu Nihon*, "Editorial," February 27).

(Because the neighborhood council came to take the palm-hemp from our house, we handed it over.)

Throughout the present year, not only is the government marking off the decisive year of the war with legal reform as its objective, but the people are also thinking along the same lines. It is an example of seeing only what is before one's eyes.

I am reading Spykeman's *American Strategy in World Politics*.[45] His geopolitical viewpoint is interesting.

1. Japan must exploit the internal upheaval in China or she must exploit the collision of power politics that revolve around China.

2. The conclusion of the book argues that the consequences must be such that America will assist Japan and England.

3. Japan's strategies were completed before the Greater East Asian War. The Mandated Territories threatened America and the Chinese blockade

kept the South Pacific free. Moreover, Thailand and Indochina came under the power of Japan. Yet there was a deficiency of essential material power internally. However, those unable to see this led Japan.

March 11 (Saturday)

Honda Kumatarō is openly announcing that America is saying it will kill all Japanese (*Mainichi*, March 1).

In the afternoon I worked in the vegetable garden. Amemiya Yōzō brought an honorarium for my recent lectures. Previously this sort of income was not unusual, but I didn't pay much attention to it then. Of late, fifty yen is welcomed. The decisive battle period of my livelihood confronts me.

March 12 (Sunday)

From morning I supervised everyone planting potatoes.

America's theme of "Destroy Japan!" has been made public in the newspapers. That is to say, it has been reported by Iguchi, the head of the Third Section of the Information Board (*Mainichi shinbun*, March 11).

In October of last year, when I made my lecture tour through the Sanin area at the request of the Communications Ministry, I made a speech stating, "I would never say that Japan would be defeated even by chance, but, if by chance there were the fact of defeat. . . ." At that time my assigned companion, Yoshikawa, advised, "I wonder how outsiders will misunderstand it when they hear you say such things as when if by chance Japan is defeated." When I think about this, I have the feeling of being in another world.

People in general take "destruction of the Japanese Empire" for the same thing as "destruction of the Japanese people."

Outstanding youths are competing to enlist in the navy. These outstanding youths are all but on the brink of the evil fate of complete destruction. Japan was expecting great future contributions from these young people. These youths will be destroyed. This will bring unimagined injury to the nation. Ah! In the present war this is of the gravest concern.

The Greater East Asian War is killing humanistic studies. All research into the problem of the structure of the world is threatened as dangerous, radical, and defeatist. Ayusawa is one example of this pressure. We also do not publicly express such things at all.

March 13 (Monday)

It goes without saying that the intellectual background of the Pacific War is based on extreme feudal ideas. The celebrity of "Saigō Takamori," "Miyamoto Musashi," and the "Forty-seven Rōnin" has never been as intense as it is at present. At the same time the attitude toward war is still more reactionary than it was in the Sino-Japanese War and the Russo-Japanese War. At the time Itō, Yamagata, and Katsura all understood the currents of international circumstances, and their keynote was being civilized.

Therefore, as regards the treatment of prisoners in the Greater East Asian War, there are reasons why there is no use of the example of the Russo-Japanese War. In a lecture meeting of the Japan Club, Superintendent of Prisoners Odashima clearly explained what they were.

1. The basic idea of the Greater East Asian War is the "revenge" idea. "Savings for Revenge" circulates everywhere in neighborhood associations.

2. Such newspapers as *Mainichi* write in capital letters in their social column, "Kill the American Devils!" (It is propagandized in our country that they are publicly saying in America, "Kill Japs!")

"Control hoarding!" "Prohibit the black market!" "Obliterate the black market!" Controls in all areas are being strengthened by officials who have nothing else to do but this. However, in the area of production they pay no attention to ideas at all. Most recently they have merely come to talk about cultivating empty land. They think that things will be produced spontaneously.

Sundays have been abolished since March 5. The reason was to have continuous operation of machinery for 24 hours a day and make possible human labor for 365 days a year. Depending upon the nature of the work, this is fine. Our circle never had Sundays free anyway. However, the problem is whether or not this will raise efficiency.

The chief of the Army Air Force Headquarters, General Terada Seiichi, returned from the recent Burma battlefront and reported that there were twenty enemy planes downed to none of ours on January 20, and fifteen enemy planes downed to none of ours on February 5. He spoke of the planes being manufactured of wood (*Yomiuri*, 13th).

In reality, even the machines for the manufacture of wooden planes have not been installed. Those in charge say, "Because orders are handed down from above, one spends two or three hours waiting to see the office head, and on top of that one is treated like a criminal."

I attended a directors' meeting at *Tōyō keizai*. After a long absence, Rōyama Masamichi was in attendance. This group is just about the only place where we can speak relatively freely. Elsewhere, even in gatherings of two or three people, one cannot speak frankly. This is because in these groups there are always spies, and yet our talks always discuss national welfare and the solution of problems related to it.

March 14 (Tuesday)

An editorial in *Tōyō keizai* (written by Ishibashi), stated, in effect, "The essential focus of strong government is that the Premier must seek outspoken ministers."

and cannot be exclusively appropriated by one party inasmuch as they are needed by competitors to describe their goods. Thus, TOP RAMEN® serves as a trademark but "noodles" does not because it is a generic name. In some cases, marks that were once valid have become generic through misuse. Examples of words that were once trademarks but are now generic terms are *aspirin, cellophane, escalator,* and *thermos.* Thus, owners of many well-known marks take great pains to ensure their marks do not become generic. The familiar refrains "SCOTCH® brand adhesive tape" and "Q-TIP® brand cotton swabs" encountered in advertising are meant to protect marks and to ensure that consumers do not use the term *Scotch tape* to describe all adhesive tape or the term *Q-tip* to refer to any cotton swab, thereby "genericizing" a once-valued trademark. Xerox's ad campaign "when you use 'Xerox' the way you use 'aspirin,' we get a headache" is similarly aimed to preserve the distinctiveness of the XEROX® mark. Generally, marks should be used as adjectives, as in "I need a KLEENEX tissue." Use of a trademark as a noun, as in "I need a Kleenex," will eventually lead to genericide of the mark and a loss of trademark rights.

- A **descriptive mark** tells something about the product or service offered under a mark by describing some characteristic, quality, ingredient, function, feature, purpose, or use of the product or service. For example, in *In re Bed & Breakfast Registry,* 791 F.2d 157 (Fed. Cir. 1986), BED & BREAKFAST REGISTRY was held merely descriptive of lodging registration services, and in *Hunter Publishing Co. v. Caulfield Publishing Ltd.,* 1 U.S.P.Q.2d 1996

(T.T.A.B. 1986), SYSTEMS USER was held merely descriptive of a trade journal directed at users of data processing systems. Because descriptive terms merely describe the goods or services, rather than identify the source of a product, they are not registrable with the PTO until the consumer links the mark with a single source. That learned association is called **secondary meaning** or *acquired distinctiveness.* Descriptive marks cannot be registered until secondary meaning is shown. The PTO assumes that secondary meaning has been acquired after five years of consecutive and exclusive use of a mark. Alternatively, secondary meaning can be shown by demonstrating a significant level of advertising, sales, and consumer survey evidence, to prove that when consumers encounter a mark such as SYSTEMS USER, they immediately identify it with its offeror. Such evidence allows a trademark owner to establish secondary meaning without having to wait five years. Laudatory terms such as *best, extra,* and *super* are also considered merely descriptive and are not registrable without proof of secondary meaning.

- A **suggestive mark** suggests something about the goods or services offered under the mark but does not immediately describe them. A suggestive mark requires some imagination or thought to reach a conclusion about the goods or services offered under the mark. For example, ORANGE CRUSH® was held suggestive of an orange-flavored beverage, *see Orange Crush Co. v. California Crushed Fruit Co.,* 297 F. 892 (D.C. Cir. 1924), and GREYHOUND BUS® was held suggestive of transportation services. A suggestive mark is registrable without proof of secondary meaning or distinctiveness.

In it he wrote, "Then why is it that great numbers of talented, intelligent people have not taken up the responsibility as outspoken ministers?... In their innermost hearts, the authorities are not prepared to welcome direct statements, and those with blunt opinions even suffer unforeseen harm to themselves." I understand that the authorities did not encourage this editorial. The Information Board does just this sort of thing.

Ishibashi said, "I am a good example of this kind of thing."

The instances of the authorities' dislike of direct statements are extremely numerous. There is a story that a certain Diet member gave advice to Tōjō. At the discussion there were only the two of them, but upon returning home he was summoned by the military police and cruelly abused. At present this situation is clear from the newspapers and magazines, and, moreover, among the people who hold important posts in the government, is there even a single "outspoken minister"?

Rōyama said it is unfortunate to have been born in a country in this state. As intellectuals we truly cannot endure this sort of degrading atmosphere and interference.

It is said that Premier Tōjō has been appointed chief of the General Staff and is extremely careful in his statements.

When he is wearing his usual epaulets he is General Tōjō, chief of staff, and he is decidedly not the premier. I understand that recently when he went to the Ise Shrine it was in the capacity of chief of the General Staff, and on such occasions he is very clear about his role. We hear he is being attacked in some way by the right wing. Even if one is not right wing, one imagines this is a delicate point.

Everywhere one goes, the core of discussion is the inadequacy of food supplies. Shimura Tamaharu (chief field investigator of the Communications Ministry), who guided me around Hokkaidō, says he has seven children; but families like his eat nothing but gruel. Because of this he says they have lost two or three kamme in weight. I hear that Rōyama gives most of his food to his children, who are still growing, and he and his wife eat what remains. Everywhere there is only rice for two meals, and a third meal is unthinkable. Even in our house Akira says he wants more rice, but of late it is rationed. Ōkuma Makoto says that in his family, "The children are hungry, but they are already accustomed to it ... and we have only gruel." During my twenty-day absence, my family ate well. In the end, no one can survive on these rations. In the magazine *Kōjin konjin* (Ancient people and contemporaries), Ubukata Toshirō writes about this with relative courage.

According to Rōyama, the rice requisition quotas in Yamaguchi Prefecture are becoming more stringent, and there are people who say, "If it comes to this, please stop the war!"

According to a letter that came to Toyoshina in Shinshū, Kesayoshi mentioned that they had been instructed to hand over everything except the family food supplies allowed until April, and he observed, "It is just like the Meiji Restoration."

As regards vegetables, half a radish must last a family of four two days. Minister of Agriculture Uchiba went to the market and confessed, "How can it go on like this?"

Food supplies will hereafter be a problem for the large cities. The reason the government is encouraging evacuation is that if there are bombings, there is the danger of food riots.

The same magazine, *Kōjin konjin*, writes such gratifying little pieces. This is the most courageous thing that it has published. Because it writes about this sort of thing, there are unexpectedly many supporters for this small, four-page magazine.

A certain person came to our house and asked if I wouldn't buy a kamme of sugar for 100 yen. When I inquired into it, I heard that it was selling for 120 yen per kamme. Of course I refused, but this is everywhere the market price. The official fixed price is about 3 yen. It is forty times this price.

The price of one straw bagful of rice is roughly 200 yen, and now it is not uncommon for three bags to be 1,000 yen.

The problem of the Jews and Freemasons raises questions even at Urakawa in Hokkaidō. It is evidence that the propaganda is spreading everywhere. It sometimes appears in magazines and sometimes in lectures, and this shows that supporting funds are coming from somewhere.

March 15 (Wednesday)

Train regulations are in effect, and hereafter, for distances of more than one hundred kilometers, the police will issue appropriate documents. Sleeping and dining cars have been completely eliminated. These are harsh regulations.

From the account of Chief of the Railway Bureau Nagasaki, it is clear that in Germany also there are such regulations.

Of late even high-class restaurants have been closed, and this is probably in imitation of Germany. Of course, it is something compelled by necessity.

This is what I always have talked about, but I think one can probably grasp what sort of meaning the word "war" has for the general masses.

Now the problem is that we cannot go to Karuizawa. However, this problem is a matter of the pressure of circumstances and transcends individual inconvenience or convenience. When one considers the commentary of Bureau Chief Nagasaki, it is a matter of action without a specific plan regarding the problem of trains—lunches and other things. This "decisive action" without a complementary plan can also be seen in the present train regulations.

On the radio this morning, an army paymaster colonel gave a five-part lecture entitled, "While You Are Eating Breakfast." It was completely a threat to the people. And then he said something about "vomiting" and the "bathroom" while breakfasting. It was dictatorial in style and one instance of his complete ignorance of the psychological characteristics of the audience. An educated person hearing this cannot but help having a negative reaction and feeling hatred. He does not understand anything.

There were many who lauded war, speaking of it as the "mother of culture" and talking about a "hundred-year war." Now, where are they? But in the newspapers as usual the kamikaze crowd named Saitō Tadashi, Kanokogi, and Nomura Shigeomi are bustling about. The stupidity of the people is beyond our reach.

The students of Tōkyō University are now at work on drainage projects at Tarui in Shizuoka Prefecture. University students doing manual labor!

I hear that the "Japonicus" who appeared recently in the *Japan Times* was Takayanagi Kenzō. It has been decided that we three—including Professor Ueda Shinnosuke—will publish under the name of "Japonicus." The next turn to write is mine.

March 16 (Thursday)

It is said that the reasons for the closing of the high-class, restaurants is the violent opposition of the laborers and drafted workers and because the metropolitan police issued a statement that they cannot maintain peace if such places are not closed. This could be true. Kobayashi of the "Silver Star" related that at their lodgings the drafted workers complained, "Aren't the officials and military going to *machiai*[46] while we are working so hard?" At the same time in this atmosphere of workers' rage against high-class, bourgeois restaurants, a policeman at a neighborhood association meeting in the area of the Higashi-chōfu police station violently attacked "rich wives" and "property owners" and incited their servants. This is a particularly common trait of young, lower-class officials. The antagonistic, revolutionary passion between laborers and officials. The foundation is already here.

In addition to this, the problem is the increasingly inflexible enforcement of draft worker recruitment. There is no work and there are no tools. The result of this sort of reckless draft labor system is that the workers fold their arms and are idle. It is natural to have many complaints and discontents.

The most important reality that has been revealed in this war is the deficiency of Japanese education. It has an idealism and formalism that cannot be believed. In the fisheries of Karafuto and elsewhere, the government controls the herring and other fish, which are in abundance. Control itself is the object. Moreover, in any order issued there is rigid enforcement without flexibility.

Because Yamada, the managing director of *Tōyō keizai*, asked me, "I wonder why this is so?" when I answered, "It is because such people as Rōyama are teachers at the Imperial University and have only been taught law," Rōyama forcefully replied, "I absolutely do not shoulder responsibility. From beginning to end, I have opposed the omnipotence of the law. However, how they can reduce the particulars of the law is the problem of their lives." We may say that with a basic education for the purpose of passing civil service exams, they cannot study anything else but law. Accordingly, they become legal technicians. The law is their single standard and objective. When this becomes the atmosphere of officialdom, lower-class officials under them and regulated companies will naturally, unavoidably, become the same.

If one does not think about the production aspect, because there is the idea that products will naturally emerge and if there is no illicit flow through the black market it is to be expected there will be more than enough, there is no responsibility regarding this aspect. When strikes occur in Japan they will be immediately and completely crushed. This way of thinking is the first step in anticipation of revolutionary upheaval.

Three or four days ago I received a letter from Shirayanagi Shūkō. He said, if one abandons virtue, even if one is victorious in war there will be ruin for the nation's immortality. Therein he commits an error. In the first place, the result of war is the destruction of the virtuous heart. In the second place, who are those responsible for the war? Among these people, are not he himself and Tokutomi Sohō the most conspicuous? Is it not these people who rashly boast of Japanese history and the Japanese spirit and who do not calculate the strength of the enemy?

Yesterday Eiko and the maid went to the center of the city. They went to Fuji Ice to have lunch and stood in line, but while waiting they were cut off. When they went to the Matsuya Department Store the lunch line filled up three or four floors completely and they were unable to eat. Thereupon they went to Fujiya and at last had lunch. Even there the line was cut off while they waited. When they had lunch there was no rice, and they were served a few ersatz noodles covered with suspicious-looking seaweed, and this cost eighty sen. A man who was sitting in front of them placed the main portion of his lunch in a box that he had brought along and meticulously ate the remaining portion. My wife said, "It's good to know what is going on outside. Eiko said she will never be finicky in what she eats." The maid also said she truly understands how thankful we should be.

Of late, cabinet meetings are taking place in the palace. From the beginning, Tōjō has hidden behind his majesty the emperor. Whenever he says anything he claims it is the benevolence of the emperor or an imperial order. This is based on his ignorance that he is unconsciously trying to hide behind the august name of the emperor. Conducting cabinet meetings at the palace is a step in this direction.

Today I heard a deeply interesting story. On February 23 of this year, the *Mainichi shinbun* issued a report in large print on the front page on the theme "Victory or Ruin." This was immediately after the publication of the sacrificial deaths of our courageous soldiers in the Marshall Islands and the great Japanese naval loss at Truk.

In the newspaper issue of the 22nd it had been reported that Premier Tōjō would simultaneously hold the position of chief of staff. The report that was published in the *Mainichi shinbun* had headlines that announced, "Victory or

Defeat," "The War Situation Has Reached a Critical Point," "Awake to the Advancing Invasion of the Enemy." In it there are the following phrases: "The decisive battles of offense and defense in the Pacific will not be carried out on the homeland shores of America and Japan. They will be fought out centered on land bases several thousands of miles distant. If the point is reached when the enemy advances to the shores of our homeland, already there is nothing more that can be done. In the case of Rabaul and New Guinea, their significance is that they are the all-important pillboxes in the defense of the homeland." After this report there is a continuing debate about bamboo spears not serving the purpose, building more airplanes, and building aircraft carriers.

Premier Tōjō read this article about three in the afternoon on the same day and was furious. He asked what was all this about—if the enemy reached the point of advancing to our shores, there was nothing that could be done? Even if Tōkyō became a charred ruin, the nation would fight to the bitter end to destroy the enemy.

A panic-stricken Information Board forbade the sale of the *Mainichi shinbun* from 3:30 P.M. on the same day it summoned the editors of the newspaper companies of the entire city and instructed them that there was to be no such article hereafter.

Moreover, the Army Ministry issued a severe rebuke to the *Mainichi shinbun*, and in addition they asked who was the reporter. The *Mainichi shinbun* refused to identify the writer, and the editor-in-chief Yoshioka Hanroku resigned.

With this it was thought that the problem has been resolved. In actuality, the aim of the writer was to argue the urgency of increasing production. Yet his hysterical writing style was excessively harsh, even for the jingoistic *Mainichi shinbun*. Yamane Shinjirō (editor-in-chief of *Tōkyō shinbun*) said at a meeting of the aforementioned Information Board that on the 22nd Tōjō said in a cabinet meeting, "Now the empire literally stands at the crossroads of prosperity or decline," and this probably crept into the writer's mind.

However, in two or three days, suddenly, the red paper of a draft notice arrived for the writer. He was a reporter who was assigned to the Navy Ministry, and as a forty-one- or forty-two-year-old man he was a militia man unconnected with military service. He was not formally drafted. He was inducted at Marugame. When the navy heard of this it was furious. It said that it was outrageous to draft a member of the Navy Information Board without notice. It negotiated with the Marugame Division and he was mustered out. The intention of the navy was to arrange immediately to take him away to the south by airplane. However, on the following day he was formally drafted. And he is now in Marugame.

A story such as this probably depicts well the character of Tōjō, the behavioral style of the army, and the army–navy relationship. This is of particularly deep interest because it is from the extremely subservient *Mainichi shinbun*.

According to Katō's account, he went to inspect an agricultural village in the Tōhoku region and became depressed. The level of rice quotas has become an acute problem; the entire farmers' output is transported to one place and there is again reapportioned. When he went to the cooperative office the senior leaders of the villages came and the farmers pleaded for assistance since they had nothing to eat. They said they could not go on and their patience was exhausted.

He said that when he attempted an interview with General Ishihara Kanji at Tsuruoka, all sorts of thought police swarmed about, and because it was inconvenient, in the end, the meeting was rejected. It is evidence of the surveillance on Ishihara.

March 17 (Friday)

I went to the funeral ceremony of Itō Masanori's wife. I stood alongside of Ueda of the present *Dōmei*—formerly *Dentsū*. The same gentleman said that at the recommendation of a certain person from Mitsubishi he had read my *History of Foreign Relations* and was impressed. Also, he said that a certain official of the Finance Ministry was ill and upon returning to his hometown requested that my book be sent to him, and he complied. The same person said, "It is something that is becoming popular among the well-informed."

Yesterday in a used-book shop I bought a book of General Satō Kōjirō published in the Taishō period entitled, *If America and Japan Fight*. Its main thesis was that in an American–Japanese war, Japan would be decisively victorious and the United States was not to be feared. Among the writing previously published in Japan, there had not been any that argued that one should be fearful of the war power of America.

Two of the so-called corrupt, greedy officials of the Nanking government were sentenced to death. It is said it was because of improper conduct in selling food supplies to the Japanese Army. When this is done in Chungking it is taken as a purge, but when the Nanking government does it, is not the shame transferred to Japan? I wish they would do the same thing in Japan.

In the Washington Conference the reduction of Anglo-American military preparations meant only the reduction of their power to protect their home waters. That is to say, it was this reduction alone that was advantageous to Japan. Lippman pointed this out (same source).

Because of its geographic circumstances Japan must be based upon the balance of power. As England had taken this policy with respect to the European continent, it is wise that with regard to the Asian continent it kept the same policy of balance of power to cope with the inevitable clash of powers that arose there. When she attempted to become a dominant power on the continent, Japan failed. In the future the foreign policy of Japan must concentrate on this one point.

I hear that the characters *gyokusai* (to die with honor) are not being used. It is related that this is because Yamane said to the head of the Information Board, Matsumura Hideitsu, "The use of this phrase is funny, isn't it?" Yamane told me, moreover, that the slogan *iki do mo oku* (one more airplane) is not being used anymore.

Necessity changes their morality.

I hear that American planes come daily to the island of Chishima.

Today, snow is falling. I am rereading Lippman's *U.S. Foreign Policy*. It is full of contradictions. However, he is a splendid critic. He stresses American imperialism.

March 19 (Sunday)

An account of Akira. In a conversation Captain Yoshida told them that an imperial messenger went to the front and explained that Japan would be patient even if Russia created a disturbance so as to avoid war between Japan and the Soviet.

This morning's newspapers prominently published two outlines that passed through cabinet meetings, entitled "Techniques for Enhancing Labor" and "The Strengthening of the Women's Volunteer Corps System." When I read these they are something that firmly establish an occupational class system based upon military regulations for the purpose of developing the highest labor efficiency. It is exactly like middle-school students with a smattering of knowledge. They are still constantly fumbling about with ideas. As to efficiency, there is nothing that approaches the inefficiency of the military.

Mankind does not understand anything outside its own experience. It is interesting that the military thinks that to have factories permeated by the military style is the best thing. They do not understand the meaning of competition. They have only faith and no knowledge.

I am not saying they always make mistakes. Yet they do not understand human psychology. When such things occasionally appear, it is likely we discover the nature of their minds (*Yomiuri hōchi*, March 19).

The newspaper articles make it clear that their view of labor is a product of the military.

It is said that the Foreign Ministry is finally moving to the Greater East Asia Building. The reason for closing the high-class Western restaurants is probably the same sort of thing. When a government resorts to trickery, this is the reason for the loss of faith in politics.

I hear that Matsuo's wife is going to their Yose villa. They say it is because when there is no one about, she is afraid that an empty house will be invaded and occupied. We have decided to go to Karuizawa.

Individual property rights do not exist anymore.

March 20 (Monday)

This morning's newspapers hesitantly wrote about "The Negative Aspect of Formalism" (*Mainichi*) or "The Necessary Thing Is Not Writing but Making Things" (*Yomiuri*). However, the young, ideologized crowd of the newspaper companies do not understand this, and along with the military they advance the strength of formalism.

March 21 (Tuesday)

I wrote an English draft for Japonicus. Under the same name three people write: Takayanagi, Ueda, and myself. Because I am the only one not skilled in English, I suppose the Japanese version will be translated by the distinguished gentleman named Obata. I was overexcited and therefore it did not come out well.

Of late there are inspections of evacuation luggage. The inspecting officer is our carpenter, Umemura. I hear that he follows our neighborhood association head and, saluting, they go about praising, "Well done!" My wife said, "Until now, even when they came to the back door they were deferential."

Here there are two problems. One is that this same thing happened at the time of the great earthquake, and now the responsibility for maintaining order has been returned to the carpenters, gardeners, and fishmongers. They are the possessors of exactly the right knowledge and activism. The second problem is the appearance of meddling by forced inspection by the police of even the individual's possessions. In the newspapers they write about whether there was a summer straw hat or piano in the evacuation baggage. Isn't it best to limit the quantity of baggage and leave the contents to the discretion of the person? The idea of what the most important thing is varies, depending upon the person.

March 22 (Wednesday)

A man from Hakodate named Imai accompanied me on the train during my trip. Since he telephoned I said we would have lunch together, but he did not come to the Economic Club. Afterward, I went to the Foreign Ministry. There was a conference at the foreign minister's residence. Takayanagi's contribution was extremely pointed, but to tell the truth my contribution was less successful. I asked Obata to make appropriate improvements in the translation. I had never felt the inadequacy of my English writing as I did today.

I attended a meeting of the People's Scholarly Arts Society. There was a talk by Tatsuno Yutaka entitled "The New Soldiers." Its theme was that soldiers who were university graduates have a new culture.

Paper for publishing has been reduced by 80 percent. What can the remaining 20 percent be used for? The publishing world will be in difficult circumstances in the future.

There was a story at a meeting that even though we explain the Spirit of the Imperial Way to the Koreans and Manchurians, they do not understand it. If they were made to read *Ninomiya sontoku yobanashi*,[47] "indeed" immediately they would understand. Thereupon in Manchuria there were 500,000 orders for this work, and at Iwanami they said in shock, "We can't handle this much at all!" It is said that there were also the same number of orders from Korea.

March 23 (Thursday)

From Katsuyama Katsuji of Kobe came some short poems:

> The mountains of my native place
> Ariake [Dawn]
> but my shadow wanes.

> When even the evening papers are eliminated
> how sad!
> No paper for my poetry collection.

To this I answered:

> Longing for the village Ariake
> I picked young fern shoots among the verdant spring grasses.

> Stop the evening papers!
> Stop the radio chatter!
> My own way of loyalty.

> In place of foolish sermons
> thirty-one syllables
> the Japanese Way.

A man named Kumon of the Police Information Bureau came by to hear my criticisms of the Tōjō Cabinet.

I hear that there is vicious slander going around concerning Premier Tōjō and Navy Minister Shimada. Concerning Tōjō, this claims that at the time he simultaneously became chief of staff, his Majesty expressed kind words to former Chief of Staff Sugiyama, but Tōjō did not convey these sentiments and was misusing the imperial prerogative of his Majesty. I hear that regarding Shimada it is said that he is completely subservient to Tōjō, and this has the appearance of dragging someone into sodomy. There is nothing more irresponsible than vicious gossip. However, the function that it performs cannot be dismissed.

It appears that animosity toward Tōjō is spread in every quarter. I don't want to criticize events that are based upon the imperial prerogative, but in the beginning I opposed the changing of premiers during the course of the war, but of late, thinking about it, if it is done in such a way that it cannot be viewed as a sign of weakness by the enemy, I wouldn't necessarily be opposed. For example, I mentioned the point that I could imagine unifying the chief of staff and premier for the conduct of the war. That the problem of the authority of supreme command will probably become an issue among the right wing and part of the military I thought of immediately when I was in Hokkaidō and heard the news.

They say that Agriculture Minister Ino was very unhappy at the time of his resignation because Tōjō asked him to stop by on his return from the broadcasting station and he was forced to resign. Even in the present case of Uchida there was hurried consultation to offer him the position, and after declining two or three times he accepted.

There is speculation that wonders whether closing the high-class restaurants is not desirable in stopping inflation. I say that the discontent of the working class is probably responsible.

Nevertheless, the undercurrent of discontent is worsening. Yesterday evening returning home on the train was completely a life-and-death struggle. This alone is enough to worsen the public spirit.

I hear that the newspaper companies are saying that because of the friction between army and navy they cannot write about anything at all. Even in this problem Japan also shows the symptoms of the last stage of an illness. For example, in the prohibition of the sale of the *Mainichi shinbun* recently, it can be said the truth was that it was too much the torch-bearer of the navy. The strong emphasis upon "bamboo spears are no good" and "increased production of naval aircraft" is touching a sensitive nerve. The *Mainichi* columns are inspired by Kurihara, the chief of the Information Board, and such columns appeared in all of the newspapers.

In Europe there is still no prospect for peace.

March 24 (Friday)

In the afternoon at the Foreign Politics Association I heard a talk by Lt. Colonel Sasaki Katsumi on the "Latest War Conditions." He observed that on the Russo-German war front the damage to Russia was extensive and Germany had the advantage. Is this only for public consumption or does he really believe this is so? If he believes it to be so, in truth, he is stupid. However, until the present these people have constantly made mistakes in their predictions.

The only optimistic place in the Greater East Asian War is the Burma front. However, whenever there is a reversal in the war situation, it is always attributed to the inadequacy of aircraft. He said, "It is written that on the anniversary of the founding of Corregidor, 'Established 1929' in the Philippines, about that time there were discussions in the Japanese Diet on military

- An **arbitrary mark** is a commonly known word that is applied to an unfamiliar product. Some of the best-known arbitrary marks are CAMEL® for cigarettes, APPLE® for computers, and OLD CROW® for whiskey. While the terms are found in a dictionary, they have no relevance when applied to the goods in question and are thus arbitrary. Arbitrary marks are registrable without proof of secondary meaning.
- **Fanciful,** or *coined,* **marks** are those that are invented and have no dictionary meaning. Marks such as KODAK®, PEPSI®, and XEROX® are examples of fanciful or coined marks. Such marks are the strongest marks of all and are entitled to the greatest level of protectability because it will be difficult for others to claim they innocently created a highly similar mark for similar goods or services.

You can readily see that companies creating marks face a commercial dilemma. The company likely wants the name to identify something about the product or service itself so that consumers encountering the new name or mark can determine what product or service is being offered. However, if the mark communicates something about the product, it is merely descriptive and cannot be registered without proof of secondary meaning. If a coined mark, such as XEROX, is selected, it tells the consumer nothing about the product or service offered, and the company will need to expend substantial sums in advertising to teach consumers to link the mark with the goods.

TRADE NAMES AND BUSINESS NAMES

A **trade name** or *commercial name* is one used to identify a business or company and its goodwill, while trademarks and service marks identify goods and services. A symbol or name used only as a business name cannot be registered as a trademark or service mark. If the business name, however, also serves to identify and distinguish goods and services, it  may be registrable under the Lanham Act. For example, when Hallmark places its business name on its letterhead and business cards, such use is as an unregistrable trade name or business name. When the HALLMARK (& CROWN)® mark appears on greeting cards, however, it is being used as a trademark and may be registered as such.

Some business owners believe that when they incorporate in a state or file partnership

Type of Mark	Example	Registrability
Generic	PEANUTS (for peanuts)	Not registrable
Descriptive	BUG MIST (for insecticide)	Not registrable without proof of secondary meaning
Suggestive	GOLDEN NUGGETS (for cookies)	Registrable
Arbitrary	POPCORN (for feathers)	Registrable
Fanciful or coined	TRALEE (for cellular phones)	Registrable

EXHIBIT 2–4
Categories of Marks

reduction." This man thinks that Japan should have been able to spend more funds on military preparations. Moreover, he did not know that at that time it was a matter of "maintaining the status quo" in the same area because of the Washington Conference Treaty. What is surprising is that there are these thirty-five- or thirty-six-year-old youths who are courageous, decisive, and self-confident. I wonder where this type of education came from. I drank tea with Obama at the "Silver Star" and then we separated. I worked in the garden throughout the morning.

March 25 (Saturday)

Today, through the day, I worked in the fields. I planted soybeans and green beans. In the evening I read about the agricultural enterprises of Professor Inagaki Otohei. Recently, the subject of agriculture has vigorously taken hold of me with the deepest interest. I was surprised at Professor Inagaki's love of learning and research, and yet he is popular. When I was a child I heard his name frequently, but I did not think he was this famous. Let a great man emerge in the scientific world! In the Meiji period, after all, dedicated researchers were numerous.

March 26 (Sunday)

The entire family has become full-time farmers. In any case, we finished one whole area. In the afternoon I wrote about my trip to Karafuto. The only place I submitted my manuscript was *Tōyō keizai*. Obama declined to contribute anything to *The Japanese Industrial Economy*. I wrote of my intention while I was traveling. Probably he has reservations about what has happened before.

March 27 (Monday)

There are all sorts of rumors among the common people regarding Premier Tōjō. If one listens to what is called barber-shop talk, Tōjō bought a piano for 50 yen, a piece of foreign goods worth 10,000 yen. They say the gossip concerning Tōjō is extremely critical. Tōjō's back-patting bid for popularity will not last long. I hear that a great number of officials of the Ministry of Home Affairs and the Finance Ministry were among those who bought foreign goods cheaply. It is said that such things are ridiculously cheap. In the future there will probably be a time when this will become a problem.

It has been announced that in addition to a rise in postal rates, from April 1 there will be no acceptance of packages of fish and food. The Hokkaidō trip was timely for me.

A story of Yamamoto Kiyoshi, the reporter who handled the "*Mainichi* case." He was drafted, but his drafting wasn't accidental, and he could not believe that he was being punished by being drafted.

March 28 (Tuesday)

A postcard from Masaki Hideri: "I read your *Japan at a Turning Point* and I admire the accuracy of your forecast of contemporary Japan. Together with lamenting the fact that so many colleagues are incapable of understanding facts that were written about fifteen years ago, I envy your intellectual sophistication in having performed this duty. Those who were not able to turn at the turning point were the failed students."

Masaki publishes *Chikaki yori*, and his "fragments of human life" are filled with epigrams that are extremely penetrating. He is one of the most powerful liberals.

Masaki talked about my book, and I took it out and read it. It was written before my trip to America in 1929.

Rain is falling. It is good for the garden. Of late, for me, the most interesting way to pass the time is reading books on agriculture. It would not be bad to manage an agricultural garden of ten thousand tsubo[48] and cultivate when it is clear and read when it rains. I wrote a political essay for *Tōyō keizai*.

March 29 (Wednesday)

The plum blossoms are fully open. In the *Mainichi* newspaper there was a letter to the editor that demanded the confiscation of detached villas in the countryside. Of late it is thought to be suitable to appropriate individual property rights.

Seven policemen came to Dobashi's house. It is said they entered his storehouse and demanded the surrender of his goods. The authorities do not permit the personal possession of commercial goods.

March 30 (Thursday)

Yamamoto Kiyoshi came by and said, "I will leave everything up to you." It is a matter of the marriage. He is not enthusiastic. This despite the common opinion that men have all the advantages. . . .

March 31 (Friday)

I hear that a fishing treaty with the Soviet Union has been concluded. I understand that in exchange, rights in northern Karafuto were returned.

They say that as regards this treaty with the Soviet Union, people such as Secretary Kase went to see the senior statesmen, and none of them opposed this. There have been three imperial conferences regarding Soviet–Japanese relations, and national policy was decided to be the avoidance of confrontation with Russia. Secretary Kase said, "We have never had such a definite national policy in Japan."

It is said that the newspapers do not make much of this because of our relations with Germany.

Hereafter the major problem is that the best foreign policy would be if we could develop relations with England and America as the other parties while the Soviet Union acted as mediator.

There are two points of significance in this. One of these is internal. Even now there are many people who hope for a Russian–Japanese conflict. I was frequently asked this, even in Hokkaidō. Two, is there the possibility of a rapprochement with a Soviet Union, which is inseparable from America and England?

April 1 (Saturday)

I received a thousand yen in the name of Kobayashi as a token payment for the *Tōdenshi*. It was done at the prompting of Miyake. In view of the fact that our family finances are unstable, expenditures expand at an extraordinary rate. Hereafter, financial matters are hard to estimate. There is absolutely no payment for manuscripts. Also, the *Ginsei* is not doing well because it has carried on till now, there is only optimism that it will probably go on somehow.

I walked along the Ginza to see how things are. Nearly half of it has closed doors, and even if one passes in front of food shops there are long lines of about one hundred people. All this noise to eat food that is not satisfying (*Mainichi*, "Miscellany Notebook," April 2).

A tale of Professor Hozumi Shigeto. A certain man went to the bathhouse carrying his rationed soap. Because he had heard that there were many thieves at the bathhouse, he was careful in placing the soap beside the hot water basin. Suddenly he was splashed with hot water, and when he again turned away the soap had vanished. He seriously believes there is a causal relationship between the hot water and the disappearance of the soap.

A story of the same person. A maid was sent to his married daughter. She sent the maid back. When she was asked the reason, she said that she took pleasure in licking the containers in which sugar had been stored, but the maid always washed these out thoroughly. She said it was better not having a maid.

Hasegawa Nyozekan said our present lives are licking-lives.

There is no maid in the home of Professor Kuwaki Genyoku; there is an old married couple. Hasegawa Nyozekan cooks his own meals. This is because his younger sister, who lives with him, cannot work because she has *byoso* [a finger infection] or something. I was told that among roughly ten households in the neighborhood association, nobody has a maid.

Hasegawa said that he was cooking rice for the first time at the age of seventy. Yesterday when he was cooking rice with a paper fire, someone came by and the fire went out, and when he tried cooking again he produced some-thing completely inedible. The problem is that he cannot study properly. Professor Hozumi said that in the end, "We'll be eating by using paper, won't we?"

Professor Makino Eichi said he thinks about moving out to the country-side, but those who are experienced tell him he will be harassed by the local residents, and it may be that he cannot be a permanent resident. Professor Makino Eichi came wearing a wartime khaki-colored cap. He said that other hats are extremely costly and he bought this one because it was cheap. He said that when he is wearing it, people do not respect him.

Yanagida Kunio said the talk in the streets of late is extremely interesting. He wishes to make notes on such things, but he lacks the patience now.

The inadequacy of rice is a topic of conversation. Talk of its inadequacy.

From today onward, costs will rise in every direction—it doesn't matter what it is—mail, trains, taxes, and other things. Moreover, it has come about that one needs permission certificates from the police for the trains. Yester-day, as a result of a 30 percent reduction, the newspapers wrote about the "Great Success." If the number gets smaller they talk about success.

It is said that with Shimada as navy minister, internal unity is difficult. The fact that he is dissatisfied with Tōjō's leadership is one reason. However, it is not reasonable to expect there will be opposition to Tōjō at the center. This is the painful position of Shimada.

The hostile feelings between army and navy are already reaching the boil-ing point. There are a great many things in this that symbolize the future of Japan (*Yomiuri*, "Paper Bullets," April 2).

An account of General Araki. He said the Japanese Army has overextended itself. As in the case of the attack at Imphal in Burma, they wasted valuable ammunition and it was useless. As a consequence, he said leave the front as it is, and, as in the Mongol Invasion, we will await the enemy assault on the beaches and beat them back with bamboo spears.

The aforementioned first statement is true, but the bamboo-spearism is the inevitable old refrain. It is unclear if this is his real thinking or just a meta-phor. Previously this was his basic tone. Even now it seems to be so.

I hear that a certain carpenter came along and said, "Is it possible to eat if one doesn't make at least a thousand yen a month?" (an account of Professor Makino). This is the extent to which black-market prices pervade everything.

April 2 (Sunday)

There was a family gathering at the *Tōyō keizai*. However, because Hirakawa Yūichi promised to repair electrical appliances for us, I did not attend. A literature graduate of an American university, Hirakawa is able to repair things that cannot be repaired by the Tōkyō electrical shops. Refrigerators, waffle irons, and other things—he can repair everything.

Here is the difference between Japanese education in formalism and education that teaches thinking.

One can be surprised by the sincerity, correctness of manners, and deep sense of obligation of youths who have studied in American universities. On this point, can Japan look down on America?

April 3 (Monday) (Clear)

The total of American casualties has been published as 173,239.

With regard to the rationing of vegetables, of late it is said to be one sen a person for one day. But one sen is not worth one green onion.

For the ration for our family we pay eighteen sen for a three-day share. It is six sen for a one-day share, and because there are six members in our family this is one sen per person. I was told that we obtained taro and bean sprouts.

However, on the one hand, the newspapers only attack the confusion of passengers on the streetcars and trains, and regarding the small number of riders they speak only of "self-control" or "good results." Japanese newspaper reporters are the megaphone of the bureaucracy. Herein is an instance of forgetting to make use of their own minds themselves. They do this while knowing themselves that one cannot eat under rationing.

In Hayama there are people who are eating only the ration. A nutritionist who was impressed by this went to see these families. I understand that all the people had become "night-blind." It appears to be a really true story.

From this April a tax at the source of 7 yen 50 sen, will be withheld from a monthly salary of 100 yen. Having to maintain the livelihood of a five- or six-person family on 92 yen, 50 sen, is by no means uncommon. This at a time when the consumer's price of 120 yen for 1 kamme of sugar is called cheap!

Understanding what this thing called war means is important for the future of Japan.

The Japanese people have had faith in the war. Since the Sino-Japanese incident, even in the stratum of intellectuals in my circle, each and every one is a supporter of the war. This is so of Obama Toshie and Ōta Eifuku. Indeed, I think that those who are seriously opposed to it are only Ishibashi Tanzan and Baba Tsunego. More than anything else, the present war is probably a realistic education for such Japanese.

April 4 (Tuesday)

A colonel said, "I thought that an attack on Pearl Harbor would awaken the sleeping lion called America. At that time I was considered out of my mind. We must shoulder the responsibility for this." It is extraordinary that there is someone in the military who says such things!

The steam trains and electric trains are in homicidal disarray. The instances are not few that recount children having died when disembarking from electric trains.

If one relies upon an editorial in today's *Mainichi*, the betrayal of Italy is the result of the manipulation of Jewish power. When I see the men who use Semitism to interpret international relations, my immediate reaction is contempt. The man Uehara, chief writer of the great newspaper called *Mainichi*, has one lance—the secret Jewish conspiracy (*Mainichi*, "Editorial," April 3).

This morning I sent off a book, but the postal fee was fifty sen, and to send a manuscript express delivery was forty-five sen. It is one example of income and expenditures where a salary of a hundred yen a month is common.

Someone came from the Higashi-chōfu Police Office to ask my opinions on the "Japanese–Soviet Fishing Treaty." I said it was one of the things that most pleased me and it was a success. However, this alone is meaningless, and one must obtain a final good result. For this the thought police and military police should not treat the Soviet Union with harshness. And one more thing, I said it would even be better if Japan used the Soviet Union to bring the war to a conclusion.

An order came from the Soviet Embassy to *Tōyō keizai* for twenty copies each of the magazine in Japanese and English. I hear that they said that they would not sell any. Previously, there had been the suspension of sales at the demand of the authorities, but this was the latest new request that had come. The embassy made the request again. I hear that *Tōyō keizai* told them there were to be no sales. The authorities said, "We wish to bind the Soviet Embassy hand and foot." If awareness of foreign relations does not extend to the lower reaches of government, foreign relations are impossible.

Premier Tōjō suddenly visited a certain aircraft factory. He took along as gifts eggs and money for food and drink. Is he possibly taking eggs and money to the entire body of the Japanese people (*Yomiuri hōchi*, April 3)?

(If one can speak of "Those Responsible for Production," they are the established middle-aged gentlemen.)

Suzuki Jūzō came to visit. In October of last year he returned on an exchange ship. He was interned in Ontario and other camps for twenty-one months. It is said that the Canadian government encouraged the movement of Japanese to its eastern provinces and that French Canada in the East also welcomed the Japanese. In the end it was a plan to keep the Japanese from living in large concentrations.

Books and reports on agriculture are more interesting than anything else. While both the government and newspapers are encouraging for cabinet discussion the development of empty land as a fixed national policy, there is no allotment of seed potatoes, and if they are not planted within two or three days it will be unfortunate. Because we are told to plant leeks, even I searched everywhere for leek seeds, but in vain. I merely planted what was given to me by a neighbor, Temmei.

There is only propaganda and nothing is done. This is called bureaucratic regulation. Because the people are stupid they still do not comprehend this.

They still talk of the "nationalization of private railways" and the "strengthening of regulation." One cannot imagine such a formalistic people existing anywhere else.

April 5 (Wednesday)

Hackneyed writing has become typical. The authorities will not accept writings if they do not talk about their "very extraordinary strategy." These people cannot go a day without being praised from morning till night.

When one looks at the Indian campaign from the larger political viewpoint, it is clear that it is producing results that must be regretted. If Japan takes Imphal temporarily, what will it matter? They do not advance beyond this, yet they cannot withdraw. It will be a stationary war front. And then the sacrifices will probably be enormous.

The newspapers are extravagantly referring to "Japanese-style salaries" or the "labor for the empire ideal." It seems to be that they are saying because the salary system is Anglo-American style, create something Japanese. The something called Japanese is feudalism. The boss protects the livelihood of the employees, and in exchange for this it is possible to strengthen absolute submission. These people do not understand at all why there had to be the Meiji reforms. Moreover, the possessors of minds that understand such things are unable to do anything about it.

In the afternoon I went to the Foreign Ministry. Professor Ueda finished his essay. He is even more stiff than Takayanagi. In the evening we all had supper near the Ginza. It is rather uncrowded because people assume they cannot eat out anymore. However, we were not able to have cooked rice. Returning home, I ate bread. This style of eating is wasteful in terms of the national economy.

The Railway Ministry is extremely unpleasant. I myself have previously not had this kind of experience. They have shelved their personal responsibility, and everything has been made the responsibility of the passengers. Such things as excessive fines for going past one's station or upon returning having to buy another ticket are extreme punishment. It is a country ruined by officials.

There should be the application of an inspection system to the railways, and I think the railways are operating extremely inefficiently.

April 6 (Thursday)

I read a speech by Smuts. It was a speech given in November of last year, and I received it from the Foreign Ministry.

It stated, "There are two dangers. One is oversimplifications and the other is following slogans." In Japan there are also these two shortcomings. One sees that the former is in the fashion that talks about the "menace of the Jews," and the latter is in the fashion of circulating slogans and then not investigating contents.

As regards Greater East Asia, in the future the intrusion of America and Russia and the awakening of China are inevitable. Facing these circumstances, Japan must control this three-country balance of power.

An account of Professor Ueda. The inability of the Japanese officials who travel to China and Manchuria to talk about world problems, big problems, is particularly conspicuous. They are simple officials. This is certainly true. They do not have this kind of training. They merely play with articles of law. In the South Seas areas that have been occupied briefly, the fact that they do not have this training is the basic reason for Japan's failure.

It is necessary to have education that trains people with a wide-ranging perspective.

In America and England during the war, those with opposing opinions are valued. In England this is true of all such people as Cripps, Morrison, and Shinwell. In America Lindberg is used in the Ford factory. In Japan the so-called pro-Anglo-Americans—if those who had not supported the war at the beginning had been employed in important positions, I wonder if their attitude would naturally have still been "Anglo-American leanings"?

However, in Japan differing ideas are absolutely unacceptable.

Kaji Kōichi sent me copy of Yoshida Tosuke's *Toward a Complete Understanding of the Japan-China Problem*. It made me wonder how there could be a liberal theorist such as this among the people of Japan. The writing style is also skillful. I hear he is trusted among the Chinese, and I can see why. Among the things I have read recently, this is the most surpassing work. It is written with great discretion, but, at any rate, in something like this being put out at all, one can see a reconsideration of Japanese policy toward China.

April 7 (Friday)

The Japanese Army continues to advance on Imphal. This is the latest great strategy of General Tōjō after becoming head of the chiefs of staff. This strategy has as its main purpose the political aim of agitating India and the rise of anti-English movements. Whether or not Tōjō's forecast is correct will probably become clear from the results of the war.

Two people who are connected with the stock market came to ask my opinions on foreign affairs problems. The meaning of the new Soviet–Japanese Treaty is after all becoming a topic of conversation.

One of these people is a man from Toyama Prefecture. Until now the farmers have been cheated by the government, and they worked believing that they could dispose of their barley crop freely. He said that if this time they are cheated again, they will probably not produce after this. He says that the stock market predicts the future, and the peaks of its pessimism take excessive form, but it still faces up to the problems of daily life.

Today's ration of vegetables in a house with six people is five or six sen. This is only a handful of bean sprouts. When I was cultivating the fields two or three days ago, young women in the flower of their youth asked me to share my vegetables. The newspapers talk of nothing but vegetables. However, notwithstanding the encouragement to increase production, there is no ration of seed potatoes and seed leeks. From this one probably understands how unproductive bureaucratism is. However, the Japanese who have no flexibility do not understand this. Whenever an impasse is reached, they say it comes down to an "inadequacy of regulations"—I am always writing the same thing, but . . . .

April 8 (Saturday)

With yesterday evening's rain, young buds are sprouting. The owner of a bean curd shop occupying the land in front of our house asked to cut down the trees around it, and if we did not he would demolish our stone wall. He came to the house that we have occupied for twenty years and demanded the trees be cut down. In regard to the field in which nothing had yet been planted, he demanded the trees be cut down completely. This is the manner of thinking common to Japanese. It is the mentality of extraordinary times. Our fields are also in the shade, but I have not requested the same thing of my neighbors.

In the depths of the mountains in the countryside, there is no charcoal or firewood. When one asks the reason why, it is government regulations on cutting wood and the manufacture of charcoal. This regulation. It blocks the outlet of production, which should be growing.

Reading the April issue of *Chūō kōron*, a serialized work entitled "On the History of Japanese Reform" by a man named Terada Inajirō viciously maligns Ōkubo and praises Saigō, and, moreover, he praises assassins. It is directed at such people as Kurushima Tsuneki, who attacked Ōkuma, and the act that killed Mori Arinori. Moreover, he says that if the *Seikanron* had been carried out, treaty revision would have been possible twenty years earlier.

Such people do not understand international relations at all. They do not understand the dominant current in which the predictably famous Saigō was defeated and in any case Ōkubo became the key figure until the last. With this sort of crowd it is not possible to expect that the conditions of the times will be surmounted in a right-wing controlled society.

In it there is a symposium entitled "The World Situation and Inevitable Japanese Victory" in which Professor Yabe Teiji of the Imperial University stresses that Germany is extremely advantaged. A Tōkyō University professor says this when the Ukraine has been seized and the Germans are blocked in every direction. From this one can judge what the average person thinks. Among them Kase Shunichi of the Foreign Ministry is well-informed on conditions.

April 9 (Sunday)

Because it is raining I cannot work in the fields. This year has been extremely cold, and after a whole month the potatoes are not sprouting. Today my schedule to try planting taro was thrown off.

April 10 (Monday)

The position of general secretary of the International Relations Research Society is being pressed upon me. Rōyama has been carrying on this role, but because he has work in the Diet he previously announced his resignation. I accepted upon the condition of advancing research in the history of foreign relations.

I hear that the *Tōyō keizai* is in difficulties because its people have been reduced by repeated military conscription and the labor draft. It is said that in such places as Seoul there is not a single person left, and Yamada has gone off to official duties. Moreover, it is said that as regards this conscription, while the people are absent from home they are paid a monthly wage, and after they return home from military service they do not resettle in the company, and most of them leave it completely.

The former fascist foreign minister, Ciano, has been sentenced to death, and other leaders are on trial. In fascism there is no freedom of "opposition." What would be the consequence if Mussolini were criticized? At least in a democratic country they would say—is this not an assembly?

I wrote an essay for *Tōyō keizai* regarding the transportation of travelers and criticized the administration of the government. Regarding this essay, there was a formal warning that spoke of "criticizing the authorities." Once one has been warned about doing this sort of thing, one is pressured as "attacking the authorities." This shows the special characteristic of bureaucratic politics.

I hear that with regard to my travel record, "To Karafuto and Hokkaidō," and "The Members of the Diet Have Pride and the Government Responds to the Hopes of the Diet," which I submitted to *Tōyō keizai*, a letter praising me came from Ashida Hitoshi to *Tōkei*.

Rōyama is researching the subject of nutritional food. Both Ishibashi and I are researching the same subject. I have high respect for Rōyama's well-organized research.

papers with a state agency, such filing serves to protect their names because the state agency will check to ensure that no similar name is already being used within the state. Thus, for example, if the secretary of state of California allows Diamond Engineers, Inc. to incorporate in California, the corporation may later have to cease using the name if it is found to infringe on a trademark. Merely allowing a company to incorporate under a name does not result in trademark rights. Approval by a state to use a name in connection with a business is merely that—the company is entitled to use the name in connection with the business itself within that state. Using the name on goods themselves or in connection with services, namely, as a trademark or service mark, is far different. Once the mark is so used in commerce, the company acquires trademark or service mark rights.

PROTECTABLE MATTER

Introduction

The definition of a trademark or service mark is that it is a word, name, symbol, device, or any combination thereof, used to identify products or services. Clearly, words such as B. DALTON BOOKSELLER® and designs or symbols such as Mercedes Benz's segmented circle or the Mr. Peanut design can function as trademarks. There are, however, a host of other items that can be protected as marks, generally because of the flexibility in the language of the Lanham Act allowing for registration of a "symbol" or "device." A symbol or device might include anything capable of conveying meaning to a person, such as sounds, smells, and shapes.

Slogans, Letters, and Numbers

A slogan can constitute a trademark if it is distinctive. Thus, the slogan HAVE IT YOUR WAY® is protectable. Alphanumeric

symbols (letters and numbers) may be protectable as long as they are not merely descriptive. Thus, broadcast station call letters such as NBC or CNN are registrable. Similarly, numbers can function as marks. For example, Ford Motor Company has registered ZX5® for trucks and vans. If the numbers or letters describe something about the product or service offered under the mark, however, they will not be registrable unless proof of secondary meaning is shown. Thus, the mark "VT220" for computer hardware peripherals was held merely descriptive and unregistrable because "VT" stood for "video terminal" and "220" was a mere model number. Similarly, an application for registration of "888 Patents" was refused because it was merely descriptive of patent-related legal services. However, once such a telephone number achieves secondary meaning, it may be registered. Thus, the mark 1-800-CALL-ATT has been registered.

Logos and Symbols

Some of the most famous trademarks in existence consist solely of logos or symbols. Thus, registrations exist for Nike's famous "swoosh" mark, McDonald's golden arches, and Ralph Lauren's figure of a polo player on a horse. Some symbols, however, such as a peace symbol or smiley face, do not serve a trademark function and would not be registrable. Similarly, as discussed below, logos that are purely ornamental or are mere background material may not be protectable.

Names of Performing Artists

A mark that merely serves to identify an artist or entertainer is not registrable. However, if the owner of the mark has controlled the quality of the goods or services, and the name of the artist or group has been used numerous times

April 11 (Tuesday)

In the afternoon I was in the fields planting potatoes. In past years an old gentleman did this, but this year I encouraged the maids Toyo and Natsu to work with the whole family. We applied a large amount of compost.

I delivered a manuscript to Japonicus, but it was difficult to write. My logic does not accept the theory of isolating Greater East Asia and making it all-important. China, Philippines, Malaya, Java—is it not the case that nowhere is there submission to the virtue of the Japanese? Will there remain any trace after the war of the Co-Prosperity Sphere, which has been maintained by means of the sword throughout the war? A Greater East Asian Co-Prosperity Sphere will grow naturally as an assembly of small nations with Japan as the core. The Japanese do not have this unifying capacity. The realities determine the logic.

April 12 (Wednesday)

Little by little the newspapers are writing about discontents. First of all, there is the complaint about the overshooting of stations by the railways and the inconsiderateness of railway authorities. The *Mainichi shinbun* brought up the problem in the contributors' column and elsewhere. This is a point I have also written about in the *Tōyō kezai*. An example of formalism (*Mainichi*—hard-working factory employees unable to buy tickets, "Miscellany Notebook," April 12).

This morning's *Asahi* took up various problems and handled them as a lot. Hitherto discontent and dissatisfaction were hidden behind phrases such as "extraordinary circumstances" and "living under war times" and were matters that could not be published. Also, if actual conditions were known by foreign countries, this would give a bad impression. However, the people feel extremely put out by how little attention is paid to such things.

There are no textbooks, there is no fertilizer, the distribution of oil for the fishing fleet allows only a few days work, and the problems of transportation connections go without saying—these sorts of things at last have come to press down upon us. These are the result of the war, but at the same time things have come to this pass because the government does not understand the delicacy of economic relations in such things as absurd requisitioning, military conscription, and the so-called priority system.

Japan has finally come to an internal stalemate. This reveals how and where the next problems will be.

Ishibashi said, "We have never had a prime minister remain in office as long as Premier Tōjō when everyone is fed up with him."

In the afternoon I went to the Foreign Ministry. A consul named Ichikawa Yasujirō wished to have an interview with me. He is a man who served under

Ambassador Kawai Tatsuo. He is in the midst of research into world postwar plans. I received a copy of these.

In regard to Japanese–Soviet relations, at the beginning Japan proposed a price of four-hundred million yen for interests in Karafuto. To that the other party made a counterproposal and offered three million rubles. As a result, a compromise was reached on five million yen. It is said that Ambassador Satō was little appreciated until then but suddenly acquired high praise for these negotiations. Moreover, it appears that the Foreign Ministry turned toward a readjustment in German–Soviet relations. I went further and am insisting upon a readjustment of Japanese–Soviet relations and the withdrawal of the army prepared against the Soviet, but there was no support for this. It is as if the Japanese think it is a sin to think about anything but the government's policy. The people who think this are either the right wing or the left wing, and this is troublesome.

Four of us who wanted supper searched high and low in the Ginza neighborhood but finally were unable to eat. In one place we were in line only thirty minutes and were cut off while waiting.

April 13 (Thursday)

Morning, I wrote a letter to Takayanagi resigning from the Takayanagi committee. At that very movement a telephone call came from Takayanagi. He said because my manuscript of the other day was extremely good, I should continue writing. One of the reasons for my resignation was there was no mention of financial remuneration. However, I could not bring myself to write about it. I wonder why Japanese will not talk about this kind of thing.

The newspapers are writing as though India and Chungking are in extreme agony because of the fall of Imphal. As usual they are full of self-satisfaction.

The senior statesmen and Premier Tōjō consulted on the 12th. In the past, Premier Tōjō and the cabinet ministers came as a group in order to shut off questions, but this time he came alone. It was possible that when the senior statesmen asked the question, "How is the war going?" they were answered, "What would you do hearing this sort of question?" I hear that the answer was previously prepared. It appears that nobody knows how to cope with Tōjō.

In the Meiji period the senior statesmen had the real power to speak freely. They graciously accepted the confidence of the Meiji Emperor, and they were in the position of scrutinizing the prime minister. They exercised the function of checks and balances. However, now it is a situation in which the senior statesmen are merely *daimyō* lined up in a row and cannot even put questions to the prime minister.

In the name of the emperor's confidence, Tōjō has become a complete dictator as prime minister, army minister, munitions minister, and chief of staff. Various sorts of problems and omens can be seen in this.

The price of rationed vegetables today is six sen.

For a six-person family, this is a three-day ration. This means that a handful of green vegetables is not even enough for a single meal for our family. Despite this it is said that Tōkyō rations are not bad.

I hear, according to Hirakawa's account, that the broadcast stations do not have preparations for complete second and third alternate systems. When there is an air attack or something else, if there were facilities for short-wave it would be possible to show the healthy state of Japan, but if this does not exist, the confusion of internal conditions would probably be assumed. And yet it is said that there is a second spare facility at Atagoyama and a third is in the basement of the First Life Insurance Company and at Komoro in Shinshū. But this is only talk and there are no facilities at all. This is the result of bureaucratic organization in which no one has responsibility. It seems that such newspapers as *Asahi* and *Mainichi* have fairly adequate evacuation preparations. This is because they have responsible people.

The deficiencies of bureaucratism and controlism have become completely clear as a result of testing over a number of years. The test of direct experience throughout my life became my final firm conviction. Bureaucratism and controlism will destroy Japan.

The payments we collect for a house that we rent to others are deposited, but in order to redeem these my wife went back and forth for two days to put our seal on innumerable papers. The complications of judicial administration are beyond words.

April 14 (Friday)

A golf competition. After the lapse of many months I have taken up the clubs again. I was utterly defeated. The golf courses have all been confiscated and Koganei is just about the only one left. Instead of being taken for use, they are being destroyed. It is a reaction against bourgeois recreation. Such things as taking what is already established, jealousy, discontent, and possessiveness are characteristic of the "Japanese spirit."

April 15 (Saturday)

The rationing structure has again been changed in a cabinet meeting. The cabinet seems to be a place where there is discussion on retail purchases of tickets and fish. In any case, the officials have nothing else to do and they are taken up by their fascination with drafting regulations. This has been the style from about the time of the ascendance of the left wing. It is a relic.

Yesterday the Imperial Bank and the Jūgo Yasuda, Shōwa, and Daisan banks were merged. The premise is the national management of capital. However, the merger of Mitsui and Daichi has not been neatly fitted; rather, the situation seems to have a great number of problems. In the interests of achieving a healthy control system, the government should wait before advancing to the second step. Here there is the dilettantism of "regulation entrepreneurs."

Obama Toshie always says that the fellows called officials only worry about how they can possibly destroy the country. These are ominous words but true.

The crowd that is now making pessimistic arguments is the crowd that thought at the time of the Pearl Harbor attack that this one blow would crush America. Miyake Seiki is one of these and has viciously attacked me. At the Thursday Society, Nishinoiri of the *Tōkyō nichinichi shinbun* lectured proudly on the fact that the war began under the leadership of the *Tōnichi* (*Mainichi*).

Because of rumor, Professor Watanabe Tetsuzō was suspected of violating Naval Criminal Law, and on the 14th he was prosecuted. The content of his lecture in Ōsaka was bad. Watanabe is a man who makes courageous statements.

It is very difficult for businessmen to read and understand all regulations. About the time they commit them to memory again, a new one has been issued.

April 16 (Sunday)

Today we all worked throughout the morning in the fields. We prepared soil that had been put in from our next-door neighbor. It was real farm labor. The first fine weather and a Sunday off for a long time.

April 18, (Tuesday)

Again today I worked in the fields all morning. We transplanted the maples. There were far too many, and it was difficult to manage them. Before we knew it, the plants had become huge.

In the afternoon I finished a manuscript for Japonicus. The main point of it was quoting a speech of Smuts, that the pressure of European power politics made the Greater East Asian Co-Prosperity Sphere inescapable. Explanations for the existence of the Greater East Asia Co-Prosperity Sphere are difficult to make.

The government has begun propagandizing the slogan, "Let's plant castor beans again this year!" The people will accept propaganda once or twice. However, these castor beans are produced at great effort, and once the people have experienced the hard fact that the government is not collecting them, probably the crop this year will decrease.

It is said in newspaper reports that the vacant houses designated as evacuation areas unbelievably are still just as they were. A good example of bureaucratic government.

The seeds for pumpkins and spinach-beet are rationed. Potato seeds have not arrived at all. For the places that require lots of seed and the places that do not need them, the ration is the same. The waste of a controlled economy and its standardization are the best reasons for the flexibility of economic liberalism.

They are sticking up posters that say, "Plant pumpkins at any cost!" Eiko said, "How about rather telling us, well, let's produce some pumpkins." As a result of disseminating trivia nationally, there can only be partiality. Particularly the result of petty matters being decided by the cabinet is the narrowing more and more of the scope of free judgment.

April 19 (Wednesday)

The governor of Ehime, named Aikawa, has moved to the position of welfare deputy. It is impossible to expect good results when everything is always changed. To know a single problem thoroughly, one needs a whole lifetime.

Together with Takayanagi Kenzō I went to a Japanese eating place in the Ginza area. There was a place in the restaurant with benches to sit on and we moved there. After two or three minutes I suddenly wondered about my hat, which had been put on a chair, and when we looked for it, it was gone. It had been stolen. It was a new soft cap. It was taken by a man with the look of a gentleman. Japan has become a nation of thieves. The country that is the "land of the gods" doesn't mind at all if it has thieves.

Thieves are becoming very common. This will probably become increasingly serious as times goes on—Ah!

April 20 (Thursday)

There was a warning by the Police Headquarters about an editorial entitled "The Adjustment of Japanese-Soviet Relations," which I had written for *Tōyō keizai*. The editor was summoned to be admonished on the following points:

1. Do not write in such a way as to say that the present treaty (a five-year-extension of the fishing treaty and the return of Karafuto) involved Japanese concessions. This agitated the emotions of the people.

2. Do not write in such a way as to say that the current decisions are successful and would be "celebrated." This is because Germany would be agitated.

3. Do not write in such a way as to say that the interests in Karafuto were the result of the Nikō Indicent.[49] This is because people will once more think about those times and about the problems in this relationship. That is to say, don't write history.

If this is the case, when one asks what may one write about, the answer is one may write only about what makes Japanese–Soviet relations brighter.

In general, this explains the operating style of the present censorship and speech control. With respect to the things I have written, a "severe warning." And when it goes a little farther, the prohibition from publishing is waiting for me.

A story from the barbershops. In Tōkyō there were over eight thousand barbershops, but already eight hundred of them are closed.

When I walked around the Ginza area after a long absence, the shops are closed and it looks literally as if teeth have been extracted.

I had a meal in the Imperial Hotel with Akiyama Takashi and Shimanaka Yūsaku. Akiyama rented a room in the Imperial Hotel. He made reservations for ten guests. However, in reality, there were only three people. Since there is no place for three people to socialize, he paid the room charge and meal cost of ten people. It was probably seventy or eighty yen. He said, "It is cheaper than going to a private room in a fancy restaurant." It was an intimate meeting to discuss the marriage of Akiyama's second son and Shimanaka's eldest daughter.

April 21 (Friday)

Day after day the newspapers are writing about evacuation. There are no trucks for evacuation, the trains are not available, and the communications between evacuation sites have not been made. It is current politics to bind people's legs and command them to jump and then ask, why don't they jump?

According to Akiyama's account, itinerant workers come from the area of Ogikubo, and in that locale "Premier Tōjō" does not exist. When one asks why he is so unpopular, the response is, "It's because the rationing is intolerable!"

With respect to views on the war, the radio and newspapers are typically circulating the expression "Both optimism and pessimism are forbidden" with respect to the war strength of America. This probably means not to think anything at all.

Among the admonitory instructions of the Police Headquarters are such things as follows:

1. Discussion of the problems of postwar structure and the introduction of the American-English position is not permitted.

2. The introduction of the American-English position regarding Japan is not permitted. However, in case it is, if it is in the direction of increasing war enthusiasm it is permissible.

To resolve everything with the argument of Judaism and Jewish ideas is the tendency, and this tendency exists even in the world of scientists (*Asahi*, April 21).

After a long while I am reading *Kaizō*. There is an opening essay by Sohō. He says we should objectively view current conditions without pessimism or optimism. After that he attacks contemporary conditions in Japan as "unkind" and "formalistic." In this man's mind, two Japans exist separately. These are the divine Japan and the declining Japan. And then he thinks the declining Japan is a result of the influence of Western individualism. Now, having entered the war as he wished and Japanism having become pervasive, why is Japan not getting better?

The main writers of *Kaizō* have simply become Patriotic Speech Society members such as Nomura Shigenobu and Saitō Tadashi. They have succeeded in cutting out everyone else. They have obtained their position with the support of the military.

The manner of argument of lower-level middle-school students is widely accepted throughout the country.

In Japan there are several forms of *lèse-majesté*:

1. The Imperial House
2. Premier Tōjō
3. The military
4. Tokutomi Sohō.

Regarding these, one cannot permit the slightest criticism.

In the afternoon I conferred with Rōyama concerning matters of the International Relations Study Society and we decided to establish an office. A reporter of the *Asahi* came there. He said that in a conference between Tōjō and the senior statesmen, Tōjō lectured for an hour and a half. Among the senior statesmen who are active, there is only Abe Nobuyuki and Okada Keisuke. At the present moment it does not seem that Tōjō will resign.

April 22 (Saturday)

The thing called the "Japanese wage" has come to be vigorously debated (*Yomiuri*, April 22).

In the end, whether one is an efficient worker or not, a fixed wage will be given. We may say "Soviet-like" without saying "Japaneselike." However, "wages" are a matter of concern for munitions companies, and the people in general, of course, do not receive them.

Society is rapidly, constantly changing. In this, Communist symptoms are emerging from all directions.

A story of Ōta Eifuku. Fuji Ice cannot continue its business operation. There is only a little business before noon, and then the employees rest from two o'clock in the afternoon. With strong police pressure in the background, they were made to convert their first floor into a gruel restaurant. This is a very great loss, but they are going to try to go on through the present year despite the losses.

It is said that, on the one hand, the enclosed pastures in Chiba Province that had begun to increase Fuji Ice's capital are being expropriated for the purpose of pasture control by Chiba Province. If that is the case, it is to be expected that Fuji Ice will no longer stay in business. In any event, income from Fuji Ice occupies a fairly important part of my income, and the road ahead is worrisome. From now on, I should also not expect much income from the Silver Star. From now on, those connected with nonwar production will not even be able to eat.

As in the case of the pasture administration of Chiba Province, we will see direct management of all the provinces. Even here, we see one manifestation of Soviet "state management." What is different is that the great capitalists are still in great shape. Combining with others, they make them their creatures. Of course, the great capitalists do not like the present state of affairs. However, it can be said that those who manipulate the officials are the capitalists, just as Marxism states that the capitalists do not have this degree of power and are led by the officials.

Something called "lumber companies" have been established in all the provinces. They are companies that cut down timber resources, and recently there was an order allowing the free cutting of standing trees. The mountains along the railways will probably be stripped bare. This too is the tendency toward "state management."

The revolution continues to advance at the fundamental level.

April 23 (Sunday)

The Imphal attack in the beginning was secret, and the newspapers have been pressing for the penetration of the Indian border. However, there has been positive reaction for the most part to this crossing of national borders, and there are such reports from western Asia. At this time, Tōjō himself has become aggressive and taken the lead in ordering propaganda. This is very much Tōjō's behavioral style, which lacks intelligence, and he acts from what he sees.

I have noticed that the radio news on the war situation in Imphal is broadcast first, and news concerning the Imperial House is broadcast next.

April 24 (Monday)

Thieves are circulating everywhere, and the farm families are being pillaged. "Foremost thief nation of the whole world" is the title of honor that has been given to Japan during the war (*Mainichi*, April 24).

Kiyoaki returned from the countryside. It is said that in the countryside one increasingly hears the question, "When will the war end?" According to the account of a certain soldier who returned from Rabaul, on our side against the airplanes of the enemy there was absolutely nothing, and there was only shooting from the ground. Moreover, as for food supplies, there was only canned food and a little bit of vegetables. Because this is the sort of tale told by a soldier who himself had come from the countryside, the war situation is rather well-known in the rural areas. Here also is something that will produce uneasiness.

An account of a doctor. He is a recruitment inspector but he was told to take up to 98 percent of those of suitable age. When he looks at them, some are unable to work, and if they remained at home it would serve the purpose of increasing production more or less. If they are recruited, it is inevitable they will become ill, and because of that the expense to the nation will be one thousand yen, and it appears that hospital costs will be in the hundreds of millions. He said that because it is an order, nothing is to be done about it, but he does not understand what he is doing.

I wrote a piece as "Japonicus." Because Foreign Minister Shigemitsu saw it and thought it splendid, he said he wished to have it appear in an English newspaper while special Philippine Ambassador Aquino was in Japan, and so I went to the Foreign Ministry. After that I went to *Tōyō keizai* and Rōyama and Ayuzawa were there.

Following that we opened a general meeting of the International Relations Research Society. It was formally decided that I would be secretary for the society. Fukai Eigo said, "I have no objection." After that Arita Hachirō led a retrospective discussion of his diplomacy. Arita is not brilliant, but he is extremely sincere. And regarding the particulars of the past, he held back absolutely nothing at all.

Premier Tanaka knew absolutely nothing regarding the assassination of Chang Tso-lin. Rather, he was aghast with surprise and hopelessness. The reason for this was his intention to have Chiang Kai-shek rule the China headquarters and Chang Tso-lin rule Manchuria. Ambassador Yoshizawa urged Chang to do this, but Chang returned to Mukden and it was at this time that he was killed in an explosion. Therefore, there were some who thought Tanaka planned it, but it was not true. The head of the second section of the Imperial Headquarters, Matsui Iwane, and the military affairs chief of the Army Ministry, Abe Nobuyuki, did not know. It was the plan of those who were there on the scene.

The Anti-Comintern Pact was carried out by Arita after talks with Mushanokōji. The military carried on negotiations, but they probably negotiated from a different approach. At the very beginning both Japan and Germany had the objective of including England. Ribbentrop was sent to England for this purpose. However, Ribbentrop failed and then became anti-English. At the time of the Hiranuma Cabinet there were deliberations for the purpose of strengthening the Anti-Comintern Pact, but Arita was opposed to making England a party to it.

A Japanese–Soviet Neutrality Pact was proposed in Arita's time, but the

Soviets did not accept. The fact that they did agree to this was because the attitude of Germany was changing rapidly and they felt the necessity of joining hands with Japan (recorded by a stenographer and retained).

April 25 (Tuesday)

Rain is falling. This year's continuous rain should be extremely bad for the crops. I am worried.

I understand that the parts that government censors warn against are only phrases such as "celebration." This is the typical censorship attitude. Quoting two or three words and making a problem out of them is a Japanese habit. In the end they do not have the ability to understand the whole.

Speaking of problems of formalism, the tragedies that have recently occurred at Christian schools are extremely numerous. It is said that the resignation of President Yuasa of Dōshisha University was because he misread an imperial rescript. Also, when President Kimura of Rikkyō University read an imperial rescript, he was standing on the middle level of the platform. Even the recent incident concerning President Sasamori of Aoyama Gakuin was all tangled up with patriotism. I hear that after this the head of the Library Department of Rikkyō University had some sort of connection with the Carnegie Foundation. Being cruelly pressured by the authorities, he committed suicide.

April 26 (Wednesday)

The problem is not the fact that fixed market prices are low. The point is that when one talks about this low price, one is "marked by the authorities." That is to say, it is power politics and economic political policy. In this way there is no reason to expect production to increase.

I went to the Foreign Ministry. The "Japonicus" that I have written has been appearing since yesterday in the *Times*. Nara and others said, "Very good!"

Since I presented my curriculum vitae, I might be able to get part-time work.

Sasaki Mosuke said that yesterday a healthy-looking man came to the house and said, "Give me something to eat!" When he answered, "We have nothing!" the man replied, "Is that so?" and disappeared without incident.

Miyake Seiki said that recently in Shimbashi Station, when he was walking along carrying a huge piece of luggage, somebody said, "I have not eaten anything since this morning—won't you please give me something to eat?" He also told us that "when a canvasser for a cleaners came to a certain house, he asked the maid to sell him one sho of rice for five yen." The maid did not

on different records (thereby representing an assurance of quality to the public), the name may be registered as a trademark. Thus, GOO GOO DOLLS® and BOB DYLAN® have been registered for musical sound recordings.

Domain Names

Domain names, for example, www.ibm.com, are registrable as trademarks or service marks only if they function as an identification of the source of goods and services. Thus, www.oakwood.com has been registered for real estate leasing services. In many cases, however, applications for domain names are refused because the domain name merely describes the goods or services offered under the mark or merely serves as an address where the applicant can be located. Thus, www.eilberg.com was refused registration because the mark merely indicated the location on the Internet where the applicant's web site appeared and it did not separately identify the applicant's legal services.

Another complication with domain name registration is that the PTO has held that businesses that create a web site for the sole purpose of advertising their own products or services cannot register a domain name used to identify that activity. Thus, www.amazon.com is registered for providing online chat rooms and bulletin boards. It is *not* registered in connection with offering books or other goods for sale. Similarly, the law firm Holland & Knight has registered www.hklaw.com in connection with its legal newsletter and *not* in connection with the offering of legal services.

The PTO itself has recognized that Internet domain names raise unique issues, and, thus, cases relating to registration of domain names continue to evolve.

Foreign Terms

Foreign terms are registrable as long as they comply with the requirements of the Lanham Act. Foreign wording will be translated into English and then examined by the PTO for descriptiveness. Thus, the word *vino* would not be allowed for wine inasmuch as its immediate translation is "wine," the very product offered under the mark. Similarly, the word *optique*, a French word meaning "optic," was refused registration for eyeglasses because it was merely descriptive. *In re Optica Int'l,* 196 U.S.P.Q. 775 (T.T.A.B. 1977).

Shapes and Containers

Shapes or configurations can function as trademarks if they are distinctive rather than functional. Thus, the famous Coca-Cola bottle shape is registered with the PTO, and a competitor who adopts a confusingly similar shape container for its product will likely be enjoined from use. The shape is not functional because it is not essential to the use or purpose of the product. If the shape aided or promoted better functioning of a bottle, such as a more efficient lip or handle, it would not be registrable. Thus, a container configuration having the appearance of an ice cream cone was found registrable as a trademark for baby pants because the shape of the container did not promote better functioning of the product.

Trade Dress

The total image of a product, such as size, shape, color, texture, packaging, and graphics, may be protected through a trademark registration. This total image is called **trade dress.** In the famous case *Two Pesos, Inc. v. Taco Cabana, Inc.,* 505 U.S. 763 (1992), the U.S. Supreme Court protected the overall image or trade dress of a Mexican restaurant chain from infringement by a competitor who used similar colors, seating configurations, and décor. When an applicant applies to register a product's design, product packaging, color, or other trade dress for goods or services, the PTO will con-

tell the master and sold it. When the event had been repeated two or three times, as was to be expected, the maid feared it would be discovered and refused. The canvasser made threats to the maid and demanded more rice, saying, "If I tell about it, you too will be arrested." Shortly after this the man was arrested, and the mistress and maid were summoned by the police and reprimanded.

Tsurumi Yūsuke said, "When I was ill I wanted to eat our stored-up white rice but couldn't find it. When I asked the maid, she said, 'Since there wasn't very much rice, the two of us have eaten it up already.'"

Sasaki was evacuated to Itō, but only Sasaki and the maid had identification papers for transfer. When his wife went to Itō, there was too little rice to feed her. When she asked to have a little more rice, the maid answered, "I have only rice for your husband and myself." The same mentality is expressed by the maid at Yamanouchi's house, who, when she left their service, selfishly took sugar from the sugar bowl "because it is my ration."

It appears that because the government gave travel permits to police officers, many of them are using them for unofficial business. One understands how low-salaried police officers are corrupted.

At the meeting this evening, everyone brought rice and charcoal and we ate a turtle dinner. Of late, there is no place that serves cooked rice.

April 27 (Thursday)

Working in the fields. We have planted something in just about every unused bit of land, in every corner.

Hull, in a speech he delivered on the April 9, stated, "In the matter of Japan returning the territories it has stolen and never again attacking its neighbors, it will return Chinese territory to China and give independence to Korea."

Moreover, in a speech by Churchill on March 26, he said, "The ruling class of Japan which activated the surpassing power of America by way of their complete surprise attack are probably some kind of fools." And again he predicted, "From all expectations, the war will conclude quickly within a year." And he made promises on postwar housing. He views the struggle as won and already is getting started on postwar problems.

April 28 (Friday)

I understand the present state of women's clothes is 10 percent *monpe*,[50] about 16 percent national uniform, and about 10 percent slacks. A story from this morning's radio. In the end, half of the women passing through the streets of the Ginza are wearing war clothes. These clothes are strange and jumbled, and in the final analysis it is apparel that says anything will do. They are disorderly and ugly. Here we probably have a manifestation of contemporary Japan.

According to a story of Suzuki Bunshirō, I hear that at a high-class restaurant such as the Toyotaya in Ōsaka and others, signs are hung inscribed "Navy Club." Probably as before they are going to have geishas. The local intelligentsia says that although the navy is popular, such behavior is harmful.

A story of Ishibashi Tanzan. A high-class restaurant was bought by a munitions company—the Nakajima Aircraft Company—and geisha are working it. After all, it is a fact that high-level executives who do not pay taxes monopolize the *monpe* geisha.

Some high-class *machiai* (houses of assignation) in the Shimbashi area have become the lodging houses of laborers—they are called production soldiers, and the words "laborers" and "factory workers" have disappeared—and some have become munitions company "clubs" and again are monopolizing the geisha and the restaurants.

The officials wedge themselves into the structure, and everywhere they go they obtain food. A certain person said that this was the sort of immorality that existed before the Russian Revolution.

Admiral Suetsugu, one of those responsible for the war, still retains the leadership of "societies"—he became the head of the Chūō Dōhōkai (Central Compatriots Society)—and is a cool customer.

I heard that the enemy has invaded Hollandia in New Guinea from both sides. According to the enemy communiqué, the Japanese Army fled and there were only twenty or so prisoners, and great amounts of food were captured. However, this has still not been announced.

Is the reason for this flight of the soldiers based upon "new orders," or, along with that, is it due to independent action on the spot? I previously mentioned that those who reflect upon dying-with-honor and will change it are the military people themselves. It is because they themselves are the greatest victims. I think circumstances such as the present ones will necessarily occur frequently in the future, and from these facts at least one of these feudal points of view, dying-with-honor, will probably be destroyed.

A man named Endō, the editor of the *Karafuto shimpō*, also manages other civil engineering companies and recounted the following tale of his experience. "In the period of about two years I have done just what the military bureaucracy told me to do, and the result is that I have lost 800,000 yen. I cannot follow them anymore!" The special characteristic of bureaucratic control is the complete disregard of individual profit. The result is the present deadlock.

Of late, to collect the deposit rent for a house we lease, we must travel to the court for three days, have notaries fill out seven or eight pages of applications, and then at last we get only about two hundred yen. Even to register takes at least two or three days. This is evidence of bureaucratic formalism.

188 • *APRIL 1944*

April 29 (Saturday)

If one relies upon a study of the Shanghai Chamber of Commerce and Industry on commodity prices in Shanghai—the cost of living for November of last year for the single person was 2,161 yuan, 9 chueh, and for a family of three it was 3,954 yuan—the yen and yuan are on a par. Because commodity prices have risen in January and February of this year, the cost of living for a single person is 2,800 yen. For a three-person family it is about 5,000 yen. As for income, officials receive five or six times their basic salary—for example, 200 yen means 1,000 yen. Two hundred yen signifies high-income people. How can one make sense of these figures?

Domestically, there is the same tendency in the inflation of commodity prices. No one is selling sugar at 150 yen per kamme. According to the account of Nanao of the Radio Equipment Manufacturing Company, construction costs in munitions factories are 1,000 yen per tsubo. Naturally, in the factories it is openly being said to the army superintendents that there is nothing that which is not from the "black market." However, at present, those who use this black market are spoken of as hustlers if they produce good results.

In other words, the "black market" is not a black market anymore. The regulations and meddling that exceeded economic principles did not move standards in the direction of an "official fixed level," and the "black market" became general. The crime is ceasing to be a crime.

They say that gasoline is about forty yen a gallon. Everything has become about twenty or thirty times its value. Moreover, the rise in rate is extremely fast.

In dictatorships, "opposition" receives the death penalty. The way in which Ciano was killed is one example of this. On top of this, Mussolini and Ciano were related as son-in-law and father-in-law.

April 30 (Sunday)

When Japan began this fatal great war, there was probably some number of people who knew this, led the way, thought about it, and engaged in negotiations about it. They probably did not exceed several tens or so. We understand how dangerous such things as secretiveness, bureaucratism, and the principles of the leaders were.

In the organization that must come in the future, freedom of speech absolutely must be maintained. The exclusion of interference with all official elections must be clearly established in principle. The improvement of politics probably cannot be hoped for if the officials do not shoulder their responsibilities to the people.

In the *Japan Times* there was an accusation from the London *Economist* whose theme was that without considering the people, Churchill took on the responsibility of carrying out the Atlantic Charter, a treaty with the Soviet Union, and other things, and because the execution of the treaty in the end depended upon the cooperation of the people, not having considered them, it was insupportable. In the future, the weak point will probably be expressed as the point when the war was begun without obtaining the unmistakable support of the people. However, the people actually desired the war.

The special feature of these times is the demonic strength of spiritism. Everyone knew the material strength of America. However, it was thought that America, with its "liberalism" and "individualism," would have to collapse immediately and that Japan, on the contrary, because it had the Japanese spirit, would be able to obtain miracles that could not be expressed in mere numbers. This is the great motivator of the war.

May 1 (Monday)

I went to a directors meeting at *Tōkei*. Because the appendix materials were to be handed over to the printer, first of all, I scanned them again and made the last changes. Itō is putting it in order. He is suitable for this.

Rōyama also attended the meeting. Ishibashi said that because draft labor is being recklessly used in great numbers, in every factory people are excessively idle. He insisted at the Finance Ministry upon the complete discontinuance of draft labor in half a year from now, and the officials of the Finance Ministry supported this.

In the evening there was a directors' meeting of the People's Scholarly Arts Society. This society includes the highest scholars of our nation. However, no matter whom I ask, they say "scholarship" truly appears to be worthless. The people who assembled this evening were Kuwaki Genyoku, Hozumi Shigeto, Makino Eichi, Takahashi Seiichirō, Hasegawa Nyozekan, Masamune Hakuchō, myself, and others. The fact that from ancient times war did not respect culture is true, but that both Napoleon and the Kaiser paid considerable respect to it is also true. The leaders of Japan are completely without understanding of the value of "scholarship." From a combination of uneducated leaders and bureaucrats who only see a part, what can be born?

A story from the meeting. In the neighborhood of Nerima seedling potatoes are quickly stolen. It is said that, of late, after the theft an envelope containing two yen is left behind. Also, at the home of a certain farmer, two youths riding bicycles came by and said that because they had an acquaintance who was ill, he should sell them potatoes. When he brought out seven or eight kamme he was asked to provide still more. When he put a ladder down into the basement storeroom to get them, the youths took up the ladder from above and fled. When the family returned from the fields, the father was not there. They said that when they caught the sound of a voice, they discovered he was in the basement room.

The second front in Europe—it is being transmitted that there is pressure for an invasion of the continent, and the news from Europe is full of this.

May 2 (Tuesday)

I am writing on the problems of the second front for *Tōkei*. Aoki Mansuke of the Miura Peninsula came to call. He is a land manager. He says that recently in that area, houses and villas are not being built. I hear the increase in the value of land is relatively small.

I am working in the fields. I planted green beans. Of the five-hundred tsubo of land, the three hundred tsubo I am working is already filled with vegetables. The soybeans and green beans are sprouting. We put additional fertilizer on the potatoes and are cultivating around them. Producing things is pleasant. I did not think that "earth" would be so appealing. With three or four chobu,[51] I think if it were possible to cultivate in fine weather and read when it rained, such a life would certainly be desirable—if only I live long enough. Of late, I am thinking about the limits of my life. I have anxious thoughts, which say, "finish your work quickly!"

May 4 (Thursday)

I worked in the fields. This year I failed to cultivate the corn in its earlier stage of development. The seed was bought at a shop in Oimachi, and it was all bad. It is important for seed shops to be trusted by their customers.

May 5 (Friday)

I went to the Foreign Ministry and requested lists of ambassadors and ministers that should be put into the *Chronology*. Afterward I listened to a speech at the Economic Club. It was by a Colonel Odajima Kaoru, the prisoner-of-war inspector, and I had already heard him previously at the Japan Club.

He said the Philippine people should be held in contempt. They take on only the bad features of the Americans. On a certain train, Filipinos, Americans, and our army were divided into three sections. When it stopped at a certain station, the Philippine vendors threw all of their wares into the American section of prisoners. Moreover, the women noisily welcomed the Americans, and they paid no attention to the Filipinos. Again, in a certain town three Americans had been taken in, and Filipino women went there to live with them. When they were asked why after having been arrested, it is said they answered, "When one has the child of an American, the child of a god is born."

Both in the Philippines and in China, there is no limit to the welcome extended to the Americans. In direct proportion to this, there is no limit to the hatred of the Japanese. It should be reflected upon.

A story of Colonel Odajima. In the Philippines a lt. colonel named Daisu escaped. He returned to America and spread stories of the cruelty of the Japanese Army. This created an enormous reaction in America. Because of this it was possible to sell war bonds successfully. The prisoners of war work extremely well. They are extremely well-organized. They are not fussy about the kind of work. Of late, a prisoner-of-war camp building in Niigata collapsed and something like ten people died. Because of the inadequacy of nutrition, the rate of prisoners' deaths is 10 percent.

Colonel Odajima's manner of talk is typically about "The Deficiencies of the Japanese." Though he is a military man, he has the opportunity to be in contact with foreigners, and this is the difference. In short, he concludes that Americans and English are superior to Japanese. This is a rare case.

Not only in Japan are they advocating the use of "bamboo spears," but also in Burma. Spies and bamboo spears are Japanese-style (*Mainichi*, May 6).

Students—they are called *gakuto*—are being hunted down for labor. University students are transporting earth in civil engineering projects and are loading and unloading commodities. This general plan was decided upon by cabinet discussion, and the basic rule is, more than six hours a week in academic study in addition to ten hours of labor daily. The personnel chief of the Foreign Ministry said that the results of the civil service exams were extremely poor. The special characteristic of wartime Japan as usual is not to think about either scholarship or the future.

May 7 (Sunday)

I came to Karuizawa. The train was unexpectedly uncrowded. Now, after a number of years, it was very relaxed. Speaking of trains, recently even those trains that run along the Tōkaidō are deserted. So there are officials who are proud of this. This is representative of the thought patterns of officials, and these officials do not notice that this is harmful to the so-called increase-and-strengthen-war-power slogan.

If the politicians do not think in terms of "politics in the interests of the people," administration will be bad. However, this is extremely difficult for the feudalistic Japanese. One must trace the source of this back to contemporary institutions and education.

Why did the meritorious retainers of Meiji Europeanize? As samurai, were they not the forerunners of the expel-the-barbarian advocates? Someone like Inoue Kaoru in the Rokumeikan period was the embodiment of such people. The meritorious retainers of Meiji differed from the leaders of the Greater

East Asian War and were flexible in their manner of thinking. To make Japan great, they followed the highest ideals.

Day before yesterday there was the report of the death of Admiral Koga Mineichi. I felt deep emotion because I had met him once. I had not the slightest objection to him, but why he was promoted to admiral of the fleet without having the merit of "victory"? This is true of everyone. Promotion in the military is carried out with respect to "seniority," "loyalty," or "death."

May 8 (Monday)

I dug in the garden and planted pumpkins and other things. In light of the fact that straw mats and ropes in storage huts are stolen, I hope my farmer neighbors will not steal my farm goods.

May 9 (Tuesday)

I finished reading the *Hodaka Plateau* by Sōma Kokkō. You can see how fascinating the contents are by my having stayed up until midnight. Thanks to it, I know the facts of my own countryside.

May 10 (Wednesday)

Both the newspapers and radio are talking about the recent unpleasantness and unkindness of human nature. All things Western have been banished, and romanization has been changed to Chinese characters, so is there any reason not to expect that the roots of evil are completely eliminated? And yet why are there so many undesirable things in the country.

In the evening I invited Rōyama and his wife to supper. I bought a chicken and made sukiyaki. It has been a long while since I had chicken sukiyaki. No matter when, no matter where, conversation is always nothing but the subject of food shortages. It is also because this is a fine topic for discussion including women. It is said that at the home of Ide, four agricultural workers from Gumma Province said they would do any work if they were promised to return home with one go[52] of rice. It is said that workers in Gumma Province are paid only one go of rice per day.

Tōkyō City is handling its own rationing. For this facilities are necessary. Sometimes it must engage in business. Thus, the socialist tendency more and more comes to thrive. Moreover, officials were a race who previously did not think about production. They think that things are produced by themselves just like the welling up of a spring. Accordingly, the only thing they think about concerning goods is their price. And it is natural that this produces a shortage of things.

May 11 (Thursday)

Rōyama came by to tell me he is returning home. We discussed the previously talked about Food Supply Problems Research Society and decided to ask Mitsui.

To study the facts of the new world order, first of all I read "Various Problems of the East Asia Co-prosperity Sphere" from Chūō Kōronsha. I read the pieces of both Rōyama and Tōhata as well as the piece by Hosokawa Karoku. Notwithstanding the fact that Rōyama has an extremely keen mind, his writing is dull. The things he writes are flat. The piece of Hosokawa is interesting, but it only indicates the problems.

The Japanese are completely incapable of governing other people. As to whether there is anything that can be learned from the present war, probably we Japanese will not be wise and will say we are preparing for the future and continue to nurture revenge.

I hear that because Hosokawa Karoku is considered a Marxist, he has been interned in a Yokohama detention center. It has been six months since some people of *Chūō kōron* who have no relation to Marxism have been imprisoned.

May 12 (Friday)

I stayed home for a day reading Carr's *Conditions for Peace*. I received it from the Foreign Ministry. The works of Englishmen are easy to read—even more than works in Japanese.

May 13 (Saturday)

Last year I bought a hoe at the Yaofuku store and they said they do not remember it. The shortage of commodities makes the merchants tell such lies. They charge many times the usual price and demand gratitude.

I received strawberry and rhubarb seedlings from Ide's place and planted them.

May 14 (Sunday)

According to the account of Tsuyuko, of late, many children who are born are extremely deformed. It is said that the child of a certain person had stomach and abdomen in reverse positions. My wife said that the father of the bride of Uehara is a famous pediatrician, and according to his story there are numerous children who do not suckle at the breast. That is to say, they do not have the strength to breastfeed. In Germany during the First World War there was the same experience. In Japan, with so much undernourishment, I have wondered why this condition has not occurred more.

Tōjō firmly decided upon war and exhibited dictatorial power, and in history until now only Mussolini and Hitler both exercised such great power. I wonder where his power was obtained?

The bureaucracy is oblivious of production. This is the more acute in a country like Japan in which the family does not have the custom of producing things. This bureaucracy cannot make production flourish. What is achieved now is because there is no competition with foreign countries. Herein, after the war there is nothing else but two prospects: (1) Will the bureaucracy become production oriented? (2) Will there be a restoration of competition?

Japan will probably take the latter path.

In the study of international relations there is the need for the most widely coordinated knowledge. Religion, ideas, politics, and economics, of course, are indispensable to the judgments of conditions. It is to be expected that these judgments are inept because in our country they are made by the most ignorant military people.

A story of Tsuyuko. Mitsui Takai is managing a boys' middle school and a girls' school. There were more teachers than students, and extreme sacrifices were necessary. There was intense pressure from the military toward such schools. The military used a man who had worked at Mitsui for years to say that they were all spies and to circulate rumors. It is said the military wished to seize the fine building that was being used as a school. They said it was because the villa of an imperial prince that was next door had already been turned over for use and the building could not be used as a school.

Sumo wrestling has already begun at the Kokugikan (National Sports Hall), but the military is also using the building. It is a well-known fact that because they wished to use the building, they abolished the Bunka gakuen.

In the area of Chigataki, twelve or thirteen villas were vandalized. In order to capture the thieves, volunteer guards have been sent out. I hear they have not yet been captured.

May 15 (Monday)

A man named Gyoda has a villa in Chigataki. This morning when his wife went to their villa she discovered that the kitchen was smashed up and thieves had broken in. Inside, everything had been scattered around; shirts and bedding and the main household items had been cut up so as to make them useless. The bedding was spread about, and such things as canned food had been opened and eaten. Judging from the fact that nothing was missing and things such as books had been pulled out, read, and scattered about, it is quite clear that they were not ordinary thieves. They were the so-called intellectual thieves, and this was the behavior of reaction against the bourgeoisie. Gyoda is the guest of Ide, and this is an actual account of Ide's daughter.

A story of Tsuyuko. Also, the Hakone villa of one of her friends was broken into, and clothes were cut up in the same way. In one room the thief was still there. "Forgive me," he said and hid his face. When he was forcibly made to show his face, he turned out to be a youth of nineteen. The master of the house felt sorry for him and had him stay over that evening and even take a bath. When the master tried questioning him, the boy said he was a draft laborer, but with the wages he received he could not eat. He was not turned over to the police, and now he is employed in a factory that is managed by the master of the house. A story of about a month ago.

There is a reaction against the bourgeoisie. The worsening of the war and the shortage of food supplies. Because of such conditions, the fact that an explosive upheaval is coming just one step ahead can be seen on all sides.

There was a bridal procession for the imperial prince, Mikasa. A very large amount of furniture for the bride was transported. I heard the story that the chauffeur expressed his annoyance, saying, "And we are not even able to eat!"

There is an overflowing of feudalistic, destructive dissatisfaction.

A woman named Hitotsuyanagi is the wife of an American named Voorhees. She is in charge of Mitsui's school in Karuizawa. When she was teaching in Tōkyō, she said, "The child of an upper-class person does not do this sort of thing." I understand that in the children's families this also invites ill-feeling. In England it is not in the least unusual to hear, "The children of aristocracy do not do this sort of thing." Moreover, it is common to hear, "The children of samurai do not do this sort of thing." However, in present-day Japan, saying this sort of thing would be strange and would inflame resentment. I feel fearful for the future of this country and its people.

May 16 (Tuesday)

Throughout the morning I worked in the fields. Ide came at 5:30 this morning to help. We planted potatoes and cabbages. We were tired out.

Tsuyuko sent me off on the 3:30 afternoon train and I returned to Tōkyō. When we had passed through Usui ten days ago there were still withered trees, but now it is all greenery. The vitality of the forests on the plateaus is quickly restored.

May 17 (Wednesday)

I went to the Foreign Ministry. Takayanagi Kenzō told me that I have been included on the military police blacklist because I have leaked secret information to the outside. I do not know any secret information whatever, but in my lectures at meetings I spoke of things appearing in an English paper, and the crowd that knows nothing thinks it to be "secret" and probably reported it this way. However, hereafter I intend to be more careful.

It is said that two part-time employees of the Foreign Ministry were arrested during the past two months. It is said that regarding one of these

sider whether the trade dress is functional or distinctive. Only nonfunctional trade dress can be protected. Because trade dress is often protected through the law of unfair competition, it is discussed more fully in Chapter 23.

Color

Until relatively recently, a single color was not protectable as a trademark. This general rule was based on the color depletion theory: there are only a limited number of colors in the world; if businesses could appropriate a color and exclude others from using it, competition would be impaired. The present rule is that a trademark may consist of color as long as the color is not functional and the color is shown to have acquired distinctiveness either through long use or a high level of consumer recognition. Thus, Owens-Corning was allowed a registration to protect the pink color of its insulation. *In re Owens-Corning Fiberglas Corp.,* 774 F.2d 1116 (Fed. Cir. 1985). Pink has no functional or utilitarian purpose when applied to the goods and does not deprive competitors from using other colors. Similarly, in 1995, Qualitex Company was allowed to protect its green-gold ironing board pads on the basis that there was no competitive need in the industry for the green-gold color, inasmuch as numerous other colors are equally usable for similar goods. *Qualitex Co. v. Jacobson Products Co.,* 514 U.S. 159 (1995). Similarly, the colors yellow and green used by John Deere & Co. on its machines were held registrable because the colors had become distinctive of John Deere's machines and equipment. However, the color pink for surgical wound dressings was held not registrable because the color of the goods closely resembled Caucasian human skin and was thus functional. Likewise, the makers of the pink PEPTO-BISMOL® stomach medicine were unable to protect its pink color. The court held that the color pink was functional when

used in connection with the medicine because the pink color had a pleasing appearance to one with an upset stomach. *Norwich Pharmacal Co. v. Sterling Drug, Inc.,* 271 F.2d 569 (2d Cir. 1959). In sum, protecting color is still a complex and evolving legal field.

Fragrances, Sounds, and Moving Images

A fragrance can function as a trademark if it is distinctive and not functional. For example, in *In re Clarke,* 17 U.S.P.Q.2d 1238 (T.T.A.B. 1990), a floral fragrance was allowed as a trademark for sewing thread and embroidery yarn and was not functional when used in connection with those goods. A fragrance used in connection with products known for such features, such as perfumes or air fresheners, however, would likely be held functional and not registrable. Similarly, sounds can function as trademarks. The famous three-note chime used by NBC was the first registered sound trademark. The roar of the MGM lion and Woody Woodpecker's distinctive laugh are also registered. Finally, the Internet has given rise to applications for marks that consist of moving images, such as Microsoft Company's spinning EXPLORER globe.

Designs and Ornamentation

A design can function as a trademark as long as it is distinctive rather than merely functional or ornamental. Some designs are protected on their own, such as Nike's famous "swoosh" design, the alligator that appears on shirts, and Betty Crocker's spoon. If the design is merely background material, however, and does not create a separate commercial impression, or if it consists solely of some simple geometric shape, such as an oval or square, it cannot be protected without proof of secondary meaning. For example, the PTO refused registration of two parallel colored bands placed at the top of socks as pure

people it was reported to the military police that he had talked to a middle-school child at his home, and that child talked to a friend who was the daughter of a naval officer, and that child talked to her own family. It concerned the war conditions in the Pacific.

From three o'clock in the afternoon a meeting of the International Relations Research Society was held. There was a talk by Yamada Yoshitarō, chief of the Foreign Ministry Investigation Office.

"The Soviet Union carries on realistic politics to the point of being detestable. It seems to view its neighbors in terms of first and second power zones. The Soviet does not oppose England's plan to control Belgium, Holland, and others, but if there were to be an Anglo-American occupation army in Norway, the Soviet would also insist upon an occupation army. Moreover, as regards Algeria and the problems of the Mediterranean, the Soviet reserves the right of discussion."

According to a tale of Mitsui Takai, when his wife was cooking something in the kitchen, in a flash a pan they bought in England was stolen with the vegetables still in it. I heard that Western clothes were also carried off.

Mitsui told me that the military rudely asked for the loan, at no cost, of a villa that was being used as a school. Already half of it was taken, but they requested the remaining half. But the family still stubbornly occupies it, though official departments keep demanding the space. If they had conducted this fairly and directly it would have been fine, but they merely intended to take it with intrigues and fault-finding.

In Nagano Province since it is the "fashionable thing to do," the authorities are investigating various possibilities. Such things as collective farming are one example of this. If the guidance were competent, new techniques would probably be developed. However, the problem will be decided upon, whether the results increase production or not.

May 18 (Thursday)

Ide said that in the countryside the wages for a day's work are five yen. If one hires people for six days, this is equivalent to a bale of rice. One cannot do anything with such a situation, and he said there is no outstanding personality in the government. Because such things as government policy concerning rice are directly related to the farmers, the farmers are able to criticize the policy of the government.

After a long while now, again I am working in my fields in Tōkyō. The potatoes are growing, and already they have small tubers. If I could have learned three or four years ago of my taste for being a farmer, I would have bought twenty or thirty thousand tsubo somewhere, settled down as a farmer, and cultivated in fine weather and read when it rained. If I had done so, I would not at present have the feeling of being unsettled. Despite the fact that there are no worries confronting us, uneasiness is the prevailing lifestyle of people.

I hear that youth crime has increased enormously. It is said that up until April of this year it is the equivalent of last year's crimes, and the crimes of last year were about double those of the year before last (an investigation of the Nagoya police).

I went to *Tōyō keizai*. I heard talk of an Indian specialist named Kimura Nikki. I heard he is a Buddhist priest, but he is conceited, narrow-minded, and dull. Because the Japanese share his level of "world knowledge," they cannot become great. He cried out, "Why did we not achieve rapport with India?" This crowd does not understand what role the Anglo–Japanese alliance served at that time (the Katō Foreign Ministry period).

May 20 (Saturday)

From three in the afternoon I attended a meeting of the directors of the Economic Club's Central Branch. This group is a special workforce of *Tōyō keizai*, but previously the names of the directors were submitted to the Information Board. At that time the candidates for such a group, whether large or small, were discussed by the Information Board—that is to say, the military. However, I understand that about that time a major named Suzuki seized dictatorial power, and my name was withdrawn from the list. About that time this Suzuki was the dictator of the intellectual world, and in publishing there was not a single thing that did not depend upon the approval of this man, and it is said that Kodansha published the work of this same person and he was awarded enormous royalties.

The Greater East Asian War was inevitable when the administration and politics were handed over to the young crowd. The current of *gekokujō* had to lead the nation into dangerous ventures. This has been so since the Manchurian Incident. If politics and diplomacy pass through the proper channels, even the dull-witted will be prudent.

At the Central Branch of the Economic Club there was a talk by Wakimura Yoshitarō (formerly an Imperial University professor). Regarding the problem of oil, there is no researcher who has the authority of this man. He has meticulously conducted research into the world situation exclusive of Japan. He explained, using statistics, that 95 percent of the world's oil production is on the side of the anti-Axis countries.

May 21 (Sunday)

I worked in the fields in the afternoon. During the morning I wrote a manuscript for the *Continental Asian Economy*. The strawberries are ready to eat.

The Police Department has been issuing air-raid warnings since yesterday. Even today the warnings are still in effect. Yesterday evening I returned home and packed food supplies and other things in a rucksack. This is for the purpose of flight when the need arose.

The propaganda directed against the "American Devils" is thriving, but somehow in general no anti-enemy hatred has emerged. However, it is possible that this exists only among the intellectual class. A somewhat dated article in the *Mainichi shinbun* (*Mainichi*, February 19).

According to a story of Akira, the minister of education, Okabe, went to the Jiyū Gakuen and said, "The Japanese carry on the bad politics of good intentions," and the English "carry on the bad politics of good intentions." [Note: "Good" in the second quote probably is bad, and good should be reversed.] This is the same as saying peace and public order in China and the Philippines would be extremely bad. It is the same as acknowledging excessive interference. I wonder in the imperial-war-spirit of the education minister, what is the "bad politics of good intentions"?

May 22 (Monday)

At the invitation of Segawa, I went to a restaurant in Ueno Park called "Meigetsu." There was also a "young lord" of a wealthy person in Toyama Province named Takahiro, and with his connections we had a lavish meal.

This man operates a factory connected with airplanes, but the young military men interfere with him and nothing at all can be accomplished. He said because of this it is impossible to increase production.

This evening we had invited the managing director of the *Mitsui hōkai* together with Ishibashi, Rōyama, and Mitsui, and we held a meeting to establish a Food Supply Research Society. But I was unable to attend because of the aforementioned gathering.

I stood on the street at the Meigetsu waiting for a friend. In front of me there was a shrine to the God of Wealth, and students who passed along here one by one politely bowed their heads. Without exception they all bowed, and moreover it was never done just formally. As it occurred regularly, I could imagine the thoroughness of their education. However, what were these young people bowing their heads to? If they see either the God of Harvest or the God of Wealth, a *torii* or shrine, they bow their heads. This also is an expression of formalism.

I forgot my cigar case at a restaurant called the "Maruya." When I telephoned they said it was there. However, today when I went there they said they did not have it. Little by little, the things I bought in foreign countries are being lost. Because they are rare items, if someone picks them up they are not returned.

May 23 (Tuesday)

Uehara Akiko came to call. We talked tête-à-tête. She tried to confer with Professor Nitobe, but a meeting did not take place. She wondered if she should go to Professor Hozumi's place, but it was inconvenient and she came to me. I feel extremely sympathetic toward Uehara's situation.

On the morning of May 27 I set out on a lecture tour for the Kyūshū area Economic Club. I returned to Tōkyō on the evening of June 11.

Diary Supplement

The following is a composition of ten pages on manuscript paper that contains 200 spaces per page with the name "Kiyosawa Kiyoshi," written during his trip for the five-day period from May 26, 1944, to May 30, 1944.

May 26 (Friday)

From the day before, Minagawa Eiji of Hong Kong came to visit. He told me about conditions in Hong Kong. The government has expended five million dollars on war dead memorials and ten million dollars on Hong Kong shrines and is flaunting its support, but these projects have not been completed. Shrines and war dead memorials are two standard practices.

In the evening Usui Yae came to call. She said that if we are defeated in war it will be a disastrous thing. She meant that because the Japanese behave barbarically in China, then if the Chinese and Koreans came to Japan, we don't know what they will do to us. It appears she truly believes this.

May 27 (Saturday)

I still feel bad. But if I do not go today, I will not be on time for my lecture at Shimonoseki. Eiji and Eiko came to see me off and I left. At Tōkyō Station Hagiwara Kasahara came along carrying a sandwich for me. The train was not excessively chaotic.

Aoki Tokuzō is here. He told me that in the newspaper this morning it was related that Professor Watanabe Tetsuzō received a sentence of one year of penal servitude (a three-year postponement of enforcement). There were two aspects to the crime, and one was the fact that he said, "Even in the announcements of the Imperial Headquarters there are mistakes, and they speak of the ruin of the enemy but publish little or nothing of the injury inflicted on them." The second was that he said Germany will be defeated. We understand that in regard to the former it corresponds to some article of the Naval Criminal Code, and as to the latter it is probably a violation of the speech law of last year. I hear that if his lawyer, Iwata Chūzō, even made an appeal, he would not win. If there were acquittal, there would be people who would say the same things he did, and this is because control is the rule of the government.

Outside the train the wheat was ripening. Here and there, groups of young men were practicing bayonet drill and charges.

In Ōsaka, Yamamoto Kiyoshi came to welcome me. We went to the New Ōsaka Hotel by electric train. The room had not been cleaned, there was no hot water, and this in the foremost hotel in Ōsaka? Except when checking in or checking out, bellboys and maids were nowhere to be seen.

May 28 (Sunday)

My stomach still has not recovered. I am still a little dizzy. At the hotel office they said, "You will never make your train!" There was a rickshaw available and I galloped away to the station. I stood in line for an hour; otherwise it was impossible to obtain a seat. The stringent controls have been effective, and it appears that the train will not be overcrowded. Since leaving Tōkyō there was not a single person standing.

When we approached Shimonoseki there was a traveling policeman who requested my name card. Among the great number of passengers, why did I stand out from the others? Probably it was because the title of the book of Miura Tetsutarō, *History of the World Crisis*, which I was reading did not have *furigana*[53] attached to it. When I produced a name card without my social status—I had nothing else at all—he said, "Don't you have proof of your position?" I showed him my itinerary plan. Previously, also at the time I was returning from Korea, I rode with a police detective and talked with him. He said, "This is the first time I have had this sort of fine conversation!" and then we separated.

At 8:15 in the evening I reached Shimonoseki as I had planned. I was surprised at how much better the Sanyō Hotel was than the New Ōsaka Hotel. It was a place noted for its bad service in the past, but this time there was bathroom paper, towels, and, even more, bath facilities. Because it is managed by the Railway Ministry, it has not been taken over and it receives special treatment.

May 29 (Monday)

Food supplies are still more abundant here than in Tōkyō. There is a place that serves its customers sweet *mitsumame*.[54] But this restaurant is always filled with customers. I was invited to a luncheon by Makino. A sea urchin shop and close to half of the others have closed down.

The Koreans here are extremely numerous. It is said that a certain man came back from the peninsula and stopped over at the Sanyō Hotel and said, "Is this Korea too?" It certainly has that sort of atmosphere. The trains are full of the Korean language. In the future, they will be the greatest social problem.

The government makes Koreans change their names to Japanese names and by doing so allows them to gain the trust of the Japanese. One can hardly bear to speak of the foolishness of the politics of the governor-generalship. If freedom of speech existed, this sort of low-level thing would probably not occur.

From 4:30 in the afternoon I gave a lecture. In the beginning I made an explanatory statement to the effect, "My materials are based on English papers." And I was really cautious. I could not express my real thoughts. My stomach was still bothering me and my performance was not good, but it appears the audience was satisfied.

May 30 (Tuesday)

In the morning I walked a little around town. Places such as food shops were closed. In all areas in the town one feels keenly the possibility of engulfing fires from falling bombs.

In front of the hotel, people were training for air raids. The police were giving orders one after the other, and I could see from my room naive young women thrusting with rifle butts. Shouting at people is the duty of the police. I wonder how useful this training will be when something actually happens. If there were no orders from the police—that condition will emerge with the air raids—I wonder what would probably happen. Going to the station and showing my ticket when I entered the platform, a young man of disheveled appearance said to me, "I am a policeman, so give me your name card." When I said, "I might be in trouble if there is any mistake, so give me your name card." He said, "If you feel so suspicious, please come along with me." He escorted me to the Detective Waiting Room. They asked me, what is your social position? What is your purpose? I told them, "Yesterday evening even the head of your police department came to listen to my lecture." With these words they became a little bit more courteous. Because it was coming to be the departure time of the train, I began to fret. If there was a quarrel and I were late in boarding the train, my plans would be upset. It is nothing new for the police to behave as if nobody was there. I got off at Hakata. Kishimoto had gone to Korea and was not available. I lunched at the Hakata Hotel. I ate things that could not be found in Tōkyō. I occupied a splendid room in the hotel. They said it had been kindly arranged by Kishimoto. From four in the afternoon I lectured, and because an army colonel was in the audience it was difficult to speak. It was partly based on innocuous fact.

I had supper in the company of a man named Amemiya. The restaurant was like the other places that had become munitions factory clubs. It was an extraordinary feast.

Returning from the trip, I did not take the diary notebook with me. One of the reasons was my baggage, but more than this it was because making an unfortunate slip of the tongue anywhere, I was afraid this diary notebook might be seized and examined. Our lives are under constant threat.

On June 11, after eight in the evening, just as I planned, I returned to Yokohama. My wife and the maid Natsu were at the station. When we returned home the fields were covered with grass. I was busy with field and other work, and after a week had passed, I wrote my impressions of the trip.

1. In Kyūshū, particularly southern Kyūshū, food supplies are abundant. The abundance of Hokkaidō is the remnants of stored goods, but Kyūshū is a productive area. I hear that near the sea coast all the fish cannot be eaten, and even bream are difficult to dispose of. One feels all the more the imperative need for transportation facilities.

2. When I looked out from the train, the people working in the fields were only women and children. Occasionally, when I saw a man it was really an old man. Military conscripts and draft laborers are very numerous, this practice still continues.

3. In Nagasaki there were no geishas, but there are a great many prostitutes and low-class geishas. If such people did not live here, the "production warriors" would not settle down here. The old Maruyamachō district is full of these houses. The houses of Chinese, splendid private villas, all are becoming the dormitories of the production warriors. There were great numbers of them.

4. When I went to Sasebo there were people called "security police" at the station. Here there is no power of the army and the navy commands. Places such as restaurants pay no taxes. I hear that when the tax office complains there is the counterattack, "Will you let the navy die without helping?" This is the talk here, and reports that in the navy the thrashing of young recruits is widespread. It is particularly extreme toward student conscripts. I hear that they thrash them with clubs and a great many suffer broken hip-bones. While I walked around the town I was surprised at the great number of traditional kimono stores and big stores that were closed down. I thought about it. If there was somebody who incited the people, it would probably ignite the fire of civil strife.

5. The second-class seats on the trains have become thread-bare and show their insides. This made me think that Japan is finally coming to the last stage in material goods.

6. In the inns there are no keys or doorknobs. Later, when I thought about it, everything made of metal has been turned over to the government. Because the people in the countryside are honest, in the future probably nothing at all will remain.

7. A tale of a director of the Kagoshima Chamber of Commerce and Industry. Recently he went to Kumamoto and some farmers noisily crowded into the second-class car. They were holding third-class tickets and looking askance at the second-class passengers. They said, "We are eating white rice every day! We have vegetables and everything else! Look at the people in the towns!" This is the resistance of the farmers.

8. Maps of both Japan and Kyūshū do not exist anywhere. Available maps are only those of Burma and the Dutch Indies.

9. Kagoshima is filled with Saigo worship, and it is filled with his photographs. Okubo is considered bad. The director of the Economic Club said,

"Today, because the intellectual class is large it is acceptable to praise Ōkubo." Based on this kind of comment I can presume many things.

As in the countries that honor Hitler and Stalin, in Satsuma Saigō is universally praised.

If it were proper for heroes not to be accepted in their native place, Great Saigō would not be a hero.

10. From Kagoshima I went to Ibusuki. It is a place where Arima Junsei lives. This area is abundant in material goods.

> Traveling south ten miles from Kagoshima, the blue sea, one does not see beautiful maidens.
> And I count the shapes of female faces as this one is Malay and that one is Indonesian.
> Where did the Satsuma people come from?
> The men are dark-skinned and the tone of language resembles Chinese.

11. A story from Miyazaki Province. It is said that the transfer of military divisions or the military establishment to their locale was a policy of the towns to enrich themselves, but of late when the army comes to a place they gobble up large quantities of commodities. The towns hope insofar as possible they do not come at all.

12. In the area of Sasebo the publication of population figures is "secret." One should understand from this how stupid secretiveness has become. The present leadership cannot understand the reality that publication provides progress.

13. In Miyazaki Province they ask in all seriousness, "Is what the central government doing all right?" Tōjō and the government have been deserted by the leadership class of the regions. From their point of view the government is too jittery.

14. I felt again this time that Matsue is a splendid place because of the character of its people and its local attractions. At the Izumo Shrine Station I wanted to fill my water canteen, and someone saying he would do it leaped from the train. There is no other place like this.

15. When I went to the New Ōsaka Hotel I truly felt for the first time these are "war times." The fine inns were the Kaibikan at Matsue, the Iwasakitani sō at Kagoshima, the Togiya shiten at Kumamoto, the Sanyō Hotel at Shimonoseki, and the Aburaya at Sasebo. One that disappointed me was the Uenoya at Nagasaki.

16. The feudalistic phenomenon known as the maldistribution of material goods is a phenomenon that commands attention in every region.

June 14 (Wednesday)

When I went to the Foreign Ministry, Takayanagi had received an honorarium of one thousand yen. He said he received this from Foreign Minister

Shigemitsu out of a slush fund. I went to a meeting of the International Relations Research Society. There was a speech by Takahashi Kamekichi. It was a consideration of the Greater East Asian Co-Prosperity Sphere, but it was full of contradictions. This whole idea, after all, is worthless.

June 15 (Thursday)

Recently, after a lecture at Kokura, a member of the audience stated that America would massacre all the Japanese, and he said my conclusions were lukewarm. It is unclear whether he really believed this sort of thing.

June 16 (Friday)

On the radio this morning I learned that twenty American planes attacked the northern Kyūshū area. At the same time it is reported that the enemy is planning an invasion of Saipan Island.

There was a board of directors meeting of Fuji Ice. The pastures of Chiba have been completely confiscated. It is said that the estimated price was 380,000 yen. Meiji Confectionery became the center of the operation, and it was hurrah for big capital. A central personality in the operation, the governor of the area, is connected with the Meiji Confectionery. It is the strategy of the capitalists and the officials.

June 17 (Saturday)

It was merely reported that there were air raids in "northern Kyūshū," but where they came to is not clear. However, it appears to be the case that there was only a little damage at Yawata.

With this secretiveness at the moment of danger, false rumors probably fly about wildly.

As usual with the newspapers, there is a talk by the "Venerable Tōyama Mitsuru" (*Yomiuri*, June 17; *Yomiuri hōchi*, June 17; *Mainichi*, June 17).

June 18 (Sunday)

Judging from the current feelings of the Japanese, in the event that American soldiers descend upon Japan by parachute, they will probably not be taken prisoner. This is reflected in contributors' letters to the *Mainichi shinbun*. These were questions from air-raid wardens (*Mainichi*, June 18).

In the evening I invited Hayashi, an officer from the Home Ministry's security force, to the Economic Club. There were others, including Ishibashi, Rōyama, and Ōta Eifuku. Hayashi was sent to New Guinea as a navy civil administrator. He is a relative of Ōta. As he wished to hear about economic problems, I introduced him to Ishibashi.

He said that the Japanese operation in New Guinea was inept. He said that emotional clashes between the army and navy occurred constantly. Today the "air-raid warnings" were called off, and again in the evening around nine o'clock air-raid warnings were issued. There is a great enemy invasion force against Saipan in the Marianna Islands. Some fairly powerful battleships have come there, but there were no Japanese battleships to go out and repel them. When will the battle of the main forces be?

Of the damage in northern Kyūshū and other places, there is absolutely no report. It is the usual secretiveness. However, it is said that the number of casualties is eight hundred plus. It has been reported that enemy planes have attacked Yamaguchi Province and other places.

June 19 (Monday)

There was a *Tōkei* board of directors meeting and Rōyama attended. From about four in the afternoon the air-raid warnings were called off. During the air-raid warnings someone stands watch all night and everyone darkens their rooms. I understand that as a result of this situation, efficiency is extremely diminished.

Where are the Japanese warships? . . . This is the question among the intellectuals. The Japanese Navy previously spoke of a "decisive battle" in the area of Bougainville and is now awaiting the enemy at the central area in the South Seas, but where is this leading force?

All the newspapers are saying a new German military weapon is giving London pain.

Of late, I do not write things that are major works. I have anxious thoughts about this.

June 20 (Tuesday)

A story of Yamamoto Kiyoshi. A certain person who had written on "Increasing Naval Aircraft Production" and been conscripted was a close friend of Yamamoto. There is no doubt that this certain person was drafted because of the crime of having written this article. It appears he was at Marugame for three months, and on the last day of the period the regimental commander said, "Now your case has been settled." The fact that by this effort of the navy he was released in one day and he was again drafted is just as previously related. While he was in the army he was well treated. I hear that as a result he left with a rather good impression of the army. I hear that the navy was deeply grateful since important people intervened because of this problem. The same person is a nephew of Hayashi Kiriku.

Mastering Research

CHAPTER FOUR

Whom You Want to Be Your First Readers

From the preceding chapter you will understand that faculty judgment is a fact important to the successful completion of your thesis/dissertation project. In this chapter we will further discuss how to deal with your academic/research advisor and your thesis/dissertation committee. These will be significant people around you, in addition to the significant others you have had before you came to school, during some of the most important years in your life.

Who is your ideal advisor

Upon your entry into a program of study leading to the honors or a graduate degree, you may be given some time to select an academic advisor for yourself. Or you may already have been assigned a faculty member as your advisor, but having the opportunity to ask for a change. Policies governing advisor selection are usually recorded in your program manual and/or other official documents. Arrangements like such seem perfect: For the student, he has his own choice which is supposed to best serve the student's need and interest. For the university or college, the student should be responsible for his academic progress under the guidance of his advisor whom he has accepted or has chosen for himself. Mentorship is often highly valued, and in practice there are numerous advisor-student pairs where satisfactory relationships have been built up and lasted long beyond the students' career in school.

There are also cases, however, showing that both advising and being advised is an unpleasant or even disastrous experience. Few, if any, studies have been

EXHIBIT 2–5
Protectable Matter

Protectable Matter	Example
Words	REAL TIME (for wearing apparel)
Letters	WROC (for radio broadcasting services)
Numbers	1054 (for cleaning products)
Foreign terms	CHAT ROUGE (for computer programs)
Shapes	Distinctive shape for coffee filters (as long as not functional)
Trade dress	Overall commercial impression of packaging, label, text, and graphics (for a can of chili)
Color	Blue (for container for wine, so long as not functional)
Fragrance	Floral fragrance for bookmarks
Design	CHECKERBOARD DESIGN (for food products)
Literary title	PARENT'S PARADE (for serialized magazine)

ornamentation. Merely decorative subject matter and pure ornamentation cannot be registered because they do not identify and distinguish goods or services and thus cannot function as trademarks.

Serialized Literary and Movie Titles

The title of a single book or movie title is generally not protectable. The title of a serialized work, such as THE BRADY BUNCH® or NEWSWEEK®, however, can be protected as a trademark or service mark.

(See Exhibit 2–5 for further examples of protectable matter.)

EXCLUSIONS FROM TRADEMARK PROTECTION

Not every word, design, or slogan can function as a trademark. It has already been noted that generic matter cannot be registered and that merely descriptive marks cannot be registered unless secondary meaning is shown. There are several additional bars to registration found in the Lanham Act (15 U.S.C. § 1052).

Disparaging or Falsely Suggestive Marks

The Lanham Act (15 U.S.C. § 1052(a)) forbids registration of a mark that disparages, brings into contempt or disrepute, or falsely suggests an association with persons, institutions, beliefs, or national symbols. Thus, WEST-POINT for guns was held to falsely suggest a connection with the U.S. Military Academy and was refused registration. *In re Cotter & Co.,* 228 U.S.P.Q. 202 (T.T.A.B. 1985). Similarly, a registration for BAMA for shoes and stockings was canceled because the Trademark Trial and Appeal Board found that BAMA pointed uniquely to the University of Alabama and thus falsely suggested a connection with the university. In April 1999, the TTAB canceled seven trademark registrations owned by the NFL football team the Washington Redskins, including the mark REDSKINS, on the basis the marks disparage Native Americans. *Harjo v. Pro Football Inc.,* 50 U.S.P.Q.2d 1705 (T.T.A.B. 1999). The ruling does not prevent the team from using the marks, but it could jeopardize the revenue generated by licensing the marks because the team can no longer sue for infringement of the marks under the Lanham Act, thus

The queues at the *zosui* restaurants remain even during the air-raid warnings. *Zosui* is rice cooked with vegetables and is a messy dish in which chopsticks will not stand up. It is not supposed to be delicious. And yet there are lines of people trying to eat it. As usual, the police say practice "self-control" and it appears that they force the closing of restaurants as their countermeasure. Why don't the police say, "Live without eating!"?

The Second Front and Germany's future produce extreme pessimism. On the English and American side there are three times as many airplanes as in Germany. In production, as a consequence of the raids on Germany, the figures have fallen from three thousand to two thousand planes, and now it is said there are only six hundred fighter planes. The final conclusion is it is just a matter of time.

Arakawa, who is vice-president of the Bank of Japan and a representative of the Finance Ministry, returned to Japan six months after the outbreak of the Second World War. He said,

> What surprised me after being absent from Japan for about three years was the fact that the leaders of Japan had developed a state of mind of ignoring what was said by others. Occasionally, if there were exceptions who listened carefully, these were people who were completely excluded outside the sphere of power. I also was an official but I thought this behavior bad. Because I could not believe the newspapers, these sorts of meetings (meetings to hear speeches) are extremely popular.

June 21 (Wednesday)

There has been an enemy invasion of Saipan in the Mariannas. Our army delivered a blow to the enemy, but the Imperial Headquarters announced that "There has been considerable damage inflicted on our warships and planes."

In the *Mainichi*, as usual, there is writing by Sohō, and there is also his speech in the *Asahi*. Didn't the army have him write this because of its expression of hope for navy action? Sohō is unquestionably a reporter in the employ of the army. (*Mainichi*, June 21).

June 22 (Thursday)

Whenever there is an incident, the reaction is "Restore Sundays" and "Cancel Holidays." Also, during the night-time air-raid warnings the neighborhood wardens stand at the street corners, and the following day there is emergency training. They do not anticipate the physical impact of these events. This still goes on even after the air raid on northern Kyūshū.

Conscription, draft labor, continues on a large scale (*Yomiuri*, June 1).

Chiba Hiroshi, a consul general, entered the army as a second-class private.

I hear that he was abused because he speaks quickly and the word *dono* as title of respect for *jōtōhei-dono*[55] was not clear in his speech. Probably he was beaten. It is a sad fact that a consul general is beaten by ignorant higher-rank soldiers.

The rumor that says that I have been seized by the police has already been put out dozens of times. Last year Shimanaka telephoned about it. It was also a subject of discussion in the Central Branch of the Economic Club. Arakawa, the vice-president of the Bank of Japan, said, "I heard this was so, but is it untrue?" In fact, I have not even been called once. Ishikawa remarked, "The fact that nothing has been done to you and me is because we are poor." It may be that not having professional titles is the reason we are not harmed.

June 23 (Friday)

England's Lyttleton[56] said that the Japanese–American war was the result of American pressure on Japan. The right or wrong of this aside, I envy a setting in which it is possible to say such things.

I hear that the rationing of vegetables is extremely tight, and for a six-person family for one day it is eighty sen worth. We made a two-day portion of *shitashi* (a boiled vegetable salad dish) of *shungiku* (spring chrysanthemums) and there was not enough even for me.

Of late, everybody is extremely emaciated. When I encountered Ohata of the Foreign Ministry after an absence of one month, he was completely emaciated. When I met my neighbor Koike on the street he was so thin I didn't recognize him. It seems that everybody is like this. The reason is the inadequacy of nutrition. In my circle people with respiratory illnesses have appeared in some numbers.

In Tōkyō the total distribution system is fine, but it still aims at only "equality." The mentality of the young officials is to declare, "We do not worry about those who are not poor!"

In a letter from Dobashi of Matsumoto I learned that the sale of shirts and the like is forbidden. Recently, officials and policemen suddenly appear and force merchandise to be handed over.

It is said that the casualties of the Red Army since the beginning of the war are 5.3 million. In actuality they are probably twice this number. Japan and Germany alone do not publish casualties for their own countries.

Ayusawa came to express her thanks because we had taken care of her at Karuizawa. The conscientiousness of this young lady! Her account: It is said that on the electric trains passengers are beaten for talking about the war.

I hear that now doctors do not provide medicine for the elderly. I hear that Okada Yachiyo is in difficulties and came to Ayusawa's home to explain her situation.

Yamauchi says a certain woman married and then became tubercular. In the husband's family they gave her nothing, saying, "With a disease that is not curable, it is worthless to provide sustenance. This is a time of shortages!" And yet with the circumstances in her own family she could not return there. When Yamauchi went to inquire about her health, the woman said, "I was born in such difficult times . . ." and broke into tears. Yamauchi also cried in sympathy.

Previously, Professor Koizumi related that even in the matter of nursing patients, at the time of air raids the doctors were ordered not to look after the elderly. This is thorough practicalness.

Because the sparrows eat the barley, when I spread a net over it, in about two days they were trapped in it, and afterward they did not come again. In the end, it is only human beings who cannot learn from their experience.

Deputy Nara said if it came about that Japan was defeated, he would later take revenge.

Saijō Yaso said if it came about that Japan was defeated, he would commit suicide. When Saijo spoke to the wife (a French woman) of a certain Japanese, she said this was why Japanese are weak; shouldn't they firmly endure and then seek revenge? The account of Tsuyuko is that Saijō was baffled by this.

If it comes about that Japan is defeated, there will probably indeed be various social phenomena of this sort revealed.

June 24 (Saturday)

They say that in the sea battle in the vicinity of Saipan, Japan called into action her most powerful battleships, but the American broadcasts claim they fled after a single battle. Because of the differences of so-called quantity—the term quantity is understood as materialism, and in present-day Japan this word is used to ridicule—it seems that Japan does not have the power to cope.

Nimitz is saying that the objective of the American fleet is to reach China. Okazaki, the Information Board official, said that it would be admirable if America actually carried out what it is saying. The intent of America is to shut off Japan from the South.

At the time I traveled in Karafuto and Hokkaidō there was confidence, but also when I traveled recently to Kyūshū there was not a single person who raised questions that asked, "How will Japan come out in the war?" "Will Japan be victorious in the Greater East Asian War?" In the first place, the reason is that they do not have the foresight even to think of such a thing, and in the second place, it is because if they raised such questions there is the strong possibility they would be in trouble. Merely asking questions, one will be taken in.

It is said that in the Ōiso neighborhood of Yoshida Shigeru (former ambassador), anything said is recorded, and the recordings are kept by the military police or the civilian police. The fact is that an apparatus has been installed in his room, and whenever Yoshida talks to anyone about foreign affairs, this is recorded. A story of Shimanaka.

I helped all day in the wheat harvest. I thought the wheat grains would be large but they were not; they were still small. When one tries growing crops oneself, one understands how much effort this takes.

June 25 (Sunday)

My forty-three-year-old next-door neighbor Temmei Ikuo received a draft notice. As head of the investigation section of the planning section of the agricultural association, he is a man who is extremely influential. Here also, I see a scheme for recruiting without considering the individual's circumstances. Because he is a neighbor, I saw him off in the morning. Several tens of people of the neighborhood association saw him off. However, this is a regular ceremony and an example of the waste of energy. Also, yesterday evening I attended a farewell party at the Hachiman Shrine.

Ōkuma Makoto came to visit me in the fields. Seeing me work as a farmer he said, "To see Kiyosawa Kiyoshi working as a farmer is regrettable," and "However, one cannot publish one's opinions at all, and it may be all right to escape the way Tō Emmei did."[57]

Today I worked in the fields almost all day. Of late I am not doing intellectual work and I feel extremely deprived.

June 26 (Monday)

I attended a board of directors meeting of *Tōyō keizai*. Wakimura Gitarō came and there was talk about the war conditions. It is said that there has been a two-division invasion of Saipan by the enemy. It is said that our side lost three hundred airplanes and there is unavoidable reorganization. (This is not the account of Wakimura.) We discussed the problems that would arise after the war.

June 27 (Tuesday)

The Japanese think being abusive about the enemy is a solution to problems. This was so up until the Greater East Asian Declaration. Even regarding the visit of Wallace to Chungking, there is the same tone of talk.

June 28 (Wednesday)

Ōzaki Yukio has been acquitted by the Supreme Court. It is a judgment with regard to lèse majesté. The fine prose of judge Miyake is outstanding (*Mainichi*, "Inkstone Drops," June 29).

Saipan has been invaded by a powerful enemy force. The shadow of pessimism is at long last apparent throughout society.

I went to the Foreign Ministry. There are policemen ostentatiously stationed at the prime minister's residence, which is in front of the Foreign Ministry residence. Later I learned that German Ambassador Stahmer visited the residence at four in the afternoon, and three people including Shigemitsu met over a period of three hours there.

It appears that the arrival of the American Army in Saipan occurred too suddenly for the authorities. It is said that evidence of this is the fact that Chief of Staff Obata went to Palau and did not stay in Japan. If he had been a bureaucrat it would have been a question of resignation. With the invasion fleet at Saipan, also Tsurumi for the first time was impelled to say, "I was chilled to the bone." He was an optimistic exponent of the Greater East Asian War, and at Karuizawa he opposed my views, saying, "Let's see what the future brings."

Both Japan and Germany have regarded the enemy with contempt. Now, for the first time it seems they understand the strength of the enemy. Impressions of the American Army's invasion of Cherbourg (*Mainichi*, June 29).

After the speech by Tsurumi Yūsuke, everybody was scheduled to debate on "The Postwar Diplomatic Policy of Japan." However, even among the people one could trust there was no one who would discuss the premise, "If Japan is defeated." I hear that if any discussion involves more than three people, it is always divulged to the military police. The representative named Koyama Kuranosuke had this experience. The truth is not spoken even between the senior statesmen and cabinet officials. In Japan the opportunity to discuss politics honestly is completely absent. This is the distinctive characteristic of Japan since before the Greater East Asian War.

June 29 (Thursday)

It is said that the Tōjō Cabinet is on the verge of a crisis. The chief of the Combined Fleet, Toyoda, said that he could not act if the navy minister was also the chief of the naval General Staff. Moreover, I learned that as regards airplanes, there are five to five for army and navy each. Thus the disruption came in the first place from the navy. It is being said that on top of this, because Home Minister Andō announced cabinet reforms, there was no way to stop this even on the part of the police.

Tōjō as usual was hysterical, and when Minister of Agriculture Uchida recently said in a cabinet meeting concerning increased food production that the use of white rice, because of its bran, was more advantageous than unpolished rice and other things, Tōjō reddened and angrily shouted, "Why are we talking about this kind of thing right now?" I understand that Uchida said it was "no good." However, it appears that Tōjō himself has absolutely no intention of stepping down. Yet under these circumstances, can Japan continue to go on?

June 30 (Friday)

It is said it has been decided to abandon Saipan. The only problem is in what form the newspapers will announce this fact, and within the Information Board there are those who are wondering how it would be if they were allowed to write freely, without the detailed instruction that has been employed until now. At present there has been guidance on the columns of each and every article. For example, in the case of the fall of Rome there was discussion as to whether there should be three or four columns, and something like two columns was decided upon. The newspapers have never been regulated from the center as they are at present.

Masamune Hakuchō came to visit. Recently he was invited by the chief of the Naval Information Bureau, and among the guests were also Hasegawa Nyozekan and Baba Tsunego. Everyone talked in a rather open manner, and the chief, Kurihara, said, "This will not be reported to the military police."

Masamune has decided to evacuate. He is going to Karuizawa soon. He said, "Even such things as the Patriotic Literary Society only talk about things ceremoniously. Why don't they talk about how difficult our daily life is?" He says the lackeys called writers are stupid. Insofar as this concerns Japan, it is truly so. Our people are a people who cannot talk about truth.

Even though such conditions have come about, the optimistic way of thinking is still apparent in the newspapers. Because of this, the general population is rather optimistic (*Yomiuri hōchi*, June 30).

Yoshida Shirō of the Asahi Glass Company and his wife came to call. His account. According to the talk of a doctor in their factory, he hears that of late beriberi is widespread, but the patients are allergic to the treatment injections. However, he said that in a test case, if they were given one egg, they immediately improved.

He said that recently the American air raids on the Kyūshū factory of Asahi Glass struck only the vital parts and were not "indiscriminate bombing."

On the island of Saipan, fifty naval planes that were lined up on the ground were destroyed without a single fight. While the planes were fine, the pilots did not know how to handle them.

July 1 (Saturday)

The financial record of Fuji Ice is poor; the pastures of Chiba Province have been completely confiscated. Recently I feel it was a mistake of judgment to borrow close to fifteen thousand yen and invest in it.

Shimanaka has been hospitalized at Minami Intestinal Hospital. I went to visit him at the hospital. He said that finally he would resign from *Chūō kōron*. The pressure upon him is in fact beyond words.

After a long lapse I attended a meeting of the People's Scholarly Arts Society. If one relies upon Professor Makino Eiichi's arguments, the judgment concerning Ōzaki Yukio was a proper interpretation of the law. The words of Ōzaki were lèse majesté, but there is no doubt concerning his loyalty. In the case of publishing laws, their objective influence and other things will be in question, but lèse majesté is not the same thing.

The circumstances following Saipan are extremely discouraging. It is said the destruction of warships and planes was enormous, and this was to a degree that it is not possible to continue the war as it has been conducted.

There is widespread propaganda claiming that women are taking up guns.

An account of Hasegawa Nyozekan. "I listened to a talk of Tomizawa Kiyoshi, but for him there is no questioning the inferiority of Japanese planes. I heard that the military weapons of Japan at the time of the Great East Asian War were extremely inadequate. The scholars who spoke of this weakness of Japanese armaments were quickly and completely dismissed. And then the government hired those who spoke like officials but were not. Consequently, there was no reason to adopt new knowledge. In the Meiji period, the authorities restrained the noisy crowd. Now, it is the opposite."

An account of Wakimura Yoshitarō. Opinions on national defense are divided into two kinds. One is from those who think that Saipan and the Philippines are the lifeline. The others think that even if these are seized through China, we will be able to take in the essential resources from the South Seas. The former idea is the navy's; the latter, the army's. To this the government-attached scholars say, "Because there are legions of coolies in China, they will be able to carry Japan from one shoulder to the other."

The army is vigorously printing in large type, "Attack Hengyang" (a city in Hunan). As usual they are arraying the largest banners, stating, "The Superior Execution of Strategy" and "Noble Courage since the Dawn of History." It appears this is spitefully directed against the navy.

For the first time since he was born, Professor Kuwaki is emaciated. This is also true of Professor Makino. Everybody is talking about becoming emaciated. It is clear that it is a matter of inadequate nutrition.

As usual, the newspapers are writing about the theme of the role of the Mongol Invasion in articles provided by either Akiyama Kenzō or Noma Kaizō.

July 2 (Sunday)

An Imperial Headquarters announcement reports a great sea battle in the southern area of the Ogasawara archipelago. If one relies upon what was transmitted, the damage to our warships was great, and it is an impossible situation for the continuation of the war if circumstances continue as they are. Yet it is said that America seems not to know how much damage has been done to the Japanese side.

The American air raids on Tōkyō we feel are exerting tremendous pressure.

No matter whom I meet, they all say how extremely emaciated I am.

The famous Imperial University professor named Hayashi Haruo has written on his admiration of the Japanese race (*Yomiuri hōchi*, July 2).

A house in front of Yūrakujo Station was taken away and a work squad of university students demolished it. The older son of Ayusawa worked on the demolition of a house in Asakusa and said he was eaten up by fleas.

On the previous 28th, Prime Minister Tōjō, Shigemitsu, and Stahmer have had meetings lasting three hours. The *Yomiuri* publicized this in capital letters. In society there are those who wondered, "Well then. . . ." Several people asked me about this. Obama said, wasn't this about the problem of peace between Germany and the Soviet? In this morning's *Asahi* it was again reported, "The strengthening of cooperation between Japan and Germany." Indeed, what they discussed was the worsening conditions for both the Japanese and German sides.

July 3 (Monday)

Early in the morning I came to Karuizawa. The grasses and trees of Usui are taking on the aspect of summer. Unexpectedly on the train I encountered Matsuo Harumi, and again, from Takasaki, I met Rōyama Masamichi, who had boarded the train. From Rōyama I heard about the resignation problems of Shimanaka as company head.

1. There were negotiations to have Shimanaka serve as substitute company head, but he declined.

2. When the Kanagawa thought control police chief finished his interrogation, he formally stated, "In the end, either way, we want you to cease being the company head." Shimanaka was then summoned to a separate room. After this he was summoned about once a week. Even when he said he was ill, the tone was, "Does it matter if you are ill?" If he did not comply with the summons, it looked as if he would be taken into custody.

3. At the time Shimanaka entered the Minami hospital, his wife, accompanied by Fujita, went to explain this to the Police Bureau of Kanagawa Province.

4. It is said that Shimanaka invited Sugimori Kojirō, Ōkuma Nobuyaka, Rōyama Masamichi, and Baba Tsunego to the hospital, previously having informed the police of his resignation. And then he told these people of his decision, and they discussed future plans. (I, who was regarded as the closest, was not invited.)

5. Making use of the authority of the government with young officials in their thirties as its core, there was a plan to take over the *Chūōkōron*. In the beginning Shimanaka intended to decide himself to step down and put a personal representative in his place as company head, but to this the "government" would not agree. They wished to put forth a government-

selected company head. It appears they wished themselves to run an organ of public opinion. Actually, at that moment, Yamamoto Sanehiko of *Kaizō* issued a notice of the discontinuation of *Kaizō's* publication, but the government, it is said, did not accept this. What is the "government"? Is not the government the "bureaucratic clique" of young officials and their followers?

6. It appears that the reason they interfered in the publishing world in this manner was that the Home Ministry had the object of providing the opportunity to have drinking parties. Ministries such as Finance and Agriculture-Commerce had great numbers of extradepartmental bodies, but there was none for the Home Ministry. Thereupon they fixed their attention on the publishing world. They cut themselves in because of their power in an area where they were able to interfere directly. For example, the Communications Ministry meddling in broadcasting stations and the electrical industry world is like the Foreign Ministry meddling in the *Nippon Times* and the Foreign Politics Association. They created problems on behalf of their aims, changed people, created the occasion to take on personalities who suited their convenience, had the opportunity for drinking parties, and sold favors to friends. Thus, their auxiliaries were expanded. Because their objectives were the above-mentioned, even in cases where there was no need for regulation they regulated unreasonably.

7. When the Home Ministry thought control police begin to do such things as this, there is no means to correct this. *Chūō kōron* from the point of view of trustworthiness is a splendid thing, and support for it is widespread. However, there is nothing one can possibly do against the pressure of summons and interrogations by low-class detective animals. Even a fine private secretary, the man named Fujita, says, "They are not human, they are animals!" Herein is the last stage of Japan completely degraded. This being the case, there is nothing to be done. We can't help but be threatened by uneasy feelings.

A story of Matsuo Harumi on the train. The friend of his second son who is in high school came to have supper. In the discussion he said that the present war came about because of the cooperation between the military clique and the bureaucracy, and the general population had no part in it. This is why the people are not enthusiastic. He said whether Japan was victorious or defeated, he would build the foundation of a new Japan. Even among eighteen- and nineteen-year-olds, there are perceptive observations on the times.

July 4 (Tuesday)

I have been saying for a long time that when the air raids come, society will probably fall into a turmoil that cannot be handled. It is likely that there will be theft, and rape and pillage will be a strong possibility.

The shortage of food supplies is natural, and probably for families that hoard food supplies there will be strict forced deliveries or else outright seizure by other people. Because I feel personally threatened, I sent carpets and various clothing to Karuizawa. Fortunately, a moving company named Shimada provided assistance. This one portion was sent on July 2. Of course it is just a part of our things.

Revolution will soon be inevitable. It won't be too long in coming. After defeat in war, the destruction of order will inevitably appear, and what follows will be violence, revolution, and assassination. I don't know how many people will be involved in making a treaty with the enemy, but they will probably be killed by assassins. In the situation that follows, no one can definitely say with certainty "a new Japan," "a Japan that has hope." For the people there is the danger of Japan becoming like Greece or like Italy. Nevertheless, there will be self-reflection after the revolution, and this will be the turning point for the future.

According to an account of Ide, in the Shinshū area the belief in victory is still unshaken. I hear they think they will deliver a devastating blow when the enemy approaches. The way of thinking in the regions is the same as that of the common people in Tōkyo. They are completely ignorant of both the world political situation and modern war.

This is something I talked to Rōyama about. That circumstances have turned out this way is our predictions hitting the mark. It may be not unpleasant emotionally to see the consequences of ignorant leadership revealed. However, at the same time, it is very difficult to bear the tragedy for our country. Here, there is a contradiction.

According to the account of Mitsui, those in middle school and above the third-year level in elementary school are sent to munitions factories and made to work. They are drafted student workers. Their study time is six hours a week. That is to say, about one hour a day. Mitsui's school (Keimei Gakuen) has contact with the navy's headquarters of battleship administration, and the school has become a mica factory and the students work in the same place. The union of labor and study is a point I have emphasized for many years. However, with this, Japanese scholarship will be completely eliminated. University students have no time at all to study. This means that the military ideas of "Defense State" and the like are achieved. Nonetheless, Minister of Education Ōkabe listens abjectly to what the military says and what a coward he is. However, he is a man who caught Tōjō's attention with his single theme of rejection of the metric system. It should not be expected that such a man understands educational administration. If Japan goes on just as it is, it will plunge into darkness.

I asked Rōyama to insert two explicit provisions in the Japanese Constitution, which would probably be constructed in the days to come.

These are freedom of speech (and regarding this severe punishment for individual attacks upon it), and from this a policy of severe punishment for assassination.

severely limiting its ability to preclude knockoff or counterfeited items bearing the team's logos. [*Recent News:* In late 2003, the district court for the District of Columbia overturned the TTAB decision on procedural grounds. Thus, as of the writing of this text, there is no definitive court ruling on the question of whether the RED-SKINS mark is disparaging.]

Insignia

Flags, coats of arms, and other insignia of the United States or any state or any foreign nation cannot be registered.

Immoral or Scandalous Matter

Immoral or scandalous matter cannot be registered. For example, a graphic depiction of a dog defecating that was used on clothing was refused registration as scandalous. The mark was also found to disparage Greyhound Corporation because the dog was reminiscent of the Greyhound dog used by the company in connection with its transportation services. *Greyhound Corp. v. Both Worlds, Inc.,* 6 U.S.P.Q.2d 1635 (T.T.A.B. 1988).

Names and Portraits of Living Persons

A mark comprising a name, portrait, or signature of a particular living person cannot be used without his or her written consent, and a name, signature, or portrait of a deceased U.S. president cannot be used without his widow's written consent. Thus, the portrait of the actor Paul Newman that appears on various food products must be with his written consent.

Deceptive Matter

Marks comprising deceptive matter cannot be registered. Thus, SILKEASE was held deceptive when applied to clothing not made of silk in *In re Shapely, Inc.,* 231 U.S.P.Q. 72 (T.T.A.B.

1986), and CEDAR RIDGE was held deceptive for hardboard siding not made of cedar. *Evans Products Co. v. Boise Cascade Corp.,* 218 U.S.P.Q. 160 (T.T.A.B. 1983). In most cases, marks are found to be deceptive because they falsely describe the material or content of a product or are geographically deceptive. Thus, SHEFFIELD used on cutlery not made in Sheffield, England, was held deceptive because of the renowned status of Sheffield for cutlery products.

Mere Surnames

A mark that is primarily merely a surname cannot be registered without proof of secondary meaning. Thus, names such as "Smith" or "Higgins" cannot be registered, while names such as "King" or "Bird" would be registrable inasmuch as they have a significance or meaning other than as surnames. A review of PTO records discloses that McDonald's Corporation's numerous registrations for its MCDONALD'S® marks routinely claim that the mark has acquired distinctiveness through its continuous and exclusive use. The PTO will examine telephone books to determine if a mark is primarily merely a surname. If the surname is combined with additional matter, such as other words or a design, it may be registrable. Thus, HUTCHINSON TECHNOLOGY® was registrable. *In re Hutchinson Technology, Inc.,* 852 F.2d 552 (Fed. Cir. 1988).

Geographical Terms

Marks including geographic terms, such as references to countries, states, towns, streets, and rivers, present special problems. When a geographic term is used to describe the place goods or services come from, it is considered descriptive and unregistrable if purchasers

July 5 (Wednesday)

I learned from the radio that enemy amphibious units have appeared close to the Agasawara Islands and Iwōjima. The air-raid warnings were because of this. Because Iwōjima was attacked by naval bombardment (they are in the midst of fighting at present), isn't the enemy probably planning to invade this area? It is said that in Saipan the Americans are advancing to the northeastern area occupied by the Japanese. It may be there will be sacrificial deaths.

The government has issued a statement. It says, "Even though there is a Chungking government army, those who reject America and England are not our enemies." This is to make it clear that the China operation does not consider China as its objective, but that America and England are the enemy. Making such a statement so late only buys the contempt of the other side. Its contents are something that we have been insisting upon for a long time. Even if it has been imposed upon us, our China policy has come to this point. However, they never engage in any soul-searching. They have never engaged in self-reflection. It is strategy. Two or three days ago there were radio broadcasts about the great quantities of munitions resources under the topic of the meaning of the Konan (Hunan) operation, and they are talking about the availability of antimony and iron. We have been fully engaged in war until now, and yet they do not understand the difference between resources "existing" and the capacity to "use" them.

July 6 (Thursday)

I finished reading Miura's *The World Historical Turning Point*. His exposition is not skillful, but it is a splendid study. I learned a great many things from it.

He has a keen eye for world order based upon a wide-scale organizational system. That is to say, it permits independence, and there is a co-prosperity sphere based upon these regional units.

I did not look at the newspapers. According to the radio I learned that there is an enemy assault upon the Ogasawara Islands and Iwōjima. However, there was a revision stating that in the Chichijima area there was no naval bombardment. It seems that the enemy left temporarily, but after about twenty days they will probably make preparations and come again. There are daily radio broadcasts from the factories that are filled with the sentiments of young men and women. They are expressions of nothing but deep emotion.

July 7 (Friday)

The weather is fine. Throughout the day I worked in the fields and garden. I am unable to read. I feel that eating takes too much work.

When I took a bath before supper I wondered if it was all right to live as I am. On the other hand, I can hear an opposing voice that says that notwithstanding the fact that I still have the desire to do something, the times have no use for me. However, I have the happy feeling of passing my days with facilities that are not found even in first-rank inns.

July 8 (Saturday)

Today I was again a farmer.

I brought in two hundred briquettes. I bought them last year and set them aside. Our total was more than three hundred, and with these my preparations for the winter period were completed. There are also the fields.

This morning in northern Kyūshū again, several tens of aircraft came. It is said that the damage was two or three half-burned houses. However, it appears that not one plane was destroyed. If one listens to the radio, one could actually imagine that there was no damage. According to the story of Ide, in the countryside it is firmly believed that we will lure the American battleships and annihilate them with a single blow. While the central government belittles the strength of the enemy, at the same time they talk about the life-and-death crisis of the country, and the people in the countryside believe only the former.

This morning the right-wing historian named Akiyama Kenzō again lectured on the radio about the role of the Mongol Invasion of 760 years before.

According to Rōyama's version, Tōjō has been trying various means to arrest Konoe. That is to say, because Konoe knew about Tōjō's war attitude, it was Tōjō's intention to throw him out of office.

Today it is two years, seven months, since the imperial rescript—the declaration of war.

Recently, when I traveled to Kyūshū the seats in the second-class train car were tattered. Japan has used up her last strength.

July 9 (Sunday)

Today I was in the fields as usual. In the afternoon I called on Sakamoto Naomichi. He had gone to Tōkyō and was not at home. I met with his wife. Her story:

Because they had been told, at Karuizawa, to build air-raid shelters, these were dug in a corner of the garden. In Paris it was all right if people simply ran away. However, here, it was said everybody must come and participate. The tools for air-raid defense all had to be placed directly in front of the entrance. However, if these could have been purchased it would have been all right, but they were told to supply those that couldn't be bought. Somehow or other these had to be bought on the black market. When they were used two or three times, they became worthless.

Their house in Yokohama was on elevated ground and the tap water would not flow there. However, they were told they would have to buy pumps.

When she returned home from foreign countries it was always said from beginning to end that Japan is number one in the world. When she made the slightest remark it was attacked as "the mania for foreign things." She said, "Just wait and you will understand."

This kind of feeling is widely shared.

The self-intoxication of the Japanese brought about the present state of affairs, and after all it is inevitable that they must pass through this stage.

I am going to leave this diary notebook in Karuizawa and return home. Indeed, because I was afraid it would be seen by someone, at times it has had to be inconspicuous.

It has become a world in which even insurance cannot be obtained.

A story of Masamune Hakuchō. Recently, the chief of the Navy Information Bureau invited representatives of various circles. It is said that even Baba Tsunego and others attended. The topic was "How is the fighting spirit of the people to be stimulated?" One fact is that it was extraordinary for the navy to invite "liberals." The second was to think, as authorities, that the will of the people was not stimulated.

At the end I will make an addendum. At the front of this diary I wrote, "A diary that was not written," but that was written when I imagined a time when it might be confiscated. There is a notebook before this diary (evening, July 9, 1944, Karuizawa villa).

July 10 (Monday)

With Rōyama I visited Shimanaka in the hospital. Shimanaka told us that the Information Board was making an announcement, the gist of which was the final dissolution of Chūō kōron.

Shimanaka's feeling was that the maneuvers such as rounding up of company members on the pretext of the Communist Party Incident were consistently intended to destroy Chūō kōron. Shimanaka had been in contact with the upper echelon of officials, and they had shown an attitude of being extremely understanding. He had come to rely upon the judgment of these people, but the machinations on the part of the young police officials made the efforts of the highest echelons altogether powerless. The Chūō kōron problem, along with the testimony taken by the Kanagawa police (Shimanaka said everything in it was lies from beginning to end), became a problem for cabinet discussion. Only Kishi said, "A dissolution order is not a peaceful solution," and Shigemitsu agreed and it became not an "order" but "voluntary."

Its paper allotment and other things were confiscated. Yamamoto of the Kaizō Company was also summoned and the same thing happened.

The editor in chief of Tōyō keizai, Satō, was summoned to the police station and given a "warning." It is said it was because he transmitted various sorts of information. I hear that because of the "rumors" concerning the Kyūshū air raids, a very great number of people are being arrested.

It is of interest that the Munitions Companies Laws have been applied to the Tōkyō Steel Works, and the latter has been attached to Nissan. (8th) Regarding this, the naval commander, Ōnishi, the general manager of the Munitions Ministry Aircraft Equipment Office, clearly stated, "What is the use of stocks if the nation is ruined?"

1. Are there not commercial laws and a constitution to prevent the ruin of the nation?
2. Herein one must see that the home front has the responsibility for the war (*Asahi*, July 7).

According to Rōyama, Chief of the Naval Information Bureau Kurihara spoke as follows at an Imperial Rule Assistance Society meeting: "The Japanese Navy never dreamed that Saipan would be seized. Consequently, at present there are no preparations for the next campaign. It is now in the midst of hurriedly studying this." Among the representatives it has not been possible to counterattack until now, and in what way was it possible for them to counterattack until now? They have questioned whether Saipan's having been taken means that Japan's production base is completely exposed. Moreover, I hear that the Imperial Rule Assistance Society has resolved to place no confidence in the government. The consequences of the war have at last shaken the mind of the people.

Evidence that the officials think of themselves as a race completely separate from the people is that a certain bureau chief brought white rice every day and inconsiderately ate it in front of everyone. One man said, of course, that rationed rice was for the other people.

The true story of a certain person. He received shoes, underwear, and other things from a young official of the Agriculture-Commerce Ministry. And then in return he brought sugar. The official handed over a receipt and said, "This sugar is used for training practice in Hong Kong." Such an accounting as this would not be in the least extraordinary. The decline and fall of officials, police, and military. Beyond words!

Watsuji Tetsurō raised a question, saying, "When there is the threat of enemy invasion, why is Japan engaged in a grandiose war in China?" Probably one reason is that the army and navy are conducting separate wars.

July 11 (Tuesday)

The dissolution of *Chūō kōron* and *Kaizō* was announced (*Mainichi*, July 11).

1. If the management operation has not been adequate, wouldn't it be better if this were changed? Why were they dissolved?
2. *Gendai* and *Kōron* are the magazines of the single-theme right wing.

According to Rōyama, the 300,000 intellectual class behind *Chūō kōron* and *Kaizō* are the opposition to the government. These people are on the black list and the government intends to sweep them away. This is one of the policies of the Tōjō Cabinet.

For the first time I picked a peach and ate it. It was extremely sweet and delicious. I have some cucumbers. Breakfasting is pleasant.

July 12 (Wednesday)

A story of Fujita of *Chūō kōron*. Hani Setsuko wrote a biography of Naval Commander Fujita. As a pilot he left behind an extraordinary record. Because this was a popular item in *Children's Science* she revised it, bound one volume, and submitted it to the authorities. The company thought this book would become a recommended work. However, it was rejected as "unacceptable for publication." This was despite the fact that the printing was completely finished. When they tried inquiring about it they were told there was a part that said that the commander was a passionate Christian and this could not be allowed.

If Commander Fujita had heard this, it is possible he would have said he was sorry to throw away his life for such stupid people. Even Christians admirably give up their lives for their country, and realizing this without altering one's perception of Christianity, on the contrary, is trying to obliterate reality on the basis of ideology.

It is said that Lt. Colonel Akiyama (a member of the Information Board) said we must be resigned to the fact that the enemy will invade our homeland (at a meeting of the Patriotic Literary Society). He behaves as if it were completely other people's business and the responsibility devolves on the home front.

Mizuno of the police came to call and said, "Although we have not previously criticized the circumstances of the operation, even in the case of Saipan they say it is the people's fault." Even this quiet man has such feelings.

I am reading Yano Jinichi's study, *A Study of the End of the Ch'ing Dynasty*. Of late, I am again reading in the area of Miura's thesis on the history of the French Revolution. The decline of the bureaucracy is the same. Moreover, even the manifestations of decline coiling about the imperial government are the same.

There is an essay of Shiratori Toshio in the *Mainichi shinbun*. It is the usual Semitic arguments. Because emotionally sick personalities are the leaders, it is not to be expected this war will be successful (*Mainichi*, July 12).

Machiai and restaurants are becoming private clubs and so-called dormitories. The *Mainichi shinbun* is taking photographs of automobiles going to these places in the evening. If one relies upon their figures—

According to the Tsukiji police station, at the end of March there were 117 *machiai* and 41 restaurants, and the larger ones among these are becoming the "clubs" and "dormitories" of the large munitions companies. There are geishas in these places as before.

Regarding the dissolution of *Chūō kōron* and *Kaizō*, there was only something in the "Kamikaze" column of the *Asahi shinbun*, and here just a little was written with great care. The tone was, "Speaking from the history of the magazines, it is possible to argue that today they cannot be allowed to continue." Only at the end of the column did it say, "It is against the basic nature of free speech that they themselves behave as if they had permission for patriotic speech, to be patriotic writers and to completely reject others." The statement on the dissolution of *Chūō kōron* and the like probably is due to the results of the stubborn activity of such groups as the Patriotic Speech Society.

Chūō kōron and *Kaizō*, the magazines that came in any event to lead the Japanese intellectual world, were buried without eulogy.

According to a story of Professor Matsumoto Jōji, his younger brother-in-law is the head of the Medical Association in Ōsaka. He attended a doctors' convention in Tōkyō (at the invitation of the government), and some Military Medical Office chief said, "Those who do not understand the circumstances of the times are the doctors and lawyers." I understand that the same person is well-read in Chinese books and quoted the ancient words, "Those who do not become angry are rare."

Professor Koizumi Tan said that in his research center (Keiō University Medical School) because he was told to submit the names of the absolutely indispensable people in such areas as Contagious Disease Research, he presented something like thirteen names, but when he was asked to reduce these, the result was seven names, and for these alone he obtained guarantees that they would not be drafted. It is said, however, that one of these had already been called up, and probably others as well will be drafted.

With regard to certain problems, a military doctor with something like the rank of lt. colonel came to a university. The professor in charge listened to his points and said, "It is completely impossible; there is nothing else to do but resign." I understand that the lt. colonel doctor said, "Well, then, please resign!" and the professor could say nothing. This is also the story of Dr. Koizumi Tan.

There is an announcement that close to the Mappi Mountains on the northern edge of Saipan they are in the midst of "fierce struggle, hand to hand, with naked swords." There is still no announcement that Saipan has fallen into enemy hands.

In the communiqués from abroad it is transmitted that the control of air power and sea power has fallen into enemy hands. America is broadcasting that Saipan fell on the sixth. On the other hand, Germany is being pressed from three directions—the East, in Italy, and northern France—and it is receiving the attack of the enemy along a thousand-kilometer front. All of these pressures are constantly directed against Berlin.

The power that is moving Japan is the military police and the civilian police. And then, in the background of these, is the military. It is true that the civilian police and military police are not compatible; however, the government officials have the distinctive feature of submitting to a stronger power for self-preservation. It goes without saying that the core of power is the military.

July 13 (Thursday)

I went to the fields to work, and on the way back I picked up peaches, cucumbers, eggplant, and other things. I have found peace in this lifestyle.

There are some who think the "enemy" is not necessarily to be feared, but we are not certain how the authorities in the country—the Kempeitai—will treat us.

There was a meeting of the International Relations Research Society, and there was a talk by Ōta Saburo (chief of the Investigation Bureau of the Foreign Ministry) on the Prime Ministers' Conference of the British Empire. After the lecture I asked questions. The overbearing attitude of this man is regrettable. But he also has a very sharp mind.

Even though it is not the talk of well-placed people, there is the opinion that the navy minister, Shimada, has submitted his resignation. It is possible it is a rumor, but it might be true.

The physician named Kasahara Jinichi has entered the military. He was a probationary regimental officer, but the crowd called lieutenants and captains do nothing but shout at these people and beat them, and they have no views or plans of any kind. And then they go to the canteen and clamor for sake and drink it. It is worse than can be imagined. He said that with such conditions there is no reason to expect victory in the war.

A professor of a higher school named Haga Mayumi at a meeting of the Patriotic Speech Society said to Masamune Hakuchō, "The war will be lost!" The reason is that "the authorities dislike the widening of general knowledge. Of late, when I went to the Navy Ministry they said, 'The situation is beyond our capacity; think of something to do!' and then when I went to the Army Ministry and expressed my opinions they were infuriated and said, 'What do you know? It is impertinent conceit!' With a crowd such as this work is impossible!" The same gentleman was a university student in Germany.

The houses alongside the railway lines have all been taken down. And yet it appears there is no intention to develop a city plan.

They say that cooking oil is being rationed. One go is twenty-three sen. It is said that if one buys it in the black market it is seventy yen. That is to say, the actual price is thirty times the fixed market price. In this way commodities do not circulate. According to a story of my elder brother, in Saitama Province one sho of rice is fifteen yen; three bales is one thousand yen. Moreover, cucumbers are around four yen per kamme. I understand that the farmers in the provinces near Tōkyō make so much money that there are many who have piled up ten thousand yen.

July 14 (Friday)

The head of *Yomiuri hōchi* has become a member of the House of Peers, and we see he lavishes empty flattery on the government. In today's *Mainichi shin-*

bun, by chance, there were somewhat prophetic statements. The president of the Tōkyō Engineering College, Yagi Hidetsugu, wrote under the heading, "Confronting the Grave War Situation" (*Mainichi*, July 14).

Certainly this Yagi is a man who stated the most intelligent things at the Kyoryokukai (Cooperative Association) (*Mainichi*, July 14).

This is an expression of the limits of what one can say at the present moment. The readers' column of *Asahi shinbun* had the same thing.

Nagai Shōzō, as the chairman of our International Relations Research Society, said when he introduced Ōta, "The government tells the people to follow it, but it does not give them either information or knowledge," and even this discreet man made a rather blunt statement. Together with the hopeless war situation, little by little, voices are coming to be raised demanding freedom of speech.

I went to the Foreign Ministry. It was been decided that Fukuda Ippei would also be a member of the committee. It is said that the bureau chief, Ota Saburō, attaches a high value to Fukuda. He equates the ability to write English with a "brain."

They say that the cabinet reforms are decided. The one who remains is Foreign Minister Shigemitsu. Greater East Asian Minister Aoki, Welfare Minister Koizumi, and others will resign, and the Army and Navy ministers will also be changed. It appears that Tōjō will remain as before.

A story of Shimanaka. Because Shimanaka had entered the hospital, his wife went to the Kanagawa police to notify them of this. A man called an assistant detective said something like, "Your husband is a bad fellow!" or "What have you come here for?" and in a shouting manner he said, "Hmm, is he sick? You are eating only excellent food—are you complaining about stomach trouble?" Because she was with twenty or thirty people who were waiting, when she wished to talk in another room she waited about an hour. "Why did you call me here?" It was all insulting, "Hey you!" and "Dumb you!"

There is talk that Hatoyama Ichiro was officially summoned and escorted by a police detective. I understand that the next one will be Rōyama Masamichi.

They say that Shimanaka wanted to go to Karuizawa, but because Karuizawa, or Atami were places frequented by the bourgeoisie, it would call attention to himself, and he was strongly encouraged to return to his hometown, Nara, where he had been born. Because he was reluctant to go to his hometown, right now he intends to take living quarters in the Hōryūji.

According to Takayanagi Kenzō, Shimanaka will probably be prosecuted. Amamiya reported that officials had taken copies of *Fujin kōron* (Woman's review) from the earliest issue. They collected them from his earliest editorship and were looking for evidence of crime. Now that the constitution is no longer operative, if one is singled out by the police, in the end there is no road of escape.

There was distribution of whiskey and grape wine by the neighborhood association. Because this was fairly distributed, our family also received a little. According to the story of the owner of Fujiya, when the factory workers who received asparagus put it into bean-paste soup, it completely melted, and even if eaten by itself it had no taste. He said, "Is there anything this expensive and tasteless?" Moreover, he said that a great deal of butter is sent to the factories, but the factory workers put it into their bean-paste soup. Fair rationingism—this, coupled with the reaction against the bourgeoisie, allows one to understand the emergence of the foundation of a destructive revolution.

July 15 (Saturday)

Yesterday a letter came from Mitsui. It said they could contribute 2,500 yen for the Japanese Diplomatic History Research Center. Mitsubishi also decided upon the same amount. In any event, it would come to a 5,000-yen contribution. According to the account of Obama, it happened that when Mitsui talked about 2,000 yen, Mitsubishi, at Katō Takeo's recommendation, said they would give 2,500 yen, and both decided to do so. Is it likely that next year there will be the conditions that will allow the zaibatsu to exist?

Because the Chūō Kōron Company no longer exists, the People's Scholarly Arts Society has no office. Given this situation, together with Professor Kuwaki I consulted with the Mitsubishi Department grounds management about whether the company's head office couldn't be lent. We are told that the military people of the Munitions Ministry have already applied to borrow the vacated space of the Chūō Kōron Company.

The people who oppressed *Chūō kōron* and *Kaizō* and forced their dissolution were after all the military. The first section of the Information Bureau is navy, the second section is army, and the third is the Foreign Ministry. Among these the one that became dominant in the *Chūō kōron* incident was the second section. Because the orders came from this section, the role of the Kanagawa Police Department was extremely prominent. It is an example of the control of society by the army's young officer clique and the underling bureaucrats.

July 16 (Sunday)

Both the radio and newspapers are daily whipping up a clamor about the army's "vigorous activity" on the Chinese continent. When one looks at the newspaper headlines, there are continuous columns of rather fulsome language about "the skill of our efficient aerial squadrons in China now have reached a point which can be called divine skill," or "brilliant continental campaigns unknown in the history of war," "surpassing masters-of-the-sky squadrons."

Going to the countryside, when I asked about the war in China I was told, "To us China is not of much interest." However, there are probably those who understand that although at sea we are being pressed, on land we are achieving brilliant military results, and this idea is probably the objective of the media.

If one relies upon the announcements of the enemy regarding the Saipan war situation, they state that some ten thousand corpses were discovered, and nine thousand prisoners were interned. These nine thousand were probably women and children.

In the critique of the newspaper of a certain third country (Switzerland?), it said that the war shows that Japan still has reserve strength, but at the same time it is costing extraordinary expenditures. What Japan must avoid is a bankrupting war. The current operations have turned out just as the enemy wanted.

A story of Obama is that it is said that one kamme of sugar is two hundred yen, and one egg is one yen. Even with these prices, many people are buying them greedily.

There is a rumor that Tōjō's villa on the embankment of the Tama River was broken into and robbery left it in disorder. Is this really true or not? Rumors are flying around in all directions.

I understand that the Wartime Defense Law was issued the day before yesterday or thereabouts. The fact that it was announced only in official statements without being mentioned by the newspapers is the style of late.

Kitada Masanori, who lives next door, was drafted. Of late, one has to say that all young persons are being drafted.

I understand that recently the Kempeitai rented the house in front of Konoe's home, and a telephone line of the Konoe house was wire-tapped. This exposes the surveillance and burial of a possible Konoe opposition.

July 17 (Monday)

All the newspapers are putting out specially outlined statements whose gist calls for total national effort. These are not editorials, and also they are not news. They are written by those around the (Military) Information Bureau and are probably forcibly required to be issued by the newspapers. These completely expose a lack of intelligence. For example, in *Yomiuri* articles entitled "The Autumn of a Total Breakthrough on the Domestic Battlefield," "The Fighting Will of One Hundred Million Seethes," "The Establishment of an Impenetrable Defense Cordon and Total Tenacity," there is the statement, "Both politics and economics benefit the domestic defense line." What does both politics and economics benefit the inner defense line mean (*Yomiuri*, July 17)?

I attended a meeting of the *Tōyō keizai* committee members. Ishibashi has returned from Lake Yamanaka. It is said that in that region there are thieves, and they seem to be sailors who are recuperating there.

According to what my wife was previously told by the wife of Ambassador Morishima, the naval marines in the Kamakura area entice the local maids,

would think that the goods or services originate in the geographic place identified in the mark. Thus, THE NASHVILLE NETWORK was held primarily geographically descriptive of various entertainment services where the applicant was located in Nashville and many of the programs it distributed were produced in Nashville. *In re Opryland USA, Inc.,* 1 U.S.P.Q.2d 1409 (T.T.A.B. 1986). Similarly, CALIFORNIA PIZZA KITCHEN was primarily geographically descriptive because the restaurant services were rendered in California and elsewhere. *In re California Pizza Kitchen*, 10 U.S.P.Q. 1704 (T.T.A.B. 1998). Such marks cannot be registered without proof of secondary meaning. On the other hand, NANTUCKET® for shirts was allowed because the shirts offered under the mark did not come from Nantucket and consumers would not immediately associate Nantucket with shirts. *In re Nantucket, Inc.,* 677 F.2d 95 (C.C.P.A. 1982). Similarly, use of DUTCHBOY® for paint was held acceptable because of its arbitrariness: there is no known connection between paint and Holland. *National Lead Co. v. Wolfe,* 223 F.2d 195 (9th Cir. 1955).

As a result of NAFTA, the Lanham Act now prohibits registration of a geographically deceptively misdescriptive mark even if the mark has secondary meaning. Thus, PERRY NEW YORK for clothing not originating in New York was not registrable because consumers, upon encountering the mark, would be deceived into reacting favorably to it due to the renown of New York in the clothing and fashion industry.

Additionally, under TRIPS, and effective January 1, 1996, the Lanham Act bars registration of any geographic mark for wines and spirits not originating from the place identified in the mark. Thus, the word *Bordeaux* can only be used in connection with goods from the Bordeaux region of France. Finally, some geographic terms have become generic and can never be registered, for example, *French fries, Swiss cheese,* and *Bermuda shorts.*

Descriptive and Confusingly Similar Marks

Marks that are merely descriptive (such as CHEESE BITS for cheese-flavored snacks) or marks that are confusingly similar to those used by a senior user are not registrable. Refusals by the PTO to register descriptive or confusingly similar marks will be discussed in detail in Chapter 4.

Functional Devices

A mark or device that is as a whole functional cannot be registered as a trademark because it would deprive others of the right to share a needed device. Thus, trademark protection might be refused for the shape of a matchbook cover when the shape functions to make the product useful. Because competitors would need to use the same shape of cover for their products to be effective, one party cannot exclusively appropriate it in perpetuity. The functionality doctrine ensures that protection for utilitarian product features be sought through patent registration, which is of limited duration. A determination by the PTO that a proposed mark is functional is an absolute bar to registration, regardless of how distinctive a mark might be.

Statutorily Protected Marks

Finally, certain marks are protected by federal statute from use or confusingly similar use by  another, such as the wording "Smokey Bear," marks used by various veterans' organizations, the Red Cross logo, and the Olympic rings and associated wording.

and they meet secretly in the mountains at night. I understand on a certain evening about midnight a policeman accompanied by their maid told her that he had discovered that the maid was having secret meetings on the beach and hoped they would pay more attention to this kind of thing. The deterioration of public morals has reached this point.

At the Imperial Headquarters there are conferences for the exchange of opinions, but a decision-making organ does not exist. There being no opportunity for intelligence to enter into political strategy and military operations, these are decided by the intuition of such people as young advisers and Tōjō. In the Sino-Japanese War, with the Meiji Emperor at the core, senior statesmen such as Itō and Yamagata carefully deliberated. This is what differs in the current situation.

Finally, Navy Minister Shimada has resigned and Admiral Nomura has taken his office. The hostile feelings between the army and navy are profound to a degree unknown before in history. Even in the munitions factories there is a struggle for materials, and the clerks in charge are having a bad time. It is true that the navy's style is in general sophisticated, but even with that, for example, when they invaded an island it was not extraordinary for them to occupy the best part. Because the army has the Kempeitai system, the pressure on those who sympathize with the navy is increased, and it is common for the Kempeitai to behave disagreeably. It is said that it is not rare for navy sympathizers to be arrested. Despite the fact that the bad feeling between army and navy is public knowledge, there is not a single word touching upon this in either the newspapers or magazines. And if it were touched upon it would be disastrous.

In the July 1 issue of *Tōyō keizai*, it was stated regarding Saipan Island that "It can be acknowledged that this one island has such value that we will expend all our power to protect it." But I understand that the police headquarters issued an "advisory warning." When for the moment Saipan had not been taken, if it was written that "Saipan does not have a value worth total expenditure of strength," publication of this would probably have been forbidden. This was written before it was seized. Public opinion is at the convenience of the authorities.

In a cabinet meeting there was a discussion of whether the members of the Imperial Rule Assistance Society, which was opposed to the Tōjō Cabinet, should be arrested. With regard to this, Vice Home Minister Karasawa Toshiki was opposed, saying they could not have the responsibility for doing such a thing.

July 18 (Tuesday)

There is no rain. In the Chūgoku region and elsewhere, because of the water shortage it is not possible to plant rice, and the problem of food supplies should be of extreme concern.

Today there was an announcement from the Imperial Headquarters, which was not news to anybody, that the enemy had captured Saipan. It said that the army and navy forces were completely annihilated and the headquarters recognizes that the resident Japanese population suffered the fate of the military. In this instance the media did not use the phrase "sacrificial death." In the statements of Premier Tōjō there are words and phrases about his great shame before His Majesty the Emperor. This is the first time Tōjō has used this sort of language. Even at the time of Attu Island, he said things that referred to "a miraculous turn of events rare in the history of war."

In the various islands of the Pacific there is probably an army of hundreds of thousands, and in China there is an army of almost millions. The fate of these soldiers is worrisome. Our armies in China are already cut off from the rear and it is not possible for them to return home, and on top of this there will probably come a time when they will have exhausted their military equipment and bullets. When the Greater East Asian War erupted, I already had grave concern for our army in China.

Revolution in Japan is already inevitable. The upheaval that will precede this strikes us with terror. Even if the "revolution" has occurred, it will probably be a destructive, reactionary thing, and because of this, prospects that Japan will benefit from this are not good. In this way the pendulum will swing to the right, and if this becomes extreme, the counterreaction will naturally probably be great.

July 19 (Wednesday)

This morning's newspapers are full of reports on Saipan. As usual, the ones who talk about "vows" and "fixed determination" are the crowd called Tokutomi Sohō, Saitō Ryū, and Ōzaki Shirō.

General Umezu Yoshijirō has been appointed chief of the General Staff. Marshall Sugiyama Gen has become inspector general of education. The civil ministers always hold many offices at the same time, but those who have the military organization in their background, such as the chief of the General Staff, cannot occupy two chairs. Saipan—the problem of the chief of the General Staff—is certainly one step toward change.

The fact that there was the sacrificial death of all the Japanese on Saipan presents us with problems hereafter. Is not this style of death a dog's useless death? Is it in the interests of Japan? Of course, living under the current military leadership, there are difficulties in finding any other path, but in the end it is as if it were fighting just to die. One can understand the impossibility of such things as "night attacks" (*Yomiuri*, July 17).

Japan works with the standard expression, "We need plane after plane." However, no one gives thought as to whether or not the substance of these planes is really superior.

I inquired about Shimanaka's health, and I went to the Foreign Ministry. Ōkuma Makoto said he had just returned home after leaving his children in the countryside. I understand that Tōjō finally presented a letter of resignation to the emperor. He tried to survive by reforms, but this was impossible. It is reported that Koiso is on his way home from Korea by airplane.

While on the train I met a certain person who previously had been with *Hōchi* and afterward had operated a printing company. He said, "Saipan fell, and the newspapers and radio do nothing more than weep as if they were suffering nervous exhaustion." Aren't they discouraging people from continuing to work?

I hear from even the man of an old couple that the rationing in Omori district was insufficient, and he said they go every day to eat lunch at Shiseidō. I understand that two days a week are foodless. He said, "If rationing were properly improved, the war spirit would rise."

Again on the evening radio there was Tokutomi Sohō. In the newspapers of the following morning (20th) his talk appeared in large print in the *Mainichi*. There was a banner headline article on his talk even in this morning's *Asahi*. It was probably at the order of the Military Information Bureau. What a stupid thing it is! Is this old man the only trump card? Why is this flattering reporter shameless?

In the Minenomachi assembly they practice air-raid drills just about every day, and there is excitement from four in the morning. I understand that this evening they also drilled, and I understand that they might say something to our group. Actually, of late, such complaints are made. I go to bed early. Whenever anything happens, the crowd who are the fishmongers and construction workers leap into action and flaunt their authority. This is the intelligence level of our country. Raising up such people is impossible.

July 20 (Thursday)

(An announcement this morning that at 11:30 in the morning on the 18th a letter of resignation was presented.)

The Tōjō Cabinet has completely resigned. The cabinet that had the responsibility for plunging Japan into misery collapsed as a result of a family quarrel. According to a story of Kasahara, there were a great many anonymous complaints, and even a secret policeman said that if Tōjō had committed suicide it would probably have been all right, but if he lives on in shame it may be that he will be killed.

Saipan—the disaster of the Tōjō Cabinet—the counterreaction—while all the Japanese were fussing—came. If the war becomes unprofitable, the people will necessarily express their discontent. Here is depicted the turning point of the Greater East Asian War. July 20 will probably be a day that will be remembered.

Anyway, there has not been in Japan a cabinet that has exhausted recklessness and ignorance to this degree. After all, the power group that manipulated him is the responsible agency. However, while Tōjō fought them he rode atop this power group and exercised total control. But simultaneously occupying the position of chief of staff, he increased his control over this power group. This becoming unbearable, he was overturned. The newspapers that previously expressed flattering words about the union of politics and war by way of his being chief of staff again are speaking of such things as "absolute confidence in General Umezu," and "intense military operations lead to the completion of the war."

Both yesterday's and today's newspapers are overflowing with words of pathetic resentment. Now, for three days during the week there were only two-page newspapers, but in these two pages there were articles stating, "The time of trial of one hundred million," "revenge on the enemy in the southern ocean," "hurry the improvement of transportation difficulties," "students who are drenched with the sweat of anger never leave their workplace," "we vow to fight the enemy throughout the land" (the above from *Asahi*), and nothing else. Because *Asahi* was like this, one can imagine what the other newspapers were like.

As to the reason for the defeat, the tone of discussion expressed in "The Basic Cause Was the Lack of Military Equipment" (July 20, *Tōkyō shinbun*) shows the military attitude.

Certainly there have been complaints from the businesspeople. From a representative businessman who expressed himself in this morning's *Nihon sangyō keizai*, there was a clear tone of accusation against the government. The president of Mitsubishi Heavy Industry, Gotō Kiyoshi (*Nihon sangyō keizai*, July 20).

(The language of the other papers was similar.)

Yoshikawa Eiji has written in the *Asahi* (20th). This novelist who wrote *Miyamoto mushashi* (this is his representative work) is one of the leaders (*Asahi*, July 20).

Corresponding to this, the opinions of Tokutomi are representative of this crowd. He still repeats what he has always been saying. That is to say, America will soon decline (a radio broadcast on the 19th).

This evening, for the first time, I learned on the radio that the Imperial Mandate had been conferred upon Koiso and Yonai. The hostile feelings between army and navy are already common knowledge to the nation. The last attempt to achieve necessary cooperation was brought about here. It indicated that representatives of one side do not listen to the other side.

July 21 (Friday)

The newspapers of the 21st for the first time are announcing the submission of the resignation of the 18th. Regarding Tōjō, *Yomiuri* was the only one that wrote favorably and the rest were silent.

On the radio this morning we hear that because of the explosion plot, those around Hitler received serious wounds. He was slightly burned and is conferring with Mussolini. Whether his wound was slight or not needs suspended judgment.

Yesterday evening a phone call came from Kiyosawa Satoru saying that the president of the Asahi Slate Company, Terakado, admires me a great deal. I understand that he says I am great and like a prophet. What I heard was that he said that the contents of what I had written in *The United States Will Not Fight Japan* predicted the present situation. Even Satoru has been rereading the books of people such as "Ikesaki Tada"[58] and says they are completely wrong. Nowadays, there are people emerging who are rereading past works. Of late, the lawyer Masaki read my *Japan at a Turning Point* and sent me a postcard. He praised my predictions.

Both Katō Takeo and Kondō Hōichirō said, "I wonder if any good will come of Tōjō's resigning? So many other people's children have been killed, I wonder if it is enough for him only to resign?"

Tōjō schemed in every way to stay in office, but in the end he did not gain his purpose (*Nihon sangyō keizai*, July 21).

In the first version of the reasons for the resignation, I understand that there were phrases to the effect that there were persons who betrayed the cabinet members and that the senior statesmen had been uncooperative. I understand that because the military was monopolized by the Tōjō clique, it opposed the resignation at that time, and there are all sorts of deadlocks. Suzuki Bunshirō's first announcement (at 7:00 A.M.) was that Abe Nobuyuki would become army minister, and the second announcement by Tsurumi Yūsuke (at about 8:30) was that General Ushiroku had decided to accept the office. Ogata Taketora was recommended for the presidency of the Information Board, but he declined.

July 22 (Saturday)

Mizuno of the police came by and showed me the final list of cabinet personnel. I hear that Vice Admiral Sakonji was negotiated with but said, "The army and navy must be military people. If they are anything else it is no good. Moreover, I declined because if I had entered the cabinet there probably would have been malicious criticism."

Tōjō was popular with the majority of people. This is probably because going to people in the street he was like Mito Kōmon[59] [Mitsukuni]. It appears that Army Minister Sugiyama Gen will simultaneously be inspector general of education.

About the time of my return home, the personnel of the cabinet were revealed. Its novelty is that Ogata has become home minister and is president of the Information Board at the same time. In any case, this is one step of progress. If one views its outward appearance, this cabinet is a continuation of previous cabinets, but in this cabinet there are personnel who are able to coolly study the matters of an "Armistice," "Peace Talks," and "Management of Current Affairs." The cabinet could extend even freedom of speech, and if they are not capable of this, one can see there are obstacles that exceed even cabinet power.

Saipan is a first step in the war, and corresponding to this the Koiso Cabinet is politically the first step toward ending the war. The enemy will invade Guam. Without anyone being told, Guam had its name changed to Omiya Island.

The Koiso Cabinet has been rounded out with seven people of the previous Yonai Cabinet. It includes the ministers Yonai, Koiso, Fujiwara, Ishiwata, Kodama, Shimada, and Hirose. In the Yonai Cabinet the war minister at that time, Hata Shunroku, on July 17, 1940, mentioned the "consensus of opinion of the army" and submitted his resignation to the emperor, and on the 16th there was a general resignation. That is to say the cabinet was fatally poisoned by the army.

The reasons for the destruction of the Tōjō Cabinet were, one, the dissatisfaction of the navy; two, the opposition of the Imperial Rule Assistance Association; three, the uncooperativeness of the senior statesmen; four, the internal conflicts within the cabinet; five, the divisions within the military itself—to the extent that the objective circumstances worsened for Tōjō, he had no power to break through them.

According to Minagawa Eiji, recently he went to express his sympathy to a family in Shiga Province that had lost a soldier son. When he said they should be proud their son is in the Yasukuni Shrine as a god, the mother was enraged and said, "When those who have lost a precious child go to the Yasukuni Shrine, they are made to squat on the white sand like beggars, and they have to bow their heads. I will never go to that stupid place!" Her reaction was almost violent.

The same source. In the area of Kasatsu in Shiga Province, the police chief assembled the ward heads of the villages and ordered them to plant their rice fields until July 20, otherwise they would be arrested. He said, "Don't all the other provinces do the same thing?" This sort of police attitude now is representative.

July 24 (Monday)

As usual the aspirations of the cabinet ministers have appeared in the newspapers. The *Yomiuri* quoted Navy Minister Yonai to the effect, "It goes without saying that the cooperative atmosphere between the army and navy is something like a chain, and when one looks at the links one by one, even though they appear to face in different directions, the chain is very strong."

And Army Minister Sugiyama, "On the basis of even greater closer cooperative union with the navy, great war strength will be produced and the enemy
will be destroyed." I wonder what the new-found emphasis on this point by
both ministers will mean.

Koiso was the gray eminence of the 2-26 Incident, and he was a famous
advocate of the Southern Advance Thesis.[60] In August 1940, at the time the
Konoe Cabinet was negotiating with the Special French Indochina Delegate,
he attempted to resolve the southern problem at one stroke, but the government did not accept this, and Commerce Minister Kobayashi, took his place
and was specially dispatched. Foreign Minister Matsuoka at the time explained, "It is merely exchanging the mask of a devil for a jolly-faced woman
[Okame]" (*Yomiuri*, 24th). The one called Koiso is this sort of man. Yet will
he be any more clever later on? He probably will not.

My wife said that when Odachi became governor of Tōkyō, because he was
a man of ability people expected he would be excellent, but things did not
improve at all, and now this man could become a cabinet minister.

More examples of the sycophancy of the newspapers toward the military.
{The lofty spirit exhibited by Tōjō and Sugiyama) (*Mainichi*, July 24). The
fact that they greeted each other is the "lofty spirit."

In what is reported to the journalists by Navy Minister Yonai, the ration
quantity inclusive of one month's rice is eleven yen per month. Moreover, he
said in this ration that the amount of cooking oil is very limited, and "How
can we help but be skinny?"

According to an account of Kiyoaki, in the countryside along the Tama
River he said tomatoes are fifty sen a piece. The somewhat better peaches
are one yen twenty-five sen. The worsening inflation does not know where
to stop.

I attended a directors meeting of *Tōkei*. Itō Masanori also attended. He said
Tōjō disliked going into reserve and to the end proposed occupying a posi-
tion such as that of "high command." Because of this, previously, when Kido
asked Tōjō how it would be if someone were appointed chief of the General
Staff, it is said he replied, "Is this the desire of His Majesty the Emperor?"
Consequently, reluctantly he appointed a navy minister for the position.

It was only the lantern-bearer Tokutomo Sohō who approved of Tōjō.
The incendiary of this war (*Mainichi*, July 26).

It is said that Tōjō in his China policy proposed cooperation with the Communists (the Yenan government) and opposition to Chungking. This is a
story of Rōyama. One understands how deviously foreign affairs are handled.

July 25 (Tuesday)

I stayed at home all day. I wrote an editorial for *Tōkei* concerning the "Shigemitsu Diplomacy."

July 26 (Wednesday)

Captain Takase Gorō of the Navy Information Bureau at the Economic Club stated that at Saipan the Combined Japanese Fleet sailed out, but the enemy had prepared three battle stages. On the basis of reports from the Japanese reconnaissance planes that the Americans were in front of them, all the aircraft had to be launched, but when they tried doing this, confronting them were American battleships, and the planes suffered extreme damage before they found the battleships. There was a battle with the American central squadron, and the Japanese exhausted their ammunition. When they withdrew toward Guam, the American left-flank squadron was waiting, and very few aircraft survived. That is to say it was almost the same as saying that the naval aircraft are "nonexistent." Even on this occasion I understand that it is said that the army planes did not appear, and they promised, "After this we plan to go out, but. . . ." The navy in the Pacific and the army on the Chinese continent has been the dilemma in this war.

In the morning I went looking for support for the Japanese Diplomatic History Research Center at the Okura Company. Afterward I went to the Manchurian Railway Office, but the response was not encouraging. I sent a letter to the company president Kobiyama Naoto, but there was no reply at all.

According to this evening's radio, it is reported that the enemy has invaded Guam (Omiyajima) and Tinian Island.

I understand that Captain Takase stated that of the forty thousand soldiers and twenty-five thousand native residents on Saipan, none were traitors. It seems that among these, even with those who had been rescued, it was certain that war deaths exceeded fifty thousand.

Even considering present circumstances, nobody is able to give the army any advice. As an example of this, there is an editorial in the *Chūbu Nihon shinbun* entitled, "The Need for a Leap Forward in the Administration of Munitions Production" regarding Premier Koiso's announcement under the title, "National Responsibility Must Be Returned to the Highest Commander." What does this phrase mean? I do not understand what he is saying, but it is a rather resolute way of speaking (*Chūbu Nihon shinbun*, July 26).

Articles with the same meaning have already appeared in the editorials of the Tōkyō newspapers. It means that the conduct of the war must go hand in hand with production. This again is as roundabout as it is unintelligible writing.

The contemporary situation is such that it is completely impossible to write anything unless it praises the military.

When Tōjō planned his reforms, Kishi did not submit a letter of resignation. He insisted on a general resignation. It appears that Tōjō considered having the Kempeitai put Kishi under arrest. However, it was his chauffeur who was arrested. For such people as Ogata and others, there was the danger of "arrest" if they insisted strongly on certain things. This is the current state of our country. Previously, Suma, chief of the Information Board, was summoned by the Kempeitai.

July 27 (Thursday)

I stayed at home all day. Because we are partially evacuating, I am arranging old letters and other things. I am recalling events of about the time I crossed from America to Europe in 1930. I am remembering the kindness of various Japanese on the American West Coast, such as Yamaguchi, Iri, Arima, and Morozumi. What is the news about Yamaguchi and the others?

Suzuki Bunshirō said that when he looks at the instructions that come to the newspapers from the Information Board, he feels extreme contempt. He said they resemble instructions for a child. However, these instructions are decided upon by young, low-class officials who would not even be admitted into a newspaper company. The fact of the low-level of breadth and intelligence in politics and diplomacy is because it is based upon such low-class officials—even the upper-level is formalistic—and national politics in practical terms was controlled by them.

The editor of *Tōkei* said that hitherto when the cabinet changed, the Information Board inquired in detail as to its real meaning and style of writing, but this time nothing at all has come forth.

July 28 (Friday)

The ration of vegetables is practically nothing, so many wives madly rush to the countryside to stock up. Tobacco also cannot be bought. I hear that in the neighborhood tobacco shops they sell at seven o'clock, but with queues like meandering snakes this morning they were sold out completely with still sixteen people left.

There was a conference of editors of the *Oriental Economist*. I understand the General Staff Office bought up five issues and sent them to friends. They understand that opinion that is not an official product has the trust of even foreigners, but they cannot think in terms of the larger perspective.

Nevertheless, the one who maintains the lonely castle of integrity in times of oppressed free speech is only Ishibashi's *Tōyō keizai*. Certainly, this is worthy of future recognition.

In the new Koiso Cabinet the ministers of both army and navy made statements, and four-point proposals were made. In these they said, "In order to promote the fighting spirit of the people, the government gave careful consideration to uplifting public morale" (cabinet meeting, 28th). The matter of "why isn't the fighting spirit high" hitherto was the question of the bureaucratic military people. The acceptance by Ogata of the Information Board presidency shows at least a concrete attempt to achieve this.

It appears in the Saipan battle that the number of those who lost their lives was exceptionally high. Yet the number of casualties has not been published even once. There is only scorn for the American publication of such figures. Probably until the end the true facts of the war will not be revealed.

July 29 (Saturday)

I wonder how it would have been if at least the ordinary people had been ordered to remain alive without forcing the Japanese residents on Saipan and other islands to commit sacrificial suicide. If that had been the case, a new economic foundation would be possible. Their present complete destruction was suitable for the American side. It is because the Americans can act freely with nothing left unfinished. However, it is absolutely impossible to discuss this matter.

There are no swift transport ships to send food supplies to the various islands in the southern area. Therefore, I understand that cargoes are transported there by submarines and warships. This is the story of Kishino's nephew. He is in charge of transporting food there. He said that because there are no ships, he is now the supervisor of shipments in the homeland.

Examples such as this are numberless. It is a matter of drafting as "soldiers" personalities central to the increased strengthening of war power.

In society there is nothing as fearless as ideas. This is because ideas do not enter the human mind without being understood. Contrarily, there is nothing more fearful than violence. This is because people cannot control it.

In the July 29 issue of *Tōyō keizai* there was an article by Ishibashi about "The Tōjō Cabinet lost the hearts of the people and was widely forsaken by the able people in society." Even during the previous cabinets there was no one else but Ishibashi who could write such things.

July 30 (Sunday)

Rain is falling. After the continuous drought, now there are floods. Many trains are not getting through. Probably the problem of food supplies will be extremely acute this year.

I understand that there was a man who came to sell candy at 150 yen per kamme. This is fifty times the price compared with two years ago.

From today onward I begin writing the "Modern Diplomatic History." I intend to go from the Washington Conference to the Greater East Asian War. I hope this will play a role in cultural history and be something left behind for later generations.

EXHIBIT 2–6
Matter Excluded from
Protection

Nonprotectable Matter	Basis for PTO Refusal
Design of international "slash" symbol placed over a portrait of President Lincoln (for place mats)	Mark would disparage or bring a person into contempt or disrepute
FLAG OF ITALY (for pasta)	Insignia of a foreign nation
Graphic pictures of nude figures (for wearing apparel)	Immoral or scandalous matter
Photograph of Brad Pitt (for salad dressing) (unconsented)	Unconsented use of living person's portrait
PETERSON (for hiking boots)	Primarily merely a surname
LEATHERETTE (for gloves made of vinyl)	Deceptive
PARISIAN EROS (for perfume not from Paris)	Geographically deceptively misdescriptive
BREADSPREAD (for margarine) (without proof of secondary meaning)	Merely descriptive
NIKEE (for athletic gear)	Confusingly similar to a registered mark
SPIROS' OLYMPIC RESTAURANT (& DESIGN OF FIVE RINGS)	Statutorily protected matter
SHAPE OF PIANO (needed for acoustical reasons)	Functional

(See Exhibit 2–6 for a table of matter that is excluded from trademark protection.)

UNITED STATES PATENT AND TRADEMARK OFFICE

The government agency responsible for reviewing trademark applications and issuing registrations is the U.S. Patent and Trademark Office (PTO). The official address for many communications sent to the PTO is Commissioner for Patents or Commissioner for Trademarks, Washington, DC 20231. The physical location of the trademark section of the PTO, however, is not in Washington, DC, but is 2900 Crystal Drive, Arlington, Virginia 22202. The PTO is currently scattered throughout eighteen buildings spread over one mile. The PTO plans to move all of its operations to Alexandria, Virginia, by mid-2005. The PTO maintains an excellent web site at http://www.uspto.gov, offering general information, updates on new issues, forms for downloading, a database of more than one million registered and pending trademarks, statistics, lists of PTO fees, and a wide variety of other valuable information. (See Exhibit 2–7 for a list of frequently called PTO telephone numbers.)

The trademark section of the PTO is divided into a variety of different departments, such as one handling assignments, one dealing with postregistration matters, and one dealing with intent-to-use applications. Due to the spread of computer and communications technology throughout the world, the workload of the PTO increased significantly in the mid-1990s. However, after years of increasing

July 31 (Monday)

Premier Koiso who went to pray at Ise related his feelings to a newspaper reporter. His statements about the time recently when he assumed office were foolish, and on this occasion his sentiments were those of a low-level official. This is really impossible. Yonai is superior. At the time Yonai was completing his cabinet, in an interview with a reporter he said, "Military people have received a deformed education" (*Nihon sangyō keizai*, July 24, July 31).

I went to a directors meeting of *Tōkei* and heard rumors about the Koiso Cabinet, which claimed that even the Imperial Rule Assistance Society has no core and will not last very long. While he was in the shadows it was said he was a "great figure" and "premier class," but when he is made to open his mouth one understands his real ability. In the end, for a military person these are not ideal circumstances. Having been army minister for close to ten years, as was true in the past, it was fine if a man became premier, but emerging suddenly like this is embarrassing.

August 2 (Wednesday)

In the evening we held the first meeting of the Kutsukake Warehouse Union. It was at the home of Ayusawa and we had supper there. The members of the association included such people as Yoshizaka, Rōyama, and Yanagizawa. We had a meal of *soba*[61] and meat.

There is a story that says that the undernourished professors of the Imperial University just barely manage to get up to their third-floor research office. It is said in the Ōsaka area that the vegetable ration is once in ten days. Yoshizaka is a product of the Home Ministry and lived at length in Geneva. He related that in the First World War the circumstances were just like the present situation in Japan. Even in the agencies in which Yoshizaka is involved (heads of financial institutions), if food is not guaranteed, employees will not come. I hear that people like night-shift work in factories because they can have a meal at night.

In the *Tōyō keizai shimpō*, Ishibashi wrote his criticisms and demands regarding the new cabinet. The Information Board ordered the elimination of these comments. The reason was they verged on "government libel." In the preceding issue he had written rather strong things but they were not noticed, and probably in the beginning with all the confusion the cabinet did not know its course, but now because they had an unobstructed view they would resort to drastic action.

Colonel Akamatsu, who acted as Tōjō's private secretary, has become chief of military affairs. A direct descendant of Tōjō has been given the most important position, and from that one can deduce his power.

August 3 (Thursday)

I visited Sakamoto together with Yoshizaka and Ayusawa. According to the same gentleman, two or three months ago two colonel-rank officers of the Imperial Headquarters came to the home of a senior statesman (probably Hirota) in the diplomatic field and because the war prospects were bad asked if there were no path for a breakthrough by some sort of diplomatic negotiations.

In the evening Rōyama came to visit. I hear Ushiba came to visit Rōyama. I understand that Ushiba said that it would have been better if the Koiso Cabinet admitted the war situation as it is, that the people should expect the worst and it was a mistake not to have done so. These facts tell us that Koiso does not have a policy direction. That is to say, for Koiso it will be, in the final analysis, a war-continuing cabinet.

According to Sakamoto, England wished to maintain an understanding with Japan until the end. At the beginning of the European war and before he returned home, an English politician named Allen came to Paris and had a meeting with Sakamoto, who was head of a branch of the Manchurian Railway. The purpose was for England to buy all the soybeans Manchuria produced. He said that Allen proposed as payment price all kinds of machinery essential to Japan. Regarding that, they talked to Butler,[62] and Butler proposed an understanding with Prime Minister Chamberlain. Because there was also the problem of face, if in the talks England was refused, it was a matter of talking with the South Manchurian Railway. If the plan was all right, they asked Sakamoto to talk with the commercial attaché at the embassy in Tōkyō. Sakamoto returned home and had various discussions, but these were totally ignored.

Last year Sakamoto went to China and had interviews with influential people. According to him, all these people said Japan would be defeated.

Ogata, president of the Information Board has the trust of the imperial court. He was one of the movers to overthrow the Tōjō Cabinet. There was trouble because Prince Higashikuni came forward, saying, "I will actively participate." It is said that to make him give up this idea was very difficult. (This is not the story of Sakamoto.) When we see the examples of the young soldiers actively seeking the support of the imperial court, we understand this movement as the only way to solve problems at a time in which there is a powerless Diet and the absence of public opinion.

August 4 (Friday)

I am reading *Powerful America* by Eugene Young.[63] It was published in 1936. His account of the roles played by the chief editor of the *New York Times*, Oakes, and Navy Minister Lord Lee is of interest. Moreover, following this he is just regarding the formulation of Japan's world political policy. His placing the responsibility upon the military corresponds to what others say.

It is said that since the beginning of the China Incident there have been in excess of two million casualties because of Japan. And added to military casualties are the civilian casualties. This is something relayed by Sakamoto from talks with influential Chinese.

August 5 (Saturday)

An article was inserted neither as an editorial nor as news in the *Mainichi shinbun* (*Chūbu Nihon shinbun*, August 1).

The preceding was probably supplied by the Information Board from a "canned" reporter. (The above-mentioned from *Chūbu Nihon shinbun*, 1st.) Tōjō, who possessed unheard of powers as premier, chief of the General Staff, and army minister all at the same time, was overthrown without difficulty. This Tōjō, on the same day that Koiso was performing his prayers at Ise, accompanied by General Akamatsu and other retainers worshiped at Ise. He behaved as if no one else was there. The reason for the overthrow of this dictator is that Japan in the end has as its core the Imperial House. And on the basis of this system I hope that the war will be brought to an end without necessitating a violent revolutionary stage.

My body is extremely exhausted. It could be the lack of nutrition, but the reason is not clear. When I took my temperature it was 37°. Resting.

August 6 (Sunday)

Here it is impossible for me to buy a newspaper if I do not show a coupon stating I am a subscriber in Tōkyō. Here I have no newspapers at all. I rely solely on the radio.

The Koiso Cabinet has abolished the previous "Imperial Headquarters–Government Liaison Conference" and established the "Supreme Council for the Direction of the War." While it is a small point, one notices that the *Information Bureau Bulletin* wrote "government" first in the statement, "It has been decided that there will still be weekly regular exchanges between the government and Imperial Headquarters." In this structure there are only the brains of the army and navy and the related cabinet members, and it is not clear how many people this is. It also expresses the frequently heard phrases of the army's and navy's close rapport. It is a laughing matter to say, "We will not pay any attention to what has happened in the past." The Greater East Asian War is a war between army and navy.

There is an article in the *Shinano mainichi shinbun*. It is an illustration of how inefficient bureaucratic control is.

An American girl placed the skull of a Japanese soldier on her desktop. This was broadcast by Tanaka Ichitarō as evidence of the devilishness of America.

Recently, anti-American hostility is being vigorously stirred up. The newspapers collect information about these matters and write about them. Doesn't hostility emerge in conformity with these government ideas, and is it an attempt to shift attention to the outside. (*Shinano mainichi*, August 4)?

August 7 (Monday)

My wife and Eiji returned to Tōkyō. The rain fell through the day. My system is out of order for some reason and I had the feeling I wanted to return to Tōkyō and eat raw vegetables. Every morning I think I am getting more emaciated. Compared with the spring of this year I have lost one kan, eight hundred me.[64] For two or three days I have not smoked tobacco.

Hara, the chairman of the Sūmitsuin, has died. He was given the rank of baron. A lawyer who has contributed nothing at all to national politics should be ashamed of honors.

One hears attacks on Tōyama Mitsuru from all quarters. They say such things as Tōjō gave him money lavishly, or his elder son Hidezō, by claiming he was an outstanding specialist, escaped military service. It is said that Tōyama is not in a position to be a patriotic leader and the army has curried favor with him. It is a society in which hooligans flourish. The boss of the National Essence League, named Sasakawa Ryōzo or something, is said to be a millionaire. In the right wing there is no one without loads of money. Because of this they will not let the war be stopped.

August 8 (Tuesday)

Premier Koiso made a radio broadcast. I did not understand what he was saying. What is the meaning of his conclusion that "We all serve only the emperor"? Phrases like this appear understandable, but the real meaning is incomprehensible.

August 9 (Wednesday)

Previously, Konoe visited Hatoyama about nine in the evening, and he talked about the process of Japanese–American negotiations. Hatoyama does not respect Konoe, but he appreciated his predicament. Sakamoto said that the one who ruined these negotiations (in the early stage) was Matsuoka.

In the opinion of Sakamoto, the Axis objective of crushing America with its power was actually added later, and in reality it was based on the pressure of the military. Kurusu opposed them and three times sent telegrams from Berlin proposing negotiations with America. However, regarding this, I understand there was no response. It is said that in the end he said it would be better if he entered into negotiations with America.

I said the pressure of the military is probably the truth, and directly afterward both Konoe and Matsuoka spoke of "war" publicly, and they probably thought that if they put this forth strongly the other party would pull back.

Tokutomi Sohō is saying that the bitter experiences encountered by the people is punishment of Heaven.

I hear that Koreans in large numbers are returning home. "Battlefield preparations" have been completed in Taiwan (announcement of the governor-general, Hasegawa, August 5). There are anticipatory preparations regarding the threat of invasion by the enemy against Taiwan.

August 10 (Thursday)

The newspapers, of late, are lavishly writing articles about "Japanese skulls," etc., and this was in an article previously mentioned. Because I had come to Karuizawa, I did not see it.

Regarding this, all the newspapers throughout the country are writing articles about the "American Beasts." The writings, which are not understood as either editorials or articles, are written by officials, and they dictate the type size and other things. The same articles appear in the *Shinano mainichi shinbun* and the *Chūbu Nihon shinbun*. "Be at one's post against the American butchers!" is extremely forceful language. We must win the war. Yet what indeed will be the counterreaction?

It has come about that "Sumitomo" has contributed 2,000 yen to the Japanese Diplomatic History Research Center. With this the total is 7,500 yen.

August 11 (Friday)

This morning's radio transmitted the news that American planes scattered and bombed in the direction of western Kyūshū, northern kyūshū, and the Sanin area. This is the third attack. Also, the content of the afternoon radio was merely euphemisms to the effect, "With overflowing self-confidence, the inevitable victory of our air command forces . . . ," and this did not tell us anything.

In the afternoon I went to Old Karuizawa. On the way I met the poet, a friend of Tsuyuko, named Ōshima Hiromitsu. I hear that recently he was on a return train and was seated with an old navy commander who told him in great seriousness that the American Army would finally use poison gas and all the Japanese would probably be killed. And so Ōshima was in extreme despair.

Such things are the contemporary propaganda style. In the center of the *Yomiuri* there was such an enclosed article of ten columns (August 8).

On August 5 the Supreme Council for the Direction of the War was established. At that time the words bestowed by his Majesty the emperor were "Harmonious Unity." Why did his Majesty the emperor particularly use these words? I am deeply awed (*Chūbu Nihon shinbun*, August 7).

Anti-American articles come out every day. The propaganda policy is to cultivate fear of devils. In reality, the people in general (also the intellectual class) believe that the Japanese people will be killed.

August 12 (Saturday)

In the afternoon I visited Sakamoto Naomichi, and together we visited Hatoyama Ichirō. Because I had only met him once, he had forgotten me, but when I introduced myself he recalled me immediately. From about 2:30 in the afternoon until about 8:00 in the evening I listened to various stories. Particularly interesting were those concerning the circumstances from the time of Premier Tōjō's resignation to Premier Koiso's assumption of office. I said if the Senior Statesmen Conferences were a majority system, nobody would assume responsibility, and if it is not an organization in which the Privy Seal assumes responsibility to the bitter end, it will be worthless.

I will write about the content of these talks separately, but, regarding the Tōjō Cabinet, the senior statesmen first of all lost hope and then went into motion. The military opposed their action. Private Secretary Akamatsu said that if Tōjō had been replaced at that moment, the army, which had become unified at great cost, would again have been fractured. He said to Kido of the Imperial Household, that he must assume responsibility.

It appears that Hatoyama himself seems to have the aspiration of solving current problems. Moreover, in actuality, up until now his stance has been clear; he has turned his back on opportunistic groups completely, and because he has withdrawn from the Imperial Rule Assistance Society he has an independent position. Therefore the senior statesmen—particularly Konoe and others—have fixed their attention on him and cooperate with him.

One hears frequently the rumor that Hatoyama has been arrested. Once, a Kempeitai bureau chief named Tsukamoto came to Hatoyama and questioned him concerning "liberals." As a result, the policeman was thoroughly impressed and said, "While I am at my work I absolutely will not let others point their fingers at you." After that the rumor arose often, but he is completely safe. It is said the policeman said, "There are frequently letters about your affairs, *sensei*." This Captain Tsukamoto says in front of everyone, "Hatoyama is a great man and inevitably will become prime minister in the future."

On top of the quarreling of the army and navy, the unqualified formalism of the government is not the least improved. They are still rubber-stamping. And they think this is "Western style" (*Yomiuri*, August 7).

In every newspaper essays are appearing under the heading, "Demands on the Supreme Council for the Direction of the War." Because these are being written in every newspaper, they are probably forced upon them by the young military officers.

The president of the Information Board, Ogata, clearly stated that on the 9th there would be no trivial interference with the newspapers. However, I wonder whether something like this is indeed possible. The officials do not have the mental disposition of subordination to their superiors.

Hatoyama is an affectionate man and has liberal intentions. He is also intelligent. One day he will probably come onstage. He is bold and courageous. It appears that he coolly told the right wing, "I do not think the war will be victorious." He is a man of virtue. At any rate, men of conscience—for example Ashida and Uehara—are attached to him. He himself said there are also people who say that if the circumstances arise he could bring together about one hundred supporters.

August 13 (Sunday)

Early in the morning Ōshima and Yoshida Tadashi (Nichidai [Japan University] professor) came to call. They said the trains are overcrowded and there are great numbers waiting who cannot board them.

Yesterday Ide kindly bought us a chicken and we had an excellent meal. However, if he paid twenty yen for it, then the main dish for one meal could not be less than five yen.

August 14 (Monday)

I left early in the morning. From Karuizawa I traveled with Kurahashi Tōjirō.

In the evening I had a discussion with Machida Chūji, the home minister. There were also such people as Hasegawa Nyozekan, Baba Tsunego, Ishibashi, and Takahashi Kamekichi.

The Supreme Council for the Direction of the War is made up of the premier, the chief of the General Staff, the vice-chief of the Military Planning Board, the army and navy ministers and Foreign Minister Shigemitsu. The minister of munitions does not attend. They are discussing when the decisive battle of the war will take place. I will write about his discussions separately (the beginnings of Japanese–Chinese relations).

Rationing is getting worse and worse, and everyone rejoiced when I brought a single radish for everybody from Karuizawa. According to the account of Ishibashi, the cost of a ration of food excluding rice for a month is two sen, two rin, for a daily average of vegetables, and for fish and other things it is a total of four sen, two rin.[65] Moreover, according to someone's account, the cost of a month's ration for a four-person family was something like forty-two yen. According to Takahashi's account, within the 2,300 calories required by human beings, what is at present being rationed is 1,400 calories, that is to say, about 60 percent of what is required. I understand that of late everyone's loss of weight is conspicuous.

August 15 (Tuesday)

I listened to a talk at the Foreign Politics Association of the Treaty Office chief, Andō. Just like the newspapers, he stated things known to everyone. He stated no opinions of his own. To someone's question, "How is Germany doing?" he said, "I am reluctant to talk about this." In the end, naturally, he did not speak the truth. As a diplomatic official he is narrow and not at all brilliant, and as a result he is incapable of diplomacy.

I understand that the Kempeitai stubbornly asked whether former Ambassador Nomura said, "America did not have any intention of going to war with Japan." In the view of Hanzawa, depending upon the circumstances, it was their intention to arrest even Nomura.

According to Baba, just shortly before Tōjō's resignation, the situation had reached the point of a coup d'état. Those arrested by the Kempeitai were as many as forty people, and Shimozono (a reporter with access to Kido's residence) and others remain under arrest as before.

August 16 (Wednesday)

I received from Sumitomo a founding grant of two thousand yen for the Japanese Diplomatic History Research Center. They said this was limited to the present year, and they asked to negotiate again next year. The money was sent to the Mitsubishi branch office in the Marunouchi Building.

I am writing an essay for *Tōkei* on "Invigorate Diplomacy!"

August 17 (Thursday)

Shirayanagi said that Japan would probably be destroyed. On this point there is a contradiction with the fact that he has enormous confidence in the "Japanese people." However, he also says that probably because of their superiority among the colored races they would survive. In the evening I was invited by Kuroki Tarō. Nishimura Isaku and Suzuki Bunshirō were there. Nishimura was formerly the director of the Bunka Gakuin. He is a man who received a sentence of eight months under the Control of Speech Law and for lèse majesté. He is frank and interesting. He has a personality that is easily misunderstood. When he was young he studied abroad, and one sees that sort of influence on him.

August 18 (Friday)

In the morning I visited the residence of Shimanaka. His coloring was good, and by and large he has recovered his health. The fact that he hesitated visiting me was because his attitude has been changing after the loss of his job.

I went to the Foreign Ministry and talked with Takayanagi.

I talked about how it would be if Japan joined in a peace offensive with America and England now, before the final decisive stage of the war. That is to say, we speculated, in conformity with the line of the Greater East Asian propaganda, how it would be if it were clearly stated that all troops would be withdrawn from China, Thailand, and the Philippines and if this promise were fulfilled. These were the things that we should at least discuss with Foreign Minister Shigemitsu.

Shirayanagi said that someone said that as regards working with all one's might, first it was the American war prisoners; second, somebody or other; and third, the student workers.

August 19 (Saturday)

The *Times* report related to the last stage of Saipan was telegraphed to the *Asahi shinbun*. Young boys died and women died. The Americans ask, "Why did these suicides take place? Is it because they believed the statements that 'the Americans are beasts? They will kill everybody!'"

The hundred thousand soldiers and noncombatants on Saipan died in this manner. It was a sacrifice to feudal ideology. It is slavish submission to military leadership. Ah! (*Asahi*, August 19).

It is the same as Attu. This kind of dying I hope will be brought to an end with the Greater East Asian War.

August 20 (Sunday)

In this newspaper also there was a translation of the *Time* article on the last days of Saipan. It was dreadful. The reporter was at a loss for adjectives and was grief-stricken while describing such things as the death of three-year-old children or women committing suicide. A Japanese could neither write nor read such an article. Every newspaper brought up the suicides of women, and the *Yomiuri hōchi* wrote, "They are the pride of Japanese women, they are the Obako of *Shōwa*," Saitō Ryū; "Courage springs forth a hundred, a thousand-fold more, a blaze of glory, for the first time in history," Hiraizumi Kiyoshi. In the *Asahi* the following: "The essence of a great race shines brightly at the last moment; the death of women illuminates the times of war," Takayanagi Mitsunaga; "And thus we are strengthened by this, the true form of Japan," Iwata Tōyō—in this fashion they use half the newspaper. Feudalism—the influence of the *naniwabushi*—great praise for ritual suicide in an age of airplanes.

According to Eiji, Japanese aircraft in extremely great numbers are being blown to pieces all over the sky. I hear that he has many friends in the army, but even Prince Higashikuni has the extremely pessimistic view that if the Japanese airplanes get any worse, nothing can be done. Because the government demands such large quantities, the attempt to satisfy these quotas as a result produces inferior planes. In November the "special student air force corps" will take flight, but Ogasawara will probably not hold out until then. As a result, he said there was nothing else to do but await the coming of the enemy and fight. The account of a certain major-general.

There was a radio report that from five in the afternoon, for about an hour, there were air raids on Kyūshū and the western Chūgoku area. I feel somewhat humiliated by these daylight raids. The report added, "There was some damage to our area."

August 21 (Monday)

The newspapers were full of yesterday's air-raids. In the miscellaneous news columns there were articles about evacuation. As for newspapers full of preaching and figures of speech we have never had such a surfeit of this before in history (*Mainichi*, August 21).

It is reported in the newspapers that an American flier who parachuted down was "speechless with excitement," but I cannot conceive of such a level of excitement, and wasn't it because the flier was badly beaten?

I went to a directors meeting at *Tōkei*. However, nobody was there. I understand that everywhere people are eating food full of sugar. Since the enemy raids are coming closer, it is because there is the feeling that it is pointless to store valuable commodities for the future.

Lt. General Tatekawa Yoshitsugu was appointed head of the Imperial Rule Assistance Society; Colonel Hashimoto Kingorō and Kobayashi Junichirō were appointed vice-chiefs. All of them are revered for their roles in the 2-26 Incident and the 5-15 Incident and are the incendiaries of the war. I hear that these personnel decisions were made by Koiso himself, and this is enough to inform us as to what sort of person he is.

August 22 (Tuesday)

At one in the morning on the 21st (from midnight of the 20th), enemy planes again came, but nothing was dropped (*Mainichi*, August 22).

We should note that in the newspaper articles there is not a single statement about protecting the lives of American soldiers (*Nihon sangyō keizai*, August 22).

What are we to do?! Probably the military defense forces do not like being watched.

trademark filings, the PTO report for fiscal year 2002 disclosed that the trademark staff was challenged with managing a continued decline in trademark filings. The year 2002 represented the PTO's second year that the number of new filings declined. In fact, the fil-ings in 2002 were nearly thirteen percent less than filings in 2001, which followed a decline of twenty-one percent from 2000 to 2001. The decline is attributed to a combination of a slow economy and the collapse of many Internet-related businesses.

EXHIBIT 2–7
Frequently Called PTO Telephone Numbers (Trademark Matters)

Assignment Division	(703) 308-9723
Certified Copies	(703) 308-9726
Director's Office	(703) 308-9000
Fees	(703) 308-HELP
File by Fax	(703) 308-9096, 9097, or 9098
Forms	(703) 308-9000
Intent-to-Use Branch	(703) 308-9550
Oppositions	(703) 308-9300
Postregistration Information	(703) 308-9500
Search Library	(703) 308-9800
Trademark Assistance Center	(703) 308-9000 or (800) 786-9199
Trademark Manual of Examining Procedure	(703) 308-9000
Trademark Trial and Appeal Board	(703) 308-9300
Trademark Status Line	(703) 305-8747

TRIVIA

- The oldest U.S. trademark registration still in existence is SAMSON (with a design of a man and a lion) registered in 1884 for use on cords, line, and rope.
- The first registration of a shape and design of a container was in 1958 for Haig & Haig's "pinch" scotch whiskey bottle.
- Some of the famous sound marks registered include Tarzan's yell, the "Ho, Ho, Ho" of the Jolly Green Giant, and the sound of a duck quacking "AFLAC."

August 23 (Wednesday)

Koiso's speech to the Conference of Regional Governors was increasingly the extreme of ridiculousness. The reason we must have such a man as prime minister is that the military organization alone occupies the center of the political world. This is intolerable in these critical times.

Even the governor-general of Korea, Abe, has an elementary-school-level mind. Korean intellectuals return home constantly. Hirayama of *Tōyō keizai* (a Korean) says that whether Japan wins or loses this war, it will be to the advantage of Korea. Indeed, he is right.

August 24 (Thursday)

The principles of leadership, regulationism, they talk, they talk.

Were such things good for the nation?

The newspapers all write as if the foreign countries were deeply moved by the last days of Saipan. It is the same mentality that writes that the samurai of the Bakumatsu period went abroad in their native costume and the foreigners were impressed.

I went to Utsunomiya to give a lecture. To purchase a train ticket is terribly difficult. They can be obtained by only one-tenth of the customers, but the trains themselves are empty. There were seventy to eighty people in the audience. I indirectly referred to the crisis in Germany. I said that Paris would probably fall within the space of one week.

It is said that in the countryside of the neighborhood of Utsunomiya, an ear of corn is twenty sen and the usual price is fifty sen. Rice is something like ten yen per sho. It is said that in Tōkyō twenty-five yen for one kin of sugar is usual.

The problems of evacuating children from Tōkyō have become the burden of the countryside. It is said that the ration of rice for Tōkyō is something like three go, six shaku,[66] but for the countryside it is two go, six shaku. Moreover, the sugar ration also differs. Step by step this situation is becoming a problem.

August 25 (Friday)

I left Utsunomiya in the morning. It was in order to hear, in Tōkyō along with Ishibashi, a talk by the Shinonomeso group leader Hashimoto Tetsuma.

Hashimoto Tetsuma set out from about 1940 to improve Japanese–American relations, and for this purpose he asked for expenses from the Konoe Cabinet and the army and navy, went to Washington, and consulted with members of the State Department's Far Eastern Department. Originally he was right wing, but because he negotiated with such people as Grew and

Craigie he ended by understanding the good points of Americans. Now, more than anyone else, he is pro-American. We listened to his analysis of events for about three hours (separately noted).

On the 23rd Rumania concluded an armistice with the Soviet Union and withdrew from the Axis.

In the newspapers there are already attacks that say that the Koiso Cabinet is in slow motion. It appears that the military and the Kempeitai are encouraging attacks on the Koiso Cabinet. In this morning's *Asahi* there was an editorial, "Warning against the Weakening of Controls." In the *Tōkyō shinbun* there was an attack concerning slow motion. I understand that with regard to the fact that *Tōyō keizai* did not support the Tōjō Cabinet, the former eliminated its article and the latter subjected it to intense scrutiny. The Kempeitai came to the organization of Takahiro (a friend of Eiji) called Shin Nihon Remmei (New Japan League) and suggested it hold a lecture meeting critical of the present cabinet. It is clear that the Tōjō party is controlling the army and from there used the Kempeitai. The newspapers also took advantage of these circumstances. With regard to the people, is there no other technique but pressure?

I understand that the military believes to the end in a final divine wind and that the war will end with a great victory.

Hashimoto Tetsuma says that under present circumstances carrying on such things as a peace offensive and peace negotiations is completely premature. In other words, people do not grasp the actual facts just as they are. This being the case, the same gentleman believes that with the grace and help of the gods, Japan consequently will obtain victory—at least he believes everything will be all right.

August 26 (Saturday)

I went to a used-book store. Recently I bought books that I most dislike, that is to say, works of people such as Tokutomi Sohō or on "The Japanese–American War." This is in preparation for writing about matters of the past.

August 27 (Sunday)

From two in the afternoon, my wife and I and the Obama family had coffee. There is a physician named Kakiuchi. It seems that he thinks the Americans will kill all the Japanese. There are only two physicians in a large hospital called Juntendō—the aforementioned gentleman and a graduate of Taiwan. Taiwanese and Koreans are not drafted.

The fact that the Koreans are in the process of returning to the peninsula is clear in the account of Yamada. Two Koreans who worked for *Tōyō keizai* both returned to Korea.

Yamada, who is a Korean, openly stated that whether Japan is victorious or is defeated, it would be good for Korea. He said if it were victorious, Korea would probably be treated better, and if it were defeated, it would be independent. According to Uma Makoto, there are Korean officials in the Foreign Ministry, and their manner of blunt speech expresses their hope that Japan will be defeated.

August 28 (Monday)

The military says, "The government is talking about straightening out the matter of free speech, but they will do it in their own way." Therefore, the government has totally increased its pressure on any attacks on the former Tōjō Cabinet. Such warnings and deletions came about a week later. That the sources of these orders are neither the Information Board nor the Home Ministry is proof that it was the Army Information Bureau.

In the matter of the censorship of free speech, there are the Information Board, the Home Ministry, the Police Department, and the Army–Navy Information Bureaus. Each has its own jurisdiction, and they are in competition.

August 29 (Tuesday)

I have received a contract for part-time employment from the Foreign Ministry. Such things as forms, photographs, and copies of family registers are troublesome to prepare. This is bureaucratic "red tape."

It seems that the government has already decided that as regards diplomatic problems, in the Diet, in order to make public Japan's circumstances, the question-and-answer style will be used.

At the request of Yonezawa Yashushi, we had lunch together. The account of the same gentleman.

1. At the Mitsubishi Bank they employed construction workers. It cost 16 yen for a period of two hours in the morning and two hours in the afternoon. It was 4 yen an hour. However, poeple who work at the bank receive about 120 yen a month. It is natural that complaints will occur.

2. Among the Koreans there are eighteen whose wealth exceeds 100 million yen, and there are even two who have 200 million yen. They contribute money to the independence movement.

3. The total of oil production before the war was 3.4 million tons. Now we probably do not product 140,000 tons. Because all the machinery is sent to Palembang, circumstances do not allow increased production.

4. The total production of gold before the war was 40 tons. At present it is 14 tons. The inconvertible paper money in the Co-Prosperity Sphere is probably 40 billion yen.

5. Last year the production of steel was 4.31 million tons. At present it is probably about 3.4 million.

In Manchuria it has declined from 1.5 million tons to 120,000 tons.

6. At the beginning of the war there were 6.85 million tons of shipping. However, now in April of the present year it is 1.5 million tons. Besides this there are requisitioned ships, and these probably do not exceed a total of 150 tons.

August 30 (Wednesday)

Paris has finally fallen. There is a report from the enemy side that it will definitely be handed over on the 25th. (The 29th according to the German announcement.)

On every side there are prayer meetings being held for victory. I judge the level of intelligence to be no different than at the time of the Mongol Invasion crisis.

August 31 (Thursday)

In order to write about the facts of the Washington Conference, I am reading the *Oriental Economist* of 1921. The tone of argument of the *Oriental Economist* is pervaded with liberalism and is extremely fine.

September 1 (Friday)

It is earthquake commemoration day. I went on a pilgrimage to Tsurumi. The iron fence of the cemetery had been completely removed. The bronze statues of the *Sōjidera*[67] no longer exist. Each and every one has been requisitioned. There are no railings on the bridges and no metal fittings on the windows. The Greater East Asian War has completely robbed Japan of all kinds of iron.

It is a full five years since the European war began. Previously, I said that in five years the full force of the war would reach its climactic peak, but the surrender of Germany is still ahead.

Ōkuma Makoto remembers that I made pessimistic remarks concerning the future of the war and said, "When things were going well, I wondered about your statement, but I submitted to your foresight."

September 2 (Saturday)

Speaking of the Japanese Diplomatic History Research Center, I sent a letter of Ōkura Kishichirō and also visited his private secretary, but there was not even a reply. In actuality when I took charge of soliciting funds I learned that money would not be easily forthcoming. However, I thought that someone like Baron Ōkura would be more sympathetic to such a venture.

After a long while I went to the Tōjō shoe store. I understand that the shoe shops have been completely merged and the store in question has lost its self-management. And now a unified company has been established somewhere in the Ginza. The owner said, "Under the circumstances it is absolutely impossible to accumulate stock and quality merchandise is impossible, and this is because no one will assume responsibility."

Tōjō is gripped with extreme fear about the consequences of the Japanese–American War. I said, "There is nothing America can do to the Japanese race. The problem is that confusion inevitably arises domestically and the matter of being on the verge of famine is inescapable." I said that in other words internal problems were a far greater danger. It appears that his decision to buy a factory in Matsumoto was because of my encouraging remarks. He said, "Your optimistic discussion has given me courage."

September 3 (Sunday)

I came to Karuizawa. I stood all the way in second-class. This was the first time that I was not able to sit all the way to Karuizawa. It is extremely difficult to buy tickets. It was because of Kiyoaki that it was possible to purchase one, and it was a result of his using his connections. Even at that, my wife paid five yen in "thank-you" money.

The grass in front of the garden is running wild. Of late, our manager, Ide, has become rude in his self-importance. It is because the people from the city are extremely flattering and dependent on him. In general, the self-importance of the farmers in the countryside is extremely brazen. They do nothing for us.

Unexpectedly, a woman came to visit. While we were talking for a while I recalled she was Kasama. Her question was, "Isn't the war ever going to end?" It appears she came to consult about how one is to handle such things as baggage, and by herself she can do nothing at all. She has extremely emotional confrontations with Tsurumi. She talks as if Tsurumi was engaged in extremely villainous acts. This might well be true of Tsurumi, but she is somewhat eccentric.

September 4 (Monday)

From the radio I learned that Finland is carrying on negotiations with the Soviet Union and demanding the withdrawal of the German Army. Germany accepts this.

I hear of late that someone is saying that in the dispatches from Ambassador Ōshima each and every report is pessimistic and is asking for caution. Now, at this late date, what is this man saying? This man's reports and behavior are one of the reasons for the country's mistakes.

The premier is a military man; the ambassador to Manchuria and the governor-general of Taiwan are both military men; and in reality those who conduct politics are all military people. In light of this, there is no reason that things should be going well for Japan. The ignorant lead Japan.

September 5 (Tuesday)

A new subscription to the newspapers is completely impossible. When I came to Karuizawa I became "newspaperless," and the radio alone became my single source of news.

September 6 (Wednesday)

In the country area called Iwamurata, restaurants and noodle restaurants are completely nonexistent. I see that the controls have at last penetrated as far as this countryside.

In anticipation of enemy attacks, bamboo-spear training is being carried on everywhere (*Asahi*, September 6).

This is evidence that the military and greengrocers are calling the tune.

On the way home I met Rōyama Masako. She said she had come today with Ayusawa Tsuyuko but no one was at home. I came home accompanied by Masako. She has an interest in politics and appears to be a woman of extremely excellent mind. I have heard about her qualities. This is what she said.

About April and May of the present year, Tōkyō Women's College was cruelly harassed by the Kempeitai. Kempeitai with their shoes on and in uniform came into the chapel and investigated everything. The wall decorations from Canada and America were also stripped off the walls. Again they stubbornly insisted that an anti-aircraft gun be installed on top of the chapel tower. Moreover, they said that the trees on the grounds were to be cut down. When the college inquired at the Ministry of Education they were told there was no reason for this sort of thing to be done. From this one understands the arbitrary harassment of Kempeitai underlings. The school authorities tamely submitted to orders to the extent that the students frequently protested. (However, the trees were not indiscriminately cut down.)

At the time of the Tōjō Cabinet resignation, when I went to a certain factory in Yotsuya there was a huge notice, and on it was written, "Make Clear the Reasons for the Tōjō Cabinet Resignation." In front of this was a large crowd of people. I thought it was the act of people opposed to the Tōjō Cabinet but when I asked my father I learned it was the act of people in support of the Tōjō Cabinet.

September 7 (Thursday)

I went to the post office and applied for a telephone. It appears to be extremely difficult. In the case of moving a phone it is a matter of getting approval from the head of the Post Office. This is outrageous because the telephones in this town of Karuizawa are 1500 *yen* (the installation is 300 *yen*).

On the way home I stopped over at the home of Sakamoto Naomichi, and Masamune Hakuchō also came by. Among one part of the army, I hear that they are inclined to send Ōzaki Hotsumi to the Soviet Union and Sano Manabu to the Chinese Communists. The fact that Ōzaki has not yet been executed is unbelievably surprising. However, the actual facts are obscure.

When Sakamoto went to Tōkyō, several of his acquaintances gathered together. Among them a navy admiral said, "If things go on like this, there will be nothing else but the sacrificial death of the entire nation." Sakamoto said he refuted him by asking him what then would be the future of the Japanese race, but at this point sacrificial-death-ism is the ideology of the present leadership class.

Ayusawa Tsuyuko told me that on a train someone said in a loud voice, "Why did the Tōjō Cabinet come to an end?" One can imagine this was propaganda of the Tōjō party meaning, "It was a plot of the senior statesmen."

The premier of the cabinet is a military man; the governor-general of Korea is a military man; the Governor-General of Taiwan is a military man; the governor of Tōkyō is a military man; and so the actual leadership is in military men. [They are] there not because of their qualifications. They are there by rank. And yet the rank is an emblem of "ignorance." If this system is not corrected, Japan will certainly not improve.

September 8 (Friday)

All day long I researched the old newspapers of 1921. In these Suehiro Shigeo said that if there was a war between Japan and America, Japan would be in trouble over food supplies. The things he argued at that time are intellectually penetrating.

Compared with this, even in his own Kyōto University circle the scholars of late have no guts. A professor named Taniguchi Yoshihiko who insists extravagantly on a controlled economy argued his case (*Chūbu Nihon shinbun*, September 2).

September 10 (Sunday)

On the assumption we could have a Chinese meal, I invited Masamune Hakuchō, but the restaurant was closed. Of late, even the Chinese who are skilled in getting ingredients can do nothing at all.

September 11 (Monday)

In the morning a policeman of the thought control police came, and one also came in the afternoon. When I asked about it he said they had promised, "Let's hear together what Kiyosawa *sensei* has to say." But it ended up by each coming separately.

The policeman in the morning said, "In the countryside there was a question, 'Why did premier Tōjō resign?'" He answered, "That alone probably indicates General Tōjō's popularity." Because the newspapers were so much his lantern-bearers, he was probably popular among the country people.

The policeman who came in the afternoon said that the people in the countryside say, "Koiso is far more admirable." He said the reason for this was that Koiso fired Koriyama, governor of Nagano, who had been unpopular.

How really misleading it is for all to say with one voice, "In the countryside they think this way."

According to the afternoon policeman, because there was the Saipan disaster and after that the resignation of the Tōjō Cabinet, in the regional workplaces everyone worked with all their might and suddenly efficiency soared.

September 12 (Tuesday)

All sorts of plans are put forward on the premise of "Victory in War." And yet the leadership class has many people who know "There is no victory." Here also the shape of formalism and spiritism is revealed.

There are such things as coal, but their transport is difficult.

Now the number of merchant ships sunk is twice the naval construction capacity. Between Tientsin and Shanhaikwan it is said the trains are always derailed by sabotage.

September 14 (Thursday)

I went to the Foreign Ministry. Takayanagi said he had had a talk with Shigemitsu's private secretary, who asked him to write something about Shigemitsu's speech on the five basic principles to the Diet because of its extreme importance. We had supper together. We paid one hundred yen for three people.

If Shigemitsu as the engineer of peace in Japan insisted upon a pro-Chinese political policy and the Greater East Asian Co-Prosperity Declaration, he would be admired for the clarity of his foresight. On the other hand, if he seriously insists that the political policy of Japan should be the same as the Greater East Asian Co-Prosperity Declaration, he will be Don Quixote. Apart from strategy, the Japanese people do not believe in this declaration.

Takayanagi said that the essays concerning the Greater East Asian Co-Prosperity Declaration that were compiled by the Patriotic Speech Society are of the lowest intellectual level. These are essays of a crowd that believes this is the moment of their triumph.

September 15 (Friday)

The Imperial Rule Assistance Society Youth Group is the only young people's organization in the country, but its leader is General Tatekawa and its brains are a colonel named Hashimoto Kingorō, who attacked and sank the Panay in order to start a Japanese–American war about the time of the beginning of the China Incident. Military men, military men, military men.

September 16 (Saturday)

Recently Ōta Eifuku, Suzuki Bunshirō, and Kanei Kiyoshi met for lunch at the Manchurian Club—formerly the Tōtōtei. The discussion they had there has become a problem, and they were summoned by the Kempeitai. Suzuki was detained for four days, Kanei for two days, and Ōta for one day. Their talk was chitchat about nothing at all. Either someone was eavesdropping in the next room or wiretaps had been installed.

According to an account of Nanao, I understand that orders for listening devices are being received from the army.

I went to the Foreign Ministry. We had a meeting concerning a critique of Foreign Minister Shigemitsu's speech.

September 17 (Sunday)

Before the fall of Saipan, the Greater East Asian minister, Aoki, stubbornly insisted at a cabinet meeting, "The ordinary civilians there must survive without any compulsory sacrificial death. This objective will be communicated from the government to the commanding officer." Tōjō also said there was no point in killing them, and it was decided to send the telegram. However, when it came time to send the telegram the problem arose about what kind of language should be used. If there was an explanation it would be understood, but there could not be too much explanation. There was fear that it would be misunderstood. Thereupon, as a result, it was entrusted to the common sense of the commanding officer. If one puts one's trust in the common sense of military men, one produces what occurred in Saipan.

Even on the point of the possibility of a telegram, there is a gap in terms of common sense between the people in general and the leadership class.

September 18 (Monday)

I attended a board of directors meeting of *Tōyō keizai*. Itō Masanobu, Rōyama and others attended. After returning home, I wrote as "Japonicus" on the subject of Foreign Minister Shigemitsu.

September 19 (Tuesday)

Because Okamura Kesayoshi has been drafted, I saw him off as far as Shinjuku. Even in my circle Kasahara Sadao was drafted, and it was the same for Yoshikazu. Yoshikazu is thirty-six or thirty-seven and is the father of five children. Okamura Kesayoshi is a military man, third class. It is clear that indeed all the young people are being called up. We say the fields are no longer green, and in the towns and villages there are no young people. Yoshikazu, who is from Hokkaidō, is going to Yokosuka. Kesayoshi is going to Aomori. Even this shows the lack of planning in transport.

September 20 (Wednesday)

On the basis of the indirect descriptions in the newspapers, I learned that the American Army has invaded the interior of Germany. The Japanese newspapers do not include a single line concerning this (*Asahi*, September 20).

I am writing a manuscript entitled *Sensen fuko* (Put war aside), and I stayed at home all day.

September 21 (Thursday)

I wrote this previously, but the essential industries, the companies, the bureaucracy all are occupied by military men. This is also true of the premiership, the Navy Ministry, the governorship of Tōkyō, the Imperial Rule Assistance Society, and the head of the Imperial Rule Assistance Young Men's Corps. This is true of all of them (*Yomiuri*, September 21)!

I hear that the ones who profit from the present war are the right-wing organizations. They obtain rights in mining and other things in China, Japan, and everywhere else and earn large sums of money. This is because they have connections with the military people. One example is the right-winger named Kodama Yoshio, who was a candidate for the legislature from Omori ward—he is something in the Kokusuikai (National Essence Society)—and, if one relies upon today's *Mainichi shinbun*, manages molybdenum mining in Fukuoka. He was introduced along with his photograph.

Again in the Burma areas of La Meng, Teng Yüeh, an entire army has been

CHAPTER SUMMARY

Trademarks play a valuable role in our economy. They serve to distinguish one merchant's goods or services from those of another and provide assurances of quality and consistency to consumers. There are four different types of marks: trademarks (used for goods); service marks (used for services); certification marks (used to certify a quality of a good or service); and collective marks (used to show membership in an association). Rights to marks are acquired through use. There is no need to file an application for federal registration of a mark with the PTO to acquire or maintain rights to a mark, although registration does offer significant advantages to a trademark owner.

Not all words, letters, and symbols are protectable. Generic words cannot be trademarked, and descriptive marks can be trademarked only upon proof of secondary meaning. Suggestive, arbitrary, and coined marks are all registrable without proof of secondary meaning. Certain types of marks are excluded from federal protection, such as scandalous marks, deceptive marks, and geographically deceptively misdescriptive marks.

CASE ILLUSTRATION—CATEGORIES OF MARKS

Case: *Corbitt Mfg Co. v. GSO America, Inc.,* 197 F. Supp. 2d 1368 (S.D. Ga. 2002)

Facts: Plaintiff owned a trademark registration for NO FLOAT for mulch and alleged that defendant's use of NON-FLOATING for mulch infringed its mark.

Holding: There is no likelihood of confusion between the marks because *nonfloating* is a common descriptive term for mulch and refers to mulch that resists the tendency to float away due to rainfall. From weakest to strongest type of mark, marks can be classified as generic, descriptive, suggestive, and arbitrary. Plaintiff's mark is descriptive (although it has secondary meaning) and does not rise to the level of a suggestive or arbitrary mark. Moreover, many other mulch producers use a variation of *float* in a similar manner.

CASE STUDY AND ACTIVITIES

Case Study.   Watson Inc., the owner of Fantasy Fun Adventure amusement park, is launching a variety of new products and rides and would like to seek trademark registration for the trademarks under which the goods will be offered. Some of the proposed marks include the following: the design of a series of "international dolls," whose designs will be placed on children's drinking cups and each of which will hold the flag of a different country; the name WATSON for a variety of food products to be offered in the park's General Store; the distinctive "oink" of one of the park's most beloved characters, Pinkie Piggie; a new ride to be called Dynamite; and a series of books that will all have the name Fluffy Buffy Bear in them, such as *Fluffy Buffy Bear Goes to School* and *Fluffy Buffy Bear Gets in Trouble*.

destroyed. Who must be held responsible for this? However, the newspapers are made to write extravagantly every day about the "miracles of military operations" and "divinely inspired campaigns." At a critical time in the defense of the homeland, what are we doing in Burma? Moreover, there is continued lavish praise for the marvels of military operations. The ignorance of the people is also responsible.

September 22 (Friday)

From the evening radio broadcast I learned that eight hundred enemy planes attacked Manila (the 21st, extending from morning till afternoon). I understand the embassy was also bombed. Secretary Satō is there. I wonder what happened to him.

Tōkyō Commercial College has been changed to Industrial College, and Kobe Commercial College has been changed to the Economic College. I know from this that there is still the name-changing sickness.

September 23 (Saturday)

I heard something said to be the account of a certain person who returned from Kōchi to the effect that now in Kōchi the residents dig things that resemble air-raid shelters on the seashore, and people are forced to work in these. Until now people absolutely thought only of Japan being victorious, but because they dig shelters they are beginning to think, "Japan is really in danger, isn't it?" and they are in great confusion.

The fact that there is training with bamboo spears is no laughing matter, and this is going on everywhere. It may be beneficial, after all, to let people know how truly frightful modern war is if their knowledge is as rudimentary as this.

September 24 (Sunday)

In the morning Saitō Yoshiko came to call. Tomorrow she will graduate from Tōkyō Women's College. In their dorm there is enough rice, but there are no green side dishes of any kind. I understand they eat only rice. A person responsible for cooking goes to a graveyard and brings back edible greens. They put this into the soup and eat little else, it is said.

She goes with drafted student workers to a factory, but many students have bronchitis. This is not surprising. It is a matter of inadequate nutrition.

Even Eiko in our family goes to a factory called Japan Steel Pipe, but at lunch they eat rice and soup in which two or three pieces of vegetables have been added. I hear that people cannot obtain such things as pickles at all.

After a long while I wrote a continuation to the work concerning the Washington Conference. In Tōkyō my various activities are many, and this is bad for writing. Because of this I should spend half a month writing at Karuizawa.

The result of dictatorship in Italy is that the politicians and famous people are all killed one after the other. Ciano was shot and his property confiscated. He was shot by the Mussolini party and had his property confiscated by the Bonomi party.

Is there a more eloquent judgment on dictatorship than this?

The *Asahi shinbun* has written an article that damns Finland. Both at the time of the fall of Italy and at the time of the surrender of Bulgaria and Rumania, the Japanese newspapers used the phrases "stab in the back," "traitors," "cowards," and right now speaking of Bagdolio the name means "betrayal." They did not think these countries were exhausted from fighting and would break their swords and arrows. They have only the biased view that "They have separated themselves from us." This is the basic reason they do not understand international circumstances, and still more importantly they lack appeal to the popular sympathy of the world.

The daily radio propagandizes as usual the "miracles" of the military operations in China and the magnificent style that is the "pride of history." I have not researched this, but it appears these are operations to link the Canton area with the Hankow area. Even if this connection is made, didn't they consider how many people will be necessary to maintain this connection? And yet nobody criticizes this.

September 25 (Monday)

I went to *Tōyō keizai.* In the evening I was invited to supper at Mitsui Takasumi's home. My wife was also invited. Along the way I bought Seeley's *Expansion of Europe* for ten yen. Indeed, it was a find.

September 26 (Tuesday)

In the morning I went to the Foreign Ministry and attended a meeting of the *Oriental Economist.* In the evening I listened to a talk at the International Relations Research Society by a Foreign Ministry official named Kakitsubo.

One part of Kakitsubo's account:

The Japanese ambassador to Afghanistan came to Moscow. At first the Afghanistan Foreign Ministry thought the Soviet Union would probably not give Japanese ambassador a visa to enter the country. Whether they would or not would be an indicator for learning the attitude of the Soviet Union toward Japan. Originally, Afghanistan was caught between the Soviet Union and England and its position was delicate. If the Soviets gave the Japanese

258 • SEPTEMBER 1944

ambassador a visa to travel, that would signify a disregard of England (because Japan and England were at war). Because the Soviet Union permitted this, Afghanistan was surprised. After this Afghanistan became strongly resistant to England.

In the Soviet Union there was absolutely no bias in terms of race. Because foreigners are common, even when they break into a shopping line the Russians say nothing. This is respect for foreigners. Mongolians are saluted especially if they are of high military court rank. However, upon returning, the Japanese military people on the train in Harbin abused the upper-class Manchurian military people who were among the ordinary passengers, supposedly because they failed to follow the rules. If the education of the military is not corrected, there is no hope.

The relationship between the Soviet Union and Manchuria is extremely bad. The consular officials are almost all Japanese. There is nothing but quarreling on both sides. And yet the Russians are very good to the Japanese. It is said that Molotov said to Ambassador Satō, "The Soviet Union is faithfully carrying out the Neutrality Pact, and it has absolutely no intention of abolishing it or violating it." The meaning of this was to signify they had no intention of supporting Chungking.

September 27 (Wednesday)

I wrote an editorial for *Tōyō keizai shimpo* entitled, "Investigate Postwar Plans." *Nihon sangyō keizai* accepted my "Record of an Amateur Farmer."

The leader of Bulgaria has been arrested. Considering the circumstances of the times, given his relationship to Germany, he will be executed. Other than democracy, there is no path to maintain the security of mankind.

September 28 (Thursday)

I attended the graduation ceremonies of the men's division of Jiyū Gakuen.

The former minister of education, Okabe Nagakage, delivered the ceremonial address. He said, "After the present war, America and England will not instruct us as they have until now, and we will probably be pressured from all directions. After the war, making vast scientific preparations, there must be victory from the beginning of any hostilities."

As usual, former Minister of Education Okabe stated vigorously what is called the Japanese worldview. He is apparently a fine character but the *sensei* has not in the least awakened to the lessons of the war.

I was almost moved to tears that the innocence of the students of Jiyū Gakuen was sullied. They listened in rapt attention just the way blotting paper sucks up ink. Are there such pure youths anywhere else? The graduates of this school will inevitably become the strength of Japan in the future.

September 29 (Friday)

At the International Relations Research Society, Professor Yokota Kisaburō reported on postwar plans and particularly the Dumbarton Oaks Conference. After all, as I expected, he has an extremely sharp mind. From the beginning this same group had no decision-making apparatus and was a preparatory gathering. Moreover, I understand Hull's opening speech mentioned that the conference was suggested by Molotov of the Soviet Union.

In today's newspapers it was transmitted that the same group has adjourned. It can be said that it is probably a problem of the voting rights of the permanent country members.

The new structure of the postwar will be similar to the League of Nations. Mankind does not have great wisdom.

September 30 (Saturday)

In the afternoon I wrote on my continuing draft about the Washington Conference, and in the evening we attended a supper to see off Kasahara Yoshikazu, who is entering the navy at Yokosuka. He is the father of five children and is thirty-four years of age. According to friends, the recruits are cruelly beaten with clubs and other things, and because of this many become deformed. When one man said things in the wrong way, the entire squad was beaten and knocked down. Is there anywhere in the world a place as barbaric as this?

A report has been issued today from Imperial Headquarters to the effect that the entire army on Omiya Island and Tinian heroically died in battle, ending on September 27. General Ōbata Tadayoshi also died in battle. The fifteen thousand residents on Tinian and the five hundred on Omiya Island—fellow countrymen—all died sacrificial deaths.

October 1 (Sunday)

The report of the total battle deaths of armies on both Tinian and Omiya Island was covered in detail in this morning's newspapers (*Asahi*, October 1).

I hear that Ogata, as an individual, is opposed to sacrificial-deathism and, assembling the teaching group of Waseda, told them it was unfortunate.

On the occasion of this disaster, all the newspapers, as usual, put out special editions. The *Mainichi shinbun* used Suetsugu Nobumasa. He said that this is the turning point of the war. The *Yomiuri* used Kanokogi Karunobu and Sosa Tanetsugu (rear-admiral), and each of them praised "sacrificial death."

Rear-Admiral Sosa cited the battle of Shizugatake[68] in 1584 and said the present was the moment for an offensive turnabout (*Mainichi*, October 1).

The black market has absolutely no ceiling. It is said that one yen for a single egg is rather cheap. Mr. Obama said, "I bought one hundred me of pork for fourteen yen." Mr. Okamura Kesayoshi, who had returned from the countryside said, "Twenty-three or twenty-four yen for a hundred me of beef and seventeen or eighteen yen for pork is the market price there." Recently, when my wife bought potatoes at Tsurukawa they were forty yen per kamme, and slightly larger ones were worth twenty-five sen each. In Saitama Province they are already six or seven yen per kamme.

For the middle class there is nothing else but ruin. We ourselves are now confronting times in which it will be difficult to live.

October 2 (Monday)

The daily newspapers write that the Japanese Army is carrying out "attacks" and "hand-to-hand combat." This is just the same as the *kōdan*[69] tales of Miyamoto Mushashi. The war will not end in victory by such heroics.

I attended a meeting of the People's Scholarly Arts Society. Among the top intellectuals, the propaganda put out on the radio about the "devilish" American barbarians is not popular. Carrying on such propaganda is rather harmful to schoolchildren and the education of others. Yesterday evening Ebina Kazuo proclaimed that the Americans were absolutely lower than animals.

Everybody loves their country. The essential point is inescapably returning to the problem of which techniques will be effective in the destruction of the enemy.

October 3 (Tuesday)

I went to the Foreign Ministry. They said that the manuscript I had written was rejected.

Because the problem of the evacuation of children was not adequately prepared for, everywhere there is abundant criticism of this. When I go to the barbershop there is discussion of this.

Under the auspices of Ishibashi, I attended a dinner to celebrate the acquittal in the Communist Party Incident of Ōuchi Hyōe, Arisawa Hiromi, and Wakimura Yoshitaro (Imperial University professor and assistant professor). Previously, they were people who were brilliantly active in literary society. The essential point of the judgment was that the Rōnō party[70] was legal, but because the crowd that assisted it hoped for the success of the Comintern, they were guilty. However, it was decided that this group of professors was completely unconnected with them.

We discussed what would happen after the war. We considered the problem of whether private property would probably disappear. We decided that private property would probably continue to exist. However, there was general unanimity that, still, for the benefit of the nation it would be put under extreme regulations. A Nazi type thing would emerge. Notwithstanding the fact that Ōuchi is called a Marxist, his outlook is unexpectedly optimistic. He is not conventional. As is true in general of all scholars, he appears to be a splendid man.

October 4 (Wednesday)

Of late, when I write random notes about agriculture there are some ten or more letters in response. Yet aside from one letter that said, "Kiyosawa is unpatriotic. You said pumpkin-heads are the right wing, and hereafter if the *Industrial Economy* prints such things it will be treated severely," all of them were supportive. There were only a few that reacted this way.

Previously, when people got together they talked about food. Now, as there is no food, the talk is about the problems of amateur farming. Everybody is doing this. Akamatsu Katsumaro does it. Matsuoka Komakichi also does it. I hear that the venerable Hasegawa Nyozekan planted potatoes and at the harvest one seed-potato appeared. It is this kind of hobby that has brought about interest in my random notes on amateur farming.

From one reader there was a proposal he became my disciple.

October 5 (Thursday)

The fact that letters are being censored is an expression of the present mentality.

Currently, the value of one sen reveals the inflation. With one sen, one cannot buy a newspaper.

Mr. XX came to call and I learned that the military factory in which he works is set up to produce three hundred tons of materials, but in reality only seventy tons is produced. And yet every day they work with all their might assembling these materials, and without doing skilled work they carry out miscellaneous duties. Today, at least, material was delivered, and tomorrow they will operate the machines. The plans of the Cabinet Planning Board and the Munitions Ministry are irresponsible and come to nothing at all. He said production has come to a standstill.

The fact that the post office has no postcards has been the case for some time. There are no stamps. Queues are formed to buy postcards and stamps. When the rumor arises that "postcards are running out," a queue forms immediately.

A Stockholm telegram transmitted the news that, with the premise of the unconditional surrender of Germany, a plan for its occupation by America, England, and the Soviet has been decided upon by a European Inquiry Commission.

It appears that the Siegfried Line has finally been broken through near Aachen. On the German side this has not yet been admitted.

October 6 (Friday)

I hear that Tōyama Mitsuru has died. He performed the most numerous crimes under the name of patriotism. At the same time he represented accurately the weak points of the Japanese people.

A paragraph of a telegram in *Yomiuri* entitled "The Seven-Lived War Strategy of Kusunoki"[71] appeared in all the newspapers (5th). It is in the style of the energetic fighting of the army that is protecting the island of Peleliu. How many "human bullets" will be spent? Such reports come out every day along with articles entitled "Attacks" and "Hand-to-Hand Combat."

Until about a year ago, queues were forbidden for the reason that they made known to foreigners the inadequacy of our materials. Now every day the newspapers write about the fact that there are no postcards and stamps. There is no longer any concern about external appearances. That postcards have disappeared after all was surprising even to me. The inadequacy of materials and labor has extended even to this point.

Telephone calls are not getting through. It seems that the automatic telephones are defective, as I tried to reach the Yotsuya telephone office all day today without success. And yet I got through to Ōmori immediately. The next stage is that telephones will probably not function at all. It has already been some time since cars have all but disappeared in the towns.

October 7 (Saturday)

It has been raining continuously for four days. I am afraid that in the forthcoming harvest the rice will have rotted. Even our family's fields are considerably damaged. It seems as if divine winds and divine rains, out of season, are somehow besetting Japan.

This morning on the radio Itō Masanori explained that those who think there will be defeat in the war will be defeated. Japan did not in the least think about such things as defeat for many years. This is the reason that the Greater East Asian War occurred. It is only recently that pessimistic talk has occurred. There was no pessimistic talk at the beginning.

A rumor that General Tōjō Hideki has been killed has come from the army. I understand that they said, "Tōjō is no longer of this world." This probably has some sort of psychological significance. Are they saying Tōjō should be called an evil man because he started the war? Or are they saying it was outrageous that he established a party within a party? If it was the former, the significance is fairly important.

There is a naval sanatorium at Tadeshine in Shinshū. The naval personnel there come to steal the trees and rocks of the villas and appropriate these for themselves. The reason is that they say that the bourgeoisie who own these villas are outrageous. I hear it is probable that in the navy they are educated in this fashion.

The same thing is taking place at Yamanaka Lake. The canned goods and other things from the villas are often stolen. The fact that the thieves are probably navy personnel is something I heard previously in other places. Moreover, the fact that the navy beats its new recruits with clubs and other things is a well-known story.

Because such matters are completely secret and cannot be opposed these outrages cannot be corrected.

As regards such matters, in the event there is the building of a new system, there is the absolute necessity for a structure that will make opposition possible.

October 8 (Sunday)

I left Shinjuku at 10:10 and came to Matsumoto, staying over at Nishi-ishikawa. The confusion in the train was beyond words. This kind of confusion is the result of the regulations. In the train I had a slight argument with a man who jumped the line and occupied a seat.

The merchant, factory-worker, and people-who-look-like-contractors crowd occupies the second-class cars. Because of that it is impossible to maintain order. So-called social manners are worsening in the extreme.

One can see the destruction of the middle class and the emergence of the newly rich class. On the trains Koreans are traveling with enormous amounts of baggage. Their appearance resembles that of beggars. The conductor examines their tickets, but because he says nothing they are probably holding second-class tickets. The Koreans are making extraordinary fortunes. I hear that this is based upon black market transactions and that they have networks throughout the country. This problem may become like that of the Jews. The authorities encourage them to change their names, and it is a fact that most all of them have Japanese names. This also is the result of ignorant military politics. The name of their governor-general is Minami. I am not certain, but I think he was the army minister at the time of the Manchurian Incident.

While on the train I read *Free Law and Controlled Law* by Makino Eiichi, which had been presented to me. Indeed, it was interesting. He is an excellent scholar.

October 9 (Monday)

With Shirayanagi I went sightseeing to such places as the Matsumoto Museum and the Matsumoto Castle. In the evening we had supper at the Dobashi home.

The Commemoration Hall is a foreign-style museum and at the same time a museum of natural history. Certainly it was skimpy. In Tōkyō this is also true, but in Japan the poverty of such cultural facilities is truly shameful.

I recommended a great museum (an exhibition of the research materials of local history) as an enterprise to Mayor Hirabayashi Morito.

At noon I had lunch at the invitation of Mayor Hirabayashi. The same gentleman is a lt. general in the army and a classmate of Ishihara Kanji. He praised with all his might the greatness of Ishihara.

Ishihara was sent as a staff officer to Manchuria before the Manchurian Incident, but from about the time he was captain the idea of the Greater East Asian Co-Prosperity Sphere was already in his mind. At the time he left to take up his post, Hirabayashi met him and could see his determination to decisively carry out this great undertaking.

The account of Lt. General Hirabayashi:

1. In the final analysis, the Manchurian Incident was the combined operation of Major General Itagaki and Ishihara. It appears that Ishihara intended to make Manchuria the Imperial Way paradise. His idea was that both the Manchurian people and the Chinese people would look up to Japan. If this took place, a Japanese–Chinese coalition would be possible. America would be confronted by their joint power.

2. Ishihara thought from the beginning that the ultimate enemy was America. However, because Japan could do nothing to this country in her present condition, a coalition with China was necessary. He thought preparations for this were inevitable.

3. The following occurred when Hirabayashi was on his way to Berlin having passed through America. At that time he resided in Berlin and he related, "Hirabayashi, we have heard that in America there are many eighty- and ninety-story buildings, is this true?" "It is just as you say." "They are foolish fellows, aren't they? With such buildings, aren't they just targets for airplanes and bombs?"

4. At the time, Hirabayashi was a Kempeitai commanding officer and there were frequently orders that seemed to be issued by Tōjō Hideki. Tōjō frequently used the Kempeitai.

The account of Shirayanagi. Ishihara is in Tsuruoka, but the head of the Police Department of Yamagata Province prayed, "While I am in this position there will be no order, 'Arrest Ishihara.'"

October 10 (Tuesday)

I hear that the husband of the eldest daughter of Kiyosawa Hiroshi died in battle in New Guinea, and she cries while clinging to her child. Even in our neighborhood in the family of Takada Jinichi the son died during the Manchurian Incident and the eldest daughter was widowed. The eldest son of Akiyama Takashi died. This is true of Ishibashi. From now on, similar tragedies will occur frequently. It is to be expected we will thoroughly understand what the meaning of war is.

At the station in Toyoshina the huge trees and other trees are piled up. These were cut from the property of an old family named Saruta. However, on the other hand it has been decided that because the quality of wooden ships is unsatisfactory, they will no longer be constructed. Because the system of transmitting orders is not penetrating the countryside, such trees are still cut. Even the Aokemi family has been required to provide four or five great trees. This is also true of the large cedars on their northern field dikes.

Since yesterday we have been treated to dishes that are rare nowadays. Indeed, the countryside is well provided for.

October 11 (Wednesday)

On the 8th there was a telegram announcing the death of Ōkuma Makoto, an official of the Foreign Ministry's Investigation Bureau. He was an extraordinary, scholarly gentleman, and I regret this because I was looking forward to his cooperation in the future.

The telegram was marked "urgent delivery" and left the Tōkyō Post Office at one o'clock in the afternoon, but it came to the Dobashi house about eleven o'clock in the evening. That is to say, it took about twelve hours. Of late, telegrams sent to Karuizawa take more than a night and a day. This is the same as it was for letters previously.

In order to buy a ticket in the Matsumoto area, there is a sign that says there is only one ticket for one station (two tickets going down, five tickets going up). In order to go to the next station, it is not unusual to line up.

October 14 (Saturday)

In the evening Shirayanagi and his wife came to visit. It was to express thanks for a previous invitation. When we served supper they said, "If there is a treat such as this, we cannot socialize with you." Experiencing only hardships from the time he was young, he is extremely sensitive to the facts of "life." Moreover, he is surprisingly hypersensitive to my "fame" and "popularity."

There were successive air raids on Taiwan on the 12th, 13th, and 14th (they reported a cumulative total of 2,950 planes). When one sees that even when Japanese forces attacked and sank three aircraft carriers and three unidentified warship-class vessels, the enemy still continued to come and attack, one can see their considerable powerful warship fleets are divided into several squadrons. The decisive period of the war finally draws near.

As usual, the army is carrying out operations in China. It is said they will strike soon at Kweilin. This is extreme propaganda. The army may be succeeding, but on the navy side things are going badly.

CASE STUDY AND ACTIVITIES (cont'd)

Activities. Identify the type of mark each product or service represents (for example, trademark, sound mark, color mark) and then indicate any possible objections the PTO might have to each mark, if any.

ROLE OF PARALEGAL

The role of IP paralegals prior to searching and application for registration is generally limited to research, particularly research regarding whether the mark satisfies the requirements of the Lanham Act for registrability. Each element of the mark should be examined to determine whether it is descriptive, disparaging, comprises merely a surname, includes a living person's name without written consent, and so forth. Design elements of marks should also be considered to ensure the design feature is a separate and distinct portion of the mark, rather than mere background. Additionally, some preliminary discussions should take place with the mark's owner to determine whether federal registration is permissible or whether the owner will be limited to state trademark registration because the mark is not (and will not be) used in interstate commerce.

INTERNET RESOURCES

Federal statutes governing trademarks (15 U.S.C. § 1051 *et seq.*)	http://www.ll.georgetown.edu and http://www.findlaw.com
PTO trademark information:	http://www.uspto.gov (general information, trademark searching, and access to *Trademark Manual of Examining Practice* for excellent information on types of marks and what may be protected) (access http://www.uspto.gov/web/offices/tac/tmep/index.html)
General information on trademark topics:	http://www.findlaw.com and http://www.megalaw.com

October 15 (Sunday)

In the final analysis, because the sacred cows of aggressive diplomacy such as Katō Kōmei and Komura are highly prized, only that of Shidehara is deemed "weak diplomacy."

October 16 (Monday)

The queues meander everywhere through the streets. This is a very common scene recently, but the fact that they are particularly long today is because the people want to know detailed reports of war results for the three-day period from midnight on the 12th, the evening of the 13th, and noon till dusk on the 14th. It is evident from this how much the people in the streets are anxious for news.

October 17 (Tuesday)

At this time all the newspapers are transmitting the news of great victory in the eastern area of Taiwan (*Nihon sangyō keizai*, October 17).

Regarding these battle results, Premier Koiso issued a statement saying, "Particularly in this battle, the torpedo plane squadrons of the army have also participated, and with the army and navy being truly united, they took heart and made a good fight. The battle results should be announced in special capital letters."

Why should the fact that the army and navy are fighting be put into capital letters at a time of national crisis? The fact that the premier says such things probably should be put into capital letters.

A while ago, according to a story of an official of Tōkyō City, when the army used training grounds the navy did not consider them convenient in the least. The army says, who cares about the navy? He said, "The sentiments of these lower-rank soldiers are probably the sentiments of the upper level of the military."

Each and every one of the newspapers has distributed these battle results throughout their pages and is straining to raise the military spirit. After a long while they have been putting out phrases such as "Great Battle Results Rare in History" (*Asahi*). Previously the phrases expressed daily were "Unparalleled in History" or "Both Gods and Men Weep."

As regards the damage to the enemy, they say in general, "500,000 tons and 26,000 men were lost" (*Asahi*).

Yet there are problems about this:

1. The casualties on the Japanese side are not touched upon in the announcements.

2. The enemy announcements transmit enormous losses on the Japanese side.

In the future the particulars of these approximations will probably be clarified. The Navy for the most part made these announcements conscientiously.

All the newspapers are saying, "Because the reelection campaign for Roosevelt is approaching, the American warships will probably go into action." They argue that elections and military action are connected. From this, one understands that they do not know how to interpret politics (*Asahi*, October 16).

What are absolute military strategies? Can that sort of thing exist? Because such ideological discussions are carried on, there are mistakes in important matters.

October 18 (Wednesday)

Men over seventeen years of age are being registered for military service. From the first of November they will begin active service. The war has finally reached our family. Being drafted is all but inevitable.

The boastful talk of the "torpedo planes" of the army has begun again on the radio and in the newspapers. They participated in the Taiwan battle. Whatever they do, afterward this prideful talk inevitably continues at tortuous length.

October 19 (Thursday)

According to Oyazu Masao, the Mitsui general manager, a certain military man came to Mitsui and in front of a Mitsui executive said, "Even my power could completely crush Mitsui." On the one hand, when the executive wondered if he was threatening Mitsui because he could not obtain money by that means, he was intending to obtain money by exaggerating Mitsui's power. Oyazu wondered about how much money Mitsui does have. It might be 120 or 130 million, but that much money is not equivalent to the war cost for several days, and he said Mitsui has no power at all. The overstated power of the Mitsui zaibatsu in Japan is surely formalistic Marxist theory.

October 20 (Friday)

It is being said the Taiwan Sea naval battle is a victory, and an outcry is surging up from the Japanese people. Even in the time of war, it is always the ordinary people who experience joy and sorrow from this sort of single battle (*Mainichi*, October 12).

Optimistic discussions are overflowing, and when there was a ration of sake and an increased supply of vegetables, the newspaper dispatches announced that the American military was entering Leyte Gulf in the Philippines. It appears this is an invasion operation. An example of the ignorance of the enemy's strength here again is immediately apparent.

Propaganda against the "American devils" has surged up everywhere. Its core is the people who lived in America. Ebina, Mutō Seigo, and others are the center of this. Recently Mutō came to my place to ask if there were any revealing photographs of the American devils, but I didn't have any (*Chūbu Nihon*, October 17).

After the establishment of the Koiso Cabinet, speech became relatively free, and the number of those who ask me to give lectures has increased. This evening I attended a lecture meeting at the invitation of the Kaneda commercial group.

I am somewhat surprised at the bad reputation of the former premier, Tōjō. I think it is an exaggeration that there are two hundred letters a day attacking Tōjō. There is a story that when Tōjō went to the Grand Shrine at Ise to pray, there were those who made nasty remarks to his face. It seems that the reason for this bad reputation is that Tōjō made use of the Kempeitai. The story of a certain person is, "I hear that at every little gathering, the Kempeitai infiltrated all of them and spied upon them."

October 21 (Saturday)

The Japanese do not have the ability to discern the important character of a problem. This is why they are bound by formalism.

Because it is being said that victory has been obtained in the naval battle in the Taiwan Sea, there are special rations of sake. The newspapers have attacked this. They attack the things that are obvious to everybody.

The essential fact is that we need concrete information. The Koiso Cabinet is saying there are "charcoal vehicles." However, they do not say why they are any good.

At the International Relations Research Society there was a lecture by Professor Ueda Shinnosuke concerning the "Chinese Communists." The Chinese Communist party has a special section called the Japanese Liberation Committee, and it has the slogan of destroying the militarism of Japan. Moreover, it is actually active against the Japanese Army in North China. He said that among the Koreans, some are fleeing, and those throwing in their lot with the Communists are fairly numerous.

October 23 (Monday)

I understand that an older person opposed the marriage of the second son of Shirayanagi into the Dobashi family on the grounds of unsuitability of age.

Has it come to the point that foolish superstition will cause trouble for the future of children? Both parents thought the marriage proposal was completely splendid, but it appears the grandmother went to a fortune teller.

October 24 (Tuesday)

In the *Tōkyō shinbun* there is only pessimistic material on every topic that states, "Rationing is bad, and if one rides the Tōkyō trains there are breakdowns and one's life is in peril. . . ."

One frequently sees in editorials and other things attacks on the Koiso Cabinet talking about the why of "charcoal automobiles," or it is lukewarm toward them. The *Yomiuri* is the most extreme.

The Koiso Cabinet has again announced "bureaucratic procedures." Again, the people are advised to attend and pray at the shrines (*Yomiuri*, October 24).

On the 20th the German army abandoned Aachen on the Siegfried Line to the enemy. They have organized a people's shock troops corps made up of men from sixteen to sixty years of age. Of late, Himmler has been touting guerrilla war techniques. They will throw the German people into the war until the very end. Magnificent and cruel.

On the 25th about one hundred enemy planes came to attack Kusu Island, in Kyūshū.

Since the 24th, in the eastern part of the Philippines, violent attacks have begun against the American transport ships. The battle results are emerging. At last the decisive great battle has begun. The damage on our side was two cruisers and other vessels.

Because a special ration of "celebration sake" was distributed to celebrate the victory in the battle in the Taiwan Sea, there was criticism everywhere. Moreover, the Koiso Cabinet frequently gives rations to the people of Tōkyō, and this also was attacked. It is the Japanese people hesitantly grumbling over small matters.

October 26 (Thursday)

In the morning I went to give a lecture at the Ashikaga Economic Club. When I looked out from the train it was the height of the autumn harvest, and it was clear that only women are left to work in the fields.

There, at noon, I had two bowls of a soup made with balls of wheat flour called *suiton*. Everybody said it was delicious and ate it up. Previously in this area people invited guests to a meal at a first-class restaurant. But . . . it is said that elsewhere rationing and other things are far worse than in Tōkyō. We are caught between the big cities and the villages, and the resources are inadequate.

In the towns there are signboards saying, "Kill American Devils." This probably means kill those who have come down by parachute. The Bushido of the Russo-Japanese War period no longer exists. There is nothing that indicates that the Japanese have not learned modern ways of thinking and do not possess the old traditions as much as the recent atmosphere in the streets (*Mainichi*, "Contributors Column," October 26).

In Ashikaga the president of the Ashikaga Bank is named Suzuki. He worked his way up from the bottom and is a decisive person. One or two years ago a man from the Kempeitai came to see him and said, "You cannot give any lectures at all." He said if Suzuki did, he would be arrested. Suzuki signed a document promising not to lecture. Suzuki related that "He probably regarded me as a sympathizer of the *Tōyō keizai shimpō*."

In the areas beyond Tōkyō, everyone is absorbed in the battle results. For a while the talk of food was the foremost dominant subject, but recently the talk is of farmers, and this flourishes everywhere. Everybody is performing as a farmer.

October 27 (Friday)

A decisive great battle is going on at Leyte Bay in the Philippines. Three enemy divisions invaded two positions, and when they brought in more military forces, our warships attacked them. This differs from the air warfare hitherto, and our main force is activated. The enemy losses are considerable, but also on our side battleships have been sunk and seriously damaged. Depending on whether the military forces on Leyte Island will survive and be increased, the enemy attack will be halted and, moreover, the tempo of air raids on Tōkyō will be halted.

When we inflict great damage there will be the possibility of negotiated peace, but it has probably not yet reached this point. I wish we would win battles so that we could seize upon timely opportunities.

If one relies upon an announcement of the Imperial Headquarters (October 26) on the damage to the enemy planes that came to attack Saishū Island and Kyūshū, I understand that the five shot down and the nineteen destroyed were equal to one-quarter of the total number. The people believe in the announcements from the navy, but toward those of the army the inclination to doubt is strong.

Kill! Kill American Soldiers! Casualties the Vital Point of the Enemy (*Mainichi*, "Topics," October 27).

The Japanese newspapers always link American elections and the war. It is said that the Philippine campaign is election strategy. Because I receive such questions everywhere, I respond that under Roosevelt there are Republican party members and there are professional militarists. Things do not go according to the Roosevelt's intentions. I explain that the fact that the Japanese do not properly understand American politics lies in the idea of linking war and politics together. That is to say, whether Roosevelt wins or Dewey wins, it is expected that it will be the same. Special *Mainichi shinbun* correspondents in Zurich are saying that this war in the Philippines is an election tragedy (printed on the 25th, issued on the 22nd).

I hear that canvas shoes are forty yen a pair; overalls are two hundred yen a pair. Letters to the editors note that it is natural that the pay of day laborers is high (*Mainichi shinbun*).

October 28 (Saturday)

A talk of Hasegawa (a man who lived in London), who was a *Dōmei* correspondent, at a meeting of the International Relations Research Center.

1. He heard that on the American side they do not announce their losses regarding naval battles at Taiwan and the Philippine Sea, but on the contrary they make a great many announcements of the losses on the Japanese side.

Katō Kōmei did not know the facts of America. At that time I was section head for Immigration, and talks about the immigration problem produced results. However, when he became minister he came to us and immediately announced an end to the subject. He said, "Americans do not understand anything. It won't do any good if we treat them as equals."

October 29 (Sunday)

I conducted the memorial service for Chiba Toyoji. There I heard a story of Ishiguro Tadaatsu:

Count Gotō Shimpei was aware that several tens of thousands of Koreans were living within the borders of Russia, and he said that something must be done about that. At the time, the newspapers attached the label of "outlaw" to the Koreans, but the Count said, "There may be reds among so many people, but in any case, in view of the fact that people who have Japanese names are living abroad, we must protect and make use of them." And he had Chiba Toyoji make up a plan. Because I also was connected with this, I knew about these things. It was also because of this concern that Count Gotō went to Russia.

On the 27th Churchill reported to the House of Commons on his Moscow visit. He was accompanied by Eden and reached Moscow on the 9th of this month and stayed over until the 19th. He said that regarding the Polish problem he could not reach complete understanding. Discussions respecting the Balkan problem were completed. He said that soon there should be an inquiry into the French popular will in order not to give the impression that "it is a government forced upon France by other countries."

In a report he made yesterday after returning from Manchuria, Hayashi Jinnojō said the American air raids are far from blind attacks, and in Manchuria they regularly attack with great accuracy such things as railway switches. The damage because of the air raids at the present moment is 60 percent, and there is only 40 percent production.

October 30 (Monday)

During a rain I gave a lecture for a neighborhood association meeting at a place called Mitaka. It was at the request of the city of Tōkyō.

I only received about thirty-four yen (from the forty-yen honorarium a tax was deducted). I thought about this. Previously, if one received a thirty-yen honorarium, one probably could buy about five kamme of sugar. Now, because one kamme of sugar is about thirty yen, if one does not make six lectures one can't get hold of one kamme. Our daily labor only allows us to buy one hundred momme of sugar.

October 31 (Tuesday)

The previous evening Ishibashi had had dinner with Vice-Minister Shibayama. The army vice-minister said he wished that soldiers would be pulled out of the factories and other places, but now the factories do not wish to release them.

In the air raids on Okinawa Province, the governor ran away somewhere and has not yet reappeared. Because the chief of police stood his ground, it was possible to maintain order. Thereupon the people of the province said the governor should be dismissed and the chief of police should be made governor. They said that when the military was there, at any rate, order was possible. There are two types—those who think that standing in the shadow of the military they will attempt to escape responsibility, and those who think that if there is no military, on the contrary, the interference of the army will take the form of harassment.

November 1 (Wednesday)

Because I was invited by Ayusawa, I set off, taking advantage of a ride in Ishibashi's automobile. When the train reached Ōmori, station there was the cry "Air raid! Take shelter!" Everyone rushed off and hid themselves in their own way. In just ten minutes the raid was canceled. Again I boarded the train, and when I went as far as Shinagawa again there was the announcement "Air raid!" Take shelter!" Everyone became agitated and crossed the street and took shelter at the sides of buildings. When they are in such places if there were a fire they would all die. I went outside. There was extreme confusion. In ten minutes there was an all-clear, but the trains did not move. Because there was nothing to be done, I went to *Tōyō keizai* by streetcar. It was exactly at the moment that people were entering its basement. Under such circumstances, if there had been an air raid it would have been really disastrous. The fact that the formalistic training comes to nothing is understood from the events of today.

Thinking that Ayusawa was still waiting, I asked Ishibashi to go by train. The train was in extreme confusion. When one relies on what was later announced, it was said that a huge airplane came to the Tōkyō-Yokohama area and fled without dropping a bomb. Everyone is questioning whether this plane came or not.

All the newspapers are writing that the air raids are being conducted in the interest of the Roosevelt election campaign. It is regrettable that it is the crowd that knows nothing about American politics. At New Year this year there was much noisy talk that the enemy would come when everyone was off-guard for the holiday.

Ayusawa's house is small, but it is a cozy place. As usual, we had a tasty meal. At 9:40 in the evening I returned home under full moonlight. Along the way there were air-raid warnings, and it seems that the air-raid officials are in disarray.

November 2 (Thursday)

I wrote about the Dumbarton Oaks "League of Nations" for *Tōyō keizai*.

In the evening because Itabashi Kikumatsu was promoted to "professor of economics" I went to his congratulatory party. I understand he received his Ph.D. degree from Nihon University, but I wonder what kind of knowledge he possesses. Aside from the imperial universities, even the title Ph.D. is not very reliable.

I dug up the sweet potatoes. The abundant harvest was superior to last year's crop. Digging up one quarter of the plants yielded twenty kan.

I stopped at the Foreign Ministry. I received shorthand notes of a speech delivered by Grew on Navy Day (speech of the 27th). He said that regarding Japan, "It's possible that in order to escape destruction, Japan may withdraw its armies from the occupied territories, and moreover it's possible that it will release Manchuria from its absolute control. However, whatever Japan says, we will not accept peace talks. A compromise peace is dangerous. But if it is only unconditional surrender, this is the only road she can take. Even if they prolong the inevitable, they will not avoid total defeat. If they behave in this fashion, they can avoid unnecessary loss of life and destruction. Let them consider their day is over" [following in English, "Let them call (it) a Day"].

This is important advice about surrender. Moreover, reflecting upon Grew's attitude, it may be a suggestion that Japan try making the "abandonment of Manchuria" as a condition. At any rate, reading this and ever since trying to make allowances for the obscure language, I could not rid my mind of this problem. However, the present authorities will probably not grasp these delicately phrased statements.

According to this morning's newspapers, the enemy military force invading Leyte Bay is five divisions. The Japanese success in the battle of the Taiwan and Philippines Seas has on the contrary trapped Japan in the enemy's war strategy. This is because the enemy has achieved its objective of some time past, namely, the Philippine invasion.

Of late, the "Imperial Headquarters Announcements" make use of the format of the army to the effect, "The ferocity of desperately attacking the target" (October 21) or "Human bullets also again succeed in sudden attack invasion" (Peleiliu invasion operations, November 1). The government has established a Bureau of Combined Planning and has appointed Azumi Tokuya as chief of the second section. As usual, personnel changes abound.

November 3 (Friday)

It is raining again. Throughout the day I wrote on the "League of Nations." I read about the Holy Alliance. It was because I thought the League of Nations and this alliance resembled each other. History repeats itself.

November 4 (Saturday)

The authorities and others are greatly encouraging the Kamikaze squadrons. It appears that they have gasoline for one-way trips. In other words, they have lived for twenty years to kill themselves. This style of careless use of human life has reached an extreme. And yet the ones who die in this way are just splendid youths (*Nihon sangyō keizai*, November 4).

As much as 95 percent of the Japanese think that foreigners are deeply impressed by this.

I wrote a critique of the Dumbarton proposals. As no one came to visit, I was able to study. I want a life in which it would be all right to do nothing but study.

November 5 (Sunday)

Every morning when I am working in the fields a groups of workers is going to the factory singing a military song as they go. When the leader sang, the entire group responded with the phrases, "If one is born as a Yamato man . . .

one dies like the flowers of a skirmish line." Thus, believing in a human bullet war, the young go off to die to do good for the nation.

Because the American election campaign is drawing near, probably the authorities' nerves will be especially on edge. This is also conveyed by the Berlin communiqués. The ones who are completely ignorant of American politics are the Japanese and the Germans. Herein tragedies are born.

If one relies upon a certain official, the ships attacked and sunk are extremely numerous and exceed many times our monthly shipbuilding capacity. He said, "With this poor record I am always amazed Japan can continue to fight, and when I hear this, this is what I think." Of course, he did not talk about the figures.

The announcement of American casualty figures—current to October 21, the total was 487,700—and within that, 410,000 were army and 70,000 were navy.

The wheat-planting season has come. And yet Natsuya has returned to her home and is not here. The potatoes also must be dug up. All day today I did field work.

In the morning air-raid warnings were issued.

November 6 (Monday)

I had previously written a letter to Kobiyama Naotō, but this had not been answered. Because he wanted to meet me, I went to see him. In the morning, air-raid warnings were issued. It appears that those in charge are extremely nervous.

I hear that the Manchurian Railway will give us 2,500 yen annually for five years.

Because Kobiyama is returning to Manchuria tomorrow, we met today. In the manner of Matsuoka, he is completely fierce-spirited. The tone of what he said was, "It's nothing at all! Air raids? That sort of thing can be taken care of immediately! It's nothing to beat the Americans. We can do it!"

Thereupon I said, "As someone who occupies the position of responsibility that you do, please be more careful in distinguishing between hopes and realities." And then I explained that I had met with Baron Ōkura Kimmochi and Hayashi Jinnojō concerning Manchuria. It seems he was somewhat taken aback by this. But in the end I thought him a distinguished man. I had had a bad impression when he had not even allowed me a reply. Even if for the moment I had received money from him, I probably would not have thought well of him. But of his own accord he met with me, and he sought to explain his fitting me into his busy schedule, saying, "Previously we missed each other and were not able to meet." This type of attitude probably explained his success in society. At any rate, those who harden their hearts should pause to reconsider.

DISCUSSION QUESTIONS

1. Classify the following marks as trademarks, service marks, collective marks, or certification marks:
   - AMERICAN MEDICAL ASSOCIATION (to indicate membership in registrant's organization)
   - COMET (for cleaner)
   - MIDAS MUFFLER (for car repair services)
   - CERTIFIED OCCUPATIONAL THERAPIST ASSISTANT COTA (certifying persons meet certain standards of skill)
   - OPRAH (for television shows)
   - CHEF BOYARDEE (for pasta)
2. Could the design of a microphone be trademarked if the design is the most effective way of producing sound? Discuss.
3. Could the color soft pink for hearing aids be trademarked? Discuss.
4. Henry Allen operates a computer consulting service in Portland, Oregon. To announce the opening of his business, he sends a flyer advertising the business services to a friend in Seattle. Is this use sufficient to support an application for federal trademark registration? What if Henry advertises his services in various computer journals? Discuss.
5. What is the danger of consumers saying, "Give me a Bud" when they want a beer?
6. Discuss whether a person could likely obtain a trademark registration for the following marks for the goods or services indicated, and discuss the objections, if any, that the PTO might raise.

Mark	Goods or Services
THOMAS EDISON	Light bulbs
UNITED STATES CREDIT SERVICES	Credit counseling services
TIGER WOODS'S CHOICE	Golf balls
QUICK PRINT	Photocopy services
HASTA LA PASTA	Pasta sauce
DANGEROUS	Perfume
OLYMPIC GYMNASTICS	Gymnastics coaching service
BEST BEER	Beer and ale
AVELLE	High-definition TV
KLEENER	All-purpose kitchen cleaner

For additional resources, go to www.westlegalstudies.com.

I bought a pamphlet at the Meiji Bookstore entitled "On Mineral Springs" (published in 1878) by Baelz.[72] Baelz was outstanding because he already held these opinions. Look at the perception of a young German scholar who has just come to a new country.

November 7 (Tuesday)

Having promised to lecture at Oume, I went there. At about one o'clock, just as the lecture meeting was beginning, there was an air-raid alert and immediately there were alarms. At this time a clerk said, "Enemy planes are overhead." I went outside. A single enemy plane was proceeding to the southeast, leaving a contrail. It appeared that a small plane was following it, but there was no comparison as to their altitudes and speeds. I could not somehow believe this was an enemy plane. In broad daylight the enemy was majestically passing over the imperial capital. Our military could do absolutely nothing about this. I said to the other people, "Truly, that is not an enemy plane. It's because I believe in our Japanese air defense." This was not at all intended to be irony.

Surprisingly enough, it turned out to be an enemy plane after all. It was a four-engine B-29. It probably took photographs of the entire layout of the capital.

The Japanese people still do not understand what a thing sheer mechanical power is, but they will probably understand before long.

I doubt the enemy will indeed indiscriminately attack Tōkyō. The American people might have thought that with regard to the suicides of even children on Saipan, "The Japanese think America is an evil demon," and America might assume a policy that shows that it is not such a country. Because of the war, the actual facts are not clear. If indeed America is considering this possibility, then the suicides of the men and women on Saipan performed the role of saving Japan.

I lectured during an air-raid alert. I quoted Fichte.

After the meeting sake was served. The meal at lunch was steamed bread and sweet potatoes. The evening meal was Japanese sake and white rice balls. One can assume their food difficulties from their repeatedly telling me they had prepared this exceptional meal because "Kiyosawa Sensei" had come.

The meals were attended by the influential people of Oume-machi. There were such people as the mayor, doctors, heads of associations, and the head of the Tōkyō City Training Center. With the exception of one person, they did not have the slightest doubt in saying, "Japan will be absolutely victorious." The basis for this argument was that they would use their family members to the utmost of their strength.

A young man—a man of forty-four or forty-five—understands the American productive power and its war capacity and questions whether Japan can equal these. It appears that he suspects the Philippine campaign is not going well. I did not positively support the thesis that Japan was all right, but I tried to indicate I did.

Also, in the case of my remarks about Germany the tone of my talk was, "It is a mistake to be pessimistic about the future of Germany, but it was also a mistake to be optimistic." Given this, there was no reason to expect the people to understand the true state of things. But if I had made such statements I would be in trouble.

In the talk at the meeting, I understand that a certain official of the Foreign Ministry said that at the beginning Grew referred to the Japanese as monkeys, but recently Grew said, "If it happened that Americans said they had had enough of the war and this was generally made known, because this would dampen their enthusiasm it would not be made known." People such as officials understand only this level of Grew's remarks. It is only the level of insisting that the Americans are tired of the war.

When I met with President Kobiyama of the Manchurian Railway I thought I would share Grew's statements with him. I brought the typescript, but because he was in a very good mood I did not discuss Grew's remarks at all. He said, "Such people say all sorts of things to suit their own convenience."

Because of an air-raid notice, the remarks on the Dumbarton Oaks plan of Yukawa's program were thrown into disorder and in the end could not be presented (*Mainichi shinbun*, November 8).

The so-called anti-aircraft guns are not things that shoot down enemy planes, but they are things that cause wounds to the people on our side.

"One should not look up at the enemy planes." This kind of behavior is shameful.

November 8 (Wednesday)

Because the members of the war association of Unoki were going to the Hachiman Shrine, our entire family also attended. They think only of things that exhaust people, such as drills until late in the evening and getting up at four o'clock in the morning, but no wonder they do these kinds of things. The ones who go out at such times are nothing more than carpenters and navvies. I understand that the former head of air defense in Unoki-nishimachi was a part-time worker at our house, but he fell ill and now it is X. Because we have been led by this sort of crowd, now in times of emergency they become the carriers of order.

I stayed at home all day. Policeman Mizuno came to ask about the problem of the American presidential election and Stillwell. The fact that Stillwell has clashed with Chiang Kai-shek and been recalled has stirred up the Japanese newspapers. I said America was to be admired for not being concerned about appearances in calling home their general and being willing to discuss the resignation of Ambassador Gauss.[73] If it had been Japan, it would have brought forth the problem of face and there would have been an uproar.

November 9 (Thursday)

In the presidential election Roosevelt has been crushingly victorious. I wrote about this in *Tōyō keizai*.

In the evening I attended the People's Scholarly Arts Society. There was speech of Sugimori Kōjirō concerning the statements of Stalin. Stalin's speech deserves close attention. He said that the racial superiority theory of the Germans, in the end, made enemies of all countries, and moreover Japan had made it clear she was an aggressive nation and had attacked Pearl Harbor and China; peace-loving nations such as America and China being attacked, finally stood up against her.

At the Scholarly Arts Society meeting, I said that Stalin had probably not reached the point of a declaration of war on Japan. Of course, this depended upon the moves of Japan.

According to Dr. Makino Eiichi, there are people who pull out the fence posts from the villas in Hiratsuka. And then when the watchmen complain they coolly answer, "If the air raids come, won't everyone's possessions disappear? So why are you going on and on about this?" "If the air raids come, the foundation is prepared for flagrant pillage," Dr. Makino remarked.

A destructive mood fills every area. While my office in the Maru Building was being repaired, three windows were smashed. They were intentionally broken, completely without reason. The hanging straps on the trains are repeatedly stolen and now not more than half remain. It is said that the upholstery of the seats in the electric trains and steam trains is stripped and taken home.

November 10 (Friday)

From morning until afternoon I planted wheat. I tried using the double-width technique. Unfortunately it required much hard labor.

Kanō of the Police Department came to ask my opinion regarding Stalin's speech. Probably he came on the instructions of the Police Department. I said there was nothing else to do but behave as if we hadn't heard it. I added that if Japan engages in too much positive action, the Soviet Union will obtain a pretext and there will be the possibility of a declaration of war.

According to Kanō, among the people in general there is the question why the American planes in the sky above the imperial capital for two or three days have not been shot down. If it is said that they cannot be shot down above the capital, then the reports of tens of planes being shot down outside of Japan is probably a lie.

Thus the real technological capacity of Japan cannot in fact be hidden from the people. Looked at as a practical education, its consequences will probably provide benefit to the Japanese.

The camellias in the fields are about to bloom. I thought they had just bloomed. The passage of the seasons is especially quick when one lives in the fields.

The Berlin communiqués are applauding the launching of the "V" rockets. Certainly they are successful on the Western front, and the American and English armies are not being allowed to advance.

I finished planting the wheat.

November 11 (Saturday)

Okuda Saneharu and Miss Yoneko of Hokkaidō came to visit. I heard that military units are stationed even in Uraga-machi, and in the mountains and on the coast they are digging great numbers of holes. For this purpose they are cutting down all the trees. Moreover, one military unit orders them cut down, and about the time they are being cut down another military unit arrives and has a different plan. It is a situation in which the timber piles up and rots along the roadside.

Recently a divisional commander came to visit. The soldiers rushed about looking for a gift for him and searched for a salmon to buy. Just at that time fishing was bad, and because they ran around frantically from village to village, those who had blind respect for the military people until then, of late, have come to doubt and despise them.

In the evening, on the anniversary of the death of Ōkuma Makoto, I was invited to supper. Such people as Kamikawa Hikomatsu and Foreign Ministry Section Chief Yoshida attended.

The discussion there was as follows:

There was a Taishō University professor named Hamada or something like that. I understand he submitted a plan to the Imperial Headquarters. That is to say, he proposed that 600,000 suicide troops be sent to America, and these would attack the Panama Canal and Alaska. He said half of these would be recruited from Buddhists throughout the country. Thereupon I asked him, "By what means will they go?" He answered "By aircraft carriers." I said, "If they go only by these it will be disastrous. And what will become of the troops who follow?" He was not able to respond. This is the level of common sense of a university professor who graduated from the Daiichi High School and an imperial university. To Saegusa's comment, "When is Germany likely to surrender?" Hamada replied, "Too much objectivity is annoying. Don't we have to help Germany?" When everyone asked, "If nothing happens after help is given, then what?" He did not reply.

I am surprised that things that are not questions for my circle of friends become problems for the ignorant crowd in different occupational circles. Given this, the future road is extremely distant. With regard to the B-29s flying over Tōkyō, even these people are losing hope in Japanese air power, which can do nothing about this. It is nothing more than a practical education. How lopsided Japanese education is. Among these people, the most ideological are those called Buddhists.

I had a clash of opinion with Professor Kamigawa Hiromatsu on the Dumbarton Oaks plan. He said things that sounded traitorous, arguing that because Japan is committed to the Co-Prosperity Sphere, if it accepted the Dumbarton Oaks proposal it would be disastrous. Those who follow the plans of the government are Japan's scholars.

But he said that America will not be crushed for three or four years. While the fact that he said, "We entered the war understanding this fact at the outset that the war will go on," was natural his style of expression was suggestive. In the questions after the lecture he responded to my statement, "When will America surrender?" saying, "America is a mixture of races. And because women have rights, if it suffers great damage, opposition and controversy will flourish. It will be serious if Japan does not inflict heavier damage on America." In my heart I did not think this way, and I believed that America and England would never be defeated. And yet the reason I asked this sort of question was, I was afraid if I did not ask I might be attacked for pro-Americanism and destroying our fighting spirit. Here was my "weakness." Because someone like Kamigawa was an "official scholar," he never has to consider being criticized, and this is his strong point.

November 12 (Sunday)

There is a report that Wang Ching-wei died on the 10th at Nagoya. Now that he has died, what will become of the establishment of the new Chinese political power made in partnership with Wang Ching-wei alone? How much the political policy of Japan was born under hopeful ideals was exposed today.

Kweilin in China has fallen. This was probably in order to establish a communication line through the Chinese continent from Canton. But is it indeed possible to maintain this long line of transportation? This also is a completely unreal operation. The newspaper topics put out special pages filled with such headlines as "The Destruction of All American Airforce Bases," "The Establishment of a Superior War Strategy," "Control over Southwest China," and "The Enemy, the Total Failure of Its War Strategy toward Japan" (the foregoing, *Asahi*). Regarding these, an imperial statement was handed down.

Of late the newspapers have only two pages. These are completely without news. Yet there are still "compositions."

November 13 (Monday)

I understand the execution of Ōzaki Hotsumi was carried out on November 7. There was a rumor that he would probably be used in diplomatic negotiations with the Soviet Union, but this was a falsehood. Compared to the assassination incident against Hiranuma (home minister at the time), there were sentences of seven years penal servitude. What a light sentence!

It is said that the government will send former Prime Minister Hirota to the Soviet Union—there is a rumor among the people that Kuhara [Fusanosuke] will be sent—and it had resorted to various stratagems. When it conferred with Molotov, he refused, saying, "Because Ambassador Sato is here, there is no need for anyone else to come." Previously, there was a rumor that Arita was going. It is said the objective is a Japanese–Soviet alliance. I cannot imagine that Shigemitsu is really thinking of such a thing.

In this morning's papers the pages are filled with the Wang Ching-wei affair. It is clear that even the death of the present premier would not be written about to this degree.

It is reported that Premier Koiso and Foreign Minister Shigemitsu went to Nagoya and conferred the Chrysanthemum Medal upon Wang. Konoe also went to Nagoya.

Yasuda Riheie of Yoda came to visit. I understand that in the provinces the people who are determined to be victorious in the war are still extremely numerous.

November 14 (Tuesday)

Reports of "body blows" occupy more than half of the newspaper and radio news. The army and navy competitively are loudly proclaiming special attack forces (*Mainichi*, November 14).

In the army there is the Banda Air Force and there are also the "Tokimune," "Seimu," and "Cherry Blossoms." Within the navy's kamikaze attack squadrons, there are subdivisions. I see in this nostalgia for names and simplicity of thinking. This is certainly one heroic tradition (*Nihon sangyō keizai*, November 14).

A policeman told me that they have received orders to protect the prisoners of war and to prevent them from being injured by mobs. Yet someone like Kanō is afraid that in such circumstances, won't the mobs make the police their target and create disturbances? I think he is probably right.

There was a story from Kanō Hisao at the People's Scholarly Arts Society. It is interesting. Recently the military does not write in the newspapers and does not use the radio. I wonder if the reason is a policy of the new army minister?

November 15 (Wednesday)

There was a board of directors meeting at Fuji Ice. At least the dividend was settled at 8 percent. We were resigned to no dividend at all, but this figure was because of the effort of Ōta.

Today is the fiftieth anniversary of *Tōyō keizai*. I was unable to attend the luncheon but went there in the evening.

On this occasion, if it were England, Ishibashi would probably have received the title of "Sir." In Japan, the value attached to intellect and culture is extremely low—especially as regards journalists. I have been connected with this magazine for close to ten years.

November 16 (Thursday)

Rain is falling. Those who are drafted are extremely numerous, and I see young men with sashes of the "Flag of Japan" on which inscriptions are written in black ink slanting down from their shoulders (*Asahi*, "Iron Broom," November 16).

The family that needs help cannot obtain it because the government's rules are inflexible and the government does not understand total power mobilization.

A story at the barbershop. In the account of someone returned from the fighting front, the soldiers did not have food and ate human flesh. Because it was not known how contaminated someone who had been killed by a bullet was, they killed the living and ate them. To this end they killed prisoners of war. It is said they were placed in a large cauldron, the oil was skimmed, and they were eaten. He himself said, "Everyone is silent about this, but everyone is doing it!" Because this was at breakfast time, the barber said food was completely unpalatable to him.

Even at the time of Attu, someone was telling stories with the same content. They were probably exaggerating, but I think to a certain extent it might be true.

Yesterday evening after ten o'clock there was air-raid training. I hear they came to wake everyone up, but in our house the maid Toyo said she wouldn't go because she disliked it and the head of the association scolded her. The so-called training is a matter of running around carrying buckets and is merely exhausting.

In the towns everywhere, holes are being dug at the sides of the roads. In these, naturally, water collects to no purpose. These are shelters in which one can only escape explosions.

With respect to Stalin's speech, the government does not permit any criticism at all. I thought I might write something about it for *Tōyō keizai*, but I couldn't do it. I wrote on the subject, "What are invaders?" Trivial gossip causes trouble, but why is criticism not permitted? The evils of bureaucratic controls.

November 17 (Friday)

I stayed at home through the whole day, and after a period of inactivity I wrote a little on the manuscript of my book. I understand that the Foreign Ministry thinks that Stalin will declare war on Japan as he did against Bulgaria. They say nothing threatening about this. However, even saying absolutely nothing at all is one sort of diplomacy. This is probably the first time since the opening of the country that something boastful has not been said.

November 18 (Saturday)

I gave a lecture at the Setagaya ward office. It was at the request of Tōkyō City.

According to city officials, there is in the end optimism on the future path of the war. They literally believe in the word of the military that "Everything is fine."

I received an honorarium of thirty yen. I have mentioned this before, but with the labor of one day one can only buy one hundred me of sugar.

November 19 (Sunday)

Our maid Toyo went to the air-raid drill. I understand that they said, "We must kill the enemy who comes down by parachute. Therefore we are going to have a drill on killing them." I understand that there is training in the use of bamboo spears. In fact about 150 people gathered together.

Obama is wearing Western clothes, which is unusual. He says that because he does not know when the enemy will arrive, he will be prepared. Based on the photographs, it is clear that their coming is imminent.

November 20 (Monday)

In the morning I visited Baron Shidehara Kijūrō. No matter how long I rang the bell, no one appeared. The person who finally opened the door appeared to be his wife. Because there were no maids, no tea was served. I was guided along to a study on the second floor. It was a splendid room of twenty tatami. There was an abundance of current books. I requested he lecture for the Japanese Diplomatic History Research Center. He consented readily. He was also willing to act as adviser. He dislikes having a speech taken down in shorthand. I don't know the reason for this. But it was an extremely agreeable discussion (this talk is recorded elsewhere).

In every home gas is shut off because of excessive use. There is beginning to be talk of cutting down the trees along the roadside (*Mainichi*, "Construction," November 19).

The theme of reform is strong in the Koiso Cabinet. Fujiwara [Ginjiro] of the Munitions Ministry and Maeda [Yonezo] of the Transportation and Communications Ministry are both facing difficult circumstances, but the extraordinary thing is the possible change of foreign minister, Shigemitsu. The names of Hirota and Arita have been put up as candidates. It is said that Stalin's speech cast an evil spell over Shigemitsu. As far as the Imperial Rule Assistance Society is concerned, they are making noises about Shigemitsu. When a certain person said that because these kinds of facts have been long known from *Pravda* and *War and the Working Class*, wasn't it a fact that Stalin's speech was no marvelous thing. Someone said, "It's a bad thing if the foreign minister has not informed himself on such matters." It appears that the reason it was said in the recent Diet session that, "That sort of way of looking at things is mistaken and the foreign minister is incompetent" was Shigemitsu's statement, "The attitude of the Soviet Union is extremely friendly toward Japan." It would have been better if Shigemitsu had said, "War with the Soviet Union is impossible, and there is nothing else but to say alas." But he said, "It is a fact that since the Anti-Comintern Pact, Japan has not shown good will toward the Soviet Union. Now, it cannot be hoped that good will will be shown by Russia," and this infuriated the Imperial Rule Assistance Society members of the Diet.

There are only a pitiful few among the Diet representatives who understand diplomatic problems.

Nobody comes to the Foreign Ministry committee meetings. Rōyama says if someone talks about potatoes, one hundred people will come.

In Kyūshū again there have been enemy air raids. Whether the reason for this is the Japanese attacks on "American air bases" in China is not clear, but the people do not think about such things (*Nihon sangyō keizai*, November 21).

In the foregoing, the statement, "The American fliers' clothing and medical supplies are the height of extravagance, and it shows another aspect of their self-indulgence," is interesting. Moreover, the statement, "They are raw recruits because their uniforms are brand new" is ridiculous. It is exactly the same misreading recorded regarding the foreigners about the time of the Meiji Restoration.

In the evening there was a talk by Nishihara Kamezō. This was better than his previous talks. He said he had been opposed to the military clique diplomacy, and he said this was also true of Terauchi.

November 22 (Wednesday)

I gave a lecture for the Setagaya ward office. It was a gathering of the heads of the war councils, and it was at the request of Tōkyō City.

I received a gift of three daikon. This is the current practice.

On my way home I visited with Kikuta Sadao. He is a professor at Meiji Gakuin. He had pulmonary disease and was hospitalized for ten months. He is an eminent scholar of Meiji history. He encouraged me to write a work that views Meiji diplomatic relations from the religious viewpoint.

November 23 (Thursday)

It is the Shintō Harvest Festival (*Niinamesai*, November 23, "Thanksgiving"). It is expected that there will be air raids, and everywhere watches are being maintained around the clock.

One understands from the following figures the fact that the statements of the army are nonsense. That is to say, they state that in the attacks of the B-29s on our homeland, 120 planes have been attacked and destroyed. Even Akira in our family said, "It's a lie, isn't it?" It is said that the 63 planes that came to attack Kyūshū on November 21 were shot down, and those that fled to the continent were pursued and shot down. Because the people's criticism has reached an extreme, they are concealing their predicament, so to speak. Why there is not a single piece of evidence is because there is a leadership that unhesitatingly lies to this degree. Because they are always giving out orders, when they make announcements it appears they think they will be believed.

The newspapers are putting out special reports on the daily dispatch of kamikaze special squadrons in the direction of the Philippines. The Shujaku Squadron sent to attack; attack by the Seimu Squadron (attack upon the enemy fleet in Leyte Bay). Thus the results of the climactic note of spiritism is reaching the point of substituting human lives for material substance. And yet no one is cautioning against this, and the people are not conscious of it.

Our maid Toyo told this story while giggling all the while. "At the air-raid training the young women were acting as something like squadrons and were practicing salutes. At the center was the wife of Itō, and when we marched forward in rows we turned our heads to the right and saluted and she returned the salute. Now even when I think about it it's funny."

The Chungking political power has been reorganized. Centering upon the Stillwell recall incident, the question is, is Chiang Kai-shek "deferring" to Roosevelt, or is "Chiang Kai-shek the better actor?" (*Asahi*). There is vigorous debate that argues, "No, this is not true, this is a superficial view" (*Yomiuri* editorial, 23rd). They are still understanding diplomacy as maneuvering. Those who know the circumstances of China do not know America, and those who know America do not know China.

Is it all right to destroy the airplane and the flier for a single attack by a kamikaze squadron?

It is said that the war cost for America for a si ngle day is $250 million. This was announced by Roosevelt on the occasion of the announcement of the Sixth War Loan Drive.

November 24 (Friday)

A headline in the *Mainichi shinbun* read, "Spruance the warmonger." This in an attack on Americans, but reference to Spruance as "Warmonger" is probably ironic.

Young persons' views on searching for food (*Mainichi*, November 24).

There is an editorial in the *Mainichi* entitled "Laughing at the Foolishness of Chiang Kai-shek." Nevertheless, it is said that Chiang has bowed down to the strong pressure of America. Yet the reporters do not understand the significance of the fact that Ho Ying-chin and Kung Hsiang-hsi remain as the chief of staff and vice-chief of the Administrative Ministry.

CHAPTER 3

Trademark Selection and Searching

CHAPTER OVERVIEW

As discussed in Chapter 2, not every word, slogan, or design can be protected as a trademark or service mark. Therefore, great care must be given to selecting a mark to identify one's goods or services. Once a mark is selected, a trademark availability search should be conducted to determine if the mark is available for registration. Searches are conducted of the PTO records, state trademark records, business directories, journals, telephone books, domain names, and Internet uses to determine whether a proposed mark may conflict with a mark already in use. Although no search can guarantee that a mark will be accepted by the PTO for registration, a search allows a trademark owner to anticipate problems that may arise in the registration process, provides a snapshot of other marks in the marketplace, and may help avoid liability for infringement.

SELECTING AND EVALUATING A MARK

Selecting a Mark

Selection of a mark occurs in a variety of ways. Some companies hold contests and encourage employees to create a mark for a new product line or service. Other companies engage sophisticated research and branding firms that will conduct surveys and create a mark and a **logo** or design for the company. There are name creation software programs that help individuals and companies create marks. Once the mark is selected, it must be screened and evaluated for use and registrability. Failure to exercise this due diligence might result in the expenditure of time and money in advertising, using, and applying for a mark that is rejected for registration by the PTO or, in the worst case scenario, might subject the owner to damages for trademark infringement and unfair competition.

If America engages in a "greedy policy taking off the mask of liberalism," this is to the advantage of Japan. The reason is that this always invites the resistance of China. However, the fearsomeness of America does not come out in this sort of fashion. If that is the case, the popularity of America will continue in China.

Following alerts a little past noon, air-raid warnings were issued. If one relies upon the announcements, they said seventy planes came to Tōkyō from the Mariana Islands. When the warnings are issued, children and women are herded into shelters that have been dug in the neighboring hills. On top of this there is probably an air-raid warden who rails at these people as they enter one by one. Even when they need to go to the toilet, when the children are in the defense shelters they cannot go outside. Whenever anyone walks by outside, they are rebuked, "Get into the shelter quickly." And yet from this position neither the shape nor the form of the enemy planes can be seen in the least. And with regard to the unseen enemy planes, it is "air defense" that does not permit going outside even for a moment. Most of the time I remain in my study. Of course I am suitably dressed in the event of an air raid.

In the evening, on the way to Ōkuma's house, people were getting off the trains in streams while discussing the unusual events of the day. A girl remarked, "The American planes are swift. They have splendid machinery inside, and when they pass over the great factories it detects the target, and immediately they know where it is. They are able to take excellent photographs." A boy said in response, "Don't say such things. These kinds of things are rumors!" Talking about the superiority of the American planes is rumor, and they have been made to believe this is behavior benefiting the enemy, but his tone was half-hearted and he seemed to be interested in the girl's talk.

According to Eiko, the air-raid shelters that the girls get into are beneath a machine factory and extremely small. There is only a thin layer of concrete overhead. If a bomb fell, it is inevitable that everyone would be killed. Because there was a dry river bed nearby, it would have been better if they had taken refuge there. I have the feeling even if we suggest this or object to the shelter it would be futile. To this extent we feel that everything is left to fate and any improvement is impossible.

The Soviet Union would turn Manchuria into an Outer Mongolia. I said, "Japan will probably not continue to hold Manchuria. Japan should use Manchuria as a means of diplomacy." There was opposition to this. In the final analysis, the government, those connected with it, and intellectuals are still extremely die-hard. They seem to fear thinking of advancing to the final stage.

December 10 (Sunday)

I stayed at home all day. In the afternoon I ladled nightsoil. I fertilized the wheat.

I am reading Ōkuma Makoto's *Bakumatsuki Tōa gaikōshi* (Diplomatic history of East Asia in the Bakumatsu period). Because the research is profound and there are many references of interest to me, it is fascinating. His criticism of the Bakufu runs to excess. However, at the present time, because the people understand that anything in the service of the emperor is correct, this sort of bias is produced.

Relying on the reports from the Foreign Ministry, there is a three-point Allied plan concerning XX [the emperor]. Chungking thinks there is danger in his existence and there is the need for a clean sweep. England thinks he is a stabilizing force. America hereafter will probably try to use him as a rubber stamp.

This problem is of the utmost gravity. Just as in the Bakumatsu-Ishin,[74] we must anticipate even greater changes. It is the most difficult problem.

There is an essay by a man called Pacificus in the *Nation*. He criticized Japanese political conditions and said that Tōjō was defeated because he earned the anger of the business people. Now in Japan the center is occupied by Fujihara Ginjirō and the southern areas are divided among the business zaibatsu. The plan of the Home Ministry is to have the Japanese businessmen obtain power. I understand that he attacked the Home Ministry as above-mentioned. As for Grew, it is clear that his policy toward Japan regards the industrialists as central, and moreover it can be imagined from this fact that he cannot cast off nineteenth-century liberalism.

In diplomacy there is nothing else but to play one's hand with as few concessions as possible with the cards one has. What Japan has is Manchuria and troops stationed overseas in foreign countries. Using these two, if she is able to hold in check Korea and Taiwan, this is the most she can do.

I hear that the declaration of Premier Koiso regarding Korea is now becoming a problem. That is to say, it is the problem of granting some political power to Korea. Korea is Japan's Ireland problem.

December 11 (Monday)

Last night at eight and this morning at three, enemy planes came. Even more than the damage, getting up at night upsets our lives.

I went to a board of directors meeting at *Tōyō keizai*. On the basis of the talk of various people, it became clear that the recent earthquake in central Japan had an extremely important influence on war power. Forty percent at the very least of Japanese aircraft production is in the vicinity of Nagoya. Besides that, shipyards and heavy industries are numerous in that area. Furthermore, it is said that because many of these are on reclaimed land, the damage was probably extensive. Fires were few, but machinery for which there is no repair materials was put out of order.

The steam trains run only as far as Kakegawa and no farther. There are absolutely no passengers accepted. There is nothing else but to go round on the Chūō line and the Hokuriku line.

The historians of future generations will write that the first full stop of the Greater East Asian War was the occurrence of the great earthquake in "central Japan." Just at that time it was reported that the enemy sent a dcivision (announcement from the Japanese side) to Leyte Island and have landed on Omoroku to its rear. It is said that in the matter of air strength, both parties have about 1,500 planes, but as regards tanks, the enemy has 1,000. The war in Leyte does not look favorable.

In Europe, on the 10th, an alliance and mutual defense treaty has been concluded between the Soviet Union and the DeGaulle French government. This is probably a stance toward both Germany and the Communists. England is opposed to the prime minister of the Italian government, Sforza, and America is opposed to interference in internal politics. In Greece an upheaval erupted and England is having a difficult time. England is making efforts to restore its power in the Mediterranean, and America and the Soviet Union are taking an interfering attitude toward this. They already see Germany as defeated and are entering into postwar diplomacy.

The December 7, 1:36 P.M., earthquake had its center in the Enshu open sea. It appears that the water system of Nagoya was halted, and in Izu-Shimoda there was the inundation of one area. It is said that in Shizuoka after the earthquake there was an air raid and the factory workers fled. The newspapers do not write anything at all about the earthquake disaster. The radio did not communicate anything at all.

December 12 (Tuesday)

Last night we were awakened by air raids twice.

Today, throughout the day, I stayed at home. I finished reading Ōkuma's *Bakumatsuki Tōa gaikōshi*. It is one of the best books of late. If he were alive I would have various points of discussion for him. Again I think we have lost such an important man.

In both Greece and Italy, England is taking a firm stand. There is probably the understanding that in exchange for Soviet rule in Poland they will obtain a free hand in the Mediterranean; nevertheless, the English prime minister says that he cannot permit Italy and Greece to be fascist, and it is certainly unnatural for Communist party members publicly to hold important cabinet positions. This matter cannot be expected to continue at length. The power distribution competition on the points that are the premise of the Dumbarton Oaks plan is now beginning.

Today at 1:22 the entire nation offered prayers for victory to the Ise Shrine. This was something previously advocated in a speech by Premier Koiso. He said it would be something like forcibly invoking a divine wind. The premier of Japan, who is leading a scientific war in the middle of the twentieth century, is earnestly praying for the occurrence of a divine wind.

The radio and also the newspapers day after day write of special attack squadrons and report on them. They are praising and publicizing the unity of the attack spirit and its execution.

December 13 (Wednesday)

Three times last night, at 8:00 P.M., 12:00 A.M., and 4:30 A.M., air-raid alerts were issued. In the midnight alert there was the sound of cruel anti-aircraft guns, and their fragments fell at places not far from the houses. The glass doors of the houses rattle. It won't be long before our house is destroyed. Whenever these raids occur we have to dress. The troublesomeness of this is a great strain. If this were repeated even for half a year in New York, Chicago, and other places, their residents would feel that the war should be stopped.

In solving diplomatic problems, there is the absolute necessity for flexibility of mental attitude. This the Japanese do not have. This is particularly true of the crowd that has become the core of Japan at present—the crowd that expounds the Jewish problem.

After a luncheon meeting at the Imperial Hotel with various people such as Takayanagi Kenzō, Hasegawa Nyozenkan, and Ayusawa Iwao, when we were talking there was an air-raid alert and it was reported that a fleet of about eighty planes in the Shizuoka-Nagoya area was dropping bombs. In the subsequent report it was stated "light damage," but before the damage of the recent earthquake could be repaired, there was more destruction from this air raid.

Even more than this, the waste of time is frightful. We could not move from the hotel until about three in the afternoon.

There was a "symposium" in the November issue of *Gendai*, and it was entitled "The Rising Indignation of the Land of the Gods."

This appeared in *Yomiuri shinbun*. What does pro-American mean, and who will decide it?

The editorial entitled "What Are Invaders," which I wrote for *Tōyō keizai*, was deleted. Takayanagi said the article became a point of discussion for Ambassador Kururu and others. I understand they said, "Because Ishibashi would probably not write on that sort of problem, it is probably Kiyosawa."

December 14 (Thursday)

Even now the trees and orchards are being steadily and completely cut down. It was the plan of such people as the Young Men's Association and the bureaucracy. However, in one circle it has come to be understood that this has gone too far. However, even in Karuizawa the trees are being cut down; moreover, even the trees in the fields will have to be cut down for firewood. Because this destruction serves these people, nothing at all can be done to control it (*Mainichi*, "Inkstone Drops," December 15).

December 15 (Friday)

Last night there was an air raid. One plane bombing 1.5 million people into wakefulness.

December 16 (Saturday)

Last night there were no air-raid sirens sounded. I slept extremely well. I had the feeling that something was missing.

Kiyono Michiyuki came to call. He said that he will soon go to Matsumoto. His story. There was a huge uproar because the Matsumoto station master was called a spy. Various kinds of articles were delivered at the station, and the station employees thought this strange. One day when he was out, dried cuttlefish was delivered at the station. When the station employees braised these, English writing appeared. Because they said this was the secret communication of a spy, he was arrested. Afterward there was a rumor that he had been shot. At any rate, it is a fact that he is no longer there.

Besides this, it is said there is another spy in Matsumoto. This sort of thing is a rumor even among schoolgirls. Because too many ships are sunk, it is said that there is no question that this was the work of spies. Then there is an uproar.

There is a certain person who is a graduate of the Imperial University in Kiyono's company. He is the agent of a certain person living in Kamata, and he is a follower of a man who cures illness. If one relies upon him, this world is now a battle between the spirit of good and the spirit of evil. The spirit of good is Japan and the spirit of evil is America, and its messengers are Jews. The Jewification of the Japanese is the evil spirit creeping into their bodies. Because of this, Tōkyō has become ashes. However, in the end, the spirit of good will be victorious. I understand this is what he said. If one has this man's amulets, the bombs of the evil spirit America will not strike their targets. There are many people in the navy who are investing great sums in this and buying these amulets. Among these are many who play the prophet. Some of these believe in the evil influence of the Jews. I understand that when a prediction of the *Omotokyō* hits the mark, the believers again increase.

December 17 (Sunday)

Last night there were no air raids. Since the night before last, I have slept wearing my pants, but contrary to expectation, there was no air raid.

The draft orders have come to our maids Toyo and Natsu. Two maids is certainly extravagant. It seems my wife had various discussions with Kiyoaki about this.

The newspapers report that an enemy division has invaded the island of Mindanao. The island is very close to Manila.

Churchill announced his intention of giving the area east of the Curzon Line to the Soviet Union. In exchange for giving England a free hand in Italy and Greece, there is a deal to give the Soviet Union Poland. In the present war it has become increasingly clear that peace will not come to the world. The curtain of power politics is again rising.

Of late I am buying a great number of new books. One among these is the *Shimbun to yudayajin* (Jews and newspapers) of Takeda Seigo. In the world there are countries that do not display such stupid works in their shop windows. The elevation of the knowledge of our people is the hoped-for task.

December 19 (Tuesday)

At 1:30 P.M. there was a regular meeting of the Japanese Diplomatic History Research Center at the Economic Club. Baron Shidehara Kijūrō attended. For an hour and a half he talked about the time of the Washington Conference. There was new material, and it was extremely rewarding.

Those who attended included Shidehara, Matsumoto Jōji, Kuwaki Genyoku, Ishibashi Tanzan, Baba Tsunego, Obama Tosie, Takahashi Yūhyō, Tamura Kōsaku, Nagai Matsuzō, Uehara Etsujirō, Sugimori Kōjirō, Kiyosawa, and Itō.

It is my intention to write soon about Baron Shidehara's talk. As usual Baron Shidehara behaved as if he did not especially care to attend. I understand this was just his mannerism. In the end, he does not want publicity. It's so, but it is a fact that he is an extremely able diplomat. I received one thousand yen from Professor Matsumoto for the Diplomatic History Research Center. My thanks are boundless.

December 20 (Wednesday)

Through the day I wrote an editorial for *Tōyō keizai*. It concerned the problem that Europe was being divided into power spheres. I argued the point that while all the nations are in the midst of war, preparations are being made for the third world war. Will the pragmatic diplomacy of the Soviet Union really be to the advantage of the Soviet Union? Something like the Polish problem will probably leave behind a curse for the Soviet Union.

December 21 (Thursday)

Throughout the morning I wrote about the change of the American secretary of state. It was an editorial for *Tōyō keizai* (the after New Year's number). This is American preparation for taking the lead in Asian imperialism in the postwar period.

December 22 (Friday)

I went to the Foreign Ministry. It was a meeting for the purpose of having Hasegawa Nyozenkan and Ayusawa Iwao participate in "Japonicus." We lunched at the Imperial Hotel.

Again there have been air raids. It is said that about one hundred planes attacked in the Nagoya area. The damage was reported as light, but indeed, is this true or not? It is probably not so.

After a long absence I went to the Economic Club. Tanaka Tokichi talks boastfully about a great German counteroffensive in the West. No one openly expresses pessimism.

I received, by way of Takayanagi, one thousand *yen* from a miscellaneous fund of the Foreign Ministry. I regret receiving this because I am not engaged in a big project.

December 23 (Saturday)

There was a rumor that Foreign Minister Shigemitsu would resign. As to that, Koiso negotiated with Shigemitsu. He wished to have a political party member (there was talk of Education Minister Ninomiya as candidate) as Greater East Asian minister, but Shigemitsu opposed dualism in foreign policy, and no matter who it is, the Greater East Asian minister must hold both positions. Because he strongly argued that if the Greater East Asian Minister were abolished, because there would be nothing else for him to do but resign, that was the end of the matter. According to a story of Takayanagi, Shigemitsu put his trust in the senior statesmen. The army said that the Soviet Union should be used; Shigemitsu said this was no good. They were dissatisfied with Shigemitsu, saying, "Does this stupid fellow say 'no good' without giving it a try?" With Stalin's speech, for the first time the army gave up the idea, and Shigemitsu was now unopposed.

I hear that Koiso went to Konoe's office and asked him to become head of the Sūmitsuin, but Konoe rejected the offer. It was evaluated by people in general as being due to Koiso's lack of tenacity.

I am reading Itō Miyoji's *Suiusho nikki* [Rainy leaves villa diary]. This is in connection with the deliberations of the Diplomatic Investigation Society regarding the dispatch of troops to Siberia. It is clear that Terauchi, Gotō, Itō, and others, taking advantage of the revolutionary confusion, had the intention of trying something. Regarding this, the most opposed was Makino, followed by Hara Kei. Itō was a private, shadowy politician and a distasteful person. It was better for the Diplomatic Investigation Society not to have a major failure in foreign relations. In diplomacy excessive caution is best; excessive haste creates trouble. The elderly are best in diplomacy. One, they have patience; two, they have comprehensive knowledge; and three, their judgments are sensible. The reasons for the military's suspicion of Makino are clear when one remembers Makino's ideas. Even at that time he attempted to resign.

December 24 (Sunday)

Yesterday the wife of Yoshida Shirō came to call and said that when she told him (Yoshida Shirō) that Papa Uehara and Kiyosawa said they should evacuate their baggage, Yoshida said that because both Papa and Kiyosawa were liberals, they say this sort of thing. He said we exist because of this nation and became angry. Yoshida is gentle to excess. This gentle Yoshida, while working at a Munitions Company called Asahi Glass, personally changed into someone who made completely inappropriate remarks. Because he is an Imperial University graduate, it is not a question of education. One may say that his reasoning is confused. According to a story of Yoshida Yoshie, I understand that Shirō says that Japan can destroy America immediately. The high spirit of young people and those working in munitions factories is the only thing that can be trusted. Nevertheless, one may say that young people are again being aroused. They say, "If we do not die, the nation will be crushed," and they voluntarily go to meet death with tranquility. I understand that the second boy of Kuroki, rather than doing trivial things on the homefront, wanted to try becoming a pilot, and moreover when his friend comes to visit, he talks in this fashion.

A little while ago Itō of the Research Center assembled students to be mobilized and said, "Even if there are air raids, students are calm!" We certainly feel the high spirits of the young. One should think about the temperament of the young. The period in which students idled in coffee houses is certainly different from this.

December 25 (Monday)

Every evening one or two, planes come to bomb Tōkyō. However, even with this, Tōkyō and the neighboring provinces were kept awake. Last night and the night before last, for three or four hours the planes were in the vicinity of Tōkyō.

The air-raid alerts were first issued by "Order of the Commandant of the Eastern Army." After that they were "Issued by the Commandant of the Yokosuka Admiralty." The fact that these did not come from the same source is due to the opposition of the army and navy.

In the Diet Premier Koiso proclaimed "Improved Treatment of the Korean-Taiwanese People." I understand that because of this statement many problems are arising in Korea, and in this morning's newspapers there has been the establishment of a "Political Management Investigation Society." Rōyama is one of the people selected to serve on it.

The so-called Rundstedt attack, which began December 16 by the German Army, is advancing successfully. How far will it really go?

I invited Hasegawa Nyozekan, Baba Tsunego, Kuroki Jitarō, and Doctor Watanuki. Baba and Hasegawa are already seniors of seventy years of age. It is doubtful whether or not they will survive this war, and this was on my mind when I invited them. Yet the two of them are in extremely good health.

Baba's temper has been aroused. He is full of indignation at the absence of conscience in the people and government. Even when he uses twenty matches, they will not light. Yet the radio broadcasts that one match can be used for two. He wonders what they are talking about.

Of late, people assemble and the main topic of conversation is bombs and incendiaries. Under wartime conditions, the varieties of topics, such as food, farming, and bombs, have come to change. This means there are changes in life-style.

December 26 (Tuesday)

At the International Relations Research Society, Ishibashi announced a plan for world order. His idea is that because a political solution could not be expected, there would probably be a solution from the economic side. Uehara said in the end that the "economy" is a political problem and that there was the danger it would end as a fine dream. The gist of the plan was the division of the world into three spheres and to create two bodies, a regional director-ate and a world directorate. However, in any case, it is a plan only Ishibashi could have thought of.

After the meeting there was sukiyaki party. It was a year-end party for the *Tōyō keizai* board of directors. Everyone talked about whether this sort of thing would really be possible in the coming year.

When I said that if the war ended just as it is now, wouldn't the Japanese people reminisce that everything in the war was easy, and for the most part they would not have received real injury other than loss of freedom. Ishibashi said, "The other day, this sort of thing was said! Those who have had the worst of it are all dead; those who survive do so because they are bystanders, aren't they?"

Possibly because of the celebration of Christmas, there were no air raids since last night. I understand that according to the newspapers, while we were focused on Christmas even Saipan was attacked. It would have been better if both sides had mutually decided to do nothing about Christmas and New Year's, but. . . . However, those who think about this sort of thing are proba-bly people who have nothing better to do. Particularly because surprise attack operations are the basic Japanese strategy, there is no possibility that this sort of thinking will be realized. According to what the newspapers are transmit-ting, the fact is that we should have bombed the places where they are cele-brating Christmas.

December 27 (Wednesday)

Today the enemy came in rows of silvery wings. Among these, one plane fell. Even the Koreans who were looking up nearby clapped their hands and were delighted. The fact that they raised their voices, shouting, "Hooray, hooray [Banzai, banzai]," was like their shouting for their sumo favorite at the National Sports Arena.

According to the announcement of the Imperial Headquarters, fifty planes came and about half of them were shot down. A large number of Tōkyō people probably do not believe this. The fact that these exaggerated announcements are continued should be regretted for the sake of continued confidence in the Imperial Headquarters.

December 28 (Thursday)

I understand that a man knowledgeable about England named Ito Kei was seized and received a sentence of one year from a military court martial. Itō worked part time at the Foreign Ministry, and it appears that the fact that his wife is English brought him under suspicion. He had some sort of discussion with a neighborhood pastor, and this pastor also talked with someone, and this was investigated. Moreover, the parents secretly informed on his conversation with a girl student. By chance the same man was drafted into the military and then was turned over to a military court. While he was in prison, the military police sympathized with him since he was a model prisoner, and I hear they found work for his wife. A diary that he had written was examined, and the fact that he had written that Japan would suffer some sort of defeat brought calamity upon him.

Churchill, accompanying Eden, flew to Greece. The fact that this seventy-year-old gentleman went to Athens on Christmas day speaks of the seriousness of the problem. But doesn't he fly around a little too much?

The good thing about parliamentary government is that if Churchill falls he will take the responsibility and there would be no recourse. That is to say, they recognize facts as facts, and it will never happen that the unreasonable will defeat the reasonable.

December 30 (Saturday)

Last night there were three air raids. I understand that about one hundred houses were destroyed at Kuramae in Asakusa. Because the alerts were later in the night, it is said that there were probably a great many killed.

Kataoka Teppei has died at the home of a friend in Wakayama. As the funeral services were to be conducted privately at his home, I went there. I

Reviewing a Proposed Mark

Once a mark is selected, it should be carefully scrutinized to ensure that it will not be excluded from protection under the Lanham Act. Considerations include whether the mark contains scandalous material, whether consent from a living person will be required, whether the mark is generic, whether it is statutorily protected, and whether the mark is descriptive of some feature of the goods and services offered under the mark. If the mark includes foreign terms, these should be translated to ensure they are not scandalous, deceptive, or merely descriptive. Many law firms specializing in trademark work use a questionnaire form or data sheet to gather basic information from clients about their marks and to aid in determining registrability (see Exhibit 3–1 for an example).

THE TRADEMARK SEARCH

Once a proposed mark has been selected, a trademark search should be conducted to ensure that the proposed mark is not confusingly similar to a mark that is the subject of a registration or pending application at the PTO or that is in use on a common law basis.

In addition to disclosing potential conflicting marks, a search will provide some indication of the relative weakness or strength of the mark. If there are numerous marks including words similar to the proposed mark for the same or related goods, the field is said to be "crowded," and the mark, while it may achieve registration, may be weak and entitled to a narrower scope of protection than a strong,

unique, and distinctive mark. For example, a review of the PTO database shows the following registrations issued to different owners:

PARAMOUNT® (for hardwood flooring)
PARAMOUNT® (for paper napkins)
PARAMOUNT® (for bowling balls)
PARAMOUNT® (for chocolates)
PARAMOUNT® (for entertainment motion picture services)

These numerous registrations for PARAMOUNT® show that the mark is weak, and an application to register PARAMOUNT for some distinguishable goods (for example, cigarettes) would likely be allowed. The owner of PARAMOUNT (for cigarettes) would be able to stop later users from using PARAMOUNT for cigarettes and related products but would have to share the field with the existing PARAMOUNT registrations and later PARAMOUNT marks used for nonsimilar goods.

A review of other marks also enables the IP team to anticipate some of the problems that may arise during the registration process and possible objections the PTO may have to the application.

Duty to Search

A party who adopts a mark and begins using it without previously searching its availability runs the risk that a senior user will allege infringement. If the later user has begun using the infringing mark, it may need to stop using the mark and any of its marketing materials and brochures that display the offending mark. Such an error is costly and time-consuming because the party will then need to adopt another mark and begin the process of establishing consumer recognition all over again.

There is, however, another reason to conduct a trademark search prior to use or application of a trademark, namely to avoid litigation alleging

hear that he had 100,000 yen in life insurance, and his widow at any rate ought not be thrown into the streets. His house is located ten minutes from Ogikubo Station. Bombs had fallen nearby, and I understand that the glass in Teppei's house was smashed. It appears that the damage in the vicinity of Nerima was extensive, and those killed were not few. According to Teppei's brother-in-law, 60 percent of the enemy bombs struck their mark and 40 percent fell at random.

There is a report of the death of Admiral Suetsugu Nobumasa. He was one of the leaders of the war-with-America advocates. He used to say that American planes absolutely could not attack Japan. Previously, he also said that Lindbergh landed in Hokkaidō in order to spy in the northern regions. I wanted to show Tokutomi and Suetsugu the reality of what kind of consequences this war would bring Japan. It is deplorable that in a certain sense he died with an aura of popular acclaim. In looking at the newspapers I burst out, "Regrettable!"

My wife was returning home after visiting Ayusawa. While on the train, this was the story of a certain woman. She said that recently the wife of a member of the neighborhood association said, "It is about time for the American guests to come." The military police heard this and cruelly slapped the woman and injured her. The woman said, "It's not possible to say anything at all while on the trains."

It seems that such examples are commonplace.

December 31 (Sunday)

The year is finally coming to an end. We have decided to stop our usual yearly visits to Atami, and this year we will greet the new year at home. In actuality, train tickets cannot be bought. For example, yesterday the trains were murderous.

According to my wife, someone was pushed against someone's helmet and two ribs were broken.

I continued my manuscript on the Washington Conference. Writing history is complex. The pen is stubborn and will not advance. The opinions of the naval theorist Bywater[75] are liberal and splendid. Liberal theories in the final analysis are becoming worldwide. A country such as England is one example.

This year is ending. Even economically we have reached the limit of our income. Our income is twenty thousand yen. This is the income from my labors, and I think it is very good for what I do. However, if one uses the black market, the expenditure is tenfold. I feel uncomfortable about the future. In my case, the situation will never be completely impossible because we also have real estate.

1945

January 1 (Monday)

From last night until tonight there were three air-raid alerts. There were places where incendiary bombs were dropped. Under these circumstances, one cannot sleep through the night. Someone like myself sleeps despite this, but there is danger in doing so.

Eating rationed rice cakes when one exchanges congratulations . . . it indeed appears to be New Year's. Cloudy sky.

For the first time now, the Japanese people are experiencing the thing called "war." Praising war as the "hundred-year war" and talking about war with such phrases as "the mother of culture" has gone on for a long time. The reason that I have been harassed is my pacifism. Is war some sort of picnic in the mountains? The people now understand this fact. However, even with that, the question is, will they learn a bitter lesson from the war experience? I think the results will be quite the opposite. For most Japanese, one, they think that war is inescapable. Two, they are intoxicated by the glory of war. Three, they have no understanding of international affairs. This lack of knowledge should be shocking.

From now on, because feelings of hatred for war will arise, during this period there must be correct education. And hereafter, too, there is the need to elevate the status of women.

In Japan the total lack of freedom is the single reason that it is impossible to explain the position of the other party in international problems. In Japan there is only Japan's position. There should be education to change this mental attitude or Japan definitely cannot become a first-class world nation. All problems must arise from here.

I fervently hope from my heart that Japan will somehow advance in a healthy way. I was born in this country, I will die in this country and my descendants will follow the same fate. Abandon the way of thinking that up until now has said that brute force makes a nation great and the people remember that only knowledge is the thing that instructs the nation. If the vengeance idea becomes the peoples' motive for rising again, there is no future.

I will probably devote my remaining literary years to changing the ways of thinking of the people. This year also I will continue to write history. Fortunately we have donations to make this possible. Aiming at later generations, I will exert myself to the utmost.

My speculations for the present year: Germany will probably be defeated during the present year. The Greater East Asian War will probably not be brought to conclusion during the present year. The Dumbarton Oaks Plan will probably be established. I can guess that if this is the case, circumstances will probably be produced in which only Japan will fight fiercely in isolation.

January 2 (Tuesday)

The other day when my wife visited Ayusawa at a small station a man who looked like a laborer dropped a bundle of hundred-yen notes. I understand that he put it, without a wallet, into his pocket, but this was extremely bulky. When a woman nearby said, "You dropped something," he put it just as it was in the front pocket of his trousers with quite a nonchalant expression. This is one expression of inflation.

How will the Japanese people and the military try to attain a full victory against the enemy? They still hope that there will be a mood of war weariness in the barracks of the enemy camp (*Mainichi shinbun*, January 1).

On the same day, January 1, in *Asahi* there was an article entitled "The Funeral Procession of B29s" and the Japanese Army said, "550 B29s have been smashed." One understands that it is believed and hoped that within America a mood of war weariness will arise (*Asahi shinbun*, January 1).

The way of thinking that says that a mood of war weariness will arise within America and after that it will be ruined has existed from the beginning of the war. With this in mind, the war was begun. Even now it appears that this thinking goes on.

Tokutomi Sohō is writing in the *Mainichi*. His title is "Let There Be a People of One-Hundred Million Heroes" (*Mainichi shinbun*, January 1).

The meaning of this can be explained as signifying that because the Japanese people are not awakened, "There is no other way to awaken the Japanese except by bombs falling dead center in Tōkyō." While Tokutomi is one of the people responsible for the outbreak of the war, he lays the guilt for this crime on the people. Even previously he wrote such things as this.

For the Japanese night attacks, expressions such as "assault troops" and "shock troops" and others are used. It is a fact that I wrote about this previously, but in this morning's *Yomiuri* there is writing stating that it is distasteful because it is like gangster language. According to the same newspaper, I understand that the Japanese word *shōidan* [incendiary] means "punishing the enemy," "removing the evil people," "suppressing the barbarians."

In the newspapers there are only dispatches that state, "The Japanese soldier is strong" and "Japan cannot be defeated." Either the secretary of navy, Forrestal, said something like this or the under secretary of the navy reported something like this.

Today a reporter for Reuters named Kimute wrote a piece that stresses that because Japan is still strong, the war strategy should be rebuilt. Having no peace of mind unless they are praised by others is since ancient times a special characteristic of the Japanese, and particularly of the military. We Japanese are not trying to learn what the enemy's state of mind is in saying these kinds of things.

Usui Yae came to visit. On about the 30th on the radio, Yasuoka Seitoku said something like "The China problem will be completely resolved this year

(1945)," and again because there was an article in this morning's *Asahi* conveying the expectation of a settlement this year, Usui had come to ask my opinion. I said this was utterly impossible. There are three alternatives: (1) the liberation of Manchuria, (2) the complete withdrawal of troops, and (3) forcing the termination of the Japanese–American war by way of Chiang Kai-shek. As regards the first, there is no readiness to do this; as for the second, if there is the withdrawal of our troops, there is the fear that the areas will become bases of the American Army; and as for the third, Chiang Kai-shek as he is now will probably not listen. I answered that if Chiang tentatively took a stand, it would probably be with the stipulation of the limits of the unconditional surrender provisions. Moreover, I told Usui a story that Akira heard from Hani Setsuko. In Peking it is completely impossible to walk about freely, and I understand that when everyone goes to bed they place a bamboo spear at their pillow. Those who do not place a spear are only those at the Peking Seikatsu Gakkō (Improved Livelihood School). I said if the war goes badly there would be incidents of brutal killing, and these would probably occur everywhere. I said that previously I had said this sort of thing and warned about it. I said that a deadlock in the war would not come from the food supply problem but would probably come from the fact that there would be no bullets to shoot.

January 3 (Wednesday)

Today there was an Imperial Headquarters report on the radio, the gist of which was that in the afternoon ninety enemy planes came to Nagoya, Hamamatsu, and Ōsaka. "Damage was light" and forty-two planes were destroyed. I hear that the damage on our side was two aircraft. Always these extraordinary battle results! These air battles are not being fought in outlying areas, and the air battles are seen by everyone at home. Whether or not the battle results of the Imperial Headquarters announcements are correct will be known by the people very soon. There are some who wonder why the air raids occur in spite of the fact that the Japanese Air Force has destroyed Saipan.

Usui came again. He brought meat. According to the story of the same gentleman, ten ships went to Kita Chishima and only three arrived at their destination. And it was the story of a certain army doctor that of the three, on the return trip only one remained.

January 4 (Thursday)

The ministers of the army and navy are strongly emphasizing the special attack spirit. This was echoed in a paragraph of a report made to the Diet by General Sugiyama on December 27.

The spirit of Navy Minister Yonai.

Premier Koiso addressed a cabinet meeting (at the beginning) and spoke of the gravity of the war situation.

January 5 (Friday)

Throughout the day I wrote diplomatic history. Ukaji Yōji came to visit. Diplomatic history is not simply the mere facts, and I decided to insert my individual views. This mode is appropriate to me and is also easier to write. Baron Shidehara said he would stop writing after part three.

Baba Tsunego agreed to write a Greater East Asian War political history. Ashida refused.

January 6 (Saturday)

I looked at the clippings of Ōkuma and other things throughout the morning. Because his widow will be evacuated, I will accept these. He was a born organizer, a scholarly type, and those who do not have this inherent talent, like myself, envied him for this.

I hear that General Tatekawa Yoshitsugu has resigned from his executive position in the Imperial Rule Assistance Society. It is a breach in right-wing ideology.

As association of supporters for the evacuation of children has come into existence in Tōkyō. This shows that the bureaucracy alone cannot handle this.

January 8 (Monday)

There was an inaugural meeting of the board of directors of *Tōyō keizai*. Rōyama, Taira, Ayusawa and others who attended.

At the gathering pessimism was expressed regarding the future course of the Philippine war. The invasion strategy by enemy mechanized forces that came to Lingayen Bay in Luzon is staring us in the face. One may say that once the enemy takes the town of San Fernando, the first curtain of the decisive battle will come down. On the other hand, it appears that other troops are planning to land somewhere in China. Thus, the southern areas are cut off.

Sakuda [Kotaro] (member of the House) came to the meeting. Because he has been assigned the presidency of the Free Speech Committee, he came to ask the opinion of Ishibashi. The same person is extremely optimistic regarding the war. He believes that Germany will be strong. Already great damage has been done to the Americans. If they were soundly defeated in the Philippines, the weak points in the racial makeup of America would appear. He meant they would be defeated by these weak points. Optimism is still widely shared by the majority in Japan.

If one relies upon hearsay, it is said that even members of the imperial family are extremely optimistic. Everyone close to it talks to them in this fashion.

To Sakuda I merely said that the German war and the Japanese war must be thought about separately.

According to Ayusawa, the section heads of around colonel rank in the General Staff are loudly stating that it has been inevitable that Japan will be crushed and that the present war is nothing more than one problem. Previously Major Maki said the Sino-Japanese Incident was expected to have this result, and because China now has been preparing for this, if Japan does not fight things could go badly in the future.

It is said that the German counteroffensive in Alsace is full scale and in several places has crossed the Rhine River.

January 9 (Tuesday)

There was a talk at the Foreign Politics Association by the ambassador [Nakamura] who has returned from Finland. During the talk there was an air-raid alert and we stopped midcourse. The essential point was that, judging from its trains, the Soviet Union is in excellent shape. From the outside they do not look as if their system is exhausted. Previously, the trains in Manchuria were fine, but now the opposite is true. Korea is worse than Manchuria, and Japan is the worst. He said that the transportation system is worse to the degree that one approaches Japan.

About August of last year, the Finnish foreign minister requested the ambassador to come to Finland. It was directly upon his return from Moscow. Nakamura had a premonition, but because the Finnish foreign minister could not say anything he wrote it out. He said please look at this and handed it over. When Nakamura read it, it stated that because diplomatic relations had been severed, resident Japanese were to withdraw. The Finnish foreign minister made the excuse, "Well, it is because of the pressure of a foreign nation." When the ambassador asked, "Which nation is interfering?" the foreign minister clearly answered, "England."

Nakamura said that the Soviet Union treated him politely.

Vice-Foreign Minister Sawada spoke with Takayanagi. He said that in *Tōyō keizai* they write as if the relationship between the foreign minister and the prime minister were bad. It appears to him that this was written by Kiyosawa, and his having written such a thing has baffled the minister. There would be a problem for someone connected with the Foreign Ministry who wrote such things.

This was probably something entitled "The Way Diplomacy Should Be," which was written by Rōyama. I was indignant and said, "I was just thinking

I would critique the foreign minister and the vice-minister. For the good of the nation I wrote what I thought was the case, and why is it so bad to write something like that?" Seeing that Shigemitsu uses petty bureaucrats, "I doubt his quality as foreign minister." I said this with some vehemence.

Because I hold the position of "part-time employee," it was as if by this they were trying to control my writing. Of late I have the recollection of turning down their invitations in the past, and my feeling of distaste continues. The one called Sawada is absurd.

Takayanagi wishes to bring this war to some kind of negotiated peace. He says that for that purpose, because he is friendly with an influential person named Jessup,[76] president of the American Institute of Pacific Relations, how would it be if he met with this person and talked to him? Yet where and how are they to meet? I said if it were somewhere in Sweden it would be fine, but there would probably be no way to go there except by submarine.

Nara said that during the present year there would be a compromise between Germany and America-England, and the Soviet Union would declare war on Japan. I said that Germany will probably make an unconditional surrender. Is such a thing as England-America and Germany shaking hands impossible?

In the evening at the Imperial Hotel there is no heat and it is unspeakably cold there. At eight o'clock almost all the lights are turned off. The premier Tōkyō hotel under wartime conditions.

January 10 (Wednesday)

I was at home all day, and I am writing a manuscript for *Tōyō keizai*. In the afternoon I wrote history.

January 11 (Thursday)

While going through the things left behind by Ōkuma, I found a typescript book written by Shigemitsu. I understand it had been written in London. It seems he liked writing in this form. It has a generalized knowledge. Doesn't his attention to fine points insufficiently touched upon make him an able official?

On January 9 the American Army invaded Lingayen in Luzon and San Fabian in the Philippines. We cannot bear thinking about the future.

The thing called "special attack spirit" is being repeatedly stressed in the newspapers and on the radio. It is true that in Japan there is a philosophy of death and there is no philosophy of life. The consequence of this is that everywhere forced labor prevails and health continues to be damaged. For example, look at the experience of students (*Nihon sangyō keizai*, January 11).

January 12 (Friday)

There is not a day when there are no evening air raids. In the beginning the neighbors next door went into the air-raid shelter, but now no one goes into it. When one becomes accustomed to the raids, one cannot go on repeating this.

The newspapers are talking extravagantly about "aggressive government." They say such things as Japan can carry out "complete mobilization" like Germany. Apparently they think everything will be fine if there is mobilization. Of late, the Japanese people are barking senselessly without knowing what they are saying. They are not making concrete suggestions. Tokutomi Sohō, as we well know, is saying that the invasion is a bolt from the blue. I would like to put this down as the opinion of a right-wing representative.

This sort of attack strikes Sohō as a bolt from the blue. Even for Tokutomi the military is too secretive.

It appears that in America they do not report on the special attack forces. As viewed by the enemy, because the aim is to give the other side a devastating blow, no matter what it is, it is nothing special. Only Japan attached such emphasis to abstract spiritual force. It does not realize that materiel and invention are part of the spiritual forces. The opinions of someone like Tokutomi are Don Quixoteism. He is completely devoid of a scientific way of thinking (*Nihon sangyō keizai*, January 12).

January 14 (Sunday)

I went to the funeral service of Kataoka Teppei, and on the way home I stopped at the residence of Rōyama. In fact, I had made a bet with Rōyama whether Germany would last to the end of 1944, and because I lost I went bearing some canned goods.

I went to a New Year's Greetings party at the home of Uehara Etsuji. I had a rendezvous to meet my wife there. Uehara had gone to Atami and was not there. Everywhere without exception rice cakes are served. This year, as there are few social affairs, no rice cakes will come to hand. Even in our household these are rationed.

After that, I went to the home of Harumasa. He is a young count. We had a talk about whether he would publish the "Rainy-Leaf Villa Diary" (of his father, Count Itō Miyōji). I was treated to supper. He said, "If the war continues, we probably will not be able to live in this fashion." All in all it was extremely lavish. Itō Miyōji obtained considerable wealth because of his greedy nature. He was a person who would do anything depending on bribes from the political parties. However, Harumasa appears to be a fine young man. One can imagine that he will probably do something with himself later. This young man is the master of a fortune of close to a million yen. Socialism

done to explore the reasons why this happens. Maybe the students really had some kind of big problems. Maybe the faculty should take the major responsibility for failing to help the students or to treat the students fairly. Or maybe it is just a matter of matching: The wrong persons were paired up, or the right persons came together in a wrong time and/or wrong place.

Whatever the specific reasons, a common lesson to learn for both the advisor and the student is that before they choose and accept each other, they should consider certain kinds of things and carefully assess the possibility for them to work as a team properly. Generally speaking, the faculty should set no condition for helping the students to maximize their chances of success. Yet different faculty members have different strengths, skills, interests, needs, and difficulties. As a student you should not only be clear about what kinds of help you will need from your advisor, but also have some idea as to what types of assistance you can reasonably expect from him.

In the educational process, probably the thing of foremost importance is to clarify the individual needs of the students. As a student, you should know what you want better than anyone else, though it is not always that easy for you to understand or to be aware of your own needs. Usually, in setting up your goals and thinking about your plans, you will find what you need in order to achieve your various objectives. For your educational pursuit, specifically with regard to the role of your advisor in the thesis/dissertation process, you might feel that you need her assistance in every aspect of your research project. Or you may just need her advice in some critical steps or points, and believe that you can handle the rest well by yourself. Or, you may simply wish that nobody would stand in the way, and should anybody set the hurdles the role for your advisor would be to help you overcome or remove them.

There are different personalities and backgrounds within the faculty. Some may appear to be so eager in offering advices and supervision that you as a student would sometimes feel a little too pressured. Some others may be happy leaving you alone, yet if you sense a kind of indifference you may gradually lose your enthusiasm. Although most faculty members are prepared to aid students, you may be disappointed when you see some professors who show no interest in you, or in your project, and do not provide the kind of assistance you seek.

The selection of an advisor for your study is extremely important, and could be complicated indeed. Generally speaking, you need an advisor who:

(1) Understand your needs and is willing to provide the assistance. The ideal advisor will always show empathy for your situation, and make you really feel

EXHIBIT 3–1
Trademark
Data Sheet
(U.S. Applicant)

Please provide the following information to enable us to prepare and file an application for registration of your mark with the United States Patent and Trademark Office (PTO).

1. Describe the mark.
   a. Words: _____

   b. Logo: _____ [describe and attach sample logo] _____

   c. Are the words "stylized" (for example, should they be displayed in any particular manner, script, or typeface or is standard printing acceptable)?
   _____

2. Describe the Applicant.
   a. Full name: _____

   b. Full address: _____

   c. Type of legal entity (corporation, partnership, etc.) _____

   d. Organized under the laws of the state of _____

   e. Name of authorized person who will sign the application and other documents and his/her title: _____

3. Describe with particularity all of the goods and/or services that are or will be offered under the mark or for which protection is being sought.
   _____

4. Consult your records and state, with respect to use of the mark by you (or any predecessor) on or in connection with any of the above-described goods or services:
   a. Has the mark been used in intrastate sales or advertising? If so, give date of first use anywhere.
   _____

   b. Has the mark been used in interstate commerce within the United States? For example, has there been a transaction with an out-of-state customer or has media advertising the goods or services offered under the mark been conducted across state lines? If so, give the date the mark was first used in interstate commerce in the United States (or in foreign commerce between a foreign country and the United States). Note that use of the mark in advertising preparatory to opening a business is not sufficient.
   _____

   c. Is there a bona fide intent to use the mark in the United States if it has not yet been used in the United States? _____

5. Provide information as to how the mark is actually used (if it is in use).
   a. Newspaper or other media advertising: ____ Yes ____ No
   b. Signs or store displays: ____ Yes ____ No
   c. Direct mail, such as brochures: ____ Yes ____ No
   d. Labels, tags, packaging: ____ Yes ____ No
   e. Other (describe): _____

6. If the mark is in use, please provide at least three original specimens showing the mark as it is actually used in connection with the sale or advertising of the goods or services. If the mark is used in connection with goods, labels, tags, boxes, or other packaging are acceptable *as long as they show the mark*. If the mark is used in connection with services, brochures and other advertising materials are likely acceptable *as long as they show the mark*. If the specimens are bulky, you may provide photographs of the specimens as long as the mark is clear and legible in the photos.

will also probably emerge. This is the most disquieting thing for the rich regarding the consequences of the war.

The enemy that has invaded Lingayen Bay in the Philippines is progressively growing stronger. Everywhere one goes, there are questions regarding this problem (*Yomiuri*, January 14).

Are the young Japanese who are dying in the Philippines doing so for the limerick-type sentiments heard in frivolous poems and songs? Ah! (*Mainichi*, January 14).

Needless to say, it is too tedious to talk about the clenched fist of the army. It is being applied even in the factories. Japan is a world of violence.

January 15 (Monday)

In this morning's newspapers I learned that the Toyouke Shrine at the Ise Shrine was damaged by enemy aircraft. The newspapers are writing about this in huge type. This is also true of the Imperial Headquarters' announcements.

Did the enemy planes calculatedly drop their bombs on this place? Along with that, did they mistakenly drop their bombs there? Along with this, again, was this indeed the work of enemy planes? According to the statements of the American prisoners of war and what is popularly heard, it is said their mission is not to attack such places as the Imperial Palace, Meiji Shrine, and Yasukuni Shrine. What reason is there to do this now? The newspaper headlines are "America Reveals Its Real Demonic Nature," "The Unclean Bombs Dirty the Ise Temple Precincts," "We Will Never Forgive This Outrage" (*Asahi*, and following these there were inserted the enraged commentaries of famous people).

January 16 (Tuesday)

In this morning's newspapers there was a whole page devoted to editorials on the air raid on Ise Shrine. There were editorials, articles, and critiques. Of course, it goes without saying that this was the result of guidance by the authorities. It is said that, thinking the Information Board somehow did not want to touch on it at all, these were issued by the General Staff.

First of all, Premier Koiso and his respectful remarks of apology to the emperor were published (*Yomiuri hōchi*, January 16).

Also, the home minister went to Ise Shrine and apologized to the gods. Following that were the titles of the editorials: "The Extremity of the Enemy's Tyrannical Barbaric Behavior" (*Yomiuri*), "The Enemy's Intentions Are Clearly Revealed" (*Mainichi*), "Clear Manifestation of the Power of the Gods" (*Asahi*) (*Yomiuri*, "Editorial," January 16).

Beginning with the preceding editorials, the newspapers have addressed themselves in more than half the paper to "Destroy the Irreconcilable Violent Enemy!" or "The Anger of One Hundred Million at the Profaning of the

Sacred Precincts Explodes," "God Damn You! From Now On Watch Out!" It is clear that this activity is used to promote the will to fight. In the *Yomiuri* there are photographs of people doing obeisance in front of the Ise Shrine. *Asahi*, in large letters outlined in black, writes of the barbaric behavior of America, saying, "Nothing But the Death of the American Devils." Moreover, as usual, Tokutomi Sohō has been brought out and made to give talks. The title of these is, "For Human Beings There Is the Way of Human Beings; the Enemy Is Not Human." It seems that Sohō, instead of assuming responsibility himself, attacks the authorities.

The problem is whether the people, as the government wanted, become enraged in their hearts. Someone listened to what housewives and ordinary people were saying. I understand they say, "Aren't the factories more important than shrines?" This is the talk of the commercial district.

The authorities are at their worst in their inability to consider the people's minds. However, the city people and right wing with whom we have been in contact are probably individually distinct from the regional people.

There was a members' meeting of "Japonicus" and I had a meal with Viscount Kanō Kurō. As might be expected, he has a sharp mind. We discussed the Greater East Asian Sphere from the standpoint of economic problems.

In the evening I was invited to a meeting at Sagono with Akiyama Takashi, Sugihara Gunzō, Yamano, Suzuki Toppa, and others. Sugihara returned to Japan from America on the last exchange ship. He related on the basis of actual experience how kindly American officials managed personal property. I understand they did it better even than the lawyer for his own family. He was grateful for this solicitude by an enemy country. This kind of behavior makes the enemy strong.

Why are the Japanese not able to do this kind of thing? Will not Japan in due course, after some fifteen years of caring even for the enemy, present itself favorably to the world?

The trains are breaking down into total wrecks. There are no windows and there is no upholstery on the seats. The windows are intentionally smashed by the passengers, and they are stealing the upholstery. I understand that if it is announced a train will be late, there is destruction on the grounds that the trains are late for other reasons.

Anger against the enemy is first of all directed inward.

January 17 (Wednesday)

The newspapers are saying forceful politics, forceful politics. And then at the same time they attack the irresponsibility of the bureaucracy. Doesn't emphasizing aggressive government finally induce bureaucratic politics? The ignorance of the newspapers is disgusting.

After the office was completed, as my time was taken up there I could not study. Itō is not businesslike, and, contrary to expectation, I have been made to carry on all the business there.

January 18 (Thursday)

There was a lecture by Baron Shidehara at the Japanese Diplomatic History Society. It was the third time he spoke. Those who attended were Kuwagi, Ishibashi, Takahashi Yūhyō, Takaishi Shingorō, Shinobu Jumpei, Ashida, Tanaka Kōtarō, Takei Taisuke, Makino Eizō, Matsuda Reiichi, and one person from Mitsui, Amemiya.

The meeting continued past three o'clock.

January 19 (Friday)

Luncheon expenses at yesterday's meeting were fifteen yen. It was totally inadequate. The cost of commodities has risen more than ten times.

Today my wife went to the home of Ayusawa and bought some rice cakes. One, not very large, was fifty sen. It is said that one batch is more than sixty yen. For the funeral party of Kazuhiko, the family of Ishibashi purchased vegetables, but I understand that these cost two hundred some yen.

In the afternoon Mizuno from the police station came to call. He came to ask about the war situation in the Philippines. I said that I'm afraid that, contrary to expectation, the battle at Luzon Island would be settled rather quickly.

I hear that the Germany Army withdrew from Warsaw on the 16th. Moreover, I hear that in Krakov there has been a shift to street fighting. The optimism about the Western war is not shared about the Eastern front. The attack of the Soviet Army should be feared. With this there is the possibility of its advancing even closer.

Ishibashi said a piano teacher is his wife's friend and has only two alternatives in her present life: dying of starvation, as she has nothing to eat, or losing all her possessions buying things on the black market. This is how things are.

The cost of postage and train fares will be raised on April 1. A letter is ten sen; a postcard, five sen.

January 20 (Saturday)

We invited people to a gathering of the Japanese Diplomatic History Research Society. These included Maruyama Kunio, Fukaya Hiroji, Hori Makoto, Itō Kōichi, Sōguchi Morikichi, and Hamada Kumeo.

Meetings such as these always fall into chitchat. It was true on this occasion. Yet Fukaya is an extremely fine man and scholarly. He is already arranging the collected letters of Mutsu. I should like to employ this man in place of Itō. To the same gentleman I sent an additional two hundred yen.

January 21 (Sunday)

I had the chills and am lying in bed. My temperature is 38.8 degrees. This is the fist time I have stayed in bed all day.

January 22 (Monday)

Among the articles in this morning's *Asahi shinbun* there is an essay by a professor of the Jingukan Daigaku (*Asahi shinbun*, January 22).

Today I stayed in bed all day. I am bleeding from the throat. I asked the doctor to visit me. He said there was prevalence of influenza and it takes this form.

Lying in bed, I finished reading in one day the short work of Professor Yoshino Sakuzō entitled *The Relationship with China*. Just as I expected, it was interesting. It was probably written just before the professor's death. Meiji cultural research is included in the work, and particularly citations of works on the history of the Chinese Revolution. This is his special interest. In the end, I am able to be sympathetic with Professor Yoshino. His style of looking at things is the same as mine. I myself am the successor in the Shōwa period to Professor Yoshino from the Taishō period on this subject. In writing diplomatic history and leaving behind scholarly works, I will bring about the further development of the work of Professor Yoshino.

It is said that the cost of applying night soil is one yen per load (two buckets). Up until last year they didn't charge for it, and this produced problems. According to an article in Chūbu Nihon, I learned that the labor charge for one day's work is about sixty-five yen (*Chūbu Nihon*, January 22).

People asking for night soil removal pay one yen per bucket, and the worker can easily remove fifty buckets in half a day.

The Diet closed its session yesterday, but neither the premier nor the foreign minister nor the finance minister actually spoke the truth.

The Diet of 1945. At this time, when people are talking about the settlement of the war this year, the ministers do not publicize conditions that should worry everyone. The Diet speeches, questions, and answers, as well as the newspapers and radio, all report that everything is fine. Look at a leadership style, ways of thinking, and education that tell lies up to the very time the nation is about to be ruined. The Japanese are able to live their lives positioning themselves in spiritual confusion between lies and truth.

January 23 (Tuesday)

There was a funeral ceremony for Ishibashi Kazuhiko. Because I had a cold, my wife attended in my place. He was a splendid young man. Hundreds of thousands of such young people must be killed. I understand that the day before yesterday, because Kasahara Yoshikazu would be boarding a tanker, he received two days leave and came to say he was staying with Kiyoaki and to extend his greetings. On my wife's excuse that I was in bed he was turned away, and how regrettable it was. I understand that because no gasoline is coming from the southern areas, they are sending out so-called civilian corps, and these are for the most part unprotected. It is completely a matter of dumping humans into their graves, because if two or three ships get through, it is regarded as successful. This is violence that the people of any foreign country would not allow. If it were a foreign country, such things as civilian service corps would not be permitted, but in Japan the parents are the first to become outraged.

The speeches of the ministers and the newspaper editorials of late are using words such as "volunteer civilian service corps soul" or "civilian service corps spirit" in place of "suicide missions."

The mother of Kojima of the neighborhood association died. I understand that with the difficulty of obtaining a coffin, he was given one on the condition it be returned. In other words, one borrows coffins for the dead but cannot buy them. They are used any number of times.

The fact that the dead cannot be cremated has been true for some while. But in this example the fact that there are few coffins and these are used many times reflects the conditions of the period. I think that very soon there will be no automobiles, and with the inability to move the bodies it is possible there will be burials in a corner of the garden in about half a year.

I am reading *Dreams of Thirty-three Years* by Miyazaki Tōten. It is unfortunate that Sino-Japanese relations were begun relying upon the *rōnin*. One fully understands the pure sentiments of Miyazaki, but. . . .

January 25 (Thursday)

Yesterday President Yagi Hidetsugu of the Technological Committee made a response in the Diet.

"There has been talk of sure-hitting suicide missions; to produce military weapons that were sure-hitting without certain death was our hope for some while; but before these could be put into action, war circumstances necessitated the dispatch of certain-death, sure-hitting kamikaze special attack squadrons. As a member of the Technological Committee, I am truly unbearably ashamed, and there is no excuse for this."

This reply produced an extraordinary reaction in the Diet. It is said there were even those who were sobbing. (*Yomiuri* allotted an amazing amount of space and conveyed the event.) That produced an outburst of opposition from the intellectuals against this feudal patriotic view (a morality of glorifying death). I had been thinking it would be good if someone would say this. Professor Yagi finally expressed this view.

Aren't the Japanese a people who understand so long as they are talked to? Aren't they a people who have the quality of naturally moving in the right direction? And because there is concern that the Japanese people will go in the right direction, don't the bureaucrats think only of obstructing their ears? Therefore won't Japan become better if freedom of speech is established? In the future social order that must come, freedom of speech above all else must be retained.

January 26 (Friday)

The resentment of the intellectual is not spontaneous, it is brought forth exploiting some provocation. An instance of this is certainly the reaction to the current Technological Committee incident.

January 27 (Saturday)

Nakano Tadashi came to call. I hear the salarymen are uneasy. I hear the positive-minded young people are attempting to prepare for the forthcoming new world by going into politics, and on the other hand the passive-minded young people are considering withdrawing to the countryside because of the difficulties of making a livelihood. I hear that even among ordinary people, at least opposition toward military people is appearing, and women in their seventies are saying, "I wonder why the politicians cannot take hold of the military people at all?" A certain friend, looking at an American magazine, said, "I want to eat chocolate soon; wouldn't it be nice if the war was over?"

Yesterday there was an express letter from Itō Yasuji (my assistant). I told Itō to take care of things in a businesslike fashion, and he even sent back postage money. Because I was in the throes of a cold, I erred in mentioning postage stamps. One reason is that Itō works badly. The other reason for my impatience is that Itō does not work at all. In the end, I am not skillful at using human beings. I would like to think that the research center will not become a mental burden.

January 28 (Sunday)

After a long while, close to two months, I went out into the fields. I am one man alone. I think this year there will be no helping hands, and there will not be a harvest like last year.

There was a telephone call from Kiyosawa Satoru. He told me that in yesterday's air raid the neighborhood of Ginza yonchōme was attacked, and places such as the Tōjō Shoe Store were burned. The office of Okamura Kesayoshi was soaked. Finally, the destruction of war presses closer to us.

A story that Eiko heard from a friend. She related that a little while ago, because the questions of Rōyama Masamichi were not adequate, he was pulled down from the Diet platform. In the next election he will probably be in difficulties. In referring to this I recall that the phrase "disturbance" was used in the newspapers. There are Diet members who do not hesitate to go as far as making critical remarks regarding Shigemitsu or talk about the peace offensive. The Japanese people are low-keyed, and at the same time the Diet members as well are low-keyed. If it were the time of political party rivalry, a single party would not be tolerated.

January 29 (Monday)

Intending to make a call at Fuji Ice and the Tōjō Shoe Store, I got off at Shimbashi. There were ropes stretched across Ginza Street and one could not pass through as far as the Imperial Hotel area because of the bombing. There is broken glass, and there are many buildings that are half-demolished. It is said that there are four hundred completely and half-demolished houses and more than three hundred dead (one thousand casualties). In one day's bombing, the damage is extremely great. I went to *Tōyō keizai* and we talked about the fact that within this year about half of Tōkyō would probably disappear.

A story of Yamazaki Seiju, told to the elderly Miura Tetsutarō. A certain senior statesman met his Majesty the emperor and respectfully inquired whether he had the desire to negotiate peace. His Majesty said that this would probably involve unconditional surrender. I understand that after a while his Majesty said, "If it reaches this point, I will go to the front line and sacrifice my life." Awe-inspiring, awe-inspiring!

A certain person said, "Why didn't the senior statesman advise his Majesty, even at the risk of being rude, that his Majesty's way of thinking is incorrect, and instead of becoming a model for one hundred million deaths it was his duty to instruct these people on how to live?"

A story that comes from Shanghai from a former assistant professor at Kyūshū University named Takahashi (Masao). In Shanghai a bale of rice was sixty thousand yen, but now it is forty thousand yen. In Shanghai at present the Japanese civilian population is about seventy thousand and it is quickly decreasing. If there is a decrease in the number of Japanese soldiers, there is the possibility of the occurrence of a problem like the Tsūshū Incident.[77]

Twenty-two enemy B-29s that came to raid on Saturday were destroyed. Imperial Headquarters announced that more than half of the remainder were damaged. I hear on the American side they said that four planes did not return. It appears the announcements on the Japanese side, even in common-sense terms, are excessively exaggerated.

January 30 (Tuesday)

I am working in the fields. Our maid Toyo dislikes working in the fields and goes out in white socks. Young unmarried women are becoming slightly strange psychologically. I hear that when my wife asked Toyo to take the land tax she said, "I don't like going because I don't like being thought of as part of your family." She also said today, "Because I greatly dislike field work, I wonder if I will stay until summer." Of late, this is the mentality of the maids. Their attitude is, "I am doing you a favor staying here." "I'll leave whenever I want to."

The absenteeism of women employees in business is extremely great. I hear that they take time off from business and visit men, and when it is time, as if nothing had happened, they return home. This is a story of Deputy Nara. It is enough for me to imagine the changes in ideas of chastity of young women unknown to me.

The people of Japan are not informed about anything. Why did the war occur? In the war, how much damage has there been, how many casualties have there been? There is no one in Japan who knows these things completely. One part of the bureaucracy knows certain things, but they do not know other things. Even in the current Diet, some questions are more or less taken up, but as usual there are no answers.

January 31 (Wednesday)

I am surprised at the unexpected damage received by Tōkyō in Saturday's air raid. From Ginza yonchōme to places close to the Imperial Hotel, the area is full of demolished houses and broken glass is everywhere. Until now only one part of the people knew about damage to the factories, but now, with the damage to the heart of the city, once again the war power of the enemy will be understood by all the people. In Ginza yonchōme the water pipes have broken down and it is impossible to travel by subway. To the south, from the Kyobunkan of Fuji Ice, the area is burned out. The solid reinforced concrete buildings are certainly strong. It was just like this at the time of the Great Earthquake. The Hattori Clock Shop is still standing. With regard to this damage, the government is able to do absolutely nothing. It is a situation in which individuals are left to their own misfortune. What shall we call this, irresponsibility or powerlessness?

I paid a call on Kasahara Kiyoaki at the Greater East Asia Hospital. This hospital had changed its name from "St. Luke," and the cross on top of the building has been completely removed. I hear that now the greatest number of air-raid casualties are transported here.

February 2 (Friday)

I met at *Tōyō keizai* with Lt. General Isogai, who was the governor-general of Hong Kong. He has recently returned to Japan. When Ishibashi asked him what generated the misunderstandings in the war, he said, "From the army view, we think the navy could do more, and so we bring our troops out to the islands." When Ishibashi asked, "It appears that the army wanted to carry on the war but the navy didn't want to fight," he answered, "One part of the navy had the feeling it wanted to avoid the war, but the larger part was anxious to fight." According to the same lt. general, there is the possibility that the American Army will invade the homeland. Because he is in contact with the Chinese people, he said the Chinese were a great people. The way of thinking of those who have contact with Americans will probably differ.

This morning's newspapers announced that a number of Military Control Districts were created. These are probably in preparation for the invasion by the American Army. Lt. General Isogai said we hear of "one hundred million honorable deaths," but he criticized the honorable-deaths thesis and said, "We soldiers understand by that phrase that our honorable deaths are necessary to preserve the nation."

Whereupon I said that I wished this idea would emerge from the heart of the army because if we said it, we would be called defeatist.

If one relies upon what was said by a certain right-winger, he stated that if the Imperial House were permitted to continue, acceptance of the American peace conditions would be fine. What kind of right-winger is he?

February 3 (Saturday)

I wrote on a manuscript all day long. I am researching the Chinese overseas students in the 1890s and Sun's revolutionary preparations. I am quoting Professor Yoshino Sakuzō.

The American Army is pressing upon Manila. I understand that in the heavy artillery being used by the American Army, they are also using rocket launchers and it is a situation in which the Japanese Army cannot move. The Japanese Army has not yet engaged its full battle strength. I understand the American side is saying this is a mystery, but is it a matter of watching for a chance, or with the disparity in weaponry is a counterattack even possible?

According to a story brought by Hirakawa, in the countryside in places such as Okayama everyone is digging pine roots for turpentine. It appears that this is being used in place of gasoline.

February 4 (Sunday)

Kiyosawa Satoru and Okamura Kesayoshi came to call. They both recently had narrow escapes in air raids. Of late, Satoru is thriving and brings us chocolate and other things. The two of them both say the power struggles of the military put us in a fix. Again, they are the same in their pessimism regarding the war. But they say that the young military people and swaggering youths are still stubborn and have no doubt that Japan will be victorious. I understand that even someone like Terakado of Asahi Slate Company is saying that Japan necessarily will be victorious. Those who are pessimistic about the state of the war are a small number of intellectuals among the Japanese masses, and even if the fall of Manila becomes a reality, still the masses will believe in victory (*Yomiuri*, "Editorial," February 3).

From the afternoon I had stomach trouble and stayed in bed. My throat, skin, eruptions and upset stomach are evidence that my body has no resistance.

February 5 (Monday)

Yesterday evening I had diarrhea and it was extremely unpleasant. I worried whether I had a serious illness. I was absent from *Tōyō keizai* and stayed in bed.

February 6 (Tuesday)

I hear that a member of the Economic Club named Yamada is saying that my predictions are as accurate as those of a god and publicly spreads this around. That is to say, the Greater East Asian War, the fate of Germany, Manila, unconditional surrender, etc.

It is always the same faces that appear (7th).

February 7 (Wednesday)

One man said that already there is absolutely no studying in the schools. There is no studying. The students are all in factories.

Finally, on the third, the American Army entered Manila. For some time it has been propagandized that Manila has no military value. It is propaganda style the same as Germany's.

trademark infringement. Liability for trade-mark infringement rests on a finding that two marks are likely to be confused. One factor many courts consider in determining whether two marks are likely to be confused is the intent and good faith use by the second user. Recent cases have begun examining whether failure to conduct a proper search is evidence of bad faith. In *SecuraComm Consulting Inc. v. Securacom Inc.,* 984 F. Supp. 286 (D.N.J. 1997), *reversed on other grounds,* 166 F.3d 182 (3d Cir. 1999), the court referred to the defendant's failure to con-duct a trademark search and suggested that such "carelessness" was a factor showing intent to infringe. Similarly, in *International Star Class Yacht Racing Ass'n v. Tommy Hilfiger U.S.A., Inc.,* 146 F.3d 66 (2d Cir. 1998), the court noted that a limited search of PTO records should not excuse infringement by the defen-dant, particularly when the defendant was advised by counsel to conduct a comprehensive search. Finally, in *Frehling Enterprises, Inc. v. International Select Group, Inc.,* 192 F.3d 1330 (11th Cir. 1999), *cert. denied,* 531 U.S. 944 (2000), an infringement case, the court held that a failure to conduct a trademark search before attempting to register a trademark was "intentional blindness" and was evidence of improper intent.

Because liability for trademark infringe-ment rests on a finding that two marks are likely to be confused, a client may be able to avoid liability by showing it acted in good faith by conducting a thorough trademark search prior to using a mark. In sum, a comprehensive trademark search can save time and money, avoid litigation, ensure a mark is available, and assist in developing a strategy to avoid possible PTO objections.

Scope of Search

There are a variety of sources that can be reviewed to locate potentially conflicting marks. Because there are literally millions of

marks registered or applied for at the PTO, and thousands of journals, trade magazines, direc-tories, telephone books, Internet sources, state records, and state trademark registrations that might contain other marks or business names, a computer-assisted or online search is the most effective method of searching. Moreover, an online search can be constructed to search only for similar marks used in connection with similar goods and services. Thus, if the client in our case study wishes to use WILD DYNA-MITE for a roller coaster ride, there is little to be gained from looking for similar marks used in connection with candy inasmuch as con-sumers would not likely be confused by the coexistence of two similar marks for such dis-similar goods.

Both LEXIS® and WESTLAW®, the computer-assisted legal research systems, offer access to vast databases that may point out con-flicts. One of the best known databases is TRADEMARKSCAN®, a product of Thomson & Thomson. TRADEMARKSCAN (federal) con-tains information on active registered trade-marks and service marks as well as applica-tions filed at the PTO (for active marks since 1884 and inactive marks since 1984), while TRADEMARKSCAN (state) provides similar information on marks registered with the secre-taries of state of all fifty states, the District of Columbia, and Puerto Rico. Other online data-bases include journals, magazines, and periodi-cals. Most of the databases are also offered on CD-ROM format, allowing IP practitioners to purchase discs and conduct their own searches. The discs are then periodically replaced and updated.

Conducting the Trademark Search: A Two-Step Process

In nearly all instances, trademark search-ing is a two-step process: a preliminary search is conducted of the records of the PTO to make

February 8 (Thursday)

In every part of the world it is said that this year is the coldest in fifty years. Water inside the houses being completely frozen is something unknown in Tōkyō life for thirty years. There is no charcoal, and this year's cold effects everyone. Through the present winter there was a ration of only one bag of charcoal. Fortunately, there is still some at our house.

February 10 (Saturday)

As previously promised, I had a meeting with Baron Shidehara at the Japan Club. I received a manuscript from him. He wasn't satisfied with what I had written and he wrote something for us. I put this into the Shidehara material separately.

At that time there were air-raid warnings. Ninety planes were attacking the aircraft factory at Ōta in Gumma Prefecture. The Kempeitai and others are exhaustively investigating why the enemy knows the location of our aircraft factories, and, assuming that this is the strategy of spies and that information comes from Russians, they go over every Japanese close to Russians with a fine-tooth comb. Our whole neighborhood has been disturbed by this.

I talked with Takahashi, the assistant editor of *Yomiuri*. I heard that the problem of how the war was being managed worried him, and investigating this, he wished to know Shidehara's opinion. The talk that says that the senior statesmen are having audiences with his Majesty is a lie, but it is a fact that Count Makino is on the move. This morning when I telephoned Count Makino on the matter of the Diplomatic History Research Center he said, "This morning I have a previous engagement, but because I certainly wish to meet with you I will telephone you later." In the evening there was a telephone call for a meeting at his home.

There was a story from the chief of the Investigation Bureau of the Foreign Ministry to the effect that in the Philippine area the enemy has control of the sky and there is not a chance of even an ant escaping. Consequently, it is being said that the young crowd of the Foreign Ministry will by no means be coming back home. The fate of Satō [the Japanese ambassador] is of great concern to me.

I understand that guerrillas are active in all the areas of the Philippines.

February 11 (Sunday)

It is National Foundation Day. As usual there are talks by Tokutomi Sohō in every newspaper.

February 12 (Monday)

There was a meeting of the board of directors of *Tōyō keizai*. Rōyama also attended. I understand that the emergence of a new political party is becoming an issue. I said I did not have great interest in this sort of thing. According to Rōyama, the government is abandoning the war effort. Consequently, the fact that it does not make clear statements is because of this. Rōyama said, "I am an advocate of fighting to the end." I said that one way is to have the Japanese who like war experience it thoroughly or try to bring it to an end because the sacrifices are costly. I said I have no determination to go on. Anyhow, little by little, the latter position will prevail.

February 13 (Tuesday)

The officials of Japan can only speak formally. Until the bitter end. There are reforms in the cabinet, and there was a speech of the new minister of education, Kodama (*Mainichi*, February 12).

Regarding the "treatment" problem concerning "fellowship" for Korea and Taiwan, Premier Koiso made an announcement in the preceding Diet. A committee was also established on that occasion. As a show of "thanks," members from Korea came to Tōkyō. In the present war, in exchange for making Korea independent, if it were possible to return Koreans in Japan to their homeland this would be the best thing.

February 14 (Wednesday)

The absenteeism in the factories is extremely high. I understand that one reason is that people work somewhere else and another reason is that even if they go to the factory, they do not work. According to a story of _____ the nephew of the said gentleman went to his factory, and because there was no coal he only worked three days in a month.

In today's newspapers the contents of a Big Three conference of America, England, and the Soviet Union were announced. The conference meeting opened on February 4 at Yalta in the Crimea. Yalta is the homeland of Chekhov and his house is there.

The punishments to be meted out to Germany are extremely severe. Given this, the Nazis will probably resist in a struggle to the death. The Soviet Union is decisively in the lead, but there is a question whether this will signify victory in the end for the Soviet Union. The only strong point of the Soviet Union is that it has soldiers under its command in all countries because of its proletarian ideology (*Mainichi*, "Kenteki" [Inkstone drops], February 14).

All the students are being driven into the factories. This shows that the leadership class—the military, does not recognize the value of education and the officials of the Education Ministry are completely lacking in self-confidence. Hitherto such people as Hashida, Okabe, Ninomiya, and Ko-dama were merely right-wing ideologues and they groveled to the military. I am fearful of the results ten years hence. Even turning students into workers cannot be argued about. If there were intelligent guidance in the factories, even this would be all right, but as it is now it is a sorry state of affairs (*Nihon sangyō keizai*, February 14).

February 15 (Thursday)

There are air-raid warnings, and I hear the enemy planes come to attack the Shizuoka, Nagoya areas.

Browsing in the bookstores, I bought Murdoch's *A History of Japan*[78] (sixty yen) and the diplomatic history of Japanese–Chinese relations of the Black Dragon Society.

I attended a meeting of a society named North Survey of Sagono. It was a group directed by Akiyama Takashi. As a guest, there was a Meiji University professor, Takinoto Shōzō, who has returned from the Philippines. He is second-generation American-born Japanese who entered Meiji University and as a valuable person became a professor. His talk was extremely profitable.

1. In the Philippines the Filipino people are attached to the American side and guerrillas are extremely numerous. Even the women think Japan is the enemy.

2. One basic reason is that because, needless to say, America will be victorious, if the small-numbered intellectual class sides with Japan, sooner or later they will encounter censure, and also they are being pressured by the masses.

3. However, the most influential reason is that the Japanese soldiers do cruel things. They frequently slap the Filipinos with the palm of their hand. The Filipinos think the worst insult is to be slapped in the face. And relatives and friends pass around reports of these events.

Not only that, but also the Japanese lynch Filipinos. That is to say, they tie Filipinos to trees, build a fire at their feet, or douse them with water until they die in agony. But they do this in broad daylight in front of great numbers of people. This cannot but help to bring about hostile feelings.

4. In the dining room of the Manila Hotel, those who take pains about their appearance are only the diplomats of neutral countries, the manager of the hotel, himself, and the waiters. The Japanese stick out their legs and while they eat pick at the hair on their legs. This sort of crowd is what the Filipinos saw for the first time.

5. Before returning to Japan he had a meal with the chief of the Military

Information Bureau. Because the chief told him to discuss any subject, he spoke of this behavior. The Chief said, "The Japanese have brains but they have no culture. I also experienced this in Malaya."

6. If anyone asks Filipinos if all the Japanese are bad, they do not think this is necessarily so. In the Spanish prayers in the Philippine churches there is the word "Wachi." When he tried inquiring about this the Filipinos answered, "Please keep General Wachi [Takaji] in the Philippines forever." General Wachi had been in China and frequently had contact with the masses, and he has been popular among them. Citing two or three examples of this sort of thing, he said that Japanese who thought about the interests of the Filipinos were held in high esteem.

7. He said that Japanese who had stayed at length in foreign countries had better understanding.

In the final analysis, from the foreign viewpoint it has the look of Japanese piracy. The medieval phenomenon called the advance of the barbarians is now manifest.

Education has been defeated. This is the result of learning without ideas and cultivation and mere acquisition of "skills." Education does not exceed the chivalrous warrior tradition, and particularly the crowd below the middle class called "military" push themselves forward in large numbers. Hitherto those sent overseas were a small number of selected people. Now, because "real Japan" has gone to foreign countries, they are introduced to the other side just as they are.

February 16 (Friday)

From seven in the morning air-raid warnings were issued. Raids continued until four in the afternoon. Carrier-based planes came to attack. I hear they bombed the airfields. The carrier-based planes struck, but there was nothing at all that could be done about them. I understand that trains were also attacked.

Finally, problems of food supplies will arise because of the cutoff of transportation.

Japan now is doing nothing productively. Our entire strength is being sacrificed in the interest of war. Because this strength is being destroyed, Japan is losing its power at a frightening rate.

Being in the center of Tōkyō, we are not informed at all where and what sort of destruction has incurred. This secretism will probably be true to the very last.

"The enemy is impatient." The radio is saying this, the newspapers are saying this, and the military is saying this. This probably means the enemy is already weary and if Japan can make one more push. . . . This perception has hitherto brought about a lot of mistaken observations.

February 17 (Saturday)

Today also, carrier-based aircraft came to bomb. It went on until about two o'clock in the afternoon. Carrier-based planes come and nothing can be done. One should understand that the navy has been completely destroyed.

February 19 (Monday)

I attended a board of directors meeting of *Tōyo keizai*. According to Rōyama, in the Diet Ando Masazumi raised questions about the location of "war responsibility." The response of Koiso was that if it is government business, it is the responsibility of the prime minister. If it is war strategy, it is the responsibility of the High Command. Koiso said, however, that he did not wish to answer concerning matters of the war. According to the constitution, no one else but the emperor assumes this responsibility.

It is a country without responsibility even for war.

February 20 (Tuesday)

In the afternoon I visited the office of Masaki Hiroshi. Last night there was a telephone call from him reporting that the magazine has been returned to him. He thought I had probably been evacuated, but when he asked Baba and Shimanaka he learned that I was in Tōkyō, therefore he decided to telephone. Because Baba said he would come, we decided to meet. Shimanaka also came. It had the appearance of a meeting of nothing but oppressed liberals. Masaka has been publishing *Chikakiyori*. He is a lawyer and a fighter such as is rarely seen in Japan. Last year there occurred a torture death incident by the police. That is to say, he brought an indictment against the police. He carried on a dispute with the police bloc as the enemy. The police, for their part, harassed him by every means, but he is fighting them vigorously.

Fujita Chikamasa of *Chūō kōron* was in prison for a year. In fact, he is out of jail, but while in his cell the police beat him brutally. His body was all swollen. After he was beaten he was made to do calisthenics. Even hearing about it makes my blood boil. In Japan if there is not a constitution, Japan is not a country of legal rule. It is a country of gangs. I hear that whatever the police do, there is nothing to be done about it. Masaki told me so. Masaki says he is fighting with the readiness to die. That is probably likely. Masaki criticized the former premier Tōjō. He is probably the only person who made an accurate critique. The conversation was a pleasure.

February 21 (Wednesday)

I went to lunch at the home of Kuroki Tokutarō. Kodaki was there. He is a section chief at the Foreign Ministry. Although I had been invited, I brought a lunch. Moreover, he did not object to my bringing a lunch. Of late, a single meal of rice is extremely precious. Kodaki served with Yoshida Shigeru and Shigemitsu. I hear that Yoshida used up as much as 200,000 yen in London. Kodaki said that as his private secretary, he had managed this money. Yoshida is a willful man. Shigemitsu is a simple bureaucrat. These were his observations. Of course, there is nothing wrong with Shigemitsu's mind.

On the 19th the enemy invaded Iwōjima. We are being pressed upon more and more.

The enemy plan for dealing with Japan was published in all the newspapers at the same time on February 19. They are also writing that the enemy has the plan of changing the national polity, that is to say, the matter of the imperial family, which has been completely concealed until now. This is rather an extreme disposition. What will be the repercussions of this? I wish to know. I wrote a piece for *Tōyō keizai*.

Tokutomi Sohō is writing again. One can see even someone like Tokutomi cannot ignore the friction between army and navy.

February 22 (Thursday)

I had a meeting with Baron Shidehara. I will write about this meeting separately. I was treated to lunch by Takahashi, vice-president of *Yomiuri*.

February 23 (Friday)

There was snow from yesterday evening, it accumulated to almost a foot. There has been no year as cold as the present year; moreover, it is the first time in about thirty years of living in Tōkyō that there has been as much snow as this.

February 24 (Saturday)

While I was viewing the Old Book Exhibition I browsed in Kanda's second-hand bookshops. I bought a very great deal (close to 500 yen).

I bought Adams' *History of Japan* (125 yen for two volumes) and Brinkley's *Japanese History* (65 yen).[79]

These were not immediate necessities, but they were things my mouth had been watering for from a long time before. But I who am now setting forth to write a history of the Greater East Asian War wonder whether it is the moment to write about the Meiji Restoration period.

But I am preparing my collection by degrees. God do not let the fires of war burn it.

February 25 (Sunday)

Today, from morning, there were air-raid warnings and the carrier-based planes came to bomb. After this, in the afternoon also, 130 B-29s came to attack. According to a story I heard afterward, these figures are conveyed as less than they are in order to announce "battle results." In the end, in order to make the battle results proportionately higher, it is convenient to announce them in this fashion.

While I was writing a manuscript I thought that if unfortunately a bomb fell, everything would be over for me.

February 26 (Monday)

Snow. As much as a foot accumulated. As it is already close to March, such a heavy snow is amazing.

When I went to *Tōyō keizai*, Nozawa was standing at the entrance and said, "It is completely overwhelming. When I see people pulling bedding from the fiery ruins, they are trembling while they stare at the ashes. I am miserable. The sacrifices of this thing called war are much too great." Without knowing to whom he was talking, his speech was overcome with grief. At *Tōyō keizai* there is no gas and no water. Their damage is even greater than at our house. The electric trains also are almost all immobile.

After the meeting I went to Kanda to pick up the books I had bought on Saturday. The whole area of Kanda has burned out. It extended from the vicinity of Kanda Station to Surugadaishita, and places that had not been bombed before were burning now. They are still burning.

The total damage is nineteen thousand houses. I understand the dead are 130 or so. I hear the Ueno area is burning. The fire fighters come and they run around asking, "Where are the hydrants of the water mains?" It is apparent they are untrained.

Jinbōchō was not burned out, and I picked up the books I had bought. It was a day of heavy snow. The city streetcars were not moving, and this made me even more miserable. Occasionally there were people who were transporting loads of baggage.

Now there are not even any transport wagons. Moreover, the nation cannot provide aid of almost any kind to the casualties.

February 27 (Tuesday)

In the morning Amemiya came to call and said he had fired Itō Yasuji. I was relieved. We paid four hundred yen to Itō for absolutely no reason, but it couldn't be helped. He is a fine man, but he is unbusinesslike and is not scholarly. It is difficult to obtain good people.

The other day, at the home of Kuroki, when I said that Japan would probably become like Greece or Spain, he said we will not be like these countries. Japanese culture will never reach their level, and we will probably become like Egypt.

The morning radio program, as usual, is military people talking. This morning a lt. general named Nakai Ryōtarō said America was a devil and vigorously attacked the advocates for peace, loudly insisting upon one hundred million honorable deaths.

February 28 (Wednesday)

I am writing an essay entitled "Politics and Diplomacy" for *Tōyō keizai*. In the afternoon I made progress on my book.

March 1 (Thursday)

I went to the Kanda used-book shops and bought things on Chinese relations and other English works. Because I will be in a fix if these shops are burned, I am buying for future use. Although books are becoming expensive, compared with other items they are cheap. However, in the not-too-distant future they will probably become costly.

There are outraged Diet members who spoke of the castration of the Japanese (*Asahi*, March 1).

March 2 (Friday)

The term "direct connection" is circulating. It is like saying that the political parties have direct connection with the masses. This probably came out because those who do not have direct connections are numerous.

March 4 (Sunday)

From about eight in the morning, 150 B-29s came to attack. The weather was so bad that the radio announced, "They are making use of the bad weather." Consequently, it appears that on the Japanese side no planes at all were dispatched. I understand Sugamo and other places were bombed, but as usual nothing at all was announced. In Japan, while it was being said that "Damage was light" and "The enemy suffered heavy damage," before one knew it more than half of the great capitol was completely destroyed by fire. On the way home I stopped at the residence of Meiji University Professor Matsumoto Ryūzō to inquire about Dobashi.

March 5 (Monday)

A story of Ishibashi. According to a story of Ichiriki, head of the *Kahoku shinpō* (North China news), just recently a military commander was appointed, and when he assembled the influential people he made a speech. He said if the enemy invaded he had confidence in Japan. In the first place, the enemy supply lines are overextended. In the second place, finally, the army can fight with their most skillful strategy. I hear that he said that in such places as the Philippines and Iwōjima, they cannot fight with full power because of the constricted area, but in the homeland they can perform adequately. I understand that everyone was flabbergasted, and the fact is that the army people are really thinking of a scorched earth policy.

There is not a single announcement concerning either the recent cabinet reforms or the domestic situation. National politics are handled in the dark. I doubt if politics were conducted like this before.

March 6 (Tuesday)

Yesterday, as Uehara Etsujirō wished to talk I met with him in the afternoon at the Sannō Hotel. If one relies upon the story of the said gentleman, he has been having talks with the senior statesmen regarding the conclusion of the war. He also met with Wakatsuki as well as talking with Okada Keisuke. He met with Shidehara, and because Shidehara thinks only of external matters, that is to say, he thinks only of resistance to the bitter end and does not think about internal politics, he said I should talk to Shidehara if there was the opportunity. Okada also understands that Koiso is inadequate and says that something should be done about him. Yet there is no one else. I understand that Konoe also is aware of Koiso's unfitness, but when he meets him he leaves without being able to ask for his resignation. I hear that his Majesty commanded an audience with the five senior statesmen and asked questions about the current state of affairs or something, and among those present was Makino.

Uehara feels that unconditional surrender itself is not to be feared. If this is the situation, he said it is possible to put forth conditions from our own side.

After all Uehara is a patriot.

On my way home I detoured to the secondhand bookstores and bought a few things.

March 7 (Wednesday)

I wrote an editorial for *Tōyō keizai* entitled "Addressing Tokutomi Sohō." It accused him of not understanding responsibility and merely placing responsibility upon others. Ishibashi's suggestion about writing something was the reason I did this. (Ishibashi said that paper was already scarce and we should write with audacity.)

March 8 (Thursday)

Fukaya kindly lent me diplomatic documents of the Hara Cabinet period. These are valuable materials. As to my forthcoming history, I can write it with better materials than those previously available.

I went to Maebashi, having been invited to speak at the Savings Section of the Ministry of Communications. There were no second-class tickets. Yet I found a seat.

In the conclusion of my speech, I stated the aim that Japan must fight until the very end. This is the sort of thing Baron Shidehara would say. This has never been my real sentiment.

The atmosphere of Japan is such that it is impossible to speak the truth. Unless this atmosphere changes, foreign relations will be impossible. I wonder if this will be possible because of the war. It will probably not be possible quickly.

March 10 (Saturday)

Yesterday evening the train was about two hours late. When we reached Kamata, air-raid warnings were issued and it was completely dark. Groping about, I boarded a train. Even when I reached home there were no lights and I went to bed.

I was awakened by air-raid sirens. There was the noisy sound of artillery. When I went outside, the B-29s were flying at low altitude, and their silver wings were revealed in the searchlights as they flew at a leisurely pace. The anti-aircraft guns were firing vigorously, but they were of little effect. But not even one of our planes was sent up. The B-29s were clearly outlined against the sky and indeed pretty. Immediately the sky in the north became pure red. The wind was blowing very strongly. With such a wind there was probably not any possibility of stopping the fires. There was the smell of burning in the wind, and I grieved over the enormous damage, though I didn't know to which areas. I heard afterward that the 130 planes did not come in formation but attacked one by one. According to a later story, Kaneda said that even though it was the enemy their strategy was splendid. They came pushing in from every direction.

a quick determination as to whether the mark may be available or whether there is a direct conflict that would preclude use of the mark. The preliminary search is often called a **knockout search** because its primary purpose is to eliminate identical or nearly identical marks. If the results of the preliminary or knockout search indicate a mark may be available, a comprehensive search of other sources (including state trademark records, telephone directories, Internet records, and trade journals) is then conducted.

Step One: The Preliminary Search

There are a variety of sources that can be used to conduct an initial trademark search, including online subscription services, CD-ROMs, the Patent and Trademark Depository Libraries, and the PTO web site search services. Following are some resources commonly used for conducting a preliminary search:

Electronic Databases and CD-ROMs

- TRADEMARKSCAN is a database owned by Thomson & Thomson, a renowned trademark search firm (discussed below), which provides information on all active registered trademarks and service marks and applications for registration filed at the PTO. The TRADEMARKSCAN database is primarily used as a quick screening tool to determine the availability of a new mark.
- DIALOG® is another database offered by Thomson & Thomson. Its database includes trademarks from the United States plus numerous foreign countries as well as patent and copyright information. DIALOG offers free online training and practice (its ONTAP® service) and free practice searching at the following web site: http://training.dialog.com/onlinecourses/trademarks/.

- SAEGIS™ is an entire suite of services provided by Thomson & Thomson that allows online worldwide trademark searching as well as searching of domain name registries and web sites to locate common law uses of proposed marks.
- TRADEMARK.COM™ is an online search service offered by MicroPatent LLC (discussed below), offering a variety of searchable databases, including federal marks, state marks, and common law uses of potentially conflicting marks.
- LEXIS and WESTLAW, the computer-assisted research systems, offer access to vast trademark databases that may disclose potentially conflicting marks.

Many law firms subscribe to one or more of these services so they can perform an initial screening search in-house. Many of the databases can be purchased in CD-ROM format, allowing IP practitioners to purchase discs and conduct their own searches. The discs are then periodically replaced and updated. Alternatively, most IP practitioners access the various databases online, on a "pay-as-you-go" basis.

In conjunction with a preliminary or knockout search, most practitioners conduct a simple Internet search using a standard search engine. For example, entering the word mark BUDDY BEAR into a search engine such as Google (http://www.google.com) may disclose some common law uses of the mark. Often paralegals conduct the knockout search and provide an initial review of the marks revealed. The results are communicated to the client along with recommendations for the next step to take. If a mark is intended to be used only for a short time, perhaps during a limited promotional campaign, a knockout search may be sufficient by itself.

Patent and Trademark Depository Libraries. For those located near Washington, DC, the PTO maintains a Trademark Search Room

In the morning I went to the center of the city to attend a meeting of the People's Scholarly Arts Society. I was told the train was only going to Shinagawa, but I was able to go to Hamamatsuchō. At Kamata Station there was a couple with reddened eyes and smeared with mud. When I asked them about it, they said that the area of Asakusa was burned and the Kannon statue was incinerated. As one approached Tōkyō, there were many people from Hamamatsuchō wrapped in bedding. The crowds of people walking on the railway tracks were exactly like the time of the previous earthquake. The areas to the right and left near Shimbashi Station were burning.

Particularly, Shiodome Station was furiously erupting in fire. Here is the most important freight station in Tokyo, and it is to be expected commodities were piled up in great heaps for two or three blocks in all directions. These were being reduced to ashes. But what should be surprising was that very precisely only the freightyard had been specifically struck, and one could only be astonished at the precision of the bombing.

From Ginza sanchōme to ichōme, everything is in flames. The fires have even penetrated the Shiroki Department Store of Nihonbashi. The Meijidō used-book store to which I always go was completely burned out. I had bought books on Thursday and expected to pick them up. Only Maruzen is undamaged. Is the fact that everywhere one goes the Mitsubishi branch banks are standing something that explains the confidence in them? What is unbearable to see is large numbers of old ladies and the sick who, while being propped up by others, are going somewhere. People carrying in one hand bedding left from the fire, people carrying buckets that have been scorched. These people hobble aimlessly down Ginza Street. The eyes of each and every one are reddened. It is probably because of the smoke and heat.

When I met with Itabashi he said that the Itabashi house had been completely burned out and his wife had gone to *Tōyō keizai*. When I went to inquire after her she was in an exhausted state. Yesterday Ishibashi went to Kamakura, and his wife and the maid were the only victims. They were unable to save anything. This person who opposed the war previously lost his son Kazuhiko, and now his house has been burned up. What sacrifices!

I hear that Asakusa, Honjo, and Fukagawa are almost completely burned out. Moreover, because of the violent wind, certain people entered the water and drowned to death, and certain people who entered air-raid shelters were overcome by smoke and their corpses were lying here and there about the road. It was a horrifying sight, truly unbearable to look at. The Yoshiwara also was completely consumed.

On my way home, when I approached the Ginsei, the wife of Kasahara Sadao, my nephew, was holding onto three children; having been burned out by the fire, they were left with nothing. Shūji was in a quandary as to what was the best thing to do.

I hear that all of Hongo, Shiba sankōchō, and other places are completely burned out, and I learned at the police station that 200,000 houses were burned up. If this is the case, it means that there are one million victims, and is this indeed true or not? One part of Tōkyō Imperial University has been lost to fire. With respect to this, the nation can do nothing at all. In the evening there was an appeal from the neighborhood association to donate clothing, food, and bedding.

My god, is this war? Premier Koiso expressed his confidence in "inevitable victory" and attacked the indiscriminate bombing by the enemy. Toward Koiso's attitude that he is merely humiliated about the burning of the stables of the Imperial Household Ministry, there will probably be a hostile reaction from the people.

In today's morning editorials there was news that two more people were promoted to general. It is a matter of ten thousand bones drying up and turning into two generals. These two are utterly arrogant.

According to a story I heard at Maebashi, a colonel of the same city spit out big talk, saying, "Something like Iwōjima is simply nothing more than an electrical spark, and the war begins now." The ignorance of military men becoming a problem in every area is our harvest.

I learned from a communiqué in effect that because French Indo-China says it will not maintain its military alliance with Japan, the Japanese Army is disarming the Indo-Chinese forces and will defend it independently.

When I was looking out from the train on the way to Maebashi, in the countryside there was still air-raid training with buckets. If one sees the actual conditions in Tōkyō, I suppose that one must understand immediately that this sort of thing is not easy and the diffusion power of knowledge is slow.

If one looks at the fire ruins of Tōkyō, again one understands the enemy is bombing on the basis of mechanical power. Accordingly, in the extreme regulation of lights that has been exercised until now, one should understand the stupidity of, for example, behavior such as going around shouting about the light from one cigarette. After all, the fact that we are led by a crowd completely without intelligence brings about this sort of thing.

The army is making clear more and more that it is in the midst of preparations for war operations within Japan. The single key that will determine problems hereafter is, what are the people thinking about this, and what kind of reaction will they have?

March 11 (Sunday)

Notwithstanding the fact that the air raids teach the essential necessity of a rational mental attitude and the power of science, the newspapers and radio are full of the official quacking of the ideological Japanists. Is this not the road finally of salvation for the Japanese people?

The miserable state following the B-29 air raid after one o'clock in the morning of the 10th day by day is becoming clear. The Ginsei employees are burned out. It is said that in the Asakusa area the corpses are piled up. They failed to escape injury when a violent wind was stirred up. Probably there, casualties are not less than the time of the great earthquake. I think they will exceed twenty or thirty thousand. (*Chūbu Nihon*, March 5).

If the dead are 100 million, what will become of the nation afterward? For this is the present ideology of the military and right wing. (*Chūbu Nihon*, March 6).

The enemy's propaganda. We can see that the people are becoming discriminating toward our propaganda.

The decisive battle of the homeland is being earnestly thought about. Already, even the head of the Information Board, Matsumura, is saying this, the commander of Sendai is saying this, and again the newspapers are propagandizing this. The only problem is, what are the people thinking (*Chūbu Nihon*, March)?

After all, it may benefit the people in general to learn how lightly those whose occupation is war treat human life. Ah!

One should see that the provision prohibiting Jewish government officials, etc., is the Nazi style. With this, whoever they are, they definitely will not obey. It is the mentality of children.

Grew fans anti-Japanese war spirit. Know the strength of Japan. An enemy who will carry on even a generation of war.

Grew clearly overestimated the war power of Japan. I think that it's probably not that he did not know. It was a warning to prevent slackness. Nevertheless, if the Japanese open their mouths, they merely view the enemy disparagingly, or they merely bad-mouth them. This is extremely lower class, and I wonder if the Japanese people understand all this.

The crowd called Kanokogi and Tokutomi Sohō, while they are two of the greatest ringleaders who brought on this war, are now saying the same things. In their clamoring for the appearance of the young, they are attacking others with regard to the current state of affairs.

The Japan ruled by these kind of people is in trouble.

March 12 (Monday)

I went to *Tōyō keizai*. Whomever one meets, one encounters the statement, "What on earth is the government trying to do?" This serious tone expresses considerable agitation. In a report in the Diet by Interior Minister Ōdachi, he stated the damage in the Tōkyō air raids was 1,040,000 casualties, more than 23,000 houses, 32,000 deaths, and the number of missing persons was not clear. When a member asked, "How many missing persons are there?" he answered, "Because it is unclear, I said unclear." I understand the Diet member said, "You stupid fool!"

I understand that in the Honjo and Fukagawa areas, after three days of air raids the corpses were still scattered about on the roads, and the air-raid wardens are transporting them by truck. It is said that because of the fire, hair and faces lose their original form and have become like blackened posts. It was not possible to distinguish men from women.

The fact that my nephew Kasahara Sadao had departed for the front and his wife with their three children had been driven out by fire I have previously written about, but when Shūji went to the war office they said, "There is nothing else to do but evacuate to relatives" and turned him away. What she received was only a food ration ticket for a five-day ration of rice and a free train ride. He said that because nothing could be done he accompanied her to a basement in the Maru Building and planned to send her off to Shinshū. Piling two quilts on a bicycle, he accompanied her. What is called aid to the victims of the nation is merely a five-day ration of rice and soy sauce.

I hear that his Majesty invited the senior statesmen and suggested the achievement of unity between the government and the high command. It is said that with regard to this the military was absolutely opposed; also, even among the senior statesmen, there was no one who spoke out against the military boldly, positively. It is not known whether or not the Lord Privy Seal, Kido, was in support of the emperor, and along with that whether the emperor spoke out, but Kido would probably have spoken out.

I understand that the Kempeitai are extremely watchful. This concerns the advocates of peace. In a Japanese-language broadcast from Saipan, the enemy said, "The plight of the people is unfortunate, but it is because the government is evil," and so on.

The government is finally resolute about invasion military operations.

In the reports on the military war situation of the army minister, Field Marshal Sugiyama Gen, there is not a single word mentioned about such things as numerical inferiority, regret, or danger. He said, "We must seize the opportune moment to decide victory at one stroke." With respect to this, the navy minister said, "We are sorry for the present situation." In an *Asahi* editorial there was praise for the "frankness" of Navy Minister Yonai, but in a certain sense this was cynical in respect to the army minister. The strongest opposition is of this level.

In Nagoya from 12:30 on the 12th until 3:20, 130 B-29s came to attack. Because it is said it burned until 10:00 in the morning, it is probably just like Tōkyō.

The imperial stables of the Imperial Household Ministry (morning of the 10th) and the Atsuta Shrine (12th) were damaged. Both the radio and the Imperial Headquarters repeated and strongly stressed this. I pray that it does not bring distress to the imperial family.

March 14 (Wednesday)

Learning from experience is the most effective way, and there are more and more of those who wish to return to the countryside. I have pretty much decided to go to Karuizawa. When I spoke to Ishibashi he said *Tōyō keizai* would rent our house.

I understand Foreign Minister Shigemitsu invited four people—Ishibashi Tanzan, Obama, Kanō of the Specie Bank, and Yanai—in an effort to find a way to stop the war and wondered if there is any way to do this by way of the business community.

I understand that the new finance minister, Tsūshima, does not understand anything at all. He utterly refuses even to consider peace talks, saying that if the American Army advanced, because it appears that our army has self-confidence, it will repel them. If it is not possible to repel them at sea, at the time of an invasion how is it possible to destroy them? Assuming that temporarily they are destroyed, how is it possible finally to crush America? If they are not destroyed, how is it possible to conclude the war? This sort of logic is intelligible to anyone; why is it not intelligible to the intelligentsia? The first reason is that they do not like to think things through. The second reason is that they are afraid that calamity will reach them if someone says this sort of thing.

In our circle those who think about the end and aftermath of the war are only Ishibashi Tanzan and Uehara Etsujirō. I hear not only this, but when the ministers talk about this those around them conform with lip service. Because the present state of affairs has occurred, they are a crowd made up of those lacking morality and valor.

The government does not put out a single announcement regarding the damage and specific details of the air raids. They talk only of how many aircraft have been shot down. If anyone calculated the number of those shot down, one would say that it is by far greater than the B-29s manufactured by America (*Yomiuri*, "Editorial," March 14).

March 15 (Thursday)

When I went to the restaurant called Sagono for a scheduled meeting of the North Survey Society, it had been burned out by the recent air raids. It was a splendid building, constructed at a cost of 300,000 yen or so. When I looked out from the mountaintop, before me was an entire area of scorched grass.

I hear that on the morning of the 14th Ōsaka was burned out in an air raid. According to a report from the Bank of Japan, twelve or thirteen thousand houses were burned out. It means that they came once for two days to Tōkyō, Nagoya, and Ōsaka.

Why is it bad to pick up the propaganda leaflets of the enemy? Why doesn't the government come to grips directly with enemy propaganda? (All the newspapers write about "sharp pencils," etc.[80] This indeed can probably be considered propaganda.)

There was a board of directors meeting of Fuji Ice. The warehouses and cold storage buildings at Fukagawa have burned up. In these the newly purchased commodities had been placed. Moreover, the Fuji Ice house properties were completely burned up. It was a discussion as to whether there should be a dissolution of the company or what. (The Ueno branch store was also lost to fire.) Ōta, the manager, is pessimistic about the future, and if from

America there are unconditional surrender stipulations, he said no commerce at all would be possible, and now there should be dissolution.

In the past I was more pessimistic than anyone else regarding the war, but now I am more optimistic than anyone else, and I tried to convince him that there were extremely bright prospects for trying to start life from the bare necessities, and for such things as a Western food and bread industry in the future. However, Ōta, because he had frequently argued with me and was a supporter for beginning the war, knew my position well. We have decided to try to keep a modest operation in the shop.

According to Watanabe, in August of last year he talked to a military man above the rank of major about the circumstances in America and that Tōkyō would inevitably be raided and because of that would become a burned-out field, but afterward when they were drinking sake he warned, "Because that sort of thing will never happen, your talking in this fashion will cause trouble." The perception of military people is of this level.

In front of Kamata Station, the Kempei carried off two persons of respectable appearance. Kempei are also stationed in front of Tōkyō Station. There is always talk that martial law will be imposed. Military government is finally coming into existence. In the newspapers and in the Diet there is talk of "strong government," but in Japan this means military rule. One should see military order and military politics as a mystique.

According to the evening radio, there was a report, the gist of which being that Premier Koiso attended a leadership conference and with the army and navy ministers mutually discussed military operations. I thought war leadership conferences already existed, but they still have not been carried out. Premier Koiso said that he was thankful for this. It was an order of his Majesty. What was done at the beginning of the Sino–Japanese War and the Russo–Japanese War has only now been done.

French Indo-China's Annam and Cambodia have declared their independence. The king of Cambodia stated that France was unable to protect them, and consequently they abrogated the Treaty of 1863. The fact that this was due to the manipulation of the Japanese goes without saying. The problem is, to what extent do these countries really wish to be independent?

A story of Nanao (businessman, director of Fuji Ice). Victims have no feeling of hatred toward America; rather, because of their miserable conditions they have the feeling they should curse their own government for not providing a single piece of bedding. Ikeda (Fuji Ice director), who had been burned out, showed the same sentiment. The same gentleman barely escaped with just what he was wearing (*Chūbu Nihon*, March 13).

The photograph of the emperor is in the elementary and other schools and has been a revered object more important than life itself. Because of this, great numbers have lost their lives.

According to Ikeda, in his township association there were 756 dead. This out of a township association of 4,200 or 4,300 people. If one relies upon this, it is generally about 16 percent or 17 percent dead. This is not too excessive.

I understand that in the Kamimachi neighborhood association of Ishibashi Tanzan there were 7 dead. When one considers these kinds of facts, based upon the air raid of March 10 the dead probably exceeded 100,000 persons (*Asahi*, March 16).

All effort is being exerted in cautioning against enemy propaganda. The contents of news articles conveyed subjects that are written about in the enemy propaganda leaflets.

One understands from this how much anxiety there is about sharp pencil bombs and other things (*Yomiuri*, March 16).

The news articles are of interest. They are skillful propaganda to prevent people in general from picking up the things dropped by the enemy (*Chūbu Nihon*, March 12).

In every direction, in expectation of the enemy invasion, there is preparatory training beginning.

March 17 (Saturday)

Because I altered the internal structure of my book, I am rewriting. As one volume, there will be the history before the Washington Conference and I will write in comparative detail, for example, on the China problem.

A report heard on the radio yesterday was that Premier Koiso attended an Imperial Headquarters Conference. If one relies upon the *Asahi*, Koiso at the time of the formation of his cabinet had three plans: (1) he would attend the Imperial Headquarters Conferences; (2) he would return to active service and carry on the coordination of essential national affairs and high command; and (3) He would manage problems with completely new ideas. He negotiated about these plans, but the military opposed both the first and second plan and (this fact is not in *Asahi* but I heard it from others) the third plan became the Supreme War Leadership Conferences. Of late, such people as the senior statesmen participated in these, and at last something of this level has been achieved.

The preceding report makes special mention of "special temporary management," and one should note Koiso putting the Imperial Headquarters in a higher position in "Imperial Headquarters, Government." This is enough to know the views of Koiso.

March 18 (Sunday)

From the morning, Usui Yae and Kamiya and Satō Ihei came to call. Because Satō wanted to rent a house at *Tōyō keizai*, he had come to look. He accompanied his family. Kamiya is a principal of an elementary school and an excellent man. I understand recently he quit and is returning to Azumi. Many of the

people in the countryside still believe Japan will be victorious. This is probably so because they have no sources to make judgments.

In southern and eastern Kyūshū, eight hundred planes came from enemy
carriers to attack

March 19 (Monday)

I understand that within the military they are saying that six months from
now, invasion operations by the American Army are completely impossible.
On the European continent England was a power but had no equivalent
power to attack Japan. In the Philippines about 200,000 are necessary, and
against Japan an army of one million probably is necessary. One man requires
from sixteen to twenty tons of ship space, but there are not that many ships.
In view of this, they will probably first invade China. In China, Japanese
troops will be rapidly withdrawn from the south and concentrated in North
China. And then Japan will tighten its hold on Manchuria, North China, and
Korea. Transportation lines can be defended because they do not use planes
for distant places. Naturally, the South Seas areas will be abandoned. I hear
this is the style of thinking.

As for oil, only 10 percent of the tankers from the southern areas (sent from
Japan) return home. Consequently, it appears it is now a question of obtaining alcohol from sugar and pine root oil. But as regards pine root oil, it takes
three hundred people to obtain one ton of it. To obtain 100,000 tons requires
thirty million people, and yet it is a fact that at the present moment cauldrons
are being set up in the mountains. In America, one ton of oil is ten dollars, and
it takes two people. When one speaks from this viewpoint, one says that the
war power of Japan is 150th.

As for the misery in Fukagawa and Honjo, the more one hears of it, the
more it is beyond words. Yesterday his Majesty conducted an imperial tour of
the disaster areas. Should not Japan appeal to America over this pitiful situation, the fact of bombing women and children? I hear that they kill people in
the fire ruins with machine gun fire. However, Japan has done this in Chungking, Nanking, and other places, and even Manila is not a case for praise, but
the immoral behavior of America cannot be permitted. According to Usui,
the men he used were drafted and they went to collect corpses. Being burned,
there was no way of knowing whether they were men or women. I understand
that there were about fifteen thousand of these, and holes were dug in Ueno
and they were buried in them.

It was decided in a cabinet meeting yesterday to close all schools (except
elementary schools). For the coming year, all schools will close. If they are the
kind of schools that have existed till now, it may be just as well if they no
longer exist.

Premier Koiso said in the Diet that the air-raid damage would be announced in as much detail as possible. Yet there were no reports on the wards,

casualty numbers, or places. As a result, there were no details at all. To say that those who know the true facts of the enormous damage are only a part of the bureaucracy is damaging to bureaucratic politics in the extreme. If there is no reform of this at the very root there will probably be no improvement. Yet, given the tendencies of the Japanese does one know if this is possible?

March 20 (Tuesday)

I stayed at home and wrote a manuscript for a magazine called *Keikoku* (Administration). The subject was "On Diplomacy in Wartime" (*Mainichi*, March 20).

It appears that the enemy is widely scattering propaganda leaflets. Regarding that, our official position is three-monkeyism: see nothing, hear nothing, say nothing. Germany is also the same, but does this attitude work?

One phenomenon of politics during wartime: It was decided on the 17th that with respect to Korea, Taiwan, and Karafuto, there was a request by the Sumitsuin to send no more than ten members from Korea and Taiwan to the imperially appointed House of Peers, in the House of Representatives from Korea twenty three members and five from Taiwan, and from Karafuto one prominent person to the House of Peers and three to the House of Representatives. It went to the Diet as a bill.

Elections have been completely suspended for a whole year. This also is being legalized.

March 21 (Wednesday)

Now all the newspapers are writing that rumors and gossip are flourishing, and the reason for this is that the government is not publicizing the facts. An instance of this is an editorial in today's *Asahi* entitled "Construct an Essential Foundation in the Depths of the People's Heart." In the same editorial they circulate the same nonsense, saying, "If one eats rice with red beans and shallots, one will escape the bombs." The fact that it states, "The reason Germany suddenly collapsed from within in the previous Great War was that it could not recognize the danger pressing upon it since it lacked political judgment and a sense of reality," was a considerable advance.

Today on the noon radio it was transmitted that the courageous warriors on Iwōjima with the highest officers leading them died honorable deaths. Relying upon the announcements of the enemy itself, there were certainly close to twenty thousand casualties, and one understands how much the Japanese Army exerted itself to the utmost. Ah!

The stupidity of the *Mainichi* editorials is not new. They base everything uniformly on the theme of Jews. They are saying that it is a false rumor that Germany is requesting a cessation of hostilities. It may be a false rumor. But the childishness of the reasons is just like all German propaganda (*Mainichi*, "Editorial," March 21).

This, in general, is the enemy state of affairs as conceived by the Japanese bureaucracy. It is a fact to say that the enemy is overwhelmed with war weariness. "Liberal countries," "individualistic countries" are incapable of war. The way of thinking before the beginning of the war is still in existence.

March 22 (Thursday)

At Maruzen I bought the three-volume *Record of the Perry Expedition* for 500 yen. Previously it was only 150 yen. But after all, because it is something I must possess for future use, I bought it once and for all.

March 23 (Friday)

Since yesterday a violent wind has been blowing. If the B-29s bomb in this kind of wind, I am apprehensive that it will be a serious matter.

Communications from Iwōjima were cut off at midnight on the 17th. Enemy casualties were thirty-three thousand (announcement on our side), and Premier Koiso said, "Our people's confidence in inevitable victory is not disturbed even in the least" (*Yomiuri*, March 22).

Today I visited Ayusawa in Tsurugawa village. The bedlam on the train was beyond description. I was carrying one suitcase, and because of this I suffered the hardships of life and death. My body was in a stooped position for an hour. With absolutely no order, it was the free competition of being jammed together as we were. The car bodies are more and more worn, and their number is diminishing. There is absolutely no hope of improvement.

A law has been promulgated on the compulsory dismantling of houses. Maruzen in Nihonbashi will be forced to move in four or five days. The wooden structures of *Tōyō keizai* will be dismantled. Moreover, Yamanaka's place has received an evacuation order (*Asahi* March 22).

Thus preparations for the defense of the homeland are gradually progressing.

The current problem is, to what extent is the Japanese Army capable of effectively resisting the invasion military operations of the enemy? In other words, will Musashino Plain become a battlefield or not? The reason someone like Ayusawa will evacuate is that he thinks there is this possibility. At the same time there is strong doubt whether indeed a counterattack is possible after the skies and seas have been seized. In modern war something like guerrilla war is impossible to carry out.

The Soviet Foreign Ministry proposed to Turkey that it should abrogate the Soviet–Turkish Neutrality Pact (*Nihon sangyō keizai*, March 23).

This attitude toward Turkey hints at the Japanese–Soviet Neutrality Pact.

in Arlington, Virginia, that contains a copy of every registered U.S. trademark. The Search Room is open to the public every weekday. For information, call (703) 308-9800. Additionally, more than eighty libraries throughout the United States (mostly in major cities) are designated as **Patent and Trademark Depository Libraries.** These libraries receive a wealth of information from the PTO, and trademark searching can be done at these libraries. See the PTO web site at http://www.uspto.gov for a list of the Patent and Trademark Depository Libraries.

PTO Web Site.   Perhaps the easiest and least expensive way to conduct a very preliminary search is to review the records of the PTO (http://www.uspto.gov). The PTO offers free public searching of its trademark database through its service called **Trademark Electronic Search System (TESS),** which allows searching of more than 3 million pending, registered, abandoned, canceled, or expired trademark records. TESS offers four search strategies:

1. **New User Form Search (Basic).** This basic search strategy is useful for finding marks made up solely of words or by searching by a trademark owner's name. Simply type in the name of the mark in which you are interested (for example, BUDDY BEAR), and you can then review records containing those terms. Thus, results would include both BUDDY BEAR and BEARS N' BUDDIES. A search for BEAR alone would disclose more than 4,000 entries that include the term *bear*.

2. **Structured Form Search (Boolean).** The Structured Form search allows a searcher to narrow the search by locating marks relating to certain goods and services (for example, BUDDY BEAR used for toys) or to locate assignments or

renewals of marks. The use of Boolean connectors also helps to narrow results. Thus, a search for "BUDDY and BEAR" would retrieve documents with both BUDDY and BEAR.

3. **Free Form Search (Advanced Search).** The Free Form search strategy is for more complicated searches and is generally most successful when Boolean connectors are used.

4. **Browse Dictionary (Advanced Search).** Browse Dictionary strategy allows one to review about ten items in the PTO's database around the search term. Thus, a search for "BUDDY BEAR" would disclose BUDDY BANK and BUDDYBEEPER.

The PTO database does not allow phonetic searching. Thus, a search for BEAR would not disclose any marks with the term *Bare*. Additionally, searching for designs is fairly difficult. However, the site offers help and numerous strategies and tips for searching. As an alternative to TESS, the PTO offers another searching option: the **Trademark Application and Registration Retrieval System (TARR),** which allows one to search for pending and registered marks by application or registration number. Thus, TARR cannot be used unless one already knows an application serial number or a trademark registration number.

The PTO site itself acknowledges its limitations and counsels users as follow: "After searching the USPTO database, even if you think the results are "O.K.," do **not** assume that your mark can be registered at the USPTO. After you file an application, the USPTO must do its own search and other review, and might refuse to register your mark." Nevertheless, despite their limitations, the PTO search systems TESS and TARR are excellent sources for obtaining initial information, and with practice, one can become fairly proficient in conducting a knockout search or obtaining basic information about the marks owned by any one party. Although a search of

There was a response to a question of Diet member Tanaka Mitsugu in the House of Representatives budget meeting on the 22nd. It was strange for the premier to say "As prime minister, it is not for me to answer." Who is going to answer this question? This is not even a High Command matter (*Asahi*, March 23).

One understands Premier Koiso behaves circumspectly toward the High Command. It's possible he is shifting responsibility for his mistakes to someone else.

March 24 (Saturday)

There was a telephone call from Kodaki. Because he had bought tickets, he said he was going to Matsumoto on the evening train.

Because train tickets can be bought only by the military and for official business, buying them is as difficult as a poor man buying a diamond. When I asked about it later he answered, "As an official business trip." (Bombing victims are an exception.)

When we went to Shinjuku Station two and a half hours before the train departure, the platform was packed with people and it was impossible to move. Everyone was entering the train through the windows. Kodaki and I fortunately boarded the train, but Seki was unable to board in the usual manner and entered through a window. The small washroom was filled with six people, and baggage and legs were floating in the air. From eight in the evening until six in the morning we stood all the way, and of course it was impossible to sleep even a wink. People were packed in the bathroom. I complained, but no one listened. Because of that, women needing to go to the bathroom complained of abdominal pains. Children were reduced to bowel movements on the mats. Quarrels and disputes occurred. Such miserable means of transportation was a first for me.

According to a lady who was standing in the same way, she had proof of being a bombing victim and waited in line for twenty-one hours to buy a ticket. After that she boarded the train, and because she continued to stand for eight or nine hours, in the end she had stood thirty or more hours. Again she will wait for the three o'clock bus from Tadeshina, and it was not clear if she would be able to board this. This means that to return to Shinshū it takes more than two days and nights of not lying down or sleeping. It appears that everyone thinks of this as natural.

March 25 (Sunday)

We were about twenty minutes late in arriving past 6:30 and reached Matsumoto. We went to Nishi-ishikawa at Asama. There was a reservation by Dobashi. First of all, the maid, emphasizing the favor done, said, "This sort of thing is unusual; it was because fortunately the room was available." Actually this morning we tried to notify Dobashi of the three ways we might come. Kodaki would telegraph by urgent telegram from the telegraph office of the Foreign Ministry. Seki went round to all the telegraph offices and was accepted at Tsukiji or somewhere. Ordinarily they would not have accepted personal messages. I understand it was telegraphed about 2:30 in the afternoon but arrived at 2:00 in the morning. An urgent telegram is slower than a train journey. At my home they tried calling every five or six minutes, but there was no long-distance line available. In the end, this third possibility did not work.

At noon I took Kodaki's brothers to Dobashi's. The fact that the bridegroom goes to the house of the prospective bride is unusual for Japanese custom. However, in the inns they do not provide lunch, and in the restaurants there are no meals. So unavoidably we decided to do this.

The arranged marriage meeting was a success. There was no opposition on either side, and there was an evening dinner party. About 9:30 in the evening we decided to leave, and when there was discussion of when to present the betrothal present, it was said that today was a lucky day. Therefore the betrothal gift was presented tentatively and the proceedings were complete. The fact that the marriage ceremony was completed from 1:00 in the afternoon until 10:00 in Japan is probably an extraordinary case. It has been decided that Seki will go to Tōkyō and come to Matsumoto.

March 26 (Monday)

Nowhere was there a place to eat lunch. Again I went to Dobashi's house. If one can speak of lunch, Kodaki gave three go of rice to the Nishi-ishikawa Inn and we received only two rice balls. I hear that no matter which inn it is, they serve only about half the amount of the rice they receive. To stay at the Nishi-ishikawa Inn, Dobashi helpfully provided me with rice. No matter what kind of work it is, rice is expected. Rice, rice, rice!

In Matsumoto, evacuation is also going on. The uproar in the trains is almost all from people coming from Tōkyō. They all frantically buy food in this region, and inflation must follow. The compulsory quartering with regional families is something that will destroy familialism at the root. However, this already is beginning.

I went to Aoki Hanami's parents' house. The talk in the evening:

1. Many soldiers are quartered in the elementary school. Half is for children and half is military barracks. I understand they are "suicide corps," and when the enemy comes to invade they will immediately charge. They march around training in the neighborhood.

2. Because the requisitioning of rice is fierce, the farmers have nothing left over for their own use. Therefore, if they labor elsewhere they earn a

great deal of money. Because of this, there being no tenant even in his parents' farm, almost one thousand tsubo of rice fields have been returned. However, if the family cultivates these fields, because they must deliver quotas to the government, they decided to leave them uncultivated. Thus, this farmland is steadily diminishing, and food becomes harder to obtain.

March 27 (Tuesday)

I left for Tōkyō on a train that departed Matsumoto at 10:19 in the morning. The confusion was as usual. There was no way in or out except through the windows, and the railway employees were encouraging this. In a talk during the train ride it was said there were those transporting chests on their shoulders. Everybody was carrying excess baggage in both hands because it was not possible to send it separately as freight. This is the reason for the confusion. With Kodaki and the oldest son of a friend named Yasudai helping, I returned.

When I returned, Nakano was arranging my books. My preparations for evacuation are progressing.

March 28 (Wednesday)

On the 25th the enemy announced the invasion of Okinawa and the Kerama Islands.

Kanō of the police came to visit. He told me that his own eldest son volunteered to be a pilot and entered the barracks, but he was beaten with green bamboo. There is a rumor that there is a proposal from the Soviet Union to Japan for a cessation of hostilities, and if Japan does not respond, the Soviet will begin hostilities. It is probably demagoguery. Following him, Okamura Kesayoshi came. I hear that the parents of Kataoka, accompanying the widow of Teppei, are transferring to the countryside, and they transported all of their baggage by freight train. We will not see them again.

March 29 (Thursday)

There was a meeting of the International Relations Research Society. I expressed my intention to resign, but this was rejected; however, there were only the two directors, Ishibashi and Mitsui, in attendance. "In order to answer the passion for the protection of the empire of newly picked, lively young ex-soldiers," it is possible to call together according to need seventeen and eighteen year olds. Akira is exactly draft age.

The shoes of Mitsui Takai are worn. Even a member of the big-name Mitsui family of the zaibatsu does not freely obtain the necessities of life.

Germany is standing at a critical juncture. I understand the English news-papers are writing about a German Resistance Corps, and only the *Times* is saying that the German main line is broken. It appears it has a life of ten days. At that time, what will be the reaction of Japan?

How far will Japan resist? This is the topic of the moment (*Asahi*, February 29).

Everywhere there is training with bamboo spears. Probably the Japanese spirit encourages the idea that when one sees B-29s, they can be dealt with bamboo spears or judo. I hear that the people of Okinawa are resolute. "If there are no rifles, bamboo spears will do fine; if the bamboo spears are broken, karate will do fine" (*Asahi*, 29th).

Will the enemy invade the homeland (before the war ends)? Or will it happen before that?

The enemy will invade Okinawa and will cut the connecting lines between the southern area and the homeland. As a result of this, it will probably come about that Japan must rely upon the resources of the northern areas. It will rely on a line that links North China, Manchuria, Korea, and the homeland. With respect to this, isn't it likely that the enemy will invade in the area of Tsushima or the southwest islands to be able to intercept this?

March 30 (Friday)

According to Tomita of Dōmei News Service, opinions within the army and navy are divided regarding the peace talks problem. From navy and army air force is the advocacy of peace negotiations by way of England or the Soviet Union, but in other parts of the army they reject this as absolutely impossible and insist upon a stubborn-resistance position. In a country in which the cen-tral power is corrupt as in Japan, military infighting may bring about the solution of the war. I hear that because of the conflict of opinion noted above, there was momentary fear there will be something like the 2-26 Incident. As a result, it appears that even the Koiso Cabinet carries on resolutely. The authorities are always resolute because if they stress the stubborn-resistance position there will be no assassinations. If one can speak in terms of numbers, those who do not understand this are few. Organizations to strongly control them are necessary, and therefore this is the reason that on the enemy side they are beginning to speak of the repression of "secret societies." The fact that Japan's problems must be solved in the hands of a foreign enemy is some-how regrettable.

Army General Minami Jirō has been chosen as the head of a new political party. This stupid man becomes the party head of a new political movement! Seeking something, the political parties dissolve, and yet the existing condi-tions make them rely on an army general.

The *Yomiuri* is inserting the talks of Navy Admiral Sosa. Although there is no one whose observations are as wrong as his, it is the same old thing.

Hysterical clamoring as usual in the newspapers, but recently it has come to increase. Two points are worth noting. One is the inevitable rapture over the imperial army and navy. Two is the point that states that the American aim is profit (*Mainichi*, March 30).

If money making continuously brings about hardships, one must say that money making is also a basic force influencing the life and death of all human beings.

The minds of the executive journalists of the great newspapers in Tokyo are generally of this low level. It is a problem of education.

I heard that Shimanaka's family has received a compulsory evacuation order. The houses with streetcars on both sides are rapidly being dismantled, and roof tiles and other things are demolished. Anyway, because they have only five days to finish, they do not have time to do a thorough job. They smash everything.

I am thinking about the "power" called war. In one evening tens of thousands of homes are burned out, and afterward what remains is broken up by a single official order. Without even waiting for the postwar plans of America, Japan is already progressively returning to its financial condition preceding the Sino-Japanese War.

The military pamphlet, "War Is the Mother of Culture," is being propagandized. Because we criticize this, we are treated as "traitors." Now try repeating these words! Is war indeed the mother of culture (*Mainichi*, March 30)?

March 31 (Saturday)

In the *Oriental Economist* I wrote about the pitiful conditions resulting from the air raids. I wrote an article admonishing the Americans (*Asahi*, March 31).

The ignorance of the people is beyond imagination.

The Asakusa Kannon was not burned up in the great earthquake, and because this was considered a miraculous virtue, many who think it will not be burned this time run to the Kannon. It is said that this is the primary reason that those who die in the Asakusa ward are numerous. One woman who was at the Keizai Club was in the neighborhood close to Ueno, and nearby there was some temple or other. Even though she was advised by others to leave, because she lived beside the temple she thought she would be all right. She did not even think of sending off her belongings, and thereupon everything was burned up. Foolish beliefs such as those in the letters to the editor column are frequently heard. The common sense of the people is of this level.

Of late, telephone calls do not get through no matter where one is calling. Operator-assisted calls are turned down. The transportation system is in a half-paralyzed state. Because of a telephone call that finally got through, I talked with Shimanaka. I learned that his new residence was completely burned out. There are probably not many who have experienced the impact of the war to the degree he has. I hear that he is evacuating soon.

April 1 (Sunday)

Matsumoto Jōji came to the house to visit. He has several grandchildren living in his house but must evacuate them somewhere. However, his villa at Kamakura and also his villa at Gotemba have been confiscated. They cannot be used. There was a villa to be rented at Karuizawa, but he was warned by others that there were problems about food. This also was no good. He is distressed that he may have to evacuate to Niigata or someplace like that.

After this we discussed the conditions of the times.

1. Matsumoto said it would be all right if we return to the conditions prior to the Japanese–Chinese Incident as a conclusion to the war. I said it is impossible to stay at this level.

2. He said something probably would be done about the constitution, and it probably would be all right if the Japanese added the provision of approval by the Diet of declarations of war and peace talks. This also is optimistic.

3. He said that with a great blow delivered against the enemy in the Okinawa area, it would be all right to aim at the moment for peace. I said I hope for this, but there is a question whether we are able to deliver so great a blow that the enemy would sue for peace. However, I agreed with him that there is the need to make the Japanese people acknowledge that we are already checkmated.

4. Matsumoto said that the war would probably continue till the fall of this year and no longer. I said that it would probably be a little bit longer. We were united on the point that the likelihood of ferocious fighting against enemy invasion troops in the Kantō area probably would not occur. At that time our side would probably not have adequate war strength.

5. Matsumoto said that because the Japanese people are a gentle people, there would not be a great violence. I said that the Japanese people are not gentle. I said that in China and other places, the behavior of the Japanese shows this.

6. Professor Matsumoto says that the four people—Tōjō, Konoe, Matsuoka, and Kido—responsible for the war will not escape.

Dr. Matsumoto said, "There is no use worrying. Of late, I am reading novels. I am reading Dickens, and it is completely fascinating." If one relies upon the same gentleman, as minister of industry-commerce in the Saitō Cabinet, there were negotiations to have him remain in the next cabinet, but he refused. Moreover, I understand that at the time of the abortive Ugaki Cabinet there were negotiations to make him home minister; if it had been justice minister, he would have accepted. It is a waste for this sort of talent to be reduced to reading novels. But this is the current situation.

Tōjō Shō came to visit. His whose shop in Ginza was burned out at the very beginning. He said that many of the large shoe factories have been burned, and probably they can no longer meet the demands of the military. He said rubber is completely nonexistent, even though there are hides. I understand that he is evacuating to Azumi.

Dr. Matsumoto has villas in Gotemba and Kamakura, but the villa in Kamakura has been seized by the military and he is unable to use it, as previously noted. The houses on both sides of the streetcar tracks are ruthlessly knocked down, and as soon as the order is given by the bureaucracy, the property handed down by ancestors is confiscated. Times such as these probably can never be possible again.

April 2 (Monday)

Yesterday evening fifty B-29s came to attack. They raided the Tokorozawa area.

I understand that according to Ayusawa an American pilot fell in his area and was killed with bamboo spears or something. An acquaintance of his had a rusted spear, but many wished to buy it and came to negotiate. When he asked what they were doing, there was unanimity that "it would probably be better than a bamboo spear."

The Japanese side is much concerned about the enemy propaganda.

The fact that the colonies of Korea and Taiwan can send representatives (Peers and Representatives) has been announced by imperial edict (*Chūbu Nihon*, March 27).

Higashi Ryōzō came to visit. He said the Japanese are completely disgusting.

He has had dealings with Americans for a long time, but he is shocked and angry at the corruption of the Japanese, particularly the military. When people who are familiar with both sides attack the Japanese, this shows that the Japanese are bad (*Chūbu Nihon*, March 27).

The American enemy invaded the islands of Kamiyama and Maejima (Kerama Island chain) on the morningof the 31st and the main island of Okinawa on April 1.

I hear that among the military there are two positions: making Okinawa the decisive battle, and reserving for future use their main strength in order to defend the homeland. The Okinawa military operations will be carried out only by the army, and the Navy is not participating. Until the end, the army and navy stand opposed.

It is said that because of the air raids in Tōkyō, the damage will probably cost ten billion yen.

Both account books and money of the banks in this area have been destroyed, and there is no way to restore these. The deposits have not been forgotten, and there is no fear about these being returned. The nation cannot but assume responsibility for the balance of the accounts of the banks. Thus the inflation in currency is inevitable. Already at the end of the previous month the level of issuance of convertible notes is nineteen billion, and it is going to increase at an accelerating rate. As for commodity prices, it is said that one kamme of sugar is six hundred yen, and one bale of rice is similarly six hundred yen. Inflation of the same level as China is inevitable.

Near the station there was a girl who said, "I'm selling a piano for 150 yen." When I tried asking why it was so "cheap," she said if it were not picked up before three in the afternoon of this day, it would do her no good. This speaks of the present absence of transport facilities.

April 3 (Tuesday)

Today is the commemoration of the Emperor Jimmu, but there is no elation about this at all. Morning, in the fields.

Because of a previous promise I visited Hasegawa Nyozekan. He wants to evacuate his library. He has about five thousand excellent volumes. Were these to be burned, it would be a great tragedy, and it was of this we talked about together. Baba Tsunego also came. How enfeebled he appeared since I had seen him last. He says he has a cold, but he gives the impression of being quite fragile. Such people as Hasegawa and Baba are pure, incorruptible gentlemen who are rarely seen in the world. The crime of war is difficult for such pure gentlemen, while less admirable men think of making money and behave as if the world were their very own. Baba said he will send his wife to Shinshū and stay in Tōkyō.

In Hasegawa's home there are scrolls and paintings done by his younger brother, Ono Shizukata, who is an unknown painter. There are also paintings in great number by his master, Terukata, and other people such as Kiyokata and Shoen. If he sold these, they would probably be worth several thousand yen. Nyozekan says that because they are works of his younger brother, he has already spoken to Yashushi Sekiguchi about donating them somewhere. Is it likely that there are many such honest men in the world? He said that if he didn't sell his house, there would be no money to transport his library. While smiling, he said that because the Nyozekan family did not buy in the black market, the neighborhood association assumed it was in difficulties and until now brought them various things, but these people have gone to the countryside, and as they had few acquaintances, they were in trouble.

Baba says that the war will probably end in August. Professor Matsumoto also shares his opinion. Hasegawa says it will probably not be so simple. I said that the speculations on victory and defeat were clear, and the war would probably continue for about a year. Because of his good nature, Baba is always optimistic about problems.

April 4 (Wednesday)

The predawn enemy air raid was the greatest sight I have ever seen. Until now the enemy air raids have been northeast of the city and elsewhere, and I have not been able to actually see them. Today they were something that I could look down upon. The planes bombed the factories in the Tōkyō-Yokohama area, and I was able to see with my own eyes the destructive power of war.

The entire family was awakened from its dreams. There were thuds and earth tremors. It is unclear even now whether these were earthquakes or bombs. We put on our clothes and went outside. In the moonlight there were bombs falling everywhere and there were fires. They were spread over the numerous factories in the Tsurumi and Kawasaki areas.

Suddenly two illumination bombs fell, and everything became bright as midday. The bombs made a continuous ferocious noise and exploded. The sky suddenly became red as a sunset.

Today not a single enemy plane was visible, and accordingly no action on our side was evident. What could be seen was only a scene of leaping flames like signal fires. Sometimes there were flashes of illumination like lightning. Was it the enemy bombs or our anti-aircraft guns?

The attack extended from about 1:30 in the morning until before 5:00 in the morning and then stopped. After this there were frequent explosions due to delayed-action bombs.

In the morning both the Ikegami line and Mekama line were impassable, and the telephones were not getting through. According to Seimei, the Denenchōfu school was operating and the telephone company adjacent to it was probably damaged.

There were radio reports that said that early this morning the damage to the military factories because of the enemy B-29 raid was not too bad. The several tens of thousands of people who saw the actual events of the air raid probably do not believe the announcements of the authorities. Those who are in the position of being the most responsible are the ones who tell outrageous lies concerning the war.

In a commentary on the internal conditions in the enemy country in the *Yomiuri*, it is claimed the feeling of war weariness is swelling up in America. This has been the view of America from the beginning.

According to a story of Kasahara Seimei, a military doctor who is a relative is receiving training, but his instructor reports that things are bad at sea. It would be best to carry out a pincer attack, luring the enemy to either the Shizuoka area or the Kyūshū area. The military does not understand the sacrificial cost, and it appears they actually think this way.

According to an editor in charge at the Military Information Bureau, conditions in the homeland were still somewhat bad for dealing with an American invasion now. Therefore he was expected to write that the American Army was on its way to the Chinese continent. If we let Americans do what they wish to Japanese, then people throughout the world will believe they can do likewise anywhere in the world.

Because the military man's war of thinking is relative and mechanical, he cannot reason things synthetically. That it is possible to engage the enemy on the Japanese homeland is something they still believe, but at that time there will be no Japanese planes or warships, and they do not understand the fact that the military equipment of the enemy will destroy all planes and is absolutely all-powerful. The mentality of the Japanese is generally of this cast, and to correct it there must be a complete change in education.

According to a military relative of Seimei, a wartime friend of his flew back from Okinawa. I understand that since it was believed just a week ago that the Americans would bring new military equipment for the Okinawa invasion, he came to the Home Ministry to do research on this. After three or four days in Tōkyō, given the invasion of Okinawa, he could not return. The man who told this story said that because even when the enemy came to the little island called Okinawa it attacked with new weapons, there was nothing to be done.

April 5 (Thursday)

The entire Koiso Cabinet has resigned, and Suzuki Kantarō has received the imperial mandate. At noon I went to the Economic Club, where it was rumored that Suzuki Kantarō would be pushed as premier in the new cabinet. Ōta says that Suzuki is the leader of the hundred million honorable deaths thesis. From things that I had heard previously, this was not true. Moreover, speaking from the perspective of the senior statesmen, I thought there was no reason to put forth such a person. Suzuki Bunshirō previously met and talked with Suzuki, and I recall he was extremely admiring of him. He said Suzuki was not a hide-bound right-winger but a gentleman of true liberal loyalties. There is nothing else but to see, based upon the facts, what he really will be as prime minister. It is because the title "leader" makes people assume a disguise.

I remember a talk by Machimura, governor of Niigata, in Toyama Prefecture. I am certain he was secretary to Suzuki after the 2–26 Incident when Suzuki, hearing that naval officers had been implicated, said that if the navy was addicted to political machinations of this sort, the nation would be ruined, and thereupon he forced the dismissal of the crowd called Suetsugu and Masaki. Moreover, when he received a report that a submarine sank because it was top-heavy, he said there should be an investigation of "under what conditions the sailors died at their posts." It is said he reacted, saying, "Knowing that, I am relieved. If I know this was the case, no matter how many submarines or other things sink, there will be no regrets." Hearing this kind of story, the fact that he is a sincere gentleman is just as these details reveal. The problem is, to what extent does he have political perception?

In the regions, everything is reduced to one newspaper. In Tōkyō also, one paper is distributed (*Asahi*, April, 5).

Articles are inadequate on the war situation and other things, substituting instead excessive amounts of letters and gossip. Because of this, many innocent people will suffer. The habit of exchanging objective fact for hopes until now is very widespread (*Yomiuri*, April 4).

Of the popular scholars who led us into the Greater East Asian War, the

these databases can provide a quick answer to very basic questions about availability of marks (much the same way a knockout search does), it is no substitute for a thorough search of other possible uses of marks, such as those used as Internet domain names, unregistered marks, and those registered with individual states. Moreover, trademark applications are not immediately entered into the database, resulting in incomplete data.

Step Two: The Comprehensive Search

The most complete analysis of potentially conflicting marks is provided by professional trademark search firms. These companies review the records of the PTO for existing registrations and pending applications, review state trademark office records for state trademark registrations, and they perform a "common law" search of various journals, directories, press releases, domain names, and Internet references to locate unregistered names and marks. Such a search is called a **comprehensive,** or *full,* **search.** Because there are literally thousands of journals, directories, telephone books, and other publications in which names and marks may appear, these professional search firms can save considerable time and money and, more importantly, provide a more thorough search than that which an individual can conduct on his or her own. Some of these companies advertise that their databases include more than one million marks that can be checked against the client's mark for potential conflicts. These companies will check for identical and phonetically equivalent marks for similar goods and services and will also check for foreign equivalents. Thus, a search for KARCOAT will disclose marks such as CARCOAT and CARKOAT. Marks with design elements also must be searched; these searches are usually a bit more expensive than searches for marks comprising solely words

due to the time-consuming task of comparing other design marks to the proposed mark. Professional search firms can also customize searches and conduct investigations as to how a potentially conflicting mark is used in the marketplace.

Costs for full availability searches can run from $400 for results available in four business days to approximately $1,100 for same-day searches. These costs do not reflect an attorney's time in evaluating the results and providing a report to a client, but rather reflect only the costs of obtaining a report that discloses potentially conflicting marks. Some companies will send the report by express mail or other overnight service or may send it via facsimile (although due to the voluminous nature of many reports, this is not a common practice). Another more recent alternative is that the report may be sent to an office via electronic transmission or e-mail. The search company will post the report to a bulletin board server, and the law firm then retrieves the search. The report is typically divided into three sections: results gained from reviewing PTO registrations and applications; results gained from reviewing state trademark records; and the common law results (references to marks in magazines, telephone directories, Internet domain names, and so forth).

Most of the professional searching firms will tailor the search to specific requirements, so that they will conduct only common law searches, or only an Internet domain name search, an international search, and so forth. Intellectual property practitioners who engage the professional searchers on a routine basis often obtain volume discounts.

International Searching

A client interested in protecting his or her mark in foreign countries should conduct a search of the records of each country in which

346 • APRIL 1945

foremost are two. They are Tokutomi Sohō and Akiyama Kenzō. These two are unofficial responsible people. The *Yomiuri* still publishes these people (*Chūbu Nihon*, March 23).

In a newspaper editorial, Itō appears to have attacked the stupidity of the strategy of awaiting the enemy invasion.

April 6 (Friday)

All of the newspapers are asking for the "concurrence of national affairs and High Command" in the succeeding cabinet.

The *Yomiuri* and the *Mainichi* editorials are stupid. Yet both are the same in talking about the consolidation of politics and High Command.

All the editorial articles (a recent characteristic of the newspapers) see the necessity for the consolidation of politics and High Command (*Yomirui*, April 6).

April 7 (Saturday)

The fifth, just as the Koiso Cabinet resigned, was the day the imperial mandate was handed down to General Suzuki. It appears that Admiral Suzuki is a gentleman of true loyalty. But as there are no ministerial candidates at hand, they will be selected from a narrow sphere, and there is no reason to expect that decent people will be assembled.

In the succession of forty-four cabinets, eighteen were military cabinets (comprised of the same people).

In the fourteen cabinets in the Meiji period, there were four with military premiers (comprising the same person).

In the ten cabinets of the Taishō period, five had military premiers.

In the sixteen cabinets in the Shōwa period, nine cabinets had military premiers. (However, Tanaka was president of the Seiyūkai.)

One should be aware that the system in which it is not possible to become premier if one is not a general has continued to the end of the Greater East Asian War, and thereby we should understand how unnatural it is.

Regarding the discontinuation of the Japanese–Soviet Neutrality Pact, all the newspapers were extremely reserved, and not a single nasty word has slipped out. This was planned by the Foreign Ministry, but if it had been its natural reaction, the old arguments would have surged forth, demanding, "We should attack Russia!"

According to Tamura Kōsaku, if Japan approaches the Soviet Union, America will become nervous and offer its hand to Japan. Or if Japan creates a peace structure with America, the Soviet Union will pay court to Japan. It is said that this way of thinking among the Japanese intellectual class is extremely widespread. It is just so. In looking at international relations, Japan is extremely balance-of-power oriented, and this attitude is especially wide-spread among the right wing and military. It is not realistic; rather, it is self-destructive.

April 8 (Sunday)

The personnel of the cabinet was settled last night and publicly announced. In the final analysis, it is the rule of etiquette to carry out *giri* in all quarters. The brain trust of the cabinet formation was Admiral Okada Keisuke, and because of his connections his son-in-law, Sakomizu Hisatsune (44) (chief of the Finance Ministry Savings Bank office), was his aide. In the end he became chief secretary. Ōta Kōzō has been brought in as education minister because of his special relation to Hiranuma. From the Greater Japan Political Association, the only political organization, Okada and Sakurai have been taken in. The rest are friends of Sakomizu and the younger generation of his own naval connections.

Because Foreign Minister elect Tōgō Shigenori was in Karuizawa, he was not announced along with the rest. The choice of this man is not bad. Someone said that the people of Kagoshima are mediocre when young, but some become impressive when they are mature. Tōgō is one of these people. Kobiyama Naoto is on the way to Tōkyō from Manchuria.

The structure is varied, and yet, naturally it is right wing and so-called reformist. In the end it has no focus. These people will represent Japan.

The true loyalty of Suzuki cannot be doubted. Yet politics cannot be carried out with just sincerity and loyalty.

It is a situation like a river ready to fall, which makes whirlpools. This sort of cabinet cannot achieve anything. Pushed by circumstances, it only waits for suitable times.

In the army the Supreme Command is complete, but to this two people have been appointed. Field Marshal Sugiyama and Field Marshal Hata. Two supreme commanders is strange. What will be done if there is a difference of opinion? However, there might be one supreme commander each for the East and West.

Fukai of the Foreign Ministry came to call. I heard that until about yesterday, in the ministry they were saying Hirota would become foreign minister.

April 9 (Monday)

Premier Suzuki told a newspaper reporter, "From the beginning I disliked politics." The fact of having to pull out a navy admiral who dislikes politics is the present situation in Japan (*Nihon sangyō keizai*, April 9).

A certain person called this the cabinet of substitutes. Finance Minister Hirose is the son-in-law of Katsuta Kanae. In place of the senior statesmen, the second-generation successors are emerging. If one relies upon a report of the *Mainichi*, Koiso will return to active service and probably become army minister, but the Army is opposed to this. A spokesman of the Foreign Ministry in Berlin is saying, "We don't know if the Japanese political changes are related to reports of the abrogation of the Japanese–Soviet Neutrality Pact." On the American side they broadcast that of course there was a connection (*Asahi*, "Shinpufu," April 9).

Rōyama said that just like ourselves, the ones who grieve for the nation are only the senior statesmen. He said that consequently they should be institutionalized and should oppose the military. I said that because the location of responsibility in parliamentary politics is unclear, the election of the premier by the parliament is impossible.

At Okinawa the combined fleet has been sent out. I understand that this was the last time it would do battle. If one relies upon the broadcasts of the enemy, they claim a 45,000-ton-class Japanese ship was sunk, and Japan has admitted this.

Inui Yasumatsu came to visit. I agreed to broadcast my critique of the Dumbarton Oaks Plan. He said that the Foreign Ministry, the Information Board, the Broadcasting Bureau, and Dōmei News Service would broadcast a critique of the San Francisco Conference. They will also broadcast something of Ishibashi. He said that they will also broadcast Kagawa Toyohiko.

April 10 (Tuesday)

I have not felt the decline of the intelligentsia under wartime conditions as I do today. Accepting the conditions of the times, we decided to send off thirty pieces of baggage, and today two packers came. Yesterday, relying upon a carpenter, lids for boxes and other things were prepared, and there was only the packing to be done. At noon, because there was a meeting of the Japanese Diplomatic History Research Society, we listened to a talk about the Russo-Japanese War period by Professor Shinobu Seizaburō. When I returned home at five in the afternoon, just then the packers finished. When I asked what the charge was, they said 17 yen 50 sen. This in spite of my having provided all the materials. This meant their wages for one day were 110 yen. This was for a period from ten in the morning till four in the afternoon, and in that time we served sake and lunch. Their wages for about an hour were 20 yen. The honorarium for Professor Shinobu was 50 yen. He is a member of the Japanese Academy, and the honorarium for one day of the most prominent scholar of Japan was 50 yen. And even this is not to be expected every day; there are only occasional requests. Our highest intellectual labor fee for a single day is 50 yen. This is the difference between the present intellectual class and the laborer. Our incomes decline more and more, and contrarily the income of the laborers becomes as high as the ceiling.

When Uehara Etsujirō said, "What a submissive people the Japanese are!"

both Professor Shinobu and Nagai Shōzō agreed with this. This judgment meant that with forced evacuation, houses smashed unreasonably, they remain silent all the while. If one looks out of either side of the streetcar, residences are smashed to pieces. It is the same after all the air raids. Walls are broken and ropes are attached to the houses, and they are pulled down. Things such as tiles are completely smashed to pieces, and at a time when resources are inadequate, tatami and chinaware are scattered everywhere. It is impossible to look at this. According to an account of Uehara, at a talk at the Kojunsha Club a chief engineer said the earth belongs to the emperor, and in the interest of national policy the destruction of houses is unhesitating. Uehara could not bear to listen and left before the affair was over.

Because a desktop plan had been drawn up, the authorities dismantled places where there were fireproof buildings and preserved places where houses were made of wood. One example according to Hirakawa, who came to visit the house of Bureau Chief Mutō, was a completely splendid building constructed before the war. This has been utterly destroyed. The government police chief came, and because he did not confer with anyone about this, this is what happened. I understand that if he had talked with us, there was a way to save the house.

I understand that the military is building enormous roads for the purpose of constructing aircraft runways in Tōkyō. This thing called war does not recognize individual rights or anything else.

In today's rains the shattered ruins were saturated, and things such as tatami are strewn in all directions. In this morning's newspapers it was announced that it had been decided to sell to individuals the things that had been damaged, but until now even this has not been done. Moreover, because there are no means of transportation, on the one hand, although there are no materials for building air-raid shelters, on the other hand, such useless things are being accumulated. Why can't the neighborhood associations make use of them? Bureaucratic and military politics thus will cause the utter ruin of Japan! Alas!

April 11 (Wednesday)

Ukaji came to call and we prepared the draft of my book. The said gentleman is prudent and an extremely fine assistant. He is taking care of the office of the Japanese Diplomatic History Research Society.

Foreign Minister Tōgō Shigenoru talked to a newspaper reporter about his "hopes." The contents are extremely formalistic (*Yomiuri*, April 11).

1. He does not touch upon the Greater East Asian Declaration of Foreign Minister Shigemitsu.
2. An *Asahi* editorial said hopes were being placed on Foreign Minister Tōgō, and there must begin a critique of Shigemitsu's diplomacy.

Until the last I did not discover the humanity in Shigemitsu, and also not sensing what was called his political genius, I thought of him as simply a dutiful bureaucrat. While he knew that I was working as Japonicus, the fact that he treated only Takayanagi as his sole ally perhaps made me biased against him. Even if it is true, I don't care. The fact that he provoked such feelings in Rōyama and myself shows his bureaucratic manner. But leaving out feelings and making a fair judgment, I was not able to discover the reasons for the superiority of his diplomacy.

Of late I am buying trashy books. It is for the purpose of trying to investigate what sort of inferior publications are spreading under the Greater East Asian War. However, it is the most disagreeable work. I dislike using my shelves for these works. I have the feeling that I am having a beggar sleep in my guest room.

Air-raid warnings were issued. Once they are sounded, the electric trains stop and nothing can be done. With this alone, the decline of Japanese industry is inevitable.

April 12 (Thursday)

Together with Fukai, I went to the home of Ayusawa. It was the idea of Fukai that Tsuyuko would be introduced to someone. There is a gentleman who is said to be the grandson of Asabuki Eiji. He teaches at Keimei Gakuen, and he attended a lecture of mine some time ago. It was an exceptional meal. The hospitality of people who have lived in the West creates a good feeling.

Kobiyama Naoto (president of the Manchurian Railway) has been appointed minister of transportation-communication. Army Lt. General Yasui Tōji has been appointed state minister. It appears that the reason is merely that he is an intimate fellow classmate of Army Minister Anami Korechika.

The judicious researcher of Meiji history Kikuta Sadao (45) passed away. He is the author of the work *Seikanron*. We have lost Ōkuma Makoto, and now we have lost this sober scholar. I myself am despondent. Recently I sent a deposit of three hundred yen, but it did not serve any purpose.

1. The fact that the Greater East Asian War arose from the people who carried out the 2–26 Incident is trying to be brought under control by the people who were targeted by these rebels.
2. An article like the one entitled "A Military Premier" will probably incite the violent passions of the Japanese.
3. The change in war ministers one after the other is a recent conspicuous characteristic. Previously army ministers continued from cabinet to cabinet.

Everywhere one goes, the topic of conversation turns toward the point of asking when the war will probably end. One can infer from this that everyone has had enough war.

Opinions are being expressed that perceive that the nonextension of the Japanese–Soviet Neutrality Pact foretells war. This is true of the *Japan Times*; it is also true of a *Chūbu Nihon shinbun* editorial (*Chūbu Nihon*, April 8).

April 13 (Friday)

With the sudden heat I am weary and have decided to do nothing (there are night air raids).

There is a report that President Roosevelt has died of a cerebral hemorrhage.

April 14 (Saturday)

I think it was midnight of the 13th or early morning of the 14th. Some 170 enemy planes came to attack the capital. One part of the palace grounds burned.

As usual, the location of the fires was completely unclear, but it covered a rather wide area. I hear that bread was prepared for thirty thousand; therefore the casualties probably reached about that number. The fire burned out one-sixth or one-seventh of the capital overnight. The miserable conditions of war are truly beyond words.

I went to the *Chūō kōron* company and paid five hundred yen to Matsubayashi as down payment for the furniture of the Diplomatic History Research Center.

One portion of Meiji Shrine and the palace grounds was burned. The electric trains are not getting through the Yamanote line. The Shinetsu line is running only from Ōmiya. One imagines the extent of the damage in this area.

April 15 (Sunday)

Today was the most memorable day of my life. This day I received my air-raid baptism. I did not suffer a wound myself, but I received pieces of an incendiary bomb on my body.

We had been asking everywhere for tickets to Karuizawa for this very day. Yesterday Mizuno of the Police Department was able to provide us one. Of late, train tickets are of a value comparable to diamonds. When Akira went to get that ticket at the station, he was told that apart from the air-raid victims from the day before, no tickets at all were being issued, and he was refused.

I transported baggage to Minagawa. After supper when we returned to our home, Kōtaki was there. While we were talking to him, there were air-raid warnings. He returned home hurriedly and I, as usual, went to bed. Like many people, I could not be bothered about it, but this is my bad habit. When I was drowsing because of lack of sleep from last night's air raids, there were air-raid warnings again. Hurriedly I made preparations and went outside. It was about 10:30 in the evening. There were stars, but the night was dark. This was different from the previous air raids, and the planes were overhead wave after wave. Their targets were the factories on both sides of the Tamagawa River. The anti-aircraft guns roared, and the bombs that were falling from the enemy planes sent up flames like a red lotus in the curtain of darkness. The B-29s were silver-colored and reflected in the brilliance of the searchlights— it was like a picture. One plane at a time flew past. They continued to drop incendiary bombs as if the sky were a checkerboard, and nothing was left behind. My wife was worried about the security of Eiko and Toyo, who were living in the Minagawa house, and left for there. Akira and I were going in and out of a small bomb shelter. Already, at the Ōmori and Kamata areas the sky became pure red, and the enemy attack was increasingly pressing closer to us. Akira said, "I have never been so anxious to hear the all-clear as tonight!" I went out to the road in front of the gate for shelter. There was a sound like the swish of rain. Reacting immediately, I hid myself at the protected side of the road. At the moment an incendiary fell slowly on the roof of the house, the neighboring pine grove and the bamboo fence burst into flames. "Father!" Akira's voice called. "Oh" I answered. I noticed my overcoat had caught fire. "Oh my God!" I said, and I tried to extinguish it but could not put it out. I took off the overcoat and beating it extinguished the fire. At that time the whole area was covered with fire. When I came to the entrance, Akira said, "Father, let's put it out!" "Yes, let's put it out," I answered. There was a feeling of being engaged in a "desperate fight to the death." With the overcoat I had taken off, I beat out the bamboo fence fire. The concrete walls of my library were burning. Because coal tar had been used, I thought it was burning, but afterward I understood it was not so, and it was because of the enemy oil and incendiary bomb. I threw water on this. The fence fire was extinguished, but the fire on the roof continued to burn. "This is bad," I said and abandoned the idea. The feeling that my library and personal belongings will be completely burned up went through my mind. Bringing a ladder, I looked at the roof, but the fire was out. About that time the house of another party across the fields and an apartment-style house across the street were burning. Also the pickle shop, which was beyond the woods, was burning. The unfortunate thing was that both were not on the leeward side of the wind, but actually there was a little wind. The fire was already coming to an end when the wind came up, but this was probably because of the fire.

Seeing the fire, we fought it and I was filled with hatred and indignation. I experienced an "overflowing with anger" feeling. But it seems that it was not only because of the enemy "America." I said, "American swine, damn you!" Clearly these were words I wished people to hear. Because I had the fear of being called "pro-American," I particularly made the point forcefully. If I were to say that I did not feel anger toward something, it would be a lie. Asking, "Who are those carrying on this sort of war?" I was indignant toward this kind of stupid politics and leadership.

After the fire was extinguished, I felt as if I had conquered the world. Actually, if I had not been there, no doubt the fire would have been prolonged. The grass of the woods flared up and the fences were burning. About two in the morning I went to bed.

April 16 (Monday)

There is talk of a "phantom killer," but the fiery sky of the B-29s is the "phantom killer." Wherever they pass over, about a city block of space is burned up. A straight line from south to north is burned, and it is still burning. Digging in the ruins, people search for things such as china. In the spreading fires there is time to take out household belongings, but where incendiary bombs are dropped, nothing is saved. Even looking at it from my experience of yesterday evening, there has absolutely never been such a time. At the moment I was thinking, shall I take out the household belongings or make efforts to put out the fire, when Akira said, "Let's extinguish it!" I regained my strength and turned to fire fighting.

Returning home, when I looked at the neighboring pine grove there were many incendiary casings. In a short time I had picked up seven of these. When those that had been dug up were collected by the neighbors, there were more than ten in an area of less than one hundred tsubo. And when these were all collected together on a low nearby ground, there were more than thirty. One had fallen to the east of the house. This had revealed itself by setting fire to the roof of the well. The ones that had fallen to the west were at a place separated two or three shaku from the roof, and there was a piece of cloth entangled in the pines. The house was saved by only three or four shaku.

Collecting these things together, we finished clearing up, and on the way home, where we went for breakfast, I had the urge to say, "There is a God!" Even though so many incendiaries had fallen, the fact that not even one had hit the house roof was extraordinary. I had the inclination to say, "Isn't God helping me?" When I gave it some thought, it was totally unexpected good fortune. Because Akira said, "Let's go into the bomb shelter since nothing can be done even if the house burns," I said, "That's so, isn't it?" and we went to look at it. Just at the moment we set out, a bomb fell on the house. Also, the fact that Akira from the east and I from the west, without noticing the passage of time, worked strenuously at fire fighting is probably the most important reason we were able to put out the fire. It may be that if we had been there five minutes later, there is no doubt the fire would have shifted to the bamboo fence. Even the fact that we had not set out for Karuizawa was fortunate. The faith of Christianity, which I had formerly believed in, moved my heart deeply, and bowing down, I wished to express my gratitude.

After breakfast, together with Eiko, I went to see the area from the Tama River to Shimomaruko. Countless numbers of incendiary bomb casings had fallen on the riverbank. Also, the dormitory of the Mitsubishi had burned. The newly built factories of Shimomaruko had become nothing more than burned fields. In some places we heard thumps and the explosions of time-delayed bombs. With this bombing alone, the manufacturing of Japan will fall to some small fraction. Yesterday evening, from our elevated location I saw the burning of the Kawasaki industrial area and Shimomaruko and was astonished at the totality of the destructive power of modern war. Now I see its burned remains. This all happened in a period of less than ten hours. The electric trains stop, and electricity no longer flows. The water system and gas are halted. According to Akita's account, people who fled to the riverbank of the Tama were killed by bombs, and corpses without heads and trunks were transported away.

Experiencing these kinds of air raids, the one outstanding fact is that the Japanese people, despite these city air raids, never resent these indiscriminate American attacks or are indignant. When I say, "Isn't this outrageous?" they say, "It's because of the war!" They think that because it is war even if old and young, men and women, are bombed, it can't be helped. I hear the words, "Because it is war," even when I am on the train, and I hear them also in the streets. Also, yesterday evening, two men who had been burned out came to stay for a couple of hours and said, "Nothing is to be done about a residence being burned up; it's because of the war. The destroyed factories are to be regretted." The Japanese view of the war is such that human indignation does not arise.

In the afternoon, Shiina, a director of Nomura Life Insurance, came to inquire about us. He said, "I am truly disgusted with the Japanese people!" He said there was a German Jew living in his area. This lady is the sister of the wife of Thomas Mann, and until now, because in the Senzoku area there were no military targets, it had been peaceful, and even air-raid shelters had not been built. Last night she was looking for a shelter, and so he guided her to one nearby. However, the head of the neighborhood association said, "There are foreigners here!" and drove out two people, causing them terrible distress. Shiina said, "What is this war for? Beginning a war without purpose. . . ."

April 17 (Tuesday)

There was an announcement concerning the air raid from the evening of the 15th to the 16th (*Mainichi*, April 17).

Every day endless rumors are flying about. Yesterday evening there were rumors that air-raid alerts would be issued or that carrier-based planes came to attack. In the electric trains as well, there are those who say this sort of thing. Not withstanding the fact that no alerts were announced, everybody believed these rumors. We are confronting a period of ruin, a period of disorder. From their very beginnings, the Japanese people have been attached to the habit of believing things uncritically. Once people's talk turns into vicious rumors, everything is possible. This was true of the rumors concerning the Koreans at the time of the great earthquake. Even now the possibility of such an incident occurring is extremely great.

It is clear that everyone has completely lost hope concerning the battle in Okinawa, but the newspapers speak of divine opportunities. As usual, they rely upon the announcements of the military. The Japanese people, even the foolish country folk, probably do not believe this. The matter of writing things that nobody believes has been true of Japanese newspapers for a long time.

The funeral ceremony for Roosevelt was carried out on the 15th. He died on the 12th at 3:30 in the afternoon. It was one day before Black Friday (Friday the 13th), and this forestalled an outpouring of superstition. Eiko said, "He deserved it!" when she heard the news. According to Akira's account, I understand that at mealtime at school everyone cheered hearing the news, but when he talked to groups of two or three people they expressed regret. Akira kept saying it was regrettable, regrettable.

On the following day when I went to the Economic Club, those who cursed him were few, and there were certainly a great number who talked as if they wanted him to carry out the postwar management of Japan. It was extraordinary the few who hated him after having suffered such terrible experiences.

There is a report, the gist of which is that an armored spearhead of the American Army has already approached as close as twenty kilometers to Berlin. Yet this is not definitely acknowledged on the American side. Goebbels has admitted the danger. However, he is saying Hitler will save them at the last minute.

The damage due to the air raids on England: 1.2 million homes.

It goes without saying that the Japanese damage in an extremely short time is by far greater than this.

Japan did not have the conditions to be able to carry on modern war. The military until the last said, "We will never allow enemy planes to enter Tōkyō," and, "We will not allow enemy planes to enter Kojimachi-ku." Now what are they saying? I think the resentment of the people toward the military is unbelievably slight. It is because criticism regarding the military is not at all possible. Common people are stupid until informed. And then, if nothing is said, that they are insensitive to the degree they notice nothing.

But I wonder if they will not notice things forever.

April 18 (Wednesday)

Everywhere one goes, the story one hears is that the food supplies of the soldiers are insufficient, and they go to homes and food shops to solicit handouts.

an application will be filed. Although the U.S. search firms can conduct such searches, interpreting the results and predicting how a foreign trademark office would view the application is very difficult for U.S. practitioners who typically are not experts in foreign trademark law. Therefore, most law firms that do trademark work have established relationships with their counterparts in foreign countries and rely upon these **associates** to conduct a search and report the results. The foreign associate then files the trademark application and prosecutes it, while the U.S. attorney generally supervises the process and communicates the progress of the application to the client.

In a recent development, some foreign countries have been allowing free searching of their trademark office databases, much the way one can search for U.S. marks through the PTO's TESS or TARR systems.

The International Trademark Association (INTA) offers direct linking to the databases of trademark offices for Australia, Canada, the European Union, Japan, and the United Kingdom (among other countries) through its web site at http://www.inta.org/links/ipoffices.html. Additionally, experts have provided brief reviews of these sites so one can determine how thorough and user friendly these sites are.

Professional Search Firms. Some of the better-known search firms include the following:

- Thomson & Thomson, 500 Victory Road, North Quincy, MA 02171-3145; (800) 692-8833 (http://www.thomson-thomson.com). Thomson & Thomson is a well-known trademark services firm, offering a full line of services, from trademark searching, to monitoring of trademarks to protect them from infringement, to investigations, to retrieving documents at the PTO. Thomson & Thomson is the owner

of the TRADEMARKSCAN, DIALOG, and SAEGIS products described above. In a recent development, Thomson & Thomson will not only mail the results of a trademark search but will post them to a user's in-box, allowing colleagues to share trademark results and cut and paste search results into letters to clients.
- MicroPatent LLC, 250 Dodge Avenue, East Haven, CT 06512; (800) 648-6787 (http://www.micropatent.com). MicroPatent offers full professional searching as well as access to its TRADEMARK.COM database described above.
- Government Liaison Services, Inc., 200 North Glebe Road, Suite 321, Arlington, VA 22203; (800) 642-6564 (http://www.trademarkinfo.com). Government Liaison Services offers full professional searching as well as document preparation and retrieval services.
- CCH Corsearch, 111 Eighth Avenue, 13th Floor, New York, NY 10011; (800) 732-7241 (http://www.corsearch.com). CCH Corsearch offers a full suite of trademark searching services, including professional searching, document retrieval, and monitoring services to ensure a client's trademark is not infringed.

Evaluating Trademark Search Reports

Once the results of the search have been obtained, they must be evaluated so that the fundamental questions whether the mark is available for use and registration can be answered. The evaluation begins with an analysis of each mark or name provided in the report and a comparison of it to the proposed mark to determine whether they are confusingly similar. This analysis requires one to take into account the overall commercial impressions presented

Also, in the Ginza area, people are hard-pressed to refuse soldiers when they come almost daily and demand food, saying they are hungry. Yesterday there were also people arguing with such soldiers.

Ayusawa's son Jun is in a regimental officers training school, but because he says he is experiencing hunger, his mother and Tsuyuko always carry food to him. The wife of Mizuno of the Police Department who comes to the house frequently takes food to her son, but she puts rice in a tub and the son cannot accept it in front of the others, and so she returns with it. As a result, Kanō took food in bite-size pieces, which his son could eat without being noticed. He said his son eats while carrying on a conversation. It is common for soldiers on "food detail" to steal and eat food with their hands when they are serving.

In the afternoon I went to see the area of Denenchōfu. Both sides of the military road was lost to fire. I went to inquire about the residence of Ōtake Masatarō. Its glass had been ruined by the bombs, but the house still survived. In the neighborhood great holes have opened up, and the houses that have collapsed are numerous. The house of Shiba Ometarō burned. The minister of state and president of the Information Board, Shimomura Hiroshi, was just returning home by auto and we met in front of the gate. He said, "The damage is extremely great!" He was in a good mood. I merely said, "Thank you for your efforts."

There is no gas, there is no water system, there are no lights. We eat meals by candlelight.

April 19 (Thursday)

Today a rumor was conveyed that "In Okinawa enemy troops have surrendered unconditionally." I also heard this; Akira heard it. In the end, it appears it was not so.

The strategy of the army is to make the enemy invade the homeland and attempt to destroy them here, but Yonai insisted on his plan and decided to have a decisive battle in the sea neighboring Okinawa. Until the end, the military conceives of such stupid ventures. I wonder how much of this is true.

Isn't the claim that the unconditional surrender position of the American Army is directed toward the munitions companies probably military propaganda? All the articles in each newspaper are talking of a "golden opportunity."

Mainichi, 19th, an editorial entitled "Training for the Winning Chance," and beside that there are two articles, one entitled, "The Moment to Grasp the Winning Chance Is Now," and the other entitled, "Naval Power Is Finally Declining." The papers have only two and a half pages, but more than half of the first page Is on Okinawa. Judging from this, this is the decisive battleground.

From today the lights are on.

The *Nihon sangyō keizai*, under a horizontal headline title, "The Annihilation of the Enemy's Pacific Naval Force Near," said, "The opening of a divine opportunity for inevitable victory."

In *Yomiuri* in horizontal black outline frames there is "Now We Grasp Victory" (*Yomiuri*, April 19).

Based on the foregoing, it is clear that the army is pouring in strength, considering this the last stage.

The sacrificial victims of the air raids are emerging. A *Tōyō keizai* reporter named Kamata on foot during an air raid had both his feet cut off and died as a result. There was no coffin in which to put the body. Thereupon, with old lumber torn off an annex of *Tōyō keizai*, the members constructed one. There are difficulties in even using crematories, but it appears this man was transported by dray or something. It was utterly pitiful.

Wakimura Gitarō has hitherto fought bravely and survived, but recently I understand he has finally been burned out completely. Akashi Teruo also has been burned out.

April 20 (Friday)

I hear that Obama came to the house in the morning and said he would buy train tickets for me. However, because of the total confusion on the trains with the evacuation of air-raid victims, he wondered how it would be to leave on the 24th. I told him it was fine.

According to the same gentleman's story, the casualties of the raids on the 13th were 580,000 persons, and the number on the 15th was 600,000. He said that when this is combined with those of March 30, it exceeds 3.2 or 3.3 million.

In England the damage because of the German air raids from the beginning of the war until February 28, 1945, is 144,542. Among these, the dead and missing are 59,793; the patients in hospitals, 84,749. The casualties in commercial shipping are 34,161.

Because it is said that things are fine in Okinawa, optimistic theories frequently emerge everywhere. I have heard that the enemy on Okinawa has surrendered conditionally, and Akira also heard this. Among some people there are some who say that America is proposing peace talks. One understands how ignorant the masses are. It is evidence that they swallow the newspapers whole. This is not just in Tōkyō but in the regions as well. The newspapers are saying that everything is fine, and yet others say don't believe it.

April 21 (Saturday)

I went to the center of the city. When I tried going to the Marunouchi Building it took two hours, and not finishing my business, I went to Fuji Ice to visit Ō. I heard that the fires came quite close to him, but he has survived. The spreading fire has reached such people as Abe Nōsei and Kahira Kenichi. I hear that also the home of Admiral Okada Keisuke was burned.

On the way home I took the Tōkyō-Yokohama line. The area from the seacoast between Ōmori and Ōimachi was lost to fire. But the most pitiful was the way the fire burned, with Kamata at the center, the entire area. Kamata Station had burned and collapsed, and as far as Hasunuma there was not a single house. The damage was beyond imagination. I was disheartened standing on the elevated platform of the station, which had burned.

In the places that Akira had seen he said in the Sugamo, Otsuka Nakamachi area there is nothing left standing as far as Ueno Station.

However, what should be stressed is the fact that the people who have been burned out are serene. This is probably because they find consolation in saying, "Today it was on me, tomorrow it will be on someone else." It is probably also the fact that the same fate shared by so many serves the role of alleviating the grief (*Yomiuri*, April 21).

The army minister, Anami, has announced the final battle. President Minami of the Greater Japan Political Society, which is a political body, has issued the statement that they support Anami's statement. Is it the army general, Anami, or the party president? It is a declaration of defense of the homeland to the death (*Yomiuri*, April 21).

I understand that on the American side they are insisting upon the punishment of Japanese cruelty to American soldiers, and Dr. Shinobu said why doesn't Japan make a public statement regarding the treatment of prisoners of war.

April 22 (Sunday)

This morning's newspapers reported that the Ministry of Home Affairs has transferred 125 officials (*Yomiuri*, April 22).

It was for the purpose of reforming personnel who had been stagnant for a long while. Politicians who carry out these kinds of changes are stupid, but the reporters are also stupid. Even if one looks at Machimura, commissioner of police, whom I have known, (newly appointed) at the beginning of the war he was governor of Tōyama Prefecture, changed to civil guard chief, was on leave for a while, then governor of Niigata, and then police commissioner. Someone like Azumi Tokuya was head of the Economic Bureau of Tōkyō, governor of Tochigi Prefecture, chief of planning, and after that vice-governor of Aichi Prefecture, and these were shifts in only two years.

It is an official-centered politics. One understands that this so-called reformism, in reality medieval idealism, is the core of politics.

The person considered the "great man" among the great men is said to be Yasui Eiji, fifty-six years old, former state minister. Indeed, the *Mainichi* is saying, "Stop the shifting of officials," and *Yomiuri* criticizes this under the title "The Shifts of Regional Officials." This is the first time that a newspaper has criticized the policies of a cabinet.

Because Premier Suzuki was appointed by the senior statesmen, the new cabinet is thought to be commonsensical, liberalistic, and mature. However, in what this cabinet does it is extremely reactionary and must be completely rooted out. For example, when one considers the talk of Education Minister Ō Kōzō (the protégé of Hiranuma), it is evident one does not understand what he is talking about. Consequently, one cannot see satisfactory results. However, if one could reverse this condition, something might be done. I cannot believe this is possible with Suzuki. After all, he is a mere soldier.

Look at these stupid, divinely inspired ideas!

I was invited for tea at the home of Satō and dined on *ohagi*.

Of late, *ohagi*[81] is particularly the greatest of treats. It is said that one kamme of sugar is about 750 yen.

I called to inquire about Dr. Matsumoto Jōji. In his area more than ten splendid houses have burned. The residence of Kinoshita Shin also burned.

April 23 (Monday)

The Red Army is invading Berlin. The Nazis will die in suicidal stands to the bitter end. Is such a style of warfare to be praised? Even the American and English principles of war, which insist upon unconditional surrender, will probably be criticized in the future, but the war principle of honorable death will probably be disputed by later historians.

In Japan this precedent must probably be the model of the "Japanese spirit." The problem is that the imperial family exists in Japan, and the Nazi war style will probably not necessarily receive the support of the upper class.

I went to a directors meeting of *Tōyō keizai*. According to Rōyama, Shigemitsu is trying to remain in the same position. Rōyama says he is also seeking support for his own premiership.

April 24 (Tuesday)

Thanks to the help of Furuta Tamotsu of *Nihon sangyō keizai*, and also with the efforts of the elder son (a student at Japan University) of Hori (my neighbor), two second-class round-trip tickets came into our hands. For second-class tickets I pay a thank-you gift of fifty yen. The ticket to Kutsukake costs fifty yen because of the thank-you money here and there. I hear that at the ticket window they openly take such thank-you gifts.

Hori, with a friend, came to visit. We talked about all sorts of things. Even students think that if the Japanese attack the enemy in the Ryūkyū Islands, Japan will be victorious in war.

In the end we intended to go by the 5:00 train tomorrow (if possible we would board this evening), and we left the house at 6:30 in the evening. My wife and I, Akira, and Eiko were going, and Tàyō saw us off as far as Ueno. All the train passengers were burdened with luggage that was more than they could handle, and they made a procession three or four blocks long. Among them were those shouldering chests. It is probably not possible ever to see such a scene anywhere else. When we arrived at around 7:30, we were already at the end of the processions. The people at the front were probably waiting from about 3:00 or 4:00. Because it was said that a special train would leave at 10:45 in the evening, we boarded this. Boarding the second-class cars, we found them quite empty, and this was also true of third class. The fact that it was Nagano-bound was one reason, but also the station personnel did not advise anyone that it was a "special train." Fortunately, due to the wise advice of Kasahara Seimei, we boarded this train. This sort of inefficiency—on the one hand, the life-and-death confusion of not being able to board, and on the other hand, running empty trains due to the inconsiderateness of the Railway Ministry.

When I looked outside from the train on the right side to the north of Ueno, because of the air raids of April 13, the whole area was like a barren field. It is beyond imagination.

April 26 (Thursday)

Akira and I went immediately to the fields. We went to the home of Ide to receive seed potatoes and manure. I returned pulling a large wagon. I picked up pieces of manure along the way. Unfortunately, because there was nothing to pick them up with, I took them by hand and put them in the wagon. Because schoolgirls were passing by, I was embarrassed to do this by hand and used a nearby scrap of paper. But even for girl students to see someone picking up manure is not unusual, and they did not look back even for a second.

While picking up manure, I wondered if doing so was for the benefit of the nation. There is absolutely no more division of labor, and we ourselves must do the work of coolies.

Despite all of that, we finished planting one part of the potatoes. It is still cold when night comes in the mountains.

April 27 (Friday)

Because of the time limit on the ticket, today Akira returned to Tōkyō. I am working at farming by myself.

April 28 (Saturday)

In the afternoon I visited Masamune Hakuchō. Even without his present hardships, he was never an impressive-looking man. Now he spends his time in the cold mountain area and has become a shabby country fellow. He treated me to rare items such as pure American coffee, walnuts, peanuts, and doughnuts.

He cursed his life-style.

He spat out, "I am barely existing, fighting hunger and cold." He said that ignorant farmers and laborers obtain money from the overpriced black market but still move about as arrogantly as kings. He said everybody is a "beggar." When I encouraged him to write about his life for future reference, he said, "I don't have any such idea in mind. I am still only living like an animal." He had bought land next door. It cost something like twenty yen for one tsubo. It is the price in the suburbs of Tōkyō. He said, "I hate to work!" but if one did not work one did not eat. I advised him to cultivate the easier parts of his land, and he decided to do so.

Afterward I stopped over briefly at the home of Sakamoto. Hatoyama Ichirō was there. He related that it was certain that Yoshida Shigeru (former ambassador to England) had been seized by the Kempeitai about April 15 or 16. I understand that Count Kabayama Aisuke had his house searched. It appears that since they did not arrest him, they thought that Yoshida might be there. Again, he said the critic Iwabuchi Tatsuo was also seized by the Kempeitai. I said, "How is Baba Tsunego?" He said, laughing, that in a cabinet discussion or somewhere, there was talk of rounding up all the "defeatists," but as six million people would have to be collected, the matter was dropped. I also thought for a long time that the government would drop this idea. This is the last gasp of the government.

Nevertheless, it is strange that nothing happens to me. Yet there was a strange affair when on the evening of the April 15 air raid two men came to my house and talked for a while. "We were in a factory at Shimomaruko and had our family flee to an air-raid shelter. It appears that the house was burned." Their appearance was not that of the ordinary workers. While I was trying to put our own fire out, I had repeated many times, "I hate the American enemy," and to these people I cursed the enemy who bombed innocent city people. They said, "Since it's wartime nothing can be done about this injury to city people, but it's regrettable to lose the factories." I never think this sort of thing, but I can't deny it was a question of self-preservation. I do not know who these two men were. However, it's true that in many instances the Kempeitai engages in spy behavior.

According to a story of Masamune, the Soviet ambassador was evacuated to the Manpei Hotel in Karuizawa, but he said all the boys at the hotel are Kempei.

April 29 (Sunday)

A National Public Spirit Group has been organized, and they are advancing preparations for the defense of the homeland. It is the same behavioral style as the honorable-deathism of Germany.

Bureaucratic organization is penetrating the countryside by degrees, and it is reaching the point where nothing functions any longer. At Masamune's place, when he tried to employ workers, first of all, he informed the Town Labor Office and received permission. Along with the laborers came supervisors, and there was meticulous point-by-point interference on what sort of work would be done and what sort could not be permitted. The officially fixed wage per day was six yen, but ten yen is usual, and it is said that among workers there are those who demand eighty yen a day. It can be presumed that there is one supervisor, who is of the salaried class, for several workers.

April 30 (Monday)

I finished planting the seed potatoes. It was exhausting, and my whole body ached.

This evening's radio transmitted the report that Germany's Himmler proposed unconditional surrender to America and England. It is said that England and America say that Germany must accept the unconditional surrender terms of the Allied nations, which include the Soviet Union. Moreover, they reported they had arrested Mussolini together with his gang. It is a fact that the Second World War has taken exactly five years, eight months. If compared with the four years, four months, of the First World War, it is one year, four months, longer. It was extended about a year and a half longer than I predicted.

Despite this, what do the Japanese think about the fact of Mussolini having been seized without his committing suicide? Moreover, what do they think will be the end of Hitler?

And so the most important thing is, what will Japan do?

The enemy planes come to attack in Kyūshū every day, and they strike Kagoshima, Miyazaki, and other places. I heard that today two hundred planes came to attack Tachikawa. The question of why they are not bombing Tōkyō is somewhat unclear. But in Japan there is no popular political activity and public opinion that appeals to America to question the reckless bombing of cities. In the thing called war, do the Japanese assume that it involves this sort of thing, or, along with that, is there a special fatalism?

The burning of Tōkyō and other people's homes in the American air raids imposes unnecessary misery on the people, and no matter what is said, it is a crime. If they realized this and stopped, everybody would be better off.

May 1 (Tuesday)

Nothing new and working at farming. I made a flower bed. Life is not only a matter of eating. Even in times of trouble, I hope there will be some cultural enjoyment.

The daily radio reports that the damage sustained in Okinawa is heavy. This is the style that has been pervasive since the China Incident. What the people wish to know is not this kind of report.

On the evening radio they noted that the Emperor Frederick of Prussia was finally victorious in the Seven Years War, and continuing,

1. In Japan until Shōwa 12 (1912) there were politicians who talked of the reduction of military preparations. The Diet applauded this.

2. In idea-propaganda America was aggressive. It would make all mankind American.

3. Material development in Japan was obstructed. For example, gasoline was imported cheaply, and one-yen taxis were operated cheaply, and this made the Japanese people succumb to a luxurious life-style and discouraged the development of synthetic oil. It is said that at the Washington Conference and the London Conference, Japanese war power was reduced, and such people as General Katō Kanji were praised. I understand that there were such articles in the latest "weekly reports." This sort of thing is not something that could be published and broadcast without the permission of the military.

Ide came and reported that in the town the subject of discussion is unconditional surrender. When Ide came yesterday, because he said, "Germany seems to be in danger doesn't it?" I said, "Germany is already finished!" He refused to believe it. Upon returning home, he heard this on the evening radio. I understand that people are saying, "I wonder why Germany did not persist somehow" and discussed this incredible situation everywhere. Because the newspapers always conveyed Germany as appearing to be a superior power, people in general did not understand this. And they thought of it as if it were an event that suddenly appeared (*Shinano mainichi*, May 1).

There is no limit to the complexities of procedures of late. Moving necessitates seals from places such as the Ward Office, the Town Assembly, and the Neighborhood Association, and when I came to Karuizawa for such things as submitting these to the squad leader, Neighborhood Association, and Town Office, this requires two or three days.

On the day of my arrival I requested the Town Hall kindly to turn on the water, but someone came the following day and then said, "Very soon the water supply will be limited only to kitchen and bath." When I said that the flush toilet was not used but I wanted water only in the washroom, he said in a commanding tone, "In wartime we have to accept inconvenience," and "If one grumbles about that, the water will be completely shut off."

This is not unusual in Tōkyō, but with the war the country people are absolutely rude in making excuses. Because I requested an extra water supply when the iron pipes in our house leaked and water spilled out under the floor, even though we begged countless times, no one came. It was a defeat for being foolishly reasonable.

May 2 (Wednesday)

Rain. I wrote concerning the surrender of Germany for *Tōyō keizai*.

In regard to Eiko's transfer of schools, I went to the Karuizawa Girls Middle School. My wife ran about countless times but did not settle it. Finally, the school administration said we should petition our wish to move her to Komoro Girls High School.

Our water system overflowed and we requested repairs from "Morikaku." They said, "We hear what you are saying." Everything is red tape. They said, "We can't do it." Every time there are dealings with people, there is no limit to the disagreeableness. If one has to deal with this every day, one risks nervous collapse. I decided to concentrate on farming.

I well understand Masamune's feeling of cursing Karuizawa.

I stopped over at the residence of Sakamoto. Unexpectedly, Hatoyama Ichirō was there. We were served tea and there was a very pleasant talk.

The circumstances of Admiral Suzuki Kantarō's achieving the premiership.

At a conference of the senior statesmen, it was Tōjō who was the first to speak. He said, "At this time it is necessary to decide whether we should end the war by compromise, or if not fight out the war to the end. This is the basis for choosing the prime minister." Hiranuma agreed with this and Suzuki echoed it, saying, "We must absolutely fight to the finish." Konoe was asked his opinion, and he said that the matter of how the war will turn out is something that should be decided by the succeeding prime minister. It should not be discussed there, and Okada agreed. Wakatsuki stated, "Because the emperor's question is the choice of a premier, these other matters are out of order." After that they moved to the selection of a premier. When Suzuki said, "It would be splendid to have the youngest man perform the office," his words meant Konoe, but on this there was no agreement, and following this Hiranuma said, "Admiral Suzuki!" and with that the matter was settled.

Before this the army recommended Sakomizu as chief secretary and laid down conditions for supporting the cabinet. Yonai was opposed to Suzuki and reported his opposition, but Suzuki was already too deeply entrenched, and it was impossible to do anything. The military submitted three conditions to Suzuki, and he was made to agree to them. Among these was a condition that stated, "The army is to be respected."

Hatoyama said the "Reds" are becoming the center. Along with Sakamoto, he avidly detests the "Reds."

Sakamoto had a talk with Tōgō Shigenori before he became foreign minister. According to Sakamoto, Tōgō seems to have hopes for a conclusion of the war by way of the Soviet Union. In order to make the Soviet negotiate, Tōgō said that if we stipulate returning Karafuto and public recognition of the Communist party, this would probably be sufficient. Sakamoto opposed this and said that if such a thing were done, Communist party members such as Okano would make their entry into politics and probably generate political disorder. Hatoyama said that if the Soviet Union agreed to this, would America and England make any kind of concessions on the basis of this? As for himself, he thought not. He said it would be better to put forward frankly Japanese conditions to England and America.

At any rate, I said there was the necessity of bringing the war to an end. For that purpose:

1. Unconditional surrender
2. Either the mediation of the Soviet Union
3. Or the mediation of Chiang Kai-shek
4. Beginning of talks with America (this would be unsuccessful based on experience with the Soviet)

If any one of these paths is possible, it should be taken.

Again, I said the Christians in Japan should join together and appeal to the public opinion of the world regarding the indiscriminate American bombing. I said, wouldn't it be ideal if an investigation announcement were allowed to be made by the people of a third country? Sakamoto said the military would probably oppose such a thing.

The conversation was extremely pleasant. We all agreed how criminal ignorance is. There is the need to enlighten the people. And in this, freedom of speech is a preordained problem.

There is a report that Hitler is dead. It has been communicated that Mussolini has also been murdered. Indeed, this evening's radio transmitted these speculations.

May 3 (Thursday)

The radio reported that Hitler died while directing the war. It should be said that this "accomplished villain" came to a good end. Himmler proposed unconditional surrender, and Hitler's successor Doenitz declared total resistance. This shows the internal upheaval within Germany.

The Soviet Union announced that they are occupying Berlin.

In the evening Premier Suzuki broadcast "On the rapidly changing European situation." I did not receive any special insight from this.

The wedding ceremony of X and Dobashi Yayoi will be tomorrow, and taking Eiko along, we went to Matsumoto. Yesterday evening we had a difficult time buying tickets. We were refused at Kutsukake and then went to Karuizawa and finally purchased some. For some reason, at Karuizawa Station they only sell three tickets a day in the same direction.

The damage due to the air raids was reported on April 25. In twelve air raids there was greater damage than in England in five years, eight months (*Yomiuri*, April 25).

Kotaki Ōshiro (second brother) and others came from Tōkyō, and everyone was there.

by the marks; their similarity in regard to sight, sound, and meaning; the relative strength or weakness of the marks based on their descriptiveness or suggestiveness; and the goods or services offered under each mark.

A typical search entry will appear as follows:

Mark	BITTY BEAR
Reg. No.	1,990,314
Reg. Date	July 30, 1996
Filing Date	June 2, 1994
Date of first use	Sept. 11, 1995
Goods	Toys and stuffed animals
I.C.	28
Owner	Pleasant Company Corp.
	8400 Fairway Place
	Middleton, WI 53562

Using our case study, if the owner of the amusement park wished to introduce a new line of children's books called BUDDY BEAR, the existence of BITTY BEAR for toys and stuffed animals may present a conflict. The marks are similar in appearance (with only a few letters being different) and similar in sound, and children's books may be viewed as related to children's toys. Consumers who encounter the BUDDY BEAR books might believe they are somehow connected with BITTY BEAR or that BUDDY BEAR is a new line of books sponsored by the makers of BITTY BEAR. On the other hand, if there are numerous other marks including BEAR for related goods (as in fact there are, such as BUBBLE BEAR and BOOMER BEAR), this is likely a sign that marks including BEAR for toys and related goods are weak and they have been allowed to coexist. If numerous similar marks for similar goods or services coexist, it is less likely that a mark will be refused or attacked. Consumers become adept at distinguishing similar marks for related products as seen by the coexistence of MICROSOFT® and MICRO STRATEGY® for related goods and services.

In many instances, paralegals provide the initial review of the search report and flag potential problems or "hits" for an attorney's later evaluation. Paralegals also play a key role in investigating some of the sources revealed in the report. By contacting the owner of a mark, it may be discovered the mark is no longer in use or that the company has ceased doing business. Marketing materials can be reviewed to determine the actual manner in which the mark is used. The file for a conflicting mark can be obtained from the PTO to determine what objections were made to the application by the PTO and how the owner overcame them.

Reporting the Results to the Client

A formal written report will then be prepared for the client. The letter, often called an "availability" or "clearance" report, typically includes the following elements:

- a description of the mark that was the subject of the search;
- a description of the method of the search, the databases that were checked, and the dates applicable to the search parameters;
- a section describing limitations on the search report, such as a disclaimer or statement that the results of the search cannot be guaranteed and that, due to errors in cataloging records and files and time delays in entering marks into databases, some marks might not be disclosed in the search;
- a discussion of potentially conflicting marks;
- the opinion in regard to availability of the mark for use and registration; and
- recommendations for further action or investigation, if needed.

The heart of the report is the attorney's opinion in regard to whether the mark is avail-

The enemy is invading the island of Tarakan. It is probably to seize oil resources.

In the shops in the Matsumoto area there is not a single thing that functions. In the evening there are no lights at all. Even the darkness is dark.

I hear that the inns in Asama with the exception of two or three are completely closed down. Even in Nishi-Ishikawa, if the guests bring their own rice they cannot stay more than two days. However, according to Satoru, the rice provided by the guests is equally divided between the maids and the manager.

May 5 (Saturday)

A history of fire in Tōkyō (Edo) (*Yomiuri*, April 26).

Saying, "A marriage is something not looked for but something to find," I made the go-between's greeting.

Matsumoto still has a feeling of normality, and everyone was wearing morning clothes and crested kimonos. However, as for the banquet meal, though the Dobashi family had brought all the charcoal, what was cooked with this was no more than half of what they brought. Of late things disappear en route.

NOTES

1. A long epic song.
2. A form of ballad drama.
3. A song from the classical Nō theater.
4. The musical recital of ancient tales.
5. The period 1883–1887, associated with a Western-style pavilion (the Deer Cry Hall) to encourage contact between Japanese and foreigners, to display Japan's Westernization, and thereby hopefully to accelerate the revision of the unequal treaties.
6. *Chūgai shōgyō shinbun* (National/international business news), the predecessor of the *Nihon keizai shinbun* (Japan economic news). Kiyosawa began his journalistic career with *Chūgai* in 1918 after a twelve-year stay in America. During most of that time he honed his newspaper talents with several Japanese-language papers.
7. Kakei Katsuhiko (1872–1961), nationalist ideologue and professor of law at Tokyo University until his retirement in 1933. Thereafter he lectured at various universities on his special interest in Christianity, Buddhism, and primitive Shinto.
8. Published in English as *The Makioka Sisters* in 1957.
9. The Silver Star, a tea room in which Kiyosawa had a financial interest.
10. The pseudo-totalitarian national organization, Imperial Rule Assistance Society, heralded a "new political structure" in 1940 and invoked imperial service as the collective way of the subject. Such local subgroups bespoke its mass political party aspiration. In Tōjō's premiership, as the entry reveals, these merely exercised Big Brother surveillance.
11. *Reconstruction*, another well-known journal of intellectual opinion of increasingly socialist persuasion, and consequently object of official censure. Finally halted in July 1944.
12. A reference to the color-coded makeup of the popular Kabuki theater indicating emotion or disposition. Red signaled, among other qualities, a choleric temperament.

13. John Henry Longford, an early Japanist and author of *Japan of the Japanese* (1915) and *Japan* (1923).
14. Onoe Taganojō III, a noted Kabuki actor especially celebrated for his role as the wife of Kikugoro VI and his depiction of older women.
15. Onoe Kikugorō VI, a Kabuki actor known particularly for his accomplished dancing and plebeian characterizations.
16. Namba Daisuke attempted to assassinate the Taishō Regent (who would become the Emperor Hirohito) in 1923.
17. A failed military officer coup in 1932, and one of a series of such outbursts intended to induce national reconstruction (the so-called Shōwa Restoration) by military violence. Considered the finale to party politics.
18. The commander who authored the anti-Semitic article noted in the June 20 entry.
19. One koku is slightly more than five bushels.
20. Forty-seven Ronin, probably the most celebrated and enduring of the samurai vendetta legends dating from the Tokugawa period, enshrined as an indestructible item of the Kabuki repertory. Miyamoto Musashi, legendary seventeenth-century fencing master and all-around samurai virtuoso of painting, poetry, calligraphy, and mental discipline.
21. The former Tokugawa territories of Satsuma and Chōshū, which provided the dominant leadership of the Meiji Restoration.
22. Probably *A Diplomat in Japan: An Inner History of the Japanese Reformation*.
23. Referring to the two Chinese characters with the same pronunciation.
24. The formal Tokugawa social stratification of warrior, farmer, artisan, merchant.
25. "The Greater Foundation Teaching"— an influential cult religion originally dedicated to the reconstruction of the world and creation of an ideal society. Because of its growth especially among discontented farmers and its

leader's claim to national leadership, it was much harassed in the prewar period and then reemerged in 1950 as Ōmotokyō Aizenen (Great Foundation of the Community of Love and Virtue).

26. Actually *Peace and War* by the American secretary of state, Cordell Hull.

27. Nakamura Kichiemon I, contemporary and rival of Kokugorō VI during a golden age of young stars. The theatrical "rivalry" of the two generated their joint nickname Kiku-Kichi.

28. A work of George Ward Price published in 1938.

29. Satō Issai (1772–1859), prolific Confucian scholar and long-time teacher at the Shōheikō, the Tokugawa Confucian College.

30. The Japanese title of the already noted Kabuki classic, *The Forty-seven Ronin*.

31. John Robert Seeley (1834–1895). A work published in 1906.

32. An in-floor foot-warmer covered with a quilt.

33. An incident in which a British merchant and two others were fatally cut down in 1862 for breaking through a procession of the daimyō of Satsuma. A naval bombardment of Kagoshima followed, demonstrating once again Western military prowess.

34. An earlier work of Kiyosawa's, *Jiyū Nihon o asaru*, published in 1929.

35. A Scottish journalist whose work *Young Japan* (1880–1881) covered the years 1858–1879 and who published the first regular newspaper in Japanese, the *Nisshin shinjinshi*.

36. The Order of the Golden Kite.

37. Tokugawa Keiki (1837–1913), the last of the military dictators known as shoguns. Seikanron, the invasion of Korea debate in 1873 that split the early Meiji leadership on the question of military chastisement of Korea for diplomatic affronts as against the primacy of the national effort for modern development. The latter position prevailed.

38. Probably the *London Daily Telegraph*, an earlier title of which included the letters N.P.

39. The second of the two earliest mytho-historical records that chronicled the beginnings of Japanese civilization.

40. Philbul Songkram, the military leader of Siam.

41. The geisha mistress of Townsend Harris, the first American consul to Japan.

42. Ichimura Uzaemon XV (1874–1945),

Kabuki actor who excelled in romantic roles of the late Edo period.

43. A light cotton informal kimono for the summer or after bathing.

44. The short-lived (1251–1284) but brilliant Kamakura regent, considered to be the hero of the Mongol Invasions of Japan, particularly the second of these, launched in 1281.

45. Nicholas John Spykman, *America's Strategy in World Politics, the United States and the Balance of Power* (1942).

46. Houses of assignation.

47. *Ninomiya Sontoku's Night Talks*, Ninomiya Sontoku (1787–1856), founder of the Hōtokukai (Repayment of Virtue Society) and a self-made plebeian ideologue who reasserted the traditional agrarian virtues of thrift, diligence, and cooperation, virtues later opportunistically manipulated by landlords and the modern political establishment.

48. One tsubo, about four square yards.

49. An episode from January to May 1920 during the Japanese intervention into Siberia in which a Japanese defense force stationed at the Amur River mouth and Nikō (Nicholaesvsk) was destroyed in a clash with partisans. Exploiting the turmoil of the Russian Revolution, Japan had dispatched troops into the area in 1918, where there followed repeated confrontations with partisan forces. The Japanese government referred to these as the Nikō Incident and used this as a pretext to make northern Sakhalin a protectorate, with the navy guarding the oil fields there. The protectorate continued until amity was restored with the Soviet Union in May 1925.

50. Pantaloon-like women's work pants, which were gathered at the ankles.

51. A hectare is 2.45 acres.

52. 384 U.S. pint.

53. The italicized syllabic script adjacent to characters to indicate their reading.

54. A summer dessert of boiled beans, and agar-agar cubes covered with treacle.

55. Roughly "Private first class, sir!"

56. Raymond Arthur Lyttleton, English minister of production.

57. T'ao Yuan-ming (T'ao Ch'ien), a celebrated third-century Chinese poet who helped develop the style of voluntary, gentlemanly rural retirement.

58. Ikesaki Tadataka (1891–1949). A literary critic and influential commentator on military affairs. Among his faulty judgments, he

stressed the Chinese inability to resist Japan, Japanese military invincibility, and the lack of American warlike zeal. As a prewar member of the Diet, he contributed to the military buildup of the 1930s. All of which earned him a class A war criminal status in the postwar period.

59. One of the several names of Mito Mitsukuni, feudal lord of one of the families collateral to the Tokugawa ruling house. He would be remembered for his pioneering historical work, the *Dai Nihon shi*, his passionate nativist preferences in literature and religion as well as his championing of the imperial house.

60. The February 26 Rising (1936). Another notorious failed military coup precipitated by the clash of purposes between the two dominant factions within the military establishment, the Kōdoha and the Tōseiha. The latter prevailed, paving the way for the ascendancy of Tōjō. The Southern Advance Theory was one of two disputed national grand strategies of Japanese international ambition. It favored advance into the raw-material-rich Southeast Asian areas as against a Northern Advance strategy against the Soviet Union.

61. A dish made from buckwheat noodles.

62. Richard A. Butler, under secretary of state for foreign affairs, 1938–1941.

63. Eugene Jared Young (1874–1939), *Powerful America: Our Place in a Rearming World.*

64. A little more than fifteen pounds.

65. 1/1,000 of a yen.

66. .0384 pints (U.S.).

67. A Zen Buddhist temple in the Yokohama (Tsurumi ward).

68. A celebrated military victory of one of Japan's sixteenth-century unifiers, Toyotomi Hideyoshi.

69. Narrated battle stories.

70. The Rōdō Nōmintō, labor farmer party. A political party engendered by the proletarian movement of the 1920s that fell under Communist domination. Its leadership was harassed and many arrested, whereupon the party dissolved itself in 1928. It passed through subsequent reincarnations.

71. Kusunoki Masashige (1294–1336), an exemplar of military prowess and imperial loyalty and devotion.

72. Edwin Baelz (1849–1913), German physician and one of the most famous of the Meiji foreign "employees." Teaching in what was to become the Medical Faculty of Tokyo University, he made significant contributions to the advance of modern medical practice in Japan.

73. Clarence E. Gauss, who resigned as American ambassador to China on November 1, 1944.

74. The last years of the Tokugawa period and the ensuing Meiji period of modern transformation.

75. Hector Charles Bywater (1884–1940). Kiyosawa is reading either *Sea Power in the Pacific: A Study of the American Japanese Naval Problems* (1921) or *The Great Pacific War: An Historical Prophecy Now Being Fulfilled* (1942).

76. Philip Caryl Jessup (b. 1897), a prolific scholar of international law.

77. July 29, 1937. The incident that committed the Japanese Army to all-out war in China after the scuffle on the Marco Polo Bridge on July 7, 1937. After the Chinese general refused the demand of his Japanese counterpart that he evacuate Peking, heavy fighting broke out. Chinese soldiers of a Japanese-sponsored security force then killed their Japanese officers and massacred 230 Japanese civilians.

78. James Murdoch (1856–1921). An early, massive three-volume work.

79. Sir Francis Ottiwell Adams (1825–1889), *The History of Japan* (1875); Frank Brinkley (1841–1912), *A History of the Japanese People from the Earliest Times to the End of the Meiji Year* (1915).

80. Booby-trapped mechanical lead pencils allegedly mixed together with the candy and chocolate dropped during air raids.

81. A rice dumpling covered with bean jam.

BIOGRAPHICAL GUIDE

ABE KENICHI (b. 1890)   An economist educated at Waseda University and then an instructor there. Later became managing director of *Mainichi shinbun* preceding World War II. Subsequently purged and depurged.

ABE YOSHISHIGE (1883–1966)   A Tōkyō University graduate specializing in philosophy, which he taught at private universities. Traveled extensively in Europe in 1938. Later president of Gakushūin University and education minister in the postwar Shidehara Cabinet.

AKAO BIN (1899)   Ideological activist in the cause of ultra-nationalism. Led the wartime National Foundation Association and the Greater Japan Imperial Rule Association. Also one of the directors of the International Anti-Communist League. Elected to the House of Representatives in 1942. Despite depurging, failed to achieve elective office after the war.

ANDŌ MASAZUMI (1876–1955)   A Tōkyō University–trained politician who became editor-in-chief and manager of the *Tōkyō asahi shinbun*. Frequently elected to the House of Representatives. Served as counselor to the Education Ministry and parliamentary vice-minister for education. Subsequently state minister in the fifth Yoshida Cabinet (1953) and education minister in the Hatoyama Cabinet (1954).

AOKI KAZUO (1889)   A statesman who held a succession of offices in the prewar and war period, including finance minister in the Abe Cabinet (1939), ambassador to China in Nanking, supreme Adviser to the Nanking government, and Greater East Asian Minister (1942) in the Tōjō Cabinet, from which position he resigned in 1944. Imprisoned for several years as a war crimes suspect.

ARAKI SADAO (1877–1966)   A graduate of the Military Academy, he held a number of military posts. Assumed the position of war minister from 1931 to 1934, when ill health prompted his resignation. During his tenure he initiated reforms that entrenched his own cronies in important posts, pressed vigorously for military appropriations, and advocated an independent Manchuria. He was identified with the restive young officers of the February 26 coup. As minister of education in the Konoe and Hiranuma cabinets, he accentuated the military content of teaching.

ARISAWA HIROMI (1896–1988)   Professor of economics at Tōkyō University, where after study in Germany he taught statistics. In 1930, he was a central figure in the so-called Professors Group of 1930, which opposed militarism. Punished with dismissal in 1938, but resumed his chair after the war.

ARITA HACHIRŌ (1884–1965)   Graduated from Tōkyō University in 1909 and entered the Foreign Ministry in 1910. Acted as ambassador to Germany, Austria, Belgium, and China and served as foreign minister in the Hirota Cabinet in 1936. He was also foreign minister in the Konoe, Hiranuma, and Yonai cabinets.

ASHIDA HITOSHI (1887–1959)   After studying law at Kyōto University, entered the diplomatic service. Served in France, Russia, Belgium, and Turkey. When elected to the House of Representatives in 1932, he abandoned diplomacy. Became president of the *Japan Times and Mail* (1933–1940). Subsequently minister in the postwar Shidehara Cabinet, and himself premier in 1948. Known also for his diplomatic history works.

AYUSAWA IWAO (1894–1972)   A specialist in labor problems and history. A graduate of Columbia University, where he was a student of sociology. A member of the Labor Bureau of the League of Nations for fifteen years. Later served as director of the Tokyo Bureau, International Labor Organization.

BABA TSUNEGO (1865–1956)   A journalist who worked for fourteen years in America and upon returning to Japan joined the *Kokumin shinbun*. A liberal political activist identified with the franchise movement. In the early postwar became president of *Yomiuri shinbun*. Produced a variety of works on political subjects.

FUJIYAMA AIICHIRŌ (1897–1985)   Businessman and politician educated at Keiō University. Assumed the presidency of Dai Nihon Sugar Company and was linked with other enterprises. Weathering the postwar purge, he held directorial posts in numerous companies. Was foreign minister in the two Kishi cabinets from 1957 to 1960.

FUKUCHI GENICHIRŌ (1841–1906)   Journalist, politician, playwright. An early student of Dutch and participant in the earliest missions to the West, including the Iwakura Embassy in early Meiji. In the same period founder of the *Kōko shinbun* and *Tōkyō nichinichi shinbun*. Following frustrated political party ambitions, he resorted to theater management in 1898. Subsequently adapted Kabuki plays for the new theater. Author of a number of reminiscences on the twilight of the Tokugawa period.

FURUGAKI TETSURŌ (1900–1987)   Until 1956 president of Japan Broadcasting Corporation. A graduate of Lyons University in 1923, he returned to Europe as an officer of the General Affairs Bureau of the League of Nations. Became a staff member of *Asahi shinbun* in 1929 where he was a frequent foreign correspondent. Assumed the presidency of NHK in 1949.

HASEGAWA NYOZEKAN (1875–1969)   The doyen of prewar Japanese journalism. One of the most perceptive analysts of Japanese culture and eloquent enthusiasts of the liberal political persuasion. The author of essays, novels, and essays for the *Nihon shinbun* before becoming a staff member of the *Ōsaka asahi shinbun* in 1908. Upon leaving the newspaper in 1918, he continued to contribute to a wide spectrum of periodicals.

HASHIDA KUNIHIKO (1882–1945)   A medical doctor trained at Tōkyō University. After further preparation in Europe, he returned to teach at Tōkyō University. He would become minister of education in the second and third Konoe Cabinets and the Tōjō cabinet. Committed suicide after the war.

HASHIMOTO KINGORŌ (1890–1957)   Notorious army officer prominently involved in the February 26 (1936) Incident and the bombing of the American gunboat *Panay* (1937). Organizer of and linked to ultra-patriotic societies. Condemned to life imprisonment in the war crimes trial.

HATOYAMA ICHIRŌ (1883–1959)   A Tōkyō University Law School graduate who went on to the House of Representatives, became a member of the House of Representatives and education minister in the Inukai and Saitō cabinets (1931). Leader of the Seiyūkai party and president of the postwar Liberal party. Surviving purging and depurging he led two cabinets of his own in 1954, 1955, and 1956.

HAYASHI TADASU (1850–1913)   An early student of the West who studied in England from 1867 to 1868. Joining the Meiji government upon his return, he provided interpreter services to the Iwakura Mission. Then moved on to a diplomatic career as deputy foreign minister under Mutsu Munemitsu, special envoy to China, and ambassador to Russia. From 1900 to 1906 he was ambassador to England and participated in the conclusion of the Anglo-Japanese Alliance. In his capacity as foreign minister, 1906–1908, he consummated agreements with France and Russia.

HIRANUMA KIICHIRŌ (1867–1952)   A major figure in the legal world who eventually became head of the Supreme Court. He was minister of justice from 1923 to 1924, when he became a member of the House of Peers and the Privy Council. His presidency of a nationalist society established his eminence in right-wing politics. Succeeding Konoe in 1939 as prime minister, his tenure saw deepening hostility with America and Britain and the temporary suspension of a military alliance with Germany. Died in prison as a war criminal.

HONIDEN YOSHIO (b. 1892)   A doctor of economics from Tōkyō University, to which he returned in 1921 after serving in the Agriculture and Commerce Ministry. Authored works on a variety of economic subjects.

HORI MAKOTO (b. 1898)   A well-known socialist publicist and politician trained in law at Tōkyō University. A protégé of Yoshino Sakuzō. At various times an instructor at Tōkyō, Keiō, and Hōsei universities. A postwar member of the Labor-Farmer party and the House of Councilors.

HOSODA TAMIKI (b. 1892)   A novelist and Waseda University graduate. His earliest work depicted military life in the ranks. Associated with the Labor-Farmer Artists League, in 1927 he was identified with the "proletarian literature" movement. Contributed later to the bomb literature dealing with Hiroshima.

HOSOKAWA KAROKU (1888–1962)   A social critic and member of the Japan Communist party. Connected with the Ōhara Social Problems Research Institute and concentrated on the study of international and labor issues. His vociferous antiwar sentiments and writings prompted his arrest in 1942. The postwar director of the Social Sciences Research Institute.

ICHIKAWA FUSAE (b. 1893)   Social worker, women's rights activist, and suffragette. A participant in the Japan Labor Federation in 1919 after having taught and practiced journalism. Studied women's social conditions in the United States from 1921 to 1924. She was the Japanese representative at the Pan-Pacific Women's Conference in 1928.

IMAI TOSHIKI (1886–1950)   A Tōkyō University trained historian who returned there after 1919 to teach English society and history. Continued his researches in England, and upon returning became professor and then dean of the Faculty of Literature.

INUKAI KEN (TAKERU) (1896–1985)   A politician who began his career with literary aspirations. Shifting to politics in the 1930s, he was involved in the creation of an anti–Chiang Kai-shek government. His implication in the Sorge spy scandal led to his arrest. His career resumed in the postwar with successive elections to the House of Representatives and appointment to the Justice Ministry in the fifth Yoshida Cabinet (1953).

ISHIBASHI TANZAN (1884–1973)   Liberal theoretician, journalist, economic specialist, and later politician. A philosophy graduate of Waseda who served in the *Tōkyō mainichi shibun* staff from 1908 to 1911 while also contributing to assorted periodicals. Joined *Tōyō keizai shinpō* in 1911 and became chief editor. Established a reputation for his trenchant critiques of economic affairs and particularly the so-called national emergency finance. In 1934 began publication of the English economic journal *Oriental Economist*. Served in multiple official capacities and as finance minister in the first Yoshida Cabinet (1946).

ISHIGURO TADAATSU (1884–1960)   Entered the Agriculture and Commerce Ministry upon graduating from the Law Department of Tōkyō University in 1908. Later became director of the Industrial Cooperative Union Bank. A noted authority on agricultural and forestry administration. Served as an executive of the Imperial Rule Assistance Society. Was minister of agriculture and forestry in the Suzuki government (1945).

ITAGAKI TAISUKE (1837–1919)   A prominent activist in the Restoration movement who abandoned the new political establishment to act as founding father of the popular rights movement after 1874. Created one of the two first political parties and continued his party activism after the establishment of the Diet. Despite his antigovernment efforts, he was home minister in 1898 under Okuma.

ITŌ HIROBUMI (1841–1909)   Preeminent statesman of the Restoration period. From the outset a central figure in the clique leadership who held important positions, including a succession of premierships at the beginning of parliamentary-party style politics. A member of the Iwakura Mission, he later conducted a constitutional study trip in 1882 to Europe, which produced what is considered his career masterpiece, the Meiji Constitution. While he was not enthusiastic over Korea annexation, his residency there saw increasing Korean subjugation to Japanese interests. He was assassinated in 1909.

ITŌ MASANORI (1887–1962)   A Keiō University graduate who served on the *Jiji shinpō* and became editor in chief (1927) and director. Also a director of the Dōmei News Agency. Afterward he was editor in chief of *Chūbu Nihon shinbunsha*. Returned to *Jiji shinpō* as a director and then president. Recognized as an authority on naval affairs.

ITŌ MIYOJI (1857–1934)   A statesman who began his career as an interpreter. Traveled with Itō Hirobumi to Europe for the examination of Western constitutions and social systems. Following the Sino-Japanese War, acted as ambassador plenipotentiary to China to ratify the treaty settlement (1895). Elevated to count in 1922, privy counselor in 1899, and vice-resident of imperial household affairs.

IWAKURA TOMOMI (1825–1883)   A court noble prominent in the anti-Bakufu movement preceding the Restoration. Occupied important positions in the new administration, but perhaps best known for his leadership of a celebrated mission to America and Europe in 1871–1873 which bore his name. An opponent of early plans for an invasion of Korea that fractured the clique leadership. He remained thereafter a powerful presence in the government espousing a dominant imperial state and an emperor-bestowed constitution.

IWANAMI SHIGEO (1881–1946)   Founder of the celebrated publishing house of his name. This press boasted the publication of sixty-five million volumes in thirty years covering philosophy, science, and literature.

IWATA CHŪZŌ (1875–1966)   A well-known lawyer of the prewar period and active member of the Tōkyō Lawyers' Association. A postwar minister of justice in the Higashikuni and Shidehara cabinets.

KAGAWA TOYOHIKO (1888–1960)   Christian thinker, social critic, and graduate of the Kōbe Theological School. Practiced his faith in the slums of that city, preaching to the poor and establishing a clinic. Pursued his studies in philosophy at Princeton in 1916. Subsequently was engrossed in social service activities. One of the founders of the Japan Farmers' Union and Agricultural Cooperative Union. His passionate advocacy of peace earned him a trip to America in 1936. The author of more than fifty books, including novels.

KAMIKAWA HIKOMATSU (b. 1889) A Tōkyō University scholar who was professor there from 1923 and went on to twenty more years of service. In postwar was professor at Meiji University. A prize-winning specialist in Japanese diplomatic history.

KAMITSUKASA SHŌKEN (1874–1947) A novelist with only primary school education. After an interval of teaching, he joined the editorial staff of *Yomiuri shinbun* in 1897, where he was to become chief editor of its literary department until his retirement in 1916. Acquired some reputation as a novelist. His early works focused on local life in Ōsaka but later conveyed socialist leanings.

KANŌ HISAAKIRA (1886–1963) A businessman employed by the Yokohama Specie Bank after his graduation from Tōkyō University in 1911. Advanced to the management of the bank's branch in Toronto. At the war's end he was manager of branches in Manchuria and China.

KANOKOGI KAZUNOBU (1884–1949) Philosopher and ideologue originally trained at the Naval Engineering College (1904). After serving briefly, he moved to America and Europe to pursue his studies. Assumed a professorship at Kyōto University in 1926. A rabidly nationalist thinker, he propagandized energetically for the military during the war.

KARASAWA TOSHIKI (1891–1967) Statesman and imperial nominee to the House of Peers. Upon graduation from Tōkyō University's Political Department in 1915, he entered the Ministry of Interior. Thereafter he occupied a series of important offices. During the war he acted as deputy chief of the Far East Research Institute. Became minister of justice in the first Kishi Cabinet in 1957.

KATAOKA TEPPEI (1891–1944) A novelist who left Keiō University before graduating in order to concentrate entirely on his writing. Achieved some measure of notice with works that began as innovative, but later became increasingly popular.

KATŌ TAKAAI (1860–1926) Statesman, politician, diplomatist. He enjoyed a distinguished career that began with his entry into the Foreign Office. He was minister to England during the Sino-Japanese War. Held the position of foreign minister four times. Elevated to baron for his role in Anglo-Japanese Treaty of 1912. Thereafter he was deeply involved in party formation and leadership, ten years of opposition to the Seiyukai, and his final premiership in 1924. He was awarded the title of viscount for his political labors.

KAZAMI AKIRA (1886) A politician who began as a journalist on the editorial staff of the *Ōsaka asahi*, Kokusai News Agency, and the *Shinano mainichi*, where he was editor. Plunged into politics in 1934 and was repeatedly returned to the House of Representatives. Acted as chief secretary to the Konoe Cabinet in 1937 and was justice minister in the second Konoe Cabinet in 1940.

KIKUCHI KAN (HIROSHI) (1888–1948) A novelist whose early schooling was marked by frequent expulsions. Despite these flamboyant beginnings, he passed through Kyōto University and moved on to the editorship of *Jiji shimpō*. Concurrently a series of successful novels encouraged him to launch the magazine *Bungei shunjū*, which attracted writers such as Kawabata Yokomitsu and Kataoka. The instantaneous success of the magazine accounted for his celebrity in contemporary literary circles.

KINDAICHI KYŌSUKE (1882–1971) Literary scholar and professor at Tōkyō University. An eminent authority on the Ainu people. One of his studies earned him an

able. Because this is the portion of the report in which the client is most interested, the opinion should be stated clearly and should outline any risks in using the mark. The attorney may state, "We believe the BUDDY BEAR mark is distinguishable from the references disclosed in the report and may be available for use and registration in connection with fountain pens," or, conversely, may state, "Based on our review of the results, we do not recommend that you use or apply for registration of BUDDY BEAR." The attorney may even go so far as to inform the client that use of BUDDY BEAR could subject the client to risk of an infringement action.

Providing the opinion is often a difficult and time-consuming task. Clients are often in a rush to launch a new product or service and are eager to adopt a mark. They may have already begun an advertising campaign. There may be significant pressure from the client to obtain a favorable response. All of these factors, coupled with the uncertainty inherent in subjective comparisons of marks, makes trademark opinion work difficult and stressful.

Investigating and Resolving Conflicts

The report of the trademark search results may disclose several potential conflicts, and the IP team may seek the client's permission to investigate these conflicts further. Alternatively, some investigation may be done before the report is provided to the client. If the client is wedded to a mark that may be barred by another mark, several options can be explored.

- **Investigation and Research.** Further investigation can be conducted using other databases, such as Dun & Bradstreet, to determine the amount of business conducted by the potential opposer. Private trademark investigators may be hired to go to the place of

business and see how the mark is being used, by obtaining the toys bearing the BITTY BEAR mark. A search can be conducted of records at the PTO or through *Shepard's Citations* to determine if the owner of BITTY BEAR has aggressively protected its mark through litigation. It is possible that while a conflicting mark is registered with the PTO, it is no longer in use. Under the Lanham Act, there is a presumption that a mark has been abandoned if it is not used for three years. Similarly, failure to file various maintenance and renewal documents with the PTO will result in cancellation of a registration. Thus, an investigation into how or whether the conflicting mark is used may reveal that the mark has been abandoned and is now available to the client to use. As discussed earlier, many of the professional search firms identified in this chapter will conduct investigations to determine how a mark is actually being used in the marketplace.

- **Consent to Use.** The owner of BITTY BEAR can be contacted to obtain consent to use and register the client's mark. The client may pay some money for this consent or may agree to display the mark only in connection with specified goods or in a certain typeface and format.
- **License and Assignment.** The client might seek to obtain a license to use a mark from another or might seek to acquire the other mark through an assignment for a certain sum of money.
- **Revising the Mark.** If none of these alternatives are fruitful, the client might revise its mark, in which case a new search must be conducted for the new mark.

imperial prize and a doctorate. Later he was professor at Kokugakuin University and the recipient of the Medal of Culture (1954).

KOBAYASHI ICHIZŌ (1873–1957)   One-time president of Tōhō Film Company. After sixteen years with the Mitsui Bank, he engaged in a succession of entrepreneurial ventures with remarkable success while acting as director of Tōkyō Electric Light Company. Dabbled with equal success in the theatrical world, founding the Taka-razuka Girls Troupe. His company Tōhō, with its movie houses and theaters, be-came a major presence in the entertainment world. In the political sphere he was minister of commerce in the second Konoe Cabinet.

KOISO KUNIAKI (1880–1955)   A graduate of the Military Academy, he rose to full general by 1937. He was minister for colonization and then governor of Korea from 1942 to 1944. He succeeded Tōjō as prime minister, and while persuaded of the futility of continuing the war, he resorted to various stratagems to improve cabinet military liaison. His efforts to strip the military of control were as profitless as his conduct of the war. He resigned in April 1945 and died later as an imprisoned war criminal.

KOIZUMI MAKOTO (1882–1952)   A physician trained at Tōkyō University and then specializing in zoology. Granted an official position in Taiwan, he was also profes-sor at a medical college. Returned later to Keiō University as professor. Authored works on medical topics, especially parasitical diseases.

KOIZUMI SHINZŌ (1888–1966)   A graduate of Keiō University who continued his studies in sociology and economics in Europe in 1912. Assumed a professorship at Keiō upon returning in 1919, and then was president from 1933 to 1947. Perhaps most noted for his tutorship of the former crown prince, whom he accompanied on a world tour in 1953.

KUME MASAO (1891–1952)   A novelist whose first play attracted attention while he was still a student. After graduating from Tōkyō University, began a magazine titled *Shinshichō* in which other literary luminaries participated. He was also a student of Natsume Sōseki. At one point he managed the art and literature section of *Tōkyō nichinichi shinbun*.

KUWAKI AYAO (1878–1945)   A historian and product of Tōkyō University, where he became committed to the "scientific" study of history. Held a professorship at Kyūshū University in 1914 and later became president of Matsumoto Higher School in 1938.

KUWAKI GENYOKU (1874–1946)   A scholar and literateur trained at Tōkyō University who became professor at Kyōto University in 1906. After two years of study in Europe and America (1907–1909), returned to a professorial post at Tōkyō Uni-versity. Conducted two inspection tours of Europe and America in 1926 and 1930. His devotion to the Kantian school of philosophy is reflected in several of his works.

MAKINO EIICHI (1878–1970)   A lawyer and scholar of the law trained in French law at Tōkyō University. Served briefly as judge and prosecuting attorney and then became professor at Tōkyō University until retirement in 1938. Had previously spent four years inquiring into the penal codes of various European countries.

MAKINO NOBUAKI (COUNT) (1862–1949)   A graduate of an American university, where he spent the years 1871–1879. Entered the Ministry of Foreign Affairs and then served in a number of positions: minister of education 1907, privy councilor 1909, minister of agriculture and commerce 1911; minister of the imperial house-hold 1920. Considered a key "senior statesman" and stigmatized as pro-British and pro-American. His narrow escape from assassination in the February 26 coup prompted his retirement.

MASAMUNE HAKUCHŌ (1879–1962)   A novelist who began his career as literary critic for *Yomiuri shinbun* in 1903. Achieved acclaim the following year for his first novel. Leaving *Yomiuri* in 1910, he turned to full-time creative writing. After touring Europe and America, he went on to establish himself as a respected literary critic and versatile novelist.

MATSUMOTO JŌJI (1877–1954)   A lawyer and authority on commercial law. After graduating from Tōkyō University, worked briefly in the Ministry of Agriculture and Commerce. Pursued further studies in Europe for which he was awarded a doctorate. In the following years he was a director of the South Manchurian Railway Company, president of Kansai University, a member of the House of Peers, minister of commerce and industry in the Saitō Cabinet 1934, as well as holding directorships in a number of businesses.

MIKI KIYOSHI (1897–1945)   A student of philosophy at Kyōto University and in Europe 1922–1925. He was a professor at Hōsei University from 1927. He was a close associate of the Marxist historian Hani Gorō, and his close identification with Marxist philosophy prompted his arrest in 1930 for six months as a Communist supporter. His work in the 1930s on the philosophy of history established him as a significant influence in modern Japanese thought. Arrested again in March 1945, he would die in prison in September of that year.

MINAMI JIRŌ (1874–1957)   General who began his career in the Russo-Japanese War and went to command Japanese Garrison Forces in China. Made full general in 1930 and appointed minister of war in the Wakatsuki Cabinet in 1931. Commander-in-chief of the Kwangtung Army and at the same time ambassador to Manchukuo. Held responsible for the February 26 Incident but made governor-general of Korea (1936–1942). Sentenced to life imprisonment in the postwar war crime trials, but released owing to ill health.

MITSUI TAKASUMI (1901)   A pedagogue trained in economics at Tōkyō University. Later became director of Keimei Gakuen and the International Peace Association. Postwar director of Tsuda Women's College. Also director of the Public Service Office of the Mitsui complex.

MIURA TETSUTARŌ (1874)   A financier who graduated from Waseda University in 1896. In addition to his presidency of the Japan Tariff Association, has held the posts of chief director of the Economic Club and the Japan Economic Research Institute.

MIYAKE SETSUREI (1860–1945)   A journalist and philosophy graduate of Tōkyō University, he began with a brief tenure in the bureaucracy. From 1887 he was associated with the journal *Nihonjin* (afterward *Japan and the Japanese*). Politically oriented, he was a fierce critic of clan clique leadership, and his disgust with the government turned him toward journalism entirely. Ideologically he was a fervent Japanist, opposing Westernization and its attendant follies. Defended Japanese culture in terms of its unique contribution to world culture.

MIYAZAKI TŌTEN (1870–1922)   Political activist and long-time friend of the Chinese republican revolutionary Sun Yat-sen. His real name was Miyazaki Torazō, and he was born in Kumamoto. He was a student at the Ōe Gijuku, where he was first exposed to the freedom and popular ideas that were already in vogue. Later he attended the Semmon Gakkō (now Waseda University). He evinced very early what would remain a lifetime passionate interest in China and advocacy of East Asian unity. In 1899 he was commissioned by the Foreign Ministry to gather information on anti-Manchu revolutionary movements. Following his return to Japan, he met Sun, whom he viewed as a hero, savior of China, and cultivated his friendship. He labored in behalf of Sun's cause, soliciting funds for the nascent Chinese revolution. He visited China in 1911 to continue serving revolution in China. His autobiography, "My Thirty-three Years' Dream" (Sanjūsannen no yume), was published in 1902.

MUROBUSE KŌSHIN (1889–1970)   A journalist who would establish himself as a political critic. Associated with a series of newspapers, including *Niroku shinbun*, *Jiji shinpō*, and *Asahi shinbun*. In the aftermath of World War I, he traveled in Europe as the correspondent of the magazine *Kaizō*. Thereafter worked as an independent cultural critic.

MUTSU MUNEMITSU (1844–1897)   An early loyalist in the pre-Restoration period who held official posts in the new government until 1874. After brief tenure in the Genrōin, he was imprisoned for his efforts to create a military force after the Satsuma Rebellion. Following a trip to Europe, he entered the Foreign Ministry, becoming ambassador to America. After a succession of official positions, he became foreign minister from 1892 to 1896. His ministry aw the fulfillment of the long-sought treaty revision.

NAGAI RYŪTARŌ (1881–1945)   A politician educated at Waseda who had continued his studies in Britain and France. After serving as professor of colonial and social policy at Waseda, he entered the House of Representative in 1920. Was reputed for the skill of his speechifying. Held several cabinet posts, including minister of overseas affairs, communications, and railways. Sent to Nanking in 1942 as special envoy to develop closer connections with the government of Wang Ching-wei.

NAKAJIMA KENZŌ (1903–1979)   A literary critic, graduated in French literature from Tōkyō University in 1928. Later taught at the same institution. A founding member of the Japan Writers Association, established in 1946. Was a member of the Japan PEN Club.

NAKANO SEIGO (1886–1943)   A politician and journalist who graduated from Waseda University in 1909. Worked at journalism as a reporter for *Tōkyō mainichi* and *Asahi shinbun*. Following a study period in Britain, acted as editor of several magazines. Elected to the House of Representatives in 1920, but later abandoned the traditional parties to inaugurate his own party, the Kokumin Dōmei, and then the Tōhōkai, a Fascist group. Served as secretary-general of the Imperial Rule Assistance Society in 1940. Following a political confrontation with Tōjō, he committed suicide.

NITOBE INAZŌ (1862–1933)   An internationally renowned pedagogue and agricultural specialist noted for his efforts for international peace and his presentation of Japanese culture to the West. His cultural analysis, *Bushido*, was translated into several languages and was widely appreciated. A graduate of Sapporo Agricultural School in 1881, he continued his academic preparations at Johns Hopkins in 1884. Later he would be professor at Kyōto University and Tōkyō University, under secretary general of the League of Nations (1920–1927), and a member of the House of Peers.

NOGUCHI YONEJIRŌ (1875–1942)   A poet who early in his studies in California came under the sway of the American writers Joaquin Miller and Edgar Allen Poe. His first collection of poems was published in San Francisco. Moving to London, he published a collection of poems there and established his reputation. Returned to

Japan to become professor of English literature at Keiō University. In 1913 lectured on Japanese poetry at Oxford. Was also a biographer of Japanese artists.

OBAMA TOSHIE (1889) A journalist trained in political economy at Waseda University. Joined *Nihon keizai shinbun* and later became its president. Once depurged, in 1952 he continued to produce commentary on economic and political issues.

ŌKUBO TOSHIMICHI (1830–1878) One of the main architects of the Restoration and dominant political presence from the beginning of the Meiji period. Many of its revolutionary projects were at his prompting. A member of the Iwakura Mission, he rejected pressure for a Korean invasion, assigning priority to domestic development. Instigator of the initial stages of economic modernization but also conspicuous in diplomatic affairs. Along with Itō and Ōkuma, one of the most powerful statesmen in the early Meiji government until his assassination in 1878.

ŌKURA KIMMOCHI (b. 1882) Public official, businessman, and engineer. Trained at Tōkyō University, he was chief of various sections of the Railway Bureau and then vice-chief of the Transportation Department of the South Manchurian Railroad and then director. Member of the House of Peers in 1933. Associated with a wide range of research organizations and railway and transportation enterprises.

ŌSHIMA HIROSHI (1886–1975) Prewar ambassador to Berlin and architect of the Japan-Germany-Italy Anti-Comintern Pact of 1937 while military attaché in Berlin. Reappointed ambassador in 1940, he was party to the establishment of the Tripartite Alliance. Later imprisoned for a life sentence by the Military Tribunal, he was released in 1955.

ŌUCHI HYŌE (1888–1980) A graduate of the Economics Department of Tōkyō University in 1913, whereupon he entered the Finance Ministry. This was followed by an official tour of America in 1916. Subsequently ascended to a professorship at Tōkyō University. In 1938 he was arrested along with Arisawa Hiromi and Wakimura Yoshitarō and others in the infamous "Professors' Group Case" for Communist sympathies. Resigned in 1944 but returned to the university for several years after the war.

OZAKI HOTSUMI (1901–1944) Poet, journalist, and provocateur, educated at Tōkyō University. In the employ of *Asahi shinbun*, worked in China as a correspondent. Quickly acquired a reputation for expertise in Chinese affairs. Acted as adviser to the South Manchurian Railway Company's Research Bureau. This same expertise catapulted him into the Shōwa Kenkyūkai—Konoe's brain trust. Attempted to forestall war with the Soviets. Fatally implicated in the Sorge spy case, he was arrested in 1942 and executed in 1944.

OZAKI SHIRŌ (1898–1964) A product of the Political Economy Department of Waseda University who spent the next ten years as a literary Bohemian. While pursuing novel writing, joined a national socialist movement. Was also known for his historical novels.

OZAKI YUKIO (1858–1944) A "freelance" politician, liberally educated. At twenty-two he was already editor in chief of the *Niigata shinbun* and later moved to *Hōchi shinbun*. After a European jaunt, became a counselor at the Foreign Office and education minister in the Itagaki-Okuma Cabinet of 1898. Elected mayor of Tōkyō and appointed justice minister in 1915. From 1890 he was elected consecutively to the House of Representatives twenty-four times. His parliamentary career lasted almost a half century.

ROYAMA MASAMACHI (1895) Academic, journalist, and political commentator who was professor at Tōkyō University. Publisher of the magazine *Shakai shisō*, where he expounded British socialism. A member of the Konoe expedition to the United States in 1934, and there lectured on Far Eastern problems. During the war resigned from the university when Kawai Eijirō was dismissed. Became a member of Konoe's research coterie and was prominent in that premier's wartime administration.

SAIGŌ TAKAMORI (1828–1877)   The antihero figure of the Restoration. An early and leading force in the anti-Tokugawa movement and central actor in the Restoration coup. Quickly included in the upper circle of Meiji leadership, he shared power with Ōkuma and Itagaki in the hiatus created by the Iwakura Mission. When his fervent commitment to invading Korea was rejected, he went into exile in Satsuma, where his dedication to the future status of the samurai class ended in the failure of the Satsuma Rebellion of 1877. His suicide only guaranteed his subsequent enshrinement as the personification of traditional samurai values.

SAIJŌ YASO (1892–1970)   A student of and professor at Waseda University. In 1924 studied at the Sorbonne in Paris. Produced a profusion of romantic poetry for assorted magazines and edited many of the same. Later turned to children's poetry and lyrics for popular songs.

SANO MANABU (1892–1953)   A political scientist trained at Tōkyō University. While a professor at Waseda, organized an antimilitary training student movement. Became a member of the Communist party and Comintern and journeyed to the Soviet Union. Returning to Japan, he was arrested in 1930 and underwent a classic conversion, repudiating Communism and sanctifying the emperor system. In the postwar he was reappointed as professor at Waseda.

SAWADA RENZŌ (1888)   A law-trained diplomat at Tōkyō University. He would be an embassy consul in France, consul general in New York, and councilor to the embassy in Manchukuo. Afterward he became vice-minister of foreign affairs in the 1938 Konoe Cabinet. During the war he was involved in territorial agreements between Burma and Japan. In 1953 selected as ambassador heading the Japanese delegation to the United Nations, where he labored to gain Japan's admittance to membership.

SHIDEHARA KIJŪRŌ (1872–1951)   A major prewar diplomatic figure who came to prominence as ambassador to the United States from 1919 to 1922 as Japanese representative at the Washington Conference. As foreign minister from 1924 to 1927 and 1929 to 1931, he became identified with a distinctive conciliatory style of diplomacy, which acquired his name and which his opponents labeled as weak. He sought to promote Japanese interests by economic and diplomatic strategies in contrast to the aggressive antics of his nemesis, Tanaka Giichi. Retired to the political wings after 1931, but returned as premier in 1945.

SHIMANAKA HŌJI (1923)   Publisher and president of Chūō Kōron Publishing Company who succeeded his father, Yūsaku, in 1949. The company produces the prominent journal of intellectual opinion, *Chūō kōron*, and a women's magazine, *Fujin kōron*.

SHIMAZAKI TŌSON (1872–1943)   A literary giant in the development of the modern Japanese novel. Regarded as a founding father of the so-called naturalist school of writing. Began as a lyric poet whose flow of works exerted normative influence in the world of poetry. His novels have become standard classics in the Japanese literary repertoire.

SHIMANAKA YŪSAKU (1887–1949)   A publisher who joined the Chūō Kōron Publishing Company and assumed its presidency in 1928. During his directorship, the company produced books and magazines of high standards and was committed to the intellectual edification of the masses.

SHIMIZU IKUTARŌ (b. 1907)   Sociologist and writer educated at Tōkyō University. Had been professor at Gakushūin University and Sophia University and an editor on the *Yomiuri shinbun* staff. In the postwar period he assumed the directorship of the Twentieth Century Research Institute.

SHIMOMURA KAINAN (1875–1957)   A statesman and journalist trained at Tōkyō University. His career began as a functionary of the Ministry of Communications. Received financial training in Belgium, which he applied to the ministry's Savings Bureau. Served as civil governor of Formosa (1915–1921). Following a trip to Europe and America, became vice-president of the *Asahi shinbun*, where he served for a decade. In retirement he was president of the Japan Broadcasting Corporation. Late in the war he was state minister and director of the Information Bureau in the Suzuki Cabinet.

SHINOBU JUNPEI (b. 1871)   Jurist, diplomat, and journalist who entered the Foreign Office after graduation and served abroad in Europe and the United States. He left the diplomatic service for an appointment at Waseda University and then turned to editorship of the *Shin aichi shinbun* in Nagoya. A specialist in international law and diplomatic history. One of his works received an Imperial Academy prize.

SHINOBU SEIZABURŌ (b. 1909)   A historian specializing in diplomatic and economic studies. A graduate of Kyūshū University (1934), his postgraduation publication *The Russo-Japanese War* was officially banned. Prior to his becoming professor at Nagoya University, he was in charge of the Industrial Labor Investigation Bureau. He authored a considerable number of works on diplomatic and economic history themes.

SHIRATORI TOSHIO (1887–1949)   A diplomat who passed his foreign service exams while still a student in the Economic Department of Tōkyō University. Went on to become ambassador to Rome. Later, in conjunction with the ambassador to Germany, Ōshima Hiroshi, he helped concoct the Tripartite Alliance between Japan, Germany, and Italy.

SHIRAYANAGI SHŪKO (1884–1950)   A historian trained in the Philosophy Department of Waseda University. As a student, his interest in literature and social problems led to his contributions to the magazine *Shakaishugi kenkyū* (Researches in socialism). A disciple of Kōtoku Shūsui, Sakai Toshihiko, and Kinoshita Shōkō, he devoted his creative energies to social problem stories for the masses. He was especially adroit at simplified historical expositions.

SŌMA AIZŌ (1870–1954)   Founder and proprietor of the Nakamuraya Food Store in Shinjuku, Tōkyō. His humble bakery and confectionery turned into a major enterprise. Was known for his patronage and protection of artists and foreign political refugees, the most notable of these protégés being the Indian Independence Movement leader, Chandra Bose.

SUEHIRO IZUTARŌ (1888–1951)   A jurist and labor expert who was the son of a famous judge. A product of the German Law Department of Tōkyō University (1912), he taught there from 1914 and then studied civil law in Switzerland, France, and Italy (1918). Returned to a professorshipb of civil law at Tōkyō University. Until purged after the war, he was dean of the Law Department from 1933 to 1946.

SUZUKI KANTARŌ (1868–1948)   Admiral, statesman, and wartime premier. He served as privy councilor from 1929 to 1940 and also grand chamberlain from 1929. He became vice-president and then president of the Privy Council from 1940 to 1945.

In April 1945 he succeeded Koiso as premier and contrived the final surrender of Japan, resigning the following day.

TAIRA TEIZŌ (b. 1894)   A publicist with several pseudonyms. A graduate of the Tōkyō University Law Department. He was a specialist on political and economic problems.

TAKAGAKI TORAJIRŌ (b. 1890)   An economist and banker trained at the Tōkyō Higher Commercial School (1915). Was an overseas student of the Ministry of Education in Europe and America from 1916 to 1919. Subsequently became professor at the Tōkyō University of Commerce. Retired from service at national institutions and would later (1953) become director of the Mitsubishi Bank.

TAKAGI RIKURŌ (b. 1880)   Businessman who graduated from the Tōkyō Commercial and Industrial School in 1897. Studied in Nanking and later acted as interpreter for the Japanese troops stationed in China. Participated in various business organizations in China and was founder and president of the Far Eastern Trading Company (1914). Assumed the presidency of the South Manchurian Mining Company in 1923. Thereafter occupied a number of chairmanships of a varied collection of enterprises.

TAKATA YASUMA (b. 1883)   A pedagogue who graduated from Kyōto University in 1910. A succession of professorships followed in his career, including Tōkyō Commercial College (1921), Hiroshima Higher School (1919), and Kyōto University (1930). A specialist in sociology and economics and the author of several works in these fields.

TAKAYANAGI KENZŌ (1887–1967)   A scholar educated in English law at Tōkyō University. Rose to full professorship there in 1920, when he was sent to Europe. When he returned he assumed direction of the university's library. Retiring in 1946, he accepted the presidency of Seikei University.

TATSUNO YUTAKA (b. 1888)   Literateur and leading figure in the French literature field in Japan. A product of both the Law and French Literature programs at Tōkyō University. From 1918 taught at Keiō University, Waseda University, and then Tōkyō University (1921). A prolific essayist and translator of French literature.

TOKUDA SHŪSEI (1871–1943)   A novelist who abandoned his school training to work for Hakubunkan Publishing Company in 1892. Became a disciple of Ozaki Kōyō, a major figure in the development of the modern novel in Japan. His early work and those that followed established his repute in the realm of realism and the "I" novel.

TOKUTOMI SOHŌ (1863–1957)   Cultural critic, idealogue, and journalist. Founder of the Minyū Publishing Company in 1887. Created the *Kokumin shinbun* in 1890, where as its director and chief editor he established his reputation as opinion maker and social critic. Increasingly an avid exponent of aggressive nationalism, he later moved on to special contributor to the *Ōsaka mainichi shinbun* and *Tōkyō nichinichi shinbun*. Before and after the Manchurian Incident, he was the intellectual darling of the military ultranationalist extremists.

TSUCHIYA TAKAO (1896–1988)   Distinguished economic historian and professor at Tōkyō University from 1921. Received further training in Europe in 1927. Ironically in the postwar he was purged for a work "On Total War" bearing his name but authored elsewhere.

TSURUMI YŪSUKE (1885–1973)   Sometime freelance diplomat, government official, and politician who entered government service after graduation from Tōkyō University in 1910. Began as chief of the Archives and Documents Bureau of the Railway Board and traveled sporadically to Europe, America, and China to investigate railway systems. Resigning from government service, he traveled to America in the hope of promoting peace, which motive he pursued as delegate to Pacific conferences beginning in 1925. Active in politics from 1928 and a Diet member several times.

UEDA TATSUNOSUKE (b. 1892)   An economist educated at the Tōkyō Higher Commercial School and professor there in 1917. Was a student in Europe and America, receiving a doctorate from the University of Pennsylvania. A specialist in the economics of medieval Europe. Later dean of the Economics Department of Hitotsubashi University.

UESUGI KENSHIN (1530–1587)   Spectacular warlord of the sixteenth century during the height of Japan's civil war period. Reknowned among his comtemporaries as exemplar of valor and purity of motive.

UGAKI KAZUSHIGE (1868–1956)   Originally a protégé of Tanaka Giichi, he held various posts in the general staff and then became war minister from 1924 to 1927. He was again war minister from 1929 to 1931. His policies in both instances earned him the title of "political" general. Senior statesmen support and the approval of the political parties made him candidate for cabinet leadership in 1936, but this was thwarted by the Army. While minister of foreign and colonial affairs he resigned, protesting China policy, and withdrew politically. Restored as a political presence in the postwar, he was precluded from continued activism by illness.

WAKATSUKI REIJIRŌ (1866–1949)   Began his career in the Finance Ministry, where he served from 1912 to 1913 and 1914 to 1915. A vigorous participant in party politics, he became prime minister in 1926 and would be much maligned for his financial policy, and especially Shidehara's foreign policies. As delegate to the London Naval Conference he provoked hostility over his agreement to naval ratios. He returned to the premiership in 1931, but the world depression, military fractiousness, and international tension following the Manchurian Incident led to his resignation. Thereafter he was elevated to the status of senior statesman.

WAKIMURA GITARŌ (b. 1900)   An economist trained at Tōkyō University who was an authority on commercial history and commercial policy. Began a professorial career at Tōkyō University in 1938, but shortly thereafter resigned because of his participation in a popular front movement. Specialized in marine insurance, shipbuilding, petroleum geology, and merchandising. Resumed his academic post at Tōkyō after the war.

WATANABE TETSUZŌ (1885–1980)   Businessman graduated in law from Tōkyō University, where he became a member of the faculty of economics. Later director of the Tōkyō Chamber of Commerce and Industry. After retirement he was elected to the House of Representatives and there was a member of a number of committees. In the postwar he was president of Tōhō Motion Picture Company.

YAMAMOTO SANEHIKO (1885–1952)   A publisher who began as editor of *Moji shinbun* and later served as London correspondent for *Yamato shinbun*. Upon returning, he became president of *Tōkyō mainichi shinbun*. Later established the Kaizō Publishing Company, which published the magazine *Kaizō* and literary, social, political, and economic works. A member of the Tōkyō City Assembly and the Diet in 1930.

YAMAURA KANICHI (b. 1893)   A journalist who wrote for a number of newspapers, including *Jiji shinpō*, *Tōkyō asahi*, *Shin aichi*, and *Kokumin shinbun*. Acted as adviser and political commentator for *Tōkyō shinbun*. Especially concerned with the new constitution and parliamentary politics in the postwar period.

YANAGITA KUNIO (1875–1962)   A celebrated folklorist who was trained in political science at Tōkyō University and began his career in the Bureau of Legislation and Imperial Household. From 1914 to 1919 he was secretary to the House of Peers, after which he entered the editorial staff of *Asahi shinbun*. Established the Japanese Manners and Customs Research Institute, devoted to the study of local history and customs. A cross-disciplinary virtuoso making contributions in cultural studies, philology, dialects, and social studies.

YANAGIZAWA KEN (b. 1907)   A medical doctor trained at Tōkyō University, he graduated in 1927. Afterward he became a specialist in the study of tuberculosis and a director of the Bacteriology Department of Tuberculosis Research Institute in 1942.

YOKOTA KISABURŌ (b. 1896)   Received his degree in German law from Tōkyō University, whereupon he continued his studies in both America and Europe (1926). Returned to serve as professor at Tōkyō University. He was regarded as an authority on international law.

YOSHINO SAKUZŌ (1878–1933)   Major intellectual figure of the early twentieth century and professor of political science at Tōkyō University. He became a theoretical authority for the intelligentsia in the period of Taishō democracy and eventually the target of both right and left. He attempted to reconcile Western democratic ideas within the limitations of Japanese history and culture.

INDEX

TRIVIA

- Among the marks registered by celebrities for entertainment services are BON JOVI® and DIXIE CHICKS.®
- The PTO has registered more than 2 million trademarks since the first trademark law was passed in 1870. Approximately 1 million of these are still in effect.
- In 2000, the mark CARNATION BRAND (& DESIGN)® used for condensed milk celebrated its one hundredth year of trademark registration.
- Elvis Presley Enterprises, Inc. has more than 100 pending applications and registrations for marks related to Elvis Presley, including registrations for JAILHOUSE ROCK®, BLUE SUEDE SHOES®, and HEARTBREAK HOTEL® for a variety of goods (including cigarette lighters and shot glasses).

CHAPTER SUMMARY

Once a client has selected a mark, the mark should be subjected to a search to ensure that no other party has secured rights to the mark or to a confusingly similar mark. Failure to conduct a search or failure to conduct an adequate search may be characterized by a court as carelessness and weigh in favor of a party who alleges infringement. Reviewing search results and reporting results to clients is difficult and time-consuming. Often follow-up investigation is needed to determine whether potentially conflicting marks remain in use or are in use with related goods or services. Conducting a search, however, will result in a snapshot of the marketplace, providing information about competitors, conflicting marks, and how the PTO has handled applications for similar marks.

If the search "clears" the mark, an application should be filed promptly with the PTO for registration of the mark if the mark has been used in commerce or the client has a bona fide intent to use the mark in commerce.

CASE ILLUSTRATION—NECESSITY OF TRADEMARK SEARCH

Case: *SecuraComm Consulting, Inc. v. Securacom,* 984 F. Supp. 286 (D.N.J. 1997), *aff'd,* 244 F.3d 273 (3d Cir. 2000)

Facts: Plaintiff owned a trademark for SECURACOMM for consulting and alleged that defendant's later adoption of SECURACOM for similar security services infringed its mark.

About the Editor and Translators

Eugene Soviak is Professor of History, Emeritus, at Washington University at St. Louis. Kamiyama Tamie is Professor Emeritus of Japanese Language at Washington University at St. Louis and Professor of Japanese Area Studies at Obirin University, Japan.

Printed in the United States
129511LV00002BA/73-300/P